# Together They Fought

## Gandhi-Nehru Correspondence 1921–1948

*edited by*

Uma Iyengar
Lalitha Zackariah

NEHRU MEMORIAL MUSEUM & LIBRARY

OXFORD
UNIVERSITY PRESS

OXFORD
UNIVERSITY PRESS

Oxford University Press is a department of the University of Oxford.
It furthers the University's objective of excellence in research, scholarship,
and education by publishing worldwide. Oxford is a registered trademark of
Oxford University Press in the UK and in certain other countries

Published in India by
Oxford University Press
YMCA Library Building, 1, Jai Singh Road, New Delhi 110001, India



First published in 2011



ISBN-13: 978-0-19-807058-0
ISBN-10: 0-19-807058-6

Typeset in 10.5/13.1 ITC Legacy Serif Std
by Excellent Laser Typesetters, Pitampura, Delhi 110 034
Printed in India by Rakmo Press, New Delhi 110 020

Photographs courtesy of Nehru Memorial Museum and Library,
Teen Muti House, New Delhi 110 001

Together
They Fought

## Contents

## Chronology of Events 1869–1948

| | |
|---|---|
| 1869 | |
| 2 October | Birth of Mohandas Karamchand Gandhi at Porbandar |
| 1882 | Gandhi married Kasturba |
| 1888 | |
| 4 September | Gandhi sailed for England from Bombay |
| 1889 | |
| 14 November | Birth of Jawaharlal Nehru at Allahabad |
| 1891 | |
| 10 June | Gandhi called to the Bar, London |
| 1893 | |
| April | Gandhi left for South Africa |
| June | Gandhi ordered off the train while travelling to Pretoria, Petermaritzberg; vows to dedicate himself to active nonviolent resistance |
| 1897 | Gandhi returned to India |
| 1898 | Gandhi went back to South Africa |
| 1905–7 | Nehru studied at Harrow, Middlesex |
| 1907–10 | Nehru studied at Trinity College, Cambridge |
| 1908 | Gandhi wrote *Hind Swaraj* |
| 1910 | Nehru left Cambridge; joined Inner Temple, London |

| | |
|---|---|
| 1912 | Nehru returned to India and started practising law at Allahabad High Court |
| 1914 | |
| 18 December | Gandhi sailed for England, leaving South Africa permanently |
| 1915 | |
| 9 January | Gandhi's final return to India |
| 1916 | First Meeting between Gandhi and Nehru, Lucknow session of Indian National Congress |
| 8 February | Nehru married Kamala Kaul, Delhi |
| 1917 | Champaran struggle |
| 19 November | Birth of Nehru's daughter, Indira Priyadarshini |
| 1918 | Kheda Satyagraha; Montague-Chelmsford Reforms |
| | Nehru elected member of All-India Congress Committee |
| 1919 | Establishment of Satyagraha Sabha |
| 13 April | Agitation against Rowlatt Act; Jallianwala Bagh Massacre |
| | Gandhi announced 3-day penitential fast |
| | Nehru assisted C.R. Das in collecting evidence for Congress Inquiry Report on Jallianwala Bagh Massaacre |
| 1920 | Khilafat Agitation; beginning of noncooperation |
| | Nehru joined Noncooperation movement |
| 1921 | Boycott of foreign cloth; Gandhi presided over bonfire of foreign cloth in Bombay |
| | Gandhi fasted for 5 days in protest against communal riots following visit of Prince of Wales; mass Civil Disobedience campaign began |

| | |
|---|---|
| 6 December | Nehru arrested for participating in boycott of Prince of Wales's visit |
| 1922 | |
| 4 February | Chauri Chaura disturbances; withdrawal of Civil Disobedience |
| 3 March | Nehru released |
| 10 March | Gandhi arrested; later sentenced to 6 years' imprisonment |
| 11 May | Nehru arrested again for organizing picketing against sale of foreign cloth |
| 1923 | |
| 21 September | Nehru arrested for defying ban on entry into Nabha State<br>Nehru elected Secretary, AICC |
| 4 October | Nehru released |
| 26 November | Gandhi began writing *Satyagraha in South Africa* |
| 1923–5 | Nehru was Chairman, Allahabad Municipal Board |
| December | Formation of Hindustani Seva Dal |
| 1925 | Formation of All-India Spinners' Association |
| January | Nehru resigned as AICC Secretary |
| 1927 | |
| 10–15 February | Nehru represented INC at the Congress of Oppressed Nationalities at Brussels |
| 1928 | Boycott of Simon Commission |
| 12–13 December | Nehru presided over Bombay Presidency Youth Conference at Poona |
| 1929 | |
| March | Gandhi arrested for burning foreign cloth |
| December | Nehru presided over Lahore session of INC |
| 31 December | Gandhi declares complete Independence; flag of free India raised |

| | |
|---|---|
| 1930 | Salt Satyagraha and countrywide arrests |
| 12 March | Gandhi began historic Salt March from Sabarmati to Dandi |
| 6 April | Gandhi and volunteers broke Salt Law |
| 14 April | Nehru arrested |
| 5 May | Gandhi arrested at Karadi and imprisoned in Yeravda Jail without trail |
| 11 October | Nehru released |
| 19 October | Nehru re-arrested |
| 1931 | |
| 26 January | Gandhi released unconditionally |
| 6 February | Death of Motilal Nehru |
| 4 March | Gandhi–Irwin Pact signed |
| 29 August | Gandhi left for London to attend Round Table Conference |
| December | Gandhi sailed for India after visiting Romain Rolland in Switzerland |
| 1932 | |
| 3 January | Satyagraha renewed |
| 4 January | Gandhi arrested in Bombay and detained in Yeravda Jail |
| | Gandhi began fast unto death in protest against separate electorates for untouchables |
| 24 September | Gandhi's fast ended; Yeravda Pact signed |
| 1933 | |
| 8 May | Gandhi began fast for self-purification in prison and was released |
| 26 July | Individual Civil Disobedience inaugurated |
| 1 August | Gandhi arrested and sentenced to a year's imprisonment |
| 6 August | Gandhi began fast as he was not allowed to work for untouchables while in prison; released later |
| 7 November | Gandhi tour of India for untouchables began |

| | |
|---|---|
| 1934 | |
| 15 January | *Glimpses of World History* published by Nehru |
| | Bihar earthquake; Nehru toured Bihar for relief work |
| 12 February | Nehru arrested and sentenced to two years' imprisonment |
| 7 April | Civil Disobedience suspended |
| 12 August | Nehru released on parole |
| 23 August | Nehru returned to jail |
| 3 September | Nehru released |
| 1935 | |
| December | Congress Golden Jubilee |
| 1936 | |
| 28 February | Death of Kamala Nehru in Lausanne, Switzerland |
| | *An Autobiography* by Nehru published |
| 12–14 April | Nehru presided over INC at Lucknow |
| 27–8 December | Nehru presided over INC at Faizpur |
| 1937 | AICC adopted resolution authorizing acceptance of office |
| 1938 | |
| 10 January | Death of Swarup Rani Nehru |
| | Nehru visited Spain, France, Britain and some other European countries |
| October | Nehru appointed Chairman, National Planning Committee of INC |
| | Gandhi tours NWFP |
| 1939 | |
| 15 February | Nehru presided over All India States People's Conference, Ludhiana |
| 3 March | Gandhi began fast unto death at Rajkot to protest refusal by local prince to keep promise made to people; broke fast 4 days later |

| | |
|---|---|
| July | Nehru visited Ceylon |
| August | Defence of India Bill, issued as an Ordinance passed in Central Assembly |
| August–September | Nehru visited China |
| 1940 | Nehru's *China, Spain and the War* published |
| 17 October | Gandhi launched Civil Disobedience campaign |
| 31 October | Nehru chosen second satyagrahi; offered Individual Satyagraha; arrested |
| 1941 | |
| March | Cripps Mission |
| 4 December | Nehru released<br>Meeting between Gandhi and Madame and Marshal Chiang Kai-Shek |
| 1942 | |
| March–April | Nehru–Sir Stafford Cripps talks |
| 7 August | Quit India resolution moved by Nehru at AICC meeting |
| 8 August | Quit India resolution passed; Gandhi led nationwide Satyagraha campaign—'Do or Die'<br>Gandhi arrested, imprisoned at Aga Khan Palace, Poona |
| 9 August | Nehru arrested; countrywide arrests and all Congress WC members arrested |
| 15 August | Death of Mahadev Desai |
| 1943 | |
| 10 February | Gandhi began 21-day fast as an appeal from Government to God for justice |
| 1944 | |
| 22 February | Death of Kasturba Gandhi in Aga Khan Palace |
| 13 April | Nehru began writing *The Discovery of India* |
| 6 May | Gandhi released |
| 9 September | Gandhi begins talks with Jinnah |

| | |
|---|---|
| 1945<br>15 June | Nehru released |
| 1945<br>25 June | Simla Conference began; Gandhi attended |
| 1945<br>November | Nehru appeared, as lawyer for the Defence, at the trial of Indian National Army officers |
| 1946 | *The Discovery of India* by Nehru published |
| March | Nehru visited Singapore |
| April–June | Nehru held talks with members of British Cabinet Mission |
| May | Nehru elected President of INC |
| 23 September | Nehru resigned from presidentiship |
| 20 June | Nehru arrested at Domel following the defiance of ban by the Jammu and Kashmir government on his entry into the state; released next day |
| 15 August | 'Great Calcutta killing' lasted 4 days |
| 2 September | Nehru joined the Interim Government as Member for External Affairs and Commonwealth Relations; nominated Vice President of Viceroy's Executive Council |
| November | Gandhi begins 4-month tour of East Bengal |
| 13 December | Nehru moved the 'Objectives Resolution' in Indian Constituent Assembly |
| 1947<br>3 January | Nehru presided over Indian Science Congress, Delhi |
| 22 March | Lord Mountbatten, last Viceroy, arrived in India |
| | Gandhi on tour of Bihar |
| 23 March | Nehru inaugurated Asian Relations Conference, New Delhi |

| | |
|---|---|
| 3 June | Nehru's broadcast to the nation accepting Partition |
| 22 July | Nehru moved resolution on 'National Flag' in Constituent Assembly |
| 15 August | India partitioned into Hindustan and Pakistan; Gandhi in Calcutta; Nehru became first Prime Minister of India |
| | Speech by Nehru—'Tryst with Destiny' |
| 1948 | |
| 13–18 January | Gandhi fasted in New Delhi for communal unity |
| 1948 | |
| 30 January | Gandhi assassinated by Nathuram Godse<br>Broadcast by Nehru to nation—'The Light has gone out of our lives' |

# Introduction

This book tells the story of two men, Mohandas Karamchand Gandhi and Jawaharlal Nehru, through their letters to each other—two exceptional Indians divided by age, custom, tradition, faith and beliefs, yet bound by a passion for the country of their birth.

These two men were major actors, among many other important dramatis personae of the era, who continue to provoke endless interest and wonder in every generation of men and women, not just for what they achieved for India but also for their extraordinary relationship. The lives of both Gandhi and Nehru were the very fabric of the political and social life of an India struggling to come into its own. If Gandhi became the father of the nation, through a turbulent historical process, Nehru came to be regarded as his political heir, his chosen son.

Nehru was called to the Bar in the summer of 1912 and returned to India in the autumn of that year after a stay of over seven years in England. In his own words, he was, when he landed in Bombay, 'a bit of a prig with little to commend' him. Gandhi, older than Nehru by twenty years, was no novice to politics when he arrived in Bombay in 1915 from South Africa. A Bar-at-Law from London, Gandhi had fought the cases of Indians in South Africa and had initiated their struggle against apartheid with a unique weapon of 'fair' war—'Satyagraha'.

It was a year later, in December 1916, that the two first met. Nehru, recounting this first encounter in his *Autobiography*, says, 'All of us admired him for his heroic fight in South Africa, but he seemed distant and different and unpolitical to many of us young men. He refused to take part in Congress or national politics then and confined himself to the South African Indian question. Soon afterwards his adventures and victory in Champaran ... filled us with enthusiasm.'

Nehru, somewhat adrift at this time, had been perfunctorily practising law, even as his mind was agonizing over the conditions of India in servility, and still more, the lot of the peasants. In 1919, an ailing Gandhi's appeal to the Viceroy not to pass the dreaded Rowlatt Bills went unheeded, culminating in Gandhi's spear-heading the first all-India agitation against the Government. He issued a call to the nation to observe 6 April as 'Satyagraha Day', with prayers and fasting, and with the pledge of Civil Disobedience. Nehru records that when he first read about this proposal in the newspapers, his reaction was, 'Here at last was a way out of the tangle, a method of action which was straight and open and possibly effective. I was afire with enthusiasm and wanted to join the Satyagraha Sabha immediately.'

But for Nehru it was not all plain sailing. Motilal Nehru's intense and protective love for his son proved an impediment. The elder Nehru scarcely believed in the efficacy of the 'new-fangled plan of action'. Gandhi himself advised Nehru not to take any hasty decision and thereby upset his father. Nehru waited in the wings.

A great national tragedy drew people into the thick of the struggle, kindling in them a new fire and dynamism. The massacre of April 1919 at Jallianwala Bagh and the Martial Law imposed thereon meant a sea change in the perceptions and attitudes of national leaders. The Punjab Relief and Inquiry work in which Nehru became involved brought him in closer contact with Gandhi. Nehru writes: 'Very often his proposals seemed novel to our committee and it did not approve of them. But almost always he argued his way to their acceptance and subsequent events showed the wisdom of his advice. Faith in his political insight grew in me.'

By the year 1920, with the death of Bal Gangadhar Tilak, Indians, more and more, had come to look up to Gandhi for leadership and guidance in their struggle for liberation from British rule. Around the time of the Amritsar Congress presided over by Motilal Nehru, Gandhi's influence began to dominate the political scene. Shouts of '*Mahatma Gandhi ki jai*' greeted him wherever he went, conferring on him the title of 'Mahatma', that is, one revered as a Great Soul.

Gandhi observes in his *Autobiography*, 'I must regard my participation in Congress proceedings at Amritsar as my real entrance into Congress politics.' This self-told story of Gandhi rings down the curtain soon after—about the time the Gandhi–Nehru Correspondence begins—marking the watershed year of 1921. 'My life,' he writes, 'from this point onward has been so public that there is hardly anything about it that people do not know. Moreover, since 1921, I have worked in such close association with the Congress leaders that I can hardly describe any episode in my life since then without referring to my relations with them.'

Most of these leaders, Motilal Nehru, Chittaranjan Das and Lala Lajpat Rai, to mention a few, were persuaded to abide by Gandhi's prescription of self-suffering and nonviolence for the common cause. So powerful was this current sweeping over India that at Gandhi's call for boycott of foreign cloth, the nation stood all too ready for the symbolic act of making a bonfire of foreign cloth.

To Jawaharlal, the fledgling political disciple of Gandhi, the door had opened to unexplored areas in his chosen path of service. He grew in admiration and respect for the political astuteness and moral strength of Gandhi; at the same time he also began to feel a discontent and irritation over some of Gandhi's decisions. The discontinuance of Civil Disobedience in 1922 was one such instance early in their association.

Nevertheless, the two men began to bond through letters, the growing closeness evident in the changed subscription from 'Gandhi' to 'Bapu' from 1925 onwards; Nehru became dearer to Gandhi as 'Jawahar'. The friendship continued to strengthen even as differences and disagreements grew. Nehru's visit to Europe from 1926 to1927 gave him a maturer understanding of world affairs. His radical views found expression through the resolutions passed at the Madras Congress at his behest. These, however, did not find favour with Gandhi, whose pungent criticism of the Independence Resolution as 'hastily conceived and thoughtlessly passed' caused him deep hurt and much mental anguish.

Regardless, in 1929, when a large majority in the Congress desired that Gandhi should accept the presidentship of the organization for that year, he recommended Nehru for the honour of the 'crown of thorns', saying, '... his being in the chair is as good as my being in it. We may have intellectual differences but our hearts are one. And with all his youthful impetuosities, his sense of stern discipline and loyalty make him an inestimable comrade in whom one can put the most implicit faith.'

It was testing time for Nehru. He signed the Delhi Manifesto, but under moral pressure. Nehru wrote to Gandhi, 'Your appeal to me on the ground of discipline could not be ignored by me. I am myself a believer in discipline. And yet I suppose there can be too much of discipline .... Something seems to have snapped inside me.' Gandhi replied with affectionate concern, 'How shall I console you? Hearing others describe your state, I said to myself, "Have I been guilty of putting undue pressure on you?"... Resist me always when my suggestion does not appeal to your head or heart. I shall not love you the less for that resistance.'

And resist, Nehru did. He found difficulty in coming to terms with Gandhi's reasoning behind some of his actions, as also his concepts, Ramarajya and brahmacharya, for example. He records, 'To some extent I resented Gandhiji's preoccupation with non-political issues, and I could never understand the background of his thought.' He wrote to Gandhi, '... I neither think that the so-called *Rama Raj* was very good in the past, nor do I want it back. I think the western or rather industrial civilization is bound to conquer India, maybe with many changes and adaptations, but nonetheless in the main based in industrialism.'

The inner rebellion notwithstanding, the time had come for him and for the nation to march as one with their leader. 'Salt suddenly became a mysterious word, a word of power.' Gandhi's call to his fellowmen to march to Dandi in protest against the Salt Tax did at first bewilder many—Nehru among them—who could not quite fit in the national struggle with common salt. But Nehru submitted later, 'The young men and women of India were indeed awake and they thundered out their welcome to revolution and the will to do and die. Who could doubt the meaning of this cry? And who was not filled with enthusiasm at this great awakening and resolve?' With rising awe he described the sight of Gandhi marching staff in hand along the dusty roads of Gujarat: 'But the fire of a great resolve is in him, and surpassing love of his miserable countrymen. And love of truth that scorches and love of freedom that inspires.'

None was more aware of the potency of this enormous wave of nationalism that swept across the country than Gandhi himself. Referring to the scepticism that the idea of the march had engendered, he said years later, 'Pandit Motilal Nehru and others did not know what I would do; and I could tell them nothing, as I myself knew nothing about it. But like a flash it came, and ... it was enough to shake the country from one end to the other.'

Arrests followed defiance. Nehru, who overtook his preceptor in getting imprisoned, announced triumphantly, 'I have stolen a march over you.' Prison life for both meant much reading and introspection and fresh plans for the working of the Congress machinery towards freedom. Nehru, whose mind was ever in ferment and whose views were growing increasingly progressive, had little patience with Gandhi's religious and apparently sentimental approach to political issues. And every time Gandhi announced a fast, the younger man was thrown into a state of great mental turmoil. Nehru commented on Gandhi's decision to fast for self-purification and for purging Hinduism of the sceptre of untouchability, with evident chagrin, 'he even seems to suggest that God had indicated the very date of that fast.'

The fast had indeed been prompted by Gandhi's 'Inner Voice', with dramatic suddenness, on 30 April 1933. 'The night I got the inspiration', he was to explain later, 'I had a terrible inner struggle. ... Then, suddenly, ... the Voice came upon me. I listened, made certain that it was the Voice, and the struggle ceased.' Nehru, pitted against this metaphysical struggle, declared in unequivocal terms, 'Not being a man of religion, my interest is largely confined to the social aspect [of untouchability] and to the wider issues involved.'

For Gandhi, the propagation of khadi undoubtedly was pivotal to the national movement, and Nehru had enchanted Gandhi by describing khadi as the 'livery of freedom'. The *takli*, Gandhi's 'twirligig', as journalists lampooned it, had also brought much mental solace to Nehru in jail where he occupied himself daily with spinning, reading and writing. However, this did not alter his position regarding the economics of khadi, holding as he did the view that 'in the ultimate solution of the nation's economic problem', the khadi movement had only a limited place.

Nehru's socialist ideology began to lock horns with Gandhi's firm stand that 'things of fundamental importance to the people are not secured by reason alone, but have to be purchased with their suffering'. Religion to Nehru seemed 'to lead to emotion and sentimentality' which were 'still more unreliable guides'. While one was growing intensely international in his ideas of progress for India, the other continued to be rooted in 'the rock-bottom doctrine of Advaita' which knit his universe in oneness. To Gandhi the estoric path had necessarily to be from the personal to the international and there could be no compromise on the means to the end. Swaraj was to be achieved only through 'Truth and Nonviolence' as embodied in khadi.

Despite their differences, clashes, conflicts and confrontations, at no time did either let the widening rift diminish their respect or love for the other. They extemporized in letters their pain and sorrow over the growing dissonance, but were firm in the belief that together they would carry the nation forward towards freedom.

In September 1934 Gandhi announced his decision to retire from the Congress in a letter to Vallabhbhai Patel, who was then its President. 'After much deliberation and discussions with friends ... I have come to the conclusion that the best interests of the Congress and the nation will be served by my completely severing all official or physical connection with the Congress, including the original membership. ... I miss at this juncture the association and advice of Jawaharlal who is bound to be the rightful helmsman of the organisation in the near future. ... Hence in leaving the organisation I feel that I am in no sense deserting one who is much more than a comrade and whom no amount of political differences will ever separate from me.'

Gandhi's retirement marked outwardly, in Nehru's words, 'the end of a great chapter in Congress and Indian history', though Gandhi continued to guide the decisions and resolutions of the Congress.

The dynamics of the Gandhi-Nehru relationship yielded nothing to the shifts in the political space. There were of course the usual tremors rocking it from time to time. There was discord, for instance, in their perception and reaction to men and matters. In a letter of 1938, Gandhi pointed out to Nehru, 'We seem to be weakening from within. It hurts me that, at this very critical juncture in history, we do not seem to see eye to eye in important matters. I can't tell you how positively lonely I feel to know that nowadays I can't carry you with me. I know that you would do much for affection. But in matters of state there can be no surrender to affection, when the intellect rebels.' Yet, Gandhi would not give up his efforts to understand the rebel. He would expostulate with him, 'Why is it that with all the will in the world I cannot understand what is so obvious to you? I am not, so far as I know, suffering from intellectual decay. Should you not then set your heart on making me understand what you are after?'

The letters no doubt reflect shared thoughts and feelings, their oneness and their individualities. Yet, they also reveal areas where both took care not to tread. Their discussions barely touched on topics such as brahmacharya, God, etc., all of them subjects close to the mind of Gandhi. There was but one occasion when Nehru felt compelled to broach the subject of brahmacharya in a letter, during a controversy surrounding his 'Bapu'. In another letter he wrote, with startling candour, about his deceased wife, 'My conception of marriage and sex may strike you as odd; they certainly differ from yours. ... while I might be irritated with Kamala or quarrel with her, her touch would always thrill me. ... It is rather odd that I should make this confession to anyone, and more especially to you, whose ideas of the relationship between man and woman seem very extraordinary to me.'

Their roles were sometimes reversed. The master never failed to recognize the superior knowledge of the student with regard to international affairs and was ever ready to be guided by him in his own understanding of world events. He wrote to Jawahar in June 1937, 'I wonder if the Spanish bombing and the British are exactly alike? Has the extent of the British damage been known? What has been the ostensible reason given for the British bombing? Don't smile or be angry that I do not know these things as well as you do. I can learn very little from the little I see in the newspapers.'

Gandhi, continuing to repose faith in the indivisibility of their partnership in a great cause, commented in a speech in 1942, 'Jawaharlal has been resisting me ever since he fell into my net. You cannot divide water by repeatedly striking it with a stick. It is just as difficult to divide us.' He further declared, 'Jawaharlal will be my successor. He says that he does not understand my language, and that he speaks a language foreign to me. This may or may not be true. But language is no bar to a union of hearts. And I know this—that when I am gone he will speak the same language.'

This conviction was vindicated when Nehru observed a quarter of a century later during a Lok Sabha debate in December 1963, 'I begin to think more and more of Mahatma Gandhi's approach. It is odd that I am mentioning his name in this connection. I am entirely an admirer of the modern machine, and I want the best machinery and the best techniques, but, taking things as they are in India, however rapidly we advance toward the machine ... the fact remains that large numbers of our people are not touched by it and will not be for a considerable time. Some other method has to be evolved that they become partners in production ...'

The fate of India hung in the balance while the world was in the grip of World War II. The failure of the Cripps Mission necessitated an effective way of not only resisting enemy invasion, but also of wresting freedom from foreign rule. It fell to the lot of Gandhi once again to attempt to change the course of history. 'History,' he had once observed with perspicacity, 'is for the most part a record of armed activities. Natural activities find very little mention in it. Only uncommon activities strike us with wonder.' India had entered yet another phase of a most uncommon activity in her freedom struggle with the launching of the Quit India campaign.

Explaining the origin of this nonviolent strategy to Louis Fischer, Gandhi said, 'My first feeling was, we need an answer to Cripps' failure. What a diabolical thing if the Cripps Mission were without any redeeming feature! Suppose I ask them to go. This idea arose from the crushed hope that had been pretty high in our minds. We had heard good things about Cripps from Jawaharlal and others. Yet the whole mission fell flat. How, I asked myself, am

I to remedy this situation? The presence of the British blocks our way. It was during my Monday of silence that the idea was born in me.' Nehru for his part commented, 'Sir Stafford Cripps meant well for India and hoped to see her free and united. But this was not a matter of individual views or opinions or personal goodwill.'

The book then falls silent for three long years, for the correspondents and their colleagues in the Working Committee had been arrested and imprisoned following the Quit India resolution. When they reopened communication in mid-1945, the rumblings of a serious Hindu–Muslim divide had begun to be felt. Meanwhile, the Muslim League's demand for Partition, ever more strident and insistent, brought Gandhi and Nehru closer, to parley and prepare the country for the inevitable. Nehru commended the proposals to the nation, but with no joy in his heart: '... for generations we have dreamt and struggled for a free and independent united India. The proposals to allow certain parts to secede, if they so will, is painful for any of us to contemplate.'

Gandhi rued the impending doom, baring his soul to Manu Gandhi, his niece, 'I shall perhaps not be alive to witness it, but should the evil I apprehend overtake India and her independence be imperilled, let posterity know what agony this old man went through thinking of it. Let not the coming generations curse Gandhi for being a party to India's vivisection. But everybody is today impatient for Independence. Therefore there is no alternative. This is like eating wooden *laddoos*, if they eat it they die of colic, if they don't they starve.'

Old now and broken in spirit, Gandhi could no longer arrest the tidal wave of events following Partition—death and destruction, and untold human suffering. He prepared to pass the burden of leadership to the younger shoulders of the future Prime Minister of India who, he was confident, would one day come to share his own worldview.

'He fights with me,' he conceded, but, 'because I am there. Whom will he fight when I am gone? And who will suffer his fighting? Ultimately, he will have to speak my language. Even if this does not happen, I would at least die with this faith.' His last letter to Nehru anointing him as 'the Jewel of India' was an affirmation of that faith.

Sardar Vallabhbhai Patel, often described as the 'Iron Man' of India, was Gandhi's other hope for the building of Independent India along with Nehru. But the disaccord between two of his most trusted deputies, whom he saw as the two pillars of democratic India, was a continuing worry for him. With the devout wish of a patriarch eager to see unity in the family between brothers, he would advise Nehru, 'You should not dispense with the Sardar, or he you'.

'He tried but signally failed' was the epitaph Gandhi had scripted for himself long before the journey of his life on earth ended. It was left to the heir to complete the script. Standing alone at the denouement of a holy union, Nehru said of his beloved 'Bapu': 'Even in his death there was a magnificence and complete artistry. It was from every point of view a fitting climax to the man and to the life he had lived.... He died in the fullness of his powers and as he would no doubt have liked to die, at the moment of prayer.'

* * *

The idea for the book was born years ago when we were both associated, one with the project of The Collected Works of Mahatma Gandhi and the other with the Selected Works of Jawaharlal Nehru series. Our fascination with the personae of Gandhi and Nehru, our individual heroes, had since been growing. The uniqueness of their relationship became a subject of obsessive interest to us. The paradox and the drama inherent in it—the unity in their polarity—was a constant topic of discussion between us. Distance, we saw, lent it more clarity, and there were lessons in it for the twenty-first century. And then one day we decided to act upon it. The end in sight was to create an exclusive epistolary space that would help throw new light on two eminent men of history—on the intersection of their lives, and the ignition of their minds, each by the other.

The correspondence, admittedly, is discontinuous in parts. The main reason for this is that both leaders served frequent, and sometimes long, terms in prison. Some letters were lost, some others destroyed, some fell into the censor's net, and some were eaten by termites, as Nehru himself explains in his preface to the

*A Bunch of Old Letters*: 'On return from a long period in prison, I often found that termites and other insects had made a feast of many of my papers.'

Given this, not all the major forces at work during the pre-Independence era, nor all the prominent leaders of the time, find mention in the pages.

The collection largely from printed sources is supplemented with additional material from the Nehru Archives that fell our way, as it were, by sheer serendipity. The Pyarelal Collection, which has yielded a considerable number of unpublished letters had just been classified and made accessible. The volume encapsulates all available correspondence between Gandhi and Nehru to unfold a tale, told in their own words.

For the completion of this work, our thanks go to the Director of the Nehru Memorial Museum and Library, Mridula Mukherjee, who lent us institutional support for the research that went into the making of this volume. Thanks are also due to Bhashyam Kasturi, and the staff of the Library and the Manuscript Section for their help in conducting our passage through the Archives, and equally to the research staff of the Jawaharlal Nehru Memorial Fund for their unfailing help and support throughout. We would like to say a big 'Thank You' to Gita Parameswaran for her patient assistance at the keyboard. Our special thanks go to the editorial team at Oxford University Press for their perseverance in ensuring that the book saw the light of day.

March 2011 UMA IYENGAR & LALITHA ZACKARIAH

# Note to the Reader

In collecting material for the book, no effort has been spared in obtaining every extant letter exchanged between Gandhi and Nehru. Our sources are the volumes of The Collected Works of Mahatma Gandhi and Selected Works of Jawaharlal Nehru, Pyarelal Collection and Jawaharlal Nehru Papers in the Nehru Memorial Museum and Library, and *A Bunch of Old Letters* (Revised Edition, 2005).

With regard to annotations bearing Collected Works of Mahatma Gandhi volume references, there is a possibility of a one-page discrepancy, here and there, between page numbers referred to and those in the editions consulted by the reader. This has been unavoidable as only available editions of the volumes were used at various stages of research. It is however, pointed out that the Revised Edition of the volumes was never used, either for extraction or for research and reference.

The section of Appendices carries matter referred to in the text, generally as enclosure, and which is not easy of access. For all other background information, readily available sources have been indicated in the annotations wherever possible.

Non-English words are in italics at their first occurrence. Names of sources, organizations, etc., have been supplied in full in the first instance and abbreviated subsequently.

Names of places as they were used in the pre-Independence times have been retained. Variant spellings of names of persons and places have been retained as in the original.

## 1. Telegram to M.K. Gandhi

Allahabad
9 May 1921

Das[1] wires from Chandpur impossible leaving. Chandpur situation critical having important bearing on all India movement.[2] Case of general noncooperation and not labour strike. Matter not settling soon. Must be placed before Working Committee meeting. Pray adjourn or hold another Committee meeting about twenty-first June Calcutta. If meeting Working Committee inconvenient have small sub-committee appointed to meet Calcutta. Pray no big question should be settled in ignorance of situation here. Have important

[1] Chittaranjan Das (1870–1925); leading barrister of Calcutta; joined the Indian National Congress, 1906; with Motilal Nehru formed the Swaraj Party within the Congress in 1922 to contest elections; President, INC, 1922

[2] In 1919 a very large number of agricultural labourers from Gorakhpur and other districts of eastern United Provinces (UP) migrated to the tea gardens of Lower Assam due to scarcity conditions in their own districts. However, the employment situation in the tea gardens deteriorated with the Depression immediately after World War I, and many retrenched workers began to return home in 1921. By the beginning of May 1921, large numbers had collected at Chandpur, a transit point near the borders of Assam. The plantation owners, worried by this great exodus, sought to enlist both official and non-official assistance to prevent this large-scale migration. C.R. Das, C.F. Andrews and other leaders who had gone to Chandpur to help the workers were accused of instigating labour strikes. The local authorities tried to prevent the labourers from leaving Assam and even ordered troops to prevent them from boarding the steamers.

proposals to make.[3] Father[4] unwell in Almora. Unable to go Bombay.

Jawaharlal

Selected Works of Jawaharlal Nehru, *Volume 1, I Series, p. 173*

## 2. Telegram to M.K. Gandhi

Allahabad
17 May 1921

Chittaranjandas wires coolie difficulty matter of finance. Provincial Congress Committee ruled Tilak[5] Fund cannot be spent for this.[6] Wire advice Calcutta. Have accordingly wired Bengal committee suggesting advance necessary funds subject to Working Committee's decision about allocation. Wire further instructions if necessary.

Nehru

SWJN, *Vol. 1, I Series, p. 173*

[3] Nehru, who played an important part in organizing the noncooperation movement in UP, his home province, was not prepared to recommend a no-tax campaign in Allahabad city until the other items of noncooperation had been completed. He believed that this could not be carried out properly without consulting their leaders.

[4] Motilal Nehru (1861–1931); lawyer, Allahabad; President, INC, 1919 and 1928; leader of the Swaraj Party in the Central Assembly, 1924–6

[5] Bal Gangadhar Tilak (1856–1920); teacher, social reformer and freedom fighter; was conferred the honorary title of 'Lokamanya', which means 'Accepted by the people (as their leader)'

On his death on 1 August 1920, Gandhi had said that 'no man preached the gospel of swaraj with the consistency and the insistence of Lokamanya' and that Tilak who had proclaimed 'Swaraj is my birthright', had hoped to see it 'fully established during his lifetime. ... he certainly brought it nearer by many a year.'

[6] The Congress, in its annual session at Nagpur on 26 December 1920, had resolved to set up the All India Tilak Memorial Swaraj Fund. On 31 March 1921, the All India Congress Committee meeting at Bombay decided upon a target of one crore rupees for the Fund.

## 3. Letter to Jawaharlal Nehru[7]

Bardoli
19 February 1922

My dear Jawaharlal,
I see that all of you are terribly cut up over the resolutions of the Working Committee.[8] I sympathise with you, and my heart goes out to Father. I can picture to myself the agony through which he must have passed but I also feel that this letter is unnecessary because I know that the first shock must have been followed by a true understanding of the situation. Let us not be obsessed by Devdas's[9] youthful indiscretions. It is quite possible that the poor boy has been swept off his feet and that he has lost his balance, but the brutal murder of the constables by an infuriated crowd which was in sympathy with noncooperation cannot be denied. Nor can it be denied that it was a politically-minded crowd. It would have been criminal not to have heeded such a clear warning.

I must tell you that this was the last straw. My letter[10] to the Viceroy was not sent without misgivings, as its language must make it clear to anyone. I was much disturbed by the Madras doings, but I drowned the warning voice.[11] I received letters both from Hindus and Mohammedans from Calcutta, Allahabad and the Punjab, all these before the Gorakhpur incident, telling me that

[7] This was sent to Nehru, in Lucknow jail, through his sister, Vijayalakshmi Pandit. Nehru had been arrested on 6 December 1921, his first imprisonment, for participating in the Volunteer Movement and urging the boycott of the visit of the Prince of Wales to India. He was released in March 1922.

[8] In February 1922, at Chauri Chaura, a village in Gorakhpur district in UP, an angry mob set fire to a police station, killing 22 constables. Following the incident, Gandhi called off the Civil Disobedience movement. Resolutions were passed at the Congress Working Committee meetings at Bardoli on 11 and 12 February 1922. See *CWMG*, Vol. XXII, pp. 337–81.

[9] Devdas Gandhi (1900–1957); youngest son of Gandhi; editor, *The Hindustan Times*, 1939–57

[10] Of 1 February 1922 to Lord Reading, the then Viceroy and Governor-General of India

[11] Gandhi's article 'Hooliganism in Madras', *Young India*, 19-1-1922, condemned disturbances during the hartal observed in Madras on 13 January 1922, to boycott the visit of the Prince of Wales.

the wrong was not all on the Government side, that our people were becoming aggressive, defiant and threatening, that they were getting out of hand and were not nonviolent in demeanour. Whilst the Ferozepur Jirka incident[12] is discreditable to the Government, we are not altogether without blame. Hakimji[13] complained about Bareilly. I have bitter complaints about Jajjar. In Shahajanpur too there has been a forcible attempt to take possession of the Town Hall. From Kanouj too the Congress Secretary himself telegraphed saying that the volunteer boys had become unruly and were picketing a High School and preventing youngsters under 16 from going to the school. 36,000 volunteers were enlisted in Gorakhpur, not 100 of whom conformed to the Congress Pledge.[14] In Calcutta Jamnalalji[15] tells me there is utter disorganisation, the volunteers wearing foreign cloth and certainly not pledged to nonviolence. With all this news in my possession and much more from the South, the Chauri Chaura news came like a powerful match to ignite the gunpowder, and there was a blaze. I assure you that if the thing had not been suspended we would have been leading not a nonviolent struggle but essentially a violent struggle. It is undoubtedly true that nonviolence is spreading like the scent of the otto of roses throughout the length and breadth of the land, but the foetid smell of violence is still powerful, and it would be unwise to ignore or underrate it. The cause will prosper by this retreat. The movement had unconsciously

[12] Of shooting on 23 December 1921

[13] Hakim Ajmal Khan (1865–1927); physician and politician who took a leading part in the Khilafat Movement; President, INC, 1921

[14] Based on the resolution of the Working Committee at Bombay on 23 November 1921. It was enjoined upon every volunteer to take the pledge to become a member of the National Volunteer Corps. The declaration of the pledge in essence read as follows: 'So long as I remain in any volunteer organisation I shall faithfully and diligently carry out all the instructions received from my superiors. I shall observe the pledge of nonviolence in words and in deed and shall inculcate the spirit of nonviolence amongst others. I shall regard the pledge as binding upon me so long as the policy of nonviolence is continued by the nation. I shall run all risks attendant upon the performance of my duty.'

[15] Seth Jamnalal Bajaj (1889–1942); wealthy financier and close associate of Gandhi; Congress treasurer for many years

drifted from the right path. We have come back to our moorings, and we can again go straight ahead. You are in as disadvantageous a position as I am advantageously placed for judging events in their due proportion.

May I give you my own experience of South Africa? We had all kinds of news brought to us in South Africa in our jails. For two or three days during my first experience[16] I was glad enough to receive tit-bits, but I immediately realised the utter futility of interesting myself in this illegal gratification. I could do nothing, I could send no message profitably, and I simply vexed my soul uselessly. I felt that it was impossible for me to guide the movement from the jail. I therefore simply waited till I could meet those who were outside and talk to them freely, and then too I want you to believe me when I tell you that I took only an academic interest because I felt it was not my province to judge anything, and I saw how unerringly right I was. I well remember how the thoughts I had up to the time of my discharge from the jail on every occasion were modified immediately after discharge and after getting first-hand information myself. Somehow or other the jail atmosphere does not allow you to have all the bearings in your mind. I would therefore like you to dismiss the outer world from your view altogether and ignore its existence. I know this is a most difficult task, but if you take up some serious study and some serious manual work you can do it. Above all, whatever you do, don't you be disgusted with the spinning-wheel. You and I might have reason to get disgusted with ourselves for having done many things and having believed many things, but we shall never have the slightest cause for regret that we have pinned our faith to the spinning-wheel or that we have spun so much good yarn per day in the name of the motherland. You have *Song Celestial* with you. I cannot give you the inimitable translation[17] of Edwin Arnold,[18] but this is the rendering of the Sanskrit text. 'There is no waste of energy, there is no destruction in this. Even a little of this dharma saves one from many a pitfall.'

[16] In January 1908. For Gandhi's book *Satyagraha in South Africa*, see *CWMG*, Vol. XXIX, pp. 1–269.

[17] Of the Bhagavad Gita

[18] Sir Edwin Arnold (1832–1904); an English poet and journalist

'This dharma' in the original refers to Karma Yoga, and the Karma Yoga of our age is the spinning-wheel. I want a cheering letter from you after the freezing dose you have sent me through Pyarelal.[19]

Yours sincerely,
M.K. Gandhi

Collected Works of Mahatma Gandhi, *Vol. XXII, pp. 435–7*

## 4. Letter to Jawaharlal Nehru

[12][20] March 1924

Panikkar[21] first class MA Oxford sometime professor Muslim University is free to replace Gidwani.[22] Is here now. Mahomedali[23] knows him well. Needs three months salary advance. Will need 100 monthly three months personal expenses which later may be deducted from fourth month at rate 100 monthly. Will require travelling expenses Amritsar. Wire Andheri if required.

Gandhi

CWMG, *Supplementary Vol. I, p. 263*

[19] Pyarelal Nayar (1899–1982); brother of Dr Sushila Nayyar; joined the noncooperation movement as a student, worked with Gandhi, and became his private secretary after the death of Mahadev Desai in 1942; author of *Mahatma Gandhi: The Last Phase*

[20] Inferred from Nehru's reply dated 12 March 1924

[21] K.M. Panikkar (1895–1963); historian and diplomat; Ambassador to China, USA and France; Member, States' Reorganisation Commission

His name was recommended for taking charge of the Akali Sahayak Bureau at Amritsar, and for editing *Onward*, the official organ of the Akalis.

[22] A.T. Gidwani (1891–1935); educationist from Gujarat; Principal of Gujarat Vidyapith for many years; had been arrested with Nehru at Nabha in 1923

[23] Maulana Mohammad Ali (1871–1931); younger brother of Shaukat Ali; journalist and politician; led the Khilafat delegation to England, 1920; President, INC, Cocanada Congress, 1923

Writing about the Ali brothers, Gandhi said, 'Mohammad Ali is his brother's alter ego. I have not seen such implicit faithfulness to an elder brother. ... He has reasoned out for himself that there is no salvation for India without Hindu–Muslim unity. Their pan-Islamism is not anti-Hindu.'

## 5. Letter to M.K. Gandhi

Allahabad
12 March 1924

My dear Bapuji,

I received your telegram late this evening on my return home. It was a great pleasure to hear from you again after such a long time. I have not dared to intrude by another visit or by letter during your convalescence.[24] But your telegram emboldens me.

I have just wired to you in reply[25] and have also sent a telegram to Mohamad Ali.[26] I did not wish to trouble him so soon after his bereavement but I thought it was due to him to know about your telegram.

I have known Panikkar by repute for several years and I met him for a short time in Cocanada. I am sure his presence will be very useful in Amritsar. His ignorance of Hindustani will be a drawback but this will be more than compensated by his other attainments. He will be an excellent man for publicity work. Perhaps, owing to his language difficulty, he might not be very helpful in bringing the Sikhs and Hindus nearer to each other. But on the whole Panikkar will be an acquisition in Amritsar.

As regards terms, anything that you consider reasonable will surely be agreed to by all others. Technically the Working Committee appoints but the Committee will not meet till the 21st April. The terms suggested in your telegram are rather complicated but that is for you to decide. I am glad to notice that Panikkar contemplates a lengthy stay at Amritsar. Personally I doubt if it will be necessary for him to stay for many months. There is just a possibility of Gidwani coming out sooner and an equal possibility of Gidwani's successor going in. Of course Panikkar will not unnecessarily invite jail, but neither did Gidwani.

[24] Gandhi had been operated upon for appendicitis at Sassoon Hospital, Poona, on 12 January 1924. He was convalescing at Narottam Morarji's Juhu residence in Bombay from 11 March.

[25] Not available

[26] Mohammad Ali's daughter Amina had died on 11 March 1924.

Owing to Joseph's[27] inability to go I requested the Punjab Provincial Congress Committee to make temporary arrangements to carry on the work at Amritsar. Only this morning I heard from them that they had appointed a certain gentleman, whom I do not know, to take charge of the work. This was of course a temporary arrangement only.

If Panikkar decided to go to Amritsar and if it is not inconvenient for him, he might spend a day here on his way up. Perhaps I might be able to give him some useful information. I shall be away from the 15th to the 20th.

With regards,

Yours affectionately,
Jawaharlal Nehru

SWJN, *Vol. 2, I Series, pp. 144–5*

## 6. Letter to Jawaharlal Nehru

Post Andheri
15 March 1924

My dear Jawaharlal,

I have your letter, and I had your and Mohamed Ali's telegrams regarding Panikkar. Your letter embarrasses me a little. I have not intended, nor do I intend now to form any decided opinion about making appointments, fixing salaries, etc. As I shared Joseph's opinion that he should be by his wife's side when she was so much troubled, and as the Sikh friends who came to see me seemed to be very anxious to have a substitute for Gidwani, a substitute who could also edit their paper *Onward*, I was on the look-out for one. They wanted Sundaram[28] who used to be on the *Independent*[29] and suggested that he could do both the things—publicity and editing. On my arrival at the retreat near Andheri, I saw Panikkar who had

[27] George Joseph (1897–1938); barrister of Madurai; editor, *Young India* and *Independent*; took part in Vaikom Satyagraha; left Congress, 1924, and rejoined in 1935. He was at Chengannur during this period by the side of his ailing wife.

[28] V.A. Sundaram

[29] Daily newspaper started by Motilal Nehru at Allahabad, and closed in 1923

come to see Mr Andrews[30] in order to discuss the advisability of an offer that was made to him by the *Indian Daily Mail.* He had hesitation in accepting the offer because the *Mail* politics were not his. I then thought of the publicity work and asked Panikkar whether he would shoulder the burden, and as I did not know him well, I consulted Mr Andrews too, and when Panikkar was prepared to go to Amritsar if you wanted him and as Mr Andrews thought he would make a very good substitute for Gidwani, I wired. But I had no desire that you should be influenced in any way by the wire because it was from me. If I was well and could acquaint myself with all the details, I should certainly have given my advice and opinion as to the selection, but for the present beyond interesting myself in the few things in which I must, I really do not want to tax my energy.

With reference to the salary the position was this. Panikkar was in the *Swarajya*[31] office at Rs 700 per month, but as the paper is not self-supporting, it has not been able to pay him a few months' salary. He left it because he could not hit it off with Mr Srinivasa Iyengar.[32] He has to discharge a debt of Rs 900 in Madras. He needs Rs 300 per month. I therefore thought that if he was paid Rs 900 in advance, he could discharge the debt and proceed to Amritsar. He would still want his expenses (to be met) at Amritsar. For this Rs 100 monthly should be paid to him by way of loan. At the end of 3 months' service, therefore, he will be owing to the Congress Rs 300. This may again be deducted from his salary at the rate of Rs 100 per month. That means that he has to serve for 6 months in order to discharge the loan he would be receiving. I am now perturbed because I gather from your letter that he may not be wanted for that length of time. I would not like to be the instrument

[30] Charles Freer Andrews (1871–1940); British missionary, who came to India in 1904 as a member of the Cambridge Brotherhood; worked closely with Rabindranath Tagore and Gandhi; honoured as 'Deenabandhu' (friend of the poor).

[31] Official organ of the Swaraj Party

[32] S. Srinivasa Iyengar (1874–1941); Advocate-General of Madras who resigned in 1920 and joined the Congress; deputy leader, Swaraj Party, in the Central Legislative Assembly; President, Guwahati Congress, 1926; resigned from Congress in 1930

of useless expense to the Congress. I propose, therefore, to place the whole situation before Panikkar, and he will probably agree that if his services are dispensed with before 6 months, he should be liable for the unpaid balance of the loan. He is not here at the present moment, or I should have sent you a more decisive letter.

I do not feel that you would want me, if it was possible, to cancel the engagement with Panikkar and am therefore letting it stand and sending him to Amritsar tomorrow. In accordance with your latest telegram, he will be going direct to Amritsar. Please authorise the Treasurer to reimburse to me the amount that I shall be paying Panikkar.

Indeed, if I was minded to influence you, I should ask you to reconsider the question of each appointment for two reasons: (1) Should the Congress spend money on non-Congress work? (2) What should be the maximum the Congress should pay its servants?

So much for business. My wound is completely healed, but the affected part is yet tender and requires care and attention. The seaside convalescence is likely to suit me. I propose, if all goes well, to stop here for 3 months. During the time I shall be doing as much writing work as I can and conferring with the leaders upon the Council-entry, etc.[33] Father, Hakimji and others are expected here by the end of the month. You need not hesitate to come down for consultation whenever you wish. I expect in any event to see you on the 20th prox. as I understand the Working Committee meets on that date. I do hope you are keeping well and taking care of yourself.

[33] After week-long discussions, from 29 March to 5 April 1924 in Bombay, with Motilal Nehru, Lajpat Rai and other Swarajist leaders, Gandhi formulated his stand on the question of Council-entry, which to sum up in his words was 'an utter waste of time. I would enter the Councils only if I believed that I could make use of them for the advancement of the country.'

For Gandhi's draft statement of 11 April 1924 regarding Council-entry, see *CWMG*, Vol. XXIII, pp. 414–18; for Motilal Nehru's response rebutting Gandhi's arguments against Council-entry, ibid., Appendix XIV.

Panikkar has seen this letter and he will hold himself ready to be relieved whenever you think it necessary and would be liable for repayment of the loan.

Yours sincerely,

CWMG, *Vol. XXII, pp. 254–6*

## 7. Letter to Jawaharlal Nehru

Sabarmati
27 July 1924

My dear Jawaharlal,
In my opinion, you should enter into correspondence with the Government and ascertain the reason for the prohibition and say that, if anything can be pointed out to the committee as really objectionable, your committee would be prepared to delete the passages.[34] If the Government returns an unsatisfactory reply, you should intimate to them that the words will not be withdrawn from circulation.

The Government are not likely to bother the children and, even if they do, the only thing they can do is to remove the books from the children. The latter may be advised then not to mind and hand over the books to the police. I do not think there is any other penalty. Please look up the law and let me know. I feel that no matter

[34] On 15 July 1924, the UP Government had issued a notice proscribing Pandit Ramdas Gour's Hindi Reader Nos. III, IV, V and VI as seditious and in breach of Section 124 A of the Penal Code. Gandhi wrote in *YI*, 31-7-1924, under the subtitle 'School Books Proscribed', 'I have taken the trouble of going through the contents of the volumes. They appear to me to be perfectly harmless, i.e., from the Government standpoint. ... the conclusion is irresistible that the Government do not like the growing popularity of the readers and are seeking by questionable methods to favour its protégés whose readers may have suffered a check in competition with Professor Ramdas Gour's. ... I invite the Government of the United Provinces to tender to the public full reason for its decision. ... I advise too the president of the committee to ask the Government to state its reasons and offer to advise Professor Gour to amend his books or withdraw them from circulation if the committee is satisfied of the justness of the Government decision.' The UP Congress challenged the Government to specify the passages that were objectionable.

how much we may have become demoralised, we may not shirk a battle that may be given to us. We need not take up aggressive civil disobedience, we may not take up mass civil disobedience; but we must face that which comes our way and tests us. Don't you think so? How to give battle will be a question for you to decide as the situation develops.

Yours sincerely,
M.K. Gandhi

[PS]
Pray do not worry about my health. It is all right and answers my purpose. You must be resourceful enough to mend the charkha. For the handle all you need is an iron inset. Wood always noncooperates with iron and gives in. Immediately you fix in an iron ring, you will find it will work all right. Please note that mere nails will not do. No part of the handle should have friction with the iron axle.

Yours,
MKG

CWMG, *Vol. XXIV, pp. 460–1*

## 8. Letter to Jawaharlal Nehru

6 September 1924

My dear Jawaharlal,
I have your wire.[35] I had heard from Father already. I am so sorry. I thought I was writing a harmless letter showing the depth of my feeling....[36]

I have therefore implored Father to let me have his views on the merits of the proposal.[37] I have discussed it with many friends

[35] Not available

[36] Omissions in the letter are as in the source.

[37] The situation with regard to the position of the Swarajists in the Congress was complex. The orthodox party in the Congress known as the No-changers wanted the original noncooperation programme of the Congress to be scrupulously adhered to, whereas the Swarajists had adopted a programme of obstruction from within the Councils. After the AICC meeting in June 1924, 'a tug of war' had developed between the two sections for control of the Congress.

among the Swarajists. I can see no other honourable solution of the difficulty. Please tell me what you think about it.

The Nabha answer is from its own standpoint conclusive. The only answer that can be returned is to take up the challenge to be arrested.[38] In the present state of things it seems to be unwise. The best thing, therefore, is to be silent and wait for better times ... I have your very prompt report on Amethi.[39] It makes very painful reading. I do not know what to do. I have sent Shuaib[40] and Kristodas[41] to Gulbarga also privately to ascertain facts. Do please go to Nabha as soon as you can. You may take Hayat and Moazzam. They should

---

Gandhi issued a statement on 31 August 1924 which said, 'I have resolved that there should be no opposition from me either at the Belgaum Congress (26–27 December 1924) or before that, so as to divide the country. I have already told Pandit Motilal Nehru that my attitude was of perfect surrender, because we have become a house completely divided.' For Gandhi's letter of 30 August to Motilal Nehru proposing alterations in the Congress Constitution see *CWMG*, Vol. XXV, pp. 53–5.

[38] Gandhi wrote in *YI*, 11-9-1924, '... Pandit Jawaharlal wrote to the administrator of Nabha on the 25th July telling him that he knew nothing of any conditions being applied to his, Acharya Gidwani's and Pandit Santhanam's discharge before the expiry of their sentence. It has taken the administrator 27 days to send the following reply: "... you are under a misapprehension with regard to the meaning of the word 'suspension'. The suspension of a sentence obviously implies conditions. If this were not the case and if your argument was sound, the suspension of a sentence without the mention of any conditions would be equivalent to remission which is obviously incorrect."

It is all very well to lecture to Jawaharlal on the meaning of the word "suspension". Unfortunately for the Administrator however the Pandit did not ask him to tell him what the word "suspension" meant but he wanted to know why he was not told of the conditions of his discharge. Is not a prisoner entitled to know the conditions of his discharge upon "suspension" of his sentence? May the Administrator be also informed that a remission may also carry conditions?'

[39] A large village about 20 miles from Lucknow where communal riots had taken place

[40] Shuaib Qureshi, Editor, *New Era*; also of *Young India* during Gandhi's imprisonment in 1922

[41] Krishnadas, whom Gandhi addressed as Kristodas, had been his secretary in 1922, and wrote *Seven Months with Gandhi*. Gandhi wrote of him elsewhere, 'Kristodas is a yogi. With him I think I am in good company. His modesty, calm thoughtfulness and seriousness are qualities of a high order.'

know the place. As M. has not been able to make headway it is difficult to try anything regarding any movement. I am here at least till Monday.

Yours sincerely,
M.K. Gandhi

CWMG, *Vol. XXV, p. 98*

## 9. Letter to M.K. Gandhi

Allahabad
12 September 1924

Respected Bapuji,
I returned from Sambhal[42] yesterday and am sending you two copies of the report prepared there. I received your letter yesterday. I have also received your telegram and am replying to it separately. It would have been better had Mohamad Ali or Hayat come to Sambhal with me, but I just forgot about them. I had taken Badruzzaman[43] with me. He is related to Khaliquzzaman.[44] He was quite helpful.

Lucknow is in a bad state and every day the tension is increasing. Some talks to secure an agreement are proceeding and I hear that the Amethi Mohamadans are prepared to apologise to the Hindus. But this alone will probably not satisfy the Hindus. Some people have asked me to go and arrange a compromise, but I have no desire to do so and I have refused to go point blank. Whom would I represent? The Hindus are not going to accept me, and why should the Muslims do so?

Yours obediently,
Jawaharlal

SWJN, *Vol. 2, I Series, p. 169*

[42] A town in Moradabad district where in a population of 50,000, two-thirds were Muslim. In 1924, the annual fair coincided with the Mohurram festival and sparked off communal rioting. Nehru and Sheikh Badruzzaman visited the town to report on the cause and nature of the riots.

[43] Sheikh Badruzzaman of Barabanki district; joined the noncooperation movement in 1920

[44] Chaudhuri Khaliquzzaman (1889–1973); friend of Nehru and a prominent member of the Congress in the UP till 1937 when he joined the Muslim League

## 10. Letter to Jawaharlal Nehru

15 September 1924

My dear Jawaharlal,

I have your most touching personal letter.[45] You will stand it all bravely I know. Father is just now in an irritable mood. And I am most anxious that neither you nor I should contribute an iota to the irritation. If it is at all possible you should have a frank chat with him and avoid such action as may offend him. It makes me unhappy to find him unhappy. His irritability is a sure sign of his unhappiness. Hasrat[46] was here today and I find from him that even my proposal about spinning by every Congressman ruffles him. I do so feel like retiring from the Congress and doing the three things quietly.[47] They are enough to occupy more than all the true men and women we can get. But even that ruffles people. I had a long chat with the Poorna Swarajists. They will not agree to spin and they will not agree to my leaving the Congress. They do not realise that I shall cease to be useful as soon as I cease to be myself. It is a wretched situation but I do not despair. My faith is in God. I know only the moment's duty.[48] It is given to me to know no more. Why then should I worry?

Shall I try to arrange for some money for you? Why may you not take up remunerative work? After all you must live by the sweat of your brow even though you may be under Father's roof. Will

[45] Not available. Nehru however observes in his prefatory note to the letter in *A Bunch of Old Letters*: 'I had written to Gandhiji and said that I was unhappy to be a financial burden on my father and wanted to stand on my own feet. The difficulty was that I was a whole-time worker of the Congress. My father when he heard of this was greatly annoyed.'

[46] Maulana Hasrat Mohani (1875–1951); poet, scholar and ardent nationalist; founded the Urdu paper *Urdu-e-Mualla*, President, Muslim League, 1921; Member, Constituent Assembly

[47] Gandhi had written on 2 August 1924 to Motilal Nehru, 'I have no interest in anything but promoting a peaceful atmosphere, khaddar and Hindu-Muslim unity and removal of untouchability.'

[48] Gandhi finally 'surrendered' to the Swarajists signing a joint statement with them on 6 November 1924, greatly relieved to have come out of the 'whirlpool of doubt regarding my duty'. For the Joint Statement see *CWMG*, Vol. XXV, pp. 288–9; also pp. 310–14.

you be correspondent to some newspapers? Or will you take up a professorship?

Yours sincerely,
M.K. Gandhi

CWMG, *Vol. XXV, pp. 148–9*

## 11. Letter to Jawaharlal Nehru

17 September 1924

My dear Jawaharlal,
Please tell the Gorakhpur Committee[49] that I dare not make any appointments at present. I am glad the 'mahatma' is out of our minds.[50] Can you give concrete instances of Mussalmans having objected to *chamars*? Do they allow other Hindus?

Yours sincerely,
M.K. Gandhi

Gandhi-Nehru Correspondence, JN Papers, *Nehru Memorial Museum and Library*

## 12. Letter to Jawaharlal Nehru

19 September 1924

My dear Jawarlal [*sic*],
You must not be stunned.[51] Rather rejoice that God gives strength and direction to do my duty. I could not do otherwise. As the author of noncooperation a heavy responsibility lies on my shoulders. Do give me in writing your impressions of Lucknow and Cawnpore. Let me drink the cup to the full. I am quite at peace with myself.

Yours sincerely,
M.K. Gandhi

CWMG, *Vol. XXV, p. 180*

[49] For the Provincial Conference for which Nehru was to go on 29 October 1924. See pp. 28–9.

[50] On 31 August 1924 while speaking at Excelsior Theatre, Bombay, Gandhi had expressed his aversion for the prefix 'Mahatma' and had appealed to the public not to address him thus. He said, 'the word "Mahatma" stinks in my nostrils. ... in the Ashram where I live, every child, brother and sister has orders not to use the word ....'

[51] Gandhi had begun a twenty-one day fast for Hindu-Muslim unity on 18 September 1924. See *CWMG*, Vol. XXV, pp. 171–2.

## 13. Letter to M.K. Gandhi

Allahabad
19 October 1924

My dear Bapuji,
I must apologise for the delay in writing to you. I have hastily scribbled some impressions and enclose them. I have not had time to re-read them or to complete them.

I have had a telegram from Nagpur asking me to go over there but I feel I must not leave Allahabad.[52] Besides I have fever today and father will not let me go for some little time.

Yours,
Jawaharlal

*Confidential*

### Some Impressions of the Disturbances at Allahabad

I have delayed writing a report on the Allahabad disturbances as I have so far been unable to form a clear idea of the occurrences as a whole. A large number of incidents happened almost simultaneously in various parts of the city and it is by no means easy to arrange them in proper order or to understand their sequence. I have also had to give a great deal of my time to activities, other than conducting an enquiry, connected with the recent troubles. My close connection with Allahabad has been more of a hindrance to me than a help and I have had to move warily in order to prevent harm resulting from some of my activities. To mention an instance, I arrived in Allahabad on the 10th afternoon and went immediately from the station to the city where I wandered about till 6.30 p.m., the curfew hour. I saw a number of shopkeepers and they suggested that we should take steps to have the big shops opened from the next morning. I welcomed the proposal and arranged a meeting of the Hindu shopkeepers for the next morning. I was told that the shopkeepers did not want to open their shops in

[52] The local leaders had sent telegrams to Gandhi, Nehru and other leaders asking them to visit the area following an outbreak of communal riots in Nagpur and Kamptee.

obedience to the directions of the authorities but a hint from us might be acted upon. The proposed meting of shopkeepers however fell through and hardly anyone turned up. I found that the idea that my advent should be followed by a quick opening of shops was not liked by some people and they succeeded in influencing the shopkeepers. As a result of this and one or two other causes the main shops did not open till the 13th. It is possible that if I had remained away in Delhi for another day or two the shops might have opened earlier.

The idea of our carrying an enquiry also somehow jarred on the nerves of many—both Hindus and Muslims—perhaps as each party thought that we would take up an attitude antagonistic to it. Dr Syed Mahmud[53] kindly broke his journey here on his way back from Delhi and spent 4 or 5 days in Allahabad. He is in perhaps a better position than I am to form definite conclusions about some aspects of the troubles. But even he was handicapped. There is a proposal now that a joint and detailed enquiry should take place on behalf of both communities. This proposal has made it difficult for us to prejudge the issues. As a matter of fact I have had to change my own conclusions in regard to many incidents several times as fresh information came in, and I am not prepared to say that I will not again change them in the light of fresh facts. These impressions should therefore be treated as impressions only liable to change even in material particulars. Dr Mahmud has now gone to Nagpur but I understand that he will also put down his impressions of the occurrences here. In view of these facts it will perhaps be desirable to keep these reports confidential for the present at least.

Both the communities are wholly and honestly convinced that the other is almost entirely in the wrong. Each accuses the other of premeditation and careful preparation, and each points to the almost simultaneous outbreaks in various parts of the city on the evening of the 7th in proof of their contention that the other

[53] Syed Mahmud (1889-1971); a contemporary of Nehru at Cambridge and a barrister of the Patna High Court; joined the noncooperation movement in 1921; General Secretary, Khilafat Movement and the Congress; Minister in Bihar, 1937-9 and 1946-52; Minister of External Affairs, 1954-7

organised them. There is an extraordinary ignorance of the other's viewpoint and losses, and hence both at present court an enquiry.

The troubles started on the night of the 7th October (the *Dussehra* day) and continued on the 8th & 9th. From the 10th onwards, there has been no disturbance of the peace, except an incident relating to a temple in Katghar (a *mohalla* of Allahabad) which took place on the early morning of the 10th.

The contributory causes here have been the same as elsewhere—*Sangathan* and *Aligol*, separate *akharas*—and the deliberate preaching of distrust and fear. The local Hindu Sabha consists of a number of narrow-minded persons with little ability or power even to organise the Hindus but able enough to increase the dislike of the Musalmans. Muslims are very poor in their leaders. There are hardly any with whom one can discuss such matters on an intellectual level. Their most prominent leader is Mr Vilayat Husain.[54] Hindus are very bitter against him and imagine that he is at the back of everything. As a matter of fact I doubt his capacity to do much. He is a timid person often used as a tool by unscrupulous persons, but I do not think he is bad at heart. I have been favourably impressed by him during the last few days.

Soon after the *Janma Ashtami* there is *Datkanda* procession. This used to be an insignificant affair but latterly it has assumed some importance. The Mohamadans say that this year it was celebrated on a large scale and many lathis were exhibited. This is possible, but nonetheless it did not create any excitement in the city. I was in Allahabad at the time and I did not even know of the procession and heard of it for the first time a fortnight or more after it had taken place.

The *Chehlum* was to follow this and there were rumours of trouble. Admittedly large numbers of Mohamadans were sent for from the adjoining villages to swell the procession and display lathis, swords, etc., because it was said that the Hindus had done something similar on the occasion of the Datkanda. Just a few days before the Chehlum a few Hindus and Muslims met and decided to issue a joint appeal and also arranged that Hindus should accompany the Chehlum procession and Muslims the Ram Lila

[54] A leading Congressman of Allahabad

procession. This had a quietening effect and the Hindu Sabha eventually agreed to it. Quite a large number of prominent Hindus including the president and members of the Hindu Sabha took part in the Chehlum procession and everything passed off successfully—the procession ending with speeches and mutual congratulations. The procession itself was a long one with a great crowd of *lathiwalas* and a fair sprinkling of swords, spears, daggers, etc. Almost every Mohamadan thought it his duty to bring some weapon and it was ludicrous to see the very old and the very young strutting about with rusty weapons and even in some case with open penknives! And the little boys with their penknives were patted on their back for their zeal and enthusiasm! However, everything passed off successfully and it was hoped that the Dussehra would also end peacefully. The next day—22nd September—I went off to Delhi. It appears however that the tension again increased and everyone looked forward to some trouble. There was no question of any conflict between the Ram Lila processions and Muslim processions. None the less there was this general apprehension. The Muslims accused the Hindus of inviting large numbers of lathiwalas from the villages and the Hindus repeated the same charge against the Muslims. Ordinarily great crowds come from the rural areas to see the Ram Lila. In times of tension, every big banker or *rais* engages some of these professional fighters to defend his house. In the result a considerable number of such persons must have been in Allahabad. I do not think the Hindu Sabha might have expected that the lower classes—chamars, *pasis*, etc., would be useful in a conflict with the Muslims. These classes, for the last few years, have been asked to take part in the Ram Lila processions.

It is highly probable that Muslims also made special arrangements to get their *budmashes* and lathiwalas in. But I hardly think it likely that they would choose the Dussehra day when in point of numbers, the Hindus are strongest, to take the aggressive on any large scale. But they did prepare themselves for a conflict if such occurred.On the morning of the 7th—the Dussehra day—a rumour was circulated that the Muslims had issued invitations to the surrounding villages for a *kabaddi* party on a large scale. This game was to take place on the outskirts of the town and on the route of the procession. The time also was the evening when the procession was to pass that way. The choice of the time and place is certainly significant. There could not have been a worse choice. Information of this was immediately sent to the police station and apprehensions of coming trouble increased.

There are two Ram Lila processions, one following the other. The first one passed without any special incident, except that it is said that when they passed the Muslims gathered together for kabaddi or any other purpose, to the extent of 500 men with lathis, the Muslim attitude appeared to be threatening. The second procession reached this place just at 6 p.m.—the time for prayers. The *Kotwal* was with it, so also Purushottam Das Tandon[55] and others. As the *azan* was heard at the request of the Kotwal, who is a Muslim, the procession was stopped for a few minutes, and music stopped also. After about 5 minutes the Kotwal apparently made a sign although the prayers were not quite over. The music started. Thereupon there was a commotion amongst the 500 or so Muslims gathered together across the road (not on the mosque side) and one man hit with his lathi a drum. Some stones were also thrown from the mosque. No one was however hurt and the Kotwal immediately scolded the Muslims. It is also said that some Muslims themselves gave a slight beating to the man who had thrown stones from the mosque. The procession started without any further mishap—went to the river and returned. It is said, probably with truth, that the news of this contretemps reached various parts of the city in various shapes and forms and was the spark which started the blaze. *Chal gai* was repeated by everybody, and the long expected conflict began in earnest in several places.

The Hindus say that Muslims started it everywhere. The Muslims deny the charge and accuse the Hindus. I am not at all clear about the events of the 7th night. There was fighting in the heart of the city, not far from the Kotwali and murders were committed soon after 7.30 p.m. The *kunjras* (Muslim vegetable sellers) are said to have attacked Hindus inside the vegetable market as well as

[55] Purushottam Das Tandon (1882–1962); a Congressman of Allahabad; Speaker, UP Assembly, 1937–9 and 1946–50; President of INC in 1950 but resigned because of differences with Nehru; was actively associated with Servants of the People Society, Hindi Sahitya Sammelan and Rashtra Bhasha Prachar Sabha.

outside. They wounded some Congress workers, including a clerk in the PCC office. But this clerk gallantly remained with them and reasoned with them and actually succeeded in calming them a little. They are said to have apologised to him when they discovered that he was a Congress worker. At least one Hindu was killed that night, and many wounded.

About the same time a Hindu band dashed down the main street of the city killing a harmless Mohamadan, cutting off the hand of another and wounding others.

At night a great effort was made to have the usual illuminations as this, it was believed, would have a calming effect. There was considerable stone throwing from houses—chiefly occupied by prostitutes—at Ramchandra & Laxman.

During 8th and 9th, assaults, free fights, stone throwing, etc., continued, groups of both Hindus and Muslims taking the offensive by turns. Deaths also occurred, usually of innocent passers-by. The two or three main incidents were:

1. The looting by a Muslim crowd of a village (Mirapur) on the outskirts of Allahabad. One Hindu was killed here.
2. The attack by some Muslims on Gangagunj—a Hindu mohalla facing [a] Muslim mohalla. A temple was desecrated here.
3. A fight in Shahgunj also accompanied by a desecration of a temple.
4. A Hindu *bania* shooting at a Mohamadan crowd and killing 2 men and a woman.
5. General and very shameful assaults on individuals and on groups both by Hindus and Muslims.

I shall write more in detail about these incidents tomorrow as the time for catching the mail is nearing. I may add however that apart from the mosque incident, I am inclined to think that Hindus took the initiative on the night of the 7th and (apart from Gangagunj and Mirapur) the Hindu middle-class attitude was deplorable. Several very unfortunate incidents happened in Hindu mohallas where well-to-do people live.

Jawaharlal Nehru

SWJN, *Vol. 2, I Series, pp. 181–91*

## 14. Letter to M.K. Gandhi

Allahabad
20 October 1924

My dear Bapuji,

I enclose the second installment of my impressions. They are very hasty and sketchy and I hope you will excuse their many imperfections. I am sending you my only copy. Could you kindly show it to Mohammad Ali?

Father is going to Nagpur.[56] He is the most suitable person. I would have been hopeless so far as Dr Moonje[57] and his party are concerned.

I have still some fever but I hope to be well soon.

Yours sincerely,
Jawaharlal

SWJN, *Vol. 2, I Series, pp. 191–5*

### Impression of the Disturbances at Allahabad

I wrote yesterday about the incident at a small wayside mosque where the Ram Lila procession stopped for a few minutes and there was a little stone throwing. This mosque is situated on the outskirts of the city and the main procession—so far as the crowds are concerned—gradually gets lesser and lesser before the mosque is reached and soon after it practically ends. The following plan may help to explain the position:

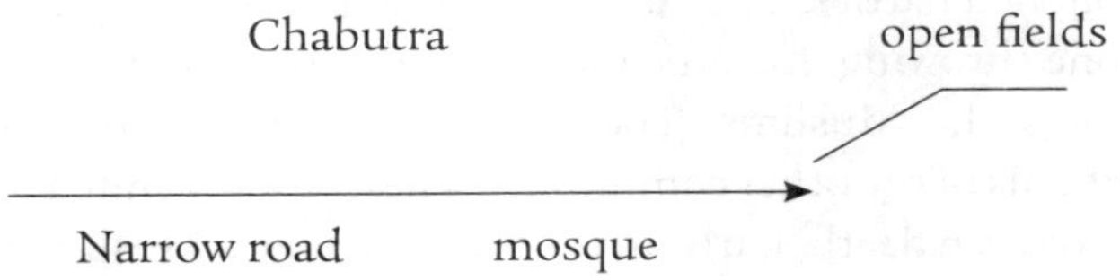


[56] Motilal Nehru and Maulana Abul Kalam Azad visited Nagpur on 26–7 October and succeeded in bringing about an agreement between the rioting Hindus and Muslims. See also *CWMG*, Vol. XXV, pp. 166–9.

[57] Dr B.S. Moonje, eye surgeon, Nagpur; leader of the Hindu Mahasabha; attended the Round Table Conference in 1930

There were only a few persons in the mosque at the time of prayers—perhaps half a dozen. On the Chabutra opposite there are said to have been about 500 Musalmans. Many of them are armed with lathis, etc. There are some detached Muslim mohallas in the neighbourhood.

The procession went on after this incident to the river Jamuna where the usual ceremonies were performed including some fireworks. People then returned in twos and threes. It is said that there was some stone throwing on the passers-by in the Muslim mohallas.

Before this, however, trouble had occurred in the heart of the city and elsewhere. Probably the cause of this trouble was an exaggerated account of the mosque incident and a belief that fighting had begun between Hindus and Muslims.

The vegetable market is situated in the busiest quarter of the city. The kunjras (vegetable sellers) are Musalmans and are supposed to be a rough lot. It is said that they took the initiative and started attacking and beating all Hindus they came across. I am unable to say who began the attack but I doubt if the kunjras are solely to blame. There can be no doubt that in one case at least on the night of the 7th a Hindu band rushed through the principal streets, killing one Mohamadan and wounding several. There was also a stone-throwing and bottle-throwing contest between Hindus and Muslims near the *subzimandi*. The fighting of the 7th resulted in the death and wounding of both Hindus and Muslims.

On the 8th and 9th there were many fights, some developing into pitched battles. They usually resulted in some injuries caused by stone throwing. In some places Hindus were on the aggressive, in others the Muslims. There were also attacks by groups or individuals of the other community. These usually ended in serious injury or even death. Early on the 8th morning, a Muslim passer-by was seriously injured very near Bharti Bhawan, not far from Pandit M.M. Malaviya's[58] house. The news of this attack spread in the Muslim mohallas in exaggerated forms and there was a general

[58] Pandit Madan Mohan Malaviya (1861–1946); President, INC, 1909 and 1918; founder, Banaras Hindu University

belief amongst the more ignorant Muslims that a slaughter of Muslims had taken place near Bharti Bhawan. This roused them to fury and they attacked a number of Hindus passing near their mohallas. As spears and daggers were used not infrequently by both parties, there were several cases of serious injuries.

Apart from these general incidents there were some special occurrences.

Mirapur—This is a village on the fringe of Allahabad. A group of Muslims from a neighbouring mohalla led by a notorious budmash took advantage of the prevailing disorder and swooped down on the village for purposes of loot. The Hindus resisted them for a while but then owing to the superior number of the Muslims the Hindus retired. It is stated on behalf of the Hindus that this was a pre-arranged affair and a drum was beaten to summon Musalmans from the surrounding villages. A sad feature of the occurrence was the joining in by the Muslims of that village in the attack on their Hindu neighbours. The village was thoroughly looted and one Hindu was killed.

Gangagunj—This is a Hindu mohalla facing several Muslim mohallas—Nai Basti, Atala, etc., largely inhabited by butchers, etc. It is stated that a band of Muslims invaded Gangagunj and after a fight with the Hindus succeeded in injuring a number of Hindus and in desecrating a temple. The temple was immediately desecrated and the idols had been broken. Some idols under a *peepul* tree were also broken.

Ram Krishna's firing—This gentleman is a rich bania who fired at a Muslim crowd and killed 2 men and a woman. It is his case that he was in grave danger and fired in self-defence. I am inclined to think that the danger was not [as] great as he imagined and he might well have done without the firing, specially as the Kotwali was almost within a stone's throw.

Temple incidents—I have already referred to the desecration of the temple at Gangagunj. There was also a desecration in another mohalla—Shahgunj, but I think it was not premeditated here. During one of the street contests the Muslims pushed back the Hindus and reached this small roadside temple. They entered and used various idols and stones there as missiles to be thrown at Hindus.

Another temple incident is said to have occurred at Katghar on the morning of the 10th. The Hindus state that early in the morning a number of Mohamadans came to this temple quietly and removed the idols and threw them about near the temple. As soon as the Hindus observed this they raised an alarm and the Mohamadans immediately withdrew. The Hindus have named a number of Muslims whom they claim to have identified. These persons are some of the leading (though poor) Muslim residents of the mohalla. There can be no doubt that someone did remove the idols, but after an enquiry I have come to the conclusion that the case started against the Muslims is wholly false. Most of the persons named are innocent, but they have been reported against to terrify the Muslim community! As a result, the Muslims have brought an entirely false case of grievous hurt against the principal Hindus there. I think the work of displacing the idols must have been done by one or utmost two persons, and it is not wholly impossible that a Hindu did it. There has been an ancient feud between some Hindus and Muslims in the village over gambling transactions and the matter has gone to court more than once. I think that one of the persons concerned with this dispute must have misbehaved in this matter at the temple.

An interesting point came out in connection with the temple. It is dedicated to some *devi* and it is freely patronised in times of sickness, especially smallpox, by many of the poorer Musalmans, who make offerings and take the earth of the temple floor to apply to the body.

I learnt of this Katghar temple incident on the 11th. At that time I did not know about the far more serious case at Gangagunj. I thought that the desecration of a temple would irritate the Hindus very much and make matters worse. We therefore went to the principal Muslim leaders and suggested they might do something to ease the situation. Thereupon they issued a notice condemning the act and saying that whoever had done it had erred against religion. No press was open to print this notice so it was duplicated and a few hundred copies distributed.

I have been surprised to find that there is no deep feeling amongst the Hindus regarding these temple desecrations. A few of them were deeply grieved but most of them attached far greater importance to personal injury and mentioned the temple incidents almost casually.

A deplorable feature of the disturbances has been the treatment received by Muslims in the better-class Hindu mohallas. On the night of the 7th a poor Musalman, resident of the mohalla, was nearly killed with daggers by some well-to-do Hindus in their mohalla. The next day another Mohamadan, Hafizuddin, a Congress worker, tried to go through the principal Hindu mohallas. He was asked not to risk it but he refused to believe that any resident of those mohallas would attack him as he was personally known to all of them. He lived nearby and used to pass that way daily. So he went with another Mohamadan. They were attacked and it is very doubtful if they would have escaped with their lives, if a Hindu, the executive officer of our Municipality, had not jumped to their rescue and smuggled them into his house.

On the 9th a group of Hindus and Muslims—P.D. Tandon, Manzar Ali,[59] Zahur Ahmad, etc.,—made a tour of the affected areas. In the Hindu mohallas they had to face a very threatening attitude and in spite of Tandon's presence, the Muslims present narrowly escaped a bad beating. Even Manzar Ali, although he almost looks like a Hindu and is very well known there, was advised by a friend or two to retire quietly into one of the houses. This experience was repeated near Bharti Bhawan. In both these places the Hindus who threatened belonged to the better classes.

A very large number of men and women go to see the Ram Lila procession. These people found it difficult to go to their homes owing to the outbreak of the disturbances. Thousands were thus holed up in small houses, in some cases for two or three days. Two large Municipal lorries, meant for the removal of rubbish, were used on the 8th, 9th, 10th and 11th to take these people to their homes. One of the petty grievances of the Muslims is that the Municipality thus favoured the Hindus and removed their lathiwalas. As a matter of fact women were chiefly taken. In one or two places stones were thrown at the lorries. The drivers of both the lorries are Musalmans and Hindus were at first not willing to

[59] Manzar Ali Sokata, Muslim leader; Congressman from UP and friend of the Nehru family

trust them. But both the drivers worked very hard and even the Hindu Sabha proposes to show an appreciation of their work.

The position now is that the minor cases have been disposed of. A number of major cases—murder, dacoity, etc.,—are still pending, and fresh reports are made daily. A large number of these reports are probably false. Most of the persons arrested so far are Musalmans chiefly because of the Mirapur incident. Police officers are almost obviously partisan, each one trying to favour his own community. The Kotwal and most of the sub-Inspectors being Muslims, there is a general impression amongst the Hindus that great favour is being shown to the Muslims by the authorities. I think this is an exaggerated impression.

The Mohamadan leaders now propose that all cases be withdrawn. This course was adopted in 1917 when a Hindu-Muslim riot occurred here. The Hindu Sabha strongly opposes this.

I have written these impressions in great haste and under fever. I am afraid there must be repetitions in them and vague statements which the context may not justify. But I did not wish to delay sending a report any longer. I do not think it will be desirable for the present to give publicity to my conclusions or impressions.

Jawaharlal Nehru

SWJN, *Vol. 2, I Series, pp. 191–5*

## 15. Letter to M.K. Gandhi

Allahabad
24 October 1924

My dear Bapuji,

I forgot to mention in my record of impressions of Allahabad one fairly important matter. A headstone from a supposed grave was removed secretly one night during the disturbances. This 'grave' has a short history. A small area in the heart of Allahabad has recently been the scene of operations of this local Improvement Trust. Many houses have been demolished, a road widened, and it was proposed to have a small park. A grave was however discovered under one of the houses and it was alleged by many Mussalmans that there were other graves also, and that the place was in fact a graveyard. As such they laid claim to the land. It is said that the grave in question is not a real one and was made in the course of a few hours to give strength to the Muslim case. The Magistrate enquired into the matter (long before the riots) and held that the grave was a recently made one and the headstone had been brought over from some other older grave. I am myself inclined to think that it is a fictitious grave. However, whether the grave is real or not, the headstone was undoubtedly removed during the riots. It is not known who did it but very probably some Hindus must have done it.

The attempts to bring the Hindus and Muslims together have failed on account of the cases. The Hindus would not agree to the withdrawal of the main cases.

Meanwhile an attempt is being made by some Hindus to boycott Muslim vegetable shops (kunjras). Hindu kunjras have started shops. Hindu butchers have also applied for licences.

Father is going to Nagpur tonight. Maulana Abul Kalam Azad[60] will meet him there tomorrow. I shall go to Gorakhpur for the Provincial Conference on the 29th.

Yours affectionately,
Jawaharlal

SWJN, *Vol. 2, I Series, pp. 196–7*

## 16. Letter to Jawaharlal Nehru

Delhi
12 November 1924

My dear Jawaharlal,
It does appear to me to be necessary to have a flying column of workers, Hindu and Mohammedan, who would on a moment's notice be ready to go to afflicted parts for investigation. We may not wait always for distinguished men to go. Take for instance the case sent to you yesterday. If the statements made are true, the culprits should be exposed. If they are false, newspaper reporters

[60] Maulana Abul Kalam Azad (1888–1958); nationalist and scholar of Koranic theology; served long prison terms; President, INC, 1923 and 1940–6; Minister for Education, Government of India, 1947–58; author of *India Wins Freedom*

should be brought to book. The investigation should be prompt and thorough. I am preparing Mahadev[61] for the work and am trying to induce Pyarelal. The latter is unnecessarily diffident. Will Manzar Ali do the work? He may be paid for it. He should have no objection to accepting remuneration. His spinning work need not be disturbed. His activity may be confined to UP[62] only though I would prefer not to have any restrictions unless we get an army of workers in the field. For the case sent to you yesterday, I hope you will send someone at once. What about the case that was sent to you some weeks ago?

Yours sincerely,
M.K. Gandhi

[PS]
I take it you will be in Bombay with Father on Thursday morning if not earlier. I reach there that morning. Mrs Naidu[63] is leaving here tomorrow morning.

MKG

CWMG, *Vol. XXV, p. 305*

[61] Mahadev Desai (1892–1942); lawyer, journalist and author; Gandhi's private secretary for twenty-five years and his biographer; arrested along with Gandhi on 9 August 1942 and died on 15 August in Yeravda prison.

Describing Desai in his chosen role, Gandhi said, 'I have by me a co-worker called Mahadev Desai who is striving to out-Boswell Boswell and thus whenever he is near me, takes down whatever he considers wisdom dropping from my lips. I can't repel his advances, even if I would, for the relation is, like the Hindu marriage indissoluble.'

[62] The former United Provinces of Agra and Oudh, now Uttar Pradesh state.

[63] Sarojini Naidu (1879–1949); poet, politician and social reformer; first woman President, INC, 1925; Governor, UP, 1947–9. She was sent to South Africa at this time with B.D. Chaturvedi by the Congress Working Committee to advise the Indians settled there.

On her death on 2 March 1949, Nehru in a broadcast tribute on All India Radio, described her as 'a nationalist and a great internationalist figure .... She was a dreamer of dreams, singer of songs, a crusader of a great cause .... What I am today is partly due to the inspiration from Sarojini Devi.'

## 17. Letter to Jawaharlal Nehru

[14][64] November 1924

My dear Jawaharlal,
Just a line to wish you many happy returns of the day for the service of the motherland and for self-realisation.

If it is possible do come with Father.

Yours sincerely,
M.K. Gandhi

CWMG, *Vol. XXV, p. 326*

## 18. Telegram to Jawaharlal Nehru

Sabarmati
28 November 1924

Sorry about baby's death.[65] God's will be done.

Gandhi

CWMG, *Vol. XXV, p. 369*

## 19. Letter to Jawaharlal Nehru

*Magh Sud 6*
2 December 1924

Dear Jawaharlal,
I have written in *Young India*[66] about the textbooks of Professor Ramdas Gour. So I am not replying separately. I hope Kamala[67] is well. I am going to the Punjab.

Blessings from
Mohandas Gandhi

JN Papers, *NMML* (Original in Hindi)

[64] The source has '16', evidently an error. Nehru's birthday was on 14 November.

[65] Nehru's infant son died a week after birth.

[66] Of 4-12-1924; see *CWMG*, Vol. XXV, pp. 394–5. See p. 11, *fn.* 34.

[67] Kamala Nehru (1899–1936). For Nehru's article 'Kamala', see *The Discovery of India.*

## 20. Letter to Jawaharlal Nehru

25 April 1925

My dear Jawaharlal,

I am in Tithal, a place somewhat like Juhu, resting for four days to fit myself for the Bengal ordeal.[68] I am trying here to overtake my correspondence in which I find your letter referring to the article 'God and Congress'.[69] I sympathise with you in your difficulties. True religion being the greatest thing in life and in the world, it has been exploited the most. And those who have seen the exploiters and the exploitation and missed the reality naturally get disgusted with the thing itself. But religion is, after all, a matter for each individual, and then too a matter of the heart, call it then by whatever name you like, that which gives one the greatest solace in the midst of the severest fire is God. Anyway, you are on the right track. I do not mind reason being the sole test even though it often bewilders one and lands one in errors that border on superstition. Cow-protection to me is infinitely more than mere protection of the cow. The cow is merely a type for all that lives. Cow-protection means protection of the weak, the helpless, the dumb and the deaf. Man becomes then not the lord and master of all creation but he is its servant. The cow to me is a sermon on pity. As yet we are merely playing at cow-protection. But we shall soon have to grapple with the reality.[70]

I hope you have received all my previous letters. I have a doleful letter from Mr Satyapal.[71] I wish you could go to the Punjab even if it is only for a few days. Your visit will hearten him. I wish Father would have two months in a quiet and cool place. And why will you

[68] Gandhi left Tithal on 27 April 1925 for Bombay on his way to Calcutta to attend the Bengal Provincial Conference at Faridpur.

[69] See *CWMG*, Vol. XXVI, pp. 222–5.

[70] Gandhi reiterates this faith in his article on 'Cow-Protection' for *YI*, 7-5-1925. The All-India Cow-Protection Association was formed on 28 April 1925. For the draft constitution prepared by Gandhi, ibid., pp. 35–7.

[71] Dr Satyapal, a medical practitioner and a prominent Congressman of Punjab; took leading part in the Rowlatt Act agitation and was deported from Amritsar in 1919 with Kitchlew; imprisoned several times; President, Punjab PCC for many years; Speaker, Punjab Assembly, 1952; died in 1954

not go to Almora for a week or so and combine work with a breath of cool air?

Yours,
Bapu[72]

CWMG, *Vol. XXVI, pp. 545–6*

## 21. Letter to Jawaharlal Nehru

30 September 1925

My dear Jawahar,
We are living in strange times. Sitla Sahai[73] may defend himself. Please keep me informed of further developments. What is he? Is he a lawyer? Had he ever any connection with revolutionary activity? As for the Congress, it would be better to make it as simple as possible so as to enable the present remaining workers to cope with it. I know that your burden will be now increased. But you must not endanger your health in any way whatsoever. I am anxious about your health. I do not at all like these frequent attacks of fever you are having.[74] I wish you could give yourself and Kamala a holiday.[75]

[72] Gandhi signs himself 'Bapu' henceforth.

[73] A farmer and a Congressman of Rae Bareli district; Secretary, UP branch of the All India Spinners' Association; took a leading part in the no-rent campaign.

[74] Nehru had contracted typhoid when he was incarcerated in Nabha Jail in 1923. Referring to it in his *Autobiography* he writes: 'I was unused to illness or lying in bed with fever or physical weakness. ... And during this period I felt a strange detachment from my surroundings and my day-to-day work. ... But for me it was in the nature of a spiritual experience—I use the word not in a narrow religious sense—and it influenced me considerably. ... But more and more I moved away from the religious outlook on life and politics. ... I remember well it had a lasting effect on me and my way of thinking, and for the next two years or more I went about my work with something of that air of detachment.'

[75] Referring to Kamala's illness Nehru writes, 'This was in 1925. In the autumn of that year my wife fell seriously ill, and for many years she lay in a Lucknow hospital. The Congress was held that year at Cawnpore, and, somewhat distracted, I rushed backwards and forwards between Allahabad, Cawnpore, and Lucknow. (I was still General Secretary of the Congress.)'

Father has written to me. Of course, I never wanted to go as far as he supposes. I would not think of asking anyone to support Father. But I would not hesitate to ask a friend or friends who would consider it a privilege to pay you for your public services. I would press you to take it from public funds, if your wants owing to the situation in which you are and must be were not extraordinary. I am myself convinced that you should contribute to the common purse either by doing some business or by letting your personal friends find funds for retaining your services. There is no immediate hurry but without fretting about it, come to a final decision. I will not mind even if you decided to do some business. I want your mental peace. I know that you will serve the country even as manager of a business. I am sure that Father will not mind any decision you may arrive at so long as it gives you complete peace.

Yours,
Bapu

[PS]
I see that I must reserve the right hand for *YI*.[76]
CWMG, *Vol. XXVIII, p. 255*

[76] Nehru explains the postscript in his note: 'Gandhiji had practised writing with his left hand in order to give his right hand rest. This letter was apparently written with his left hand.'

'*YI*' stands for *Young India*, the English weekly that Gandhi edited from 1919, and which he described as 'a clear mirror through which anybody who cares can look at me'.

## 22. Telegram to Jawaharlal Nehru

Ahmedabad
1 December 1925

Jawaharlal Nehru
Anand Bhavan
Allahabad
Fast broken.[77] Condition perfect. Hope Kamala steadily progressing. Sarup[78] here.

Gandhi

CWMG, *Vol. XXIX, p. 296*

## 23. Letter to Jawaharlal Nehru

21 January 1926

My dear Jawahar,
I am glad you are taking Kamala with you.[79] Yes, if both of you cannot, you at least should come here before you go. About the Deshbandhu Memorial,[80] your letter to Jamnalalji will be enough. About AISA, you will remain Secretary but if an assistant is required, Shankerlal[81] should have one.[82] I cannot blame you for

[77] Gandhi had undertaken a week-long purificatory fast by way of atonement for lapses among boys and girls in the Satyagraha Ashram. He was 'anxious to see the Ashram free from errors which are sapping the manhood of the nation and undermining the character of the youth.'

[78] Vijayalakshmi Pandit (1900–1990); Nehru's older sister; married Ranjit Sitaram Pandit, 1921; Minister, Local Self-government and Public Health, 1937–9; Indian Ambassador, Soviet Union, 1947–9, United States and Mexico, 1949–51, High Commissioner, United Kingdom, 1955–61; elected first woman President, United Nations General Assembly, 1953; Governor, Maharashtra, 1962–4

[79] In March 1926, Nehru sailed for Europe accompanied by Kamala and Indira. A stay in Switzerland was expected to improve Kamala's health. They returned to India in December 1927.

[80] The All-India Deshbandhu Memorial Fund. C.R. Das, popularly known as 'Deshbandhu' (friend of the nation), had died on 16 June 1925.

[81] Shankerlal Banker, social worker and labour leader of Ahmedabad; printer and publisher of *Young India*

[82] The All-India Spinners' Association was constituted on 24 April 1925, for the purpose of promoting khadi as a means of trade in providing employment to thousands.

not preparing the chart. You have not idled away your time. You should have clothes that would answer in Europe.

Yours truly,
Bapu

CWMG, *Vol. XXIX, p. 425*

## 24. Letter to Jawaharlal Nehru

Ashram, Sabarmati
5 March 1926

My dear Jawaharlal,
I received your note of the 1st. Though you have left a note for Dr Mehta,[83] I have also written to make assurance doubly sure. I hope Kamala kept excellent health on board. Did you all profit by the voyage? No time say anything more.

Yours sincerely,
M.K. Gandhi

CWMG, *Vol. XXX, p. 77*

## 25. Letter to Jawaharlal Nehru

Ashram, Sabarmati
23 April 1926

My dear Jawaharlal,
I have been thinking of writing to you every week and every week I have failed. I must not let this week however pass by. I have had the latest news about you from Father while he was here with the Responsivists.[84] You will have seen the agreement that has been arrived at.

[83] Dr Jivraj Mehta (1887–1978); son of Dr Pranjivan Mehta; physician and nationalist; Chief Minister, Gujarat, 1960–3; Indian High Commissioner, United Kingdom, 1963–6; Member, Lok Sabha, 1971–6.

[84] On 20 April 1926. The next day a solution acceptable to Congress leaders, Swarajists and Responsivists (of the Responsive Cooperationist Party) was evolved. For the clauses of the agreement referred to as the Sabarmati Pact, see *CWMG*, Vol. XXX, Appendix II. The Pact, however, broke down owing to 'irreconcilable differences between the signatories of the Sabarmati Pact regarding the interpretation of its terms'.

Hindus and Muslims are going more and more away from each other.[85] But this thing does not disturb me. Somehow or other, I feel that the separation is growing in order only to bring them all closer later on.

I do hope Kamala is benefiting.

Yours,
Bapu

CWMG, *Vol. XXX, p. 345*

## 26. Letter to M.K. Gandhi

Clinique Stephani
Montana s/Sierre, Switzerland
15 March 1927

My dear Bapuji,

I have not written to you for a very long time. I have purposely avoided doing so, so as not to add to your work, and have contented myself by sending you news of us through Mahadeva and Devadas. But neither of them has been, so far as I am concerned, an extraordinarily good correspondent. Of this I do not make the slightest complaint, as I can fully realise how busy Mahadeva must be with his numerous activities, and Devadas, I am very sorry to learn, has not been keeping well. Besides, *Young India* has been keeping me supplied with news about you. But the effect of not hearing often or frequently from any person is a slackening at this end also. And so I have not written as often even to Mahadeva or Devadas as I might otherwise have done.

I presume you have been in some sort of touch through father with our movements here and the state of Kamala's health. It is a year, almost to a day, since we landed at Venice, and it must be confessed that the results of the year's treatment have been far from satisfactory. At present Kamala is keeping well and latterly she has

[85] This period perhaps marks the beginning of Muslims moving away from the Congress. About this time, there was a small conference of leaders of Hindu and Muslim communities that met in Delhi. Mohammad Ali said in an interview (to the Associated Press) that none except Gandhi and Sarojini Naidu had condemned the Hindus for communal disturbances. He also said that all Congressmen except Gandhi and the Nehrus were anti-Muslim.

made real progress. I am hoping that this will continue but still I have a feeling that although she may be outwardly cured care will be necessary in future to prevent relapses. She goes out for fairly long walks now and so far as appearances go looks healthier than she has done for some years.

I had hoped to return to India in spring this year but this is not likely now. It is hardly wise to go during the monsoon. So it seems that we must stay on here till late August. We propose to remain in Montana for another five weeks and then to go down to Montreux, quite near the place where M. Romain Rolland[86] lives, and later to France and England. If necessary we shall return to Montana for another few weeks' rest and treatment in the summer.

Indira[87] has been living at a little school two or three hours' journey from here. We see her about once a month. She will join us when we go down from Montana. Krishna[88] is with us and is well.

You must have read of my going to the Brussels Congress.[89] I had the pleasure of meeting a number of very interesting persons there. Among these was Ernst Toller,[90] a young but famous German dramatist. I have only read one of his works—*The Machine*

[86] Romain Rolland (1866–1944); French novelist; awarded the Nobel Prize for Literature in 1915; close friend of Gandhi and his biographer

In a letter of 26 September 1926 to Mirabehn, Romain Rolland had written: 'The fact is that YCU has seen in Gandhi the purest Christian (without knowing it) of today—the man who, over and above all the priests and pastors resumes the direct tradition with the spirit of the Gospel.'

[87] Indira Priyadarshini Gandhi (1917–1984); Nehru's daughter; married Feroze Gandhi in 1942; President, INC, 1959–60; Minister, Information & Broadcasting, 1964–6; was Prime Minister of India for three consecutive terms from 1966 to 1977 and for a fourth term from 1980 until her assassination in 1984.

[88] Krishna Hutheesing (1907–1967); Nehru's younger sister; author of *We Nehrus, With No Regrets, Nehru's Letters to His Sister* and *Dear to Behold*.

[89] Nehru had been invited to participate in the International Congress against Colonialism and Oppression held at Brussels in February 1927. The Conference founded the League against Imperialism and for National Independence, appointing Nehru its honorary President as well as a member of the Executive Committee.

[90] Ernst Toller (1893–1939); personal friend of Nehru; imprisoned for participating in the Bavarian revolution; left Germany in 1932 and lived in exile in Europe and the United States; ended his life seven years later

*Wreckers*[91]—but this I liked. It deals with the early industrial period of England and the hostility of the workers to machinery. It would interest you. Toller asked me specially to send you his respectful regards.

We have all been very glad to get reports of your good health.

Yours affectionately,
Jawaharlal

SWJN, *Vol. 2, I Series, pp. 311–12*

## 27. Letter to M.K. Gandhi

London
22 April 1927

My dear Bapuji,

I did not send you any cable last week, as I could not hit upon a sentence short enough and intelligible enough to convey my meaning. With more thought I adhere to my opinion expressed last week that on the whole it will be better if I am not chosen President.[92] This disinclination is perhaps not due to the reasons you mention. Whether I am President or not I do not suppose I shall keep apart from political activity when I return home. I have begun to feel strongly that a *laissez-faire* attitude and trusting to Providence to right matters is a very feeble way of combating evil. I do not of course imagine that any individual can do much but if everyone decided to wait and see, nothing would ever be done. Here, far away from India, it is exceedingly difficult to appreciate fully the position at home and I cannot therefore say exactly what I ought to do on my return, although I have general ideas on the subject. Under the circumstances and for the reasons I mentioned briefly in my last letter I do not feel inclined to welcome the proposal about the presidentship. You and others in India are likely to be better judges. Personally I should have thought that Ansari[93] would be the best choice.

[91] Published in 1923

[92] There was a suggestion that Jawaharlal be elected President of the Madras session of the Congress that was to be held in December 1927.

[93] M.A. Ansari (1880–1936); leading doctor of Delhi; participated in the Home Rule and Khilafat campaigns; organized a medical mission to Turkey; President, Madras Congress, 1927

I fancy that you have got a wrong impression about my idea of the utility of the League against Imperialism. I do not expect much from it and indeed I am quite sure that none of the members of the so-called imperialist or oppressing nations will help us in the least whenever their interests conflict with ours. I have no illusions about their altruism. But I welcome all legitimate methods of getting into touch with other countries and peoples so that we may be able to understand their viewpoint and world politics generally. I do not think it is desirable nor indeed is it possible for India to plough a lonely furrow now or in the future. It is solely with a view to self-education and self-improvement that I desire external contacts. I am afraid we are terribly narrow in our outlook and the sooner we get rid of this narrowness the better. Our salvation can of course come only from the internal strength that we may evolve but one of the methods of evolving such strength should be study of other people and their ideas.

I have so much that I wish to write. I have refrained from doing so in the past as I did not want to add to your work. But perhaps if you will permit me I shall write more fully a little later.

We are leaving London and England after about 3 weeks' stay today for Belgium. Kamala has been tolerably well in spite of the fatigue of living in a great city. But she is tired out. I hope she will be fresher after a few days on the Continent. We are all tired of staying in foreign parts and want to go back home. It was my intention to return in September but now father is coming here in August and we can hardly go immediately after his arrival.

Yours affectionately,
Jawaharlal

SWJN, *Vol. 1, I Series, pp. 325–6*

## 28. Letter to Jawaharlal Nehru

Nandi Hill, Mysore State
25 May 1927

My dear Jawaharlal,
I had your letter while I was on the sick list and unable to do much correspondence. I am still convalescing and am able to do only a

moderate amount of work; but I am making steady progress. You have been there a long time now; but I know you have not wasted it. I hope however that Kamala will become completely restored when you return. If her health requires a longer stay, I presume that you will remain there.

I read most carefully your public as well as private confidential report[94] about the doings of the Oppressed Nations' Conference. I myself do not expect much from this league, if only because its free activity depends upon the goodwill of the very powers that are partners in the exploitation of the oppressed nations, and I feel that the members of the European nations that joined the league will not be able to sustain the last heat. For, they will not be able to accommodate themselves to what they would consider to be an injury to their self-interest. On our side there is the danger of our people again looking to external forces and external aid for salvation instead of seeking to achieve it by evolving internal strength. I am not carefully following European events. You are on the spot and you may see an altruistic improvement in the atmosphere there which I miss altogether.

There is some talk of your being chosen President for the next Congress. I am in correspondence with father about it. The outlook here is not at all happy in spite of the unanimous resolution[95] of the AICC on the Hindu–Muslim question. I do not know whether the process of breaking heads will in any way be checked. We have lost hold upon the masses, and it seems to me that if you become President, you will be lost for one year at any rate to the masses. That, however, does not mean that Congress work has to be neglected. Someone has got to do it; but there are many who are willing and eager to do that work, may be due to mixed motives, even selfish motives; but they will keep the Congress going on somehow or other. The institution will always be, at their wish at the disposal of those who may be qualified for mass work and may

[94] Of 19 February 1927. See *SWJN*, Vol. 2, I Series, pp. 278–97.

[95] Of 15 and 16 May 1927 at Bombay. See *Indian Annual Register*, Vol. 18, pp. 15–16. For Gandhi's article with reference to it, see *CWMG*, Vol. XXXIV, pp. 2–4.

have gained control over the masses. The question then is how your services can be utilised. What you yourself think, you should do. I know you are capable of taking a detached view and you will say quite unselfishly like Dadabhai[96] or MacSwiney[97] 'put the crown on my head', and I have no doubt that it will be so put. I do not myself see the way so clear as to make me force the crown on you and plead with you to wear it.[98] Father will be writing to you also by this mail, if he has not done so already. I am sending a copy of this to him.

It might be as well for you to cable your wishes. I am likely to be in Bangalore till the end of July. You may therefore send your cable directly to Bangalore, or to be absolutely certain send it to the Ashram and it will be repeated to me wherever I may be.

With love to you all,

Yours,
M.K. Gandhi

G-N Correspondence, JN Papers, *NMML*

## 29. Letter to Jawaharlal Nehru

Kumara Park, Bangalore
20 July 1927

My dear Jawaharlal,
I have both your letters. Events have moved fairly fast between the dates of my letter and of the arrival of your letters. Sarojini Devi

[96] Dadabhai Naoroji (1825–1917); Professor of Mathematics and Natural Philosophy, Elphinstone College, Bombay, 1854; author of *Poverty and Un-British Rule in India*; Member, Bombay Legislative Council, 1885–7; President, INC, 1886, 1893 and 1906; Member, British Parliament, 1892–5; Member, Royal Commission on Indian Expenditure, 1896

Venerated as the Grand Old Man of India, he was to Gandhi 'one of the great men who have moulded my life' and from whom he had 'learnt the lessons of regularity, single-minded patriotism, simplicity, austerity and ceaseless work'.

[97] Terence MacSwiney, Mayor of Cork in Ireland, who died in 1920 after a long hunger strike in a British prison

[98] See also p. 70, *fn*. 164.

suggested under pressure from Mahmudabad[99] and Mr Jinnah[100] that I should press Father to accept the presidential chair for the coming year. I totally dissented from her view and told her that Dr Ansari was the only possible President, though even he will be able to do precious little.[101]

Things are going from bad to worse, and it is quite plain that we have not yet drunk the last dregs. But I regard all this rising of the poison to the surface as a necessary process in national up-building [*sic*]. It is quite true that what was burrowing under the surface has now broken through the crust and allows itself to be seen by the naked eye.

I saw the other day in the daily press portraits of yourself, Kamala, Krishna and Indu, or was it you three without Indu, I now forget. You all seem to have grown fuller in the face and all over. I hope that the appearance coincides with the reality.

Though I am not yet physically quite strong, I have resumed the interrupted tour with considerable modifications and in gentle stages. I will not have resumed it but for the fact that collections were locked up and could not be freed unless I presented myself for receiving them.

Shankerlal and Anasuyabehn[102] are just now with me in addition to the party mentioned by me in my previous letter.[103]

CWMG, *Vol. XXXIV, pp. 207–8*

[99] The source, however, has 'Muhammadabad'.

[100] Mohammad Ali Jinnah (1876–1948); barrister of Bombay and President, Muslim League, 1916, 1920 and 1934–48; Indian nationalist who later campaigned for the creation of Pakistan; Governor-General of Pakistan, 1947–8

[101] Gandhi sponsored the election of Dr M.A. Ansari in the hope that he would be able to activate Hindu–Muslim unity. See also *CWMG*, Vol. XXXIV, pp. 304–5 and 403.

[102] Anasuya Sarabhai (1885–1972); sister of Ambalal Sarabhai; owner of several mills in Ahmedabad and leader of the Ahmedabad labour movement

[103] Not available

## 30. Letter to Jawaharlal Nehru

Satyagraha Ashram
4 January 1928

My dear Jawaharlal,

I feel that you love me too well to resent what I am about to write.[104] In any case I love you too well to restrain my pen when I feel I must write.

You are going too fast. You should have taken time to think and become acclimatised. Most of the resolutions you framed and got carried out could have been delayed for one year.[105] Your plunging into the 'republican army' was a hasty step.[106] But I do not mind these acts of yours so much as I mind your encouraging mischief-makers and hooligans. I do not know whether you still believe in unadulterated nonviolence. But even if you have altered your views you could not think that unlicensed and unbridled violence is going to deliver the country. If careful observation of the country in the light of your European experiences convinces you of the error of the current ways and means, by all means enforce your own views

[104] Nehru in his prefatory note to this letter had written: 'I returned from Europe in December 1927 and went straight to the Madras session of the Indian National Congress. A number of resolutions were passed there at my instance. This letter was written by Gandhiji because he did not approve of my activities at this session.'

[105] The important resolutions passed by the Madras Congress, held in December 1927, pertained to Independence, boycott of the Simon Commission, the war danger, the situation in China, the League Against Imperialism, restrictions on issue of passports, drafting of the constitution and Hindu–Muslim unity.

[106] The reference is to the Swadhin Bharat Sangha (Republican Congress) set up for the establishment of complete national independence as early as possible. Nehru was president of the executive committee. He writes in his *Autobiography:* 'One of the sideshows at Madras was a Republican Conference that held its first (and last) session that year. I was asked to preside. The idea appealed to me, as I considered myself a republican. But, I hesitated, as I did not know who was at the back of the new venture, and I did not want to associate myself with mushroom growths. I presided, eventually, but later repented of this, for the Republican Conference turned out to be, like many others, a still-born affair.'

but do please form a disciplined party.[107] You know the Cawnpore experiences.[108] In every struggle bands of men who would submit to discipline are needed. You seem to be overlooking this factor in being careless about your instruments.

If I can advise you, now that you are working secretary of the INC, it is your duty to devote your whole energy to the central resolution, i.e. Unity;[109] and the important but secondary resolution, i.e., boycott of the Simon Commission.[110] The Unity Resolution requires the use of all your great gifts of organisation and persuasion.

I have no time to elaborate my points *verb sap.*[111]

I hope Kamala is keeping as well as in Europe.

Yours,
Bapu

*A Bunch of Old Letters, p. 59*

[107] Nehru comments that after his return from Europe his 'outlook was wider, and nationalism by itself seemed to me definitely a narrow and insufficient creed. Political freedom, independence, were no doubt essential, but…without social freedom and a socialistic structure of society and the state neither the country nor the individual could develop much.' (Ibid.)

[108] In January 1926, hundreds of young men undertook all manner of tasks at the Volunteer Conference at Cawnpore but were not efficient as units or as an organization as they were not properly trained.

[109] The Hindu-Muslim Unity resolution recommended joint electorates, reservation of seats, introduction of reforms in NWFP and Baluchistan, redistribution of provinces on a linguistic basis and the immediate formation of Andhra, Utkal, Sind, and Karnataka; no legislature to interfere with liberty of conscience or intervene in inter-communal matters without the consent of three-fourths of the members of either community. Hindus and Muslims were urged to respect each other and not to undertake forcible conversions. See *CWMG*, Vol. XXXV, Appendix IX.

[110] On 8 November 1927 the Conservative Government had announced the appointment of a commission, consisting of members of the British Parliament with Sir John Simon as Chairman, to report on the working of the Act of 1919 and to inquire into the desirability of introducing a responsible government. The exclusion of Indians and the notion that an investigation should be undertaken to see whether India was fit to govern herself caused indignation, resulting in a general determination to boycott the Simon Commission.

[111] Abbreviation of the Latin *verbum sapienti sat est*—a word is enough for the wise man

## 31. Letter to M.K. Gandhi

Allahabad
11 January 1928

My dear Bapuji,

The Working Committee is now meeting in Benares and so I cannot go to Bombay or Sabarmati for some time.

I am loath to inflict another letter on you so soon after my last[112] but I am very much troubled by your criticism of the Congress resolutions and I feel I must write to you again. You are always very careful with your words and your language is studiously restrained. It amazes me all the more to find you using language which appears to me wholly unjustified. You have condemned in general language the proceedings of the Subjects Committee and specially selected some resolutions for greater criticism and condemnation. May I point out that it is always unsafe to judge on hearsay evidence? You were not present yourself and it is quite conceivable that the opinions you may have formed after a personal visit to the Subjects Committee may have been different. Yet you have chosen to condemn and judge unfavourably the whole Committee, or at any rate a great majority of it, simply basing your judgement on the impressions of a few persons. Do you think this is quite fair to the Committee or the Congress? You have referred to discipline and to the Working Committee as the National Cabinet. May I remind you that you are a member of the Working Committee and it is an extraordinary thing for a member, on the morrow of the Congress, to criticise and run down the Congress and its principal resolutions? There has been a general chorus of congratulations on the success of the Madras Congress. This may be wrong or without sufficient basis but undoubtedly there was this general impression in the country and atmosphere counts for a great deal in all public work. And now most people who thought so feel a bit dazed at your criticism and wonder if their previous enthusiasm was not overdone or mistaken.

[112] Not available

You have described the Independence Resolution[113] as 'hastily conceived and thoughtlessly passed.'[114] I have already pointed out to you how the country has discussed and considered this question for years past and how I have personally thought over it, discussed it, spoken about it in meetings, written about it and generally been full of it for the last five years or more. It seems to me that under the circumstances no stretch of language can justify the use of the words 'hastily conceived'. As for 'thoughtlessly passed', I wonder if you know that the resolution was discussed in the Subjects Committee for about three hours and more than a dozen speeches for and against were made. Ultimately as you know it was passed almost unanimously both in the Committee and the open Congress. Were all the people in the Committee and the Congress who voted for it 'thoughtless'? Is this not rather a strange assumption? And why should it not be said with greater truth that the small minority opposed to the resolution were mistaken? You mention that last year the resolution was rejected by the Committee. I do not know what inference you draw from this but to me it seems obvious that this can only mean that the Committee and the Congress have been eager to pass it in the past as in the present but refrained from doing so out of regard for you. I hope you will agree with me that it is not healthy politics for any organisation to subordinate its own definite opinion on a public issue out of personal regard only.

I am not referring here to the merits of the resolution. But I shall only say this that after prolonged and careful thought a demand for independence and all that this implies has come to mean a very great deal for me and I attach more importance to it than to almost anything else. I have thought over every word you said the other day in Madras on this question and it has merely confirmed me in my opinion. But I doubt if anyone outside a small circle understands your position in regard to this. I am sure that none of the others–liberals, etc.,–who want Dominion Status

[113] Moved by Nehru at the open session of the Congress on 27 December 1927, which read: 'This Congress declares the goal of the Indian people to be Complete National Independence.'

[114] For Gandhi's article, 'The National Congress', *YI*, 5-1-1928, see *CWMG*, Vol. XXXV, pp. 438–41.

think in the same way with you. Yesterday Sir Ali Imam[115] addressed a meeting here on the Simon boycott. I also spoke for a few minutes[116] and like King Charles' head[117] independence cropped up and I laid stress on it. After the meeting Ali Imam told me that I did well in laying stress on this; he and his friends would probably come round to this position sooner or later but for the time being they had to be a little restrained as they wanted to carry many people with them. I am sure most liberals welcome the independence resolution, whatever they may say about it, as they feel that it strengthens their position. But whether they like it or not, it passes my comprehension how a national organisation can have as its ideal and goal Dominion Status. The very idea suffocates and strangles me.

I took no special interest in the resolution on the boycott of British goods[118] chiefly because I felt that it would meet with your strong disapproval and the boycott could not succeed unless a

[115] (1869–1932); President, All India Muslim League, 1908; Law member, Viceroy's Executive Council, 1910–15; Judge, Patna High Court, 1917; Member, Executive Council of Bihar and Orissa, 1918; one of the signatories of the Nehru Report, 1928

[116] On 10 January 1928. Nehru had said, 'when Sir Ali Imam himself finds it difficult to swallow the Simon Commission, you can imagine my feelings when I have to face such a proposition.... we should not only boycott the Simon Commission but at the same time decide to boycott now and forever the whole conception behind it, the whole conception that the British Parliament is there to give us what it wills and keep away from us what it likes, and the whole conception that we are parts for ever and ever of the British Empire.'

[117] Using this analogy later in his speech on 28 December 1928 at Calcutta, while moving the compromise resolution on the [Motilal] Nehru Report at the Subjects Committee, Gandhi said: 'This resolution is really without its crown, but we are today suffering from what is known in psychology as inferiority complex. We have King Charles' head dangling before our eyes every five minutes. You know the celebrated Mr Dick who could not possibly think of anything without imagining the head of King Charles. This brand of inferiority is marked on our foreheads, on our breasts.... Do not consider the Nehru Report as an excrescence to be deplored but regard it as an integral part of the struggle.'

[118] Which read: 'With a view to bring [*sic*] about as effective a boycott of British goods as possible, this Congress calls upon Provincial Congress Committees to organise a boycott of selected British goods having regard to the conditions of each province.'

more or less unanimous effort was made. But I have no doubt that it can be made into a partial success if there was some unanimity in our own ranks. You must have read about the wonderful effectiveness of the boycott in China.[119] There was nothing special in China which we have not got and there is no fundamental reason why we cannot succeed where they succeeded. But granting that it is not likely to succeed, is it such a laughing matter after all? Has our boycott of foreign cloth by khaddar succeeded so remarkably—has our spinning franchise succeeded? They have not but you did not hesitate to press them on the country and the Congress because you felt, and rightly, that they would be good for this nation even if they did not wholly succeed.

I remember how Kelkar,[120] Aney[121] & co., even as members of the Working Committee, used to make fun of the Congress resolutions on khadi, and it is very painful for me to think that you are also ridiculing important Congress resolutions. The Kelkar's & Aneys do not count and I do not care what they say or do. But I do care very much for what you say and do.

Having singled out two resolutions for your special condemnation you casually refer to the others as 'several irresponsible resolutions'. Excepting the Unity Resolution every other resolution of the Congress may come under this heading. And so the labours of the 200 and odd persons in the Subjects Committee and the larger numbers in the Congress are summarily and rather contemptuously disposed of. It is very hard luck on the unhappy persons who, though wanting perhaps in foresight and intelligence, did not spare themselves and tried to do their best. We have all 'sunk to the level of the school boys' debating society' and you chastise us like an angry schoolmaster, but a schoolmaster who will not guide us or give us lessons but will only point out from time to time the error of our ways. Personally I very much wish that we were more

[119] In 1925 a boycott of British goods organized in China had lasted for months and caused heavy losses to British traders.

[120] N.C. Kelkar (1872–1947); editor of *Mahratta*, 1896–1918; later became a Responsivist

[121] M.S. Aney (1880–1968); acting President, INC, 1933; Member, Viceroy's Council, 1942; representative of Indian Government in Ceylon, 1943–7; Governor, Bihar, 1948–52; Member, Lok Sabha, 1959–67

like real school boys, with the life and energy and daring of school boys, and a little less like the right honourable gentlemen who are for ever weighing the pros and cons and counting the cost.

You know how intensely I have admired you and believed in you as a leader who can lead this country to victory and freedom. I have done so in spite of the fact that I hardly agreed with anything that some of your previous publications—*Indian Home Rule*, etc.—contained.[122] I felt and feel that you were and are infinitely greater than your little books. Above everything I admire action and daring and courage and I found them all in you in a superlative degree. And I felt instinctively that however much I may disagree with you, your great personality and your possession of these qualities would carry us to our goal. During the noncooperation period you were supreme; you were in your element and automatically you took the right step. But since you came out of prison something seems to have gone wrong and you have been very obviously ill at ease. You will remember how within a few months or even weeks you repeatedly changed your attitude—the Juhu statements, the AICC meeting at Ahmedabad and after, etc.,—and most of us were left in utter bewilderment.[123] That bewilderment has continued since then. I have asked you many times what you expected to do in the future and your answers have been far from satisfying. All you have said has been that within a year or 18 months you expected the khadi movement to spread rapidly and in a geometric ratio and then some direct action in the political field might be indulged in—several years and 18 months have passed since then and the miracle has not happened. It was difficult to believe that it would happen but faith in your amazing capacity to bring off the improbable kept us in an expectant mood. But such faith for an irreligious person like me is a poor reed to rely on and I am beginning to think if we are to wait for freedom till khadi becomes universal in India we shall have to wait till the Greek Kalends. Khadi will grow slowly, and if war comes it will grow very fast, but I do not see how

[122] *Hind Swaraj* or *Indian Home Rule*, written in Gujarati during Gandhi's return journey to South Africa from England in 1909, was a severe indictment of western civilization.

[123] See pp. 12–13.

freedom is coming in its train.[124] As I mentioned before to you our khadi work is almost wholly divorced from politics and our khadi workers are developing a mentality which does not concern itself with anything outside their limited sphere of work. This may be good for the work they do, but little can be expected from them in the political field.

What then can be done? You say nothing. You only criticise and no helpful lead comes from you. You tell us that if the country will not even take to khadi how can we expect it to do anything more difficult or daring. I do not think the reasoning is correct. If the country does not go ahead politically by one method, surely it is up to our leaders to think of other or additional methods.

Reading many of your articles in *Young India*—your autobiography, etc., —I have often felt how very different my ideals were from yours.[125] And I have felt that you were very hasty in your judgements, or rather having arrived at certain conclusions you were over-eager to justify them by any scrap of evidence you might get. I remember how in an article on the 'Two Ways'—or some such title—you gave some newspaper cuttings from America about crime and immorality and contrasted American civilisation with India. I felt it was something like Katherine Mayo[126] drawing conclusions from some unsavoury hospital statistics. Your long series of articles,[127] based on the French book, *Towards Moral Bankruptcy* also made one feel the same way. You misjudge greatly I think the civilisation of the West and attach too great an importance to its

[124] Ironically enough, Nehru was later to describe khadi famously as the 'livery of freedom' in a statement to the Press on 10 July 1937. See also Letter no. 255 (p. 308).

[125] Gandhi's autobiography entitled *The Story of My Experiments with Truth* had started appearing serially in *Young India* from the first week of December 1925.

[126] An American author who sought to show that India was socially backward and therefore unfit for freedom. Her book *Mother India* was written with the active assistance of British officials in London and India. For Gandhi's pungent critique of the book in the article 'Drain Inspector's Report', *YI*, 15-9-1927, see *CWMG*, Vol. XXXIV, pp. 539–47.

[127] Which appeared in *Young India* from 1 July to 19 August 1926, was based on M. Paul Bureau's *D'Indiscipline des moeurs*, condemning the use of contraceptives

many failings. You have stated somewhere that India has nothing to learn from the West and that she has reached a pinnacle of wisdom in the past. I entirely disagree with this viewpoint and I neither think that the so-called *Rama Raj* was very good in the past, nor do I want it back.[128] I think the western or rather industrial civilisation is bound to conquer India, maybe with many changes and adaptations, but nonetheless in the main based on industrialism. You have criticised strongly the many obvious defects of industrialism and hardly paid any attention to its merits. Everybody knows these defects and all the utopias and social theories are meant to remove them. It is the opinion of most thinkers in the West that these defects are not due to industrialism as such but to the capitalist system which is based on exploitation of others. I believe you have stated that in your opinion there is no necessary conflict between Capital and Labour. I think that under the capitalist system this conflict is unavoidable.

You have advocated very eloquently and forcefully the claim of *daridranarayana*[129]—the poor in India. I do believe that the remedy you have suggested is very helpful to them and if adopted by them in large numbers will relieve to some extent their misery. But I doubt very much if the fundamental causes of poverty are touched by it. You do not say a word against the semi-feudal zamindari system which prevails in a great part of India or against the capitalist exploitation of both the workers and the consumers.

But I must stop. I have already exceeded all reasonable limits and I hope you will forgive me. My only excuse is my mental agitation. I did not want to become Secretary of the AICC as I wanted perfect freedom to say and do what I considered necessary.[130] But Ansari pressed me on the ground that many of my resolutions and specially the Independence Resolution, had been passed by the Congress and I thus had full freedom to work on my own lines. I could not answer this argument and had to accept. Now I find

[128] For Gandhi's views on the ideal of *Ramarajya*, or the kingdom of Rama, who symbolized Righteousness, see *CWMG*, Vol. XXV, pp. 489–90.

[129] God in the form of the poor

[130] Nehru was again elected General Secretary in January 1928 and held the post till December 1929.

that every effort is being made to belittle and ridicule these very Congress resolutions and it is a painful experience.

Yours affectionately,
Jawaharlal

SWJN, *Vol. 3, I Series, pp. 10–15*

## 32. Letter to Jawaharlal Nehru

Satyagraha Ashram, Sabarmati
11 January 1928

My dear Jawaharlal,
Your letter.

I hope Chand[131] is out of the wood.

My point is not that you have not thought out any of your resolutions, much less the Independence one; but my point is that neither you nor anyone else had thought out the whole situation and considered the bearing and propriety of the resolutions. The finest resolutions may be irrelevant or out of place. But you should read carefully my articles on the Congress. The special article on Independence[132] will be out tomorrow.

The Unity Resolution needs much working out.

Do come whenever you can and when you come bring your work here and give yourself enough time.

This is scrappy but can't give more time now.

Yours,
Bapu

G-N Correspondence, JN Papers, *NMML*

[131] Chandralekha, Nehru's niece and the eldest daughter of Vijayalakshimi Pandit

[132] Entitled 'Independence *vs.* Swaraj' (*YI*, 12-1-1928); see *CWMG*, Vol. XXXV, pp. 455–7.

## 33. Letter to Jawaharlal Nehru

Satyagraha Ashram, Sabarmati
15 January 1928

My dear Jawaharlal,

I have your letter[133] which I appreciate more than anything else you could have written me, because you are absolutely frank and I am glad for having written the article if only to draw from you what you have been keeping to yourself all these long years. But of this later.

This I am dictating merely to tell you that poor Brockway[134] is in a bad way. I understand that he will have to undergo another operation of a more serious nature and might have to stay in India for many more months. I understand too that he has come to an understanding with the AICC arrived at by Father that his passage to and fro should be paid by the Congress. If that is so, I suppose we should defray his hospital expenses also and perhaps these in any case seeing that he was coming to the Congress. Will you please inquire and do the needful, even set the wire in motion if necessary.

I understand that the Madras Committee has already paid nearly Rs 400. The hospital charges alone are said to amount to Rs 12 per day. I am writing to Srinivasa Iyengar also.

Yours sincerely,
Bapu

G-N Correspondence, JN Papers, *NMML*

[133] Of 11 January 1928; see pp. 46–53.

[134] Fenner Brockway (1888–1988); British anti-war activist and politician; for many years Secretary of the Independent Labour Party; attended the Congress session at Madras, 1927

## 34. Letter to Jawaharlal Nehru

The Ashram, Sabarmati
17 January 1928

My dear Jawaharlal,
I must dictate and save time and give rest to my aching shoulder. I wrote to you on Sunday about Fenner Brockway. I hope you got the letter in due time.

Do you know that it was because you were the chief partner in the transactions referred to that I wrote the particular article you have criticised, except of course about the so called 'All India Exhibition'?[135] I felt a kind of safety that in view of the relations between you and me my writing would be taken in the spirit in which it was written, however, I see they were a misfire all round. I do not mind it. For, it is evident that the article alone could deliver you from the self-suppression under which you have been labouring apparently for so many years. Though I was beginning to detect some difference in viewpoint between you and me, I had no notion whatsoever of the terrible extent of these differences. Whilst you were heroically suppressing yourself for the sake of the nation and in the belief that you were working with and under me in spite of yourself, you would serve the nation and come out scatheless, you were chafing under the burden of this unnatural self-suppression. And, while you were in that state, you overlooked the very things which appear to you as my blemishes. I could show from the pages of *Young India* equally strong articles written by me when I was actively guiding the C., with reference to the doings of the All India Congress Committee. I have spoken similarly at the All India Congress Committee meetings whenever there has been irresponsible and hasty talk or action. But whilst you were under stupefaction these things did not jar on you as they do now. And it seems to me therefore useless to show you the

[135] For Gandhi's comments on the Exhibition that 'represented not the rural civilisation of India, but the exploiting city civilisation of the West', see *CWMG*, Vol. XXXV, p. 439.

discrepancies in your letter. What I am ow most concerned with is future action.

If any freedom is required from me I give you all the freedom you may need from the humble but unquestioning allegiance that you have given to me for all these years and which I value all the more for the knowledge I have now gained of your state. I see quite clearly that you must carry on open warfare against me and my views. For, if I am wrong I am evidently doing irreparable harm to the country and it is your duty after having known it to rise in revolt against me. Or, if you have any doubt as to the correctness of your conclusions, I shall gladly discuss them personally. The differences between you and me appear so vast and radical that there seems to be no meeting ground between us. I can't conceal from you my grief that I should lose a comrade so valiant, so faithful, so able and so honest as you have always been; but in serving a cause, comradeships have got to be sacrificed. The cause must be held superior to all such considerations. But this dissolution of comradeship—if dissolution must come—in no way affects my personal intimacy. We have long become members of the same family, and we remain such in spite of grave political differences. I have the good fortune to enjoy such relations with several people. To take Sastri[136] for instance, he and I differ in the political outlook as poles asunder, but the bond between him and me that sprung up before we knew the political differences has persisted and survived the fiery ordeals it had to go through.

I suggest a dignified way of unfurling your banner. Write me a letter for publication showing your differences. I will print it in *Young India* and write a brief reply. Your first letter I destroyed after reading and replying to it, the second I am keeping, and if you do not want to take the trouble of writing another letter, I am prepared to publish the letter that is before me. I am not aware of any offensive passage in it. But if I find any, you may depend upon my

[136] V.S. Srinivasa Sastri (1869–1946); politician, administrator and educator; acclaimed for his oratory and command over the English language; Member, INC, 1908–22; one of the founding members of the Liberal Party

removing every such passage. I consider that letter to be a frank and honest document.

With love,

Yours sincerely,
Bapu

Pandit Jawaharlal Nehru
Anand Bhavan
Allahabad

G-N Correspondence, JN Papers, *NMML*

## 35. Letter to M.K. Gandhi

Allahabad
23 January 1928

My dear Bapuji,

Your letter came as a bit of a shock and was painful reading. Painful because with relentless logic you had contemplated certain eventualities which I had not considered possible or even thought of in their entirety. You talk about my carrying on 'open warfare' against you and of 'unfurling my banner'. I have no particular banner to unfurl nor had I thought of the possibility of any warfare between you and me. I had certainly thought of differences of opinion, which may be fundamental, and of my following a line of action in regard to certain matters which may not meet with your approval. But I felt that you would certainly desire me to follow that line, even though you disagreed with it, if you thought that I was quite clear about it in my own mind. And even if there were possibilities of conflict on some points, there appeared to me absolutely no necessity for this difference or conflict to spread to the many other points on which I presumed there would be considerable ground for common action. You have referred to Sastri and your relations with him. Is any assurance from me necessary that nothing that can ever happen can alter or lessen my deep regard and affection for you? That regard and affection is certainly personal, but it is something more. No one has moved me and inspired me more than you and I can never forget your exceeding kindness to me. There can be no question of our personal relations suffering. But even in the wider sphere am I not your child in politics, though perhaps a truant and errant child?

I should very much like to discuss many things with you and I cannot say whether I shall or shall not change many of my present opinions after my discussion with you. I hope I am not rigid in mind and outlook and nothing could please me more than to be convinced by you. I have wanted to have a good talk with you frequently in times past but you are always so busy and although I saw you often enough before I went to Europe I never had the opportunity I desired. I shall try to come to you as early as possible. Before I do so I shall write to you again and somewhat more fully some of the conclusions I have arrived at after some thought. I do not want to trouble you, specially in your present state of health, with long letters. But I think that if I write to you about my present views it would clarify matters and save time when we discuss them.

I do not quite appreciate your suggestion to publish my previous letter and to comment on it. Should you wish it of course you can do so. But it was an entirely personal letter and I do not see why the public should concern itself with it. Perhaps you may have been led to think that I am going to start some kind of a campaign against your ideas and it was desirable that before doing so some kind of statement should be issued. I have no such intention and if I criticise anything or defend anything against your wishes it will be done incidentally only. May I however warn you against believing everything that appears in the papers. The other day I spoke at Benares at a public meeting. I spoke in Hindi and my speech was wholly distorted in the English report and I was made to say something which I had never thought of. This was commented upon by the *Tribune* of Lahore, and maybe other papers and it was made out that I was attacking you. This was a monstrous notion as I had not referred to you or thought of you in that connection. I have sent a contradiction.[137] There is danger of this happening and

[137] See 'Letter to the Editor', 21 January 1928, *SWJN*, Vol. 3, I Series, pp. 17–18. Nehru had written: 'The report refers to "effete and fossilised" people. My knowledge of Hindi is not sufficient to include any word for fossilised. What I wished to say was that we must develop the spirit of youth and not

I would beg of you not to believe such reports and to give me credit for greater sense and courtesy.

I would therefore suggest that for the present at least you might not publish my letter. But it is for you to judge and if you think it necessary you can publish extracts from it.

The last letter I received from father was not a cheerful document. He had evidently been upset by the doctor's reports about the state of his eyes and his heart. He has been told that if he does not take great care he may lose his sight. He talks in his letter of the 'approaching end' and appears to be very dispirited. I want to meet him in Bombay on February 6 when he lands. If he agrees I should like him to go with me to Sabarmati straight from Bombay.

Please do not trouble to answer this letter. There is nothing to answer. I shall try to follow it up after a week or so by another letter.

With love,

Yours affectionately,
Jawaharlal

SWJN, *Vol. 3, I Series, pp. 18–20*

## 36. Letter to M.K. Gandhi

Allahabad
23 February 1928

My dear Bapuji,
I wrote to you a few hours ago and informed you that I hoped to be in Sabarmati on Monday or Tuesday night. Immediately after I received a summons from Delhi to go there and remain there for the next fortnight or more to assist in constitution drafting. I have

---

become unchanging embodiments of age. I laid stress on the fact that this spirit was sometimes to be found more in the elder men than in our own youth, many of whom seemed to be born old. An extraordinary inference has been drawn that I was criticising Mahatma Gandhi. This is a monstrous notion. No person who has had a glimpse of him even once, much less one who has had the high privilege of working with him and under him for many years, can call him old in spirit. He is the supreme example of latter-day India, of all that is good in youth—energy and action, courage and daring, perseverance and resolution.'

no present intention of remaining in Delhi and I shall try my best to visit you but it may be that I am delayed in Delhi a little. Personally I have had enough of this All Parties Conference.[138] After ten days of it the strain was too great for me and I fled to avoid riot and insurrection! I feel better already after a three days' absence but another dose of all the parties may go to my head. I am thus not at all desirous of attending the meetings in Delhi. But I do not know what might happen. I shall wire to you from Delhi.

Love.

Yours affectionately,
Jawaharlal

SWJN, *Vol. 3, I Series, p. 36*

## 37. Telegram to Jawaharlal Nehru

Sabarmati
26 January 1928

Jawaharlal Nehru
Anand Bhawan
Allahabad

Your letter. Mine was written merely give you relief freedom. Have no desire publish anything from you.[139] Do bring father if at all possible. Love.

Bapu

CWMG, *Vol. XXXV, p. 546*

[138] The All-Parties Conference had set up a committee with Motilal Nehru as Chairman, to draw up a constitution for India as an answer to the challenge of the Secretary of State, Lord Birkenhead, that Indian politicians were capable of no constructive suggestions. Nehru was not a member of the committee but assisted his father with the secretarial work. His suggestions that the constitution should establish a democratic socialist republic and a beginning made in election units were ignored.

[139] See pp. 56–7 and 59.

## 38. Letter to Jawaharlal Nehru

Satyagraha Ashram, Sabarmati
26 February 1928

My dear Jawahar,

I have your letters. I am sensing all that is going on in Delhi and can understand every word of what you have said in your letter. I can't give you an adequate conception of my grief as I follow the Conference proceedings from day to day and read between the lines. Father's illuminating letter[140] only confirmed my own reading from a distance. Then came Kripalani's[141] letter yesterday to Krishnadas, and yours has come today to put the finishing touch. What a miserable show we are putting up against the insolence of Lord Birkenhead[142] and the crookedness of the Commissioners? I had not expected much from Sir John Simon,[143] but I was not at all prepared for his resorting to all the known tricks of bureaucracy, and this the latest trade on untouchables adds to the ugliness of the whole picture. However, we have to be patient. You must therefore patiently go through the agony and mend where you can.

Do come as early as possible. I hope Kamala is keeping up her strength, if not actually adding to it. I wonder if Father has told you that, before you came, when Father was with me in Bangalore, he and I had contemplated your stay in Bangalore because of its magnificent climate during summer. There are just four weeks of somewhat trying weather, but you could always go to Nandi Hill only 35 miles from Bangalore where you have delightfully cool

[140] Of 24 February 1928

[141] J.B. Kripalani (1888-1982); General Secretary, INC, 1934-46, and President, 1946; later resigned from the Congress

[142] F.E. Smith, First Earl of Birkenhead (1872-1930); British Conservative MP, 1906-19; Attorney-General, 1915-19; Lord Chancellor, 1919-22; Secretary of State for India, 1924-8

About his speech on 9 July 1925 in the House of Lords, Gandhi had said, 'Every fundamental position that he takes is challenged by every educated Indian, no matter to what party he may belong.'

[143] Chairman of the Statutory Commission which had landed in Bombay on 3 February 1928

weather. In no case should Kamala be allowed to lose what she gained in Switzerland.

Yours sincerely,
Bapu

CWMG, *Vol. XXXVI, p. 58*

## 39. Letter to Jawaharlal Nehru

Satyagraha Ashram, Sabarmati
20 March 1928

My dear Jawahar,
I have received your two letters. I write just now only to fulfil the promise to send you a message for the friend you mentioned. He has now written directly to me, but as I promised the message to you, here it is.[144]

I hope you are following my articles on boycott and mills.[145] I am having conferences with the mill-owners also. Whether they will come to anything I do not know. But if anything appears to you wrong or weak you will please let me know.

How is Kamala doing? Where are you going to keep her during the hot season?

Yours sincerely,

CWMG, *Vol. XXXVI, p. 121*

## 40. Letter to Jawaharlal Nehru

Satyagraha Ashram, Sabarmati
1 April 1928

My dear Jawahar,
I have your letter.

The enclosed copies[146] will tell you what progress is being made in the negotiations with the mill-owners. I however agree with you

[144] The message to Marcelle Capy read: 'There can be no living harmony between races and nations unless the main cause is removed, namely, exploitation of the weak, by the strong. We must revise the interpretation of the so-called doctrine of "survival of the fittest".'

[145] The articles 'What Can Mills Do' and 'The Weapon of Boycott' appeared in *YI*, 15-3-1928 and *Navajivan*, 18-3-1928 respectively.

[146] Not available

that nothing will come out of them at the present moment. But the negotiations may fructify on due occasion. There was a time when the mill-owners were absolutely defiant about boycott propaganda. I shall write to you after these negotiations are finished.

Though Romain Rolland's first expected letter has arrived and [he] warmly looks [forward] to my proposed visit, it does not enable me to come to a decision. As the time for arriving at a fixed decision is drawing nearer, my diffidence is growing. There may be however a cable from Rolland next week and it may decide my fate.[147]

Meanwhile there is no going to Singapur. I am fixed up here for the time being. If I do not go to Europe, I am due to go to Burma and pass there two months, going to a hillside and making collections during my stay there.

I am quite of your opinion that some day we shall have to start an intensive movement without the rich people and without the vocal educated class. But that time is not yet.

You do not tell me where Kamala is to pass the summer months.

Yours sincerely,

CWMG, *Vol. XXXVI, p. 174*

## 41. Letter to Jawaharlal Nehru

The Ashram, Sabarmati
5 April 1928

My dear Jawahar,

You will see my article on mills in the current issue of *Young India*.[148] The latest move is on their own to start a Swadeshi League without reference to us. Do not think anything concrete is going to come out of my effort. By all means let them prosecute their own plans. So far as I can see, we must confine our attention to khadi hawking.

No final decision has yet been arrived at about the European visit. I am shirking it and making it depend upon some further indication from Rolland which I should have next week.

Yours sincerely,

CWMG, *Vol. XXXVI, p. 193*

[147] See p. 67.

[148] Dated 5 April 1928 under the title 'A Mill-owner on Boycott'

## 42. Letter to Jawaharlal Nehru

The Ashram, Sabarmati
8 April 1928

My dear Jawahar,

I have your letter. I do not remember Father having told me that he would be back in Bombay to confer with the mill-owners during the last week of this month.[149] But he and I discussed the question of foreign cloth boycott at length and he had a conference with Seth Lalji, Shantikumar, Seths Ambalal,[150] Kasturbhai[151] and Mangaldas.[152] It was a good conference, but nothing definite was done. I have now heard that the mill-owners are going to start their own Swadeshi League which means of course that we are not coming to any terms.

I had a long discussion with Lalaji[153] today, for he was here for two days. He is enthusiastic about boycott of foreign cloth. I have supplied him with literature. He even suggested that I should invite a few leaders and confer with [them] about boycott. I told him I had not the courage to do so. He is of opinion that if intense boycott propaganda is to be taken up, I must not go out of the country, wherein of course I agree; but I cannot take up intense propaganda unless politically-minded India is wholeheartedly with me and unless the agitation about temporary boycott of [foreign][154] cloth, principally British cloth, is given up. We have, therefore, come to this provisional arrangement that if anything concrete takes place by spontaneous action on the part of the known leaders, I should

[149] Gandhi had written to one of them, Shantikumar Morarji, on 31 March enunciating his eight-point programme for the mill-owners to agree upon.

[150] Ambalal Sarabhai (1890–1967); a leading industrialist of Ahmedabad

[151] Kasturbhai Lalbhai, Agent, Raipur Manufacturing Company, Ahmedabad.

[152] Mangaldas Girdhardas

[153] Lala Lajpat Rai (1865–1928); Congressman of Punjab; described as the 'Lion of Punjab'; supported extremists in 1907 and was imprisoned in Mandalay for six months; President, INC, 1920; member of the Swaraj Party, but later broke away to found the Nationalist Party; was lathi-charged by the police during the Lahore demonstrations against the Simon Commission; died as a result a few days later, on 17 November 1928

[154] 'British' in the source

give up the idea of going to Europe. On the other hand [if] nothing of that kind happens and if otherwise I see my way clear, I should proceed and that Lalaji and others who are minded like him should cultivate an atmosphere for intense propaganda about foreign cloth boycott with or without the assistance of mills. I therefore suggest that you should confer with Dr Ansari and others. I suppose they will all go to the Punjab and pass the resolution about foreign cloth boycott through khadi. I would warn you against any mention of indigenous mill cloth. You can simply say: 'Whereas the only effective means of immediately demonstrating the united strength of the nation lies through boycott of foreign cloth, this conference urges all concerned completely to boycott foreign cloth and adopt hand-spun and hand-woven khadi even though such adoption may necessitate revision of one's taste about dress and some pecuniary sacrifice.' You will also let me know the result of private discussions you may have with friends and advise me as to whether I should give up the idea of going to Europe. Dr Ansari should really be able to decide.

Yours sincerely,

CWMG, *Vol. XXXVI, pp. 207–8*

## 43. Letter to Jawaharlal Nehru

The Ashram, Sabarmati
17 April 1928

My dear Jawahar,
I have your letter. Do you know that even when you wrote to me that you were going to the Punjab, I did not know that you were going as the president of the Conference?[155] When Dr Kitchlew[156] wrote to me, he said nothing about who the president was to be. However I was glad when I learnt that you presided.

[155] Punjab Provincial Conference on 11 April 1928. For the English version of Nehru's address in Hindi as President, see *SWJN*, Vol. 3, I Series, pp. 219–30.

[156] Saifuddin Kitchlew (1888–1963); contemporary of Nehru at Cambridge; joined the nationalist movement in 1912; rose to prominence during the Martial Law Regime in 1919; Secretary, All India Muslim League, 1928; awarded the Lenin Peace Prize in 1952

Of course I notice everywhere what you noticed at the Conference. I wonder if you have noticed what I sense everywhere, utter absence of seriousness and disinclination to do any concrete work demanding sustained energy.

Do you find any hope in the Punjab for Hindu-Muslim unity?

About the European visit, I can give you no definite news yet.

The fiasco about mills you know everything [of] by this time from Father.

Yours sincerely,

CWJN, *Vol. XXXVI, pp. 237–8*

## 44. Letter to Jawaharlal Nehru

The Ashram, Sabarmati
24 April 1928

My dear Jawahar,

I have your letter. Of course you know already the calamity that has befallen me on the death of Maganlal.[157] It is well-nigh unbearable. However I am putting on a brave front.

I had not read the resolution asking the Congress to drop 'peaceful and legitimate means' and change the expression into 'by all possible means'.[158] Independence I can swallow, 'by all means'

[157] On 23 April 1928 at Patna. Maganlal Gandhi, a grandson of an uncle of Gandhi, had dedicated himself to the satyagraha struggle in South Africa; later, in India he had got deeply involved with the Satyagraha Ashram activities, especially weaving.

Gandhi wrote in *YI*, 26-4-1928, that Maganlal Gandhi had been 'my hands and feet and eyes. The world knows so little of how much my so-called greatness depends on the incessant toil and drudgery of siient, devoted, able and pure workers, men as well as women. And among them all Maganlal to me was the greatest, the best and the purest.'

[158] The Congress Constitution adopted at the Nagpur session in December 1920 had as Resolution No. 1, Article 1, which read: 'The object of the Indian National Congress is the attainment of Swarajya by the people of India by all legitimate and peaceful means.' The phrase 'legitimate and peaceful means' came to be much debated in subsequent years of constitution-drafting. Gandhi's suggestion to substitute it with the words 'truthful and nonviolent' was not accepted by the Working Committee. See *CWMG*, Vol. LVIII, p. 265 and Vol. XLII, pp. 374–5.

is unswallowable. But I suppose we shall have to develop stomachs strong enough to swallow any poison. I hope however that you will not allow yourself to be exploited beyond your wish and capacity. The mill-owners, it has now become obviously clear, wanted to do a deal with the Congress. But I am not sorry for these abortive negotiations. They have cleared the atmosphere.

The expected letter from Romain Rolland was received on Sunday. He will not bear the burden I wanted him to do.[159] So I am not going this year. But you will read about this in the pages of *Young India*.

Yours sincerely,

CWMG, *Vol. XXXVI, pp. 258–9*

## 45. Letter to M.K. Gandhi

[24][160] April 1928

My dear Bapuji,
We have just been shocked to learn from the papers about Maganlal Bhai's death. He was the last person I would have thought of in this connection. But somehow our strongest and healthiest pass away and the weak and the ailing remain. To you and the khadi movement his passing away must be a great loss. He had intended coming to Allahabad this month from Calcutta and we were all looking forward to seeing him here. But that is not to be.

We seem to be having a cup full of misfortunes. One of our best workers here, Anandi Prasad Sinha, the Secretary of the District Congress Committee and a member of the AICC died last week.

[159] Giving reasons for abandoning the contemplated visit to Europe, Gandhi wrote in *YI*, 26-4-1928, 'To European Friends': 'Owing to my distrust of myself over a general visit, I wanted to make my visit to that wise man of the West the primary cause of my journey to Europe.... But evidently he was too humble to bear the burden of calling me merely so that in furtherance of the common interest we might by mutual talks understand each other better. And I wanted him to shoulder the very burden, if he felt that truth required us to meet each other face to face.'

[160] The source has '14', evidently a slip.

He went on April 13 for a National Week[161] meeting to a village about 20 miles from here. After finishing the meeting he was in a hurry to return to Allahabad to attend the meeting here too. In trying to mount the railway train he slipped and fell and had his leg cut off. He might perhaps have lived on if he had been looked after properly, but he was neglected both by the railway people and the police and when at last he arrived in hospital here there was great delay in tending to him. To the last, with profuse bleeding going on, he kept on smiling. We have few enough people who do any national work now. They can be counted on the fingers of one hand. And the loss of one good worker is a big loss.

Yours affectionately,
Jawaharlal

SWJN, *Vol. 3, I Series, p. 405*

## 46. Letter to Jawaharlal Nehru

Satyagraha Ashram, Sabarmati
B.B & CI Rly
17 June 1928

My dear Jawahar,
I have your two letters. The news about Kamala and Indu is disturbing. I am hoping to have more definite information from you. I am tempted to suggest for both, and certainly at least for Kamala, the poor man's remedy, and that is hip-bath and sitz-bath according to Kuhne's system,[162] and dieting together with sun-bath. But I know that this is not practicable and that she will have to go through the ordinary treatment.

I hope that there will be an agreed draft constitution in a complete form brought out by the Committee.

[161] Observed from 6 to 13 April 1920 annually for many years. It was marked by fasting on the opening and closing days and engaging in constructive work during the week. In 1919, 6 April was observed as a day of protest to mark the launching of the All-India satyagraha against repressive legislation known as the Rowlatt Act by fasting, prayer and hartal. 'Black Friday', the 13th of April 1919, had witnessed the Jallianwala Bagh massacre at Amritsar.

[162] Namely, Louis Kuhne's hydropathic treatment

Mahadev had a serious fall from the platform of the Ashram well. He is bed-ridden but better.

CWMG, *Vol. XXXVI, p. 427*

## 47. Letter to M.K. Gandhi

Allahabad
30 June 1928

My dear Bapuji,
Father has I believe written to you about Kamala and Indu. Indu I am glad to say has been pronounced to be well but Kamala is supposed to be more or less as she was two years ago. Ansari agrees with the diagnosis but says that only a very small part is affected and this should yield easily to treatment. She looks well. She has a bad cough but I believe this is a separate ailment and has nothing to do with TB.

I know Kuhne's system fairly well. In fact many years ago I tried it myself. I had no special occasion to do so as I am not in the habit of falling ill. I can't say that it cured me of anything because I was not suffering from anything. But I felt fitter all the same. Kamala has also tried it in the past. I think it would do her good now, but it is difficult to arrange it just now in Mussoorie without breaking off completely with the present doctor. When she comes to Allahabad I shall start it.

The 'agreed draft constitution' seems to be as far off as ever. Indeed I think it is further off. Even in our little committee a sufficient amount of heat is engendered and it is not easy to consider the communal question dispassionately. I do not know if anything will happen next week when a final effort is going to be made to settle differences. I doubt it. Everybody thinks he is 100% in the right and the other party is a narrow-minded obstinate pig or a bigot of the worst kind. This does not produce a helpful atmosphere.

One of the wisest things I have done was to withdraw my name from the membership of the committee. As it is, my presence at committee meetings is a trial to all concerned. It is certainly painful to me to have to put up with all that is said and done there and I am sure my occasional intrusions are not welcomed. The committee will be over in a few days but the problem will however remain. The fault must be mine but anyway it results in my feeling always that I do not fit in with anything. I am always the square peg and the holes are all round. I feel very lonely.

I trust Mahadeva is quite well now.

Yours affectionately,
Jawaharlal

SWJN, *Vol. 3, I Series, pp. 49–50*

## 48. Letter to Jawaharlal Nehru

3 July 1928

My dear Jawahar,
I have your letter. Yes, Father wrote to me all about Kamala and Indu.

It is clear that we have not got the atmosphere for a proper settlement. Look at the Kharagpur horror! There will have to be more pitched battles before the parties come to their senses.

I wish you will not feel lonely. Let us recognise that the task before workers is not as easy as we thought at one time it was. I would like you not to lose patience and take up some plodding work with a living faith in it. Let the *Song Celestial* be your guidebook.

With love,

Bapu

CWMG, *Vol. XXXVII, p. 422*

## 49. Letter to Jawaharlal Nehru

29 July 1928

My dear Jawaharlal,
I do hope Kamala and Indu are flourishing. I had your wire and letter.[163] The presidential business is now finished.[164]

[163] Not available

[164] In his article 'Crown of Thorns', *YI*, 26-7-1928, discussing the issue of Congress presidentship for the forthcoming Calcutta Congress session, Gandhi wrote: 'Sardar Vallabhbhai is ... out of the question now. His hands are too full to allow of his attention being diverted from Bardoli. And before December comes upon us he may be a guest in one of His Majesty's innumerable prisons. My own feeling in the matter is that Pandit Jawaharlal should wear

I write this to consult you about Bhuvarji. He asks the Ashram to give him Rs 20 per month and for this he wants Rs 100 in advance. I would like you to tell me how he is working and whether he is giving you satisfaction. The AISA will not and cannot give him anything. Do you advise the Ashram to supply his needs? What is the nature of work he is doing?

Yours sincerely,
Bapu

CWMG, *Vol. XXXVII, p. 422*

## 50. Letter to M.K. Gandhi

Allahabad
14 November 1928

My dear Bapuji,
Shankerlal writes to me that he has sent you a letter I wrote to him some days ago. I do not know if I made my meaning clear in this letter. I suggested to him that for various reasons it would be desirable for the AISA Council to have a more competent person than myself as agent in the UP. I am painfully conscious of the fact that I am not much of a success there—partly because of my inability to go deeply into accounts and partly because of other occupations. I did not mean that I want to get rid of the responsibility or the work. I shall gladly carry on and do what I can. But if it is possible to make better arrangements I shall welcome them.

I cannot suggest many names. The only person I can think of in the UP is Kripalani. He is practically a UP man now, is well known in khadi circles here and is a wholetimer. It would have been a good thing if he was made the agent for both the UP and Delhi. This would result perhaps in better coordination between the Gandhi Ashram and the UP dept. of the AISA. I am not sure however how far this suggestion is practicable at present.

---

the crown. The future must be for the youth of the country. But Bengal wants Motilal to guide the Congress barque through the perilous seas that threaten to overwhelm us during the coming year.... It is these considerations which actuate even the dare-all Bengal patriot [Subhas Chandra Bose] to want Pandit Motilal Nehru as the helmsman for the coming year.' The Congress met at Calcutta in the last week of December with Motilal Nehru as President.

There is no immediate hurry in this matter. I wanted the AISA Council to consider it largely in view of the rumours of my impending arrest.[165] But I do not think anything of this kind is going to happen this year.

Kamala has been giving us a great deal of anxiety. Not because she is in any critical state but she is generally much weaker and liable to all manner of pains and troubles. We propose to take her to Calcutta for treatment.

Yours affectionately,
Jawaharlal

SWJN, *Vol. 3, I Series, p. 175*

## 51. Letter to Jawaharlal Nehru

Satyagraha Ashram, Sabarmati
17 November 1928

My dear Jawahar,

Your letter frees me from all anxiety. So long as you are willing to act as agent, no change need be made, and certainly not whilst there is rumour of your being spirited away. When that event happens, we shall see. Personally I like the idea of Kripalani becoming Agent when you can no longer shoulder the burden. We shall discuss the matter further if you can come to Wardha on the 18th December or we shall do so in Calcutta.

Sitla Sahai wanted to be in the Ashram for some months for mental adjustment more than anything else. He has domestic and

[165] In his *Autobiography*, Nehru writes: 'In the second half of 1928 and in 1929 there was frequent talk of my arrest. I do not know what reality lay behind the press references and the numerous private warnings I received from friends who seemed to be in the know, but the warnings produced a feeling of uncertainty in me and I felt I was always on the verge of it. I did not mind this particularly as I knew that, whatever the future held for me, it could not be a settled life of routine. The sooner I got used to uncertainty and sudden changes and visits to the prison the better. And I think on the whole I succeeded in getting used to the idea and whenever arrest came I took it more casually than I might otherwise have done. So rumours of arrest were not without compensation; they gave a certain excitement and a bite to my daily existence. ... As a matter of fact I had a long innings in 1928 and 1929, and arrest came at last as late as April 1930.'

other worries preying upon him. He wanted a quiet time and he is having it.

I am sorry about Kamala. Evidently she never completely recovered in Switzerland. I am glad you are taking her to Calcutta. She will at least have the best advice possible.

I hope you are not overworking yourself. Lalaji's death[166] is a great calamity.

Yours sincerely,
Bapu

Pandit Jawaharlal Nehru
Anand Bhawan, Allahabad

CWMG, *Vol. XXXVIII, pp. 61–2*

## 52. Letter to M.K. Gandhi

Allahabad
24 November 1928

My dear Bapuji,
Thank you for your letter. I shall of course carry on to the best of my ability with the AISA work. I have no desire to leave it. But I felt a little overwhelmed with various kinds of activities and thought that I was not doing justice to the AISA. Sitla Sahai's departure for a lengthy period made matters worse and hence I wrote to Shankerlal.

I am being dragged willy-nilly to this municipality.[167] For the last six months or more I have resisted and refused but the facts are too strong for me and I have had to give a conditional consent. It may be that I am elected the Chairman in a week or so. This is not a prospect which cheers me up. I like municipal work but the present state of our municipality is so bad that a tremendous deal of work is required.

I should very much like to come to Wardha for the AISA meeting. I shall try to do so but I doubt if I shall succeed. Anyway I hope

[166] On 17 November 1928. See p. 64, *fn.* 153. For a description of the incident by Nehru, see *An Autobiography*, pp. 173–4.

[167] For two years, from April 1923 to April 1925, Nehru had served with distinction as Chairman of the Allahabad Municipal Board. Three years later, he was drawn again into municipal politics and was defeated by the loyalist candidate by one vote in the election for the chairmanship.

to see you in Calcutta. The papers announce that you are going to Mysore in December.

It is obvious that Kamala did not get cured in Europe. She is tolerably well at present but is very weak. She will go to Calcutta and may stay there some time for treatment.

Yours affectionately,
Jawaharlal

SWJN, *Vol. 3, I Series, p. 176*

## 53. Letter to Jawaharlal Nehru

Satyagraha Ashram, Wardha
28 November 1928

My dear Jawahar,

I have your letter. I shall be sorry indeed if you have to enter the Municipality again, unless you enter it on condition of perfect obedience being rendered to you. If you have to go in for the purpose of settling disputes, it is not worthwhile. My conviction is that you cannot combine all-India work with solid municipal work. Solid municipal work is a thing complete in itself and requires all the energy that a man can give it and I would not like your work to be anything but solid.

I was to have gone to Mysore to attend the Christian Convention. That was the hope I had given to friends during the middle of the year, but I informed them about a month ago that my going was impossible, if I was to have any rest at all.

The news you had given me about Kamala is bad. I like the idea of her being under treatment in Calcutta. She will have there the best medical advice possible.

I do hope that you will find time to attend the meeting here.[168]

Yours sincerely,
M.K. Gandhi

Pandit Jawaharlal Nehru
Anand Bhawan, Allahabad

CWMG, *Vol. XXXVIII, pp. 111–12*

[168] Which was to be held on 29 November, the National Mourning Day for Lajpat Rai

## 54. Letter to Jawaharlal Nehru

Wardha
3 December 1928

My dear Jawahar,
My love to you. It was all done bravely.[169] You have braver things to do. May God spare you for many a long year to come and make you His chosen instrument for freeing India from yoke.

Yours,
Bapu

CWMG, *Vol. XXXVIII, p. 150*

## 55. Telegram to M.K. Gandhi

11 January 1929

Papers announce you touring north United Provinces. Hope you will extend tour South also.

Jawahar

CWMG, *Vol. XXXVIII, p. 337fn*

## 56. Letter to Jawaharlal Nehru

Ashram, Sabarmati
12 January 1929

My dear Jawahar,
I have your telegram. I had certainly intended to tour in some parts of the UP in response to a request made by some workers in Banda and Jhansi. But they withdrew the request, being diffident. The tour, therefore, was cancelled. There is yet another in prospect and that is near Meerut and Delhi. They want me to go there in March. But for March I have so many engagements from which I have got

[169] This refers to the exemplary behaviour of Nehru and his companions when they were brutally assaulted and severely beaten up by the police while holding a peaceful demonstration in Lucknow against the Simon Commission on 29 November 1928. For Gandhi's articles on this incident, see 'Its Gory Career', *YI*, 6-12-1928 and 'The Blood-stained Path', *Navajivan*, 9-12-1928. For Nehru's description of the incident, see *An Autobiography*, pp. 183–6.

to choose. There is Andhra, there is Karnataka and there is Burma besides Delhi and Meerut; and there is also the Punjab. Lalaji's Society[170] people want me there for their anniversary celebration. I am awaiting Father's decision as to the proposed European visit. If he cancels that visit, then the way will be open for me to satisfy all the demands upon my time. If he wants the European visit to come off, then I may not extend my tour beyond the first week of April. I cannot take the matter any further just now. But I would like you to help me to make my choice. You will consult Father about his wishes and that will enable you to guide me better.

By the time this reaches you, Father will have probably telegraphed to me his opinion. If he has not, please see that he does.

How is Kamala doing now? And how are you yourself faring? You have become Secretary.[171] I want you to throw yourself heart and soul therefore into the programme,[172] and compel obedience to instructions from the Working Committee and try to bring order out of the existing disgraceful disorder.

Yours sincerely,
Bapu

CWMG, *Vol. XXXVIII, p. 337*

## 57. Letter to Jawaharlal Nehru

Satyagraha Ashram, Sabarmati
17 January 1929

My dear Jawahar,

I have your letter. About the tour in the UP. I have written to you already. I write this about Kripalani. Jamnalalji tells me that you want Kripalani to take up organisation under you, that is to say, to take up the work that Sitla Sahai was doing and add to it as much as he can. Your letter under reply does not quite give me that impression. Kripalani himself, I understand, has written to you already, because on the strength of Jamnalalji's letter, I had begun

[170] Servants of the People Society founded in 1920 by Lala Lajpat Rai

[171] Nehru was General Secretary, INC, from 1927 to 1929.

[172] Constructive programme as laid down in the resolution passed by the Congress at Calcutta on 1 January 1929. See *CWMG*, Vol. XXXVIII, pp. 313–14.

to talk to him before receipt of your letter and so had Shankerlal. You will now write to me therefore what you exactly intend in this matter.

If I do not tour in the UP in the near future and if you can come over to Sabarmati even for a day or two, we can discuss many things.

I utterly distrust doctors' reports about Kamala whether they are favourable or unfavourable. I wish you and Father and Kamala will make up your minds for her to take the natural treatment, that means Kuhne's bath and sun-baths. Sun-baths are now in vogue even amongst the medical profession and very extraordinary results are claimed for them.

You will telegraph if necessary about Kripalani.

Yours sincerely,
Bapu

CWMG, *Vol. XXXVIII, pp. 359–60*

## 58. Letter to M.K. Gandhi

Anand Bhawan, Allahabad
21 January 1929

My dear Bapu,

Your letter has surprised me a little. Sitla Sahai has also written to me that he has been asked to give up the secretaryship of the UP branch of the AISA as a result of some arrangement arrived at between Jamnalalji and me. Evidently there has been a serious misunderstanding somewhere.

My impression of the conversation I had with Jamnalalji was and is that the status quo should be maintained for the present but that Kripalani be asked to tour round our centres and select spots and make recommendations for the reorganisation of khadi work in the province. Jamnalalji certainly referred to the possibility of Sitla Sahai doing some other work if he was not suited to his present work. But as in my opinion the question did not arise just yet, I did not discuss it. Kripalani's name was discussed for the agentship, not the secretaryship. Jamnalalji however wanted me to remain as agent. I agreed to this. My only difficulty was that I did not consider myself a competent agent.

It does not really much matter what my opinion is on the subject. It is for you and Jamnalalji and Shankerlal to decide and we shall abide by your decision. I had not contemplated the possibility of Sitla Sahai leaving the secretaryship. I feel now however that there is practically no alternative. It appears that Jamnalalji and Shankerlal are both decidedly of opinion that Sitla Sahai is not fit for this work. If that is their opinion then he must go whatever my own opinion may be. As a self-respecting person he should himself resign.

My own opinion of Sitla Sahai's capacity is different from Shankerlal's. I am fully cognisant of his failings, and specially of his remarkable capacity for rubbing people up the wrong way, but still I think that he is a very good worker. I am not aware of anyone in my immediate circle of workers in the UP who can replace him with advantage in the AISA. The Gandhi Ashram probably can supply one or more good workers for the AISA here.

Since Sitla Sahai's departure for Sabarmati I have had the greatest difficulty in doing AISA work. It was largely owing to this that I first wrote to you last year[173] suggesting my resignation from the agentship. Our annual report ought to have been sent nearly two months ago. But there is no one here who can draft it properly. I must do this whole thing myself after going into all the figures, etc. December was a heavy month and I was away for the greater part of it. January so far has also been well occupied and I have not had any time to give to the drafting of this report. I do not want to be responsible for an office which cannot do its work punctually and yet what am I to do? To find some time is not so difficult. But to find enough time and the mood to go into the business side of shops, etc., is difficult. If somebody could relieve me of this side of the work I should be very happy.

I hope you will go to Europe this year. As you know I am always in favour of your going. Father is not very keen on your going simply because he has made up his mind that I am going to be arrested within the next three or four months. I am afraid his love for me makes him take too tragic a view of the possibility of my arrest and to consider it an event of extraordinary importance. So

[173] See p. 71.

far as I can see nothing wonderful will happen, only I shall have some peace of mind and freedom from worry.

Kamala is keeping tolerably well. I shall soon begin giving her Kuhne's baths. As for sun-baths the Indian sun was not good enough for the Calcutta doctors! They have advised ultra-violent rays and given me a small apparatus to produce these rays.

Yours affectionately,
Jawaharlal

SWJN, *Vol. 3, I Series, pp. 422–3*

## 59. Telegram to M.K. Gandhi

21 January 1929

Your letter. Apparently some misapprehension. My idea Kripalani undertake thorough investigation, make recommendations for reorganisation. Meanwhile status quo continuing. But am agreeable to any course you suggest.

CWMG, *Vol. XXXVIII, p. 395fn*

## 60. Letter to Jawaharlal Nehru

The Ashram, Sabarmati
24 January 1929

My dear Jawahar,
You will see my letter[174] to Father about the European visit. I would like you to let me have your own opinion on it. It will help me in coming to a decision.

I have your telegram about Kripalani. Jamnalalji and Shankerlal, more especially Jamnalalji, have set their hearts upon Kripalani. They have no faith in Sitla Sahai being able to do much. They think that he has not been able to show himself to advantage during the three years he has been at work in UP. I am therefore going to confer with Sitla Sahai and see what he has to say. But before I decide anything finally, I would like you to let me have your own view about Sitla Sahai.

[174] Dated 24 January 1929; see *CWMG*, Vol. XXXVIII, pp. 394–5.

Here is a copy of my Sind programme.[175]

Yours sincerely,
Bapu

Encl. 1
[PS]
After writing this, your letter was received. I have now talked to Sitla Sahai. It is on the whole better for him to resign. As for his future programme I am going to confer with him tonight.

Bapu

CWMG, *Vol. XXXVIII, p. 395*

## 61. Letter to Jawaharlal Nehru

Satyagraha Ashram, Sabarmati
26 January 1929

My dear Jawahar,
I have had a chat with Sitla Sahai, and both of us have come to the conclusion that, all things considered, it is best for him to resign and that he should, for the time being, be in the Ashram with his wife. During that time he will master all the technique of khadi and take part in all such other activities of the Ashram as may be necessary. I want him also during this time of preparation and probation[176] to understand my method of work.

I agree with you that he is a valuable worker and therefore should be as efficient as possible. Immediately after my departure from Sind, he will come to Allahabad to wind up his home and to prepare the papers for handing over charge and the balance sheet to date so that whenever Kripalani is ready to go there he can take charge.

[175] Gandhi was to tour Sind from 3 to 15 February 1929 to collect money for the Lalaji Memorial Fund and to help resolve differences among Congress workers in the province.

[176] For the campaign of nonviolent noncooperation envisaged by the Calcutta Congress of December 1928

I wish you will not listen to doctors when they object to the Indian sun. You have heard of Dr Muthu.[177] Revashankerbhai's[178] son Dhiru was suffering from tuberculosis of the bone. After having tried sanatorium cure in Solon and all the doctors he could get hold of in Bombay, he sent for Dr Muthu, paid him a fee of thousand rupees per day. Dr Muthu had no better advice to offer than to prescribe open air, light food and sun treatment. The affected bone was discharging some time one pound of pus per day. The affected bone had to be exposed to the sun every morning for a few hours and he had to lie in the open air the whole day long. He was not even sent to a sanatorium. He is now completely cured. European sun may be better, but the Indian rival is by no means to be despised. Doctors here suggest the morning sun. They say that ultra-violet rays are best taken between 8 and 10 o'clock and in summer between 7 and 8. But it really depends upon the patient's condition.

Yours sincerely,
Bapu

CWMG, *Vol. XXXVIII, pp. 404–5*

## 62. Letter to Jawaharlal Nehru

The Ashram, Sabarmati
1 February 1929

My dear Jawahar,
You should carefully read the Punjab letter[179] that I have reproduced in *Young India* about what was done in Calcutta. Probably you knew everything of what is stated in the letter. I wish that you will make it your business first to put the Congress Committees in order and then organise the work in connection with the constructive programme. Unless by some unforeseen circumstances there is an honourable settlement with Great Britain, there will be

177 Dr C Muthu, a tuberculosis expert

178 Revashankar Jagjivan Mehta, also known as Jhaveri, a businessman of Bombay, and brother of Dr Pranjivan Mehta

179 Which carried a detailed description of the irregularities in the registration of the delegates to the Calcutta Congress session

practically no other party save the party of independence in the country. But the cry will be ineffective if we cannot put up a proper fight. If that fight is to be put up through the Congress, then the Congress must be a living thing. And if it is to be a nonviolent fight then the present constructive programme ought to be worked now for all it is worth. Apart from the fact, therefore, that you, as is your wont, having taken up the secretaryship, would work your office whole-heartedly, I would like you on the strength of merits also to give your undivided attention to the Congress programme. I cannot help feeling that we can do much with the boycott of foreign cloth through khadi and, if there are enough workers, also about picketing liquor shops. And if these things are to be done, I think that it is necessary for you to travel in all the provinces and first put the machinery in order.

They stopped me from leaving for Sind yesterday owing to the terrible cold winds that had suddenly overtaken Sind. It was foolish of them to have stopped me, but I was helpless. I am now leaving tomorrow. You will therefore post-date the programme by two days.

Sitla Sahai is leaving tomorrow to prepare balance sheets, etc. I expect him back by the time I return from Sind.

Now that the European visit is dropped, you will be free to take me to the UP. Andhra and Burma which must precede will prevent me from going there before the last week of April.[180]

I hope Kamala is better.

Yours sincerely,
Bapu

Pandit Jawaharlal Nehru
11 Clive Road, New Delhi

CWMG, *Vol. XXXVIII, pp. 423–4*

[180] Gandhi toured Burma from 8 to 22 March 1929. Writing about his 'Impending Visit to Burma', he said, 'I am going there principally in the interest of khadi and Gujarat Vidyapith which has always had magnificent support from the Gujarati colony in Burma. I hope to receive donations for the Lajpat Rai Memorial.'

## 63. Telegram to Jawaharlal Nehru

Jacobabad
7 February 1929

Jawaharlal Nehru
11 Clive Road, New Delhi
Your wire.[181] Can attend working committee[182] seventeenth. Wire Shikarpur.[183]

Gandhi

CWMG, *Vol. XXXIX, p. 427*

## 64. Letter to Jawaharlal Nehru

Satyagraha Ashram, Sabarmati
26 February 1929

My dear Jawaharlal,
I have your letters. I want to send you a longish thing, but I must not now. I have wired to you about Sitla Sahai. I have wired to you today that I shall be passing through Allahabad and that I shall be in Delhi for seven hours. I wish that we could see each other either in Delhi or in Allahabad and you may even travel some distance with me if it is possible.

I am trying to procure the services of Jairamdas[184] as Secretary for the boycott committee.[185] He is coming here tomorrow. If he

[181] Not available

[182] Meeting, which was to be held in Delhi, to understand and discuss Gandhi's scheme of boycott of foreign cloth before passing it. For the scheme of boycott, see *CWMG*, Vol. XXXVIII, pp. 388–9, and for Gandhi's article 'The Delhi Visit', *YI*, 28-2-1929, see *CWMG*, Vol. XL, pp. 43–5.

[183] Gandhi, who had been collecting money for the Lajpat Rai Memorial Fund, went on 8 February 1929 to Shikarpur, where he addressed students and a public meeting for contributions in the name of *daridranarayana*.

[184] Jairamdas Doulatram (1891–1979); General Secretary, INC, 1931–4; later Governor of Bihar, of Assam and Union Minister for Food. For Gandhi's letter to him, see *CWMG*, Vol. XL, pp. 20–1.

[185] Committee for the Boycott of Foreign Cloth, of which Gandhi had taken charge

consents, of course, he has to leave the Council at least for this year. We shall talk about the future programme of the boycott committee. About the use of the purses to be presented to me, what you have said is quite correct. It will be predominantly used for khadi work. The tour was to be undertaken for khadi, but naturally I will now talk about the constructive programme. But if the people give the money unconditionally as they should, and if you think that some other use might be made of a part of the purses, we shall discuss about it. But you may put down this also as an item for discussion when we meet, lest I forget when we meet.

I would like you not to arrange a hurricane tour but give more time to a few centres where people from surrounding places may gather, and not many functions at one village. If you have not read my note about this in *Young India* please do read it now.

Yours sincerely,
A. Subbiah
for Bapu

CWMG, *Vol. XL, pp. 38–9*

## 65. Letter to Jawaharlal Nehru

Satyagraha Ashram, Sabarmati
BBCI Rly
3 April 1929

My dear Jawahar,

I have your letter. As things are, the Andhra people have not left me a single day to enable me to go to the Ashram and then to come to Bombay, and as now the May part of the tour is really for my recreation, I would not like to leave Bombay for Allahabad on the 27th May. But I would like to come to the Ashram for a few days and then go to Almora. I could still do Cawnpore, Allahabad and Lucknow before leaving for Almora, and could even go to the Punjab if the people in the Punjab so require it. No announcement therefore need just now be made, but if you want to fix the date in advance for Cawnpore and Lucknow and even for Almora, let it be a date after 10th June. I would like to give a clear week to the Ashram before I move out.

I would like you to ascertain from the Punjab people what they would have me to do.

I have not got the Andhra Desh programme rigidly fixed yet.[186] For the time being therefore you would use Bezwada as headquarters. I expect to reach Bezwada on the 8th instant.

I would like Sitla Sahai to come here if he is not required there for the time being. I want him to be here with reference to his wife and daughter, especially so during my absence.

I send the measurements for Padma's[187] glasses which please hand over to him. I promised to get those measurements and have them sent over to him.

Yours sincerely,
Bapu

CWMG, *Vol. XL, p. 199*

## 66. Letter to Jawaharlal Nehru

29 April 1929

My dear Jawahar,

I never get the time to write to you. I have gone through the Bareilly report. It says nothing, so far as I can see, about the prospect of khadi. Have you read it? What do you propose about it?

As for the tour, you would arrange as you think best.[188] Prabhudas[189] wrote an urgent letter. I have told him I should be ready to go after 10th June and that he should fix the programme in consultation with you.

The tour is somewhat trying but I am taking it very well indeed.

[186] In his article 'Forthcoming Andhra Tour', *YI*, 7-3-1929, Gandhi said that 'the tour was originally conceived ... to raise money chiefly for khadi production in Andhra'.

[187] Sitla Sahai's daughter

[188] In June 1929, Gandhi went to Bareilly, Almora and Naini Tal as a prelude to a more extensive tour of the UP from September to November.

[189] Prabhudas Gandhi, Gandhi's grand-nephew

I saw a summary of your speech on the tomb[190]—I liked it.

Yours,
Bapu

[PS]
My tour programme has been sent to you.

CWMG, *Vol. XL, pp. 304–5*

## 67. Letter to Jawaharlal Nehru

Kavali
10 May 1929

My dear Jawahar,

What a weight upon your mind to have both Kamala and Krishna with the severe attacks you have described. I suppose these domestic troubles must also be taken as part of national discipline. I am glad that Krishna does not require an operation.

You may not know that Andhra Desha is noted for nature cure men and some of them are really brave fellows, brave in the sense that they relentlessly pursue the search without counting the cost. This remedy has in many cases answered where everything else has failed. And it has the merit of simplicity combined with perfect harmlessness even where it may not result in a cure. I wish you would turn your attention to these cures. Of course in this strict dieting plays a most important part. Where patients do not submit to the dietetic prescriptions, the treatment becomes valueless.

I take it that in spite of Bengal's desire for a postponement, AICC will meet on the advertised date.

I had your telegram[191] about Almora. I shall hope to leave Ashram after the tenth of June so as to reach Almora on the 15th.[192]

Yes, you can have me for UP and the Punjab and Delhi for the whole of September and October, if October is also wanted. About

[190] Evidently a slip for 'bomb'. On 8 April two bombs were thrown in the Central Legislative Assembly while the session was in progress. See also Gandhi's article 'The Bomb and the Knife', *CWMG*, Vol. XL, pp. 259–61.

[191] Not available.

[192] Gandhi toured Andhra Pradesh from 5 to 21 May. He was to return to Sabarmati on 28 June.

the Allahabad Municipal Board, you shall decide. I am fed up with addresses. You may therefore accept on my behalf if there is any political or other advantage to be derived from it. If I have received any communication from the Board I have no recollection of it.

Andhra PCC has asked for extension of time up to June on the plea that most of the Congress workers are busy in their own districts with arrangements for the tour and hence are unable to supply the information I wanted. This fact in itself is an evidence of the chaos that reigns supreme in our house. For what I see throughout Andhra is true almost of every province.

I have failed to get any satisfaction from Utkal.

I expect the Tamilnad Secretary on Sunday at Nellore.

I have written to Ghanshyamdas Birla[193] instead of Ramjeebhai to find an auditor of repute for auditing Bengal PCC's accounts.

Yours sincerely,

Bapu

CWMG, *Vol. XL, pp. 367–8*

## 68. Letter to Jawaharlal Nehru

5 June 1929

My dear Jawaharlal,

I am glad you will join me during the tour. Copies of the reports make sad reading. I suggest your sending copies to the respective committees with your observations and suggestions. The report about Bihar surprises me. But that shows the extent of our fall.

Hope Kamala and Krishna are well.

Bapu

CWMG, *Vol. XLI, p. 13*

[193] G.D. Birla (1894–1983); leading industrialist and close associate of Gandhi, who lent financial assistance to his social welfare schemes; Member, Second Round Table Conference, 1931; was during this period, Treasurer, Lala Lajpat Rai Memorial Fund, Calcutta

## 69. Letter to Jawaharlal Nehru

[After 1 July 1929][194]

My dear Jawaharlal,

I read the current *Congress Bulletin.*[195] I think that the reproduction of that statement was out of place in an official publication which is designed merely to record Congress activities.[196] Is it not like a government gazette? On merits too I understand that it was prepared by their counsel. It is not the outpourings of earnest souls as you and I thought it was.

Nor did I like your advocacy and approval of the fast they are undergoing.[197] In my opinion it is an irrelevant performance and in so far as it may be relevant it is like using Nasmyth hammer to crush a fly. However this is for you to ponder over.

I would like you to come to a decision soon regarding the presidentship. Why this hesitation? I thought at Almora it was agreed that you would wear the crown. On this, read the enclosed and hand it on to Father.

I hope Kamala is well.

Yours,
Bapu

CWMG, *Vol. XLI, pp. 152–3*

[194] Inferred from the contents

[195] Which was started as a weekly in 1922 to serve 'as a record of Congress activities all over India in all its multifarious departments, and an epitome of newspaper opinions both pro-Congress and anti-Congress.'

[196] The reference is to the statement given in court by Bhagat Singh and Batukeshwar Dutta in the Assembly Bomb case, which was published in the *Congress Bulletin* of 1 July 1929.

[197] See pp. 91–2. Bhagat Singh, Dutta and some other prisoners were fasting in protest against the treatment meted out to them in prison.

## 70. Letter to M.K. Gandhi

Allahabad
9 July 1929

My dear Bapuji,

I returned last evening. On my way back from Delhi I stopped for two days in Bareilly to keep my promise made when you were there. I visited a number of villages.

Could you kindly ask Pyarelal to let me know who will accompany you when you come here for the AICC meeting? As desired by you we shall not have any public functions which usually take place during your tours. I should like to know however if you would mind attending a public meeting which we propose having on the 27th evening. The AICC and WC are sure to take 2 days, so in any event you will be here till the evening of the 27th or return on the morning of the 28th. We should like to have a meeting or perhaps more than one meeting to be addressed by visitors. As there is always danger of rain we shall probably have our meetings in a hall, admission being regulated by tickets.[198] The meetings will take place in any event. But of course if you could go there for a short time it would be a great advantage. Please ask Pyarelal to reply. You need not trouble.

Regarding the Congress presidentship, I think it would be better if you did not write or say anything in public for another month or so. There is no hurry. I am very nervous about the matter and do not like the idea at all. The situation in the country is changing and developing and another month might give us more data to go by.

Yours affectionately,
Jawaharlal

SWJN, *Vol. 4, 1 Series, p. 155*

[198] The meeting was held in Mayo Hall.

## 71. Letter to M.K. Gandhi

Allahabad
13 July 1929

My dear Bapuji,
I have your letter. About the presidentship, I wrote to you a few days ago and you must have got my letter soon after you wrote yours. My own personal inclination always is not to be shackled down to any office. I prefer to be free and to have time to act according to my own inclinations. But for years past I have been tied down to various offices and have had to give a great deal of my time to routine and other work to the exclusion of other matters to which I would have liked to attend to [*sic*]. On my return from Europe I had the fixed intention of spending a few months at least in some village areas, more or less cut off from outside activities. I wanted to try to organise them according to my own ideas but even more so I wanted to educate myself and try to get at the back of the mind of the villagers. The Congress Secretary duties and repeated and continuous calls for other work prevented me from doing this.

Somehow or other I cannot extricate myself from the tangle of activities I have got into. It seems even more difficult to extricate myself now than it has been. Now that it is proposed to take a really serious step in the near future, it is all the more difficult to think of retirement for a while to a village.

So far as I am concerned the presidentship will thus be a burden to me. Most others also are likely to consider it a burden and a nuisance. You will not of course be deceived by various odd persons here and there expressing their confidence in me. It is very good fortune that I have won the goodwill of a number of people but with this goodwill there is also a lack of confidence. I represent nobody but myself. I have not the politician's flair for forming groups and parties. My one attempt in this direction—the formation of the Independence for India League last year—was a hopeless failure so far as I was concerned. Instead of having a group of single-minded individuals cooperating together for a common object, I found that there was neither single-mindedness nor cooperation and I was being compelled by force of circumstances to do things I was in thorough disagreement with.[199]

Most people who put me forward for the presidentship do so because they want to keep someone else out. I am the lesser evil. This kind of negative backing is hardly good enough and does not enthuse.

If there is going to be effective action next year there can be no doubt that it will make all the difference in the world whether you lead it or not. Of course you can lead, as you have done in the past, without being Congress President. But it would help matters certainly if you are also the official head of the organisation. I feel that it would be a great gain if you would preside. That would strike the imagination of the country and other countries. If I have the misfortune to be President you will see that the very people who put me there, or many of them, will be prepared to cast me to the wolves.

Anyhow, I do not see why a final decision should be made now. The AICC meeting this month is bound to have far-reaching results whichever way the decision goes. I think the best one can do is to wait till it is over.

I am sorry you disapproved of my giving Bhagat Singh and Dutt's statement in the *Congress Bulletin*. I was myself a little doubtful as to whether I should give it but when I found that there was very general appreciation of it among Congress circles I decided to give extracts. It was difficult however to pick and choose and gradually most of it went in. But I agree with you that it was somewhat out of place. I think you are mistaken in thinking that the statement was the work of their counsel. My information is that counsel had nothing, or practically nothing, to do with it. He might have touched up the punctuation. I think the statement was undoubtedly a genuine thing.

[199] Referring to it in his *Autobiography*, Nehru says, 'Indeed one of the objects of the Independence League was social freedom. We had hoped to build up a strong League organisation all over India and utilise it for propaganda in favour of independence and socialism. Unhappily, ... the League never got going except to some extent in the UP.'

Have I been advocating the fast? I had not intended doing so and I do not know to what statement of mine you are referring to [sic]. In Delhi I had stated that we could not help sympathising with Bhagat Singh and Dutt during their long fast. As a matter of fact I am not in favour of hunger strikes. I told this to many young men who came to see me on this subject but I did not think it worthwhile to condemn the fast publicly.

Kamala had another attack three days ago but it was a short and mild one this time. My mother is now laid up with dengue fever.

Yours affectionately,
Jawaharlal

SWJN, *Vol. 4, I Series, pp. 156–7*

## 72. Letter to Jawaharlal Nehru

20 July 1929

My dear Jawaharlal,

I have glanced at the programme, so far as I am concerned it is all right. I think I shall easily stand it. I have not checked it for Mondays. But I assume that you have avoided travelling on Mondays.[200]

Pyarelal, Devdas and Kusumbehn[201] will be with me. Vallabhbhai,[202] Mahadev and Manibehn[203] will reach via Jubbulpore. I do not think there will be any other company with me.

You will please not detain me on 28th. I would like to get away by the first train after finishing on 27th.

[200] In 1921 Gandhi took a vow of silence, which usually started at 3 pm on Sunday and lasted for 24 hours, with occasional exceptions. These were: a) when he or somebody else was in mortal danger, and speaking would render aid, b) when the Viceroy or a similar dignitary called unexpectedly, making speech necessary.

[201] Kusum Desai

[202] Sardar Vallabhbhai Patel (1875–1950); Congressman of Ahmedabad; organized the no-rent campaign in Bardoli, 1928; President, INC, 1931; Member, Interim Government, 1946–7; Deputy Prime Minister for Home States and Information and Broadcasting, 1947–50; hailed as the Iron Man of India, was instrumental in enabling the accession of almost all of the 565 semi-autonomous Princely States

[203] Daughter of Vallabhbhai Patel

I hope Kamala is better. I do want to see her healthy and bright when I come to Allahabad.

Yours,
Bapu

CWMG, *Vol. XLI, p. 205*

## 73. Telegram to M.K. Gandhi

23 July 1929

May I announce you will unfurl National Flag Sunday morning eight.

Jawaharlal

CWMG, *Vol. XLI, p. 218fn*

## 74. Telegram to Jawaharlal Nehru

[On or after 23 July 1929][204]

Jawaharlal
You may fix unfurling ceremony Sunday if no train available Saturday after Committee meeting.

CWMG, *Vol. XLI, p. 218*

## 75. Letter to Jawaharlal Nehru

On the train
29 July 1929

My dear Jawaharlal,
Your letters to Indu are excellent and should be published.[205] I wish you could have written them in Hindi. Even as it is there should be a simultaneous publication in Hindi.

Your treatment of the subject is quite orthodox. The origin of man is now a debatable subject. The origin of religion is a still more debatable matter. But these differences do not detract from the value of your letters. They have a value derived not from the truth of your conclusions but from the manner of treatment and from

[204] The telegram was in reply to the preceding item.
[205] They were published in 1930 as *Letters from a Father to His Daughter.*

the fact that you have tried to reach Indu's heart and open the eyes of her understanding in the midst of your external activities.

I did not want to strive with Kamala over the watch I have taken away. I could not resist the love behind the gift. But the watch will still be kept as a trust for Indu. In the midst of so many little ruffians about me, I could not keep such a piece of furniture. I would therefore be glad to know that Kamala will reconcile herself to Indu getting back her darling watch.

My article[206] on the Congress crown is already written. It will be out in the next issue of *Young India*.

Yours,
Bapu

CWMG, *Vol. XLI, p. 235*

## 76. Letter to Jawaharlal Nehru

7 August 1929

My dear Jawaharlal,

I do not like the title 'Dawn of History'. 'A Father's Letters to His Daughter' may be a better title than 'Letters to Indira', though I do not mind the latter.

I wish Kamala would be freed from these recurring pains. I should risk the operation, if the doctors would perform it.

I am keeping the clock under lock and key and shall bring it on my coming there.

I go to Bombay on the 11th to meet Jinnah.[207] I admire Sarojini Devi's optimism. But I am going to Bombay without much hope.

Yours,
Bapu

CWMG, *Vol. XLI, p. 256*

[206] 'Who Should Wear the Crown?', *YI*, 1-8-1929; see *CWMG*, Vol. XLI, pp. 239–41.

Writing eloquently for the choice of Nehru as Congress President, Gandhi said: 'I am of opinion the crown must be worn by Pandit Jawaharlal Nehru. ... older men should yield with grace what will be taken by force if they do not read the signs of the times.'

[207] To persuade him to accept the Nehru report

## 77. Letter to Jawaharlal Nehru

11 August 1929

My dear Jawaharlal,
This is an account they have sent me of the little band of satyagrahis who will present you with an address.

You may not mind the wires and protests you are receiving.[208] You will judge things for yourself when you go to Kathiawar if at all Kamala's condition permits you to do so.[209] I leave Bombay 7th September for Bhopal and reach Agra as per programme on 11th unless you want any alteration.

Yours,
Bapu

CWMG, *Vol. XLI, p. 280*

## 78. Telegram to M.K. Gandhi

21 August 1929

Beg of you not to press my name for presidentship.

Jawahar

CWMG, *Vol. XLI, p. 305fn*

## 79. Letter to Jawaharlal Nehru

22 August 1929

My dear Jawaharlal,
I am delighted over Kamala's operation. I hope she will be fully restored now.

You may depend upon my not unduly pressing your name on the country. I felt bound to express my opinion to the committee

208 A prince in the state of Kathiawar had issued an order that no young man or woman from among his subjects should take part in the Youth Conference.

209 For Nehru's address at the Kathiawar Youth Conference, Rajkot, on 31 August 1929, see *SWJN*, Vol. 4, I Series, pp. 18–19.

at Lahore in reply to their wire.[210] It is enough for your self-respect that you do not want the crown. It is an ugly business for anybody this time. I have simply pressed your name as of a principle. If the country is not ready to assert that principle, we can wait.

If you are not to be the helmsman, the only alternative I can think of at this juncture is re-election of Father, or failing that, of Dr Ansari. Can you think of any other name?

I am preparing for the UP tour. I am daily recovering lost strength. I am in no way sorry for my experiment[211] from which I have learnt a lot.

Yours,
Bapu

CWMG, *Vol. XLI, p. 314*

## 80. Telegram to Jawaharlal Nehru

Barabanki
11 October 1929

Jawaharlal Nehru
Anand Bhavan
Allahabad
As previously arranged Sikh League message[212] already sent through Sardul Singh[213] Lahore.

Gandhi

CWMG, *Vol. XLI, p. 546*

[210] Dated 19 August 1929, suggesting that Gandhi accept the presidentship of the Congress. Gandhi declined on grounds of ill health and on the plea that he was out of tune with much that was going on in the name of Congress. He urged the Congress, instead, to elect Nehru.

[211] In a diet of uncooked food, as a result of which Gandhi suffered from dysentery, and had to undergo medical treatment. See also *CWMG*, Vol. XLI, pp. 306–7.

[212] Which read: 'Please convey my good wishes to the Sikh League meeting at Lyallpur. I hope the League will have the wisdom not to boycott the Congress and realise that the question is not closed but open for discussion and adjustment.'

[213] Sardar Sardul Singh Caveeshar, Member, Congress Working Committee; Director, National Publicity Bureau, Lahore, 1925

## 81. Letter to M.K. Gandhi

4 November 1929

My dear Bapuji,

I have thought well for two days. I can take, I think, a calmer view of the situation than I could two days ago but the fever in my brain has not left me.

Your appeal to me on the ground of discipline could not be ignored by me. I am myself a believer in discipline. And yet I suppose there can be too much of discipline. Something seems to have snapped inside me evening before last and I am unable to piece it together. As General Secretary of the Congress I owe allegiance to it and must subject myself to its discipline.[214] I have other capacities and other allegiances. I am President of the Indian Trade Union Congress,[215] Secretary of the Independence for India League and am intimately connected with the youth movement. What shall I do with the allegiance I owe to these and other movements I am connected with? I realise now more than I have ever done before that it is not possible to ride a number of horses at the same time. Indeed it is hard enough to ride one. In the conflict of responsibilities and allegiances what is one to do except to rely on one's instincts and reason?

I have therefore considered the position apart from all outside connections and allegiances and the conviction has grown stronger that I acted wrongly day before yesterday. I shall not enter into the merits of the statement or the policy underlying it. I am afraid we differ fundamentally on that issue and I am not likely to convert you. I shall only say that I believe the statement to have been

[214] The Delhi Manifesto offered to cooperate with the British, provided the Government adopted a policy of general conciliation. Though Nehru was not in agreement with it, he was persuaded to sign on grounds that as General Secretary of the Congress he was bound to carry out the wishes of the majority. The All Parties Leaders' Conference held in Delhi on 1 November 1929 issued the Delhi Manifesto the following day in reply to Lord Irwin's announcement of 31 October that a Round Table Conference was to be convened after the Simon Commission had submitted its report. The second conference held in Allahabad expressed concern at the debates in Parliament but decided to stand by its Delhi Manifesto. See *CWMG*, Vol. XLII, pp. 80–1.

[215] Which was to hold its session at Nagpur on 30 November 1929

injurious and a wholly inadequate reply to the Labour Government's declaration. I believe that in our attempts to soothe and retain a few estimable gentlemen we have ruffled and practically turned out of our camp many others who were far more worth having. I believe that we have fallen into a dangerous trap out of which it will be no easy matter to escape. And I think that we have shown to the world that although we talk tall we are only bargaining for some titbits.

I do not know what the British Government will do now. Probably it will not agree to your conditions. I hope they will not. But I have little doubt that most of the signatories—excluding you of course—will be quite prepared to agree to any modification of the conditions which the British Government might suggest. In any event, it is quite clear to me that my position in the Congress will become daily more and more difficult. I accepted the presidentship of the Congress with great misgivings but in the hope that we shall fight on a clear issue next year. That issue is already clouded and the only reason for my acceptance has gone. What am I to do with these 'Leaders' Conference'? I feel an interloper and am ill at ease. I cannot have my say because I am afraid of upsetting the conference. I repress myself and sometimes the repression is too much for me and I break out and even say things which I do not wholly mean.

I feel I must resign from the secretaryship of the AICC. I have sent a formal letter[216] to father, a copy of which I enclose. The question of the presidentship is a far more difficult one. At this late hour I do not know what I can do. But I am convinced that I was a wrong choice. You were the only possible president for the occasion and the year. I cannot be president if the policy of the Congress is what might be described as that of Malaviyaji. Even now if you agree there is a possible course which does not necessitate a meeting of the AICC. A circular might be sent round to AICC members saying that you are agreeable to accepting the presidentship. I would beg of them to excuse me. This would be

[216] Dated 4 November 1929. Nehru had written to Motilal Nehru, then President, INC, tendering his resignation as General Secretary of the AICC and member of the Working Committee.

a formal matter as of course all the members, or nearly all, would welcome your decision with joy.

An alternative course is that I should declare that in view of the circumstances, and also in view of the difficulty of choosing another president now, I shall not retire now but immediately after the Congress is over. I shall act as the chairman and the Congress can decide what it likes regardless of me.

One of these two courses seems to me to be necessary if I am to retain my physical and mental health.

As I wrote to you from Delhi I am not issuing any public statement. What others say or do not say does not worry me very much. But I must be at peace with myself.

Yours affectionately,
Jawaharlal

[PS]
I am sending a copy of this letter to father. I feel a little lighter after writing this letter. I am afraid it will trouble you a little and I do not want to do so. I feel half inclined not to send it to you just yet but to wait for your arrival here. Ten days more will no doubt lessen my agitation and give me a better perspective. But it is better that you should know how my mind has been working.

SWJN, *Vol. 4, I Series, pp. 166–8*

## 82. Letter to Jawaharlal Nehru

Aligarh
4 November 1929

My dear Jawaharlal,
I have just got your letter. How shall I console you? Hearing others describe your state, I said to myself, 'Have I been guilty of putting undue pressure on you?' I have always believed you to be above undue pressure. I have always honoured your resistance. It has always been honourable. Acting under that belief I pressed my suit. Let this incident be a lesson. Resist me always when my suggestion does not appeal to your head or heart. I shall not love you the less for that resistance.

But why are you dejected? I hope there is no fear of public opinion in you. If you have done nothing wrong, why dejection?

The ideal of independence is not in conflict with greater freedom. As an executive officer now and President for the coming year, you could not keep yourself away from a collective act of the majority of your colleagues. In my opinion your signature was logical, wise and otherwise correct. I hope therefore that you will get over your dejection and resume your unfailing cheerfulness.

The statement you may certainly make. But there is no hurry about it at all.

Here are copies of two cables[217] just received. Please show them to Father too.

If you feel like talking things over with me, do not hesitate to catch me wherever you like.

I hope to see Kamala hale and hearty when I reach Allahabad.

If you can do wire that the blues are over.

Yours,
Bapu

CWMG, *Vol. XLII, p. 96*

## 83. Telegram to Jawaharlal Nehru

Muttra
6 November 1929

Jawaharlal Nehru
Anand Bhavan
Allahabad

Deeply appreciate moral difficulty your second letter.[218] But there should be no hurry arriving at decision. Resignation must not be pressed. If still agitated meet me wherever you like.

Gandhi

CWMG, *Vol. XLII, p. 101*

[217] From *Daily Express* (*CWMG*, Vol. XLII, p. 87, *fn.*1) and from Fenner Brockway (p. 161, *fn.* 1).

[218] Dated 4 November 1929; see pp. 97–9.

## 84. Letter to Jawaharlal Nehru

Brindaban
8 November 1929

My dear Jawahar,
I have your letter. You must have got my wire. You must not resign just now. I have not the time to argue out my point. All I know is that it will affect the national cause. There is no hurry and no principle at stake. About the crown, no one else can wear it. It never was to be a crown of roses. Let it be all thorns now. If I could have persuaded myself to wear it, I would have done so at Lucknow.[219] The contingency I had in mind when I would be forced to wear it was not of this type. One of them was your arrest and increased repression. But let us reserve the whole of this for calm and detached discussion when we meet.

Meanwhile may God give you peace.

Bapu

CWMG, *Vol. XLII, p. 116*

## 85. Letter to Jawaharlal Nehru

18 November 1929

My dear Jawahar,
Here is my draft.[220] I want you to consider it carefully and take your full share in the discussion tonight. I do not want you to suppress yourself in any way whatsoever except where you feel that self-suppression is better than self-expression on particular occasions. After all we must each serve according to our lights, not borrowed.

Bapu

CWMG, *Vol. XLII, p. 181*

[219] At the AICC meeting held on 28 September 1929

[220] Of Resolution for the Congress Working Committee. A conference of representative political leaders held at Allahabad adopted the resolution to stand by the Delhi Manifesto of 2 November 1929.

## 86. Letter to M.K. Gandhi

Allahabad
7 January 1930

My dear Bapuji,

I enclose some odd notes.[221] I am sure they are perfectly useless but still I am sending them. I do not quite know what kind of information you require for the statement. Probably I am sending this too late. Anyhow this will not make much difference.

I shall expect your statement and resolution for the 26th[222] in a few days. Could you also add some directions for the observance of the day? For instance, should there be speeches at meetings or just a reading of the statement? I think that it would be desirable if meetings were all held at one time—5 p.m. This may be suggested, with local freedom to change the time.

I enclose a letter from Rajagopalachari.[223] I think there is something in what he says. There are so many statements and counter-statements in the press that the issues are likely to be clouded. Personally I dislike touring on a big scale but if you think I should rush about I shall do so.

Rajagopalachari's idea that we may get some of the non-Congress members out of the legislatures seems to me to be amazingly optimistic. There is no chance of this happening. Indeed it is clear that many Congress members even will stick on or resign and then seek election. I do not think we need mind this very much, provided we can create a boycott mentality in the people and take action against all Congressmen who disobey the Congress resolution.

[221] On the exploitation of India from Sunderland's *India in Bondage*, Lajpat Rai's *Unhappy India* and other books

[222] Fixed as Independence Day by the new Working Committee

[223] C. Rajagopalachari (1878–1972); popularly known as 'CR' or 'Rajaji'; a lawyer of Madras who joined the noncooperation movement in 1919; Member, Congress Working Committee, 1922–42, 1946–7 and 1951–4; Chief Minister of Madras, 1937–9 and 1952–4; left the Congress in 1942 but rejoined in 1946; Governor, West Bengal, 1947–8; Governor-General of India, 1948–50; founder, Swatantra Party, 1959

He had written that Nehru and Gandhi should tour the country to give publicity to the decisions of the Lahore Congress.

But even apart from the Council boycott it seems desirable to make the country feel that we are in earnest. If we remain quiet for some weeks it may have a bad effect.

Father is going to Calcutta for the Bengal dispute on the 10th January.[224]

Yours affectionately,
Jawaharlal

SWJN, *Vol. 4, I Series, pp. 206–7*

## 87. Letter to Jawaharlal Nehru

10 January 1930

My dear Jawaharlal,
Here is my draft resolution or declaration for 26th instant.[225] I have nothing as yet from anybody. But I thought I would not now wait till the last moment. You will cut it up or extend and amend it as you like. The shorter the sweeter.

Ever since we have separated at Lahore, I have been evolving schemes of civil disobedience. I have not seen my way clear as yet. But I have come so far that, in the present state of the Congress, no civil disobedience can be or should be offered in its name and that it should be offered by me alone or jointly with a few companions even as I did in South Africa if you have studied the *History of Satyagraha.*[226] If you have not, you should. If I do finally see my way clear, I shall think out what part the Congress can play in that event. All this however, I have no time to discuss through correspondence. If I make further progress, I shall let you know. If you have any remarks to offer, please let me know. In any case prepare yourself to come here a day or two earlier than the Working

[224] Long-standing differences among Congressmen in Bengal and the rivalry between Subhas Chandra Bose and J.N. Sengupta had been aggravated by election disputes.

[225] The 'Independence Day Pledge' was jointly drafted by Gandhi and Nehru and released on 17 January 1930. See *CWMG*, Vol. XLII, pp. 384–5.

[226] *Satyagraha in South Africa* by Gandhi, the serial publication of which had concluded in *Navajivan*, 22-11-1925. For the English version see *CWMG*, Vol. XXIX, pp. 1–269.

Committee meeting day. Of course you can come earlier still...[227] Before 26th inst. if necessary.

I hope father is going to Bengal on the appointed day.

I am most anxious to come to grips during your year of office, but that strictly according to my lights. Please therefore feel free to criticise whatever I say or suggest. I want to do nothing that would cross your purpose or thwart your plans, if you have conceived any independently. The more I think, the more convinced I feel that it was a happy thing for the country that I did not become President. I would have felt hampered in maturing plans in complete detachment. As it is, I cannot conceive a more favourable opportunity for me for making my experiment than when you are the helmsman of the Congress.

Yours,
Bapu

[PS]
Since writing this, I have your letter. In view of what I have said above, I must not go out. The one who may travel through a few places with effect is father. The weight that he can carry in the matter of the Councils boycott is not to be rivalled by anybody. Can he go?

CWMG, *Vol. XLII, pp. 382–4*

## 88. Letter to Jawaharlal Nehru

Sabarmati
12 January 1930

My dear Jawaharlal,
I omitted to reply when I wrote to you to your important question about 26th instant. I think there should be nothing mentioned about processions. We do not want the people to hold processions under licences, nor do we want them to hold them without. The only thing, therefore, they should do is to hold meetings and devote the day, if possible, to enlisting members. I do not think that speeches are necessary or advisable. I am anxious to avoid

[227] Illegible in the source

anticipation of a crisis. I would value perfect calm for ushering in civil disobedience. I am writing about this in *Young India*.[228]

I hope you received my draft declaration in good time.

Yours sincerely,
Bapu

CWMG, *Vol. XLII, p. 392*

## 89. Telegram to M.K. Gandhi

Sabarmati
12 January 1930

Your telegram. Just in time. Thanks. Made also other changes which communicated *Young India*. Separate resolution unnecessary.

Jawaharlal

M.K. Gandhi Papers, Pyarelal Collection, *NMML*

## 90. Telegram to Jawaharlal Nehru

Ahmedabad
13 January 1930

Wire if text celebration declaration received and approved. Wish publish forthcoming *Young India*. If many changes made wire text to reach tomorrow morning.

Gandhi

CWMG, *Vol. XLII, p. 394*

## 91. Letter to M.K. Gandhi

Allahabad
13/14 January 1930

My dear Bapuji,

Your letter with your draft statement reached me late in the evening. I was under the impression that in addition to this statement there would be a resolution for the meeting on the 26th. I had issued instructions to this effect to the Provincial Congress Committees.

[228] Dated 16 January 1930 in an article entitled 'Independence Day'.

I sent to you a telegram accordingly. I am however not quite sure that a resolution, apart from the statement, will be necessary.

As the time at our disposal is limited I am typing this letter myself in the small hours of the morning. I have also just typed a slightly revised statement for your approval. This has been done in a great hurry and I am not at all satisfied with my draft. However, here it goes. Even if there is a little delay in issuing it, it will not matter so much.

I do not particularly fancy giving a quotation[229] in our statement from Trevelyan.[230] The quotation itself may be apt but it is merely an expression of opinion which seems to me to be somewhat out of place in the statement.

I presume the figures you have given have been carefully verified. I do not know where you got the figures about customs in Russia. It is probably correct. But the conditions in Russia are very different and the Soviet Government controls all imports and hardly permits anything but necessary articles to come in. In the average daily income the figures given is seven pice; the average daily tax is stated to be 2.5 pies. I presume it is correct.

I am not at all clear how you can keep the Congress out of any programme of civil disobedience. However, this can be discussed when all of us meet in Sabarmati. I shall certainly come a day or two before the Working Committee meets.

Father is still in Calcutta and must be busy with the Bengal dispute. I expect him back on the 15th. I doubt if he can travel about much just yet but he may be able to go to a few places. He has been very poorly since his return from Lahore. His blood pressure has been very high.

[229] From a paper submitted by Sir Trevelyan to the Parliamentary Committee of 1853 on Indian territories titled 'The Political Tendency of the Different Systems of Education in Use in India'. He observed: 'Educated in the same way, interested in the same things, engaged in the same pursuits with ourselves they (Indian educated youth) become more English than Hindus just as Roman provincials became more Roman than the Gauls or Italians.'

[230] Sir Charles Edward Trevelyan (1807–1886); Governor, Madras, 1859–60; Finance Minister, Government of India, 1862–5.

For the short resolution for the 26th meeting I had drafted the following:

We the people of..., assembled here to demonstrate that India must be completely free, do solemnly resolve that we will strive to our utmost capacity so that Purna Swaraj may be attained. And we will carry out the Congress instructions issued from time to time in this behalf.

I do not like this nor am I sure on consideration that such a resolution is necessary after a longer statement. But I give it for what it is worth.

I shall await your reply.

Yours affectionately,
Jawaharlal

SWJN, *Vol. 4, I Series, pp. 211–12*

## 92. Telegram to M.K. Gandhi

Allahabad
14 January 1930

Posted revised statement. Sending Press telegram. Full text *Young India*. Have suggested dropping Trevelyan quotation and other changes. But all suggestions hastily made subject your final decision. Trust all figures fully verified. Please inform me your decision.

Jawaharlal

MKG Papers, Pyarelal Collection, *NMML*

## 93. Telegram to Jawaharlal Nehru

Sabarmati
16 January 1930

Jawaharlal Nehru
Allahabad
Received wires. Figures retested. Found accurate. You may add short resolution if necessary.

Gandhi

CWMG, *Vol. XLII, p. 405*

## 94. Telegram to Jawaharlal Nehru

Sabarmati
16 January 1930

Jawaharlal Nehru
Allahabad
Your letter received after despatch wire. Resolution drafted by you wholly unnecessary.[231] Revised declaration should be circulated. Tariff ratio should read twenty-four times and eight times respectively less heavy than in United States and Germany.

Gandhi

CWMG, *Vol. XLII, p. 405*

## 95. Letter to M.K. Gandhi

Allahabad
17 January 1930

My dear Bapuji,
I received two telegrams from you yesterday. From the first telegram it was obvious that my express telegram and my press message sent to *Young India* had been stopped or delayed. I have learnt from a friend in Agra that the Government had stopped these telegrams. Apparently they allowed them to go later. But I do not know if they were censored or not. It is obvious that we cannot rely on the Telegraph Office in future, and the Post Office is almost as doubtful. I shall send telegrams to you today but to make sure that my communication reaches you I am sending this by a messenger.

Father returned from Calcutta yesterday and I have discussed the statement with him. He felt that the paragraphs of percentages, etc., were out of place. I feel this way too, but I do not wish to make any radical changes at this stage. A few changes we are making, which I hope you will not mind. I am giving these separately. I shall issue the statement to the press, to the PCCs and a number of individuals today. Probably I shall have difficulties in getting it printed because press people are very timid.

[231] See pp. 105–6.

Having regard to various developments and the news in the paper it seems likely that the Government will try to obstruct us as much as possible. I agree with you that stress should not be laid on processions. At the same time it is difficult to prohibit them. I propose to send a circular[232] today discouraging processions but at the same time leaving the matter in the hands of the local committee. I shall give them the reasons which you yourself have mentioned.

It is possible that an attempt may be made to prevent the demonstration on the 26th January either by Sec. 144 or by other means. Father thinks, and I agree with him, that express directions should be issued to provincial and district committees in regard to this matter. I feel that if such an order is made merely prohibiting a meeting we cannot submit to it. We should gather together peaceably and make the declaration and disperse. If even this is sought to be prohibited we should disobey the order and take the consequences. There is hardly time to consult in this matter. I shall not issue a public statement but I propose to send a circular to provincial committees more or less on these lines.

I am sending this letter with a young man named Murari Sharma. You may, if you like, send him back with any message or keep him in the Ashram till we come. If he remains in the Ashram I hope some work will be given to him.

Yours affectionately,
Jawaharlal

[PS]
As for the time of the meeting on the 26th an identical time is desirable and probably 5 p.m. is best. For villages however this is a late hour. I suppose this cannot be helped.

[PPS]
Changes made in the statement for the 26th January

The second paragraph to read thus:

India has been ruined economically. The revenue derived from our people is out of all proportion to our income. Our average

[232] Dated 17 January 1930, enclosing a copy of the resolution that was to be passed at the meeting to be held on 26 January (Purna Swaraj Day or Independence Day).

income is 7 pice (less than 2d) per day, and of the heavy taxes we pay, 20% are raised from the land revenue derived from the peasantry and 3% from the salt tax which falls most heavily on the poor.

5th paragraph as follows:

Politically India's status has never been so reduced as under the British regime. No reforms have given real political power to people. The tallest of us have to bend before foreign authority. The rights of free expression of opinion and free association have been denied to us and many of our countrymen are compelled to live in exile abroad and cannot return to their homes. All administrative talent is killed and the masses have to be satisfied with petty village offices and clerkships.

I have left out the figure 2.5 pies of average daily tax. This introduces comparison between pies and pice and does not help the argument much.

The tariff ratios in the 4th paragraph have been changed as follows:

24 times and 8 times respectively less heavy than in the United States of America and Germany. The figure for Russia 44 times as given in the original statement.

SWJN, *Vol. 4, I Series, pp. 214–15*

## 96. Telegram to M.K. Gandhi

17 January 1930

Your telegram just in time. Changes made.[233] Also other changes which communicated *Young India*. Separate resolution unnecessary.

Jawaharlal

SWJN, *Vol. 4, I Series, p. 215*

[233] For the final declaration, 'Things to Remember for 26th', see *CWMG*, Vol. XLII, pp. 426–8.

## 97. Telegram to Jawaharlal Nehru

Ahmedabad
17 January 1930

Jawaharlal Nehru
Allahabad
Reading three o'clock this morning para regarding customs currency. Do not like it. If declaration not sent press paragraph referred should read. Quote. Customs and currency have been so manipulated as to heap further burdens on the peasantry. British manufactured goods constitute bulk of our imports. Customs duties betray clear partiality for British manufactures and revenue from them is used not to lessen burden on the masses but for sustaining highly extravagant administration. Still more arbitrary has been manipulation of exchange ratio which has resulted in millions being drained away from the country. Unquote.

CWMG, *Vol. XLII, p. 406*

## 98. Telegram to M.K. Gandhi

Allahabad
26 January 1930

Everything here passed off most successfully, satisfactorily.

Jawaharlal

MKG Papers, Pyarelal Collection, *NMML*

## 99. Telegram to Jawaharlal Nehru

26 January 1930

Your wire. Same report here too. Huge but orderly programme. Tell father necessary his writing Viceroy and meeting Sapru[234] about discussions at interview being used for propaganda.

Bapu

Jawaharlal Nehru
Anand Bhawan, Allahabad

MKG Papers, Pyarelal Collection, *NMML*

[234] Sir Tej Bahadur Sapru (1857–1949); eminent Liberal Party leader and advocate of Allahabad; Law Member, Viceroy's Council, 1920–3

## 100. Letter to M.K. Gandhi

Anand Bhawan, Allahabad
2 February 1930

My dear Bapuji,

I have your letter with the New York cable. For some time past I have been receiving frantic messages from both Rezmie[235] and Sailendra Nath Ghose[236] asking me to send cables and articles to be syndicated in America. I have also been asked to get you to send an appeal to America. I knew you would do nothing of the kind and so I told them that we could not help them in the least and referred them to the *Free Press.*[237] Some time after my return from Lahore I got a cable from Rezmie with a reply paid form for nearly Rs 200/- asking me to send Congress resolutions and a message. Owing to a mistake, intentional or otherwise, of the Telegraph Office, I received the reply form a fortnight after the Congress. It was too late to send the resolutions by cable then. I therefore utilised the form to send the Independence Day resolution—Rezmie in his cable to you refers to this.

Both Rezmie and Ghose in New York are out for each other's blood and it is impossible to believe all they say about each other. I want to keep out of their intrigues and quarrels.[238] I shall write to Rezmie about this cable to you.

I hope to reach Sabarmati on the 12th morning.

Yours affectionately,
Jawaharlal

MKG Papers, Pyarelal Collection, *NMML*

[235] Of the India Independence League

[236] President of the Indian National Congress of America, New York City

[237] *The Free Press Journal*, a daily published from Bombay

[238] In his cable of 6 March 1930 to Gandhi, John Haynes Holmes expressed alarm over Sailendra Nath Ghose's 'wildly violent misrepresentations like announcing Indian resolve military resistance arming million nationalists'; see *CWMG*, Vol. XLIII, p. 24*fn*.

## 101. Letter to M.K. Gandhi

Anand Bhawan, Allahabad
3 February 1930

My dear Bapu,

Father has been told by Ansari to take absolute rest. He is in Delhi and is taking some injections. He will remain there till he goes to Sabarmati. Indeed Ansari has agreed to his going to Sabarmati with difficulty.

I have read with some surprise the eleven points[239] you have laid down as a test of cooperation with the British Government. I do not know how you square them with independence being our immediate objective. Indeed they fall far short of even dominion status. Important as some of them are, they are after all individual reforms and they do not touch many vital problems. At the most they can be said to be a repetition of two of the four conditions which you laid down for the acceptance of the Round Table Conference.

I have no doubt that your eleven points will not be conceded but I am afraid they will give a shock to many people. They will think that the talk of independence was mere eyewash and not seriously meant. The British will think that you are out to bargain only.

I was further surprised to learn that you have given these eleven points to Bomanji as a kind of message to Ramsay MacDonald. Bomanji is a very irresponsible person and he will pose as the accredited ambassador of India.

Yours affectionately,
Jawaharlal

MKG Papers, Pyarelal Collection, *NMML*

[239] Enunciated in Gandhi's article 'Clearing the Issue' in *YI*, 30-1-1930. These were the terms communicated to Shavaksha Bomanji, a Bombay millionaire, who undertook to negotiate with the Prime Minister Ramsay MacDonald. The points were: total prohibition; reduction of the exchange ratio to 1S 4d; reduction of land revenue by 50 per cent; abolition of salt tax; reduction of military expenditure by at least 50 per cent; reduction of high salaries; protective tariff on foreign cloth; passage of the Coastal Tariff Reservation Bill; discharge of all political prisoners, save those condemned for murder or the attempt thereat by the ordinary judicial tribunal, and withdrawal of all political prosecutions and abrogation of repressive laws; abolition of CID; free issue of licences for firearms.

## 102. Letter to Jawaharlal Nehru

6 February 1930

My dear Jawaharlal,

I never thought you would miss the importance of the 11 points. However I do not propose to waste your time by arguing when a day or two after this reaches you, you will be on your way to Sabarmati. I expect you here for certain on 12th. I hope to satisfy you that our case has been strengthened not weakened by the 11 points. Will Kamala accompany you?

Yours,
Bapu

CWMG, *Vol. XLII, p. 459*

## 103. Draft Telegram to Jawaharlal Nehru

[10 February 1930][240]

Expect you without fail Wednesday noon.

MKG Papers, Pyarelal Collection, *NMML*

## 104. Letter to Jawaharlal Nehru

24 February 1930

My dear Jawaharlal,

I have your letter. I had not read the speech. I hardly get time to read.

You will see the forthcoming issue. It will contain much. The substance has already appeared in Gujarati *Navajivan*. Perhaps we shall get a few moments to discuss things more fully when we meet on 1st March. My letter[241] to the Viceroy will also clarify the issue.

[240] This was in reply to Nehru's telegram sent to Congress, Ahmedabad, which said: 'Arriving Wednesday noon by Express. Inform Gandhiji.'

[241] Dated 2 March 1930 wherein, *inter alia*, Gandhi said: 'The Delhi interview having miscarried, there was no option for Pandit Motilal Nehru and me but to take steps to carry out the solemn resolution of the Congress arrived at in Calcutta at its session in 1928.... the terrific pressure of land revenue, which furnishes a large part of the total, must undergo considerable modification in an independent India.... Conversion of a nation that has

I am glad there is nothing serious with Kamala. But why should she not now go to a hospital and have the necessary treatment?

Yours,
Bapu

CWMG, *Vol. XLII, pp. 494–5*

## 105. Telegram to Jawaharlal Nehru

Ahmedabad
6 March 1930

Jawaharlal Nehru
Allahabad
Letter handed press for publication. Marching early morning 12th with sixty companions.[242]

Gandhi

CWMG, *Vol. XLIII, p. 21*

## 106. Letter to Jawaharlal Nehru

7 March 1930

My dear Jawaharlal,
After a talk with Sitla Sahai, I have decided to send him there. Let him see what he can do there and you will watch developments. If he and you decide that he should come back, he may do so. His wife

---

consciously or unconsciously preyed upon another, far more numerous, far more ancient and no less cultured than itself, is worth any amount of risk.... The plan through civil disobedience will be to combat such evils as I have sampled out.... If you cannot see your way to deal with these evils and my letter makes no appeal to your heart, on the 11th day of this month, I shall proceed with such co-workers of the Ashram as I can take, to disregard the provisions of the salt laws. I regard this tax to be the most iniquitous of all from the poor man's standpoint. As the independence movement is essentially for the poorest of the land the beginning will be made with this evil.' See also *CWMG*, Vol. XLIII, pp. 2–8.

242 Accompanied actually by 78 volunteers, Gandhi left Sabarmati for Dandi on 12 March 1930 to break the salt law and start the civil disobedience campaign.

and children will remain here and he can draw upon the Ashram for his bare upkeep. The rest you will hear from him.

Yours,
Bapu

CWMG, *Vol. XLIII, p. 23*

## 107. Letter to Jawaharlal Nehru

11 March 1930

My dear Jawaharlal,

It is nearing 10 p.m. now. The air is thick with the rumour that I shall be arrested during the night.[243] I have not wired to you especially because the correspondents submit their messages for approval and everybody is working at top speed. There was nothing special to wire about.

Things are developing extraordinarily well. Offers of volunteers are pouring in. The column will proceed with the march even though I may be arrested. If I am not, you may expect wires from me; otherwise I am leaving instructions.

I do not know that I have anything in particular to say. I have written enough. I gave a final message this evening to a vast crowd that gathered for prayer on the sands.[244]

May God keep you and give you strength to bear the burden.

With love to you all,

Bapu

CWMG, *Vol. XLIII, pp. 48–9*

[243] Gandhi was, however, not arrested until 5 May 1930. In a speech at Allahabad on 14 March 1930, Nehru said, 'It seems to be the intention of the Government not to touch Mahatma Gandhi so long as it is possible for it to do so, but there is evidence to show that in the meanwhile one leader or the other will be taken away gradually. ... One special feature of the struggle initiated by Mahatma Gandhi and the Congress is that there is no room for any compromise. Peace undoubtedly follows every battle and this much I can safely foretell, that the result of the present struggle will not be that we remain as we are.'

[244] Of the river Sabarmati. See *CWMG*, Vol. XLIII, pp. 46–8

## 108. Letter to Jawaharlal Nehru

13 March 1930

My dear Jawaharlal,

I hope you received what might have been my last letter. The news given to me of my impending arrest was said to be absolutely authentic. But we have reached the second stage safely.[245] We take the third tonight. I am sending you the programme. All the friends are most particular that I should not go to Ahmedabad for the Working Committee. There is considerable force in the suggestion. The Working Committee may, therefore, come to the place where we may be for the day or you alone may come.[246] The sentiment that we won't voluntarily go back without finishing the struggle is being well cultivated. My going back will mar it a bit. Jamnalalji told me he had written to you about it. I hope Kamala is keeping well.

I asked yesterday that full wires should be sent to you.

Yours sincerely,
Bapu

CWMG, *Vol. XLIII, p. 66*

## 109. Letter to Jawaharlal Nehru

Ras
19 March 1930

My dear Jawaharlal,

You are in for a whole night's vigil but it is inevitable if you are to return before tomorrow night. The messenger will bring you where I may be. You are reaching me at the most trying stage in the march. You will have to cross a channel at about 2 a.m. on the shoulders of tried fishermen.[247] I dare not interrupt the march even for the chief servant of the nation.

Love.

Bapu

[245] The second halt was at Bareja.

[246] The AICC session held at Sabarmati on 25 March 1930 authorized Gandhi to initiate and control civil disobedience.

[247] Gandhi had crossed the river Mahi early in the morning on 20 March, and Jawaharlal met him there.

[PS]
This is the place where Vallabhbhai was arrested.[248] All the hereditary officials of this village have just gone, leaving their resignations in my hands.[249]

Pandit Jawaharlal Nehru

CWMG, *Vol. XLIII, p. 103*

## 110. Letter to M.K. Gandhi

27 March 1930

My dear Bapuji,
I have received a letter from the Frontier Provincial Congress Committee stating that they are deeply pained to learn that illiterate Pathans have been engaged by the Government to obstruct you at Dandi. The Committee feel that this use of the Pathans by the Government brings discredit on the Pathans of the Frontier Province. They suggest therefore that if you are agreeable they might send some nationalist Pathans from Peshawar to Dandi. These persons will not go there primarily to offer civil disobedience but to explain, if they have a chance, to their fellow Pathans there in Pushtu the significance of the national campaign and of civil disobedience. Two names are suggested: Khan Abdul Ghaffar Khan[250]

[248] On 7 March 1930, and sentenced to three months' imprisonment. For Gandhi's 'Statement on Arrest of Vallbhbhai Patel', 7 March 1930, see *CWMG*, Vol. XLIII, p. 24.

[249] For Gandhi's article on this entitled 'About Headmen and Matadars', ibid., pp. 103–4 and pp. 153–4.

[250] Abdul Ghaffar Khan (1890–1988) of the Mohamadzai clan; brother of Dr Khan Saheb, prominent Pashtun Congress leader of the NWFP, popularly known as 'Frontier Gandhi' for his unqualified faith in nonviolence; founded the 'Red Shirt' or 'Khudai Khidmatgar' volunteer organisation in 1929; detained by Pakistan Government from 1947–55 for demanding Paktoonistan; recipient of the Nehru Award for International Understanding, 1969; awarded Bharat Ratna, 1987.

He was in Nehru's description, 'straight and simple, faithful and true, with a finely chiselled face that compels attention, and a character built up in the fire of long suffering and painful ordeal, full of hardness of the man of faith believing in his mission, and yet soft with the gentleness of one who loves his kind exceedingly.'

and Maulana Khan Mir.[251] The former, I know, is a good person. Khan Mir, I am told, has recently been released from exile whatever that might mean.

Of course, Pathans cannot be said to excel in nonviolence. They are apt to lose their tempers but I do not think one or two of them are likely to do anything harmful if they are near your group. Whether they do anything useful or not at Dandi, contact with your group will do them good and the Frontier Province will appreciate the honour. If you think it is worthwhile for these friends to be sent for, kindly send a telegram to our office here in which you might say, 'Send Muslim friends'.

Yours affectionately,
Jawaharlal

SWJN, *Vol. 4, I Series, pp. 292–3*

## 111. Letter to Jawaharlal Nehru

Delad
31 March 1930

My dear Jawaharlal,
I have your letter. I have not wired, as I do not think there are any Pathans at Dandi and, if there are, we shall cope with them. The advent even of good and true friends from the Frontier will cause complications. I want to present at Dandi, if I am allowed to reach it, the one issue without any avoidable complications.[252] Things seem to be shaping very well indeed in Gujarat.

I am surprised that they have already arrested so many in Rae Bareli. I feel you are right in confining your attention to the salt tax for the time being. We shall know during the next fortnight what more we can or should do.

[251] Secretary, Congress Committee, Peshawar

[252] The Government, however, did not arrest Gandhi but arrested others for breaking the salt law.

Referring to the dilemma of the Government in arresting him, Gandhi observed later that its 'plight is that of the serpent which has swallowed a rat. It would find it hard to resort to either course of action—allowing me to remain out or of putting me behind the bars.' For Gandhi's speech at Dandi on 5 April 1930, see *CWMG*, Vol. XLIII, pp. 181-5.

Unless you hear from me to the contrary, please take 6th April as the date for simultaneous beginning.[253]

It is now nearing 10 p.m., so good night.

Bapu

CWMG, *Vol. XLIII, p. 160*

## 112. Letter to M.K. Gandhi

Anand Bhawan, Allahabad
10 [April][254] 1930

My dear Bapu,

We have just returned from our first public manufacture of salt in Allahabad City. Yesterday we started in some villages nearby. No arrests were made in the villages but there was a great tussle between our volunteers and the police to get possession of the salt and the pan. Some people were hurt in this and burnt their hands as the pan in which the salt water had been boiled was very hot. I have just heard a rumour that several arrests have been made in the villages today.

In Allahabad City we had a tremendous show today. It was the biggest gathering I have seen here and there was very great enthusiasm. A pleasing feature was the part Muslims took in it. Many of them came to garland us and offer us pan, etc. I was the leader of the batch of volunteers and a Muslim was deputy leader. Kamala and Krishna were also with us. The crowd was so vast at the place we started making salt that we had little room to move about. In the middle of our work some policemen with a sub-inspector tried to force their way in but they could not get through the crowd. They did not try very aggressive tactics and ultimately went away. There were plenty of police at a distance but they were not utilised. So we made the salt and realised about Rs 500/- by auctioning it. A little packet sent to me by Devadas just before his arrest[255] fetched Rs 180/-. We made only a little salt in public as

[253] On this day, Gandhi symbolically broke the salt law by picking up a lump of salt mixed with mud from the coast of Dandi, thus marking the beginning of satyagraha on the first day of the National Week.

[254] The source has June, evidently a slip.

[255] In Delhi on 9 April 1930

the process was a long one and the crowd was difficult to manage. But previously in the course of the day we had made a lot in our office and we sold all this in small packets. Father helped in the auctioning.[256]

Altogether Allahabad responded wonderfully. We shall continue this from day to day and soon will have several centres in the city.

I expected to be arrested afterwards and I gave the police an opportunity to do so by remaining at our office nearby for some time but no arrest has so far been made. I think however that I shall be arrested soon.

We are breaking the salt laws in many cities and villages in the UP. Some arrests are being made—usually the leader of the group of volunteers is arrested—but no wholesale arrests have taken place in our province yet.

One of our chief difficulties is to remain in touch with our various centres. Telegrams are being held up and letters greatly delayed. We have to rely on messengers. The result of the censorship is also to prevent publicity being given. Specially in Allahabad there is no paper which cares to give full details. Our telegrams to other papers are being held up.

I have just seen in the *Hindustan Times* that there was a great round-up there when Devadas was arrested. There was no mention of this in the local papers here.

From Chapra in Bihar comes news by letter that the police are very aggressive. They broke up the volunteers' camp and carried away their tents. There is great enthusiasm in the district—indeed so great that there is fear of a conflict with the police.

Altogether the movement is developing very happily and I am quite content if they do not arrest you.

[256] Mahadev Desai in his letter dated 7 April 1930 to Nehru, had enclosed 'a pinch of salt manufactured by Bapu at Dandi on the 6th of April to be kept either as a memento or sold by auction, the upset price to be less than a thousand rupees. The little packet I have in my possession was purchased for Rs 501. I am addressing this letter to Krishna, lest the police should open your letters and confiscate the invaluable salt.'

Today as I expected arrest I nominated you as Congress President. I hope you will agree. In the alternative I suggest father but this was only if you were arrested.

Tomorrow the dedication ceremony of Anand Bhawan will take place.

I enclose a specimen of our salt.

Yours affectionately,

Jawaharlal

MKG Papers, Pyarelal Collection, *NMML*

## 113. Message for M.K. Gandhi

[Before 16 April 1930][257]

I have stolen a march over you.[258]

SWJN, *Vol. 4, I Series, p. 314*

## 114. Letter to M.K. Gandhi

28 July 1930

My dear Bapuji,

It is a delight to write to you again after a long interval even though it be from one prison to another.[259] I would like to write at length but I am afraid I cannot do so at present. I shall therefore confine myself to the matter in issue.

Dr Sapru and Mr Jayakar[260] came yesterday and had a long interview with father and me. Today they are coming again. As they have already put us in possession of all the facts and have shown us your note and letter, we felt that we could discuss the matter between us two and arrive at some decision even without waiting

[257] This appeared in *The Leader*, 16 April 1930.

[258] Nehru was arrested on 14 April. He telephoned this message from prison to Motilal Nehru, who conveyed it to Gandhi.

[259] This letter was taken by M.R. Jayakar to Gandhi who was in Yeravda Central Prison. Nehru was in Naini Jail.

[260] M.R. Jayakar (1873–1959); barrister and judge; leader of the Liberal Party, who worked closely with Sapru

for the second interview.[261] Of course, if anything new turns up at the second interview we are prepared to vary any previously formed opinion. Our conclusions for the time being are given in a note which we are giving to Dr Sapru and Mr Jayakar.[262] This is more or less brief but it will I hope give you some idea of how our minds are working. I might add that father and I are in full agreement in regard to what our attitude should be.

I must confess that your point (1) regarding the 'Constitutional Issue' has not won me over. Nor does father fancy it. I do not see how it fits in with our position or our pledges or with the realities of today. Father and I entirely agree with you that we can be 'no parties to any truce which would undo the position at which we have arrived today'.[263] It is because of this that the fullest consideration is essential before any final decision is arrived at. I must confess that I do not see any appreciable advance yet from the other side and I greatly fear a false or a weak move on our part. I am expressing myself moderately. For myself, I delight in warfare. It makes me feel that I am alive. The events of the last few months in India have gladdened my heart and have made me prouder of Indian men, women and even children (!) than I have ever been. But I realise that most people are not warlike and like peace and so I try hard to suppress myself and take a peaceful view!

May I congratulate you on the new India that you have created by your magic touch? What the future will bring I know not, but

[261] Gandhi had, for negotiating with the Government, sent a note stating his conditions for attending the Round Table Conference. These were: the Conference should discuss safeguards for the transitional period only, with the right for anyone to raise the issue of independence; CD would be called off but peaceful picketing and salt manufacture would continue; all satyagrahi prisoners should be released, confiscated properties restored, fines refunded and dismissed officers reinstated. See 'Note to the Nehrus' and 'Letter to Motilal Nehru' dated 23 July 1930, *CWMG*, Vol. XLVI, pp. 42–4 and 44–5. On the 24th, Gandhi sent another letter to Motilal Nehru where he said, 'Whatever you and Jawaharlal do is acceptable to me'.

[262] See 'Note from Nehrus' dated 28 July 1930, *CWMG*, Vol. XLIV, Appendix I(A).

[263] The quoted sentence from Gandhi's letter of 23 July 1930 to Motilal Nehru reads: 'I would be no party to any truce which would undo the position at which we have arrived at today.'

the past has made life worth living and our prosaic existence has developed something of epic greatness in it. Sitting here in Naini Jail I have pondered on the wonderful efficacy of nonviolence as a weapon and have become a greater convert to it than ever before. I hope you are not dissatisfied with the response of the country to the nonviolence creed. Despite occasional lapses the country has stuck to it wonderfully—certainly far more grimly than I had expected.

I am afraid I am still somewhat of a protestant regarding your 11 points. Not that I disagree with any one of them. Indeed they are important. Yet I do not think they take the place of independence. But I certainly agree with you that we should have 'nothing to do with anything that would not give the nation the power to give immediate effect to them.'[264]

Father has been unwell for the last 8 days ever since he took an injection. He has grown very weak. The long interview last night tired him out.

Yours affectionately,
Jawaharlal

SWJN, *Vol. 4, I Series, pp. 369–71*

## 115. Letter to M.K. Gandhi

31 August 1930

My dear Bapuji,
I enclose our joint note for you.[265] Father is improving slowly. Yesterday was the first day when he had no blood in his sputum.

[264] Gandhi had written in his letter of 23 July 1930 to Motilal Nehru: 'I know that neither you nor Jawahar were enamoured of the eleven points brought out in my first letter to the Viceroy. I do not know whether you still have the same opinion. My own mind is quite clear about them. They are to me the substance of independence.' See also p. 113, *fn*. 239.

[265] For 'Note from Nehrus', dated 31 August 1930, see *CWMG*, Vol. XLIV, Appendix V. Referring to it in his statement to Tej Bahadur Sapru and M.R. Jayakar of 5 September 1930, Gandhi wrote: 'We gave two anxious nights to these papers and we had the benefit of a full and free discussion with you on all the points arising out of these papers. And as we have told you, we have all arrived at the definite conclusion that we see no meeting ground between the Government and the Indian National Congress so far as we can speak for the

But today again there was a trace of it. So we are not out of the wood yet. Day before yesterday he suddenly felt rather irritated at talks of his release and efforts being made for it. He was so uncomfortable about it that he sent the following telegram:

Lord Irwin, Simla.

I understand efforts are being made to secure my early release for reasons of health. While appreciating kind intentions prompting such efforts I wish to say that I do not approve of them. I seek no favour or clemency.

I take it that there is no question of his release now before his term expires. The burdens on Kamala are increasing and she takes them very seriously and conscientiously. I should not be surprised if within the week she and my sisters were arrested. Hansa Mehta[266] having gone there is no reason why Kamala and others should not also be arrested. The picketing ordinance has now been applied to Allahabad. I hope you are keeping well.

Love

Yours affectionately,
Jawaharlal

[PS]
Syed Mahmud sends his respects, regards and love. Hope you are taking fruits now.

SWJN, *Vol. 4, I Series, pp. 378–9*

---

latter, being out of touch with the outside world. We unreservedly associate ourselves with the opinion contained in the note sent by the distinguished prisoners in Naini Central Prison, but these friends expect us to give in our own words our view of the position finally reached in the negotiations for peace, which you, with patriotic motives, have carried on during the past two months at considerable sacrifice of your own time and no less inconvenience to yourselves.'

[266] (1897–1995); wife of Jivraj Mehta; Vice Chancellor, University of Baroda, 1949–58; President, All India Women's Conference, 1946; Member, Constituent Assembly, 1947–50; Indian Representative on Human Rights Commission, 1947–52; was arrested on 30 August 1930

## 116. Letter to Jawaharlal Nehru

Camp Borsad
8 May 1931

My dear Jawaharlal,

I had your telegram and now I have your letter of 30th ultimo but not the previous letter.[267] There is certainly no urgent need about your returning. From your telegram I have gathered that you were all A1 in spite of the chill of which you write to me in your letter. What you read in the papers about a breakdown was not without foundation but just now in Gujarat there is no immediate danger of a breakdown.[268] I am going to Simla next week to confer with Mr Emerson[269] about several outstanding matters and he says in his letter that incidentally there would be meeting with the Government about the Round Table Conference. He expects me also to go to Nainital on or about the 18th. I do not know how things are progressing in the UP just now. But it will be as well for me to go to Nainital. Of course you were quite right in writing to me on the Hindu-Muslim question as frankly as you have done. I should have felt hurt if you had done less. You have a perfect right to unburden yourself without the least fear of being misunderstood by me. Of course I do not plead guilty to your charge. I have always taken

[267] None available

[268] Of the Gandhi-Irwin Pact of 5 March 1931 (*CWMG*, Vol. XLV, Appendix VI). Gandhi had represented to the Government prior to the Gandhi-Irwin Pact on 5 March 1931 regarding 'the lands of civil resisters sold in Gujarat in respect of revenue dues.' Ibid., pp. 245–6. Again in *YI*, 7-5-1931, he wrote: 'To sell the farmers' land and that too for a song is vivisection. The sale of forfeited lands in Gujarat was such an operation. The clause in the Settlement about these lands was for Sardar Vallabhbhai the biggest bite to swallow. But he swallowed it because ultimately he shared my faith that the lands could not long be withheld by the buyers from the original owners and in any case they were bound to be restored when full settlement was attained ... Healthy public opinion has an influence of which we have not realised the full significance. But we are not yet out of the wood. There are yet tough buyers who have not come forward. But I have little doubt that if the workers don't lose patience and the Settlement does not otherwise break down, they will also respond to the influence of that public opinion.'

[269] Herbert William Emerson (1881–1962); Home Secretary, Government of India, 1930–1; Governor, Punjab, 1933–8

good care to say that I was speaking for myself. So long as we have not evolved a concrete policy how could I help expressing my own personal views? But the occasions have not been many when I have let myself go. I quite agree with you that Dr Ansari's proposal about arbitration consisting of the many names he suggests is highly unpractical. Nothing of course has come out of it. Dr Mahmud's fear is absolutely baseless. I did see Bhopal[270] at the latter's instance and when he discussed the Hindu-Muslim question I naturally said that he might call in Shaukat Ali[271] and his other friend and then summon me to Bhopal if he thought that there was anything to be done. I could not say to him that he was not to move at all. That same day Mrs Naidu brought Shaukat Ali to Mani Bhuvan and I relate the conversation I had with Bhopal. Nothing more has happened. I have made no movement and have written not one single line beyond saying that I was praying, which I am literally doing. I wrote last week as much to Dr Mahmud when he complained that I had broken the pact that I was to be dumb. When you return completely restored, we must have a meeting of the Working Committee and if we can evolve a formula for the guidance of all Congressmen, nothing will please me more. Personally I think that we shall not be able to evolve any formula just now and I am more and more driven to the idea I adumbrated before you on the day of your departure or the day previous. When you reach Bombay of course you will first of all seek me out wherever I am. It is highly likely that I shall be by that time in Borsad or Bardoli.

No going to London without Hindu-Muslim unity.

Love to you all.

Bapu

Pandit Jawaharlal Nehru
Nuwera Eliya
Ceylon

CWMG, *Vol. XLVI, pp. 118–19*

[270] Hamidullah Khan (1894–1960); Nawab of Bhopal; Chancellor, Muslim University, Aligarh, 1930–5, Chancellor, Chamber of Princes, 1931–2 and 1944–7

[271] Elder brother of Mohammed Ali

## 117. Letter to Jawaharlal Nehru

5 June 1931

My dear Jawaharlal,

I hope you did not lose in S. India what you gained in Ceylon.[272] If you are fresh and do not mind the journey do come to Bardoli for Sunday so that we might have a quiet chat here before beginning operations on Tuesday.[273] I hope Kamala and Indu have profited by the rest.

Yours,
Bapu

Pandit Jawaharlal Nehru
c/o Sjt. Jalbhai Naoroji
Napean Sea Rd.
Bombay

CWMG, *Vol. XLVI, p. 323*

## 118. Letter to Jawaharlal Nehru

Borsad
17 June 1931

My dear Jawaharlal,

Sitla Sahai writes to me about impending repression in Rae Bareli through the taluqdars.[274]

[272] Nehru had had a month's holiday in Ceylon, on his doctor's advice, with his family and had later travelled through Travancore, Cochin, Malabar, Mysore and Hyderabad.

[273] Nehru called in on 8 June. Gandhi left in the evening for Bombay, accompanied by Nehru and Abdul Ghaffar Khan, to attend the Congress Working Committee meeting which passed a resolution on the 11th that Gandhi alone should represent them at the Round Conference in November 1931.

[274] Gandhi in his letter dated 17 June 1931 to Sitla Sahai wrote: 'Where cultivators accept our conditions and are prepared to pay the rent but the zamindars are not prepared to accept it, the amount should be received by us and deposited into the bank.'

You must have seen the enclosed notice about the flag on the University building.[275] I am receiving complaints from other places also. As soon as you have the time I would like you to go into all these things and then tell me what you think about it all. If the matters can wait till we meet at Surat for the Working Committee[276] we must discuss them then or you should write to me earlier.
Pandit Jawaharlal Nehru
Anand Bhawan, Allahabad

CWMG, *Vol. XLVI, p. 390*

## 119. Letter to Jawaharlal Nehru

20 June 1931

My dear Jawaharlal,
I have just received your letter. The incident at Dongri was bad enough but the incidents at Allahabad make matters look still worse. I came to know about the antecedents of Pannalal only two days ago. I am now making full enquiries so as to enable me to deal with it somehow or other in the pages of *Young India*.[277] These incidents perhaps affect me more than they affect you and I am being driven to two conclusions: First, during the last struggle violent people crept into the Congress ranks and they impregnated the atmosphere with violence in a very subtle manner. We are now reaping the fruit. Secondly, the position which I adumbrated at the Working Committee and which I put so unconvincingly before it

[275] Referring to this in his *Autobiography*, Nehru writes: 'In Bangalore, in the Mysore State, I had hoisted at a great gathering a national flag on an enormous iron pole. Not long after my departure this pole was broken up into bits, and the Mysore Government made the display of the flag an offence. This ill-treatment and insult of the flag I had hoisted pained me greatly.'

[276] On 13 July 1931

[277] Pannalal, son of Maganlal Zaveri, had gone to the public meeting held in early June at Dongri, especially to hear Abdul Ghaffar Khan. He was stabbed fatally by someone in the crowd of Muslims that surrounded him, his father and brother, taking them for nationalist leaders. For Gandhi's article 'A Martyr', see *CWMG*, Vol. XLVII, pp. 57–8.

is the correct position from more points of view than the one I put before the Committee.[278]

I entirely agree with you that in view of what is going on here, the Round Table Conference is a small and unreal affair and if the Settlement breaks through [sic] it will be perhaps no use my going to London.

I am very clear that we must not be in any shape or form, directly or indirectly, party to the breach. I would therefore urge you not to break any order yourself if it is served upon you nor encourage any of our workers to do so without first receiving sanction from the Working Committee. We must thrash the whole thing out fully and there are not many days left now before we meet. But I would like you to take a step, if it is at all possible, before coming here. Ask for an appointment with the Governor[279] and see him after arming yourself with the fullest details of the repression that is going on. At the present moment the Government and the Congress are supposed to be cooperating with each other and therefore they shall have to trust us and plead with us, making use of us wherever they feel there is any breach on the part of any of our workers.

I have asked Mr Emerson to consider a proposal I have made, appointment of an arbitration board to investigate all the complaints regarding breach of Settlement either on the side of the Government or on our side. The letter went three or four days ago.[280]

Pandit Jawaharlal Nehru
Anand Bhawan, Allahabad

MKG Papers, Pyarelal Collection, Subject File 5, *NMML*

[278] For Gandhi's explanation of his position, ibid., pp. 1–3.

[279] Sir Malcolm Hailey (1872–1969); entered Indian Civil Service, 1895; Member, Viceroy's Council, 1919–24; Governor, Punjab, 1924–8; Governor, UP, 1928–30 and 1931–4

[280] For Gandhi's letter to Emerson dated 14 June 1931, see *CWMG*, Vol. XLVI, pp. 379–81.

## 120. Letter to Jawaharlal Nehru

24 June 1931

My dear Jawaharlal,

I quite agree with you that the order under 144 about which you have written to Kunwar Jagadish Prasad[281] is in breach of the Truce, if not of the letter certainly of the spirit.[282] I am glad you have written to Kunwar Jagadish Prasad but I adhere to the suggestion I have made that you should seek an interview with the Governor himself.[283] I had mentioned to the Viceroy and Mr Emerson that they should seek the first opportunity of meeting you and they had agreed. The latter now enquires when you would see him. Will you see him?

I have your letter about the outstandings collected by you in Ceylon. Mahadev had written to Somasundaram about it acknowledging receipt and Somasundaram has acknowledged Mahadev's letter. Do you desire anything more to be done?

I have read the letter from Mills enclosed by you. Mills does not know nor do you that I have lost caste with Haridas Mozumdar.[284] He is so disgusted with the Delhi Settlement that he is sorry for having advertised me in America. Probably he has not proved as good as his word. But there it is. Only I have lost caste so often and with so many that I have now become a hardened sinner. My sympathies are all with Haridas. I must in fairness to him say that

[281] Kunwar Jagdish Prasad (1880–1957); Chief Secretary to the UP Government, 1927–31; Home Member, UP, 1933; Member, Viceroy's Executive Council, 1935–40

[282] On 17 June 1931, Nehru had written that the order under Section 144 appeared to be a clear breach of the truce terms (a provisional settlement between the Government of India and the Congress where even peaceful picketing was not permitted). And further pointed out that if a person was to obey the notice issued under Section 144 in Rae Bareli he must abstain from all activity, agrarian, political and labour. Thus no Congress or any other similar work could be carried out in Rae Bareli. See *SWJN*, Vol. 5, I Series, pp. 79–80.

[283] The interview sought with the Governor of UP, Sir Malcolm Hailey, was not granted.

[284] Editor, *India Today and Tomorrow*, published from New York. For Gandhi's letter of 3 May 1931, see *CWMG*, Vol. XLVI, p. 78.

in the same letter that he revises his views about me he protests his loyalty to me personally. What I can be apart from my views to evoke loyalty is another matter.

Orders from Dr Ansari and Co. have upset our plans. They want alteration both of date and of venue.[285]

Pandit Jawaharlal Nehru
Anand Bhawan Allahabad

MKG Papers, Pyarelal Collection, Subject File 5, *NMML*

## 121. Letter to Jawaharlal Nehru

Borsad
28 June 1931

My dear Jawaharlal,

I have your letter and your postcard.[286] I am glad the notice under Sec. 144 in Rae Bareli has been withdrawn.[287] It was undoubtedly due to your clear letter to the Chief Secretary. By the time you reach Bombay for the Working Committee, the Committee should be ready to give definite guidance.

I am quite convinced that in order to complete our case it is necessary for you to ask the Governor to see you. In seeking the interview you will tell him that you want to leave no stone unturned to see that the clear position is placed before the highest authority in the province. You may bring nothing from the Governor but our position will surely be the stronger for your having made the

[285] The reference is to the change of venue of the Congress Working Committee, which was to be held on 7 July 1931, from Dumas in Sachin State to Bombay. In his statement dated 29 June 1931 on the ban by Sachin State, Gandhi said: 'Let the public know that the change of venue has nothing to do with the order.... The date and venue had to be changed for the convenience of, and at the request of, Dr Ansari, Maulana Abul Kalam and Mr Mohamed Alam.' See *CWMG*, Vol. XLVII, pp. 72–3.

[286] Not available

[287] The District Magistrate, Rae Bareli, had ordered the Congress workers to abstain from speaking or writing anything on the agrarian or political situation of the district. For Gandhi's article on the subject, 'Kisan's Trouble in the UP', see *CWMG*, Vol. XLVII, pp. 92–4 and ibid., pp. 109–10.

attempt to see him and to secure fulfillment of the Settlement. We shall lose nothing by your offering to see him and seeing him if he accepts the offer.

You might have seen in *Young India*[288] what I wrote about the happenings in Unao District. I am going to write again on the material supplied by you and others.

It was unfortunate that the Working Committee had to be postponed. Vallabhbhai was strongly against going to Allahabad in the present circumstances there. I think too that what with Cawnpore and the other excitement in UP it was better that Allahabad was avoided for the time being.[289]

Bapu

CWMG, *Vol. XLVII, pp. 69–70*

## 122. Letter to Jawaharlal Nehru

Borsad
1 July 1931

My dear Jawaharlal,
I have your letter[290] of 27th June, redirected from Bardoli. Possibly you did not know that from Bombay I had come back to Borsad because it has been necessary for Vallabhbhai and me to divide our work.[291] Danger is being averted by constant presence and vigilance. But any day there might be a burst-up in Borsad. I have

288 Dated 25 June 1931. It was alleged by the President, District Congress Committee, that on 30 May 1931 a raid had been made on the tenants by the zamindars of the village along with the Sub-Divisional Magistrate; see *CWMG*, Vol. XLVII, p. 59.

289 There were allegations of harassment and coercion by Congress pickets made to the Government by Messrs Ranjilal and Bros., Cawnpore, importers and dealers of foreign piece-goods. Gandhi wrote to the local Congress Committee that picketing should be suspended if the allegations were proved correct after investigation.

290 Not available

291 Of collection of payment by the villages on account of current dues or arrears. Gandhi and Vallbhbhai Patel were touring the District of Bardoli, assuring the villagers that no coercion would be used against them 'if they paid at least the current dues'.

had difficult experiences of working settlements in South Africa and even getting the poor head broken in rendering a cent per cent account from our side, and then had to get myself arrested in making the Government render a tolerably good account of themselves.[292] But I thought that I had forgotten all about working settlements. Now, however, I am reviving old memories and many of the experiences are being repeated. My great satisfaction however is that whether war or settlement, the nation must go forward if we remain faithful servers.

I like all your letters to the Chief Secretary. I do hope that the Governor will consent to see you.

Here is a complaint against you. Please keep the typewritten sheet and return it to me if you write about it or bring it with you and you will tell me all about it when we meet.

Bapu

CWMG, *Vol. XLVII, pp. 85–6*

## 123. Letter to Jawaharlal Nehru

Bardoli
25 July 1931

My dear Jawaharlal,

I enclose a letter[293] received from CMS Parsonage, Kaviyoor. Will you please get from Congressmen in Khatauli the facts about the case?

Yours sincerely,
Bapu

[292] Gandhi refers to an incident of 10 February 1908 when he had been beaten up by Mir Alam and his companions. See *CWMG*, Vol. VII, pp. 75–6.

[293] In which the Rev. K.M. Mathan had complained that those who changed their religion and became Christians were being persecuted by Congressmen

Encl. 2
[PS]
I have a wire from Simla saying they are in correspondence with Bombay Government and that I should not take precipitate action.[294]
Pandit Jawaharlal Nehru
Anand Bhawan, Allahabad

CWMG, *Vol. XLVII, p. 205*

## 124. Letter to M.K. Gandhi

Allahabad
25 July 1931

My dear Bapu,
Soon after you left Delhi I sent the telegram to Abdul Ghaffar Khan.[295] I hope you received his reply. I have received a letter from some Peshawar Congressmen complaining of the activities of some of the red shirts.

I wrote to Jagdish Prasad, the Chief Secretary, from Delhi and asked him for an interview with Hailey. On arrival here I read in the papers that Hailey was unwell and had gone to Naini Tal. Jagdish Prasad telephoned to me from Lucknow today saying that it would not be possible to arrange an interview with Hailey soon owing to his ill health but that he (JP) would like to see me. I am going to Lucknow on the 28th to meet him.

It appears that the UP Government has issued some instructions to the district officers regarding some kind of a swift enquiry into rents and prices. But this will apply to the next kharif and not to present conditions. Probably there will be a change

[294] The reference is to H.W. Emerson's telegram dated 25 July 1931. Gandhi had earlier wired him and sent a letter to the Collector of Surat regarding 'the painful happenings in Bardoli'. Demanding an open impartial tribunal enquiry into complaints of forced collection of land revenue and repression of tenants, he had said that 'failing relief I must regard settlement and faith broken freeing me for such action as may be necessary for protection [of] people.' See also *CWMG*, Vol. XLVII, pp. 202 and 203–4.

[295] For an extract from Abdul Ghaffar Khan's letter to Gandhi detailing extreme repressive measures of the Government against the Khudai Khidmatgars in the NWFP, see *CWMG*, Vol. XLVII, p. 160.

in the law authorising the district officers or some special officer to fix rents. But this will not relieve the present tension. The official figure for ejectments in Allahabad district is about 4,000. It appears however that some at least of the persons ejected are ploughing their fields without interference. On the other hand there is interference in some cases. The general campaign against the tenant has toned down a little but a sufficient number of individual cases of oppression and ill treatment continue. There were a dozen new cases under Sec. 107 during the last few days. Two days ago a number of kisans were beaten badly by a zamindar in a tehsil of Allahabad district. Just before writing this letter some kisans came to me complaining bitterly of a beating by a zamindar. Women were also beaten. Some time ago they paid [annas] 8/-. They now offered another 4/- according to your advice but on demanding a receipt they were beaten and threatened in a variety of ways.

A primitive police tax has been imposed in two areas in the Allahabad district. In both these places there was some months ago a riot in which a zamindar and some of his men were killed. The tax is a heavy one amounting to about 20% of the rent. How this is going to be paid is a mystery. It was announced by beat of drum that if it is not paid locks will be broken and goods taken away.

I enclose copies of two notices under Sec. 144. They are old but interesting. You will observe that it is presumed that '1,000 accused persons' were Congress volunteers. In one of them all 'outsiders' are prohibited from entering the village. Thus lawyers, friends or relatives could not enter.

From Shahjahanpur comes shocking news of the ill treatment of a fine of 15 by a sub-Inspector of police.

In Barabanki a deliberate attempt is being made by the Deputy Commissioner and some taluqadas to create communal friction.[296]

We are having a meeting of the Council of our PCC tomorrow.

Yours affectionately,
Jawaharlal

MKG Papers, Pyarelal Collection, *NMML*

[296] On 21 July 1931, Gandhi had sent to H.W. Emerson a memorandum, also known as 'charge-sheet', citing instances of breaches of the Settlement.

## 125. Letter to Jawaharlal Nehru

26 July 1931

My dear Jawaharlal,

Here is a letter from Ferangimahal. Also a copy of my reply. You will see from my reply that I have told the reader that he should expect a more detailed reply from you. If they would have an outside Commission I think we should give it to him.

Pandit Jawaharlal Nehru
Anand Bhawan, Allahabad

MKG Papers, Pyarelal Collection, *Subject File 5, NMML*

## 126. Telegram to M.K. Gandhi

15 August 1931

UP Government invited Govind Ballabh Pant[297] sit on Agrarian Committee which considering future revenue policy. I consider present circumstances his joining inadvisable. Please wire your opinion to Sherwani[298] Elgin Road Allahabad.

CWMG, *Vol. XLVII, p. 298*

## 127. Telegram to Jawaharlal Nehru

[On or after 15 August 1931][299]

Pt. Jawaharlal Nehru

Your wire. Think Govind Ballabh should join Committee.[300] Have wired Sherwani accordingly.

CWMG, *Vol. XLVII, p. 298, fn.* 1

[297] (1887–1961); advocate, Allahabad; leader, Swaraj Party, UP Council, 1923–30; severely beaten up along with Nehru at Lucknow during demonstration against Simon Commission, 1928; Chief Minister, UP, 1937–9 and 1946–55; Union Minister, 1955–61

[298] T.A.K. Sherwani, landlord and barrister from Aligarh; President, UP Provincial Congress Committee, 1931

[299] See preceding item.

[300] Pant, however, declined to serve till he had received the approval of the UP Congress Committee.

## 128. Letter to Jawaharlal Nehru

Ahmedabad
18 August 1931

My dear Jawaharlal,
I send you the enclosed[301] for your information. You will destroy it after use.

Encl. 1
Pandit Jawaharlal Nehru
Anand Bhawan
Allahabad

CWMG, *Vol. XLVII, p. 308*

## 129. Letter to M.K. Gandhi

Allahabad
19 August 1931

My dear Bapu,
I enclose copies of the letter and the figure sent to me by the Japanese Consul General.[302]

Roger Baldwin has sent me a copy of a letter he has addressed to you from New York. The letter was meant to prepare you for an interview in Europe but this presumably will not come off now. I shall like however to tell you something of Roger. He is a good friend of mine and I saw him frequently in Europe in 1927. He is the most prominent worker among the American liberals and radicals. He has I think been to jail more than once as his chief job in life

[301] Not available

[302] Who in reply to Nehru's letter of 27 July had written on 9 August, giving figures regarding salaries of Government servants in Japan. Gandhi sought this information in support of the Karachi Resolution on Fundamental Rights and Economic Changes, whereby the salary of government servants was to be limited to not more than Rs 500 per month or Rs 6,000 per year. In his article for *YI,* 30-7-1931, 'Five-hundred-rupee Limit', Gandhi wrote, 'The way to examine the justness of the Congress conclusion is to find the proportion between the salaries and the average income of India's millions, and secondly to compare with the salaries and the average income of other countries. ... I have now before me some figures about the Japanese Public Service, both superior and subordinate. ... The average daily income of the Japanese per head is about four annas. Compared then with the Japan figures, the Rs 500 limit by the Congress is over-generous.'

is to defend civil liberties. He is the director of the Civil Liberties Association of America and is an expert in matters relating to prisons. He has visited prisons in almost every country in Europe and has specially investigated the conditions of politicals there. He is fairly radical in his views but because he is not a Communist he has been attacked by them specially because of his attitude towards the Congress. You will remember perhaps my showing you a letter from him to me. I should have particularly wanted him to meet you if you had gone to Europe. Indeed the main reason for his coming to Europe was to meet you.

Affectionately yours,
Jawaharlal

MKG Papers, Pyarelal Collection, *NMML*

## 130. Letter to Jawaharlal Nehru

Ahmedabad
21 August 1931

My dear Jawaharlal,

This will be given to you by Srinivasa Sharma of Meerut. He has found his way to the Ashram and as he seemed to be very importunate, he was admitted. He did not then say that he had really deserted his wife and run away from his place because he was heavily in debt. He felt penitent three or four days ago and confessed that he had left his wife and that he had creditors for nearly Rs 1,000. He is therefore afraid to return to Meerut. I have advised him to seek some work in UP. He seems to have been a volunteer also in Allahabad. I had only one chat with him and he impressed me as a sincere man wishing to do the right thing. He is now going to Allahabad and will see you. I would suggest your putting him somewhere, insisting on his sending for his wife and finding out something about his creditors. If he proves a reliable worker he might be of great use. If, however, you cannot accommodate him anywhere and consider it too much of a bother in the midst of your work you may dismiss him from your mind.

Pandit Jawaharlal Nehru
Anand Bhawan
Allahabad

CWMG, *Vol. XLVII, p. 337*

## 131. Letter to Jawaharlal Nehru

Ahmedabad
21 August 1931

My dear Jawaharlal,

Here is a copy of a telegram I have sent to the Viceroy.[303] There are so many rumours and so many misrepresentations going on that I thought I would clear the position by letting the Viceroy know exactly where we stand. Dr Sapru also sent me a wire of which I send you a copy herewith and a copy of my reply.[304]

I hope you found Indu cheerful.

Bapu

Encl. 3
Pandit Jawaharlal Nehru
Anand Bhawan
Allahabad

CWMG, *Vol. XLVII, p. 339*

[303] Freeman-Freeman-Thomas, First Marquis of Willingdon (1866–1941); British Liberal politician; Governor, Bombay, 1913–19; Governor, Madras, 1919–24; Governor-General, Canada, 1926–31; Governor-General, India, 1931–6

The Congress Working Committee endorsed on 13 August 1931 Gandhi's decision not to attend the Round Table Conference. The entire correspondence between Gandhi and the Government, together with the Congress 'charge-sheet' against the Government, which catagorised instances of breaches of truce, was released for publication. Referring to rumours that the publication of the charge-sheet had upset the Government, Gandhi sent the Viceroy a telegram dated 21 August 1931 which *inter alia* read: 'I contend that the appointment of an impartial tribunal is implicit in the settlement in the event of differences arising between the Government and the Congress regarding the interpretation of the Settlement or the working in practice. I have been prepared as I am now to waive such an enquiry if by quiet personal discussion or some such informal means reasonable satisfaction is given to the Congress.' See *CWMG*, Vol. XLVII, pp. 330–1.

[304] For the cables from and to Sapru, ibid., p. 330.

## 132. Telegram to Jawaharlal Nehru

Gujarat Vidyapith, Ahmedabad
23 August 1931

Jawaharlal Nehru
Anand Bhawan
Allahabad
Am proceeding Simla tonight.[305] Vallabhbhai accompanying. We both consider your presence and Abdul Ghaffar Khan's necessary. Please start.

Bapu

CWMG, *Vol. XLVII, p. 353*

## 133. Letter to M.K. Gandhi

Allahabad
1 September 1931

My dear Bapu,
You have gone at last and there have been great rejoicings in many quarters and five-column headlines in the newspapers.[306] But India seems to be a duller and an emptier place without you and I am afraid many will look, oftener than the pious Muslims five times a day, to the Kaaba in the West, and will pay little heed to work at home. Wireless reports tell us that you are enjoying yourself on board and are unperturbed at the frolics of the Arabian Sea, although many others have been laid low. I am glad for one reason at least that you have gone. You will rest after a fashion for a fortnight and the sea air will freshen you.

I returned to Allahabad from Bombay to find Kamala ill. She had had fever—probably malarial. She is better now but is extraordinarily fragile and weak.

[305] For talks with the Viceroy

[306] Gandhi set sail for England on 29 August 1931 to attend the Round Table Conference in London. Referring to their parting, Nehru writes in his *Autobiography*, 'I accompanied him from Simla to Bombay, and there, one bright morning towards the end of August, I waved good-bye to him as he was carried away to the Arabian Sea and the far West. That was my last glimpse of him for two years.'

I am enclosing some papers. There are copies of letters from and to the Private Secretary to the Viceroy.[307] There is a newspaper cutting giving an article[308] from an Egyptian paper. I hope you will read it, specially as I understand Shaukat Ali is going to descend on you at Port Said.[309] There is some wholesome advice in this article which Shaukat would do well to accept—but I fear he will not do so! The example of Egypt has often been thrust upon us. It is well that we should know what it was.

I am also enclosing a cutting from the *Pioneer* just to show you what your friend Newham[310]—if that is his name—is capable of. It is a shameless bit of writing and propaganda. I said something about it in a press interview yesterday but the *Leader* took special care to leave out that part of the interview. But after all it was not for me to contradict. It is for Abdul Ghaffar and I have drawn his attention to it.[311]

I have decided to send Kamala's brother, Kailas Nath Kaul, to Khan Sahib. I sent for him here and explained to him what his job was going to be. He liked the idea of going. I think the Khans will like him and get some work out of him.

I have suggested to Vallabhbhai to invite Abdul Ghaffar to the Working Committee[312] on the 8th. I hope he will come.

Another enclosure is a copy of the letter I have sent to Slocombe.[313]

In the UP conditions are bad but there are no red spots. People seem to be resigned to their fate. Cholera is raging in the Allahabad

[307] For Nehru's letter to the Private Secretary to the Viceroy, see *SWJN*, Vol. 5, I Series, p. 115.

[308] Which stated that the settlement of the minority problem in Egypt was based on the trust and goodwill of Muslims and Christians and not on reservations and safeguards

[309] Shaukat Ali joined Gandhi on 7 September.

[310] Charles E. Newham, then Editor-in-Chief, *The Pioneer*

[311] Nehru had wired to Abdul Ghaffar Khan: '*Pioneer* and *Civil Military Gazette* carrying on propaganda against Khudai Khidmatgars suggesting conflict with Congress giving misleading statements in alleged interview with you at Simla. I suggest your issuing press statement.'

[312] At Ahmedabad. See also Letter no. 136 (p. 147).

[313] George Slocombe, correspondent of *The Daily Herald* in India in 1930. For Nehru's letter dated 31 August 1931, see *SWJN*, Vol. 5, pp. 322–3.

district and helps to divert attention. Ejectments continue, and our good workers are caught here and there in the coils of Sec. 108 Cr. P. Code. But all this is being done more quietly and without any fuss. The Chief Secretary—Jagdish Prasad—writes to me long letters, courteous and detailed, dealing with the complaints I make. I present the tenant's side, he puts forward the other side and it is a little difficult to say without full enquiry where the truth lies. Probably there are exaggerations on both sides. But the solid fact remains that thousands of tenants, and specially occupancy tenants, have been dispossessed and are in great trouble. I see no obvious way to tackle this problem. I shall continue writing of course to Jagdish Prasad.

The report of the Agrarian Committee appointed by the UP Government does not appear to be at all satisfactory.[314] We do not know all the details yet but I am afraid it has produced a complicated scheme and the quantum of reduction is not enough. Much will be left to the petty revenue officials and this will mean trouble.

Meanwhile the rains are holding back and there is likelihood of a bad harvest.

You asked me to send duplicate copies of all airmail letters by the ordinary mail. This is going to be a little difficult. I cannot easily get duplicates of all the cuttings and enclosures. It is not even easy to get a copy of this letter unless Krishna gets busy with her typewriter. The AICC office here has been depleted and a little illness makes it difficult to carry on. However it does not matter very much if my letter goes astray.

With love and all good wishes,

Yours affectionately,
Jawaharlal

SWJN, *Vol. 5, I Series, pp. 28–30*

[314] Nehru writes in his *Autobiography*, 'The Government Agrarian Committee issued its report and made certain recommendations, which were both complicated and vague, and left a great deal to local officers. On the whole, the proposed remissions were bigger than in the past season, but we felt that they were not enough.... Also the report dealt with the future only and ignored past arrears, debt, and the question of the large number of dispossessed tenants.'

## 134. Letter to Jawaharlal Nehru

7 September 1931

My dear Jawaharlal,

We have just left Port Said. The Big Brother[315] joined us here. Today is my day of silence. We meet tomorrow for a talk. Here are interesting cuttings from the *Daily Mail* and *Daily Telegraph*[316] some friends from shore brought us. They are meant for your amusement and recreation. You may pass them on to Vallabhbhai after you have done with them.

Devdas has given me your further letters to Indira. I have not yet had the time to look at them. My time has been fully taken up with preparing for *Young India* and *Navajivan*, writing letters and keeping some appointments with sleep thrown in.

I hope the situation in UP has improved. I am anxious for news from you. I know you will not hesitate to use the cable when necessary.

Are you keeping touch with A. Ghaffar Khan?

How is Jayaprakash doing?

You will know from *YI* all about affectionate messages from Egypt.

Malaviyaji has been keeping very good health. The sea did not trouble him except for one day. Mirabehn[317] had the largest share of seasickness. Pyarelal and Devdas had a fair share. Mahadev has been quite free. And he has worked the most.

Yours,
Bapu

Encl. 3 cuttings

CWMG, *Vol. XLVII, pp. 401–2*

[315] Shaukat Ali

[316] Of 24 September 1931

[317] Madeleine Slade (1892–1982); daughter of a British Admiral, she arrived in India in 1925 to join Gandhi at Sabarmati Ashram. In his letter to Romain Rolland who had recommended her, Gandhi had written: 'What a treasure you have sent me! ...I shall leave no stone unturned to assist her to become a bridge between East and West. She shall be a fellow-seeker with me ... and I propose to share the honour of fatherhood with you.' Gandhi gave her the name Mira.

## 135. Letter to M.K. Gandhi

Ahmedabad
11 September 1931

My dear Bapu,
The Working Committee has been sitting for three days. It has not finished its work yet. Probably it will end today. As desired by you we considered what our minimum demands should be and a note to this effect has been drafted.[318] This is not technically a resolution but it is as good as a resolution. We are of course treating this as confidential. Vallabhbhai will send you a copy of the note. I am also enclosing it.

The note covers most of the points mentioned by you except on the type of federation desired and the division of subjects. We may consider this before we part.

According to your suggestion I wrote to Ramanand Babu[319] about the army matter. He has not replied yet but his assistant editor has done so and as this reply is interesting, I am sending it to you with this letter.[320]

In discussing the note we were to send you, Ansari was very keen on adding some kind of an assurance to the princes. Most of us were not agreeable to this. He tells me that he is writing to you on this subject.

[318] For the note, see *SWJN*, Vol. 5, I Series, pp. 33–7.

[319] Ramananda Chatterjee, Editor, *The Modern Review*, Calcutta, whom Gandhi described as 'one of the foremost among journalists'

[320] The letter read: 'The authoritative military opinion ... seems to be that it requires more time to train soldiers in India than, say in England, and that, on this account, it is not possible to raise a large army in this country within a short time.... In times of real danger and stress it requires almost as much intelligence and initiative in a private as well as a Commissioned Officer ... This initiative and intelligence, the Indian sepoy is unable to supply on account of his defective education and lopsided character development. ... This phenomenon ... has been exploited to the full by the British as an argument for the retention of the British personnel. And what is still more important, it will always remain as an obstacle to the complete Indianisation of the Indian Army unless that fundamentally vicious thing—the recruitment policy of the British Government of India is absolutely done away with.'

Bengal is troubling us a great deal.[321] Sen Gupta is acting aggressively and putting us in a very false position. The Frontier appears to be a little worse. UP is bad and indeed worse also. In Muttra district there have been over 2,000 ejectments in August. Some of our special workers have been arrested (not in Muttra).

I enclose a copy of an article on the Defence of India[322] I have given to Kumarappa[323] for *Young India*.

We propose to publish our rejoinder to the Government soon.[324]

This letter goes by ordinary post, which goes today. In a day or two I shall write by airmail.

Jinnah, just before he left, gave an interview on the communal question, which can hardly be beaten by Shaukat Ali.[325] It was an amazing farrago of nonsense and narrow-minded communalism.

Yours affectionately,
Jawaharlal

SWJN, *Vol. 5, I Series, pp. 31–2*

[321] The reference is to the rivalry between Sen Gupta and Subhas Chandra Bose.

[322] 'The Defence of India', written by Nehru and published in *YI* in two instalments—on 24 September and 1 October 1931. See also *SWJN*, Vol. 5, I Series, pp. 555–60.

[323] J.C. Kumarappa (1892–1959); Gandhian economist in charge of *Young India*, 1930–1; author of *Gandhian Economic Thought*

[324] The Government published the replies of provincial governments to the charges levelled against them in the Congress charge-sheet. Gandhi urged an impartial investigation into the charges, but the provincial governments were not open to an enquiry. A rejoinder, therefore, from each concerned province was under preparation. In his letter of 28 August 1931, Gandhi wrote to C. Rajagopalachari, 'I would like you to prepare a rejoinder to the Madras Government's reply to the Madras charge-sheet and bring the latter to date and send your rejoinder to the Sardar.'

[325] On 5 September 1931, Jinnah had said, 'The new constitution should provide for reasonable guarantees to Muslims and if they are not provided the new constitution is sure to break down.'

## 136. Letter to M.K. Gandhi

Ahmedabad
12 September 1931

My dear Bapu,
Yesterday I sent you a letter by the ordinary post, registered. I am sending a copy of this and a copy of the Working Committee's note by airmail. There are some minor corrections in the note which I enclose today which yesterday's copy did not contain.

The Working Committee finished its sessions yesterday. I am staying over for a day or two to clear up some work. The next meeting of the Committee has been fixed for October 24th—either in Delhi or Allahabad. Probably by that time we shall know tolerably well how you have been fashioning in London!

In the copy of the letter I am enclosing I have made a wrong statement which I must correct. I have stated that there have been over 2,000 ejectments in Muttra district in August. What I should have stated is that over 2,000 processes have been issued. The actual ejectments have not taken place yet.

Love.

Yours affectionately,
Jawaharlal

[PS]
The Working Committee's note is being treated by us as a confidential document. But you are at full liberty to use it in any way you like, even to publish it if you so choose.

SWJN, *Vol. 5, I Series, pp. 32–3*

## 137. Letter to M.K. Gandhi

Allahabad
17 September 1931

My dear Bapu,
I have had a letter from Mahadeva from Aden and he has told us something of the happenings on board. But we do not suffer from lack of news of you. We have the minutest details about your meals

and prayers, and the hour you get up, and your walks and above all your famous loin-cloth.[326]

I returned yesterday from Ahmedabad after a fairly prolonged stay there. The Working Committee seems to swallow up more and more time. We meet again on October 24th perhaps at Delhi.

I do not wish to trouble you about our difficulties here. I only want to inform you that at my request Vallabhbhai has written to Emerson about the distressing state of affairs in the UP. I am myself thinking of writing briefly to the Viceroy's Secretary

Next week I shall send you the report of our Agrarian Enquiry Committee.[327]

[326] Gandhi had taken to wearing only the loin-cloth from September 1921 during his tour of South India where he encountered extreme poverty. For his article 'My Loin-cloth', see *CWMG*, Vol. XLVI, pp. 54–6 and also Vol. XXI, pp. 225–7.

On 11 September 1931, in reply to newspaper representatives who questioned him on his attire, Gandhi had quipped: 'In your country you put on plus-fours. I prefer minus-fours.'

In a letter to Churchill years later, on 17 July 1944, Gandhi wrote: 'You are reported to have a desire to crush the simple "Naked Fakir" as you are said to have described me. I have been trying to be a "Fakir" and that naked—a more difficult task. I, therefore, regard the expression as a compliment though unintended. I approach you then as such and ask you to trust and use me for the sake of your people and mine and through them those of the world.'

[327] Nehru writes in his *Autobiography*, 'It was a terrible summer for all of us.... The Indian peasant has an amazing capacity to bear misfortune, and he has always had more than his share of it—famine, flood, disease, and continuous grinding poverty. ... But somehow the events of 1931 did not seem to him part of Nature's inscrutable plans... they were the work of man, he thought, and so he resented them. ...

The UP Congress committee had also appointed a small committee to collect various agrarian data, past and present, to report on the existing situation. This committee submitted a long report containing an able survey of agrarian conditions in the UP and an analysis of the havoc caused by the agricultural slump in prices.... The report which was published in book form was signed by Govind Pant, Rafi Ahmad Kidwai, and Venkatesh Narayan Tiwary.'

I am enclosing a copy of a letter I have sent to the Maharaja[328] of Patiala.

The Working Committee did not consider after all the question of federation and division of functions. But the Committee's views on this subject are clear enough. They believe in a strong central government. The list of central subjects given in the Nehru Report may be treated as a good basis for discussion. I find from the report of Shafaat Ahmad Khan's[329] speech in the Federal Structure Committee that he claims sovereignty for the provinces. This is an interesting development. Shafaat Ahmad is more than half mad and cannot be taken seriously but it is likely that some of the other stalwart Muslims may support him. I think there should be some plain-speaking on this subject.

You must have heard about Chittagong.[330] It was pretty bad but the reports you must have received were no doubt exaggerated. Sen Gupta has been openly stating that the whole affair was got up by the official and non-official Europeans. Others have said this also and there appears to be truth in the charge.

There was a lovely cartoon in *Punch* the other day about the 'Elusive Mahatma'—I wonder if you saw it. I was so taken by it that I forthwith subscribed to *Punch* as well as other English papers to read what they say about you.

[328] Bhupinder Singh (1891–1938); Chancellor, Chamber of Princes, 1926–30. In June 1931, the Maharaja had rejected the federation scheme he had supported at the Round Table Conference and proposed a 'union of the Indian States alone in direct relationship with the Crown'.

For Nehru's letter dated 16 September 1931 to the Maharaja, see *SWJN*, Vol. 5, I Series, pp. 37–41.

[329] (1893–1947); Professor of History, Allahabad University; High Commissioner of India and South Africa, 1941–4; Member, Interim Cabinet, September-October 1946

In his speech at the Federal Structure Subcommittee on 14 September 1931 he had advocated full autonomy for the provinces and transfer of some special central subjects to them.

[330] There was a complete breakdown of law and order in Chittagong (Bengal, now in Bangladesh) for three days in the first week of September 1931. The damage caused by hooliganism was estimated at Rs 1 crore.

I hope you met Roger Baldwin.[331] In a letter from him which I have just received there is a passage which might interest you. '... the new British "Dictatorship" is the creature of the American bankers. You have two enemies to fight from now on—the hidden enemy of Wall Street, backed by the American Government, and Britain. Wall Street will use all its power to save India for Britain as the chief source of revenue in trade for an economically degenerating empire.'

Yours affectionately,
Jawaharlal

SWJN, *Vol. 5, I Series, pp. 42–3*

## 138. Letter to M.K. Gandhi

Swaraj Bhawan, Allahabad
19 September 1931

My dear Bapu,
In my desire to send you duplicate of the letters I send by airmail I am getting into quite a muddle and I am afraid I must have puzzled you also. Sometimes the copy must have reached you before the original. The enclosures with the original could not all be repeated with the copy. However, I shall carry on in this haphazard way in the hope that something reaches you.

I enclose a draft trust deed for Swaraj Bhawan.[332] I shall be glad if you could let me have your approval of it. In particular I should like your opinion on the point raised by Jamnalalji and referred to in my note.

An article on Muttra District sent to Kumarappa for *YI* is also enclosed for your information.[333] Our district officers, whose salaries and future emoluments you will no doubt be asked to guarantee for ever and ever, are carrying on merrily. Only two hours ago I had

[331] See pp. 138–9.

[332] In 1930 Motilal Nehru had donated Anand Bhawan, his family residence, to the Congress. It was thereafter named Swaraj Bhawan, 'Abode of Freedom'. Motilal Nehru's decision to give rather than to sell 'was prompted by his resolve to throw his all into the battle which Gandhi had begun'. For the Swaraj Bhawan Trust Deed, see Appendix I in this volume.

[333] See p. 146, *fn.* 322.

a visit from a group of kisans from Allahabad. They bore signs of injury on their bodies and even their womenfolk had bruises and blood and broken teeth. Those who were more seriously injured could not come to us. All this was merely the result of gentle persuasion to pay the balance of the rent due. And as I thought of these gentle methods my mind went back to a well-remembered clause: 'such picketing shall be unaggressive and it shall not involve coercion, intimidation, restraint, hostile demonstration, obstruction to the public', etc., etc.[334]

It is a strange world we live in and daily we add to our experiences. In London city there is peace and harmony—and the future of India is being discussed and fashioned out. Here, the future seems so distant. The present absorbs our attention. Enough for the day is the evil thereof, and it is a little difficult to feel vastly interested in the constitutional problems that are being discussed at the RTC—direct or indirect election, second chambers, etc. I wonder when you will come to grips with the real question.

I am sending you separately by airmail one Agrarian Report. There are a number of misprints in it. I have not myself read the whole of it yet as it is just out of the press.

I went to see Chintamani[335] yesterday. He is pretty bad and he is hardly likely to be well enough to go to the RTC. He is very much cut up at not going as he apparently set his heart on taking up a strong line in opposition to Sapru!

Love.

Yours affectionately,
Jawaharlal

G-N Correspondence, JN Papers, *NMML*

[334] For the picketing rules laid down by Gandhi, see *CWMG,* Vol. XLV, pp. 291–2 and also Vol. XLVI, p. 185.

[335] C.Y. Chintamani (1880–1941); Editor, journalist and liberal politician; was called the 'pope of Indian journalism'; became Editor, *Vizag Spectator*, at the age of 18; Editor, *The Leader,* 1909 and 1934; was invited to attend the First Round Table Conference in 1930–1.

## 139. Letter to M.K. Gandhi

Delhi
24 September 1931

My dear Bapu,

I am on my way to the Punjab to attend the Punjab Provincial Conference at Jhang.[336]

Shocking incidents have happened at Hijli in the detenus' camp in Bengal.[337] You may have received cables about them if the censor has not stopped them. I enclose some newspaper cuttings. Bengal is in a bad way and the non-official and official Europeans seem to be making a dead set against Congress activities on the one hand and the detenus and their colleagues on the other. I feel we have been neglecting Bengal and we cannot afford to do so. Subhas[338] has resigned from the BPCC—and so have many others. But Sen Gupta's group is not acting very graciously.

I did not send you the UP Agrarian Report by airmail after all but sent it by ordinary post. The charge for the air was [annas] 12/- and this seemed to me to be monstrous. I felt you would not approve of this extravagance.

Love.

Yours affectionately,
Jawaharlal

[336] Nehru addressed the Conference on 26 September 1931.

[337] On 16 September the detenus at Hijli had been fired upon as they were alleged to have attacked the sentries. Two persons were killed and twenty injured. An official inquiry later said that the firing was unjustifiable. See also Letter no. 141 (p. 156).

[338] Subhas Chandra Bose (1897–1945); educated in Cuttack, Calcutta and Cambridge; qualified for the ICS but resigned in 1921; detained or exiled for long terms; President, INC, 1938 and 1939. On 18 September 1931, Bose resigned as President of the Bengal PCC on Gandhi's suggestion that his resignation would help settle the dispute between him and Sen Gupta; organized the Indian National Army in South-east Asia; died in an aircrash in August 1945

[PS]
You seem to be shifting your headquarters in London but I am continuing sending my letters to Bow.[339]

The newspaper cuttings are sent separately.

SWJN, *Vol. 5, I Series, pp. 327–8*

## 140. Letter to M.K. Gandhi

Jhang, Punjab
27 September 1931

My dear Bapu,
I grow impatient, you will think. You have hardly been in England a fortnight and I complain of you not having got the British Government and others to agree to discuss vital matters of principle. I am sure you are right and I am wrong. But when I read of the same old crowd repeating the same old pet phrases about the communal problem and you putting up with this inanity, I marvel at your patience. How wonderful you are to argue and argue and yet again argue with this motley crowd.[340] I wonder if any purgatory would be more dreadful for me than to carry on in this way. If I had to listen to my dear friend Mohamad Ali Jinnah talking the most unmitigated nonsense about his 14 points[341] for any length

[339] At Bow, London, on 3 November Gandhi addressed the annual meeting of the Children's House, run under the auspices of the Kingsley Hall Settlement.

[340] Gandhi had described the disagreement among Indian representatives on the communal question, thus: 'The attainment of unity has been rendered a task of Herculean difficulty by the composition of the Conference itself, as all the Delegates here are nominated, none of them is duly elected. ... What is offered is simply a share in the power of the bureaucracy to exploit India and this sets up an apple of discord in our mind-set. Further, the Government having made constitution-making dependent upon the solution of the communal question, every party is tempted to pitch its demand as high as possible. If the Government at all mean business, it would unhesitatingly accept my suggestion, viz., to appoint a judicial tribunal to decide the communal question at issue.'

[341] Where he had formulated his demands, of which the important ones were: a federal constitution with residuary powers vested in the provinces, separate electorates with a third of the seats in the Central Legislature reserved for Muslims, reforms in the NWFP and Baluchistan, creation of Sind as a

of time, I would have to consider the desirability of retiring to the South Sea Islands, where there would be some hope of meeting with some people who were intelligent enough or ignorant enough not to talk of the 14 points.

It is a month today since the fateful decision was taken at Simla and you rushed across India to sail for foreign lands. Four weeks you have been away and it seems so long.

Lahore
28.9.31

I am continuing this letter in a hurry during a brief stay in Lahore. I enclose a copy of a letter I have sent to Emerson.[342]

The Punjab papers were full some time ago of your having accepted Jinnah's 14 points. The Sikh League got alarmed and hurriedly summoned an All Party Sikh Conference. This conference has rejected the Working Committee's scheme and reiterated their 17 demands.[343]

There is a great deal of repression going on here and large numbers of young men are being proceeded against. Some are being

---

separate province and no bill or resolution to be passed in an elected body, if three-fourths of the representatives of any community opposed it. See also Letter no. 135 (p. 145).

[342] Nehru had written on 27 September 1931, protesting about the notice issued by the Deputy Commissioner of Shahpur district, withdrawing the salt concession from the whole area covered by the salt range. It was purported to have been withdrawn because of allegations that the people had abused the salt concession by removing surplus salt for sale in markets miles away from the salt range.

[343] The Working Committee had prepared a scheme on the communal question for adoption by the whole country. For details of the Congress scheme and Gandhi's views, see *CWMG*, Vol. XLVII, pp. 139–41.

The scheme envisaged, among other things, 'That for the Hindus in Sind, the Muslims in Assam and the Sikhs in the Punjab and NWFP, and for Hindu and Muslims in any Province where they are less than 25 per cent of the population, seats shall be reserved in the Federal and Provincial Legislatures on the basis of population with the right to contest additional seats.'

The Sikh League had, however, reiterated the rights of the Sikh community, opposed communal representation and reservation of seats, but demanded, if communal representation was adhered to, one-third of membership in the Punjab Cabinet and Legislature, 5 per cent representation in the Centre and at least one Sikh member in the Central Cabinet.

charged under Sec. 302 (the murder section) for a speech, which is extraordinary. These speeches are reported usually by police constables who know nothing about shorthand. It is easy to distort them or to introduce a particular phrase or two. There has been of course a general tendency here to use strong language. I have been going for it since I came to the Punjab and Naujawans[344] have had a severe drubbing.

This is written in a hurry as I want to catch the airmail and I am leaving Lahore soon.

Yours affectionately,
Jawaharlal

SWJN, *Vol. 5, I Series, pp. 46–7*

## 141. Letter to M.K. Gandhi

Allahabad
1 October 1931

My dear Bapu,

I returned today from the Punjab, visiting three UP districts on the way. On my arrival here I found your letter from the high seas awaiting me. The English newspaper cuttings were interesting reading. I am sending them on, as desired by you, to Vallabhbhai.

There is no marked change to report about the UP. I get occasional letters from Jagdish Prasad, the UP Chief Secretary and they are always courteous and promise enquiry into complaints made. Sometimes minor relief also comes. For instance you will remember my drawing your attention to the joint magistrate of Meerut joining an anti-picketing association. He has been asked to resign from it. The major question—the ejectments from land—continues unsolved. I am told by government officials that a fair number of the ejected tenants have been allowed to retain possession by private arrangements with their landlords but I have not been able to verify this. I have no further news of Muttra. In another three days I shall go out on a little tour of Bara Banki, Gonda, Bahraich and Rae Bareli and find out locally what is happening. Meanwhile, I have an impression that the local government is trying to restrain

[344] Members of the Naujawan Bharat Sabha

its district officials, but not wholly with success. The rains have naturally interfered with activity—both on the tenants' side and the zamindars'. Considerable damage has been caused to the crops by heavy rains, during the last ten days. The chief trouble with the ejected tenantry is their fear of losing their crops. This fear induces them to sell and borrow and do anything almost to save their crops for themselves.

I enclose some newspaper cuttings. Two deal with Hijli.[345] You will be able to judge from Tagore's speech how deeply Bengal has felt in the matter.[346] It has really been a terrible affair. There is a feeling in Bengal that the Congress executive has callously ignored their sufferings in both Chittagong and Hijli. Vallabhbhai has, I understand, written to Emerson asking for an impartial enquiry into the Hijli affair.

The other cuttings contain Aney's award in the Bengal Congress dispute.[347] A compromise has been arrived at, which seems to be fair and reasonable. There is, however, an unfortunate tendency on the part of the *Advance*[348] party to crow over it.

I have tried my best to keep in touch with Abdul Ghaffar Khan. Kailas, Kamala's brother, was sent to him two weeks ago. I have had no news of him or his work. I do not know if letters are not written or are stopped on the way. Khurshed[349] is of course there. I have been writing frequently to Abdul Ghaffar Khan and his brother Dr Khan Sahib but have only received one or two brief acknowledgements. I do not know what the present situation is so far as the Government is concerned. But the friction between the old Jirga people and the Peshawar Congressmen continues. I had a long talk with one of the latter in Lahore and he was full

[345] See p. 152.

[346] On 26 September 1931, Rabindranath Tagore at a protest meeting in Calcutta had described the Hijli incident as 'tragic and cowardly in its brutality'.

[347] The terms of the Aney Award stipulated that all complaints in the Bengal Congress elections dispute be dropped and fresh elections to the Bengal PCC be held in January 1932. Till then a joint committee consisting of an equal number from the rival factions was to carry on the Congress work.

[348] The newspaper of J.M. Sen Gupta's group in the Bengal Congress

[349] Granddaughter of Dadabhai Naoroji

of complaints. I soothed him and made various suggestions. I feel however that some one of us must go there and personally help in removing this friction. Our resolution about the Frontier PCC and the Afghan Jirga and the Khudai Khidmatgars was a difficult enough one to give effect to.[350] It becomes doubly difficult when the people concerned have little notion of constitutions and the like, and are not fond of letter-writing. Abdul Ghaffar Khan is also having some difficulties with his own people in the Jirga. Some, like Ahmad Shah,[351] have strongly criticised the Working Committee resolution. But Abdul Ghaffar's position in the Jirga is very strong and he can certainly deliver the goods. I am trying to send Rafi Ahmad Kidwai[352] to him. I think Rafi is a good man for the job.

Jaya Prakash is here. He has had a lot of trouble in his family—deaths and illness—and has been absent a lot. He is unhappy and feels unsettled and without any foundations. I do not think he is enamoured of his work with Birla.[353]

Kamala accompanied me to the Punjab but was unwell most of the time. She seems to require complete rest for a period. She has grown very weak and it is only her enthusiasm and will that carry her on.

We read daily of your fresh triumphs and conquests in the land of our rulers. Whatever happens, it seems to be quite clear that your visit has been all to the good and will bear rich fruit. Tomorrow is your birthday and we shall gather together in town and village

[350] The Working Committee had decided that the Frontier PCC and the Afghan Jirga, which had not been part of the Congress organization should merge to form a new organization on the basis of the constitution. The Khudai Khidmatgar (founded in 1929 by Abdul Ghaffar Khan to promote nonviolence among the Pathans and improve their conditions by peaceful work), was the volunteer wing of the Afghan Jirga. This became the volunteer unit of the Frontier Congress in 1931.

[351] A close associate of Ghaffar Khan and one of the founders of the Khudai Khidmatgar organization; left Congress in 1931 on the question of the merger of the Khudai Khidmatgar with the Congress; later joined the Khaksar movement

[352] (1894–1954); Congressman of UP and a close associate of Nehru; Minister, UP, 1937–9 and 1946–7; Central Minister, intermittently, from 1947 till his death

[353] As secretary

and think of you and send you our loving homage and good wishes. But a birthday is not needed to remind us of you. You have a strange way of filling the mind and stirring the emotions, and even a cold-blooded person like me feels a little less cold-blooded when thinking of you.

I enclose a copy of the letter I sent to Emerson. This should have gone to you with my last airmail letter but I could not lay my hands on it then.

I hope you received the draft of the Swaraj Bhawan Trust Deed which I sent you some time ago. I shall await your instructions in the matter. Ansari and Perin[354] are strongly opposed to any reference in the deed to a sale of the property. They say that this should not be permitted in any event. I have not heard from Bidhan[355] and Jamnalalji yet. But Jamnalalji's views I know already.

I have written to you fairly regularly since you left—twice a week, by airmail and ordinary post. I hope my letters have reached you. Sometimes I have felt that my letters must be becoming a nuisance to you. Do not trouble to write to me except when you have something special to say.

Vallabhbhai writes to me that he has sent you a cable but he has forgotten to send me a copy. Apparently the cable relates to the unholy marriage of the pound with the rupee and the drain of gold from India that is likely to take place.[356] I do not pretend to understand the intricacies of currency and finance but I am very much disturbed at recent happenings. I feel that the English people, or rather their financiers, are bent on making us a pauper and a bankrupt nation by the time Swaraj comes. You must have seen that the People's Bank has failed. I wonder if other Indian banks will follow.

[354] Perin Captain, granddaughter of Dadabhai Naoroji

[355] Dr Bidan Chandra Roy (1882–1962); physician and Congressman of Calcutta; Chief Minister, West Bengal, from 1948 till his death.

[356] In September 1931, Britain separated the rupee from the gold standard and linked it to the sterling. As the exchange value of the sterling was falling in terms of gold, the rupee also depreciated in the world market.

For Gandhi's comments on the 'Manipulation of the Exchange', see *CWMG*, Vol. XLVIII, pp. 287–8.

I was glad to read the messages of Madame Zaghloul Pasha[357] and Nahas Pasha.[358] I wish you could visit Egypt on your way back.

Yours affectionately,
Jawaharlal

SWJN, *Vol. 5, I Series, pp. 133–6*

## 142. Letter to M.K. Gandhi

Lucknow
4 October 1931

My dear Bapu,
I have had a long letter from Mahadeva from London giving an interesting account of happenings there. The newspapers tell us that Ansari, though absent, fills the picture.[359] He seems to be a little worried about it, quite needlessly, I have told him. He has called an emergent meeting of the Council of the Nationalist Muslims Party for day after tomorrow. I wonder if you have sent him a cable. The more I read about the innumerable claims for special representation the more I feel that it is almost impossible to have anything but a purely nationalist solution. Certainly there can be no peace or solution of the problem by merely agreeing to Jinnah's ridiculous 14 points.

Since I wrote to you last I have had time to find out a little more about the agrarian situation. The tenantry have lost hope to a large extent of any real relief being given to them. Their passion for land is amazing and specially the fear of being dispossessed with the

[357] Safia Zaghloul Pasha, widow of Zaghloul Pasha, who had sent Gandhi a message on 6 September 1931

[358] Mustapha Nahas Pasha (1876–1965); Egyptian nationalist leader who became head of the Wafd in 1927; served a number of times as Prime Minister between 1928 and 1951

[359] Gandhi's efforts to have Dr Ansari included among the delegates to the Round table Conference were in vain. He said in his statement to the Press in London on 14 October 1931: 'I have felt the absence of Dr Ansari a severe handicap, but he will be of no real use unless the Muslim Delegation desires or approves of his selection as a delegate.'

crops ripening has made many of them do almost anything to stock on. A large number of the dispossessed tenants in Allahabad, probably 25% or more, have raised money somehow, by sale of property, etc., and paid up the dues fully and thus got back the land. This is bad enough as they will soon find out. What is worse is the effect this is going to have on future remissions. There is a clause in the report of the official Rent Committee that these proposals will not apply to cases where the zamindar and the tenant have mutually agreed to a fresh arrangement. Altogether the position is most unsatisfactory. Stray reports of beatings of kisans continue to come. Collections also continue.

The Working Committee meets probably at Delhi in the last week of this month.

Love.

Yours affectionately,
Jawahar

SWJN, *Vol. 5, I Series, p. 137*

## 143. Cable to M.K. Gandhi

16 October 1931

Agrarian situation becoming critical. Coercive processes attachments forcible collection rent continued right through without interval. Many ejected tenants proceeded against for criminal trespass. Many for fear permanently losing land sold cattle belongings borrowed money. Paid full demand plus extras. Fresh demand now made for current season. Inadequate remissions.Threat that if full payment not made within month remission might be cancelled. Also no objection considered on behalf tenants till full payment made. Condition kisans deplorable. Thoroughly exhausted after past six months continuous harassment forcible measures. Apparently process likely to be repeated this season also. Allahabad District Congress Committee resolved under circumstances ask permission start satyagraha if necessity arises by advising withholding payment rent. Application for permission made to Vallabhbhai and provincial committee. Representative district kisan conference being held next week to decide question. Decision likely have far-reaching consequences but question payment or withholding payment must be decided soon.[360] Vital urgent problem for kisans admitting no delay.

SWJN, *Vol. 5, I Series, p. 155*

## 144. Letter to M.K. Gandhi

Allahabad
16 October 1931

My dear Bapu,

I have sent you a cable today which I am afraid will add to your worries. This cable relates to a decision of the Allahabad District Congress Committee asking for permission to advise tenants to withhold payment of rent for the current year. I am enclosing copy of this cable as well as copies of letters I have addressed to Private Secretary to the Viceroy and Kunwar Jagdish Prasad.[361] You need not trouble to read through these letters specially one of them which

[360] Nehru observes in his *Autobiography*, 'I welcomed therefore, the presence of Sherwani and others from our province at our committee meeting, for Sherwani (our Provincial President) was by no means a fire-brand. ... Every subsequent step taken by the Provincial Committee was in the closest cooperation with him, and indeed, often through him, as President Tassaduq Sherwani's pleading before the Working Committee, therefore, produced great effect on the members—a much greater effect than mine would have done. With great hesitation, but feeling that they could not refuse it, they gave the UP Committee authority to permit in any area the week's suspension of payment of rent and revenue. ... The Allahabad Committee held a big Peasant Conference, which passed a tentative resolution saying that in case better terms were not obtained, they would have to advise the peasants to withhold payment of rent and revenue.'

[361] Both letters were dated 15 October 1931. In the first letter giving facts and figures, Nehru demanded to know how poor tenants, who had been given remission because they could not pay the full demand, were expected to pay arrears. He had also written to say the revenue staff seemed to look upon the tenant as the enemy of society to be harassed in every way and made to pay up by any means. The second letter brought to their notice 'various activities of Government officials, the police and zamindars' agents.' He further pointed out that the position of the kisans had deteriorated and they continued to get reports from a large number of districts showing that the tenantry were harassed, and more importantly that the rent policy of the Government and its application was causing misery to vast numbers of people.

is full of figures. I thought, however, they should be with you for facility of reference. I have taken all these steps on my own account more or less privately. But the final communication will be sent by the presidents of our provincial and Allahabad District Congress Committee. It is really deplorable to what a pass we have reduced the tenants largely because of the advice we gave. They followed that advice for a while and talked of paying 8 annas and 12 annas and taking full receipts but it had little effect on anybody and they were proceeded against and finally ejected.[362] Meanwhile of course there were all manner of acts of oppression. Even after their ejectments they hoped that the Congress would do something for them to save them their lands. Nothing happened except numerous cases of criminal trespass. Not only were they ejected from their lands but they were sent to prison and fined for trespass. Ultimately they despaired of getting any help from the Congress and had nowhere to look to for relief. Even then they did not blame us or lose faith in our bona fides. But they certainly felt that we were not in a position to do anything for them. At last, full of despair, urged on by the one desire to save their lands at any cost, they sold up their cattle and borrowed money wherever they could and at whatever rates they could without thinking of the consequences. Only one thought obsessed them—the idea of saving their lands. So they paid not only the full sum due for the current year but often some arrears and heavy costs. They thus had to pay very much more in the end to get back their land than if they had paid the full rent without any remission to begin with. And they got back something much less than they previously had. Their occupancy rights had gone and they became life tenants.

Now they are threatened with the new season's demand and the same processes are likely to be repeated. It is a difficult problem for them and for us. After very careful consideration our district committees felt there was no way out except to advise that the rents be withheld. This advice must be given within the next two or three weeks if it is to be in time and effective. Hence the urgency of the matter. Our district and our province will of course take no steps without the permission of the Working Committee. The Working

[362] See also pp. 135–6.

Committee meets at Delhi on the 27th of this month. Our provincial committee meets immediately after.

It is clear that any step that the Allahabad district might take would have its effect on adjoining districts which are equally badly hit. The matter may become provincial. You can appreciate the other far-reaching consequences.

I do not know how this will affect your work in London. So far as I can see the Round Table Conference is as dead as a doornail and it does not matter much what effect is produced on it.

I am sending this letter some days ahead of the airmail date. I shall try to follow it up with another letter, if necessary, giving further particulars.

Yours affectionately,
Jawaharlal

SWJN, *Vol. 5, I Series, p. 156*

## 145. Cable to Jawaharlal Nehru

18 October 1931

Jawaharlal Nehru
Allahabad
Your cable. You should unhesitatingly take necessary steps meet every situation. Expect nothing here.

Bapu

CWMG, *Vol. XLVIII, p. 173*

## 146. Letter to M.K. Gandhi

Bombay
21 December 1931

My dear Bapu,
It is only a few days now when you will land on the shores of India and be welcomed back after an absence which has seemed so long to many of us and yet perhaps I may not be there to join the happy throng to see you again and gain fresh strength and inspiration from you. Many friends have tried to induce me to stay on in Bombay till you come in the secret hope that thus I might

avoid arrest.[363] But all my instincts are against this. Our provincial conference meets in Etawah this week and not to be with my old colleagues in the hour of crisis seems to me perilously near treason. I have no desire to precipitate my arrest. I want to meet you again. But I cannot keep away from Etawah. I hope to come back. In case I do not, I write this letter.

I am not writing anything about conditions in the UP. You will get to know all about them from many sources and what I write now may be out of date when you land. I shall only say this that I am quite satisfied in my own mind and heart that we have done the right thing. I hope the larger movement, which appears to be inevitable, will also be based on the well-being of the peasantry.

Kamala is unwell. I am leaving her behind. She has been told to remain in bed for some time as she has been running a temperature.

There is one matter about which I am troubled and want your advice. If I am not available kindly send word to Kamala. It is about the income tax which was assessed on father. You will remember that I sent a note to the Income Tax Officer in June or thereabouts pointing out how in the opinion of my lawyer there was no liability on me to pay. I added however that I was not prepared to contest the matter in a law court or to raise any difficulties. I left the decision to the law officers of the Government of India and said that I would abide by it. No answer came to me for two months or more. I sent a reminder and I was told that this matter had been referred to higher authorities. Again no answer for three months. Ultimately, on December 2, I received a letter from the Income Tax officer informing me that the Government of India had decided against me and demanding full payment by December 15. In my reply I accepted the decision but stated that I could not possibly pay 31,000/- so soon. I offered to pay Rs 10,000/- by the end of December or early January and the balance as soon as I could sell some railway and other shares. I suggested also that I could transfer these shares at the market rate to the Government. The Income Tax officer came to see me and more or less agreed to the payments suggested by me but said that it might be difficult for Government to take the

[363] See p. 165, *fn*. 365.

shares. He promised however to refer the matter to Government soon after I paid Rs 10,000/-. I can now pay another 5,000/- and probably I shall be able to make enough money from some jute debentures early in January to pay the balance.

My difficulty arises in this way. On the one hand I have promised to pay up. On the other we have advised the tenants and landlords not to pay rent or revenue. Any payment by me is sure to be trumpeted by Government as a payment to escape a penalty which I had brought on the tenants. It may be that very soon our motorcar may be attached and Anand Bhawan itself might be taken possession of. Under these circumstances what am I do?

This letter is written in some hurry, as I have to catch a train. Jamnalalji writes me to say that I am going to Allahabad against his wishes.

Yours affectionately,
Jawahar

MKG Papers, Pyarelal Collection, *NMML*

## 147. Letter to Jawaharlal Nehru

28 December 1931[364]

My dear Jawahar,
Indu gave me your letter. Somehow or other your arrest did not come upon me as a surprise.[365] I have not yet been able to go to

[364] Gandhi landed in Bombay on this day.

[365] Nehru and Sherwani had been served with orders under the new Ordinance for the United Provinces not to leave Allahabad city. The Ordinance was said to have been directed against the activities of the rural areas of Allahabad and the suspension of rent in some other UP districts. They were arrested on the morning of 26 December, when they were to leave for Bombay to receive Gandhi.

On the arrest of Nehru and Sherwani in UP and Khan Abdul Ghaffar Khan in the NWFP, Gandhi said at a public meeting in Bombay on 28 December 1931: 'There can be no justification for the Ordinances promulgated in the UP or the north. We cannot tolerate any of them.' He asked, 'The question now before us is: what is our duty? Shall we take the hint from the action of the Government and launch a campaign of satyagraha or shall we try some other means? ... if there is any possibility of avoiding satyagraha, I shall do my utmost to prevent it and advise you to have patience. I think after years of experience India has learnt to hold herself in patience.'

Kamala. I may tonight or tomorrow for certain. You will be glad to know that I have read your second series of letters[366] to Indu. I had some suggestions to make, but of that, when perhaps we have come to our own.

Meanwhile love to you and Sherwani.

CWMG, *Vol. XLVIII, p. 443*

## 148. Letter to M.K. Gandhi

Naini Prison
30 December 1931

My dear Bapu,
Your letter came this evening and, need I say, both Sherwani and I were delighted to receive it. We have returned to our old haunts, happy in the thought that you are back home. Sherwani's friendship with Naini is even older than mine. It dates back to 1921. We are going back gradually to our old routine, as if there had been no interruption. There is just one twinge of regret that we missed seeing you. We were looking forward to it so much. But we shall have plenty of meetings yet.

Kamala's illness worries me a little, but I am very much comforted by her being at 78 Nepean Sea Road.[367] She could not have more loving care and attention anywhere else. I am only afraid that she might decide to dash about in quest of adventure before she is fit enough to do so.

My letters to Indu can rest in a convenient drawer or pigeonhole for a few months or years as the case may be. I am sorry you gave much time to them.

We are delighted to learn that the return voyage has done you good and you are in fit condition. You will need to be!

We are told that our trial will take place on Jan. 4th.[368]

With love and all good wishes from Sherwani and myself,

Yours affectionately,
Jawaharlal

SWJN, *Vol. 5, I Series, pp. 345–6*

[366] Published as *Glimpses of World History* in 1934

[367] The residence of Jal Naoroji in Bombay

[368] For the Court proceedings and Nehru's statement at the trial, see *SWJN*, Vol. 5, 1 Series, pp. 347–8.

## 149. Letter to Jawaharlal Nehru

2 January 1932

My dear Jawahar,

I was delighted to receive your letter. You have no cause to envy us poor folk outside. But we do envy you for getting all the glory and leaving the drudgery to the outsiders. But we are plotting vengeance. I hope you are allowed to get some newspapers. In all I am doing you are constantly before my mind's eye.

I saw Kamala the other day. She does need plenty of rest. I shall try to see her once more and insist upon her not leaving her room till she is thoroughly restored. I hope you will approve of the action taken regarding Dr Mahmud. I am sure that the promise to pay the assessment on Anand Bhawan should be paid [*sic*].

Love to you both.

Bapu

[PS]

God and Government willing, I go to the Ashram tomorrow to return in two or three days.[369]

CWMG, *Vol. XLVIII, pp. 477–8*

## 150. Telegram to Jawaharlal Nehru

24 September 1932

Pandit Jawaharlal Nehru

Jail Dehradun

During all these days of agony you have been before mind's eye.[370] I am most anxious to know your opinion. You know how I value

[369] Gandhi was in Yeravda Prison from 4 January 1932 to 8 May 1933. In *YI*, 7-1-1932, Mahadev Desai reported Gandhi's arrest, writing in 'The Historic Week', that it was, as in the past, 'under Regulation XXV of 1827 for removal of inconvenient persons without assignable reasons'. See also Verrier Elwin's *An Autobiography*, pp. 66–7. Elwin was present on the scene at the time of Gandhi's arrest.

[370] Gandhi had begun on 20 September a 'fast unto death' in disapproval of the Separate Electorates (proposed by Prime Minister Ramsay MacDonald's Communal Award) for the Depressed Classes, which he felt would still further divide the caste Hindus from their brethren.

your opinion. Saw Indu Sarup's children.[371] Indu looked happy and in possession of more flesh. Doing very well. Wire reply.

Love.

Bapu

CWMG, *Vol. LI, p. 134*

## 151. Telegram to M.K. Gandhi

25 September 1932

Gandhiji
Yeravda Jail Poona
Your telegram and brief news that some settlement reached filled me relief joy.[372] First news your decision fast caused mental agony confusion but ultimately optimism triumphed.[373] Regained peace mind. No sacrifice too great for suppressed downtrodden classes. Freedom must be judged by freedom of lowest but feel danger other issues obscuring only goal. Am unable to judge from religious viewpoint. Danger your methods being exploited by others but how can I presume to advise a magician.

Love.

Jawahar

SWJN, *Vol. 5, I Series, pp. 409–10*

[371] Vijayalakshmi Pandit's daughters Nayantara and Chandralekha

[372] A conference of the leaders of all communities was convened at Poona on 20 September to consider MacDonald's Award and the consequent fast unto death undertaken by Gandhi. Under the scheme prepared by the conference, the Harijans would not accept separate electorates but be a part of the general electorate with reserved seats. As a result of this agreement Gandhi broke his fast on 26 September 1932.

[373] Nehru writes in *Glimpses of World History*, on 15 September 1932, 'News has come, terrible news, that Bapu has determined to starve himself to death. My little world, in which he has occupied such a big place, shakes and totters, and there seems to be darkness and emptiness everywhere. ... Shall I not see him again? And whom shall I go to when I am in doubt, and require wise counsel, or am afflicted and in sorrow and need of comfort?'

## 152. Letter to Jawaharlal Nehru

31 December 1932

My dear Jawaharlal,

Sarup came to me the other day to discuss her project about untouchability.[374] She said you had advised rest in Ceylon. I regard it as unnecessary. She is quite able to do some work and she is willing to do some untouchability work. I think she should be allowed to do the work so long as she wishes to do it.

She told me you had some more teeth out while she was busy growing grey hair. But eyewitnesses tell me you were otherwise keeping quite fit. You still seem to be refusing to see visitors. I wish you would see them, if it is at all possible. It will give them satisfaction.

We are now a happy team of four, Chaganlal Joshi[375] having been added unto us.[376] I do not know whether you are interesting yourself in the Harijan work. I am having a glorious time with the Shastris.[377] My knowledge of the letter of the Shastras is better but of true religion they are able to give me but little.

Bapu

CWMG, *Vol. LI, pp. 311–12*

[374] The movement against untouchability had been gathering ground at this time. Gandhi had been campaigning, through a series of articles and discussions with Hindu scholars, for the opening of the Guruvayoor temple in Kerala to Harijans on the same terms as for the caste Hindus.

[375] An associate of Gandhi and a former manager of the Sabarmati Ashram

[376] Mahadev Desai and Vallabhbhai Patel were the other two.

[377] Learned men in the Hindu orthodoxy with whom Gandhi conferred throughout this period in order to 'derive authority for reform from the same scriptures that the Sanatanists profess to believe in'. Gandhi wrote in his 'Statement on untouchability', 'There is a growing body of Shastris, well-versed in Sanskrit who believe that it is not only permissible in Hinduism to admit "untouchables" to public temples, but that it is wrong to prohibit them from offering worship in common with other Hindus at these temples. These pundits also believe that there is no such thing as untouchability, attaching to birth and incapable of being cured by any penance or purification. They do believe that there is no such thing as untouchability attaching to acts and occupations, but this is no peculiarity to Hinduism. It is common to all religions and is based upon unhygienic principles.' See *CWMG*, Vol. LII, p. 199.

Gandhi had had a discussion on 23 December with Shastris. For the posers raised before the Shastri Parishad, ibid., p. 265.

## 153. Letter to M.K. Gandhi

5 January 1933

My dear Bapu,

Your letter is always a tonic, and when it comes after a long interval, it brings a thrill with it and its effect is all the more exhilarating. I recognised Mahadeva's handwriting on the envelope. Yours did not seem as of old. Perhaps your left hand was functioning and I am not so familiar with it.[378]

I am following of course with great interest your campaign against untouchability, as far as I can from the *Statesman* and the *Pioneer*.[379] Anything that you may do is bound to interest and fascinate. The subject itself has tremendous possibilities. Not being a man of religion, my interest is largely confined to the social aspect and to the wider issues involved.

Of course Sarup should do untouchability work if she feels like it. My suggestion about a short holiday in Ceylon was made chiefly in the interest of Krishna. I am a little worried about her. After a year in prison, with our home practically broken up, she feels rather at a loose end and does not know what to do. Ever since her childhood, the poor girl has been deprived of real home life and proper education because of our preoccupations and repeated visits to prison. She grew up a rather lonely girl not having as much friendship and sympathy as she was entitled to.

Father's death shook her up a great deal. I tried to soothe her and win her confidence and I am glad to say that I succeeded to some extent. But 1931 was for all of us a year full of work and worry and anxiety. Then came a long spell of prison for her, and for a young girl this was a far greater ordeal than it could be for most of us. As her release drew near I sensed how she must be feeling and how life in Anand Bhawan, as it is today, would be no joy to her. She would feel out of joint. She would want to do something and yet not know what to do and this would rob her of peace of mind.

[378] Gandhi had started writing with his left hand from 1 March 1932, as his right hand was in pain.

[379] Gandhi's correspondence with the Zamorin of Calicut over the opening of the Guruvayoor temple to Harijans was published on 2 January 1933.

Latterly she has begun to look upon me almost as a kind of refuge in a friendless world. If I had been out I might have been of help to her but I could do little from Dehra Dun jail.

I felt that a short holiday in natural surroundings would ease her mind and remove the tension. Hence my proposal about Ceylon. Three weeks in Ceylon would not have solved any problem but she would have freshened up and returned with a brighter outlook on life. These were my reasons. I was thinking more of mental health than of physical health. But the proposal seems to have fallen through as nobody seems to be keen on it. For the present therefore Ceylon is off.

Perhaps Krishna will go to Poona to see you and you might be able to advise her about her work. I might see her also. It is easy enough to suggest odd bits of work but this must appeal to the person concerned.

As for my interview, it is now nearly seven months since I had one.[380] I have missed them greatly but the UP Government had been very discourteous to mother and Kamala and I felt that I had no alternative; besides I have not yet got rid of my obstinacy—a hereditary failing in me of which you cannot be unaware. The Government made some partial amends and the Home Member, the Nawab of Chhatari, came and expressed his concern. All this was more or less beside the point, and the graceful thing and the right thing was not done, but then the right thing is seldom done. I wrote[381] again to Government. Still I decided in my mind that should special necessity arise I would withdraw my prohibition and consent to an interview.[382] So matters have stood for the last

[380] Nehru had had his last interview on 13 June 1932.

[381] On 11 July 1932, a letter addressed to the Superintendent, District Jail

[382] Referring to this, Nehru writes: 'Our policy in prison was to observe the jail rules unless we considered them humiliating or otherwise improper. Nevertheless, incidents occurred from time to time. On one occasion when I was in Naini Central prison, some of us undertook a full three-day (seventy-two-hour) fast as a protest. We were normally allowed interviews in prison. At one time these interviews were once in three months, then once a month and at the time of this correspondence I was permitted to have fortnightly interviews. As I was kept in Dehra Dun District Jail, my mother and wife had to undertake a long journey from Allahabad for the interview. After their arrival in Dehra Dun, they were told that they could not interview me. As a consequence of this

few weeks. I did not suggest an early interview, as there was some talk of my transfer back to Naini prison.

Now that you have also written about it, what can I do but immediately to capitulate to you? So henceforth, and unless something untoward intervenes, I shall take my usual interviews. Kamala may not be able to see me for several weeks still. She is in Calcutta under Bidhan's treatment. But I shall see mother and Indu and Sarup and Krishna or such of them as can find me.

The stopping of interviews has made me retire a little more into myself, but I have had pleasing and friendly neighbours—the Himalayas. The sight of their outline against the sky, and now their summits and sides covered with fresh snow, have meant a great deal to me. They seem to rouse in me ancient memories of the long ago when perhaps my ancestors wandered about the mountains of Kashmir and played in their snow and glaciers.[383] I have had companions here but largely I have been left to myself, and I have grown a little contemplative, in defiance of heredity and family tradition and personal habit! But that is a thin veneer which I am afraid will rub off at little provocation. How can the Ethiopian change his skin?[384]

I have read a lot, and if wisdom could be had in books I would be wise. But wisdom eludes me, and big question marks confront me wherever I look. Sometimes I think of Prince Siddhartha's old question and no answer comes:

How can it be that Brahm
Would make a world and keep it miserable
Since if all powerful, he leaves it so,
He is not good, and if not powerful,
He is not God?[385]

---

incident I gave up all interviews for several months. At the same time I was more or less in solitary confinement and had no companion'.

[383] For Nehru's ruminations on mountains and rivers, see *Jawaharlal Nehru–An Anthology*, pp. 603–4.

[384] Quotation from Isiah xiii, 23, which reads: 'Can the Ethiopian change his skin, or the leopard his spots?'

[385] From *The Light of Asia* by Edwin Arnold

From all accounts in the papers you are as ever the slave of industry and are over-working yourself even in prison. The new industrial system of the West is often criticised and blamed because it makes man a machine for ceaseless work and robs him of all leisure. You are supposed to be no lover of this system. And yet, you seem to personify to me often this very industrial system!

I am intrigued at your remark that eyewitnesses have told you that I am keeping fit. The information is correct but who could these eyewitnesses be, who have managed to reach you? I have had no interviews for a long while and, except for a colleague who was discharged a month ago, I can think of no other likely recent eyewitness. It is true that I am poorer by four teeth. I have sacrificed them at the altar of modern science to appease the goddess of physical health.

This is a long letter for gaol. But this I am writing to you after over a year and I have not seen you for over sixteen months. My last glimpse of you was when you were sailing away to the far west and your figure grew smaller and smaller as the ship bore you away and left us, feeling rather lonely and forlorn, on the pier.[386]

With my love to all the happy family of four in Yeravda,

Yours affectionately,
Jawaharlal

SWJN, *Vol. 5, I Series, pp. 449–51*

## 154. Letter to Jawaharlal Nehru

15 February 1933

My dear Jawaharlal,
In the hope of giving you a good letter against your splendid letter I have been postponing writing to you. But I can do so no longer. Daily the work is increasing. I must therefore write now and do the best I can. I wonder if you are allowed an innocent paper like *Harijan*.[387] I am sending it in the hope that you will get it. If you do, you will

[386] See p. 141, *fn*.306.

[387] An English weekly that began to be published every Saturday from 11 February 1933, with Ramachandra Shastri as its Editor. It was, in Gandhi's words, 'a views-paper, as distinguished from a news-paper'.

please let me have your opinion. The fight against sanatanists is becoming more and more interesting if also increasingly difficult. The one good thing is that they have been awakened from long lethargy. The abuses they are hurling at me are wonderfully refreshing. I am all that is bad and corrupt on this earth. But the storm will subside. For I apply the sovereign remedy of ahimsa—non-retaliation. The more I ignore the abuses, the fiercer they are becoming. But it is the death dance of the moth round a lamp. Poor Rajagopalachari and Devdas![388] They are also in for it. They are dragging out the engagement with Lakshmi and weaving round it foul charges. Thus is untouchability being supported!

Sarup and Krishna saw me the other day about untouchability and Indu as part of the domestic interview. Indu was in excellent health and seemed to be quite happy. Sarup is having a brief tour in Kathiawar and Gujarat for anti-untouchability and Krishna was to have gone to Allahabad. Devdas is in Delhi helping Raja who is moving the MLAs for the anti-untouchability Bills. Our time is being wholly occupied for the anti-untouchability work. Sardar Vallabhbhai contributes all the envelopes for the ever-increasing number of outgoing letters. He is the diligent newspaper reader who digs out odd bits of information on untouchability and what not. He is also a factory for the inexhaustible supply of mirth. The inspection day is just the same to him as any other day. He never has any request to make. With me never a day passes but I have some request to make. But I do not know which is the happier. Why may I not be as happy as he, if I can take my defeats without pulling a long face!

We all envy your solitude and your studies. It is true that our burdens are of our own making or more accurately of my making. I have dashed to pieces all Vallabhbhai's hope of becoming a good Sanskrit scholar. He can't concentrate on his studies in the midst of the excitement of Harijan work and the daily dish of spiced criticism which he enjoys like the Bengal footballers their game. Mahadev

[388] Devdas was betrothed to Lakshmi, daughter of C. Rajagopalachari. As this was an engagement between a brahmin and a bania, the sanatanists, that is, the orthodox Hindus, were against it. See also p. 169.

continues to be what Shaukat described him to be—the *hamal*[389] of the party. No work is too much for him or beyond him. Chhaganlal Joshi is still finding his feet. But he is flourishing. With the spring now well on us, he cannot fail to blossom out. We are not a bad assortment. We observe the rules of the game and so make a fairly decent family strictly regulated by the code of *varnashrama*[390] which between Dr Ambedkar[391] and me will soon provide a new sensation for the sanatanists.[392] More trouble for me but none of my seeking, I assure you. I have now only space and time enough to say we all hope your progress all round continues steadily.

Love from us all.

Bapu

CWMG, *Vol. LIII, pp. 309–10*

## 155. Letter to M.K. Gandhi

7 March 1933

My dear Bapu,

Thank you for your letter and the first two copies of *Harijan*. I read through the *Harijan* of course with interest, and delighted to see the old rapier touch of overmuch kindness and inexhaustible patience which extinguishes, or as you say neutralises, the opponent. I pity the poor sanatanists. With their anger and abuses and frantic cursing, they are no match for this kind of subtle attack. And yet the power of stupidity and conservatism and entrenched privilege in this world is amazing. Even mahatmas and saints cannot easily upset this combination unless circumstances have prepared the

[389] Meaning, in Urdu, 'porter'

[390] Defining which Gandhi had said: 'My conception of *varnashrama* has nothing in common with its present distinction of untouchability and caste. ... it simply means that we must treasure and conserve all the good qualities that we inherit from our ancestors, and that therefore each one should follow the profession of his father so long as the profession is not immoral.'

[391] B.R. Ambedkar (1891–1956); Harijan leader and a signatory of the agreement of 1932 that rejected separate electorates for the Harijans; Member, Viceroy's Council, 1942–6; Law Minister in Nehru's Cabinet, 1947–51 and one of the principal draftsmen of the Indian Constitution

[392] In a rejoinder to Dr Ambedkar, Gandhi wrote on 14 February that varnashrama was an integral part of Hinduism.

ground. Have you read Bernard Shaw's[393] *Saint Joan*—the play about Joan of Arc? If not I wish you would do so, and especially the preface of the play. It is quite a little thing and will not take much time. A short while ago I sent a copy of the book to Indu and you could easily commandeer it from her.

The tribe of sanatanists is of course doomed because they are relics of a bygone age. Their very anger shows the extent of the danger that confronts them. Under strain all tolerance disappears, and their intolerance at present is a sign of the great strain you are putting on them. It is all very well for the likes of Sapru and me (a curious combination!) to talk pompously and in a superior way of our tolerance in matters of religion when neither of us has any religion worth talking about; or for us to bless the movement for temple entry when neither has the remotest desire to go within a hundred miles of a temple except, so far as I am concerned, to see the architecture and the statuary! But touch either of us on some particular subject and you will find the raw side and there will be little of tolerance then. Who is more intolerant than you are in certain matters? The fact is real tolerance hardly exists; what goes under the name of tolerance is indifference. What we do not value we make a virtue of tolerating in others. A person who is not prepared to be aggressively intolerant about something or another is a pretty useless individual. So I feel a little sympathy—of an inverted kind—for the sanatanists. They value something for which they are prepared to fight. The issue is clarified. The dangerous people are always those who are dodging and avoiding difficulties in an effort to ignore them or forget them, or are looking at them with one eye only!

[393] George Bernard Shaw (1856–1950); Irish playwright with the distinction of being the only person to have been awarded both the Nobel Prize for Literature (1925) and an Oscar (1938) for work on the film *Pygmalion*.

Gandhi had had an interivew with him in November 1931, and later described him as 'a very witty man, a lover of epigram and paradox with a Puck-like spirit and a generous ever-young heart, the Arch Jester of Europe'.

Fifteen years later, in a letter to Bernard Shaw, Nehru said, '... like many of my generation we have grown up in the company of your writings and books. ... A part of myself, such as I am today, has been moulded by that reading.'

Of course, if you will stir up stagnant matters there will be bad smell, and the Hindu social structure has stagnated long enough in all conscience. My own remedy for a stagnant pool would be to drain it completely and let the sun dry and purify the bottom and the sides. Cool fresh water can then be poured in and arrangements made for it to keep running on, so that there may be no stagnation again. Superficial drainage can never clean the accumulations of filth at the bottom. But you are emptying the tank to some extent and maybe we shall see the bottom!

The *Harijan*, I take it, will not convert a single bigoted sanatanist. But it will no doubt influence vast numbers of others whose eyes have so far been closed to our own social evils. We get used very soon to the dirt round us. I wish the *Harijan* would give detailed facts about the suppressed classes—how they are treated in various parts of the country, their disabilities, and especially their economic condition, in so far as this is due to social conditions. This mass of facts will impress the mental person and overwhelm the sanatanist. There will be no spectacular conversion of the latter in spite of your sweet reasonableness.[394] If I may give you a quotation from an eminently respectable Victorian—John Stuart Mill:[395] 'We are the last persons to under-value the power of moral convictions. But the convictions of the mass of mankind run hand in hand with their interests or class feelings. We have a strong faith, stronger than either politicians or philosophers generally have, in the influence of reason and virtue over men's minds; but it is in that of the reason and virtue of our own side of the question. We expect few conversions by the mere force of reason from one end to the other.'

You have recently had a criticism of the *Harijan*, or rather your article in it, from an old school master. As you like criticisms, here is another—a superficial one! My first view of the *Harijan* was not agreeable. Suddenly it brought to my mind by its general

[394] A phrase Nehru uses while describing Gandhi in his Prison Diary entry of 4 June: '... Bapu always talks of compromise and his sweet reasonableness deludes people and befogs their minds.'

[395] (1806–1873); British philosopher, economist, moral and political theorist and administrator

appearance—size, get-up, type, etc.,—that old and highly respected organ of pompous futility, the *Indian Social Reformer.*[396] I do not know if this worthy but utterly useless and humourless paper still carries on in its ponderous manner for the edification of the dull and sober. I have no grievance against it if it keeps away from me. Only, the outward resemblance to it of the *Harijan* was not a point in the latter's favour. Of course the resemblance vanished when I started reading the paper.

But I must protest against the apology for an envelope in which your letter came. If Vallabhbhai is responsible for it, much as I love him, I must make it clear that envelope-making is not his strong line. Or perhaps the fault is not entirely his when the raw material he is supplied with comes from the waste-paper basket.

Forgive me for my superficiality. I like my diamonds smooth and polished. You have shown us the art and style of living life in the grand manner. That is the real thing, but why should we ignore style and art in the little things of life? Most of us cannot reach the snowy heights. Would you deprive us of the flowers in the valleys?

I have written a long enough letter already and yet many of the things I wished to say remain unsaid. What is the use of my writing about the Harijan movement? You have more than enough of the subject. I would have liked to write to you of some of my interests and occupations, just to divert and refresh your mind. Being prevented from activity in the present I live a little in the future, but largely in the past. I should like to tell you of the delightful civilisation of the Gobi desert thirteen hundred years and more ago, where a strange mixture of Indian and Chinese and Russian culture flourished and even Roman culture had a look in, and Sanskrit was the language of learning, and the Buddha legend, the golden link that joined these countries of Asia; and of the origins of Gothic architecture in Gandhara or Afghanistan and Persia nearly a thousand years before the Europe of the middle ages, in a passionate fervour of faith, built up those wonderful Gothic cathedrals which go up almost like visible prayers to the sky; and of the vivid life of Central Asia in those early days and the varied caravans, full of rich and beautiful merchandise, and accompanied

[396] A weekly started in Bombay in 1890 and edited by K. Natarajan

by many a scholar and a pilgrim, which passed to and fro between western Asia and India and the Far East; and later, of another world in this very region, the Arab world, also pulsating with life; and, in the Indonesian waters, of the empire of Sri Vijaya,[397] a real bit of India abroad, where Indian culture was supreme and Indian art is said to have reached its zenith. And I could also accompany you in thought across these vast spaces of Central Asia now and see the changes that time has wrought, and unearth from under the hot sands of the deserts the relics of ancient days which tell us so much of peoples and cultures and civilisations that have been long dead. And so I could go on and on to find an outlet for my suppressed energy till my long letter drives you to distraction and the jail authorities to something worse!

Mother has decided to go to Poona. I saw her a fortnight ago and found her looking older and more shrunk up than before. I hope you will not make her travel about. She wants rest. She was not very happy about her last place of residence in Poona. If it is possible perhaps she might stay elsewhere.

Kamala has at last left Calcutta after three-and-a-half months of treatment there and yet she is more or less on ticket-of-leave. She is at Patna now staying with her brother for a few days. By the end of the month she might manage to reach here. She now intends staying in Dehra Dun for two or three months and Indu can join her during her holidays. We are a homeless and a scattered family!

As I am not a Harijan by birth or adoption I am clearly not entitled to a free copy of the paper. I am therefore asking Sarup to send a year's subscription and arrange to have the paper sent to me here direct. I understand that it is a permitted article.

I have been a sun worshipper during the winter months here and my body has put on the sun's livery. But spring has come now and the sun gets uncomfortably warm, and with the spring have come not only fresh leaves on the trees but hordes of flies, and my faith flags before this onset.

Ansari paid me a visit and thumped me about. It was good to see him again.

[397] Which spread from Sumatra to Malaya and parts of Indonesia between the seventh and thirteenth centuries. It declined after the thirteenth century.

I have presumed greatly on the indulgence of the jail authorities by writing such a long letter. But presumption is an old failing of mine.

Love to you and your companions.

Yours affectionately,
Jawaharlal

SWJN, *Vol. 5, I Series, pp. 459–62*

## 156. Letter to Jawaharlal Nehru

2 May 1933

My dear Jawaharlal,
As I was struggling against the coming fast, you were before me as it were in flesh and blood.[398] But it was no use. How I wish I could feel that you had understood the absolute necessity of it. The Harijan movement is too big for mere intellectual effort. There is nothing so bad in all the world. And yet I cannot leave religion and therefore Hinduism. My life would be a burden to me, if Hinduism failed me. I love Christianity, Islam and many other faiths through Hinduism. Take it away and nothing remains for me. But then I cannot tolerate it with untouchability—the high-and-low belief. Fortunately Hinduism contains a sovereign remedy for the evil. I have applied the remedy. I want you to feel, if you can, that it is well if I survive the fast and well also if the body dissolves in spite of the effort to live. What is it after all—more perishable than a brittle chimney piece. You can preserve the latter intact for ten thousand years, but you may fail to keep the body intact even for a minute. And surely death is not an end to all effort. Rightly faced, it may be but the beginning of a nobler effort. But I won't convince you by argument, if you did not see the truth intuitively. I know that even if I do not carry your approval with me, I shall retain your precious love during all those days of ordeal.

[398] On 1 May, Gandhi announced his intention of commencing a fast for 21 days in connection with the Harijan cause. He had said in a statement issued to the press that the fast was directed against nobody in particular but was a prayer for purification of himself and his associates. The 21-day fast began on 8 May, the day Gandhi was released.

I had your letter which I had thought I would answer at leisure. Well, God had willed otherwise. I had talks with Krishna. Of Sarup's work in Kathiawar I think I wrote to you. Kamala has not even sent me her address. There has been no letter from her for many days now. When you see her please give her and Indu my love. Kamala must not worry over the fast. If possible send me a wire.

Love from us all.

Bapu

CWMG, *Vol. LV, p. 96*

## 157. Telegram to M.K. Gandhi

5 May 1933

Your letter. What can I say about matters I do not understand. I feel lost in strange country where you are the only familiar landmark and I try to grope my way in the dark but only stumble. Whatever happens my love and thoughts will be with you.[399]

Jawahar

SWJN, *Vol. 5, I Series, p. 474*

## 158. Letter to M.K. Gandhi

5 May 1933

My dear Bapu,

Your letter came today. I was half expecting it for your large heart never permits you to forget anyone. I have sent you a telegram already.

As my telegram will indicate, I feel utterly at a loss and do not know what I can say to you. Religion is not familiar ground for me, and as I have grown older I have definitely drifted away from it. I suppose I have something else in its place, something other than just intellect and reason, which gives me strength and hope. Apart from this indefinable and indefinite urge, which may have just

[399] Nehru's Prison Diary entry of 8 May reads: 'Bapu began his twenty-one day fast today. When first news of the proposed fast came a week ago I had a shock but I recovered soon. Three days ago came Bapu's letter—a typical cry from the heart which bowled me over and I had quite an emotional crisis. I sent him a telegram which I did not like at all. My mind was in a muddle.'

a tinge of religion in it and yet is wholly different from it, I have grown to rely entirely on the workings of the mind. Perhaps they are weak supports to rely upon, but search as I will, I can see no better ones. Religion seems to me to lead to emotion and sentimentality and they are still more unreliable guides. Intuition—undoubtedly there is such a thing, though where it comes from I cannot say; perhaps from the stored-up experiences at the back of the mind, the subconscious self.

The Harijan question is bad, very bad, but it seems to me incorrect to say that there is nothing so bad in all the world. I think I could point to much that was equally bad and even worse. All over the world there is the same Harijan question in various forms. Is it not the outcome of special causes? Surely it is due to something more than mere ignorance and ill will. To remove these causes or to neutralise their effect appears to be the only way to deal with the roots of the matter. But why should I write of these matters now! I do not want to argue in this letter as the stage for argument seems to be past.

It is hard to be so far from you, and yet it would be harder to be near you. This crowded world is a very lonely place, and you want to make it still lonelier. Life and death matter little, or should matter little. The only thing that matters is the cause that one works for, and if one could be sure that the best service to it is to die for it, then death would seem simpler. I have loved life—the mountains and the sea, the sun and rain and storm and snow, and animals, and books and art. And even human beings—and life has been good to me. But the idea of death has never frightened me; from a distance it seems fitting enough as the crown of one's endeavour. Yet, at close quarters, it is not pleasant to contemplate.

The last fourteen or fifteen years have been a wonderful time for me, ever since I had the good fortune to be associated with you in various activities.[400] Life became fuller and richer and more worthwhile, and that is a dear and precious memory which nothing can

[400] As Nehru records it, his 'first meeting with Gandhiji was about the time of the Lucknow Congress during Christmas, 1916', but it was after the Gandhian era of Congress began in 1919-20 that Nehru came to be closely associated with Gandhi in public life.

take from me. And whenever the future happens to be dark, this vision of the past will relieve the gloom and give strength.

All my love to you.

Yours affectionately,
Jawahar

[PS]
Kamala is staying in Dehra Dun. I shall communicate your message to her.

SWJN, *Vol. 5, I Series, pp. 473–4*

## 159. Telegram to M.K. Gandhi

8 May 1933

Now that you are launched on your great enterprise may I send you again love and greetings and assure you that I feel more clearly that whatever happens it is well and whatever happens you win.[401]

Jawahar

SWJN, *Vol. 5, I Series, p. 475*

## 160. Letter to Jawaharlal Nehru

22 July 1933

My dear Jawaharlal,
I have often wished to write to you but I have been helpless. Every ounce of the energy newly acquired has been spent in attending to the pressing work before me.

[401] Nearly a month later, Nehru wrote in his Prison Diary, 'As I watched the emotional upheaval during the fast I wondered more and more if this was the right method in politics. It is sheer revivalism and clear thinking has not a ghost of a chance against it. All India, or most of it, stares reverently at the Mahatma and expects him to perform miracle after miracle and put an end to untouchability and get swaraj and so on—and does nothing itself! ... more and more I realise the gulf between Bapu and me and I begin to doubt if this way of faith is the right way to train a nation. ... There is trouble ahead so far as I am personally concerned. I shall have to fight a stiff battle between rival loyalties. Perhaps the happiest place for me is the gaol!'

I had a nice time with Mother and Kamala. I was not able to see much of Sarup and Ranjit.[402] Mother is anxious about Krishna. She had long talks with me about her future. If you have any suggestions for me in the matter please let me have them. Of course my movements are uncertain. But that does not matter.

Devdas and Lakshmi,[403] I left in Poona. They are due to come here now. Devdas will most probably settle down in Delhi for the time being. Mahadev, Ba[404] and Prabhavati[405] are with me. They are all soon to disperse, I expect.

I have been slow in regaining pre-fast strength. But I am slowly improving.

Love.

Bapu

CWMG, *Vol. LV, p. 287*

## 161. Letter to M.K. Gandhi

25 July 1933

My dear Bapu,

I received your note yesterday.

Mother's anxiety about Krishna is natural. It is the anxiety of any mother, more specially a Hindu mother, and it concerns itself chiefly with the desire of getting her daughter suitably married. She would have liked to see her married among the Kashmiris and failing that among Brahmins. The idea that Krishna should marry somebody who is not even a Brahmin is more than she can comfortably swallow. So far as I am concerned the question of K's

[402] Ranjit Sitaram Pandit (1893–1944); a Sanskrit scholar and a barrister of Rajkot; married Vijayalakshmi, Nehru's sister, 1921; joined the nonco-operation movement and served several terms of imprisonment; translated Kalidasa's *Rajatarangini*, *Mudrarakshasa* and *Ritu-samhara* into English

[403] Whose marriage had taken place at Poona on 16 June

[404] Kasturba Gandhi (1869–1944); wife of Gandhi, affectionately called Ba. Though she did not concur with all of Gandhi's opinions and actions in the early years she stood by him throughout her life in the practice of his ideals. Kasturba died in Gandhi's arms while they were both in Yeravda prison.

Gandhi said of her, 'Truly she has so far been my teacher. She teaches me ... patience, forgiveness, greater need for sacrifice, for love and charity.'

[405] Wife of Jaya Prakash Narain

marriage does not worry me so much, although I certainly think about it. My views about it are the exact opposite of mother's. I would welcome as wide a break from old custom as possible. The Kashmiri community as a whole (there are exceptions of course in it) disgusts me; it is the very epitome of the petty bourgeois vices which I detest. I am not particularly interested in a person being a Brahmin, a non-Brahmin or anything else. As a matter of fact, I fail to see the relevance of all this; one marries an individual, not a community. And then all this is beside the mark as the decision is going to be Krishna's, not mother's or mine, and it is quite impossible to treat a grown-up girl in any other way.

I do not quite know what any of us can do in the matter. From a letter I had from Krishna a few days ago I gathered that she was waiting for me to come out to tell me something on the subject. I can make no definite guess till I know what is in her mind. But she seems to be pleased about it. If she has a clear preference and there is no insuperable objection (and I cannot imagine any such) the matter will, I take it, be settled that way. I shall write to you as soon as I know more.

I do not know if you have heard of a proposed marriage in our family. My cousin Braj Lal's son,[406] who has been studying in the London School of Economics has got himself engaged to a Hungarian girl who is a fellow student of his. His father and mother got rather put out by this news and they hurried to London and later even to Budapest to see the girl's parents. But the girl won them over and they have returned full of praises for her!

There are certain legal difficulties in the way of such mixed marriages. Braj Lal proposes to get the Hungarian girl formally converted to Hinduism and then to get her married by Hindu or Arya [Samaj] rites. The girl herself is quite willing. Personally I dislike this change or adoption of a religion to serve another end.

I am becoming more and more hostile to the religious idea. Exceptions apart (and some of them are big exceptions), it seems to me the negation of real spirituality and only a begetter of confusion and sentimentality. I should like to keep myself away, as far

[406] B.K. Nehru (1909–2001); joined ICS in 1934; Secretary, Economic Affairs, 1957; Governor, Assam, 1968; Governor, Jammu and Kashmir, 1982

as possible, from all religious rites and ceremonials, all the hall-marks of religion—indeed to be wholly non-religious. Regard for mother and a desire not to hurt her feelings at this time of her life, occasionally make me agree to participation in some ceremony. But even so it is an unwilling and ungracious participation and I am not sure if it is not better to do without it.

I read only this morning of Sen Gupta's sudden death.[407] It came as a shock. Although never very intimate with him, I had known him for nearly 26 years. He was much older than I am but his last term at Cambridge coincided with my first, and we met for the first time at the end of 1907. How life goes by us and the scene changes as we sit surrounded by our thoughts!

Kamala is staying on in Dehra Dun. Perhaps she will remain till my discharge which is ordinarily due in the second week of September.[408]

I hope you will soon be back to perfect health.

Love.

Yours affectionately,
Jawaharlal

SWJN, *Vol. 5, I Series, pp. 490–2*

## 162. Letter to Jawaharlal Nehru

31 August 1933

My dear Jawaharlal,
So you are out before your time. I hope you got my wire.[409] I had thought that Mother was going back to Allahabad. I expect full report from you.

Indu has been with me fairly often. She is to come again this evening.

If it is at all possible, we must meet soon. But of course you will be held up there.

[407] Jatindra Mohan Sen Gupta, a prisoner at Ranchi, had died suddenly of an apoplectic stroke on the night of 22 July 1933.

[408] Nehru was released on 30 August on account of his mother's illness.

[409] Not available

If Mother remains bad. I shall expect a full letter from you. It would be as well to send it by registered post.

I am slowly regaining lost strength. I say nothing about the fast[410] as I expect you now know all about it. More when we meet.

Love.

Bapu

CWMG, *Vol. LV, p. 384*

## 163. Letter to Jawaharlal Nehru

3 September 1933

My dear Jawaharlal,

I have your letter.[411] Evidently your presence has served as a tonic for Mother. If she remains free from fever, you should be free to move out for a few days. If so, you should come to me as early as you can. I am anxious to leave here on Friday or Saturday next for Bombay and be there for about a week and then go to Wardha.

I do not know the young man[412] you mention. I know the family well. I must have met him too. But I could not identify him, if I saw him. The family has liberal traditions. Krishna is therefore likely to be quite happy with them. I have written to Anasuyabehn about him. She of course knows all these people intimately. But meanwhile I see no harm in your sending for him and seeing him and presenting him to Mother if you find him acceptable. On hearing from Anasuyabehn, I shall wire to you, if necessary. Of course, I am otherwise keeping the matter quite secret. I take it that you have not minded my writing to Anasuyabehn.

Kamala needs freedom from excitement and worry. I am inclined to think that she is the least unhappy in Bombay with Naoroji sisters. I therefore feel that you should bring her when you come here and then leave her here.

[410] Which he had started on 16 August, arising from the refusal of the Government to yield to his request for increased facilities in Yeravda Jail, where he was kept following his arrest on 1 August. He was released unconditionally on 23 August.

[411] Not available

[412] Gunottam Hutheesing

In the expectation that we must meet soon, I say nothing of the political situation or of my fasting exploits. I am steadily regaining lost strength.

Poor Mahadev is in Belgaum.[413] It is good to go through the fire. Do please tell Mother that she is continually in my thoughts. She has to live long enough to see the clouds lifting.

My love to you all.

Bapu

CWMG, *Vol. LV, p. 399–400*

## 164. Letter to M.K. Gandhi

Poona
13 September 1933

My dear Bapu,

In our recent conversations you will remember that I laid stress on the reiteration and clearer definition of our national objective.[414] The objective of political independence has been finally laid down by the Congress and there is nothing to add to it or take away from it. We stand for complete independence. Sometimes a little confusion arises because of vague phraseology and misleading propaganda and it is therefore as well to remove this confusion by a reiteration of our political demand. Even the word 'independence' is used with a variety of meanings. Obviously it must include, as the Congress has clearly and definitely laid down, full control of the army and of foreign relations as well as financial control.

In regard to economic matters, the Karachi Congress, by passing the important resolution[415] on Fundamental Rights and Economic Changes, gave a lead and pointed out the direction in which we should move. I attach great importance to that resolution but I would personally like to go much further and to clarify the position still more.

[413] Mahadev Desai who had been arrested on 1 August 1933 was in Belgaum prison at this time.

[414] Nehru had had discussions with Gandhi on 9 and 10 September at Poona.

[415] On 31 March 1931. For the text drafted by Nehru and with changes by Gandhi, see *CWMG*, Vol. XLV, pp. 370–2.

It seems to me that if we are to improve the condition of the masses, to raise them economically and give them freedom, it is inevitable that vested interests in India will have to give up their special position and many of their privileges. It is inconceivable to me how else the masses can rise. Therefore, the problem of achieving freedom becomes one of revising vested interests in favour of the masses. To the extent this is done, to that extent only will freedom come. The biggest vested interest in India is that of the British Government, next come the Indian Princes, and others follow. We do not wish to injure any class or group and the divesting should be done as gently as possible and with every effort to avoid injury. But it is obvious that the divesting is bound to cause loss to the classes or groups which enjoy special privileges at the expense of masses. It is also obvious that the process of divesting must be as speedy as possible to bring relief to the masses whose condition, as you know, is as bad as it can well be. Indeed economic forces themselves are acting with amazing rapidity today and breaking up the old order. The big zamindari and taluqdari system in the United Provinces has largely collapsed, though it may be kept up for some time longer by outside agencies. Even the condition of the zamindars is very bad and the peasantry of course are in a far worse position.

We are all agreed that the Round Table Conference and its various productions are utterly useless to solve even one of India's many problems. As I conceive it, the Round Table Conference was an effort to consolidate the vested interests in India behind the British Government so as to face the rising and powerful national and economic movements in the country which threaten their interests. Essentially, in the international parlance, it was a fascist grouping of vested and possessing interests, and fascist methods were adopted in India to suppress the national movement. And because the mere preservation of all these vested interests in India cannot possibly solve our economic ills, whether those of the masses, or even of the middle classes, the effort is foredoomed to inevitable failure. Even from the point of view of a democratic nationalism, as you yourself stated at the Round Table Conference, democracy and autocracy can ill go together.

Another aspect has to be borne in mind. The problem of Indian freedom cannot be separated from the vital international problem of the world. The present crisis in the world's affairs is having its repercussions in India. At any moment it may result in a complete breakdown or in a violent international conflagration. Everywhere there is a conflict and a contest between the forces of progress and betterment of the masses and the forces of reaction and vested interests. We cannot remain silent witnesses to this titanic struggle for it affects us intimately. Both on the narrower ground of our own interests and the wider ground of international welfare and human progress, we must, I feel, range ourselves with the progressive forces of the world. This ranging ourselves at present can of course be ideological only.

These are some of the larger issues that fill my mind and I am convinced, not only that we ignore them at our peril, but that a true appreciation of them will vitalise and give new meaning to our struggle for freedom which we must continue till the full objective is achieved. These wider issues are of great importance but at present, as you know, the minds of large numbers of our countrymen are greatly exercised over immediate national problems and specially the question of carrying on the struggle. The statements that you and Syt. M.S. Aney[416] issued some time ago to guide the country have, I am afraid, produced some confusion and there has even been some resentment in regard to particular directions contained in them. There is a vague talk, in quarters which ought to know better, that the Congress has been dissolved. It is obvious that nothing of the kind has been done or could be done under the constitution. Your directions and those of Mr Aney were, I take it, in the nature of advice or suggestions to meet a certain position that had arisen. The Congress continues as before but it is clear that it cannot function normally. When the Government declares its committees to be illegal, there can be no regular offices or open activity. To recognise this fact and to adapt ourselves to it is not to

[416] Madhavrao S. Aney, who at this time was acting President of the INC. For his statement of 22 July 1933 discontinuing mass civil disobedience, see *CWMG*, Vol. LV, Appendix IX.

wind up any Congress committee, much less the Congress organisation as a whole.

A necessary consequence from this was to avoid the possibility of a few newcomers who formed committees when the old members and other reliable workers went to prison, or even individuals, committing the Congress to an undesirable course of action. As is known, we have had to face this risk in the past and unreliable persons have come to the helm of affairs in some local areas with the intention of obstructing and even stopping the very activities they were supposed to further. It thus becomes desirable to prevent such unreliable persons from exploiting the name of the Congress committee. This of course does not prevent Congress workers in any area from cooperating together in an organised way for the furtherance of our programme.

Confusion has also arisen in the country about the implications of individual and mass civil disobedience. I appreciate, to some extent, the difference, but this difference does not appear to me to be a fundamental one, as in any event, civil disobedience is essentially an individual affair. Individual civil disobedience can develop into mass civil disobedience. Besides, you told me that if an organisation felt strong enough to undertake the responsibility and the risk, it could, of its own initiative, take up mass civil disobedience. Indeed you were of opinion that a local organisation could in this manner go ahead in any direction which was not contrary to Congress methods or policy.

Stress was laid in your previous statement on the undesirability of secrecy, although you pointed out that there was nothing inherently illegitimate in secret methods. I think that most of us agree, and certainly I am of that opinion, that our movement is essentially an open one and secret methods do not fit in with it. Such methods, if indulged in to any large extent, are likely to change the whole character of the movement, as it has been conceived, and produce a certain amount of demoralisation. Agreeing with this, some of us feel that, to some extent as for instance, in communicating with each other or sending directions or keeping contacts, a measure of secrecy may be necessary. Perhaps secrecy is hardly the word for these activities and privacy would suit them better. Privacy of course is always open to all groups and individuals. Secrecy or the avoidance of it, as you said, cannot be made into a fetish.

But secrecy is certainly involved in the production of printed or duplicated news-sheets and bulletins. These bulletins have often served a useful purpose in the past in keeping contact between headquarters and districts and in sending information or directions. You pointed out to me the difficulties and undesirable consequences of running these secret presses and duplicating machines. Many good workers are tied up and have to avoid aggressive action, money has to be invested in such machines and frequently they are taken away by the police. Even from the practical point of view this continuous drain and tying up of workers results in demoralisation. You suggested that the best way was to have handwritten copies of bulletins, etc., containing the name of the publisher. Generally, I agree with all this and appreciate the force of your argument. But I do feel that under certain circumstances it may be desirable for a local or provincial committee or group to issue bulletins of directions, etc., secretly. This must not be encouraged, indeed it should be discouraged, but a certain latitude in exceptional circumstances might be permitted.

There is one other small matter which seems to me rather ridiculous. It was right and proper, if I may say so, for you to court imprisonment by giving previous intimation of your intention to do so to the authorities. But it seems to me to be perfectly absurd for others, and even Congress volunteers, to send such notices or communications to the authorities. Any person desiring to offer civil resistance should openly carry on activities which further our cause and thus court arrest. He must not forget or ignore these activities and merely ask to be arrested.

This letter has become long enough. I do not mention here the many other matters which I had the privilege of discussing with you.

Yours affectionately,
Jawahar

SWJN, *Vol. 5, I Series, pp. 526–30*

## 165. Letter to Jawaharlal Nehru

'Parnakuti', Poona
14 September 1933

My dear Jawaharlal,
I am glad you have written so fully and frankly. When, on my return from London at the end of 1931, I found you to have been suddenly snatched away from me, I felt the separation keenly.[417] I was, therefore, most anxious to meet you and exchange views.

With much of what you have said in your letter I am in complete agreement. The experience gained after the Karachi Congress has, if possible, strengthened my faith in the main resolution and the economic programme referred to by you. I have no doubt in my mind that our goal can be no less than 'Complete Independence'. I am also in whole-hearted agreement with you when you say that without a material revision of vested interests the condition of the masses can never be improved. I believe, too, though I may not go as far as you do, that before India can become one homogenous entity, the princes will have to part with much of their power and become popular representatives of the people over whom they are ruling today. I can corroborate from first-hand experience much of what you say about the Round Table Conference. Nor have I the slightest difficulty in agreeing with you that in these days of rapid inter-communication and a growing consciousness of the oneness of all mankind, we must recognise that our nationalism must not be inconsistent with progressive internationalism. India cannot stand in isolation and unaffected by what is going on in other parts of the world. I can, therefore, go the whole length with you and say that 'we should range ourselves with the progressive forces of the world'. But I know that though there is such an agreement between you and me in the enunciation of ideals, there are temperamental differences between us. Thus you have emphasised the necessity of a clear statement of the goal, but having once determined it, I have never attached importance to the repetition. The clearest

[417] Nehru had been arrested on 26 December 1931, while on his way to meet Gandhi.

possible definition of the goal and its appreciation would fail to take us there if we do not know and utilise the means of achieving it. I have, therefore, concerned myself principally with the conservation of the means and their progressive use. I know that if we can take care of them, attainment of the goal is assured. I feel too that our progress towards the goal will be in exact proportion to the purity of our means. If we can give an ocular demonstration of our uttermost truthfulness and nonviolence, I am convinced that our statement of the national goal cannot long offend the interests which your letter would appear to attack. We know that the princes, the zamindars, and those who depend for their existence upon the exploitation of the masses, would cease to fear and distrust us, if we could but ensure the innocence of our methods. We do not seek to coerce any. We seek to convert them. This method may appear to be long, perhaps too long, but I am convinced that it is the shortest.

In the main I agree with your interpretation of Sjt. Aney's instructions and my note upon them.[418] I am quite clear in my mind that had those instructions not been issued, the whole movement of civil resistance would have collapsed through growing internal weakness; for Congressmen were deluding themselves into the belief that there were organisations effectively functioning to which they could look for guidance, when as a matter of fact, under the organised terrorism which the Ordinance Rule means, organised functioning of Congress committees had become impossible. A false belief in the functioning of organisations, rendered illegal and largely impotent, was fast producing a demoralisation which had to be arrested. There is no such thing as demoralisation in civil resistance properly applied. You have said rightly that after all 'civil disobedience is essentially an individual affair'. I go a step further and say that so long as there is one civil resister offering resistance, the movement cannot die and must succeed in the end. Individual civil resisters do not need the aid of an organisation. After all an organisation is nothing without the individuals composing it. Sjt. Aney's instructions were, therefore, I hold, an effective answer to the Ordinances and if only men and women belonging to the

[418] See *CWMG*, Vol. LV, pp. 295–301.

Congress will appreciate the necessity of those instructions with all their implications, the Ordinances will be rendered nugatory, at least so far as the resisters are concerned. They can form a nucleus around which an army of invincible civil resisters can be built up. Nothing in Sjt. Aney's instructions or in my note would warrant the supposition that they preclude organised action by Congressmen in any shape or form.

I would like to warn you against thinking that there is no fundamental difference between individual civil resistance and mass civil resistance. I think that the fundamental difference is implied in your own admission that 'it is essentially an individual affair'. The chief distinction between mass civil resistance and individual civil resistance is that in the latter everyone is a complete independent unit and his fall does not affect the others; in mass civil resistance the fall of one generally adversely affects the rest. Again, in mass civil resistance leadership is essential, in individual civil resistance every resister is his own leader. Then again, in mass civil resistance, there is a possibility of failure; in individual civil resistance failure is an impossibility. Finally, a state may cope with mass civil resistance; no state has yet been found able to cope with individual civil resistance. Nor may much be made of my statement that an organisation which feels its own strength can at its own risk adopt mass civil resistance. While, as an opinion, it is unexceptionable, I know that at the present moment there is no organisation that can shoulder the burden. I do not want to raise false hopes.

Now about the secret methods. I am as firm as ever that they must be tabooed. I am myself unable to make any exceptions. Secrecy has caused much mischief and if it is not put down with a firm hand, it may ruin the movement. There may be exceptional circumstances that may warrant secret methods. I would forgo that advantage for the sake of the masses whom we want to educate in fearlessness. I will not confuse their minds by leading them to think that under certain circumstances, they may resort to secret methods. Secrecy is inimical to the growth of the spirit of civil resistance. If Congressmen will realise that all property is liable to be confiscated at any moment, they will learn to be utterly independent of it.

I quite agree with you that it is ludicrous for individuals to send notices to the local authorities of their intention to offer a particular form of civil disobedience. We do not want to make a great movement ridiculous. Therefore when civil resistance is offered it should be offered seriously and in an effective manner, in so far as this is possible, in furtherance of the Congress programme.

I notice one gap in your letter. You make no mention of the various constructive activities of the Congress. They became an integral part of the Congress programme that was framed after mature deliberations in 1920.[419] With civil resistance as the background we cannot possibly do without the constructive activities such as communal unity, removal of untouchability and universalisation of the spinning-wheel and khaddar. I am as strong as ever about these. We must recognise that whilst the Congressmen can be counted by hundreds of thousands, civil resisters imprisoned have never amounted to more than one lakh at the outside. I feel that there is something radically wrong if paralysis has overtaken the remaining lakhs. There is nothing to be ashamed of in an open confession by those who for any reason whatsoever are unable to join the civil resisters' ranks. They are also serving the cause of the country and bringing it nearer to the goal who are engaged in any of the constructive activities I have named and several other kindred activities I can add to the list. Ordinance or no Ordinance, if individual Congressmen and Congresswomen will learn the art of contributing their share to the work of building of the house of independence and realise their own importance, dark as the horizon seems to us, there is absolutely no cause for despair or disappointment.

Finally, if I can say so without incurring the risk of your accusing me of egotism, I would like to say that I have no sense of defeat in me and the hope in me that this country of ours is fast marching towards its goal is burning as bright as it did in 1920; for I have an undying faith in the efficacy of civil resistance. But as you are aware, after full and prayerful consideration, I have decided not to take the offensive during the unexpired period of the sentence

[419] For the Congress Working Committee Resolution passed at the Nagpur session of the INC on 30 December 1920, see *CWMG*, Vol. XIX, Appendix I.

of imprisonment that was pronounced against me on the 4th of August last by the court that met in Yeravda Jail. I need not go into the reasons as I have already issued a separate statement about it.[420] This personal suspension, although it may be misunderstood for a while, will show how and when it may become a duty. And if it is a duty, it cannot possibly injure the cause.

Yours,
Bapu

Jawaharlal Nehru
Poona

CWMG, *Vol. LV, pp. 426–30*

## 166. Letter to Jawaharlal Nehru

23 September 1933

My dear Jawaharlal,
I was ready to write to you only yesterday. My inquiry was completed at 1 p.m. I have now met Kasturbhai, Mrs Hathisingh and Shankerlal who knows the family well. I am not quite satisfied with my experiences. I have missed straightforwardness. And yet I have nothing to say against the proposed match. Krishna will be happy enough in the new surroundings. What is more, she seems to have set her heart upon the match. She has been corresponding with Raja's mother. Rajababu is the pet name of her chosen one. There is no question of their leaving anything in Krishna's name. Of course I made it perfectly clear to them that the suggestion as to leaving something in Krishna's name was purely mine, and that even so, I had no intention of making it a condition of marriage. I made the proposal, I told them, because I believe in such arrangement for all girls wherever it was possible. If the match is to be finally fixed up, you have to write to Mrs Hathisingh, Ahmedabad, making the proposal definitely and she will send you her acceptance. She is quite ready for the marriage to take place as early as Krishna wishes.[421] She is desirous (and I concur) that the betrothal and

[420] See *CWMG*, Vol. LV, pp. 425–6.

[421] The marriage took place in Allahabad on 20 October 1933. See also p. 205.

marriage should take place simultaneously. You may now write to young Hathisingh and send for him when you like.

I hope Mother is better as also Kamala.

I reached Wardha this morning. Except for the high blood pressure which the doctors register, there is nothing wrong with me. Nevertheless I am not to move about for at least three weeks from today, i.e., up to 15th October next.

Mathuradas[422] is in Bombay. Chandrashankar[423] and Nayar are with me of course, apart from Ba, Mirabehn and Prabhavati. Prabhudas[424] is also with me.

Love.

Bapu

CWMG, *Vol. LVI, pp. 19–20*

## 167. Telegram to Jawaharlal Nehru

Wardhaganj
23 September 1933

Jawaharlal Nehru
Lucknow
Your wire.[425] Posted letter today. Completed inquiry yesterday.[426] Result on whole satisfactory. You will write Mrs Hathisingh formally offering hand. Glad mother better.

Bapu

CWMG, *Vol. LVI, p. 21*

[422] Mathuradas Trikumji; grandson of Gandhi's step-sister; secretary, Bombay Provincial Congress Committee, 1922–3; Member, Bombay Municipal Corporation, 1923–5, and later Mayor

[423] Chandrashankar Prabhashankar Shukla, Editor, *Harijanbandhu*

[424] Son of Chhaganlal Gandhi

[425] Not available

[426] See letter following.

## 168. Letter to Jawaharlal Nehru

24 September 1933

My dear Jawaharlal,
I had a talk today with Jamnalalji about the proposed match. He seems to know the family well. He is decidedly of opinion that the family, apart from Kasturbhai of course, is not as well off as they would appear to be. He is even of opinion that they may be actually in want. I thought I should pass this news on to you. He too is anxious that I should let you have his opinion. Personally I remain unaffected by it. But he thinks that Krishna should know it. So far as I can judge, nothing will affect Krishna's choice unless she has something definite against the young man. And she would be quite right. Kasturbhai is strongly of opinion that Krishna's choice is good.

Love to you all.

Bapu

[PS]
You may succeed in making persons like me not addressing you as Pundit but I see that the adjective will abide with you.

[PPS]
What I wanted to suggest was that if this marriage comes off and if Mother agrees, the religious ceremony may be performed at Wardha. I know the difficulty. I am thinking selfishly I know. I have simply thrown out the suggestion. Let us see what happens. I am likely to see Kasturbhai.

CWMG, *Vol. LVI, pp. 23–4*

## 169. Letter to Jawaharlal Nehru

28 September 1933

My dear Jawaharlal,
I have your several letters. I had a long chat with Rafi.[427] He will tell you all about it. I adhere to the opinion that it will do no good to have the AICC meeting. But that does not mean that it will

[427] Rafi Ahmad Kidwai

deeply hurt me if such a meeting was held. On the contrary if a sufficient number desire it, it is their duty to send a requisition for the meeting. What I feel is that we may not take the initiative. If you personally feel that it is better to hold the meeting even though there is no requisition, you should hold it. I know that I am not in touch even with the opinion of workers. Therefore, my opinion may safely be discounted by those who have a decided opinion the other way.

The other point I would like to clear apart from the impression that Rafi may give you of my talks is about the workers. Whilst I shall try to do what I can, I am firmly of opinion that every province should support its own workers and that every district or tehsil should support its. Unless we reach that state, ours must remain a house of cards. I think that you should take up the begging bowl in the province and set the pace and the example. My ideal is that every worker should find his maintenance from the area he may serve and feel proud of it. Every labourer is worthy of his hire.

The rest from Rafi.

I hope both Ma and Kamala are better. You will tell me in due course what Dr Bidhan has to say.

Love.

Bapu

[PS]
Of the personal letters I need say nothing. I hope you had my two letters written. ...[428]

CWMG, *Vol. LVI, p. 30*

## 170. Letter to Jawaharlal Nehru

7 October 1933

My dear Jawaharlal,
I have your two letters. The first did not call for a reply.

I see that Krishna's marriage comes off on 20th instant. I am glad. I must not attempt to come to Allahabad. It is much better

[428] Illegible in the source

for me to remain in the purdah till the medical men declare me to be quite fit. Herewith a letter for Krishna.

I see Mother is not yet quite out of the wood. Let us hope she will be fit enough to attend the wedding.

Your article for the *DH*[429] I like very much. I am sending it to Agatha[430] for such use as she can make of it. She is a wonderful worker.

Mira had forgotten all about the note of her prison experiences.[431] Her draft is now ready. It will be sent to you to be handed to Andrews and such other use that you may wish.

I am thinking out what is possible to do for the workers.

What is this I read about Tandon's differences? Have you seen the paragraph?

Love.

Bapu

CWMG, *Vol. LVI, pp. 63–4*

## 171. Telegram to Jawaharlal Nehru

Wardha
9 October 1933

Jawaharlal Nehru
Anand Bhawan, Allahabad
Thank God. Hope mother will be well enough attend forthcoming wedding in good health.

Bapu

CWMG, *Vol. LVI, p. 79*

[429] *The Daily Herald*. The reference is to a series of articles entitled 'Whither India', published in the Indian newspapers from 9–11 October 1933. They were later reprinted as a pamphlet. See *SWJN*, Vol. 6, I Series, pp. 1–16.

[430] Agatha Harrison, a Quaker, who met Gandhi for the first time on 2 November 1929 and became his admirer; an authority on women in industry, she visited India several times

[431] Mirabehn had been sentenced on 23 August 1932 to a year's imprisonment.

## 172. Letter to Jawaharlal Nehru

Wardha
9 October 1933

My dear Jawaharlal,
I had your wire[432] to which I sent a reply in the afternoon. I do hope Mother will be strong enough to attend the wedding.

I got today the accompanying from Saraladevi.[433] I have told her Indu is left free to do as she chooses and that she is not likely to entertain any marriage proposal as she is still studying. I have told her too that I am forwarding the letter to you. If Indu was at all prepared to consider a marriage proposal, I do regard Dipak[434] to be a good match.

Hardikar[435] and Kamala Chattopadhyay[436] came in today. Hardikar is suffering from fistula and would need an operation. I shall know more tomorrow. Jamnalalji has gone to Bombay for helping a friend who is in financial trouble. He will be back in four days.

My tour[437] commences on 8th November, all being otherwise well. I am having fair rest.

Kamala never writes nowadays.

Love.

Bapu

CWMG, *Vol. LVI, pp. 79–80*

[432] Not available

[433] Saraladevi Chowdharani (1872–1945); daughter of Rabindranath Tagore's sister, Swarankumari, and Jhanakinath Ghosal; nationalist poet, singer, educationist and orator, and a disciple of Vivekananda. She met Gandhi in 1920.

[434] Son of Saraladevi Chowdharani

[435] N.S. Hardikar, founder and Secretary-General of the Hindustani Seva Dal

[436] Kamaladevi Chattopadhyaya (1903–1988); Gandhian social reformer and freedom fighter; driving force behind the renaissance of Indian handicrafts, handlooms, and theatre in post-Independence India; worked for the uplift of the socio-economic standard of Indian women by pioneering the cooperative movement in India

[437] Harijan tour

## 173. Letter to Jawaharlal Nehru

15 October 1933

My dear Jawaharlal,

Here is a letter[438] for Mother. Let us all hope that she will be well enough to take part in the ceremony.

Have you introduced the Roman character for writing Hindi?

A typed letter is going to you (today) with a copy of my letter to Malaviyaji.[439]

Love.

Bapu

CWMG, *Vol. LVI, p. 98*

## 174. Letter to Jawaharlal Nehru

Satyagraha Ashram, Wardha
15 October 1933

My dear Jawaharlal,

I had your letter[440] enclosing a copy of your letter to Krishnamurti of Madura.

Here is a copy of my letter to Hales,[441] in reply to his letter which you must have seen in the Press. And here is also a copy of my letter to Malaviyaji. It speaks for itself.

438 Dated 15 October 1933; see *CWMG*, Vol. LVI, p. 97.

439 In his letter of 15 October 1933 to Madan Mohan Malaviya, Gandhi had expressed his conviction that if the AICC were to meet, it would by an overwhelming majority pass a resolution endorsing continuance of civil resistance movement. He argued that if on the contrary, Malaviya believed that the AICC would adopt a new programme and give up civil disobedience, he should canvass for a requisition, and that Nehru would act on it, by convening a meeting. He added '... if you would promote a requisition you should also in consultation with the requisitionists chalk out a definite policy and programme which you will prosecute unflinchingly.'

440 Not available

441 H.K. Hales, Conservative member of the House of Commons; had contacts with British manufacturing interests in India. For Gandhi's letter to Hales, see *CWMG*, Vol. LVI, pp. 84–5.

All my good wishes for the wedding. I shall be with you in spirit on that day.

Love.

Bapu

Encl. 2

CWMG, *Vol. LVI, p. 97*

## 175. Letter to Jawaharlal Nehru

Satyagraha Ashram, Wardha
16 October 1933

My dear Jawaharlal,

Herewith the resignation of Jamnalalji.[442] If you think that it must not be sent in and is likely to cause embarrassment, you need not take any action upon it. You may then return it with your reasons after you are free from the wedding arrangements. If, however, you think that the resignation may be accepted, you may publish it forthwith. I know that the Treasurer can only be appointed by the All-India Congress Committee. Therefore, the treasurership may remain in Jamnalalji's hands, for the time being. The chief thing is that he ceases to be a member of the Working Committee. I think that the step is a wise and necessary one. Constituted as he is, it is risky for him to seek imprisonment just now, that is, without taking the rest that the specialist considers necessary. But, ordinarily, fighters can't consult their health to the extent that Jamnalalji's temperament demands and as he shares the same view of a civil resister's duty that I have, he is ill at ease, so long as he holds a responsible office in the Congress organisation.

I have given you my reasoning which decided my acceptance of Jamnalalji's proposal to resign.

Yours,

Bapu

Encl. 1

CWMG, *Vol. LVI, pp. 101–2*

[442] From the Congress Working Committee

## 176. Letter to Jawaharlal Nehru

18 October 1933

My dear Jawaharlal,

Herewith two garlands made out of yarn specially spun by me today for the bride and the bridegroom charged with my blessings. Will you please put them round their necks on my behalf! I hope they will reach you in time.

I cannot help being sorry that the ceremony has been vetoed by Mrs. Hutheesing. But I suppose in these matters I am a back number.

I understand what you say about Dipak. I would write to Sarala Devi in as gentle a manner as I can.

Love to you all.

Bapu

[PS]

I would like you to wire to me when all is over that Mother was able to stand the strain.

CWMG, *Vol. LVI, pp. 104–5*

## 177. Letter to Jawaharlal Nehru

Wardha
23 October 1933

My dear Jawaharlal,

I had two wires one from you[443] and [the] other from Krishna and Raja. Thank God. Mother's bravery commands my worship. I have pictured her to be a personification of quiet, dignified bravery and sacrifice, ever since I have met her.

One thing I have been forgetting to write to you. If ever you feel that you would like to call a meeting of the AICC, you must not hesitate to call it. You need not mind my disinclination. I am disinclined, because I feel it will make confusion worse confounded and mean waste of energy, time and money. But I may be quite wrong.

Love to you all.

Bapu

CWMG, *Vol. LVI, p. 132*

[443] Not available

## 178. Letter to Jawaharlal Nehru

Wardha
26 October 1933

My dear Jawaharlal,

Herewith resignation from Dr Alam.[444] I have told him that it should have been sent to you. I advise its acceptance. It arises out of a letter of bitter complaint received against him from Lahore. I sent him a copy of it. He strictly denied some of the charges made therein. But accepted the one about practice.

Jamnalalji is anxious about his resignation. My own opinion is that his too should be accepted. He is anxious to go to prison but it worries him that he does not go at once.

I suppose Krishna is now in Bombay.

I see nothing in the papers about Mother nowadays. Is she better?

Vithalbhai's[445] death was fully expected by me but the actuality is disturbing me. His very opposition I valued. It cleared my mind and enabled me to put my position more clearly before the country than I otherwise could have.

Love.

Bapu

Encl.

CWMG, *Vol. LVI, pp. 141–2*

## 179. Letter to M.K. Gandhi

Allahabad
27 October 1933

My dear Bapu,

I should like to have your advice in the matter of Allahabad Congress Hospital. This hospital was situated in Swaraj Bhawan and functioned successfully till the end of 1931 when Swaraj Bhawan

[444] Dr Sheik Mohammad Alam

[445] Vithalbhai Patel (1871–1933); brother of Vallabhbhai; legislator and political leader, and co-founder of the Swaraj Party; died on 22 October in Vienna. For Gandhi's tribute to him, see *CWMG*, Vol. LVI, p. 137.

was seized by the police. All our expensive equipment and medicines—there were even six unopened cases of fresh medicines worth Rs 2,000/- were taken possession of by the police. An ambulance car had the same experience. After some interval, the British authorities, more for show purposes than for anything else, proclaimed that they would continue to keep a dispensary open in Swaraj Bhawan for the public. For the last year or two this dispensary has been supposed to function. But there is no evidence that even a single member of the public has ever taken advantage of it. Some policemen go there occasionally for treatment. Anand Bhawan overlooks Swaraj Bhawan and no one here has seen any patient enter or come out of the place. And yet I am told false entries are made in their books to show that many patients are being treated. However, I am not interested in this.

The Congress Hospital after being turfed out of Swaraj Bhawan had no home and for some weeks it established itself under a big tree in a public park nearby. Medicines were distributed from this open place and in the course of two months under the tree it treated 2,500 outdoor patients.

In April 1932, the hospital was established in a cottage belonging to me. This little house adjoins Swaraj Bhawan on the side away from Anand Bhawan. Previously this house had been rented out. As soon as we could get it vacated we established the hospital there and it has been functioning there ever since. Some threats were made by the authorities but they were ignored. It was also suggested by them that if the word Congress was dropped from the name they would not interfere. This proposal was rejected and the hospital continued to be described on its board as the Congress Hospital and it continued to display the national flag. The Government did not then interfere with it.

Indoor patients were not taken but during the year ending 31st March 1933, as many as 58,000 outdoor patients were treated. During the six months ending 30 September 1933, 37,034 outdoor patients have been treated. We have reduced our maintenance charges very greatly and have spent during the last 18 months Rs 8,360/- over the hospital. This worked out to about Rs 465/- a month. A great part of these funds has been received from the profits of the Allahabad Swadeshi Exhibition. We have not received much directly from the public except medicines and surgical appliances from some firms in Bombay. But a great part of the latter went to the Government. We have now almost exhausted our present resources. Some little money may come to us from the next swadeshi exhibition but such an existence is rather a precarious one and I should have liked to provide for the hospital for at least the next two years. It is doing good work and it has kept the flag flying during a period of considerable difficulty.

Would you advise us to make a public appeal for funds giving the above facts? I am afraid that many people who might otherwise help may not be keen on doing so openly under the existing circumstances although the hospital as such has nothing whatever to do with politics. If a public appeal has to be made who is to make it? The person who is most intimately connected with the hospital is my cousin Mohanlal Nehru.[446] Kamala has also been much interested in it. Of the local committee there is no one of real importance and some of them have practically dropped out during the last two years of storm and stress.

I might mention that in calculating the expenditure of the hospital I have not included house rent. The rent of the house, which used to be Rs 75/- p.m., is my own contribution to the hospital expenses.

Yours affectionately,
Jawaharlal

SWJN, *Vol. 6, I Series, pp. 201–3*

## 180. Letter to Jawaharlal Nehru

30 October 1933

My dear Jawaharlal,
I have your letter about the Hospital. You ought to be able to say without fear of contradiction that the Swaraj Bhawan Dispensary is a perfect fraud and thoroughly boycotted. Without absolute proof, I am disinclined to believe that they fabricate cases. I am anxious to have this evidence, because it is necessary for framing my opinion about the Congress Hospital, for I feel that we should be able to

[446] Secretary, Board of Management, Swaraj Bhawan Trust

take possession of the Swaraj Bhawan strictly for Hospital work, if the Government management has proved to be a fiasco. If you think that the Congress Hospital or Dispensary should be run in the place where it is now being run and that no attempt whatsoever should be made to regain possession of the Swaraj Bhawan, an appeal certainly becomes necessary and then it should be issued in the names of Mohanlal Nehru and Kamala.

I am glad that Mother is making steady progress. Evidently the successful conclusion of the marriage ceremony has also something to do with easing the mental strain she was having.

Andrews is expected here on Wednesday.

I understand what you say about Jamnalalji. When do you think it may be safely announced?

Thakkar Bapa[447] writes saying that you have prohibited Congressmen from working for Harijan cause, even though they may not be offering civil resistance. Where is the truth! I have known nothing about any such embargo.

Love.

Bapu

CWMG, *Vol. LVI, pp. 160–1*

## 181. Letter to Jawaharlal Nehru

1 November 1933

My dear Jawaharlal,

Your several letters to hand. I see you have handed to the Press the two resignations.[448] They should clear the air a bit.

I do not follow the Hindu Sabha activities. They are vicious. It is most unscrupulous if they are making use of my name in connection with *shuddhi*.[449] If you have any literature please pass it on to me. I think that the nationalist Press so called or real has not welcomed its activities and has been known often to condemn it. I do not know anything about the embargo on M.A.K. Azad's book. As to the Harijan activities, the complaint is wholly unjustified. My

[447] Amritlal Thakkar of the Servants of India Society

[448] Of Jamnalal Bajaj and Dr Alam

[449] Literally 'purificatory rite'; here, reconversion

conscience is absolutely clear. So far as you and I are concerned, we can clear our minds and hands by exchanging letters, if you like. I do not know what aggressive action is possible or desirable beyond an emphatic condemnation of specific acts.

As to Gorakhpur, I do not see what can be done. I am finding it hard to get funds for your workers and the Dal people. I am still talking about both. Baba Raghavdas[450] told me he was trying grain collections for the peasants in distress. He is under promise to send me authentic details of persecution.

Nariman[451] was here yesterday. I have advised him to see you and told him that you were my political chief! What else could I do? I stand thoroughly discredited as a religious maniac and predominantly a social worker. I told him that if I felt convinced that the AICC members desired discontinuance of CD and a council-entry programme, I would at once ask you to convene a meeting of AICC. I do not do so because I believe that the majority will insist on a CD programme and I do not want to invite the ordinance sword for it. I have told him too that I would not resist any programme that the AICC might want though I could not give my approval to the suspension of CD. I believe Kelkar's attitude to be honest and consistent. He frankly dislikes NCO and CD. He would not join the terrorists or whatever they may be called. Then for a man of political activity, Council-entry is the only programme such as it is. Hopeless inactivity is the worst of all and should be discountenanced.

I think I have now covered all the points raised in your letters and even not raised. It is nearing 4 a.m.

Hope Mother's progress continuing. Herewith note for Kamala.

Love.

Bapu

CWMG, *Vol. LVI, pp. 167–8*

[450] A peasant leader of UP

[451] K.F. Nariman

## 182. Letter to Jawaharlal Nehru

3 November 1933

My dear Jawaharlal,

My own opinion is that the atrocities such as are referred to in the Frontier Province note should first be dealt with privately, and all the means that we can employ to induce the authorities to adopt less cruel measures should be employed. I am asking Andrews to deal with the Frontier Province note. And if you have no objection I would like you to show the note to Sir Tej Bahadur and see what he has got to say and if he is at all inclined to move.

I enclose herewith a copy of my letter to the Governor of Bengal about what is going on in Hijli.[452]

Love.

Bapu

CWMG, *Vol. LVI, p. 180*

## 183. Letter to Jawaharlal Nehru

Wardha
11 November 1933

My dear Jawaharlal,

I have just returned from a heavy tour[453] programme and having read your letter telegraphed as follows:

Find unable give two days. Can give three hours any Monday afternoon. Twenty-seventh instant Raipur. Fourth December Jubbulpore.

It is impossible to give more than one day and more than three hours. It is difficult enough even to give three hours. The programme is so packed that hardly any time is given for rest. Four hours for rest, bath and dinner, have hitherto dwindled down to two. A programme in which tens of thousands of people are

[452] This was in response to Satis Chandra Das Gupta's description in his letter to Gandhi about the inhuman treatment meted out to his brother Kshitish Chandra and other prisoners in Hijli jail for their refusal to salute (salaam) the jail authorities.

[453] The Harijan tour, the first lap of which commenced on 7 November 1933

concerned cannot easily be postponed or disturbed. The enclosed copy[454] will give you an idea of the work, and where you find hours of rest, except for Friday afternoon, they have been encroached upon, changing the time from 10 a.m. to 2 p.m. to 12 O'clock to 2 p.m.

I entirely agree with you that the proposed conversation will not clarify matters to any satisfactory extent. If the AICC meeting is held, I do not know how I shall be able to attend the sittings. Will it not be better for me to abstain from attending? If it is desirable, I will send my views in writing. The opinion I have expressed in my public letter to you is becoming more and more confirmed.[455]

You must have seen Lahiri's statement about the Hijli Prison. It more than confirms Satisbabu's letter. I have heard from the Governor. His Secretary says that 'His Excellency will look into the matter to which you refer'.[456]

I have read the appeal for the Hospital. I hope it will have the response it deserves.

I carefully read your letter about the Government demand. In anything you do about Swaraj Bhawan, do you not think that you should consult the trustees and not merely inform them? I have not been able even to show your letter to Jamnalalji for sheer want of time. He twits me by saying that as I am in Wardha you are ignoring him entirely, not even acknowledging his letters. I told him that your letters to me are as much for him as for me and that just now the few of us who are out have little time for performing acts of mere courtesy.

You cannot expect rapid progress for an old patient like Mother. The wonder to me is that she has survived the attack she had. I hope the progress though slow continues.

Love.

Bapu

G-N Correspondence, *JN Papers, NMML*

[454] Of the tour programme; for details see *CWMG*, Vol. LVI, Appendix I.

[455] See pp. 193–7.

[456] This was in reply to Gandhi's letter of 2 November to the Governor of Bengal.

## 184. Letter to Jawaharlal Nehru

13 November 1933

My dear Jawaharlal,

I have just arrived in Chanda and whilst the others are coming, I have taken up your letter. It is now 9 p.m. The programme is fairly strenuous. I was in Hinganghat at 6 p.m.

Tiwari[457] has handed me your letter. I have also read yours to J.[458] So far as he knows there is probably very little left in AICC a/c. The books are not with him. He has sent for the accounts. Meanwhile I have suggested that Rs 500 might be sent at least on a/c. If the funds are exhausted, I do not know what is to be done. I have an earmarked a/c at my disposal. I am loath to part with that fund. I am drawing upon it for Hardikar and I want to do likewise for the list of workers you have sent me. It too will be soon exhausted. In the circumstances, the office staff has to be reduced if not given up altogether, i.e., if the civil resistance movement is to continue. The more I look about me, the more convinced I feel that those who are in the fight will have to do without funds except such as may remain in hands such as mine. Have just managed for Gujarat and Karnataka. The lady who was to have paid Rs 50,000 has just sent the message that she would like to pay Rs 10,000 to you. If she does, I shall expect you to pay the UP workers out of this. Anyway I think it is best for you to confer with Jamnalalji and if necessary with me as to the management of the funds that are still available. I have sent notices everywhere that no more help need be expected through me. I am trying to run through whatever is at my disposal.

Now about the informal meeting. You will see from the programme herewith that I am in Delhi between 10 and 14 December. Thakkar Bapa says I can take up the bulk of 14th for our meeting. I am supposed to entrain for Andhra on 14th immediately after 4 p.m. Ansari who was with me on Sunday suggested Delhi. You

[457] Venkatesh Narayan Tivary (1890–1965); General Secretary, UP PCC, 1914–18; Editor, *Abhyudaya*; Member, UP PCC's Committee on Agrarian Distress, 1931; Member, UP Legislative Assembly, 1937–9 and 1946–52; Member, Constituent Assembly, 1946–50; Member, Lok Sabha, 1952–7

[458] Jamnalal Bajaj, who was the AICC treasurer at this time

will now make your choice—24th instant, 4th Dec., or 14th Dec., i.e., if the conference is to come off at all.[459]

As to the Harijan tour, I am not worrying at all over the proposed boycott in UP. I am finding no difficulty here. Congressmen and non-Congressmen are cooperating in arranging for the tour. You are unnecessarily hard on the liberals whom I would include among non-Congressmen. We have to get work even from them. They work according to their lights. In any case, I do not want a single Congressman to work for this movement who would [not] go to jail. I have said this to everyone who has come to me. I am sending back some of the best workers who have just come out. Ba I hope is going soon and so is Manibehn Patel. Kakasaheb,[460] Swami,[461] Surendra are going. Those Congressmen who are too weak to go or who have lost faith in civil disobedience and who are anxious to work for the Harijan cause I am taking, but not those who want Harijan work as a mere cloak. This movement, if it is to become universal, must be able to continue even if every Congressman is in jail or it must perish. I feel too that Congressmen should not handle this movement to strengthen the CD movement or the Congress hold on the people. It would be going about it the wrong way. Such an attitude will damage both the Congress and the Harijan cause. Cases of this type have come under my notice. I have expressed strong disapproval of any such work. I think I have now sufficiently answered all your questions. If not, please ask again.

You will have noticed that the Sarkar Salaam in Hijli has stopped.[462] Shall I write to Sir Tej about the Frontier treatment?

I had a nice letter from Krishna. She seems to be happy in her new home.

I hope Mother's progress continues.

Love.

Bapu

CWMG, *Vol. LVI, pp. 220–2*

[459] Gandhi conferred with Nehru, Abul Kalam Azad, Dr Syed Mahmud and Jamnalal Bajaj at Jubbalpore on 5 December. He continued discussions with the leaders at Delhi.

[460] D.B. Kalelkar

[461] Swami Anand

[462] See p. 211.

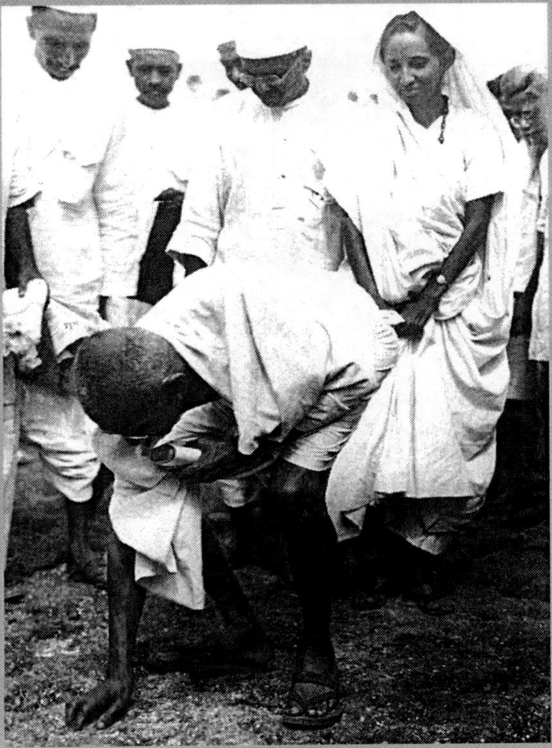

Salt Satyagraha—Gandhi picking up salt

Gandhi being shaved, Allahabad, 1939

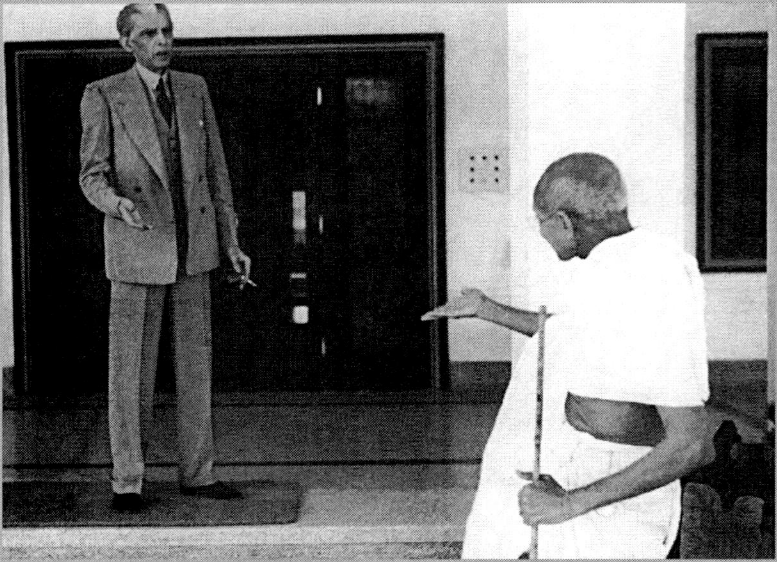

Gandhi and Mohammad Ali Jinnah meeting before talks with the Viceroy, 24 November 1939

Gandhi, with Mahadev Desai, leaving Delhi Jail after an interview with State prisoners, 15 March 1939

Gandhi and Nehru in conversation at Bhangi Colony in Delhi on Gandhi's 77th birthday

'The Elusive Mahatma'

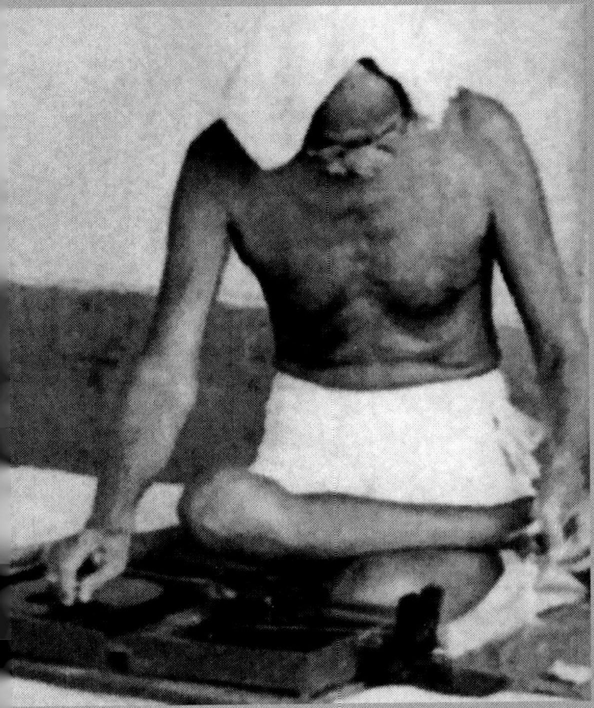

Gandhi and Nehru spinning khadi

Gandhi and Subhas Chandra Bose at the Haripura Congress, 19 February 1938

Nehru in jail, 1921

Nehru with daughter Indira, signing copies of his book *The Discovery of India*

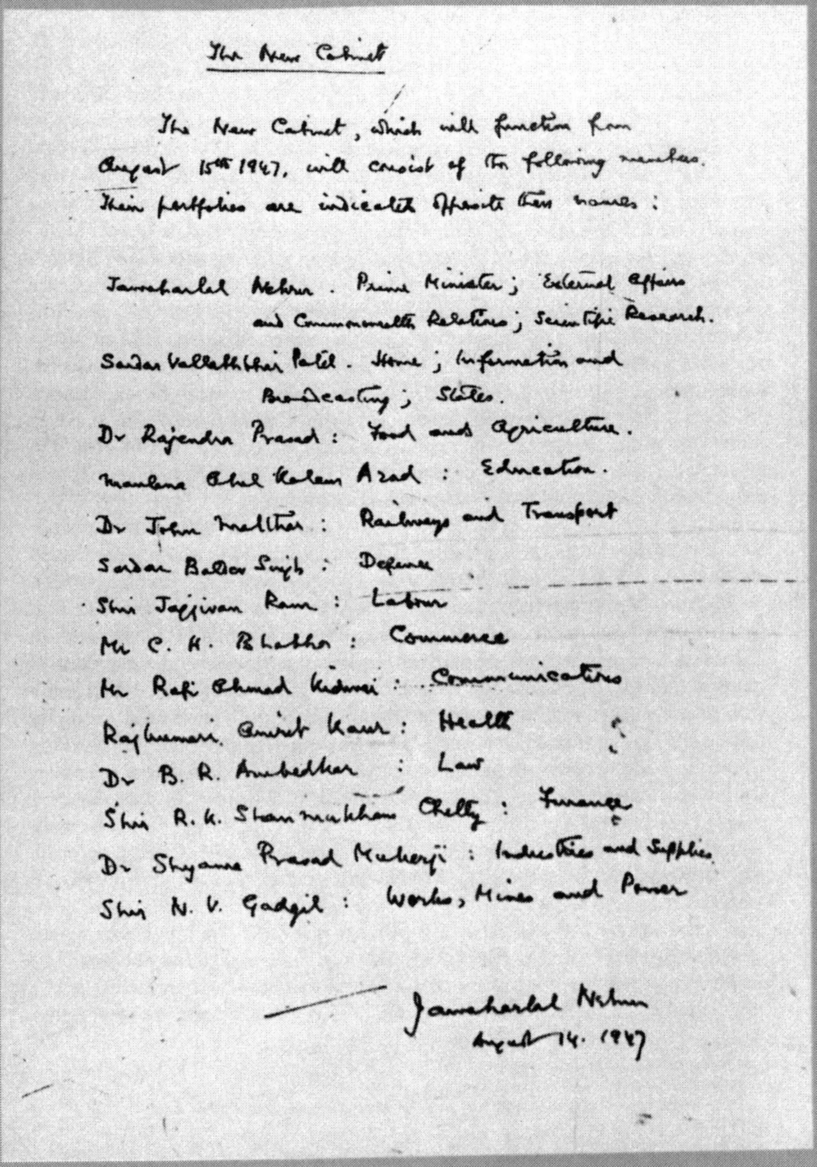

The New Cabinet

The New Cabinet, which will function from August 15th 1947, will consist of the following members. Their portfolios are indicated opposite their names:

Jawaharlal Nehru. Prime Minister; External Affairs and Commonwealth Relations; Scientific Research.

Sardar Vallabhbhai Patel. Home; Information and Broadcasting; States.

Dr Rajendra Prasad: Food and Agriculture.

Maulana Abul Kalam Azad: Education.

Dr John Matthai: Railways and Transport

Sardar Baldev Singh: Defence

Shri Jagjivan Ram: Labour

Mr C. H. Bhabha: Commerce

Mr Rafi Ahmad Kidwai: Communications

Rajkumari Amrit Kaur: Health

Dr B. R. Ambedkar: Law

Shri R. K. Shanmukham Chetty: Finance

Dr Shyama Prasad Mukerji: Industries and Supplies

Shri N. V. Gadgil: Works, Mines and Power

Jawaharlal Nehru
August 14. 1947

Jawaharlal's first Cabinet List

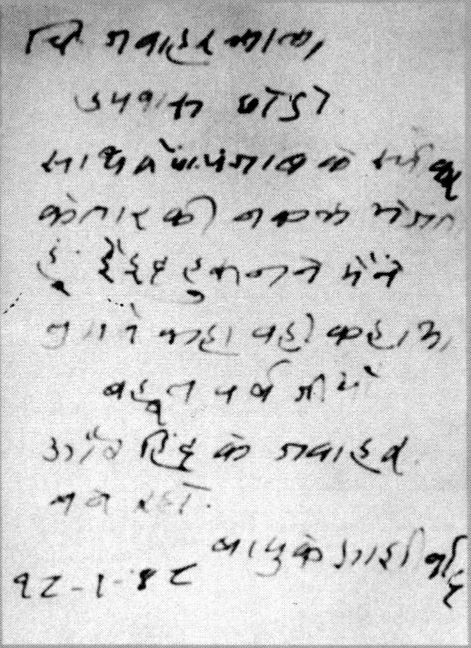

Gandhi's last letter to Nehru

'The Light has gone out of our lives'

## 185. Letter to M.K. Gandhi

Allahabad
20 November 1933

My dear Bapu,

I am sorry for the delay in writing to you. It is difficult to know where to write as you are moving about, and I have recently had a full share of work which has given me no breathing time—meetings, consultations, workers coming, peasants, etc., and there is a huge correspondence without any staff to deal with it. I am afraid I am guilty or have been guilty of not answering letters promptly and Jamnalalji is entitled to complain. But I thought that my letters to you were bound to be shared by him.

About the Swaraj Bhawan Trust matters you are perfectly right that I should refer to the trustees.[463] It was my intention to do so and I shall now take the necessary steps.

I am very sorry to learn that you cannot find time—except three hours on a Monday afternoon—to give to a consultation with some of us. I suppose we must be content with that. I feel that we must meet to clear up certain matters—not fundamental policies but procedure. I was waiting to hear from Ansari. As he did not write I wired to him and he replied that we might meet on December 4th at Jubbulpore but he preferred December 10th at Delhi. I sent an answer to him that December 4th was late enough and we should meet then. To that I have had no reply. I am now provisionally fixing 4th and informing others accordingly.

As for the AICC it still hangs in the air though a requisition is threatened from time to time. I think it will materialise. I feel that you should attend it even though you may not take an active part in it. If necessary your tour programme might be varied to fit in with it. Changes in the programme have already been made and this is not impossible. However it is for you to decide.

I have just received intimation that some old railway and other shares standing in my name have been attached on account of my income tax. The value at par of these shares was about Rs 20,000. I suppose the present value is much less—probably about 13,000/-

[463] See pp. 206–9 and 193.

or 14,000/-. Previously they had realised other moneys from a sale of a car, etc.

I wonder if you have noticed my gentle comment on the Hindu Mahasabha and the still more gentle rejoinder.[464] I have enjoyed them greatly.

Yours affectionately,
Jawaharlal

SWJN, *Vol. 6, I Series, pp. 68–9*

## 186. Letter to Jawaharlal Nehru

27 November 1933

My dear Jawaharlal,
Here is Gasavi's letter. I am telling him, I see no objection to the Party so long as it is not claimed as the Congress Party and that in any case he should seek your advice.

I note that we are to meet at Jubbulpore on 5th December. I shall try to give more time, if it is at all possible.

Have I not sent you the programme for CP?[465] More than that was not ready till now.

So you are being gradually disburdened of shares and the like. I am not sorry. From my point of view the ideal thing would be a voluntary surrender of all the property you have, either to an institution or to those members of the family who do not want to throw themselves into the battle which is bound to be prolonged

[464] Speaking at the Banaras Hindu University on 12 November 1933, Nehru had said, 'Under cover of seeming nationalism, the Mahasabha not only hides the rankest and narrowest communalism but also desires to preserve the vested interests of the group of big Hindu landlords and the princes. ... The Mahasabha shows its attachment to vested interests by openly condemning every form of socialism and social change. Anything more degrading, reactionary, anti-national, anti-progressive and harmful than the present policy of the Hindu Mahasabha is difficult to imagine.'

In a letter published in *The Leader* of 20 November 1933, Bhai Paramanand had said that owing to his [Nehru's] 'early training' and upbringing abroad 'he is incapable of thinking as a Hindu'.

[465] The former Central Provinces, the major portion of which now forms the state of Madhya Pradesh

and perhaps increasingly bitter. In the final heat only those will be able to stand who have no property and nowhere to rest their heads on. But it is no use worrying over the future. Whatever happens you will be found in the front rank.

I am glad that Mother is making steady progress. I wonder if she knows all that is happening.

Yes, I did read your attack on the Hindu Sabha. It might have been less fierce. The summary made you speak like a partisan.

Love.

Bapu

[PS]

You will find the dates in the enclosed programme.[466]

CWMG, *Vol. LVI, p. 291*

## 187. Letter to Jawaharlal Nehru

26 December 1933

My dear Jawaharlal,

Here is a cutting from the *M. Mail.*[467] Though the whole conversation practically referred to you and your views, naturally the interviewer could not reproduce it all. I was shown the proof. It is a fair presentation of the substance of what I said. Please read it carefully and correct me where you find me to have erred about yourself. There is a great deal of misunderstanding about you in our circles too. But it does not worry me.

You will find also the programme so far as it goes.

I hope Mother is progressing.

Love.

Bapu

CWMG, *Vol. LVI, p. 404*

[466] For the circular regarding changes in the tour programme, see *CWMG*, Vol. LVI, pp. 502–3.

[467] For 'Interview to *The Madras Mail*', see *CWMG*, Vol. LVI, pp. 382–5.

## 188. Letter to Jawaharlal Nehru

The Cape
21 January 1934

My dear Jawaharlal,

I have your three letters[468] before me. As to the money, I thought you had it already. I had issued instructions. I am sending a reminder.

I hope the consultation in Calcutta has resulted in some good to Kamala.

I had no desire to apologise for you. The interview represents the interviewer's impressions. But there is no apology there. I have given my full interpretation of your mind and actions. I do feel that your concrete programme is still in the melting pot. You are too honest to say: 'I know the whole of my programme today.' You have no uncertainty about the science of socialism but you do not know in full how you will apply it when you have the power.

You have unnecessarily raised the question of your place in the Congress. So far as I am concerned, you do not disturb me at all. I should be myself in a wilderness without you in the Congress.

More I need not say now. I have not the time either to give you a longer letter.

I have received your notice about 26th. I could not have issued it unless I was in a position to say definitely what to do. But I do not mind it.

A brief telegram in the *Hindu* about Government measures in Midnapur has however dazed me. The measures appear to be worse than the Punjab measures of 1919.[469] The shock is almost unbearable. Our cowardice disconcerts me. Not knowing what the papers are saying, if anything at all, I may be wrong in my analysis. I have never felt so helpless as I do at the present moment.

I have written to Dr Bidhan and to Gurudev.[470]

[468] Not available

[469] The year of the Jallianwallah massacre at Amritsar in the Punjab

[470] Dr B.C. Roy and Rabindranath Tagore to whom Gandhi wrote on 21 January regarding the Ordinances promulgated consequent upon the assassination of B.E.G. Burge, the District Magistrate of Midnapore, by three Bengali youths on 2 September 1933. See *CWMG*, Vol. LVII, p. 29.

I hope Mother is better.
What about Rafi?
Love.

Bapu

[PS]
Jayaprakash had written to me about his affair and I wrote to him at length. His brother[471] will have the scholarship. With the burdens he has, he should really begin to earn. But he won't. I am keeping in touch with him.

CWMG, *Vol. LVII, pp. 30–1*

## 189. Letter to Jawaharlal Nehru

Gauhati
14 April 1934

My dear Jawaharlal,
I got up this morning at 12.15 in order to overtake arrears.

You have been ever in my mind. I hope you will be permitted to receive this letter.[472] I would like a line from you to tell me how you are keeping and what you are doing.

You must have seen my two decisions.[473] That they are almost simultaneous is a mere coincidence. The revival of the Swaraj Party is a right step. There is no doubt that we have in the Congress a body of men who believe in Council-entry and who will do nothing else if they cannot have that programme. Their ambition must

[471] Rajeshwar Narayan

[472] Nehru was in Alipore Central Jail at this time, having been sentenced on 16 February 1934 to two years' rigorous imprisonment for sedition.

[473] Taken at a meeting held in Delhi on 31 March 1934, attended by Madan Mohan Malaviya, Dr B.C. Roy, Khaliquzzaman, G.B. Pant and other Congress leaders. It was decided to re-form the Swaraj Party and take part in the elections for the Central Assembly. (For Gandhi's letter to Dr M.A. Ansari regarding the revival of the Swaraj Party, see *CWMG*, Vol. LVII, pp. 352–3.) The other was Gandhi's decision to confine civil resistance to himself. In a statement to the press at Saharsa on 2 April 1934, Gandhi had said, 'The introspection prompted by the conversation with the Ashram inmates has led me to the conclusion that I must advise all Congressmen to suspend civil resistance for swaraj as distinguished from specific grievances. They should leave it to me.' Ibid., pp. 348–50 and 361–4.

be satisfied. The other decision about confining CR to myself so far as the goal is concerned is much the most important. It was inevitable. Having arrived at it, I can see the rightness of the decision for a thousand reasons. I have given the precipitating cause. But the decision was slowly coming to me. I do hope that you have not been upset by it. You were before my mind's eye the whole time the decision was taking shape. I concluded that, though it might produce a momentary shock, you would ultimately see the truth of it and be glad. I wonder!

We all often talk about you. We are a large party. I was with Mother and the members of the family for nearly two hours when I passed through Allahabad.

Love.

Bapu

CWMG, *Vol. LVII, p. 388*

## 190. Letter to M.K. Gandhi

Allahabad
13 August 1934

My dear Bapu,

Thank you for your telegram[474]—we are all happy to think that you have successfully passed through—or will pass through in a few more hours—your latest self-imposed ordeal.[475] My temporary discharge has undoubtedly done good to Kamala.[476] Fundamentally she may not be much better but the psychological effect has been marked and of course this is a great help in her treatment. She has really been continuously ill, more or less, for the last year or so***[477] I am in a peculiar position. On arrival at Allahabad I was met by the district magistrate who told me that the UP government had ordered that I should be permitted to visit my wife and remain

[474] Not available

[475] Gandhi had started his seven-day fast on 7 August 1934 as a penance for the acts of violence committed on the Sanatanists at Ajmer. He believed that self-purification was necessary for the removal of untouchability.

[476] Nehru was on parole from 12–23 August 1934 on account of Kamala's illness.

[477] The asterisks in the text indicate portions censored by the Home Department.

with her for two days, and for a longer period if the doctors considered that her condition was still one of serious illness. There were no conditions, he added, only my parole and that I would go back to prison at the end of this period. I told him that I was grateful to the UP government for their courtesy in permitting me to visit my ailing wife but I regretted that I was quite unable to give any undertaking on parole however this might be put. As for going back to prison it was open to them always to take me there. I was not likely to run away or hide myself, nor was I interested in raising legal quibbles. This answer of mine put the magistrate in a quandary. Eventually he allowed me to go home for the night and said that he would communicate with the Chief Secretary by telephone and let me know the next day (that is today). I reached home at about 8.45 p.m. last night. The same night at about 10 p.m. I sent a letter to the district magistrate repeating what I had told him orally. The answer to that came this afternoon. He said that he quite understood my difficulty in giving any undertaking. But I had recognised the courtesy of the UP Government in allowing me to visit my wife and in a similar manner I rely on your courtesy and good sense to do nothing to compromise the present position. The present undertaking will remain in force at least till Wednesday morning, by which time I hope to have received further instructions from the UP Government. So that is how matters stand. I am somewhere in mid-air.

It is clear that the Government do not wish to have me out of prison at any rate till the next Congress is over. I am inclined to think that I shall be taken back to prison soon. I shall be kept in Nainital this time and can be easily accessible in case of need. I am very glad, however, that I was given this opportunity of seeing Kamala, mother and others. This has done her good and done me good. Mother has been down with dysentery*** After just six months of absolute seclusion and anxiety, excitement and activity of the past 27 hours, I feel very tired. I am writing this letter to you at midnight.[478] All day there have been crowds of

[478] Lord Willingdon who had seen a copy of this letter made by the police, described it in his letter of 24 September to Hoare, as 'this very human document'.

people coming. If I have the chance I shall write to you again but I doubt if I shall be able to do so for some months. I am therefore going to indicate to you briefly how I have reacted to the various major Congress decisions of the last five months or so. My sources of information have naturally been strictly limited but I think that they were sufficient to enable me to form a fairly correct idea of the general trend of events.

When I heard that you had called off the civil disobedience movement, I felt unhappy. Only the brief announcement reached me at first. Much later I read your statement and this gave me one of the biggest shocks I have ever had. I was prepared to reconcile myself to the withdrawal of civil disobedience. But the reasons you gave for doing so and the suggestions you made for future work astounded me. I had a sudden and intense feeling that something broke inside me, a bond that I have valued very greatly had snapped. I felt terribly lonely in this wide world. I have always felt a little lonely almost from childhood up. But a few bonds strengthened me, a few strong supports held me up. The loneliness never went, but it was lessened. But now I felt absolutely alone, left high and dry on a desert island.

Human beings have an enormous capacity for adapting themselves and so I too adapted myself to some extent to the new conditions. The keenness of my feelings on the subject, which amounted almost to physical pain, passed off; the edge was dulled. But shock after shock, a succession of events sharpened that edge to a fine point, and allowed my mind or feelings no peace or rest. Again I felt that sensation of spiritual isolation, of being a perfect stranger out of harmony, not only with the crowds that passed me, but also with those whom I had valued as dear and close comrades. My stay in prison this time became a greater ordeal for my nerves than any previous visit had been. I almost wished that all newspapers might be kept away from me so that I might be spared these repeated shocks.

Physically I kept fairly well. I always do in prison. My body has served me well and can stand a deal of ill-treatment and strain. And being vain enough to imagine that perhaps I might yet do some effective work in this land to which fate had tied me, I looked after it well.

But I wondered often enough if I was not a square peg in a round hole, or a bubble of conceit thrown about hither and thither on an ocean which spurned me. But vanity and conceit triumphed and the intellectual apparatus that functions within me refused to admit defeat. If the ideals that had spurred me to action and had kept me buoyed up through stormy weather were right—and the conviction of their rightness ever grew within me—they were bound to triumph though my generation might not live to witness that triumph.

But what had happened to those ideals during these long and weary months of this year when I was a silent and distant witness, fretting at my helplessness? Setbacks and temporary defeats are common enough in all great struggles. They grieve but one recovers soon enough. One recovers soon if the light of those ideals is not allowed to grow dim and the anchor of principles holds fast. But what I saw was not setback and defeat but that spiritual defeat which is the most terrible of all. Do not imagine that I am referring to the Council-entry question.[479] I do not attach vital importance to it. Under certain circumstances I can even imagine entering a legislature myself. But whether I function inside or outside the legislature, I function as a revolutionary, meaning thereby a person working for fundamental and revolutionary changes, political and social, for I am convinced that no other change can bring peace or satisfaction to India and the world.

So I thought. Not so, evidently, the leaders who were functioning outside. They began to talk the language of an age gone by before the heady wine of noncooperation and civil disobedience had fired our heads. Sometimes they used the same words and phrases but they were dead without life or real meaning. The leading figures of the Congress suddenly became those people who had obstructed us, held us back, kept aloof from the struggle and even cooperated with the opposite party in the time of our direst need. They became

[479] The AICC meeting at Patna on 18 and 19 May 1934 endorsed Gandhi's statement of 7 April suspending Civil Disobedience by individual Congressmen excepting himself. A resolution sponsored by Gandhi was passed allowing Congressmen to enter Councils and a Parliamentary Board was constituted under Malaviya and Ansari.

the high priests in our temple of freedom and many a brave soldier who had shouldered the burden in the heat and dust of the fray was not even allowed inside the temple precincts. He and many like him had become untouchables and unapproachable. And if he ventured to raise his voice and criticise the new high priests, he was shouted down and told that he was a traitor to the cause because he spoilt the harmony of the sacred precincts.

And so the flag of Indian freedom was entrusted with all pomp and circumstance to those who had actually hauled it down at the height of our national struggle at the bidding of the enemy; to those who had proclaimed from the house-tops that they had given up politics (for politics were unsafe then), but who emerged with a jump to the front ranks when politics became safe.[480]

And what of the ideals they set forth before them, speaking as they did on behalf of the Congress and the nation? A pitiful hotch-potch, avoiding real issues, toning down, as far as they dared, even the political objective of the Congress, expressing a tender solicitude for every vested interest, bowing down to many a declared enemy of freedom, but showing great turbulence and courage in facing the advanced and fighting elements in the Congress ranks. Is not the Congress being rapidly reduced to a magnified edition of that shameful spectacle, the Calcutta Corporation, during the last few years? Might not the dominant part of the Bengal Congress be called today 'the society for the advancement of Mr Nalini Ranjan Sarkar',[481] a gentleman who

[480] Referring to the incident in his *Autobiography*, Nehru writes, 'One feature of these early months [1931] pained me greatly. This was the hauling down of our national Flag by various municipalities and public bodies, and especially by the Calcutta Corporation which was said to have a majority of Congress members. The flag was taken down under pressure from the police and the Government, which threatened severe action in case of non-compliance. ... And those who submitted in this way lowered the morale of the nation, and injured its self-respect.'

[481] (1888–1953); Mayor of Calcutta, 1934; Finance Minister, Government of Bengal, 1938–9 and 1941–2; Member, Viceroy's Executive Council, 1942–3; acting Chief Minister, West Bengal, during B.C. Roy's absence in 1949

N.R. Sarkar was elected Mayor in July 1934 defeating Fazlul Huq, with the European members voting for him. See also Nehru's note on the Congress rejoiced to entertain government officials, Home Members and the like when most of us were in prison and civil disobedience was supposed to be flourishing? And the other part probably a similar society for a similar laudable object? But the fault does not lie with Bengal alone. Almost everywhere there is a similar outlook. The Congress from top to bottom is a caucus and opportunism triumphs.

The Working Committee is not directly responsible for this state of affairs. But nonetheless the Working Committee must shoulder the responsibility. It is the leaders and their policy that shape the activities of the followers. It is neither fair nor just to throw the blame on the followers. Every language has some saying about the workman blaming his tools. The Committee had deliberately encouraged vagueness in the definition of our ideals and objectives and this is bound to lead not only to confusion but to demoralisation during periods of reaction, and to the emergence of the demagogue and the reactionary.

I am referring especially to the political objectives which are the special province of the Congress. I feel that the time is overdue for the Congress to think clearly on social and economic issues but I recognise that education on these issues takes time and the Congress as a whole may not be able to go as far at present as I would like it to. But it appears that whether the Working Committee knows anything about the subject or not it is perfectly willing to denounce and excommunicate people who happen to have made a special study of the subject and hold certain views. No attempt is made to understand those views, which, it is notorious, are held by a very large number of the ablest and most self-sacrificing people in the world. Those views may be right or wrong but they deserve at

---

Programme presumably written in August 1934 (*SWJN*, Vol. 6, pp. 270–2), where he had written, 'We have seen the disgusting antics of the Calcutta Corporation under Congress control. One Congress party there cooperates with the officials and the European group against another Congress party. That party might be called the Society for the Advancement of Mr Nalini Ranjan Sarkar. Other parties in Calcutta and elsewhere seek other people's advancement. The whole of Congress is now likely to go the way of the Calcutta Corporation.'

least some understanding before the Working Committee sets out to denounce them. It is hardly becoming for a reasoned argument to be answered by sentimental appeals or by the cheap remark that conditions in India are different and the economic laws that apply elsewhere do not function here. The resolution of the Working Committee on the subject showed such astounding ignorance of the elements of socialism that it was painful to read it and to realise that it might be read outside India. It seemed that the overmastering desire of the Committee was somehow to assure various vested interests even at the risk of talking nonsense.[482]

A strange way of dealing with the subject of socialism is to use the word, which has a clearly defined meaning in the English language, in a totally different sense. For individuals to use words in a sense peculiar to themselves is not helpful in the commerce of ideas. A person who declares himself to be an engine-driver and then adds that his engine is of wood and is drawn by bullocks is misusing the word engine-driver.

This letter has become a much longer one than I expected and the night is already far spent. Probably I have written in a confused and scrappy way for my brain is tired. But still it will convey some picture of my mind. The last few months have been very painful ones for me and, I take it, for many others. I have felt sometimes that in the modern world, and perhaps in the ancient world also, it is often preferred to break some people's hearts rather than touch others' pockets. Pockets are indeed more valuable and more cherished than hearts and brains and bodies and human justice and dignity!

There is one other subject I should like to mention. That is the Swaraj Bhawan Trust. I understand that the Working Committee recently considered the question of the upkeep of Swaraj Bhawan and came to the conclusion that it was not responsible for it. As however it had already made a grant about three years ago and this had not been paid yet, although expenses were incurred on the

[482] The reference is to the Working Committee Resolution passed on 18 June 1934. See Appendix III in this volume. See also the following item.

strength of it, a fresh grant was sanctioned.[483] This will probably be enough for some months. In regard to the future the Working Committee was evidently anxious not to be saddled with the burden of maintaining the house and grounds. This burden amounts to Rs 100 a month, which includes taxes, etc. The trustees, I understand, were also a little frightened of the burden and suggested that parts of the house might be let in the ordinary way to raise money for maintenance. Another suggestion was made that part of the grounds might be sold off for this purpose. I was surprised to learn of these suggestions, as some of them seemed to me to be contrary to the letter of the trust and all of them against its spirit. As an individual trustee I have only one voice in the matter but I should like to say that I have the strongest possible objection to any such misuse of the trust property. The very idea of the wishes of my father being flouted in this way is intolerable to me. The trust represented not only his wishes but was also in a small way a memorial to him and his wishes, and his memory is dearer to me than a hundred rupees a month. I should, therefore, like to assure the Working Committee and the trustees that they need have no anxiety on the score of the money required for maintenance of the property. As soon as the present funds, now granted by the Working Committee for some months, are exhausted, I shall make myself personally responsible for the maintenance and no further grant need be made by the Committee. I would also beg the trustees to respect my feelings in this matter and not to break up the property or to hire it out for the sake of hiring it out. I shall endeavour to maintain the Swaraj Bhawan till such time as it is put to some worthy use.

I have not the figures by me but I believe that even thus far the Swaraj Bhawan has not been, in any sense, a financial burden on the Working Committee. The grants that have been paid to it will probably not be much in excess of reasonable rent for the quarters occupied by the office of the AICC. This rent could have been reduced by occupying smaller and cheaper quarters. At the same

[483] On 28 July 1934, a resolution was passed granting money, as a special case, for the maintenance and repairs of the house.

time in the past the AICC has paid as much as Rs 150/- a month for rent of an upper floor only in Madras.

Perhaps some parts of this letter might pain you. But you would not have me hide my heart from you.

I received your short note in Alipore jail and I sent an answer. But the superintendent suppressed that answer.

Yours affectionately,
Jawahar

SWJN, *Vol. 6, I Series, pp. 277–82*

## 191. Telegram to M.K. Gandhi

[14 August 1934][484]

I have been permitted to stay with Kamala. The position is not clear. Hope you are well.

G-N Correspondence, JN Papers, *NMML*

## 192. Letter to Jawaharlal Nehru

14 August 1934

My dear Jawaharlal,

Though you are now under distressing circumstances, your release takes a great load off my mind, as it is three-fourths medicine for Kamala. I have missed you greatly during all the momentous steps I have taken. But of these when we meet.

I am well, though the last day proved the most trying of all the days and washed me out thoroughly. But I have no doubt that I shall pick up quickly.

This is however to suggest to you that you should not make any public political pronouncement. I have felt that in cases of domestic illness or sorrow the Government has acted in a becoming manner. I do feel therefore that we ought to recognise this fact by not using the liberty thus obtained for any other purpose not inconsistent with that of the Government. I feel that this is due to them and to ourselves, especially when civil resistance is suspended. If my argument appeals to your reason, you will announce your

[484] Inferred from Gandhi's reply

self-restraint in a fitting manner. When Kamala is better I expect you to come here. I shall be in Wardha up to the end of the month, except that I might have to go to Bombay to attend the delicate operation that Jamnalalji might have to go through during the month.[485]

I hope Mama is doing well and so [also] Krishna. You will let me know how you have fared this time in jail.

Love.

Bapu

CWMG, *Vol. LVIII, pp. 303–4*

## 193. Letter to Jawaharlal Nehru

17 August 1934

My dear Jawaharlal,

Your passionate and touching letter[486] deserves a much longer reply than my strength will permit.

I had expected fuller grace from the Government. However your presence has done for Kamala and incidentally for Mama what no drugs or doctors could have done. I hope that you will be allowed to remain longer than the very few days you expect.

I understand your deep sorrow. You are quite right in giving full and free expression to your feelings. But I am quite sure that from our common standpoint a closer study of the written word will show you that there is not enough reason for all the grief and disappointment you have felt. Let me assure you that you have not lost a comrade in me. I am the same as you knew me in 1917 and after. I have the same passion that you knew me to possess for the common goal. I want complete independence for the country in the full English sense of the term. And every resolution that has pained you had been framed with that end in view. I must take full responsibility for the resolutions and the whole conception surrounding them.

[485] Jamnalal Bajaj was operated upon for ear trouble on 16 August in Bombay.

[486] Of 13 August 1934

But I fancy that I have the knack for knowing the need of the time. And the resolutions are a response thereto. Of course here comes in the difference of our emphasis on the method or the means which to me are just as important as the goal and in a sense more important in that we have some control over them whereas we have none over the goal if we lose control over the means.

Do read the resolution about 'loose talk' dispassionately.[487] There is not a word in it about socialism. Greatest consideration has been paid to the socialists some of whom I know so intimately. Do I not know their sacrifice? But I have found them as a body to be in a hurry. Why should they not be? Only, if I cannot march quite as quick, I must ask them to halt and take me along with them. That is literally my attitude. I have looked up the dictionary meaning of socialism. It takes me no further than where I was before I read the definition. What will you have me to read to know its full content? I have read one of the books Masani[488] gave me and now I am devoting all my spare time to reading the book recommended by Narendra Deva.[489]

You are hard on the members of the Working Committee. They are our colleagues such as they are. After all we are a free institution. They must be displaced, if they do not deserve confidence. But it is wrong to blame them for their inability to undergo the sufferings that some others have gone through.

[487] Complaints had been made to the Working Committee that the 'loose talk' Resolution No. 13 of 18 June 1934 was a reflection upon the newly formed Congress Socialist Party and its programme. The Committee wanted it to be known that the resolution was not intended to criticize any party or its programme but was intended to affect individuals engaged in the loose talk referred to therein. For the text of the resolution, see Appendix II in this volume. See also pp. 225–6.

[488] Minocher Rustom Masani (1905–1998); better known as Minoo Masani; author, activist in India's struggle for freedom, parliamentarian and member of the Constituent Assembly

[489] Acharya Narendra Dev (1889–1956); socialist and scholar; Vice-chancellor, Kashi Vidyapith and Banaras Hindu University, 1938

Gandhi had written to him on August 1934, pointing out that he missed 'in your draft constitution acceptance of the Congress objective of attainment of *purna swaraj* by legitimate and peaceful means.' See also *CWMG*, Vol. 58, pp. 36–7 and 274–6.

After the explosion I want construction. Therefore now, lest we do not meet, tell me exactly what you will have me to do and who you think will best represent your views.

As to the trust, I was not present. Vallabhbhai was. Your attitude betrays anger. You should trust the trustees to do their duty. I did not think there was anything wrong. I was too preoccupied to concentrate on it. I shall now study the papers and everything. Of course your feelings will be fully respected by other trustees. Having given you this assurance, I would ask you not to take this matter so personally as you have done. It more becomes your generous nature to give the same credit to your co-trustees for regard for Father's memory that you would take for yourself. Let the nation be the custodian of Father's memory and you only as one of the nation.

I hope Indu is well and likes her new life. And what about Krishna?

Love.

Bapu

CWMG, *Vol. LVIII, pp. 317–9*

## 194. Letter to Jawaharlal Nehru

22 November 1934

My dear Jawaharlal,

I sent you a letter some days ago simply inquiring about your health. Mummy who came in yesterday tells me you do not get letters except what is sent in Kamala's packet. I should like to know the rules regulating your correspondence. Please let me know how you are doing and how you are passing your time.[490]

Love.

Bapu

CWMG, *Vol. LIX, p. 383*

[490] On 27 November Nehru was transferred from Naini Jail to Almora Jail, which was near Kamala's place of stay

## 195. Telegram to M.K. Gandhi

4 September 1935

Leaving this evening by air.[491] Love.

Jawahar

CWMG, *Vol. LXI, p. 385fn*

## 196. Telegram to Jawaharlal Nehru

4 September 1935

Thank God. Hope you are well.

CWMG, *Vol. LXI, p. 383*

## 197. Letter to Jawaharlal Nehru

4 September 1935

My dear Jawaharlal,

You can imagine the relief I had on receiving your wire. As usual Mahadev is taking this with him. I wish I had come myself but I must not. You will frankly give me your opinion on all the things of common interest. Unless there is an insuperable bar you should take charge of the Congress ship next year. You will wire to me Kamala's condition on reaching there. The news of your release must itself have brought her considerable relief.

I hope you were keeping well.

Love.

Bapu

CWMG, *Vol. LXI, pp. 385–6*

[491] Gandhi had sent a telegram to the Viceroy on 30 August 1935 which read: 'Regarding Kamala Nehru's health have just received express cable Germany: "Condition serious owing to persistent nausea vomiting." In view of this serious news may I appeal for Pandit Jawaharlal Nehru's unconditional discharge enabling him if at all possible to catch Dutch Air Mail flying next Tuesday.' Nehru was released on 3 September 1935.

## 198. Letter to M.K. Gandhi

Badenweiler
10 September 1935

My dear Bapu,

I arrived here night before last. It was a rapid journey and it was a little difficult to adjust oneself to sudden changes after long seclusion. I had managed to catch the Imperial Airways plane at Allahabad as it happened to be a day and a half late owing to an accident at Akyob. From Allahabad onward the plane tried to make up this lost day and a half and it succeeded in the attempt. This meant one doing a normal four-and-a-half days' flight in three days. I was glad of this speeding up but it meant our flying day and night and no proper rests. The evening after we left Karachi we reached Cairo. It seemed extraordinary to think in Cairo that I had been in India on the previous day—in Allahabad just two days earlier—in Almora jail three days before. Another day's flying brought us to Bindisi from where I came by train to Badenweiler. Having left Almora jail on Tuesday noon I was in Badenweiler on Sunday night.

I found Kamala vastly changed for the worse. It was a shock to see her. I had a long talk with the doctor of the sanatorium in spite of the difficulty of having an interpreter. It was a highly unsatisfactory talk and the doctor painted Kamala's disease in the blackest colours. It was the malign type of TB (there is such a thing as benign type of the disease!) and anything might happen at any [time].[492] Why this sudden deterioration should have occurred within the last month is not at all clear. In some days after the operation she seemed to prosper—then gradually she went down and about two weeks ago her condition became grave. In so far as the operation was concerned it was supposed to have been successful and the lung collapsed. It may be that it shook up the system and thus enabled another and more virulent aspect of the disease to grow, though this is vigorously denied by the doctor here. Anyway the pleural inflammation, which had been present in some degree all through the past year, became rapidly worse.

[492] The source has 'type', evidently a slip.

Fluid collected inside, nausea and vomiting frequently occurred, it was difficult to give nourishment and the temperature went up. This state has continued now with little ups and downs for two or three weeks and she has become excessively weak. On some days she hardly took any nourishment. The one slight improvement during the last two days has been an absence of nausea and since yesterday she has taken more nourishment. Her temperature remains high. Night before last it went up to 104.5°. Yesterday it was a little better—103.5°. It may be said therefore that there has been a slight change for the better but these little changes are not of great account. I am told that she is a bit more cheerful also.

Under the circumstances nothing can be done except to maintain and add to her strength, and to extract the pus from the inflamed area from time to time. If she manages to emerge from this present ordeal and to gain strength, perhaps the inflammation may grow less and there may be no further formation of pus. What will have to be done then, it is too early yet to consider. Perhaps the ordinary sanatorium treatment will be considered sufficient, perhaps another operation may be suggested. She is fed up with Badenweiler and I would myself like to take her to Switzerland which has a better winter climate. The chances of her complete recovery are very remote, the chances of her partial recovery are feeble; yet the odd chance always remains and one works for it.

You have asked me to send you a cable daily. I shall do so for some days but it hardly seems worthwhile unless there is a marked change to record. So if you do not get a cable any day you can conclude that she is much the same. Airmail letters of course I shall send you frequently.

I feel rather lost here in Badenweiler. I have so far no proper things with me, clothes, etc., as I came away too suddenly. The pension where I am staying has no bathroom, which is a trial, and one has to go to the public baths. Apparently most pensions here do not have bathrooms. The German Government controls the spending of money for some intricate reasons and we may only draw a fixed amount per day from the bank. It is a complicated business to get money and the amount drawn are entered in the passport which thus becomes a kind of account book. I would feel far more at home, for this as well as many other reasons, in Switzerland or France. But that must wait till Kamala is better. I find that everything on the continent is far more expensive now in terms of English money than it used to be.

I met Agatha Harrison here and Subhas Bose. They had come on learning of Kamala's serious condition. Probably Charles Andrews will also be coming here after landing at Marseilles next Friday.

Indu is here, rather at a loose end. It is difficult to fix up anything educational for her while Kamala is in this condition. But she has made good progress in German.

Kamala sends you her love.

Yours affectionately,
Jawahar

MKG Papers, Pyarelal Collection, *NMML*

## 199. Letter to M.K. Gandhi

Badenweiler
10 September 1935

My dear Bapu,
I wrote to you this morning. A subsequent visit to Kamala confirmed that the slight improvement was maintained. She was looking just a little better, had taken a little more nourishment, and her temperature though still high was showing a tendency to come down. Little enough but helpful and comforting indications. With luck she might continue this improvement and thus get over the present crisis. Of course even that would mean only a small stage in a long journey. Before I send this letter to you I shall add a few lines to say how I find her tomorrow morning.

I am sorry I did not carry out your bidding and send you a cable today. Yesterday I had cabled to you and tomorrow I shall do so again. If you will permit me, I shall not send daily cables for the day-to-day changes are slight and it is difficult to explain them in a brief cable. I should like to send cables whenever there is a marked change or other reasons. In the absence of another cable you can presume that the previous condition continues. Of course I shall send you airmail letters—probably twice a week. I understand also that Reuters are going to send frequent messages. Their agent in Berlin telephoned to the Sanatorium doctor and asked him to supply a daily bulletin.

In sending cables it seems a waste of money to send a number of cables to different addresses in India. It ought to serve our purpose to have one cable duplicated in India to various friends. I propose therefore to send a cable whenever necessary to Anand Bhawan and I am asking Sarup to convey the message by telegram to you and to some others immediately. In the event of my sending a cable to you it is likely to be unsigned—for motives of economy. You can presume that an unsigned cable from Badenweiler is from me.

In the few lines I wrote to you from the airplane I think I mentioned that I had arranged to have sent to you from Allahabad a typed copy[493] of what I had written in prison. This copy, not being revised, is likely to be full of mistakes. But this will not matter much and you can make allowances for them. When you have glanced through these pages I shall be glad if you could point out to me any errors of fact in them or any deviations from good taste or propriety. I refer especially to various references to Working Committee proceedings and private conversations. I wrote entirely from memory and it is possible that I might have made mistakes. In regard to opinions I imagine it is good to be frank to each other and for the public. That helps far more in arriving at the truth for each individual who has to face and try to solve the problems that almost seem to overwhelm us. It is often difficult to separate the personal factor from an impersonal consideration of a question and in your case that is particularly difficult for each one of us who has been and is powerfully influenced by you. I welcomed and treasured this influence but I have also felt that it is each individual's job to think out things

[493] Of *An Autobiography* brought to Gandhi by Mahadev Desai. Nehru began writing it in jail in June 1934 and finished it on 14 February 1935. Hailed as his greatest literary achievement this massive manuscript of 976 pages was written in less than nine months.

for himself and to act according to his own lights defective as they might be. I might add that certain principles and fundamental matters apart, I feel at present, after my long seclusion, unfit to pronounce definite opinions about current policies and activity. Probably I shall adjust myself after a while. Just now my mind is tired and worried and cannot easily concentrate on such matters.

It is my intention to offer what I wrote in jail to an English publisher who has long been after me.

Agatha Harrison is returning to London tomorrow. Andrews ought to be here in four or five days' time.

Love.

Your affectionately,
Jawahar

[PS]
Kamala this morning was keeping up the slight improvement. Her temperature did not go beyond 39 °C. But one unfortunate development took place which was partly our fault. In the desire to feed her up she was given a little too much to eat last night and this caused her trouble during the night. There was slight vomiting. We shall have to be more careful in future about food.

Kamala has received your letter sent through Princess somebody in Frieburg.

MKG Papers, Pyarelal Collection, *NMML*

## 200. Letter to Jawaharlal Nehru

12 September 1935

My dear Jawaharlal,
How well you have joined Kamala! It is the best tonic for her. I shall keep a note for her herewith. Your messages are being duly received here. And Sarup repeats what she receives. Let us hope all will end well. Please thank Dr Atal for his messages and letters which have been most helpful. I expect a regular mail from you whilst the crisis lasts. Typed sheets are with me. I shall go through them as soon as possible.

Mahadev had to go to Bombay to help Vallabhbhai about an inquiry. And he is still there. Rajagopalachari has just dropped in with Laxmi and her baby boy.[494] Devdas was badly ill. Ansari has packed him off to Simla. I have Mira[495] on my hands prostrate with bad fever.

I would like you to allow yourself to be elected President for the next year. Your acceptance will solve many difficulties. If you think fit, send me a wire.[496]

Has Indu been fixed up?

Khurshed is here. She will be writing to you by the ordinary mail.

Love from us all.

Bapu

CWMG, *Vol. LXI, p. 406*

## 201. Letter to M.K. Gandhi

Haus Waldeck, Badeneweiler
13 September 1935

My dear Bapu,
Two days ago I sent you a brief cable from Freiburg without signing it. Afterwards it struck me that you might have been puzzled over it, especially as it came from another city. Freiburg is quite near—about an hour's journey by local train—and I had gone there to make purchases.

I have just received an airmail cover from Mahadeva from Allahabad containing your brief notes to Kamala and to me and Khurshed's letter.[497] These were meant to catch me before I left but they missed me there.

Kamala's condition since I wrote to you last has not changed markedly. There are little ups and downs. The temperature yester-

[494] Ramachandra Gandhi (1937-2007): grandson of Gandhi and C. Rajagoplachari; held doctorates in linguistics and philosophy; taught at universities in Britain and the US; and in India at Santiniketan, Punjab University and Bangalore University; founded the Philosophy Department at Hyderabad University

[495] Madeleine Slade

[496] See pp. 243-4.

[497] Khurshed Naoroji was acting as Gandhi's secretary in the absence of Mahadev Desai, who had gone to Allahabad to see Nehru before he left for Europe.

day and the day before showed a tendency to rise again and went up to 39.5 °C. (Temperatures are taken here in centigrade and are what are called internal temperatures). Last evening she was not looking at all well. The examination of her blood was not also satisfactory and altogether I was greatly depressed by the turn events seemed to be taking. This morning however she looked brighter and her temperature was lower. This afternoon the doctor will take out pus from the inflamed pleura. As pus is being continually formed it has to be extracted. On the whole I would say that her condition is stationary and though the disease is active and virulent, her system is combating it with some vigour. The little daily ups and downs do not mean much.

In your note you have mentioned the next Congress and Mahadeva has written to me also and put a number of questions.[498] At the moment I am not in a mood to answer all these questions and to some extent I am not in possession of material facts. Later on perhaps, I shall write at greater length on these topics. Meanwhile could you kindly have a copy of the New Congress Constitution sent to me?[499] I am very vague about it.

More and more I have come to feel that many of our political and economic controversies and differences are due to the fact that people have entirely different mental backgrounds. They live in different worlds and speak different languages and have different objectives. Is it surprising that they should often disagree and distrust each other? It is natural enough for difference of opinions to arise but we in India have to contend against something more than that. It is the total inability to understand the other's viewpoint. Even worse than this is the absence of desire to understand the other. Ultimately of course all understanding of another is more emotional than intellectual or rather it must be both. We in India have deliberately discouraged the intellectual outlook and as emotionally...[500] were in entirely separate grooves, there were no points of contact or possibility of understanding. We have

[498] In a letter dated 6 September 1935; see *CWMG*, Vol. LXI, Appendix II.

[499] It was sent by Mahadev Desai as an enclosure to his letter of 25 September 1935 to Nehru; ibid., Appendix IV.

[500] Illegible in the source

imagined that by a repetition of phrases—be good, be united, be pure, be brave—and we can achieve the required results. But different people have different conceptions of goodness, unity, purity, bravery, etc.

But I must not go [on] in this vein. What I wished to state was that I am almost always far more occupied with this background of thought and emotions for I feel that only so can I decide on right actions in the present. Others I find do not think this way at all. They get vastly excited over what I consider petty matters. What has importance for me seems to have no importance for others. The policy pursued by the WC latterly has seemed to me singularly ineffective and helpless and showing no perceptions or understanding of world events or national or economic problems. I have not been in touch with events and so I cannot be definite but vaguely my feelings have been one of continuous surprise and some irritation. Often I have felt that it would be easier for me to understand a man like Winston Churchill[501] and vice versa (though we are highly likely to come into conflict), than to understand many of the well-known personalities in Congress ranks, and even less than so outside the Congress in India. For instance, I have never ceased to wonder that persons like Srinivasa Sastri exist. The ideal man should have personality, character, intelligence and knowledge. It is very difficult to find the fortunate person of all these. I am prepared to admire a person even if he possesses one of these qualities. But I am wholly unable to appreciate one who is devoid of all these and such persons seem to be common enough.

All this is neither here nor there. It is just an attempt to give you a glimpse into my mind. I do not understand this phrase at all: you must take charge of the Congress and run it as you wish without obstructions. That has no meaning for me. The question is not who is to run the Congress. The question is what policy should be adopted. The personal approach seems to me all wrong. I hope you

[501] Sir Winston Churchill (1874–1965); British politician and historian; Prime Minister, United Kingdom, 1940–5 and 1951–5; only British Prime Minister to have been awarded the Nobel Prize for Literature; second person to be made an Honorary citizen of the United States

will read the Mss book I have left in India. Kripalani promised to take it to you. This will help you to look into my mind.

Love.

Yours affectionately,
Jawahar

MKG Papers, Pyarelal Collection, *NMML*

## 202. Letter to M.K. Gandhi

Pension Ehrhardt, Badenweiler
Schwarzwald-Germany
17 September 1935

My dear Bapu,

Kamala's condition shows no marked change. Three days ago a large quantity of pus was extracted by aspirations. Her temperature fell with a bound and became normal for the first time in several weeks. This seemed a hopeful sign but our pleasure was not long-lived for the next day the temperature rose again quite high. There is enormous variation in temperature. Last night it was 104.4°F—this morning it was 98.6°F, which is normal.This indicates, I am told, an acute inflammation inside and the formation of pus. Obviously a continuing state of affairs of this kind is very bad. The doctor says that we must do nothing but wait and watch and try to strengthen her body by judicious feeding. Any heroic measures are likely to lead to disastrous results. So we wait and watch.

There are some good signs. Her appetite is slowly improving. Her pulse is good, so is her heart, and one lung is wholly unaffected. It is a tough struggle between the good and the bad in the body and it is difficult to say which is likely to triumph. One day she is looking better, the next she is depressed and looks worn out. That is natural and she is very weak. On the whole, however, she puts up a brave front.

I have not got over a feeling of tiredness of mind and body due to the sudden changes I have gone through recently. An annoying cold in the head has not improved matters. But I am growing to like Badenweiler. It is a quiet restful place beautifully situated in a kind of amphitheatre formed by gentle hills opening out towards the West with the Rhine in the far distance. The evening sun comes till late because of this opening. There are lovely walks all round and a very fine park. It is an ideal place to do quiet work. As soon as I feel better and more settled mentally, I shall take to the revision of the book I wrote in prison and I propose to revise it and alter it pretty drastically. I hope I shall have your views in regard to it also.[502]

It is my intention, as soon as Kamala's health permits, to visit a few friends round about and to fix up Indu's education. I hope to see Romain Rolland. Later I should like to go to England for a while.

Charlie Andrews was here for a few hours last week. He came almost direct from Marseilles and then returned to Geneva. He might come back here from Geneva. Subhas Bose has gone to Austria. He is much better but he still has various pains and is undergoing treatment for them.

Indu, though well, is remarkably thin and weak. She refuses to fatten.

Love.

Yours affectionately,
Jawahar

MKG Papers, Pyarelal Collection, *NMML*

## 203. Letter to M.K. Gandhi

Pension Ehrhardt, Badenweiler
20 September 1935

My dear Bapu,

I have just received your airmail letter of the 12th, enclosing a note for Kamala. I do not know if any of your previous letters to Kamala have gone astray. Kamala thinks so but in her present condition it is hard for her to remember. Two of my letters from Almora to her were not delivered to her till long after they were due. This was largely due to defective forwarding arrangements at Geneva and elsewhere. Ever since letters have been coming to Badenweiler direct there has been no trouble to my knowledge.

[502] For Gandhi's views, see pp. 269–70.

Kamala's condition continues much the same. High temperatures in the evening—up to 104°F—and a drop in the mornings, but the drop has not been as great as before. It has not come down below 100°F. It is difficult to give nourishment with these temperatures and she is so utterly weak and thin that nourishment is essential. Pulse remains good, so also the heart. Probably tomorrow there will be another drawing of the pus by aspiration. A specialist at Freiburg is being consulted. The question at issue is whether an operation should be performed to arrange for a continuous drainage of this pus. The sanatorium doctor has so far been averse to this but he seems to be wavering now as Kamala's condition is not changing and seems to have stabilised itself at a very unfortunate level.

You have asked me to send you a wire on the question of the Congress presidentship. It is difficult enough to write a letter on the subject, how then can I compress my thoughts in a brief cable? I realise that my election would for the moment at least solve some difficulties. I also feel that I have certain qualifications for undertaking the job, for, as you know, I am not an over-modest and retiring person. But with all my conceit I feel a little afraid and somewhat reluctant. The reason for the reluctance is partly my desire to be light and free on my return to politics and the presidentship is a tremendous burden which might well crush me. As for what I would do in India on the political or allied planes I have little notion at present. Not that my mind is a blank; it is full of notions and ideas, but I have so far not attempted to adjust them to actualities and to translate them into lines of action. I live still in the detached and unreal atmosphere of prison and, deliberately, I had avoided a closer approach to reality till I had come into personal contact with my colleagues. I may get out of this atmosphere after a while but those personal contacts with my colleagues and with existing conditions will be denied me to a large extent so long as I am away from India. My reluctance therefore has substantial reasons behind it. On the other hand, I do not believe in shirking a job because of difficulties or possibilities of failure. In any event on my return to India I propose to take an active part in politics. They are not for me a career or an occupation from which I can retire at will. Even if I had not had an irrepressible urge towards something, which might not be easy to define, loyalty to the past and even more so to the present, with all its tragic suffering and vulgar suppression of the best in our people, would drive me on. I have little respect for quitters and I hope I shall never be of their number.

So on the whole I feel that I must not refuse the presidentship if it comes my way. It seems rather absurd for me to 'accept' or not when the whole thing is in the air, but since you have put the question I have to answer it. I hope my colleagues realise that I am a bit of a handful, apt to behave like a bull in a china shop. But you know me well enough, perhaps better than I do myself, with all my good and bad qualities. I have pointed out to you how my mind is working at present, somewhat indefinite and undetermined, but yet not lacking in some measure of determination, and perhaps with a spring somewhere at the back of it which circumstances might release.

Indu is still here. It was difficult to send her away so long as Kamala's condition was serious. Also I have seen so little of her during the last few years that I liked having her with me. But I feel that this is not a healthy environment for her and I shall try to fix her up soon if I can at all manage it.

Love.

Yours affectionately,
Jawahar

MKG Papers, Pyarelal Collection, *NMML*

## 204. Letter to Jawaharlal Nehru

Wardha
22 September 1935

My dear Jawaharlal,

Your three welcome letters give us all accurate news about Kamala. For the time being I expect you to follow up the practice. I had telegraphed for daily wires because of the public demand. But you were right in not sending any when there was no change. You were right also in omitting the sender's name. Your presence there is a source of great satisfaction to your friends here as it is an elixir of life to Kamala. I am not writing to her separately this airmail.

I am going to take up your manuscript presently. I have no difficulty in agreeing with you in the enunciation of principles. But when we descend to the concrete, we generally use the language I have used. In the huge organisation the Congress has become, no one man can hope to run the show. But someone has to shoulder the burden. And people want some guidance. Hence my inquiry. If you are elected, you will be elected for the policy and principles you stand for. I would like you therefore to tell me whether you will allow your name to be proposed for the crown of thorns.

I suppose Indira will now wait till Kamala's condition is better known.

I am sending the Congress Constitution.[503] If you can concentrate your attention on it, I would like you to send me your considered criticism on it.[504]

As to the present policy of the Congress, whilst I can in no way be responsible for the detailed working of it, it is in the main of my shaping. It is not one of drift. It is founded upon one central idea—that of consolidating the power of the people with a view to peaceful action. But in your absence, we have been literally trekking. Now that you are free you have to give the guidance and take with you such of your old colleagues as would go with you wholeheartedly. So far as I know they will not resist you, even where they may not be able to follow you. I must not weary you with more of this kind of thing whilst you are there nursing Kamala. Missing Kamala.

Love.

Bapu

Jawaharlal Nehru
Haus Waldeck
Badenweiler, Baden, Germany

CWMG, *Vol. LXI, pp. 438–9*

[503] Mahadev Desai had said in his postscript to the letter to Nehru: 'It was too late to get enough stamps for posting the constitution. It will follow in the next mail.' It was, however, sent later by airmail; see p. 259. For the text of the new amended constitution of the Congress, see *CWMG*, Vol. LIX, pp. 245–60.

[504] See also p. 239, *fn*. 499.

## 205. Letter to M.K. Gandhi

Pension Ehrhardt, Badenweiler
23 September 1935

My dear Bapu,

Since I wrote to you last Kamala's temperature has behaved most erratically and alarmingly though I am told that in her present condition high temperatures are usual and almost inevitable reactions to the inflammation inside and by themselves need not cause much alarm. Still there is a limit to this kind of thing. On the 20th her temperature in the evening went up to 104.2 which was more or less usual for her—how we get accustomed to the most unusual occurrences and call them usual! The next day the temperature came down and continued to go down even in the evening till it reached 97.5°F which is sub-normal. A few hours later, in the early hours of the morning of 22nd it shot up to 105.8°F and then gradually came down to 100°F. It mounted again to 103°F and it has been hovering round about there since.

105.8° F seems to me a tremendous temperature. Yet the curious part of it is that even with the temperature her pulse is relatively good and as soon as the temperature comes down she feels better and even cheerful. Tomorrow it is proposed to extract pus again by aspiration. Her principal diet at present is orange juice and other fruit juices.

I have been here now for just two weeks and I do not understand at all this continuing crisis. I can understand a crisis and I can understand a chronic condition but this seems to have the evils of both, except that it may be said that the body with its amazing adaptivity has to some extent adjusted itself to a critical condition and is fighting it and just succeeding in holding its ground. I feel at sea and unhappy.

Consultations with the Freiburg specialist have so far not helped matters any further. After the aspiration tomorrow there will be more data for consultations. I might add that a recent blood test was slightly more favourable than the last.

Love.

Yours affectionately,
Jawahar

MKG Papers, Pyarelal Collection, *NMML*

## 206. Letter to M.K. Gandhi

Badenweiler
26 September 1935

My dear Bapu,
I enclose a copy of a letter which I have sent to Agatha Harrison.[505] This was in reply to hers in which she made a proposal which will appear from my answer.

Kamala is no better and the continuation of this acute stage day after day is a very bad sign. Yesterday I had another talk with the doctor in charge and he was inclined to take a graver view than he has so far done. Of course he refuses to be and cannot be definite. But it is feared that apart from the inflammation of the pleura the lung itself may become active. This indicates a serious complication, for the steps which are usually taken to pump the pleural inflammation have the effect of encouraging lung activity and vice versa. One method of treatment is in direct conflict with the other. So far it is by no means certain or even probable that

[505] In his letter of 25 September 1935 to Agatha Harrison, Nehru had written '... your suggestion that I should talk with some of the people with special responsibility for India during my visit to England has set me thinking. ... I do not feel in the mood for any public function and I have so far not succeeded in getting rid of what might be called the gaol atmosphere.... More important still is the feeling that I must take no definite step without knowing much more fully than I do now the position in India in regard to particular individuals and groups, and without consulting my colleagues there. You must remember that during the last four eventful years I have been mostly in prison and no one in prison can ever be in real touch with developments outside. The personal touch and the psychological link is absent.... That proposal affects me in a different way. I think it is always good to meet people on the other side. ... But what would I say and how could I presume to represent anybody? Am I to discuss the new Act that has been passed? It occupies a very small corner of my mind, which is troubled and distressed by a host of other happenings.'

Writing a month later to Rajendra Prasad, Nehru said that 'good people mostly Quakers', such as Agatha Harrison of the Conciliation Group of London, 'believe in bringing about contact between prominent Indians and men in authority. They work quietly and individually, frequently approaching the big noises. I like these people but ... I do not think it takes us anywhere and sometimes it might even add to our difficulties by creating confusion of issues.'

there is lung activity...[506] Perhaps the next two days will throw some light on this dilemma.

In any event it seems highly probable that Kamala is not likely to improve wholly for a considerable time. I can't even afford to leave her for a few days just at present and I hesitate to send Indu away. One good thing for what it is worth, is her improving interest in food. She had vegetables and took them with some relish.

I find that Reuter has been sending more or less unintelligible messages about Kamala's illness. Partly the fault must lie with our doctor whose English is exceedingly weak. We have tried to help him with the drafting of messages but evidently he tries to improve on the draft and then Reuter shortens them down.

Love.

Yours affectionately,
Jawahar

MKG Papers, Pyarelal Collection, *NMML*

## 207. Letter to M.K. Gandhi

Badenweiler
30 September 1935

My dear Bapu,
Your letter of the 22nd September came today. I have already written[507] to you about the Congress presidentship. If people want me I am not going to shirk the burden. But just at present my mind is confused and troubled and I do not know when I shall have the chance of renewing contacts with people and realities in India.

Kamala's condition though not deteriorating is very near it and the continuation of certain features, despite attempts to control and check them, is alarming. Her maximum and minimum temperatures during the last three days have been:

| | | |
|---|---|---|
| Sept. 28th | 104.6° | and 97.2°F |
| 29th | 105° | and 96.7°F |
| 30th | 105.8° | and 96.5°F |

[506] Illegible in the source

[507] On 20 September 1935; for Mahadev Desai's letter acknowledging receipt of it, see *CWMG*, Vol. LXI, Appendix V.

Progressively they seem to go higher and lower. It is a process which cannot continue for long without ending life itself. The temperature used to rise late in the afternoon and to go down in the course of the night. Now it is down during the day and rises at night, attaining its maximum at about 2 a.m. In the morning it is down again and in late afternoon—5 p.m.—it reaches its lowest level. As soon as the temperature begins going down there is profuse perspiration which lasts for the greater part of the day. This is exhausting. Her heart, considering everything, continues to be good. Though weak it is unaffected. It was 90 this afternoon. She has no cough or sputum to indicate that the lung is not active. The chief trouble thus is the inflammation of the pleura with pus—empyema I believe (this is called but I am almost sure the spelling is wrong). To get rid of this pus aspiration has been resorted to several times and the accumulated pus extracted. The cavity has been irrigated and some antiseptic put in. But ...[508] that this is not very helpful as the temperature goes up morning after and there is no change in the patient.

It is not clear what else we can do. It is possible to arrange for continuous drainage of the pus by a minor operation. Perhaps this may be done but it seems unlikely that this will have marked results.

Apart from the conservative treatment she is undergoing at present there is one other possible course—Sambruck's operation (named after the famous German surgeon, which involves the cutting of ribs). This is a life-and-death operation usually undertaken as a desperate measure and involving a tremendous deal of risk. I believe this operation was performed by Sambruck on King George. ... He survived. Many do not. In Kamala's case she was definitely advised against this operation soon after her arrival in Europe. A much lesser operation was suggested and this was performed with apparently successful results at the time. An adhesion was cut thus allowing the affected lung to collapse. The fact that there is no cough or sputum would indicate that the operation had this successful result. In it ... pleural inflammation. It is not possible to be sure but the probability seems to be that there is no such activity.

[508] Dots indicate portions illegible in the source.

But the operation which Kamala underwent seems to have had one unfortunate result. By shaking up the bodily organism it might have given an impetus to pleural inflammation which had existed all along since last year. The disease, though confined to one lung, is of a virulent type and any disturbance encourages it. Very probably even without the operation it would have increased, as it was slowly increasing when she left India, but the process might have been slower. The surgeon who operated on her first—and he is a famous surgeon who has specialised in that particular operation—said when he examined her that she had come too late. The operation should have been performed at least six months earlier. After the operation, however, he was so pleased that he held out hopes of fairly speedy recovery. The operation itself was successfully performed as is indicated, *inter alia*, by the fact that no outside infection was in it. The only germs found in the pus are TB germs.

The indirect effect of the last operation leads one to think that further operative treatment, apart from other dangers which are very great, might lead to greater virulence of the disease. Thus Sambruck's operation is to be avoided unless death is the only alternative.

On the other hand the only other course is to continue the present treatment with minor variations although it is not at all succeeding. There is always a faint hope that she might turn the corner. And undoubtedly her body has shown some powers of resistance.

There was some talk of taking her elsewhere—probably to a Swiss sanatorium where the climate will be better in the late autumn and afterwards. In winter especially Badenweiler is not a very suitable place. But all such talk is for the present beside the point. She is hardly in a condition to be moved. In any event she remains here for another month.

All I have written is from the layman's viewpoint. I have not attempted to express expert opinion though I have been guided by it. One of our difficulties here is the language and it is not easy to discuss fine points with the German doctor.

Indu can hardly be sent away from here under existing circumstances.

Andrew was here for a day and a half and left for England yesterday.

Love.

Yours affectionately,
Jawahar

MKG Papers, Pyarelal Collection, *NMML*

## 208. Letter to M.K. Gandhi

Badenweiler
3 October 1935

My dear Bapu,

My last two letters must have indicated to you that we considered Kamala's condition very serious and were considerably distressed about it. Indeed I have been on the verge of sending you a cablegram to the effect that she was deteriorating. Today I have to give you slightly better news.

In our anxiety we decided to consult other noted doctors. Zurich is the best Swiss centre for well-known specialists and it is only three hours' railway journey from here. Atal therefore went off to Zurich with all charts and papers with the intention of bringing a famous specialist there with him to Badenweiler. This gentleman gave a patient hearing and then pointed out some fairly obvious features of the disease, favourable and unfavourable. He said the tremendous swing in temperatures was dangerous; otherwise there had been certain developments which were hopeful, such as the cessation of nausea and the capacity to take some nourishment, also the good pulse, etc. There was nothing new in this and perhaps he could not say much else without examining the patient. When he was asked if he could come to Badenweiler he demanded the paltry sum of £140 (or rather the equivalent of it) for a visit! It was not sheer greed that prompted this monstrous demand. There are national conflicts between Germany and Switzerland in various spheres and as a result, it appears, that the Swiss doctors or some society of them had laid down this prohibitive tariff. We were of course not prepared to pay this sum in any event. To some extent even he discouraged us by saying that the case appeared to be a surgical one and he himself was a physician.

We then fixed up with a Freiburg surgeon to come up for a consultation and this took place last evening. The Freiburg man examined Kamala thoroughly and as a result gave on the whole a favourable opinion. Of course, he said, the case is a very serious one but there was no reason for immediate alarm and there was a fair possibility of the body overcoming the acute pleural trouble. He was entirely against the big operation (Sambruck's) and even against the minor operation to establish continuous drainage of the pus. He was of opinion that the greatest danger lay in outside infection entering the body and adding greatly to the virulence of the disease. This must be avoided at all cost and any operative measure would involve the danger. Otherwise too he thought that an operation was not indicated. The collapse of the lung, as a result of Unverricht's operation in Berlin had been complete showing that this operation had been a success, and when this was so Sambruck's operation was not indicated. He was clear that at present there was no lung activity. He suggested therefore that the present treatment should continue with minor variations, that is to say, every two weeks or so, there should be an aspiration and some antiseptic should be put in. The antiseptic he suggested was a stronger one than the last.

On Oct. 1st Kamala created a new record for herself in the way of temperatures. The maximum was 106.7°F, the minimum was 95°F. Such temperatures, at either end, are almost beyond the capacity of the average thermometer. And yet surprising as it was she took her food tolerably well and was not really as bad as I expected her to be. Yesterday the maximum and minimum temps were 105.2°F and 96.8°F which were slightly better. It is curious how our standards of comparisons change and a dose of the very bad makes us appreciate something only slightly less bad. And so it was with some relief that I noted that the temperature had only gone up to 105.2°F! But more important than this was the improvement yesterday in her appearance. This was marked.

The specialist's opinion as well as the better appearance do not take us very far, but they have afforded me considerable relief for the present. I am not afraid of operations, big or small, but instinctively I was feeling that a further operation should be avoided. I am glad that the specialist also said so and the reasons he gave could be understood even by a layman, despite the language difficulty (our talks are tri-lingual—German, French and English). One cannot build much on day-to-day changes but still I am glad to be able to send you something in the nature of good news today.

May I mention one thing which does not apply to you but to those who write to Kamala? Many of these letters I have been quite unable to read to her because they were full of expressions of anxiety for her serious illness. It would be far better if little reference was made to her disease in letters meant for her.

Love.

Yours affectionately,
Jawahar

[PS]
Yesterday—Oct 2nd—was I believe your birth anniversary. It was also curiously enough, the birth anniversary of the late Marshal Hindenburg[509] and all the Nazi flags were up to celebrate it.

MKG Papers, Pyarelal Collection, *NMML*

## 209. Letter to Jawaharlal Nehru

3 October 1935

My dear Jawaharlal,
Your letters come in with clock-like regularity and they are such a blessing.

I see that Kamala is putting forth a very brave effort. It will be rewarded. You know my partiality for nature-cure methods. There are in Germany itself many nature-cure establishments. Kamala's case may be past that stage. But one never knows. I know of cases which were reported to be for surgical treatment but which yielded to nature-cure treatment. I send you this experience of mine for what it is worth.

Your letter[510] about the wearing of the next year's crown was delightful. I was glad to have your consent. I am sure that it would

[509] Paul von Hindenburg (1847–1934); German Field Marshal and statesman; Chief of General Staff, 1916–19; elected second President of Germany, 1925. He appointed Hitler Chancellor on 30 January 1933.

[510] See pp. 243–4

solve many difficulties and it is the rightest thing that could have happened for the country. Your presidentship at Lahore[511] was totally different from what it would be at Lucknow.[512] In my opinion it was comparatively plain sailing at Lahore in every respect. It won't be so in any respect at Lucknow. But those circumstances I cannot imagine anybody better able to cope with than you.[513] May God give you all the strength to shoulder the burden.

I am going through your chapters as speedily as I can. They are to me of absorbing interest. More than that I must not say just now.

This letter carries the love of us to you all.

Bapu

Pandit Jawaharlal Nehru

CWMG, *Vol. LXII, p. 6*

## 210. Letter to Jawaharlal Nehru

Wardha
[10 October 1935][514]

My dear Jawaharlal,

I wanted to write to you on Sunday but I was so busy that I simply could not do it. That was to be in answer to your letter enclosing copy of your letter to Agatha.[515] Yours to Agatha gave me an insight into the working of your mind which I would not miss for anything. She fully deserved that frankness. I can endorse most of

[511] In 1929

[512] Where the Congress session was to be held in April 1936. Nehru was elected President of INC on 1 February 1936.

[513] Reflecting a similar faith in Nehru's leadership, Subhas Chandra Bose wrote to Nehru on 4 March 1936, 'Among the front rank leaders today—you are the only one whom we can look up to for leading the Congress in a progressive direction. ... I earnestly hope that you will fully utilise the strength of your public position in making decisions. ... Gandhiji will never take a stand which will alienate you.'

[514] A part of this letter is available in Mahadev Desai's Diary under this date. The original which is damaged here, however, bears the date 18 October 1935.

[515] See p. 247, *fn*. 505.

your sentiments. You do not know that I have written to her more than once in much the same strain though in my own way and my own language. Nevertheless if Kamala shows distinct signs of improvement and if you are free to go [to] London and the way is open, I would like you to see the big ones, open yourself out to them even as you have to Agatha.[516]

But your letter received yesterday shows that you may not leave Kamala's bedside just yet. After all you have been freed for that purpose and if Providence keeps you chained to Kamala's bed, we must not grumble. You have gone there to see her through the terrible ordeal. How I wish I was there to share your burden and cheer Kamala! As I saw her for two days in Bombay before her departure, I observed that she never had so much peace of mind as she seemed to enjoy then. Her faith in the benevolence of God, she said, was never so bright as then. Her mental disturbance had vanished and she did not mind what happened to her. She went to Europe because you all wished it; it seemed to be her obvious duty to do so. If she lives, she will live for greater service than she has yet rendered. If she dies, she will do so to come down to earth with a body more fitted for her task than the one she has today.

It is well too that Indu's literary studies remain suspended for a while. For me, she is having a training that is of far greater value than any she would have in a college. She is having her training in the University of Nature.[517] She may give the finishing touch by completing her literary studies.

I am going through your chapters with the deepest interest. I should like to finish them at a single sitting as Mahadev did and as Khurshed almost did. I have no such good luck. I must reserve my

[516] See also pp. 260 and 264.

[517] Indira had been studying at Visva-Bharati at Santiniketan in Bengal, an educational institution set up by Rabindranath Tagore for learning in the natural environment. She had been taken away, however, to be with her ailing mother.

Writing to his daughter on 15 June 1934, Nehru had explained his choice of Santiniketan: 'The very object of going there is to learn from the sufferings ... which surround ... the great majority of people ... and to get to know how to work so as to raise them and get them out of their misery.'

opinion till I have reached the last chapter. I am thankful that you have sent them to me.[518]

I am not going to talk to you about the politics. It is enough for my purpose that you will shoulder the burden, if it falls to your lot. That it will, seems to me to be a foregone conclusion.

You will read the accompanying to Kamala, if you think fit.[519] Indu used to write to me a few lines when you were not there. Now I suppose she thinks she is absolved from the task!

Love.

Bapu

[PS]
You must excuse my obstinacy in writing with village ink, village reed on village paper.

CWMG, *Vol. LXII, pp. 16–17*

## 211. Letter to M.K. Gandhi

Badenweiler
11 October 1935

My dear Bapu,
Your letter of the 3rd has just come. I am just writing a few lines as I am going to Freiburg in half an hour to see an eye doctor about my eyes. There is nothing the matter with them but Dr Atal insists that I have them examined. I shall return this evening.

In my last letters to Mahadeva I said that Kamala's blood examination was unsatisfactory. I am not sure yet if this was so bad as we thought at first as otherwise Kamala is much the same and has not deteriorated. Temperature has on the whole been better and nourishment is fairly good. Yesterday she had another aspiration and only a small quantity of pus came out. As for nature-cure treatment in a sense the sanatorium treatment is largely nature cure. We have ruled out further operative measures. It is difficult

[518] For Gandhi's views about the book, see pp. 269–70.

[519] Gandhi's Hindi letter read: 'Chi Kamala, What can I write to you except to say that we remember you every day? May God give you peace whatever be the circumstances. Have no worry for anything. Blessings from Bapu.'

to change treatments radically at this stage. That is also a reason why we cannot take her away to another place just yet, much as I would like to do so. If she could get over her present trouble we would have a chance of giving her a change. Anyway, she ought to be taken away for the winter. But I am told now that she ought to be taken to a high altitude.

Love.

Yours affectionately,
Jawahar

MKG Papers, Pyarelal Collection, *NMML*

## 212. Letter to M.K. Gandhi

Badenweiler
13 October 1935

My dear Bapu,

I am glad to inform you that Kamala's improvement continues and her temperature has not gone beyond 99°F for the last three days. There has been a marked change in her appearance and she has been quite jolly since yesterday. She herself feels that she has turned the corner and is getting well now. That of course is a good thing. I hesitate to make much of possibly a temporary change for the better, but I must say that she has not been so well since I came.

She will have to remain here for another month but we are already trying to fix up some place in Switzerland where she could go to for the winter. There is some slight difficulty about this as I do not fancy the place he suggests and he does not approve of my suggestions. Of course the doctor's opinion will finally prevail. But I have a feeling that natural prejudices go a long way in the formation of these opinions.

Now that Kamala seems to be on the mend I am beginning to look round a little. Probably about ten days' time or so Indu and I will go to London for a week. I do not propose to take part in anything in the nature of a public engagement there.

Love.

Yours affectionately,
Jawahar

[PS]
Today (Sunday) is Winter Help Day here in Germany. The problems of helping the unemployed becomes especially acute during winter and large collections, supposed to be voluntary but practically compulsory, are made for this purpose. There are all manner of dodges and methods to get money. One of them is to appoint one day each month during winter when everybody has a very simple one-course meal (in hotel, restaurant or household) in the middle of the day although he is made to pay for a full meal. The difference goes to winter help. So today we had such a meal.

MKG Papers, Pyarelal Collection, *NMML*

## 213. Letter to Jawaharlal Nehru

Wardha
17 October 1935

My dear Jawaharlal,
Your very important letter to hand.[520] I have wired to Rajendra Babu[521] about Swaraj Bhawan.[522] I do not know what is happening. I am entirely of your opinion that the policy of the Committee should be strictly defined.

As to our attitude on the present world situation, I do not think there is want of appreciation of it. But it is our helplessness which imposes silence on us. There is no weakness either. It is merely a matter, if you will, of tactics in the best sense of the term. Anyway I have no sense in me of weakness. But I know that I cannot speak with effect at this juncture. I cannot give the lead without knowing what the people can do. I know what they should do. And what is true of me is perhaps equally true of the majority of our workers. But I have great faith in you in these matters. You have

[520] The reference is to Nehru's letter to Mahadev Desai dated 5 October 1935, with which he had enclosed his written views on the Constitution. See Appendix III in this volume.

[521] Rajendra Prasad (1884–1963); lawyer of Patna who joined Gandhi in 1917; President, INC, 1934, 1939 and 1947–8; President, Constituent Assembly, 1946–50; first President of India, 1950–62

[522] The telegram dated 17 October read: 'Jawaharlal may [have] received Mohanlal Nehru's letter Swaraj Bhawan. Wants definition decisive attitude Congress Committee.'

undoubtedly a much greater grasp of the situation than any one of us has, certainly than I can ever hope to have. Therefore, you may be able to evolve a dignified formula for national self-expression in speech as well as in action assuming of course that at the present moment direct action is ruled out.

Your paragraph about Kamala is somewhat disturbing. But we are prepared for these ups and downs. I must await your further contribution on the Constitution before I say anything. I am glad I spent the money for putting you in possession of the Constitution as early as it was possible.

Love to you all.

Blessings from
Bapu

CWMG, *Vol. LXII, pp. 39–40*

## 214. Letter to M.K. Gandhi

Badenweiler
18 October 1935

My dear Bapu,

I have just received your letter (the date is undecipherable) in which you refer to my letter to Agatha Harrison.[523]

Kamala's condition has not been so satisfactory as we hoped, yet on the whole it has not been bad. After three days of normal temperature, a progressive rise set in. Daily it was a little more–99°-99.5°-100°-100.5°. This morning it just touched 103 and then came down. Otherwise her condition has been fair and her nourishment good. It would seem that the inflammation continues and pus is formed, though the process is slower than it was and the bodily resistance is increasing, also that the last aspiration, followed by irrigation and the putting in of iodoform in glycerine, definitely did her good, but as the effect of this wears off pus is formed. On a repetition of this process progressively better results should be obtained.

I wrote to you in my last letter that I hoped to take Kamala to Switzerland next month and keep her there for the winter. But the

[523] See p. 254.

doctor here is strongly against any removal till the pus formation has absolutely stopped and he cannot say when this will happen. He also thinks that even then a mild climate is indicated. Personally I am a great believer in the Swiss winter which although very cold is really far pleasanter and more bearable, because it is fairly dry and the sun comes out, than the valleys which are dismal and misty during winter. Kamala herself is very keen on going to Switzerland. But it is quite impossible for us to shift her in direct opposition to the doctor's advice. She feels disappointed and depressed. But I hope this will pass. In all likelihood therefore she remains on here for many weeks.

I am afraid I cannot get myself to agree to see 'the big ones', whoever they might be, in London.[524] Besides, I do not consider them big. I can put up with a good deal of cruelty, though it is a painful affair. But a combination of vulgarity, hypocrisy and unctuousness is just too much for me, and it is safest to follow my own inclination in the matter. I still propose going to England about the end of this month for a week and during this visit at least I intend confining myself to friends and those who might interest me. Probably I shall pay one or more subsequent visits to England later. As you must know, a general election is going to take place in England next month. This is not a very suitable time to meet people who are politically inclined. There is too much excitement. The election is likely to repeat the victory of the 'National' Government, though Labour will probably add to its numbers.[525] Abyssinia also is an exciting topic now all over Europe. Perhaps Germany is least affected by it and here in an out-of-the corner of Germany, life is placid enough. But not so in England or Austria or the Balkans, or Czechoslovakia–in fact in most places in Europe where all manner of complications are found and news from the Abyssinian front and Geneva is anxiously awaited almost hourly. France is in a peculiarly critical condition. Fascism is gaining strength and openly threatening a violent

[524] See p. 255.

[525] United Kingdom General Election were held on 14 November 1935. Labour leader Ramsay MacDonald was defeated, resulting in a majority for the National Government led by Stanley Baldwin.

seizure of power in the near future. It has drawn to its ranks the upper-middle classes, the upper peasantry and many ex-combatants. To counter it and meet its menace other groups—socialists, communists, Radicals (representing the non-Socialist Republicans which have been the backbone of French Republic) and most intellectuals have formed a common group. It is quite certain that if a Fascist coup comes off it will be resisted with violence. There will be no quiet submission as there was in Germany. This means civil war of a fairly virulent type and it is by no means unlikely that this may come off during the coming winter. The fascist danger has brought together a strange assortment of people and Russia today is ranged wholly on the side of the moderate groups resisting fascism.

Economically, Europe is still in the downgrade in spite of superficial appearances and propaganda. Even England puts up a brave show because of its refusal to pay the American debts and partly because of the gold drain from India. Otherwise it would be nationally in a fix. She is only carrying on on the basis of defaulting. The gold drain from India will of course stop sooner or later. The supplies are limited. Other more important factors are at work also and expert economists are of opinion that (war apart) an economic crisis of tremendous magnitude will force Europe, England included, within a year or two at the latest. Germany, of course, is in great economic difficulties. This process may be hastened by Abyssinian developments.

Love.

Yours affectionately,
Jawahar

MKG Papers, Pyarelal Collection, *NMML*

## 215. Letter to M.K. Gandhi

Badenweiler
24 October 1935

My dear Bapu,

I am writing to you after a little gap. I spent three days in Switzerland and returned last evening. I found Kamala looking a trifle better. She had maintained her progress and added a little to it. The temperature goes up somewhat still—up to 101° over—generally 100°F. Her appetite is improving and it is evident in many ways that she is on the up-grade.

In Switzerland I saw Romain Rolland and Madeleine Rolland. The former said that he had written to you many months ago, probably last year, and put some questions to you but you had not answered.

Indu and I are going to England on the 28th. We intend staying there for a week or so but if Kamala goes on improving we might stay a little longer. I had impressed on everybody there that I do not want public functions and the like. To get over this various 'receptions' are apparently being organised and I am likely to have a rather hectic time.

Masani wrote recently to the press about Abyssinia and India. I think it was a good letter—I enclose a cutting. This has given rise to some controversy in the press and Nathan Laski[526] has come out with quite an amazing defence of everything that Government does or may do.

My visit to England is not well timed. Most people are busy with the election.

Yours affectionately,
Jawaharlal

[PS]
I may not be able to write to you quite as regularly as I have so far done when I go to London. But as Kamala's condition is more satisfactory such frequent letters are not necessary.

MKG Papers, Pyarelal Collection, *NMML*

## 216. Letter to M.K. Gandhi

Badenweiler
28 October 1935

My dear Bapu,
Your letter of the 17th October. I am leaving today for London with Indu and I want to send a few lines to you before I go.

[526] (1863–1941); a wealthy Jewish cotton merchant and father of Harold Laski; Liberal Party Chairman and a staunch Churchill supporter

Kamala is keeping fairly well, the temperature on the whole keeping down. Probably there will be another aspiration after a few days. She is very restless and keen on going to some other place. It has been very dismal here with almost continuous rain. Everywhere at present there is changeable weather. She is keeping up her appetite and is full of spirit.

I shall consider the Congress Constitution carefully again on my return from London and write to you about it.

Agatha Harrison writes that Mahadeva has mentioned to her something about 'contacts' between me and the superior ones. I confess that all my instincts are opposed to any such thing and I think that one should follow one's instincts in the matter. Curiously enough I have an odd link with many of the great ones—the bond of Harrow. Baldwin,[527] Samuel Hoare,[528] Churchill, Zetland and Butler[529] are all old Harrowians.

Whether I meet the great ones or keep away from their shadow I am likely to meet more interesting people—the *New Statesman* group consisting of some of the ablest journalists in England, and an advanced group at Oxford. I am far more attracted to these people than to more [*sic*] superior folk. And I think that, in the final analysis, they are more important.

Love.

Yours affectionately,
Jawahar

MKG Papers, Pyarelal Collection, *NMML*

[527] Stanley Baldwin (1867–1947); British Conservative politician and statesman; Prime Minister, United Kingdom, 1923–4, 1924–9 and 1935–7

[528] Sir Samuel Hoare, later Vicount Templewood (1880–1959); Conservative MP, 1910–44; Secretary of State for India, 1931–5; Foreign Secretary, 1935; Home Secretary, 1937–9; Lord Privy Seal, 1939–40; British Ambassador, Spain, 1940–4

[529] Sir Spencer Harcourt Butler (1869–1938); Member, Indian Civil Service in charge of Education, 1910–15; Lieutenant-Governor, Burma, 1915–18 and of United Provinces, 1918–21

## 217. Letter to Jawaharlal Nehru

Wardha
[About 29 October 1935][530]

My dear Jawaharlal,

I have your letter. We have to be prepared for ups and downs in Kamala's health. I marvel at the resisting power Kamala is showing and so long as she has got this tremendous reserve of strength and will, we can hope for the best; at least I do. When I said good-bye to her in Bombay,[531] I did not feel that we were parting for all time, and I naturally said: 'We are going to meet again in a year's time, if I am out till then.' I claim to have that hope still and I interpret your reports in that light.

I understand the depth of feeling behind your intense disinclination to see the 'big folk', but I know that in spite of your disinclination, if there is a real approach to you, you are not going to be unapproachable. I know that at a given moment your decisions are always correct. Your firm decision, therefore, does not frighten me. I share your view, however, that during the election fever nobody would want to see you, nobody would be in the mood to discuss things that are irrelevant to their electioneering campaign, and India has ever been irrelevant on such occasions. From your standpoint you will be going to England at a safe time.

Khurshedbehn will be most probably leaving for Bombay on Wednesday. She has a bit of a literary programme before her which should keep her busy for some months.

I wonder if you have even time to look into *Harijan*, which is sent to you regularly?

Love.

Blessings from
Bapu

CWMG, *Vol. LXII, pp. 77–8*

[530] Nehru reached England on 29 October 1935. Evidently the letter was written about this time. Again, in his letter dated 7 November 1935 to Nehru, Mahadev Desai wrote that Khurshed had already left.

[531] On 23 May 1935.

## 218. Letter to M.K. Gandhi

Mount Royal, Marble Arch
London, W.1.
2 November 1935

Mahatma Gandhi
Wardha, CP
India

My dear Bapu,

I received your letter of the 17th Oct., as well as Mahadev's letter of the 20th a little before leaving Badenweiler for London.

Indu and I came to London three days ago, and we are having a busy time here seeing many friends. Owing to the General Election most of the political crowd is very busy, and I have been unable to see a number of people, but still I have had opportunities of meeting some very interesting persons.

There was a big reception here which was quite a success. I have also attended meetings of the conciliatory group and 'Friends of India' and other groups.

News from Badenweiler is fairly satisfactory, and Kamala seems to be progressing slowly. We are therefore staying here a little longer than we intended.

On the 5th we are going to Oxford for a couple of days, from there to Birmingham for a day to Horace Alexander[532] and then a day in Cambridge. I hope to be back in Badenweiler before the 12th.

About the Abyssinian situation, strange developments appear to be going on behind the scenes.[533] There is hardly any doubt that the present National Government is trying hard to let Abyssinia down by coming to some unholy agreement with Mussolini.[534]

[532] (1889–1989); English ornithologist, pacifist and crusader for Indian independence; associate of Gandhi, Member, Friends of India Society; Professor, Selly Oak College, Woodbrooke, Birmingham; author, *The Indian Ferment* and *India Since Cripps*

[533] On 3 October 1935, Italy under Mussolini attacked Abyssinia.

[534] Italian dictator, Benito Mussolini about whom Gandhi had observed nearly five years earlier, in a letter to Romain Rolland, 'Mussolini is a riddle to me. Many of his reforms attract me ... I admit an iron hand is there. But as vio-

Probably much depends on the result of the General Election here. If the labour gains are really substantial, in no event is labour going to have anything like a majority, then probably the new government will endeavour to come to terms with Mussolini over the patch of Abyssinia—if the labour gains are at all substantial there is every chance of a deal.The latter is likely.

With love,

Jawahar

MKG Papers, Pyarelal Collection, *NMML*

## 219. Letter to M.K. Gandhi

London
4 November 1935

My dear Bapu,
The attached sheet contains a specimen of typewriting done by an English stenotypist here. I am sending it to you in all its beauty without correcting it. After this experience I am reverting to my fountain pen.

I learn from a letter that Kamala had another aspiration the other day. Much less pus than usual came out, there was more water. This is a good sign and leads one to think that the pleural inflammation is going down.

I feel very tired after five days of London. It has been a continual rush and it has been quite impossible to fit in all the things I wanted to do or to see all the people I wanted to see. I have practically promised to pay a second visit—probably in January—before I return to India.

Love.

Yours affectionately,
Jawahar

MKG Papers, Pyarelal Collection, *NMML*

---

lence is the basis of western society, Mussolini's reforms deserve an impartial study. His care of the poor, his opposition to super-urbanisation, his efforts to bring about coordination between capital and labour, seem to demand special attention. What strikes me is that behind Mussolini's implacability is a desire to serve his people.'

## 220. Letter to M.K. Gandhi

Badenweiler
21 November 1935

My dear Bapu,

Kamala's condition has been on the whole satisfactory since I wrote to Mahadev last a few days ago. Temperature low, almost normal, blood examination very satisfactory. The stuff that was taken out of her pleura at the last aspiration had no bacilli or microbes. So far so good. But she has been having severe pains in her side—the affected one—and this has distressed her greatly. Perhaps these pains are a sign of the healing of the pleura as the foreign matter is discarded and new stuff is formed underneath. She has also got some throat trouble which is a nuisance. Altogether she has been very low in spirits. One of the reasons for this is the necessity for staying on here. She is so tired of Badenweiler, or rather of her room at the sanatorium, and wants to be taken elsewhere. But any transfer is bound to be a risky affair in her present condition, and in any event the present treatment would continue elsewhere. The only alternative is a bigger operation—thoracoplasty it is called—which is full of danger and which I want to avoid as far as possible. At present it is not indicated.

Climatically Badenweiler might be improved upon in winter, though climate is not the major consideration for her at present. The doctor treating her is good and Kamala is fond of him. So everything considered we are staying on here more or less indefinitely. I doubt if it will be possible to shift her for many weeks.

The question of my return to India is not too far off now to be ignored. I certainly want to go back in time for the next Congress session. Kamala is already a little worried at the prospect of my departure. Still, unless something entirely unforeseen occurs, I shall try to go back in time and Kamala, however much she might dislike it, will agree that I should. I would even prefer going to the Congress and returning to Europe sometime later—expensive as this is likely to prove—to not going at all.

Even apart from the Congress session, many things in India and particularly in my province disturb me and pull at me. The pull of India is strong even for me who am at home almost in Europe. And thus the idea that things are not well in India and the UP and I am having a quiet time here is distressing.

Today Reuters telephoned to me from Berlin saying that they had had a message from Calcutta enquiring if I was going back to India to preside over the Congress. I told them that the question was premature as to my knowledge no election of president had taken place. But that I certainly intended, my wife's health permitting, to attend the next Congress session.

Indu is going to Bex in Switzerland and will study there for the best part of the next year. After that she may go to the University—perhaps first to the Sorbonne in Paris and then to Oxford. But all this is undecided.

Love.

Yours affectionately,
Jawahar

MKG Papers, Pyarelal Collection, *NMML*

## 221. Letter to M.K. Gandhi

Badenweiler
25 November 1935

My dear Bapu,

Kamala's condition has been fairly satisfactory. The temperature thus far has kept down and that is good. It is already 11 days since the last aspiration and if it follows the usual course it ought to go up now. If it does not go up then it means that the healing process of the pleura is proceeding fairly rapidly. That would be an excellent sign. On the other hand various pains continue to trouble her greatly and she continues restless and often sleepless. She has also had some digestive trouble probably due to our attempts to overfeed her. Today she was made to fast.

It is growing cold here. There has been a heavy frost during the last two nights and there may be snow soon. It is pleasant—so I find it—in the crisp cold air. Kamala rather feels the cold.

Indu has gone to her school at Bex.
Love.

Yours affectionately,
Jawahar

MKG Papers, Pyarelal Collection, *NMML*

## 222. Letter to Jawaharlal Nehru

Wardha
19 December 1935

My dear Jawaharlal,
I wrote to you last week about the sudden breakdown in Bapu's health.[535] He is progressing well, but it will be some time before his blood pressure becomes normal again. He seems to have worked at high pressure all these months and Dr Jivraj and Dr Gilder who examined him two days ago are definitely of opinion that he must have a couple of months' rest. This he has agreed to do. For ten days now he has been in bed resting and sleeping, never reading or writing or dictating. But you will be surprised to know that he continued to do his reading on the commode even during these days! And he finished the 9th Part of your *magnum opus*—which it really is—this evening.

And as soon as he finished it he called me to his bedside and asked me to send you his impressions. If he had been well he should have written himself or dictated something but he did not want to strain himself in the teeth of the doctors' advice and so told me in Gujarati in a minute or two what he felt. What I say will, therefore, be in my language and not his. He said:

It is needless to say that it is a brilliantly written book, and a great literary production. There are parts where I have my fundamental differences with you and which I would like to criticise, but I will not do so as it is scarcely necessary or useful. For when all is said and done it is a highly introspective narrative containing an expression

[535] In his letter of 13 December, Mahadev Desai had written about Gandhi's high blood-pressure and the 'timely warning ten days ago when he had some unaccountable pain in the back regions of the head ...'

of your innermost thoughts and convictions. Even if you could be persuaded to moderate or soften that expression, I should not attempt it, as it would result in taking away from its naturalness, if not also its truthfulness. After all we are helpless actors in the mighty flow of events, we have to act according to our lights allowing or expecting the events to correct us where we err. There is just one thing where perhaps I might make a helpful suggestion. The attack on the Liberals seems to have been overdone. It seems to obtrude on the reader's attention over and over again and sometimes mars the grace and beauty of the narrative. Not that there is any venom in anything that you have said; far from it; but you should not be even unconsciously guilty of doing an injustice to them. What you have said about Sastri leaves that impression on me.[536] These friends served the country in their time according to their lights, and whilst we may have our serious differences with them we do not exactly serve the cause of the country by publicly pillorying them. If you have not, therefore, already sent the book on to the publishers, you might alter these portions ...

Yours affectionately,
Mahadev

CWMG, *Vol. LXII, pp. 171–2*

## 223. Cable to Jawaharlal Nehru

22 December 1935

Our hearts are with you and Kamala.[537]

CWMG, *Vol. LXII, p. 173*

[536] For the comments alluded to, see Nehru's *Autobiography*, under the chapter 'The Liberal Outlook'.

[537] The cable is excerpted from Mahadev Desai's letter to Nehru dated 23 December 1935, which read: 'Two cables from you in painfully quick succession have been repeated to Sarupbehn. Bapu immediately sent a cable to you yesterday. And "our" here means the whole family, including Rajendra Babu, and Jamnalalji and Vallabhbhai (who are all here) not to mention those near Bapu.'

## 224. Letter to M.K. Gandhi

Badenweiler
23 December 1935

My dear Bapu,

Four days ago I discussed the Congress jubilee with Kamala. We decided to send a joint message to Rajendra Babu.[538] The next morning I sent this by cable. As I was coming back from the telegraph office a message came for me to hurry to the sanatorium as Kamala was not well.

Before this letter reaches you the cables will have informed you of Kamala and of whatever fate is in store for her and for us. How this seemingly sudden change came about I do not quite know, nor do I very much care to know. Probably the change was, like all human changes, slow enough, but it became apparent suddenly. Latterly we had been disturbed at her growing weakness, and yet there were some indications that she was overcoming the disease. Our main anxiety was that this weakness was delaying her recovery. We did not think in terms of death. Day before yesterday morning she had a bit of coughing and immediately her condition became bad. We feared some kind of a rupture of the lung. But later this was ruled out. I am now told by those who presume to know that this crisis is caused by the heart and brain being affected by the spreading anaemia. This is serious enough and is said to end fatally within a relatively short period. The remaining period of life would depend on the vitality of the patient and as Kamala has hardly any vitality left, the consequence seems to be a quick end. Yesterday morning, indeed we thought it only a question of some hours. She was visibly growing worse. Today she was just slightly better though fundamentally the crisis continues. With the help of proper nourishment, given in various odd ways, a slight improvement might be created. But it seems to me that only a miracle can ward off the end. Still human nature being what it is, one goes on trying.

[538] For Nehru's message for the Golden Jubilee of Congress that was to be celebrated on 28 December, see *SWJN*, Vol. 7, I Series, pp. 45–6.

Your telegram and some other messages cheered her a little I think. She is not able to talk except for an occasional brief sentence, but her mind is still functioning to a large extent. She recognises people and even tries to give them messages. Nourishment is the great problem. We try to give her as much water and fruit juice as possible, fearing always that a little too much may create trouble or even suffocate.

News of your ill health came to us a few days back and, rather foolishly, I told Kamala about it. She reacts very quickly to bad news, especially when it relates to persons she loves.

She is sleeping now in the adjoining room while I write this letter.

Love.

Yours affectionately,
Jawahar

MKG Papers, Pyarelal Collection, *NMML*

## 225. Letter to Jawaharlal Nehru

Delhi
9 March 1936

My dear Jawaharlal,

So you return leaving Kamala forever in Europe.[539] And yet her spirit was never out of India and will always be your precious treasure as it will be of many of us. I shall never forget the final talk that wetted our four eyes.

[539] Nehru, writing from Ahmednagar Fort prison in 1944 says, 'Early on the morning of February 28th Kamala breathed her last.... we took her to the crematorium in Lausanne. Within a few minutes that fair body and that lovely face, which used to smile so often and so well, were turned to ashes. A small urn contained the mortal remains of one who had been vital, so bright and so full of life. ... The bond that kept me in Lausanne was broken and there was no need for me to remain there any longer... But after leaving Cairo and flying, hour after hour, ... a terrible loneliness gripped me and I felt empty and purposeless. I was going back alone to my home, which was no longer home for me, and there by my side was a basket and that basket contained an urn. That was all that remained of Kamala, and all our bright dreams were also dead and turned to ashes. She is no more, Kamala is no more, my mind kept on repeating. ... nor would we write any more chapters in the book of life.'

Heavy responsibility awaits you here.[540] It is laid on you because you are well able to bear it. I dare not come to you, as I would have if my body had regained its original elasticity. There is nothing organically wrong with me. The body has even gained in weight. But it has lost the vitality it seemed to have only three months ago. Strange to say, I never felt any illness. And yet the body had become weak and the instrument registered high blood pressure. I have to be careful.

I am in Delhi to rest for a few days. If your original plan had been carried out I would have remained in Wardha for our meeting. It would have been quieter there for you. But if it is the same thing to you, we may meet in Delhi where I should be till 23rd instant at least.[541] But if you prefer Wardha I can return there earlier. If you come to Delhi, you could stay with me in the Harijan quarters newly built in Kingsway—quite a good place. You will tell me, when you can, the date of our meeting. Rajendra Babu and Jamnalalji are or will be with you. Vallabhbhai also would have been but we all thought it would be better if he stayed away. The other two have gone there not for political discussion but for condolence. The political discussion will take place when we have all met and when you have finished domestic work.

I hope Indu bore well the grief of Kamala's death and the almost immediate separation from you. What is her address?

May everything be well with you.

Love.

Bapu

CWMG, *Vol. LXII, pp. 251–2*

[540] Nehru had just at that time been elected President of the Indian National Congress for the second time.

[541] They met in Delhi on 17 March.

## 226. Letter to Jawaharlal Nehru

21 April 1936

My dear Jawaharlal,
The notes make good reading. Your answers were fairly full and of course straight.[542]

Why do you feel worried over the forthcoming meeting?[543] If there is discussion it would only be to convince one another of the soundness of one's views. You will stop the discussion when you think a proposition has been thoroughly argued. After all you want team-work and I have great hope of this happening.

I reach Nagpur 23rd evening.

I wish Ranjit will take care of himself. I am glad he has gone to Khali.[544] I expect Sarup to accompany you.

Sardar is still suffering and is just now on buttermilk only. I am taking him to Nandi Hill after 8th May. I wish you too could come.

Love.

Bapu

CWMG, *Vol. LXII, p. 339*

## 227. Letter to Jawaharlal Nehru

Wardha
3 May 1936

My dear Jawaharlal,
My right hand needs rest. You will perhaps like to read the enclosed.[545] It need not be returned.

[542] The reference is presumably to Nehru's interview to the press, 19 April 1936. See *SWJN*, Vol. 7, I Series, pp. 200–2.

[543] Of the Congress Working Committee

[544] The estate of Ranjit Pandit, Nehru's brother-in-law, in the Kumaon Hills, where Nehru had spent 16 days in the early days of spring 1938. Describing the beauty of Khali, Nehru wrote in 1938, 'there was peace and quiet and well-being and for companions we had the snows and the mountains and the hillsides covered with a multitude and a variety of trees and flowers, and the singing of birds.'

[545] See the following item.

Khurshed has written to me about her new suggestion regarding the scope of Kamala Memorial. If it is a substitute for the hospital, it is in my opinion inadmissible. And it cannot be carried out for 3 lacs.[546]

Love.

Bapu

CWMG, *Vol. LXII, p. 366*

## 228. Letter to Jawaharlal Nehru

Nandi Hill
12 May 1936

My dear Jawaharlal,
The reason why I sent you my reply to Agatha[547] was to know whether I had correctly represented your attitude.

But I am glad you have gone for me instead. I am not guilty of supporting a system which involves a continuous and devastating class war or expressing approval of systems based essentially on *himsa*[548] or of criticising and condemning people for more or less minor faults and praising others who are guilty of far more important failings.

It is possible that I am unconsciously guilty of the things you seem to impute to me. If so, you should give me concrete instances. I have already admitted that my method of dealing with things is different from yours as I see it. But there is no difference whatsoever about looking at the existing system.

Dr Ansari's death[549] is a severe blow. For me it was infinitely more than a political friendship.

I hope you are going to Khali or coming to me to breathe a little cool air.

[546] See also p. 281.

[547] Dated 30 April 1936, in which Gandhi wrote: 'But Jawaharlal's way is not my way. I accept his ideal about land, etc. But I do not accept practically any of his methods ... Though the gulf between us as to the outlook upon life has undoubtedly widened, we have never before been so near each other in hearts as we perhaps are today.'

[548] Violence as opposed to ahimsa, nonviolence

[549] On 10 May while travelling by train from Dehra Dun to Delhi.

Please tell Sarup I had her two notes. I will write to Sir Tej.
Love.

Bapu

CWMG, *Vol. LXII, p. 392*

## 229. Letter to Jawaharlal Nehru

21 May 1936

My dear Jawaharlal,
Here are two cuttings from the *Hindu*.[550] I have refused to believe that you are correctly represented by the reporter. But I would like the correct version, if you can send me one on both the subjects. The exclusion of women was entirely your own act. Indeed, nobody else had even thought it possible to exclude a woman from the cabinet. As to khadi I have understood you to say that it is indispensable in the present economy of the nation and that when the nation came to its own, hand-made cloth might have to give place to the mill-made.

Love.

Bapu

CWMG, *Vol. LXII, pp. 424–5*

[550] The first cutting read: 'Mr Jawaharlal Nehru, addressing a ladies' meeting this evening, said that he was asked in several places why he had not included women in the Congress Working Committee. He was surprised that no such question was coming from women. He continued, "The responsibility of choosing the Working Committee members rests with the President, and you all know what the situation was at Lucknow. You know the price I had to pay for my views and I have to continue to pay such price. Choosing the Working Committee members was not easy. You are aware I, as President, encountered many odds at Lucknow and my wishes were not carried out. Possibly, another man in my place would have resigned but I propose to do my utmost."'

The second cutting read: 'Mr Nehru when he visited the Khadi Bhandar today expressed doubts as to whether hand-spinning and weaving were an economic proposition. From his experiences in the United Provinces, he could only say that it was not so. He, therefore, favoured development of machinery.'

## 230. Letter to M.K. Gandhi

Anand Bhawan, Allahabad
25 May 1936

My dear Bapu,
I returned late last night. I found one of your letters awaiting me. Another came today.

About the two cuttings from *The Hindu*. I attended and spoke at several dozen meetings in Bombay—I have lost count of them—and had no time to see reports. I spoke in Hindustani of course and reporting was no easy matter—and then condensed reports are apt to be misleading. The report on what I said on khadi, however, was pointed out to me and was corrected the same day or the next day. What I had said was that for many reasons—economic, political, social—khadi was an important item in our present programme and must be encouraged. But that I did not think that it could finally solve our poverty problem, especially if the present social system continued. This system transferred the improvements and additional earnings of the peasant to the landlord. But I pointed out that this theoretical argument did not apply today. For this I said that although I was in favour of big industry, I believed that even with the increase of industrialisation there would be considerable room for the development of cottage industries in India. At present of course they were even more important from various points of view.[551]

About women and the Working Committee I began by saying that I had received some protests for their non-inclusion. I would have welcomed even stronger protests for I wanted our women to be more aggressive and to insist on their rights, both political

[551] This paragraph was quoted in Gandhi's article in *Harijan*, 6 June 1936, 'A False Alarm', wherein he explains the purport of Nehru's observations on khadi. See *CWMG*, Vol. LXIII, pp. 15–17. He further observed in another article (ibid., p. 115), 'In common with the other believers in khadi till the country has attained its freedom he thinks khadi to be a vital necessity. His doubt about its economic value has a place, if at all, only when independence is achieved and industrialisation on a vast scale takes place in the country. Surely no wise man will give up khadi now for fear of its being overwhelmed by industrialisation which may or may not envelop India in the far-off future.' See also the following item.

and social. I invited them to organise themselves to press for their rights which they were not likely to get if they waited for the goodwill of their menfolk. About the Working Committee I said that it was formed under peculiar circumstances when I had to play an unusual part. A हयादार[552] president would probably have resigned but I being बेहया[553] stuck on even though the majority of the Congress had decided against me on some vital issues. This peculiar position was reflected in the formation of the WC which certainly could not be under the circumstances of my choice although technically I was responsible for it. When various important viewpoints have to be represented, the lesser ones go to the wall. You are perfectly right in saying that I was responsible for the exclusion of women. But yet this is not the whole matter. I would have liked to have a woman in the WC but as matters developed and numbers of other names appeared and stayed, there was little choice left. Ultimately I felt that it mattered little to me who was in the WC and who was not. The Committee as it took shape was not my child—I could hardly recognise it and to some inclusions, as you know, I reacted strongly.[554] Yet ultimately I submitted but inevitably with the thought that I was surrendering to others and almost against my own better judgement. At the very first meeting, almost without provocations, the inherent conflicts appeared. The whole purpose of a president nominating a homogeneous committee was thus frustrated.

As you know Jaya Prakash has not been elected to the AICC owing to some technical difficulty. I do not know whether this seat should be filled soon by someone else or left vacant for the present. Jaya Prakash feels that he must not hang on under these circumstances.

[552] *Hayadar*, meaning self-respecting

[553] *Behaya*, meaning shameless

[554] The Working Committee rejected Nehru's proposal to permit the collective affiliation of trade unions and peasant leagues with the Congress, and also his attempt to associate the Congress more directly with the struggle for political reform in the princely states. And Gandhi's policy of passive support was reiterated. The resolution on agrarian reform had been toned down and, while condemning the 1935 Act, the Congress agreed to contest the elections and shelved the question of office acceptance.

About your other question, it is a little difficult to answer without indulging in personalities. Perhaps when we meet I shall mention some names. But, even generally speaking, I find something incomprehensible in your pushing people whose only merit seems to be that they are moneyed or have succeeded in attaining a certain position in this cut-throat world of ours.

Day after tomorrow I am going to Delhi (to visit Zohra)[555] and the Punjab. I shall be away for 8 days. And then I shall attend the UP Provincial Conference at Unao. Perhaps afterwards I might go to Khali but even then only for a week or 10 days.

Many letters have come to me about a proposed Ansari Memorial. We are all waiting for a lead from you.

Love.

Yours affectionately,
Jawahar

MKG Papers, Pyarelal Collection, *NMML*

## 231. Letter to Jawaharlal Nehru

29 May 1936

My dear Jawaharlal,

I have your letter of 25th instant. So you are touring with almost feverish speed. May you have the requisite strength. Even a week at Khali will be a godsend.

I propose to make public use of your statement on khadi.[556] I have received so many inquiries. The distorted summary has caused consternation among our people who have faith in khadi. Our statement will ease the situation a bit.

Your explanation about the omission of a woman on the WC does not give me satisfaction. If you had shown the slightest desire to have a woman on the Committee, there would have been no

[555] Daughter of Dr Ansari, who had died on 10 May 1936

[556] The *Bombay Chronicle* report of 16 May 1936 reported Nehru as having stated that 'khaddar has benefited the people of the country to a considerable extent. We have derived as much benefit out of it as possible and should continue to do so. It is the duty of Congressmen to see khadi is encouraged. But I want to say that in the ultimate solution of the nation's economic problem the khadi movement has only a limited place.'

difficulty whatsoever about any of the older ones standing out. There was pressure if it may be so called only about Bhulabhai.[557] And the first time his name was mentioned you had no objection. There was no pressure about any other member. And then you had this unfettered choice of omitting a socialist name and taking a woman. But so far as I remember you yourself had difficulty in choosing a substitute for Sarojini Devi and you were anxious to omit her. You even went so far as to say that you did not believe in the tradition or convention of always having a woman and a certain number of Mussalmans on the cabinet. Therefore so far as the exclusion of women is concerned, I think it was your own unfettered discretion. No other member would have had the desire or the courage to break the convention. I must also tell you that in certain Congress circles the whole blame is being thrown on me, for I am reported to have excluded Mrs Naidu and to have insisted on having no woman—a thing for which as I said to you I had not even the courage. I could not exclude even Mrs N, not to mention a woman.

As to the other members too, I have been under the impression that you chose the members because it was the right thing to do for the cause. There was no question of *behaya* or *hayadar* when all were actuated by the noblest of motives, i.e., service of the cause according to their lights. I may say that your statement which your letter confirms has given much pain to Rajen Babu, CR and Vallabhbhai. They feel—and I agree with them—they have tried to act honourably and with perfect loyalty towards you as a colleague. Your statement makes you out to be the injured party. I wish you could see this viewpoint and correct the report if it is at all possible.

As to the third thing, I would love to have the thing cleared. I cannot guess what you want to say. But that must wait till we meet. I must not add to the strain you are already bearing.

[557] Bhulabhai J. Desai (1877–1947); Advocate-General; appeared on behalf of the peasants during the Bardoli Satyagraha before the Broomfield Committee, 1928 and the Bardoli Enquiry, 1931; joined the civil disobedience movement, 1932; Member, Congress Working Committee and leader of Opposition, Central Assembly; President, Bombay PCC; defended the three Indian National Army soldiers accused of treason during World War II

About Dr Ansari memorial, I have given Asaf Ali[558] my clear opinion that the memorial for the Doctor should await better times politically as it has for Papa.[559] Do you think otherwise?

The Kamala Memorial is making slow progress.

Herewith the Princess's letter containing a reference to Indu.

Love.

Bapu

[PS]
Bangalore City till 10th.

CWMG, *Vol. LXII, pp. 454–5*

## 232. Letter to Jawaharlal Nehru

19 June 1936

My dear Jawaharlal,

I was about to send you the enclosed[560] for your information when I got your letter yesterday.

I am glad Ranjit is better. He must take care of himself.

I do not want you to issue any special statement about the omission of women from your cabinet. I think that this omission does not stand on the same footing as the inclusion or exclusion of others. None of us had either the courage or the wish to exclude women altogether from the WC. If this is the correct interpretation of your attitude, it should be made clear if the occasion offers itself.[561]

As to the others I am sorry you feel still sore about what happened. You swallowed the Bhulabhai pill in the interests of the cause. And surely at the very first discussion I had said before you had mentioned the thing that there must be socialists in the cabinet. I mentioned also the names. What however I want to

[558] Asaf Ali (1888–1953); barrister of Delhi; Congress Member, Central Assembly, 1943–6; Member, Interim Government, 1946; Indian Ambassador, USA, 1947–8; Governor, Orissa, 1948–52; Indian Ambassador, Switzerland, 1952–3

[559] Motilal Nehru, who had died on 6 February 1931

[560] Not available

[561] For Nehru's statement to the Press of 6 July 1936 clarifying his position, see *SWJN*, Vol. 7, I Series, pp. 313–14.

emphasise is not who mentioned whom but that all were actuated by no other motive than that of serving the common cause.

So far as I remember, what you have sent me is not the statement I had seen. What you have enclosed I seem to see for the first time. Please ask Dr H. if he issued any other. Even the one you have sent me is at variance with what the Doctor used to tell me. I take no exception to the expression of his views, faulty, in my opinion, though they are. My complaint is that he said one thing to me and said another thing [for] publication. You are at liberty to show this to Dr H.

I hope you are well. I was following your Punjab hurricane tour not without anxiety.

Love.

Bapu

[PS]
If the writing is too faint to read, please throw away the letter.

CWMG, *Vol. LXIII, pp. 72–3*

## 233. Letter to Jawaharlal Nehru

Segaon, Wardha
22 June 1936

My dear Jawaharlal,
This is another batch of cuttings, of more importance perhaps to you than to me. My right hand is resting.

No more, since we meet soon.

Love.

Bapu

CWMG, *Vol. LXIII, p. 82*

## 234. Letter to M.K. Gandhi

Allahabad
5 July 1936

My dear Bapu,
I arrived here last night. Ever since I left Wardha, I have been feeling weak in body and troubled in mind. Partly this is no doubt due to the physical causes—a chill which has aggravated my throat

trouble. But partly also it is due to other causes which touch the mind and spirit directly. Since my return from Europe, I have found that meetings of the Working Committee exhaust me greatly; they have a devitalising effect on me and I have almost the feeling of being older in years after every fresh experience. I should not be surprised if this feeling was also experienced by my colleagues of the Committee. It is an unhealthy experience and it comes in the way of effective work.

I was told, when I returned from Europe, that the country was demoralised and hence we had to go slow. My own little experience during the past four months has not confirmed this impression. Indeed I have found a bubbling vitality wherever I have gone and I have been surprised at the public response. What this is due to I cannot say definitely. I can only make various guesses. This public response has naturally heartened me and filled me with fresh energy. But this energy seems to ooze out of me at every meeting of the Working Committee and I return feeling very much like a discharged battery. The reaction has been greatest on this occasion because of my being physically in a low condition.

But it was not about my physical condition that I wished to write to you. There are more important matters which worry me and so far I have seen no clear way out. I do not wish to act in a hurry or without giving the fullest thought to the matter. But even before my own mind is decided I want to tell you which way I am looking.

I am grateful to you for all the trouble you took in soothing over matters and in helping to avoid a crisis.[562] I was convinced then and

[562] At the Congress Working Committee meeting held at Wardha on 29 June, Nehru was out of tune with the majority of the members, so much so that seven members of the Working Committee, namely, Rajendra Prasad, C. Rajagoplachari, Jairamdas Doulatram, Jamnalal Bajaj, Vallabhbhai Patel, J.B. Kripalani, and S.R. Deo, tendered their resignations from the Working Committee. They later withdrew them on Gandhi's intervention. Rajendra Prasad, however, sent a personal letter to Nehru explaining in detail the reasons that had impelled him and the others to send in their resignations.

The differences in the WC, which had become apparent at the Lucknow Congress Session at which Nehru was elected President, revolved round the question of how the Congress could commit itself to socialism in its programme.

I am convinced now that a break of the kind suggested would have had serious consequences for all our work, including the elections. And yet, where are we now and what does the future hold for us? I read again Rajendra Babu's letter to me[563] (the second one) and his formidable indictment of me. That indictment, though formidable, is not specific, except for my speech at the women's meeting, which, as a matter of fact, has nothing to do with any wider issue. The main thing is that my activities are harmful to the Congress cause. They are doing damage to the Congress and are lessening its chances of success at the elections. If I continue in this way there is likely to be further deterioration and my colleagues do not wish to take any chances in this vital matter.

Now, obviously, if there is any truth in this charge it must be faced. The matter is too serious to be glossed over. There are no black and white shades, no delicate balancing of the resultant good or evil; it is all black and that really makes it easier to decide. For however tenderly the fact may be stated, it amounts to this: that I am an intolerable nuisance and the very qualities I possess—a measure of ability, energy, earnestness, some personality which has a vague appeal—become dangerous for they are harnessed to a wrong chariot. The conclusion from all this is obvious.

My own impression before Lucknow, and to some extent even at Lucknow, was that it should not be difficult for all of us to pull together this year. It is evident now that I was mistaken, though there has been no lack of trying on either side. Perhaps the fault may lie with me; I am not aware of it; but one can seldom see the beam in one's own eye. The fact remains, and today there is no loyalty of the spirit which binds our group together. It is a mechanical group and on either side there is a dull resentment and a sense of suppression, and that, as every student of psychology knows, results in all manner of undesirable complexes, both individual and social.

When I reached Bombay this time many people stared hard at me finding it difficult to believe how I had survived. It seemed to be common knowledge there (as reported in the *Times of India*

[563] Dated 1 July 1936; for the text see *A Bunch of Old Letters*, pp. 194–6.

previously) that a peaceful end awaited me—politely of course. All had been fixed up except the cremation. Hence the surprise. It struck me as curious that I should be wholly ignorant of all these confident rumours when many people in the street were full of them. But though I am ignorant of them, the rumours had the strongest justification. That is a measure of my present isolation.

I have written at length, both in my book, and subsequently, about my present ideas. There is no lack of material for me to be judged. Those views are not casual. They are part of me, and I might change them or vary them in future, so long as I hold them I must give expression to them. Because I attached importance to a larger unity I tried to express them in the mildest way possible and more as an invitation to thought than as fixed conclusions. I saw no conflict in this approach and in anything that the Congress was doing. So far as the elections were concerned I felt definitely that my approach was a definite asset to us as it enthused the masses. But my approach, mild and vague as it was, is considered dangerous and harmful by my colleagues. I was even told that my laying stress always on the poverty and unemployment in India was unwise, or at any rate the way I did it was wrong.

You will remember that both in Delhi and in Lucknow I made it clear that I must have freedom to express my views on social matters. I understood you and the members of the Committee to agree to this. The question now becomes one more of this freedom of expression than of the views themselves. Even more so it is a question of values in life, and if we value anything greatly we may not sacrifice it.

There is undeniable conflict. Who is right and who is wrong it is futile to argue. But after last week's incidents I am beginning to doubt if we are really following the right course. I am inclined to think that the right thing for us to do will be to put the matter briefly before the AICC at its next meeting and to take its direction in the matter. How best to do this I am not clear yet but it should be done as simply as possible without much argument. So far as I am concerned there will be little argument.

Presumably the result of this will be that I retire and a more homogeneous Committee will be formed.

You told me that you intended issuing some kind of a statement.[564] I shall welcome that for I believe in every viewpoint being placed clearly before the country.

I am not mentioning this matter to anyone as yet. Of course, prying and impertinent eyes will see this en route even before it reaches you. They have to be suffered.

In Bombay I had a talk with Mridula.[565] She came from Ahmedabad for a few hours at my request. She gave me to understand that, so far as facts were concerned, she had noticed (or mentioned) no difference between what you had told her and what I had written or said. She had indeed made this clear in her letter to you but perhaps you missed a sentence or two. She proposed to send you a copy of her previous letter so that you might see this for yourself.

I was told in Wardha that it was being said by Gujarat women that you and or Vallabhbhai or both were responsible for the exclusion of women from the Working Committee. I enquired from Mridula. She told me that to her knowledge nobody had said so or thought so.

I also had a talk with Sarojini on the subject.

I met Jivraj Mehta and Khurshed. Jivraj did not quite agree with Bidhan about the cost, etc. But he brought down his previous figure somewhat. He now says that 2 lakhs ought to be enough for the construction, equipment, etc., of the hospital. He would like to see another 2 lakhs as a reserve fund. He is also of opinion that the construction should be made not on the Swaraj Bhawan grounds, as originally planned, but on the fields to the East of Anand Bhawan. I shall make enquiries from the Municipality about this.

[564] The reference appears to be to Gandhi's article 'Are We Rivals?' which appeared in *Harijan*, 25-7-1936

[565] Mridula Sarabhai (1911–1974); daughter of Ambalal Sarabhai; Member, Bal Sena, 1920–5; youth movement, 1925–30; was imprisoned several times from 1930 onwards and worked closely with the Jammu and Kashmir National Conference after 1938; appointed one of the Secretaries of the Congress, 1946; organized relief and rehabilitation for refugees and abducted women during Partition

Gandhi once said of her, 'If I had a hundred women like Mridula, I could launch a revolution.'

I propose to convene a meeting of the Kamala Memorial trustees in Bombay about the time the AICC meets. Also a meeting of the Swaraj Bhawan trustees.

In Bombay Nargis[566] insisted on sending me to a German throat specialist and this man has told me to remain absolutely silent for a week in order to rest my throat. It is a hard job.

Love.

Yours affectionately,
Jawaharlal

A Bunch of Old Letters, *pp. 196–9*

## 235. Letter to Jawaharlal Nehru

Segaon, Wardha
8 July 1936

My dear Jawaharlal,

I have just received your letter. I was seeking time to be able to write to you on the events in Wardha. Your letter makes it difficult. I would however just like to say that the letter of withdrawal does not bear the meaning you put upon it when it was given to you. It was sent to you after I had seen it. The sending of such a letter in the place of resignation was my suggestion. I wish that you could take a juster view of that letter. In any case I am firmly of opinion that during the remainder of the year, all wrangling should cease and no resignations should take place. AICC will be paralysed and powerless to deal with the crisis. It will be torn between two emotions. It would be most unfair to spring upon it a crisis, in the name of democracy, which it has never been called upon to face. You are exaggerating the implications of the letter. I must not argue. But I would urge you to consider the situation calmly and not succumb to it in a moment of depression so unworthy of you. Why should you not allow your humour to play upon the meetings of the WC? Why should it be so difficult for you to get on with those with whom you have worked without a jar for years? If they are guilty of intolerance, you have more than your share

[566] Nargis Captain

of it. The country should not be made to suffer for your mutual intolerance.

I do hope you have accepted the very sane advice of the German doctor.

Love.

Bapu

CWMG, *Vol. LXIII, pp. 127–8*

## 236. Letter to Jawaharlal Nehru

Segaon
15 July 1936

*Unrevised by me*

Dear Jawaharlal,

(1) I hope you got my wire about the *Times of India* letter.[567] I procured it yesterday and read it through. Nobody has ever written to me about the subject matter. My reading of the letter confirms my view that you should take legal notice of the libel.

(2) If you will not misunderstand me, I would like you to keep me free of the Civil Liberties Union.[568] I do not like for the time being to join any political institution. And there is no meaning in a confirmed civil resister joining it. Apart however from my joining

[567] *The Times of India* dated 10 July 1936 had carried a letter from J.D. Jenkins under the heading 'Pandit Jawaharlal Nehru and the Muslim Party' where he had criticized Nehru for having contributed an 'offensive article to a journal of the Punjab' but had not mentioned the fact that it was originally printed in 1935. Nehru in his letter of 11 July 1936 to the newspaper had asked for details of the article attributed to him. The article 'His Highness the Aga Khan' published in *The Modern Review,* November 1935, had been written with reference to Sir Mohammad Iqbal's statement which contained a plea for the solidarity of Islam, and protest against fissiparous tendencies. Later, however, Jenkins apologized.

[568] Nehru had sent a circular on 22 April 1936, addressed to a number of prominent individuals of all parties and Editors of newspapers, proposing to start a Civil Liberties Union—the sole function of which would be the protection of civil liberties in all departments of national activity. Subsequently on 8 July 1936 on receiving positive replies to the proposal, he had in consultation with friends drafted a provisional constitution and had sent it out to a number of people including Gandhi, asking, 'May I have your permission to include your name in the foundation members of the National Council?'

or not joining the Union, maturer consideration confirms me in my opinion that it would be a mistake to appoint Sarojini Naidu or for that matter any civil resister as President.[569] I am still of opinion that the President should be a well-known constitutional lawyer. If that does not commend itself to you, then you should have an author of note who is not a law-breaker. I would also ask you to restrict the number of members. You need quality, not quantity.

(3) Your letter is touching. You feel to be the most injured party. The fact is that your colleagues have lacked your courage and frankness. The result has been disastrous. I have always pleaded with them to speak out to you freely and fearlessly. But having lacked the courage, whenever they have spoken they have done it clumsily and you have felt irritated. I tell you they have dreaded you, because of your irritability and impatience of them. They have chafed under your rebukes and magisterial manner and above all your arrogation of what has appeared to them your infallibility and superior knowledge. They feel that you have treated them with scant courtesy and never defended them from socialists' ridicule and even misrepresentation.

You complain of their having called your activities harmful. That was not to say that you were harmful. Their letter was no occasion for recounting your virtues or services. They were fully conscious of your dynamism and your hold over the masses and the youth of the country. They know that you cannot be dispensed with. And so they wanted to give way.

I look upon the whole affair as a tragi-comedy. I would therefore like you to look at the whole thing in a lighter vein. I do not mind your taking the AICC into your confidence. But I do want you not to impose on it the unbearable task of adjusting your family quarrels or choosing between them and you. Whatever you do you must face them with accomplished things.

[569] The resolution passed on it at the Lucknow Congress session in April 1936 said that 'Rabindranath Tagore had consented to be the President of the Union while Sarojini Naidu had accepted the Chairmanship of its Executive Committee.' The chief area of the Union's utility was to be that of propaganda and enlightenment of public opinion. The Union was also to 'keep world opinion about the conditions prevalent in India through the agency of similar unions in other countries'.

Why do you resent their majority being reflected in all subcommittees, etc.? Is it not the most natural thing? You are in office by their unanimous choice but you are not in power yet. To put you in office was an attempt to find you in power, quicker than you would otherwise have been. Anyway that was at the back of my mind when I suggested your name for the crown of thorns. Keep it on though the head be bruised. Resume your humour at the committee meetings. That is your most usual role, not that of a care-worn irritable man ready to burst on the slightest occasion.

How I wish you could telegraph to me that on finishing my letter you felt as merry as you were on that New Year's Day in Lahore when you were reported to have danced round the tri-colour flag.

You must give your throat a chance.

I am revising my statement. I have decided not to publish it till you have seen it. I have decided that nobody should see our correspondence, besides Mahadev.

Love.

Bapu

CWMG, *Vol. LXIII, pp. 144–5*

## 237. Letter to M.K. Gandhi

15 July 1936

My dear Bapu,

Your telegram[570] about the *Times of India* letter came last night. I dislike getting entangled in the meshes of the law but, as you so wish it, I am sending another letter to the *Times*, a copy[571] of which is enclosed. Further action will depend on their reply.

I am going to Karachi tomorrow. It is going to be a lengthy business. I enclose a tentative programme.[572]

Love.

Yours affectionately,
Jawaharlal

SWJN, *Vol. 7, I Series, p. 368*

[570] Not available

[571] Dated 15 July 1936; see *SWJN*, Vol. 7, I Series, p. 367.

[572] Of tour of Sind from 18–27 July 1936

## 238. Letter to M.K. Gandhi

Anand Bhawan, Allahabad
20 July 1936

My dear Bapu,

Your letter came last evening. Of course I want to consider the situation calmly and to act only after the fullest deliberation. That is why I wrote to you. So far I have not mentioned this matter to anyone else. I do not want to do anything in a hurry or in a moment of depression. Life has hardened me sufficiently and the process continues. But I am still sensitive enough to various kinds of approach, and as you say, I am often intolerant, though I try not to be so. I am not, I hope, devoid of humour.

I am trying to consider the matter, however, in as impersonal a manner as possible. I would beg of you to remember that it was not raised by me in the WC. On both occasions I went to the WC meeting without the least thought of it and was much surprised at the turn matters took. I became the accused person on the defensive–an accused who was charged vaguely without specific instances. A kind of trade union came into evidence against me, a combination of my own colleagues intending to take joint action against me, without even first discussing the matter with me. That was an unpleasant enough situation for me and the unpleasantness was all the greater because of the element of surprise in it. All manner of hints and insinuations appeared in the Press, specially in the Bombay Press. Subsequently when I visited Bombay all manner of people were discussing these matters....[573] escaped me to give rise to this subdued but nonetheless pointed controversy in the Press.

I pointed to you myself that the consequences of this contemplated break would be disastrous. I pointed this out to my colleagues. Yet they were firm and even you, to begin with, were inclined to accept this as inevitable. Subsequently you were much more firm and my colleagues very reluctantly... their opinions. But the background did not change. It is one of utter dissatisfaction with me (not personally) and my work; the idea that I am injuring

[573] Ellipses in the letter indicate illegibility in the source.

the common cause. Holding that view friction becomes inevitable, even though it may be suppressed.

I happen to attract a good deal of attention both from the Government and the people. On the one side large numbers of people seem to be influenced by me, on the other I am the butt of a continuous propaganda, insidious and apparent, on the part of the Government, vested interests, communalists, liberal newspapers, Responsivists, etc. That is all in the day's work and I do not mind. But in addition I have to face often veiled attacks by Congressmen and a ...[574]

MKG Papers, Pyarelal Collection, *NMML*

## 239. Letter to M.K. Gandhi

Talia-Sind
20 July 1936

My dear Bapu,

Your letter reached me yesterday in Karachi. I am not sending you a telegram as I do not quite see what I can say in a telegram. I should have liked to write at some length but that is not easy at present owing to the intricate programme which I have to follow here. But as I have told you I propose to take no step without reference to you and other colleagues. I have shown our present correspondence to no one and I do not propose to do so. But I have mentioned the fact of having written to you to Kripalani.

As for the Civil Liberties Union I think matters have gone a little too far now to suggest another name for the presidentship.[575] Invitations for the National Council have also been issued to a considerable number of persons and their acceptances are coming in. Perhaps you are right about yourself.

Yours affectionately,
Jawaharlal

MKG Papers, Pyarelal Collection, *NMML*

[574] The rest of the letter comprising four hand-written sheets is not decipherable.

[575] See pp. 288–9.

## 240. Letter to Jawaharlal Nehru

Segaon, Wardha
30 July 1936

My dear Jawaharlal,
How I wish you would put down your foot on 'insane' programmes and save your energy for the common good.

All will be well if you will never lose your humour and make up your mind to stay out your period, trying to push through your policy as much as you can through the present team. Time has arrived to think of the future, i.e., next year's plans. Whatever happens, you must not be in opposition. That is my confirmed opinion. When like Father you feel that you are ready to take sole charge of the Congress, I think that from the present company you will find no opposition. I hope you will have plain sailing in Bombay.[576]

Kamala Memorial is disturbing me. I do not know what is happening about the collections or the scheme. If Khurshed or Sarup or both are concentrating on the thing, it is well. Please tell Sarup I expect her to keep me informed of her doings in this connection.

I won't discuss here the question of socialism.[577] As soon as I finish revision of my note, you will have the draft before it goes to the Press. My difficulty is not about the remote future. It is always the present that I can concentrate upon and that at times worries me. If the present is well taken care of, the future will take care of itself. But I must not anticipate.

I hope you are keeping really well.

Love.

Bapu

[PS]
You will see the correspondence between Jenkins and myself. I too hate legal proceedings. But this seems to me to be a case where action is called for.

CWMG, *Vol. LXIII, pp. 179–80*

576 At the AICC meeting that was scheduled to be held on 22 and 23 August 1936

577 For Gandhi's views on socialism, see his letter to Sampurnanand, dated 27 July 1937; *CWMG*, Vol. LXV, pp. 440–1.

## 241. Letter to Jawaharlal Nehru

Segaon, Wardha
10 August 1936

My dear Jawaharlal,
Khan Saheb has received the usual notice to attend the meetings in Bombay. He has no desire to attend them and I do not want to press him. And in Bombay he will be asked to attend meetings and functions at which he would be called upon to speak. I do not want him to do so just now. I want him rather to pass the year with me. And he is none too strong nor invulnerable to attacks of illness. Will you, therefore, please excuse him from attendance?

Love.

Bapu

CWMG, *Vol. LXIII, p. 213*

## 242. Letter to Jawaharlal Nehru

Segaon
28 August 1936

My dear Jawaharlal,
Our conversation of yesterday has set me thinking. Why is it that with all the will in the world I cannot understand what is so obvious to you? I am not, so far as I know, suffering from intellectual decay. Should you not then set your heart on at least making me understand what you are after? I may not agree with you. But I should be in a position to say so. Yesterday's talk throws no light on what you are after. And probably what is true of me is true of some others. I am just now discussing the thing with Rajaji. I should like you to discuss your programme with him if you can spare the time. I must not write at length, having no time. You know what I mean.

Love.

Bapu

CWMG, *Vol. LXIII, p. 249*

## 243. Letter to Jawaharlal Nehru

28 December 1936

My dear Jawaharlal,

If you finish today, as I hope you will, you will perhaps let me go away tomorrow after mid-day.

If you have appreciated my suggestion about holding the Congress in villages hereafter, I would like you to ask the Congress to revert to the old rule of holding it in between February and March. The sufferings of the thousands in wintry weather should be avoided if possible. Parliamentarians should fit in with this arrangement. There is no reason why, if the Congress secures a majority in the legislatures, they should not have vacation as they have during Xmas, Easter, etc. I have told Sarup that land somewhere must be secured soon and then house-to-house collections started for Kamala Memorial.

Love.

Bapu

CWMG, *Vol. LXIV, p. 197*

## 244. Letter to Jawaharlal Nehru

3 January 1937

My dear Jawaharlal,

I wish I could have gone with you to Ajanta.[578]

Before I received your letter, I had spoken strongly to Khan Saheb and urged him to send Mehrtaj[579] to Vakil's school.[580] But he was adamant. He does not want her to go to a mixed school. I spoke to Mehrtaj too. She is undoubtedly restless. But Khan Saheb is sanguine and believes that Mehrtaj will recover her usual cheerfulness.

I do hope you will take care of yourself and not wear yourself out.

[578] Nehru had visited the Ajanta caves during his tour of India at this time prior to the general election, on behalf of the Congress.

[579] Abdul Ghaffar Khan's daughter

[580] In Bombay

I had a brief talk with Sarup over the memorial. I am sure that before anything else, at least the ground must be acquired. There need be no insistence on having the plot you described to me or another near Anand Bhawan.

Love.

Bapu

CWMG, *Vol. LXIV, p. 206*

## 245. Letter to M.K. Gandhi

Allahabad
8 March 1937

My dear Bapu,

I have your letter of the 5th March[581] enquiring about khadi at exhibitions. This matter has been repeatedly discussed by us in the course of the past year ever since my return from Europe. The UP Provincial Congress Committee organised one or two exhibitions two or three years back. Since then they have not repeated this. But occasionally some of our district committees organise exhibitions. Even this has grown rarer now. Exhibitions organised by swadeshi sabhas however continue. Last November the Allahabad Swadeshi League had their annual exhibition. As usual they exhibited mill cloth. They wanted me to open the exhibition. For several months I refused to agree because of this khadi matter. Ultimately however I agreed to do so for various reasons chiefly local. I felt that my refusal would be misinterpreted and would do us some injury. In my opening speech there I dealt largely with this question of khadi.

The question you have put is not easy to answer. The average khadi worker seems to be of the opinion that khadi should not be exhibited if mill cloth is allowed there. Other Congress workers are usually of a contrary opinion on the ground that at such exhibitions there is usually a good sale of khadi. Obviously the opinion of the khadi worker who is presumed to be an expert at his job and who is anxious to push khadi should be almost final. I would, therefore, hesitate to give my decision

[581] Not available

against him unless I succeed in convincing him. I imagine that from a certain long-distance view it is better even to incur some loss now so as to avoid producing any confusion in the public mind as to what khadi is and what it is not. This can only be done by adherence to the present policy of banning uncertified khadi sales in such exhibitions.

At the same time I find that uncertified khadi is sold at such exhibitions and plenty of people patronise it. There are quite large numbers of people, as you know, who are not particularly keen on buying certified khadi, but who are prepared to do so if it comes their way. The point is: are we to cater for these people in any special measure or are we to concentrate on holding fast to those who desire to use pure khadi only? This question has not only its business side but its psychological side also. Khadi has, on the one hand, built up a firm foundation for itself and there is a body of men in the country who must have pure khadi, whatever the cost or the trouble. At the same time, khadi does not spread as rapidly as it might among other classes who only occasionally patronise it. For khadi workers the object should be to develop the khadi habit in the latter. That habit comes largely from appeals to the mind or heart and partly from sheer habit. Ordinarily speaking, it would be a good thing to have as many casual purchasers as possible so that they may get used to buying and wearing khadi and thus develop the real habit. The present policy, to some extent, keeps away this casual purchaser and thus reduces the field from which regular khadi buyers might be drawn.

In regard to these exhibitions there is another difficulty. Often enough there is no real supervision over the stuffs that come in and textiles made of foreign yarn are taken, or even some stuffs which are largely foreign and have just a bit of Indian material and work on them. This may perhaps be got over with a more stringent control. But the usual Swadeshi League committee is not frightfully keen over this matter.

Swadeshi exhibitions often raise other issues also which cannot be ignored. For instance, last year I decided to open it because I felt that any other decision on my part would have given rise to some trouble and bitterness and thus would have come in the way of our work.

Therefore if you want my final opinion I cannot give it very definitely, and because of my not being so definite I must respect the opinions of others who are working for khadi. I am however inclined to think that it might be preferable to allow khadi to be exhibited and sold in these exhibitions under certain conditions which would prevent as far as possible (1) something else being mistaken for khadi and the distinction between khadi and mill cloth being clearly preserved, (2) the exclusion of partly foreign stuffs from the exhibitions.

I have just this morning returned from Lucknow. I hope to be here for the next six days. On the 14th I go to Delhi where I hope to meet you on the 15th. In Delhi I shall be staying at Ansari's house.

My mother is improving, I think, though the process is so slow it is hardly perceptible.

I am sending a copy of this letter to Shankerlal direct.

Yours affectionately,
Jawahar

SWJN, *Vol. 8, I Series, pp. 404–6*

## 246. Silence Day Note to Jawaharlal Nehru

[Before 5 April 1937][582]

I still maintain my objection to Kamaladevi. You can have Mridula instead if you want two women. There must be other women in the AICC. Maulana would remain if pressed. I would like Jamnalaji to be spared. But that is a matter between you, Rajen Babu and him. I do not mind too many from UP. You can't help it. I take it you will discuss the list with those whom you want to retain. I can't think of anyone else and anything else.

I think I told you that I used to like her. Her ability is unquestioned. But I have known things which have worried me about her. I should unhesitatingly take Sarup. But I can understand the delicacy. Satyavati deserves the place apart from her fanaticism which makes her sometimes a dangerous ally. You may show my

[582] Inferred from the reference to Gandhi's objection to Kamaladevi Chattopadhyaya's inclusion, presumably in the Congress Working Committee formed by Nehru in 1937. See the following item.

objection to Kamaladevi if you know her sufficiently. For I do not say this behind her back. I believe she knows my opinion. It hurts to hold that opinion, but how can I help myself?

Therefore, let not my opinion weigh with you unduly. If those you want do not object, you should have her. Of course I am partial to Mridula. But Satyavati has a longer record of service and has from the public point of view a better right. Mridula is a brick so far as work and loyalty are concerned. She will be the youngest member, if the choice falls on her. If I had to make the selection of course the choice will be Satyavati almost for the reasons that make you exclude Sarup.

CWMG, *Vol. XCIII, Suppl. Vol. III, pp. 101–2*

## 247. Letter to Jawaharlal Nehru

5 April 1937

*Unrevised*

My dear Jawaharlal,

Why should you become ill? Having become ill, why will you not give yourself rest? I thought you were going to steal away somewhere after Indu came. Please give my love to her when she arrives. I must send her a line with this.

Now about your grouse. Somehow or other everything I say and even perhaps do jars on you. Silence was impossible. I thought in the context the words courtesy and discourtesy came out all right. Yours is the first note of complaint from the Congress side about the statement.[583] I could not help myself if the complaint was universal. I am glad you have written. You must bear with me till my understanding becomes clear or your fears are dispelled. I apprehend no harm from my statement. Is there anything at the back of your mind that I do not understand?

[583] The reference is to Gandhi's statement to the Press on 30 March 1937 wherein, acknowledging that he is 'the sole author of the office-acceptance clause of the Congress resolution and the originator of the idea of attaching a condition' to it, he asks, 'Should the Governors be courteous to the Ministers or discourteous?' See *CWMG, Vol. LXV*, pp. 36–7.

Kamaladevi travelled with us from Wardha to Madras. She was coming from Delhi. She came to my compartment twice and had long chats. At last she wanted to know why Sarojini Devi was excluded, why Laxmipati was being kept away by Rajaji, why Anasuyabai was excluded, and so on. I then told her of my part in her exclusion, and told her almost all that [I] could remember of the note I wrote for you on that silent Monday. Of course, I told her I had no hand in Sarojini's exclusion at first or inclusion after. I told her also that Rajaji, so far as I knew, had nothing to do with L's exclusion. I thought you should know this.

I hope this will find you fully restored. You don't say anything about Mother.

Love.

Bapu

CWMG, *Vol. LXV, pp. 55–6*

## 248. Telegram to Jawaharlal Nehru

Wardhaganj
14 June 1937

Jawaharlal
Care Doctor Bidhan Roy
Wellington Street
Calcutta
I hope you Indu well. Come with her and Maulana during last week weather cooling.

Bapu

CWMG, *Vol. LXV, p. 304*

## 249. Letter to Jawaharlal Nehru

Segaon, Wardha
22 June 1937

My dear Jawaharlal,
Your letter[584] has just reached me. Though three days might prove too few, they would be better than nothing. It is a pity Indu can't

[584] Not available

come with you. I had thought that the operation that she had for tonsils many years ago was the last. I take it this would be as simple as the previous one.

Love to you all.

Bapu

CWMG, *Vol. LXV, p. 328*

## 250. Letter to Jawaharlal Nehru

25 June 1937

My dear Jawaharlal,

Just received your statement[585] on the Frontier policy. Khan Saheb and I have read it. I like it very well. I wonder if the Spanish bombing and the British are exactly alike.[586] How has the extent of the British damage been known? What has been the ostensible reason given for the British bombing? Don't smile or be angry that I do not know these things so well as you do. I can learn very little from the little I see of the newspapers. But don't trouble to answer my questions. I shall follow the reactions to your statement. Maybe these will throw some light. And in any case you will fill in the gaps when we meet. I hope the Maulana will come. But even if

[585] Dated 22 June 1937, issued from Allahabad under the title 'Bombing and Kidnapping on the Frontier'. For the text, see *SWJN*, Vol. 8, pp. 457–62; see also 'Impressions of His Visit to the Frontier', an interview taken by Ram Manohar Lohia and printed in *The Congress Socialist,* 6-11-1937 (*SWJN*, Vol. 8, pp. 468–72). Nehru had undertaken a seven-day tour of the Frontier Province.

[586] For Nehru's writings on Spain, see *SWJN*, Vol. 8, I Series, pp. 701–10. The *National Herald* carried a series of editorials by Nehru which were later reprinted in *China, Spain and the War*, with the following note by Nehru: 'These essays, written a year after my visit to warring Spain, were attempts to capture and imprison in the written word the impressions I gathered there. Unfortunately, as is usual with me, I had kept no record and made no notes, and impressions fade with the lapse of time and memory plays strange tricks. And yet these impressions were vivid enough and much has remained in my mind and will remain, even though the shock of fresh horror and disaster overlays them. I could not finish, as I had intended, this writing down of past experiences. This remains an unfinished document.'

he cannot I would like you to hold on to the date. Let us have the three quiet days.[587]

Hope Indu is well.

Love.

Bapu

[PS]

Khan Sahib wants you to see the enclosed.[588]

CWMG, *Vol. LXV, p. 338*

## 251. Letter to Jawaharlal Nehru

10 July 1937

My dear Jawaharlal,

I had long chats with Maulana Saheb yesterday. If he is to be consulted in the choice of Muslim Ministers in the Provinces, I think it is better to make the public announcement to that effect. The Maulana agrees. If you think that the Working Committee should be consulted, I would suggest consultation by wire.

I expect you will write on the Hindi-Urdu topic at an early date.[589]

Yours sincerely,

Bapu

CWMG, *Vol. LXV, pp. 380–1*

[587] They met in the first week of July.

[588] Not available

[589] Nehru in his article of 25 July 1937 on 'The Question of Language' wrote, 'We have had during recent months a revival of the old controversy between Hindi and Urdu and light excitement has accompanied it and charges and counter-charges have been flung about. A subject eminently suited for calm and scholarly consideration and academic debate has been dragged down to the level of the market-place, and communal passions have centred round it. Inevitably, many of the champions who have entered the field of battle have little to do with scholarship or the love of a language for its own sake; they have been chiefly concerned with the Government orders and court procedure. Those who love language as an embodiment of culture, of airy thought caught in the network of words and phrases, of ideas crystallised, of fine shades of meaning, of music and rhythm that accompany it, of fascinating history and associations of its words, of the picture of life in all its phases, those to whom language is dear because of all this and more, wondered at this vulgar argument and kept away from it.' (*SWJN*, Vol. 8, I Series, pp. 829–45)

## 252. Letter to M.K. Gandhi

Allahabad
13 July 1937

My dear Bapu,
On my return from Wardha I had to go almost immediately to Bundelkhand for Sherwani's election. I have just returned and found your note awaiting me. I am glad that a public announcement was made about the Maulana being consulted regarding Muslim Ministers. I am expecting him and Govind Ballabh this evening for consultation.

Abdul Ghaffar Khan accompanied me to Jhansi, etc., and has returned with me. Probably he will go to Bihar in a day or two. I do not quite know his programme yet.

About the Hindi-Urdu matter I shall write something within a few days. It will not be very deep. But it may help in clearing the issues and facilitating a calmer consideration of them. I shall send you a copy, also to Maulana. Just at present there is a rush of work here in the office owing to my long absence[590] and Kripalani is not here.

Sherwani's election is an uncertain affair. One thing can be said, that the majority either way is likely to be small. The electorate is 7,500. Probably 5,000 will vote and I imagine that the majority will be less than 500, probably much less. The major fact against us is a question of caste brotherhood. The Muslim League candidate[591] is

[590] Nehru writes in his *Autobiography*, 'This general election was a memorable affair for me. I was not a candidate myself but I toured all over India on behalf of Congress candidates, ... In the course of about four months I travelled about 50,000 miles, using every kind of conveyance for this purpose ... by aeroplane, railway, automobile, motor lorry, horse carriages of various kinds, bullock cart, bicycle, elephant, camel, horse, streamer, paddle-boat, canoe and on foot.'

[591] Rafiuddin Ahmad. Jinnah in an appeal addressed to the voters of the Jhansi-Jalaun-Hamirpur Muslim rural constituency bye-election had said, 'The Muslim League has been established with a view to coordinate the actions of Muslims according to the dictates of Allah and the Holy Koran. ... By defeating the Congress candidate let us give them such a crushing reply that non-Muslim organisations never dare to interfere in problems which concern our religion and community alone.' See also p. 307.

a Malkhan Rajput and 25 per cent of the total electorate consists of these Malkhan Rajputs. These people in a caste panchayat have decided to support the Muslim League candidate and they have even gone so far as to threaten with various pains and penalties those members of the brotherhood who vote against their candidate. These people are so frightened of this caste order that they dare not even come out of their houses to our meetings. They simply keep away. This is a solid block of votes and we have so far been unable to touch them.

Then, of course, there is the cry of 'Islam in danger' and this is being exploited to the uttermost by Shaukat Ali and some others. As a matter of fact we have had all the better of the argument and we have produced quite a galaxy of Muslim leaders including men like Maulana Husain Ahmad[592] and other Ulemas to support Sherwani.The general feeling among the better class Muslim is entirely in favour of Sherwani. The peasantry as a rule is also in his favour except for the Malkhan Rajputs. The whole electorate is very backward, politically speaking. Whatever the result of the election it has been a great success from our point of view in awakening the Muslim masses there, and large numbers of Muslims of the middle classes have volunteered for help to Sherwani. Students of Aligarh have come of their own accord to help him. Altogether the atmosphere created by this election not only in the constituency but in the UP generally is good. There is considerable resentment at the exploitation of religion and at the backwardness of the Muslim masses who can be misled in this way.

There are of course elements of trouble in the constituency in the sense that Shaukat Ali and others are always talking in terms of trouble. Shaukat Ali continually refers to a possible civil war.[593]

[592] (1879–1957); Islamic scholar; was against the two-nation theory; President, Ulema-e-Hind, till his death

[593] In a statement published on 9 July 1937, Shaukat Ali had said, 'I am very sorry to see Pandit Nehru and his entourage on the warpath, issuing challenges to everybody. I do not know what others will do, but I am certain that the Indian Muslims will never accept the position, which he wants to assign them. Nor would they become anybody's camp followers. If he persists in this policy I am afraid he will create great mischief, hurt the cause of freedom and the progress of India and worsen our position which will eventually end in civil war.'

He has said that he will make a Spain[594] of India and so on and so forth. His language sometimes is astonishingly vulgar. All this may delude some people. But it has produced a strong reaction among the thinking Muslims against him. Many people who were half-hearted in their support of the Congress are now much stronger and more determined.

Yesterday at Orai I had a slightly unpleasant experience. As I was coming back in a car from Jalaun accompanied by Mahmud and two others, suddenly a group of little boys, hardly more than six or seven years of age, headed by two grown-ups with the Muslim League flag, tried to stop our car and then threw stones at it. A windowpane was broken, but no one was hurt. Such incidents, small in themselves, create excitement. However, I treated it lightly and I believe the excitement passed. Some of our Muslim colleagues there were very angry and wanted to demand police action. But I stopped this. Reports from the Punjab and Sind regarding work among the Muslim masses are very encouraging.

Yours affectionately,
Jawaharlal

SWJN, *Vol. 8, I Series, pp. 159–61*

## 253. Letter to Jawaharlal Nehru

Segaon, Wardha
15 July 1937

My dear Jawaharlal,
Today is the election day. I am watching.

But this I write to tell you that I have begun to write on the function of Congress Ministries and allied topics.[595] I hesitated but I saw that it was my duty to write, when I felt so keenly. I wish I could send you an advance copy of my article for *Harijan*. Mahadev will see this. If he has a copy he will send it. When you see it, you will please tell me if I may continue to write so. I do not want to interfere with your handling of the whole situation. For, I want the maximum

594 Where a civil war had broken out in July 1936

595 See 'Congress Ministries', *Harijan,* 17-7-1937 (*CWMG*, Vol. LXV, pp. 406–8) and also 'The Fundamental Difference', *Harijan,* 24-7-1937 (ibid., pp. 431–3).

from you for the country. I would be doing distinct harm, if my writing disturbed you.

I hope you got my letter about the Maulana.

Love.

Bapu

CWMG, *Vol. LXV, p. 395*

## 254. Letter to Jawaharlal Nehru

Segaon, Wardha
22 July 1937

My dear Jawaharlal,

Maulana Saheb stopped for a day in Wardha and we had a long chat. He showed me the draft agreement between Muslim League members of the Assembly and the Congress members. I thought it was a good document. But he told me that whilst you liked it, Tandonji did not. I have written to the latter about it as the Maulana suggested I should. What is the objection?

The Rs 500 salary with big house and car allowances is being severely criticised. The more I think of it, the more I dislike this extravagant beginning.[596] I talked about this, too, to the Maulana.

How is Indu?

Love.

Bapu

CWMG, *Vol. LXV, p. 427*

[596] The Congress Working Committee meeting held at Wardha from 15–22 March had passed the following resolution: 'Apart from free provision to be made by the state for residence and conveyance, the salaries of Ministers, Speakers, and the Advocate-Generals shall not exceed Rs 500 per month, as laid down in the Karachi Resolution on Fundamental Rights and Economic Programme.'

## 255. Letter to Jawaharlal Nehru

Segaon, Wardha
30 July 1937

My dear Jawaharlal,
I hope Mahadev told you yesterday in addition to acknowledging your essay on Hindi[597] that the Viceroy[598] had invited me to Delhi on the 4th for no special reason but merely to have the pleasure of meeting him. I replied[599] saying that he had anticipated me for I wanted to seek an interview with him about the ban on Khan Saheb and my desire to visit the Frontier.[600] I am accordingly reaching Delhi on the 4th. The appointment is for 11.30. Therefore, I hope to be able to leave the same day, returning to Segaon on the 5th.

But this letter is to send you a copy of Zakir's[601] letter in reply to my letter giving my reaction to the recent riot in Bombay and the wretched Hindi-Urdu controversy. I thought that I should share with you this considered letter.

I do not regard the Jhansi election as a rout.[602] It is an honourable defeat, giving rise to the hope that if we plod away we can effectively take the Congress message to the Mussalmans. But I still abide by my opinion that the mere taking of the message unaccompanied by substantial work in the villages won't answer our purpose in the end. But it all depends upon the way in which we want to generate power.

[597] See p. 302, *fn*. 589.

[598] Lord Linlithgow (1887–1952); Chairman, Royal Commission of Indian Agriculture, 1926–8; Chairman, Joint Select Committee on Indian Constitutional Reform, 1933; Viceroy of India, 1936–43

[599] On 27 July 1937

[600] The ban on Abdul Ghaffar Khan's entry into NWFP, imposed in 1931, was lifted after six years at the end of August 1937.

[601] Zakir Husain (1897–1969); educationist, co-founder of Jamia Millia Islamia University; Vice Chancellor, Aligarh Muslim University, 1948–56; Governor, Bihar, 1957–62; President of India, 1967–9

[602] The Muslim League candidate, Rafiuddin Ahmad had polled 4,557 votes defeating N.A.K. Sherwani, the Hindu candidate, by 727 votes.

Meherally's[603] speech in Madras is an eye-opener for me. I wonder how far he represents the general socialistic view.[604] Rajaji has sent me a cutting containing his speech. I hope he has sent a copy to you also. I call it a bad speech of which you should take notice. This is going contrary to the Congress policy as I read it.

There is also Roy's speech at Madras. I take it, you get all such cuttings. Nevertheless, for ready reference I enclose the cuttings which Pyarelal has made for me. Roy has been writing to me, too. You should see his latest letter. It will go with this if I have not destroyed it. What is your reaction to his attitude? As I have already told you I find it difficult to understand him.

Your calling khadi 'livery of freedom' will live as long as we speak the English language in India. It needs a first-class poet to translate into Hindi the whole of the thought behind that enchanting phrase.[605] For me it is not merely poetry but it enunciates a great truth whose full significance we have yet to grasp.

Love.

Bapu

[PS]

Though the paragraph about Roy's speech follows the one about Meherally's it is not to suggest that it is on a par with M's.

CWMG, *Vol. LXV, pp. 445–6*

[603] Yusuf Jafar Meharally (1903–1950); participated in the agitation against the Simon Commission in 1928 and the Salt Satyagraha, 1930; Member, Congress Socialist Party, 1935–6; participated in the Quit India movement

[604] Commenting on Yusuf Meharally's speech in his letter of 27 July 1937 to Sampurnanand, Gandhi had written, 'It explains fully what the socialists are doing. The object is to start a revolt in every sphere. But a revolt has never been possible without violence.'

[605] In a statement issued to the press on 'The Decision to Accept Office' Nehru has said that 1 August should be observed as Ministry Day and also it was time that every Indian came out on India's side and cooperated with the Congress in the high tasks it has undertaken. 'I trust that as an earnest of this sympathy and goodwill every Indian, who stands for Indian freedom, will wear khadi, the livery of our freedom.' See *SWJN*, Vol. 8, pp. 109–10.

## 256. Letter to Jawaharlal Nehru

On the Train
3 August 1937

My dear Jawaharlal,

I am writing this on the train taking us to Delhi. Herewith is my Foreword[606] or whatever it may be called. I could not give you anything elaborate.

You have 'perhaps' before Pushtu and Punjabi.[607] I suggest your removing the adverb. Khan Saheb for instance will never give up Pushtu. I believe it is written in some script, I forget which. And Punjabi? The Sikhs will die for Punjabi written in Gurmukhi. There is no elegance about that script. But I understand that it was specially invented like Sindhi to isolate the Sikhs from other Hindus. Whether such was the case or not, it seems to me impossible at present to persuade the Sikhs to give up Gurmukhi.

You have suggested a common script to be evolved out of the four Southern languages. It seems to me to be as easy for them to substitute Devanagari as a mixture of the four. From a practical standpoint, the four do not admit of an invented mixture. I would, therefore, suggest your confining yourself to the general recommendation that wherever possible the provincial languages which have vital connection with Sanskrit, if they are not offshoots from it, should adopt revised Devanagari. You may know that this propaganda is going on.

Then, if you think like me, you should not hesitate to express the hope that as Hindus and Muslims are one day bound to be one at heart, they will also, who speak Hindustani, adopt one script, i.e., Devanagari, because of its being more scientific and being akin to the great provincial scripts of the languages descended from Sanskrit.

[606] To Nehru's essay on the 'Hindi-Urdu Question' published in *Harijan*, 21-8-1937. See *CWMG*, Vol. LXVI, p. 7.

[607] In the first of the seventeen-point suggestions presented by Nehru in his essay 'The Question of Languages', published in the *Bombay Chronicle*, 11–13 August 1937, the word 'perhaps' was replaced by 'to some extent'.

If you adopt my suggestion in part or in toto you will have no difficulty in laying your finger on the spots requiring the necessary changes. I had intended to do so myself in order to save your time. But I must not put that strain on my system just now.

I take it that my endorsement of your suggestions does not mean that I must ask the Hindi Sammelan to give up the use of the word Hindi. I am sure, that cannot be your meaning. I have taken it to the farthest limit possible as far as I can think.

If you cannot accept my suggestions, it would be better for the sake of accuracy to add the following sentence to the 'Foreword': 'At any rate I have no hesitation in heartily endorsing them in a general way.'

I hope Indu's operation will go off well.

Love.

Bapu

CWMG, *Vol. LXVI, pp. 7–8*

## 257. Letter to Jawaharlal Nehru

On the Train
4 August 1937

My dear Jawaharlal,

I am stupid. On receiving your letter I searched my file and behold! I found the cutting containing Meherally's speech. I referred to his, not Masani's speech.

This is being written in a terribly jolting train taking me back to Wardha. It is now 10.30 p.m. I woke up from sleep, thought of the speech and began the search. Yesterday's compartment was better.

I saw the Viceroy. You will have seen the communique.[608] It correctly summarises the interview. There were other incidental things which Kripalani will mention to you when he meets you. One thing

[608] Issued after the interview on 4 August. It read: 'The Viceroy listened with interest to Mr Gandhi's views on the matters in question and undertook to intimate them to the Governor of the North-West Province. The interview was entirely general and personal in character, the principal subject of discussion being rural uplift and improvement of the conditions of the peasantry.'

I may mention here. He might invite you as he invited me. I told him that if the invitation was sent, you were not likely to refuse it. Was I right?

I am sorry for having inflicted Roy's speeches on you. But I think you were bound to read them. However, I am in no hurry to have your opinion on them. You may take your time unless you have already read them.

I note that you are having the operation for Indu in Bombay.

Love.

Bapu

CWMG, *Vol. XLVI, pp. 12–13*

## 258. Letter to Jawaharlal Nehru

Segaon, Wardha
8 August 1937

My dear Jawaharlal,

I forgot to cover one point in your letter[609] referring to Meherally's speech. I mean Rajaji's communiqué releasing the summer school prisoners. I had read it before receiving your letter. But it did not offend me. I suppose because you approved of the action of the students of the summer school and I could not defend it any way whatsoever.[610] I think that it was necessary to draw attention to the fact that the release did not mean approval of this break or the offence, which in law it was. I fear that often when the Congress is in power it will use language which its predecessors have used and yet the motive behind will be different.

I hope you will have a nice time in Bombay over the operation. You will wire when it is over.

Love.

Bapu

[609] Not available

[610] The Government banned the school started on 1 May, 1937 by the Andhra Congress Socialist Party and the Andhra Youth League on the ground that it sought to spread communist and revolutionary ideas and also lathi-charged the students subsequently. For Nehru's statement, 'On the Ban of the Kottapattam Summer School', see *SWJN*, Vol. 8, pp. 249–50.

[PS]
If Nariman comes to you please grant him the permission to have the inquiry.[611] I am sorry you will be bothered about this affair in Bombay. Mahadev will tell you what I have been doing.

Bapu

CWMG, *Vol. LXVI, pp. 24–5*

## 259. Letter to M.K. Gandhi

27 August 1937

Mahatma Gandhi
Wardha
My dear Bapu,
I enclose a letter I have received from Hardikar.[612] This is just for your information. As you had spoken to me about this matter I wrote to Hardikar and am forwarding his reply. I do not want you to take the trouble to reply about this.

Yours affectionately,
Jawaharlal

MKG Papers, Pyarelal Collection, *Subject File 67, NMML*

[611] See p. 316.

[612] In his letter of 22 August 1937 to Nehru, Hardikar had written: 'The article in question is the same that I had sent you ... I do quite remember that I talked with Mahatmaji for about forty-five minutes between Victoria Terminus and Kalyan when I was proceeding to Poona ... He referred to the underlined sentence in the following and said that "If you do not like the leadership of today you organise your own party, have your own programme, and try to capture the Congress just as I did before 1920."

'(I quote this from my memory) "If we have to create new circumstances in the country, we will have to have new leadership, and if new leadership is to be created, *it must not be of the type that we are observing today*".'

## 260. Letter to M.K. Gandhi

Allahabad
30 September 1937

My dear Bapu,

Chaman Lal[613] has sent me a copy of a letter dated 25th September which he and Hansraj[614] have sent to you. This letter has only just reached me and I am sending him a reply immediately. I enclose a copy of this reply. I think that Hansraj and Chamanlal have acted very unwisely in this matter. I do not know what answer you have sent to them but I am sure that a meeting between you and Jinnah at this stage would not only serve little purpose but might be actually harmful. I am writing to Maulana also about this.

Yours affectionately,
Jawahar

SWJN, *Vol. 8, I Series, p. 182*

## 261. Letter to M.K. Gandhi

1 October 1937

My dear Bapu,

I have received your note with Chamanlal and Hansraj's letter. I have already written to you about it. If Jinnah wants to see you, you cannot of course say no. But I think you might make it clear to him that a mere talk between you two might not help. Perhaps

[613] Dewan Chamanlal; founder member, All India Trade Union Congress; Member, Legislative Assembly, 1923–31; Member, Royal Commission on Labour, 1928–31; Member, Punjab Legislative Assembly, 1936–45; Member, Constituent Assembly, 1946–8; Ambassador of India, Turkey, 1948–9; Member, Rajya Sabha, 1952–67

[614] Raizada Hansraj (1869–1958); leading Congressman of Punjab; Member, Central Legislative Assembly for many years; Member, Lok Sabha, 1952–6

Hansraj and Chamanlal had written that Jinnah was 'in a mood not only to discuss but also to come to an agreement regarding the communal issue as well as other issues of graver import'.

he might suggest first what he wants to discuss. There is the agreement between him and Rajendra Babu which he seems to repudiate now. If he accepts that now let him say so.

This matter is likely to come up before the Muslim League Conference at Lucknow on October 15–16. A party in the League is pressing for adoption by the League of the Rajendra Babu-Jinnah formula. They even threaten to walk out if this is rejected. There are other matters also. It is this pressure which perhaps is inducing Jinnah to take some step which will give him the position of a plenipotentiary on behalf of the Muslims. It will be easier for him then to deal with the League. Of course the League is fully with him but outside the League he is fast losing hold of any influence he possessed.

I would personally prefer that no meeting took place till the position was clearer. But if J desires it then you cannot refuse. But I do not like others to interfere.

I am writing in haste. I have suddenly been summoned to Lucknow. The Muslim Leaguers there have specially requested me to explain to them the significance of the Constituent Assembly resolution. Probably they will not oppose it if I have a talk with them. So I have accepted their invitation and am going.

Today is the last day for enrolment of members for the Congress. The Congress offices are worth seeing. All the workers from the districts coming in crowds with membership books and subscriptions. There is a regular mob. As usual the membership drive took place during the last months or so. It had a good response. In this district we have made 30,000 members. We would make another 10,000 if we had another fortnight. These are I think nearly all bona fide members as there are no rival parties at work.

I shall return from Lucknow on the 5th. On the 9th I leave for the Punjab and on the 14th I ought to be in Peshawar for 3 days.

I hope you will come to Calcutta for the WC, etc.

Love.

Yours affectionately,
Jawaharlal

MKG Papers, Pyarelal Collection, *Subject File 16, NMML*

## 262. Letter to Jawaharlal Nehru

Segaon, Wardha
1 October 1937

My dear Jawaharlal,

So far as I am concerned Pattabhi[615] is a good choice. But I suppose you will have the sense of the members of the Committee.

I don't know whether you will find time to attend the Educational Conference that is being held in Wardha,[616] for which the invitation has gone to you. If you can, I would like you to come, but I do not want you to make time for the Conference if more important work requires your presence elsewhere. Undoubtedly it will be a strain for two days, but your presence will be a solace to me if you can come.

Love.

Bapu

[PS]

You will find herewith the result of my correspondence with Syed Habib, in the shape of a cheque and letter. I simply rebuked him for getting money from here, there or anywhere, without mentioning the conversation I had with you.

CWMG, *Vol. LXVI, p. 183*

## 263. Letter to Jawaharlal Nehru

12 October 1937

My dear Jawaharlal,

I have your letter. I am trying to come to Calcutta, leaving here on the 25th. You will then tell me all about the ministerial deeds in the Congress Provinces. I do hope that the sore throat and cold were only temporary things, and that you were able to stand the strain

[615] Pattabhi Sitaramayya (1880–1959); Congress leader from Andhra who took interest in the States People's Movement; President, INC, 1948; Governor, Madhya Pradesh, 1952–7; author of *The History of the Indian National Congress*

He was being considered for Congress presidentship at this time.

[616] On 22 and 23 October

in the Punjab. The climate in the Frontier must be very delightful. How I wish you would take things easy for a time at least!

Bapu

CWMG, *Vol. LXVI, p. 227*

## 264. Letter to Jawaharlal Nehru

1 Woodburn Park, Calcutta
1 November 1937

Dear Jawaharlal,
Enclosed herewith is the judgement[617] of the inquiry committee about the two issues raised by Shri Nariman in his correspondence with you and me. I had thought that Shri Nariman's acceptance of my recommendation to make a confession which was to take the place of the judgement was a fair ending to an inquiry which gave me many an anxious moment. But Shri Nariman's recantation of the confession which I first saw only in the Press alters the position and reveals the painful state of Shri Nariman's mind. The recantation contains a patent untruth as pointed out by me in my letter to Shri Nariman which you will find in the enclosure.

I recall the fact that Shri Nariman himself courted the inquiry and deliberately wanted an investigation into the charge made on him by Sardar Vallabhbhai of a grave breach of trust in the matter of the Bombay election in 1934. In his letter addressed to you occurs the following sentence:

If the verdict of such an independent tribunal and enquiry tends to blame me in the slightest degree, then I will willingly submit to any penalty which you or any other authority chooses to impose, but at the same time hoping and expecting that, if the blame is found elsewhere, similar indiscriminating [sic] judgement should follow regardless of personalities or personal considerations.

[617] In which D.N. Bahadur had arrived at the conclusion that the 'charge against K.F. Nariman in respect to the elections in 1934 was proved and the charge made by K.F. Nariman against Vallabhbhai was not proved.' For Gandhi's 'Note on Nariman-Sardar Case', see *CWMG*, Vol. LXVI, pp. 233–4, and for K.F. Nariman's statement which followed, ibid., Appendix VI.

In his letters to me (I have not the copies with me), he went further and said that, if he was found guilty of the Sardar's charge, he would consider himself to be unworthy of holding any office of trust.

I am of opinion that by his conduct Shri Nariman has proved himself unworthy of holding any position of trust, not only because he has been found guilty of grave breach of trust in 1934 election and has failed to prove the charge brought by him against Sardar Vallabhbhai, but by his subsequent conduct as betrayed in the correpondence, and especially by his unfortunate recantation of the confession freely given by him in the presence of his counsel.

Yours sincerely,
M.K. Gandhi

Shri Jawaharlal Nehru
President, AICC

CWMG, *Vol. LXVI, pp. 284–5*

## 265. Letter to M.K. Gandhi

Allahabad
3 November 1937

My dear Bapu,
I have just spoken to Pantji on the telephone and he informs me that the situation in Cawnpore is not so bad as he had feared.[618] I am therefore staying on in Allahabad for two days and am going to Cawnpore on the 6th.

One of the Andamans' prisoners, Biswanath Mathur,[619] recently released from Hazaribagh jail, has seen me here. He was released about 10 days ago. He went to Delhi to interview B.K. Dutt, another Andamans' prisoner. Dutt, as you will remember, is well known as

[618] On 9 August 1937, 5,000 mill workers had gone on strike as a protest against alleged victimising and the breach of agreement reached between the mill-owners and the Mazdoor Sabha; for Nehru's letter dated 23 September addressed to the mill workers of Kanpur, see *SWJN*, Vol. 8, I Series, pp. 328–34.

[619] Congressman of Gaya; imprisoned for four years from 1933 in the Andamans for his part in the Gaya Conspiracy Case; later joined the Communist Party

the companion of Bhagat Singh[620] in the Assembly Bomb Case. In this case he was sentenced to 10 years. But subsequently he was sentenced to a life term in the conspiracy case with Bhagat Singh in Lahore. Mathur informs me that Dutt is in a very bad way. He is not only physically ill with various troubles but mentally he is in a state of extreme neurosis and desperation. He is practically in solitary confinement in Delhi, there being no other political prisoners there. Quite apart from the question of release, a suggestion was made to me that it would be a good thing if he was transferred to a Bihar jail. He would probably get better treatment there as well as companions. Also such relatives as he possesses live in Jamshedpur and he could easily have interviews with them. I understand that he has had no interview with relatives for a long time. I do not know what can be done in this matter as he is under the Delhi Government. Perhaps the Bihar Government might suggest his transfer in view of the fact that his relatives live in Bihar. I am sending a copy of this letter to Rajendra Babu.

Yours affectionately,
Jawaharlal

SWJN, *Vol. 8, I Series, p. 632*

## 266. Letter to M.K. Gandhi

5 November 1937

Mahatma Gandhi
1 Woodburn Park
Calcutta
My dear Bapu,
I have received the following telegram from Kusumdevi C/o Bhagwatmal Tewari, Ramnagar, Champaran: 'My husband Babu Kamalnath Tewari severely suffering from appendicitis in Lahore Central Jail. Earnestly try his immediate release for medical

[620] Bhagat Singh (1901–1931); organized revolutionary activities in the Punjab, Delhi and UP; alleged to have been involved in the shooting of a police officer at Lahore on 17 December 1928; arrested after he and B.K. Dutt had exploded a bomb in the Central Assembly on 3 April 1929; one of the principal accused in the Lahore Conspiracy Case; sentenced to death and executed on 23 March 1931

treatment and kindly save his life.' I do not know what to do in such matters. I am sending the telegram to Dr Gopichand[621] as well as the Punjab Provincial Congress Committee.

Yours affectionately,
Jawaharlal

MKG Papers, Pyarelal Collection, *Subject File 349, NMML*

## 267. Letter to M.K. Gandhi

Anand Bhawan, Allahabad
13 November 1937

*Personal*

My dear Bapu,
I enclose a letter I have received from a friend in Paris whom perhaps you know. The letter speaks for itself. In my reply I am telling him that I am referring the matter to you for your advice. I am also informing him of the existence of the Gandhi Seva Sangh.[622] If you think it worthwhile you can ask Mahadev to write directly to Mr Anupchand Shah.

Yours affectionately,
Jawaharlal

Mahatma Gandhi
Encls: 1

MKG Papers, Pyarelal Collection, *NMML*

[621] Dr Gopichand Bhargava (1890–1966); Congress leader of Punjab; leader of Opposition, Punjab Assembly, 1937–40; Chief Minister, Punjab, 1947–51

[622] The Gandhi Seva Sangh was formed in 1923 but its policy and programme continued to evolve till 1934 when they became more defined. Broadly, its aims were the removal of untouchability and promotion of village reconstruction work and village industries. At the meeting of the Sangh in April 1937, when asked whether those who entered the legislatures might be members of the Sangh, Gandhi had said that the members of the Sangh should also enter the legislatures as 'no political programme can stand without the constructive programme. ... But there should be no scramble for power. That will be our undoing. Only those will go as are asked by the Gandhi Seva Sangh to go ....'

## 268. Letter to M.K. Gandhi

Allahabad
14 November 1937

My dear Bapu,

I have just read your article on the AICC meeting.[623] Regarding the Mysore resolution[624] you have said that it was *ultra vires* of the AICC.[625] If this was so, then I had no business to permit discussion on it and should have banned it. I am not aware of any constitutional provision which leads to this result and only something in the nature of such a provision can bar a resolution moved in the ordinary way and supported by a majority of the AICC. Apart from the constitution itself, I am not aware of any previous decision

[623] Gandhi had written in *Harijan,* 13-11-1937, 'the resolution moved in the AICC criticising the Congress ministries and still more the speeches, were wide of the mark. The critics had not cared to study the facts. ... Let them study and take to heart what Jawaharlal Nehru has said in his elaborate statement on the matter. I am convinced that in their action the critics departed from truth and nonviolence ....'

[624] Passed by the AICC on 31 October 1937 at Calcutta which read: 'This meeting of the AICC expresses its emphatic protest against the ruthless policy of repression as indicated by the inauguration of various restrictive and prohibitive orders and political prosecution launched in the Mysore state and also against the suppression of civil rights and liberties by denying the elementary rights of speech, assemblage and association.

'The meeting sends its fraternal greetings to the people of Mysore and wishes them all success in their legitimate nonviolent struggle and appeals to the people of the Indian states and British India to give all support to the people of Mysore in their struggle against the state for right of self-determination.'

[625] Gandhi had observed in *Harijan*, 13-11-1937, 'Much more offensive, in my opinion, was the Mysore resolution and the pity of it is that it was carried with practically nobody to speak out the truth. I hold no brief for Mysore. ... In my opinion the Mysore resolution was *ultra vires* of the resolution of non-interference.... The resolution did not set forth the correct state of affairs, and the speeches were full of passion and without regard to the facts of the case. The AICC should have appointed, if it was so minded a committee even of one person to ascertain the facts before proceeding to pronounce judgement ....'

of the Congress or the AICC which lays down that such matters should not be considered. Even if there was some such resolution, I do not see how it could prevent the AICC from considering a matter if it so chose, unless the resolution was embodied in a rule of practice. The AICC is at complete liberty to consider a resolution which may go contrary to a previous resolution passed by itself. If however there is a rule of practice or procedure, this has to be acted upon till [*sic*] the AICC does not alter it. There is no question of such a rule, but I do not even know of a resolution which lays down a policy which the Mysore resolution infringes. In statements issued by us in the past mention has been made that the Congress desires to follow a policy of non-intervention in the states. Those statements cannot bar the AICC itself from intervening if it so chooses. I cannot understand how the legal phrase, *ultra vires*, can be made to apply.

Another question arises, what is intervention? Is a mention of a state in a resolution intervention? Is a demand for civil liberties, or a condemnation of repression, intervention? If so, the Congress itself has been guilty of it in specific and unequivocal terms during the last two years.

The Mysore resolution of the AICC is very badly worded and, in any event, I did not want it to be passed by the AICC just then. But my feelings have little to do with the matter. I have to act as the president of a democratic assembly. Are we to refrain from condemning repression in a state in future whatever the nature of this repression? If this repression consists in attacking the Congress itself, insulting our flag, or banning our organisation, are we to remain silent? These matters must be cleared up so that our office and our organisation might know definitely what line we are to take up.

You have said that the AICC should not have passed the resolution without at least hearing the other side. Do you think that it is feasible for us to appoint inquiry committees to go to the states? Will the states agree? On several occasions I have suggested this to the states—not a committee but just an individual to go there and inquire from both sides. They have invariably turned this down.

This Mysore matter has been going on for a long time. The Karnataka PCC has taken some steps in the matter. Their secretary has had a long interview with the Dewan of Mysore[626]. I have repeatedly written to the Dewan and put a large number of specific cases before him. He has replied at length without, in my opinion, justifying the state policy. For months past I have been restraining Congressmen in Mysore from indulging in any disobedience of orders and, in fact, no orders have been disobeyed, except by Nariman recently.[627] The Karnataka PCC ultimately considered the situation and condemned the policy of repression in Mysore and asked us for further directions as to what they should do. It is hardly correct, therefore, to say that the AICC condemned anybody unheard or *ex parte*. We pursued all the ordinary avenues open to us.

I am writing all this to you as I want to be clear in my own mind what our policy is. You have censured the AICC and me for the course we pursued. I have not yet understood how and where I was wrong and so long as I do not understand it, I can hardly act otherwise.[628]

Yours affectionately,
Jawahar

SWJN, *Vol. 8, I Series, pp. 567–9*

## 269. Letter to Jawaharlal Nehru

On way to Wardha
18 November 1937

My dear Jawaharlal,

I fancy I could read the personal letter in your eyes as you were hovering round me that awful Sunday night and silent Monday.

[626] Sir Mirza Ismail (1883–1959); Dewan of Mysore, 1926–41; Prime Minister, Jaipur, 1942–6; Dewan of Hyderabad, 1946–7.

[627] K.F. Nariman had been arrested in Bangalore on 24 October 1937 while addressing a students' gathering.

[628] Mahadev Desai replying on behalf of Gandhi wrote that Gandhi 'was clear that there was an infringement of the policy of non-intervention. ... Bapu wants me to assure you that he never intended to censure you ....'

The weakness has not yet left me.[629] I need prolonged rest from all mental toil, but that perhaps cannot be had.[630]

This I write to report to you what I have done about the prisoners in Bengal, and to ascertain whether it meets with your approval.[631] The negotiations have been a taxing affair. Before entering upon them I had consulted the two brothers[632] as to the desirability of securing relief through negotiations. It was possible to be indifferent as to the result and rely upon the growth of public opinion forcing release whenever it was to come. The Brothers were emphatically for negotiations, whilst public agitation continued. I unfolded my plan also and it was after the style of my telegram to the Andamans prisoners. And so I saw the repatriates, detenus brought back from Deoli and last night the Hijli prisoners.[633] The Ministers have agreed to release what they call 'village and home domiciled' detenus almost forthwith, and inside of four months to release those in the detenu camps whom they may consider to be safe. For the rest they will accept my recommendation, if they are not earlier released. My recommendation will depend upon

[629] Gandhi during this period was under stress from high blood pressure and had had a breakdown on 1 November 1937, a silence day. He was in Calcutta from 26 October to 17 November.

[630] Sarojini Naidu commenting on Gandhi's illness in her letter to Nehru dated 13 November 1937 said: 'The little man is sitting unconcernedly eating spinach and boiled marrow while the world ebbs and flows about him, breaking into waves of Bengali, Gujarati, English and Hindi. Bidhan and his colleagues are in despair over his stubborn indocility as regards his health. He is really ill ... not only in his brittle bones and thinning blood but in the core of his soul ... the most lonely and tragic figure of his time ... India's man of destiny on the edge of his own doom.'

[631] On 24 July 1937 about 225 political prisoners in Andamans Central Prison had gone on a hunger-strike. One of their demands was general release of all political prisoners and repeal of repressive laws. But the Government of India had decided not to consider any of these demands unless they gave up the strike. For Gandhi's telegram to the Viceroy dated 27 August and his telegram to Andamans prisoners dated 30 August, see *CWMG*, Vol. LXVI, pp. 74–5, 99 and 253.

[632] Subhas Chandra Bose and Sarat Chandra Bose

[633] Gandhi had met the repatriates from the Andamans in Calcutta's Alipore Jail on 30 October and issued a statement to the press regarding his efforts for their release. See *CWMG*, Vol. LXVI, pp. 281 and 286–7.

my ascertaining the present belief of the detenus. If I am able to say to the Government that they do not believe in methods of violence for the attainment of independence and that they will pursue such Congress activities, as are approved of by the Congress from time to time, they will release them.[634] A declaration of policy might be made any time. I need not go into the details of the conversations with the prisoners in the several prisons and in Hijli camp. I wonder if all this commends itself to you. If you strongly disapprove of it, I would like you to telegraph. Otherwise I shall await your letter.

The strikes in Ahmedabad of which I have no knowledge, except from what I gather from the papers, as also what the papers say about Sholapur, disturbed me.[635] If we cannot control the situation either because a section of the Congressmen would not submit to Congress discipline or because the Congress cannot control the activities of those who are outside the Congress influence, our holding of offices is bound to prove detrimental to the Congress cause.

The 'Bande Mataram' controversy has not yet died out.[636] Many Bengalis are sore at heart over the WC decision. Subhas told me he was trying to calm the atmosphere.

I expect to have to go back to Bengal soon after the assumption of office by the incoming Governor.

I hope you are keeping well. The paragraph in the newspaper about Sarup was disturbing. Is her health unequal to the strain she is undergoing?

[634] For Gandhi's statement on Bengal Government's Communique dated 21 November, ibid., pp. 303–6.

[635] For Gandhi's article on the subject entitled 'Storm Signals' in *Harijan*, 20-11-1937, ibid., pp. 300–2.

[636] Some Muslims having objected to the practice of singing the patriotic song *vande mataram* in certain legislatures, the Congress Working Committee which had met in Calcutta in the last week of October, recommended that 'whenever and wherever *vande mataram* was sung the first two stanzas should be sung with perfect freedom to the organisers to sing any other song of unobjectionable character, in addition to, or in place of *vande mataram*'. The song occurs in *Anandhmath* by Bankim Chandra Chattopadhyay. For Gandhi's views on it, see also *CWMG*, Vol. LXIX, pp. 379–81.

This is being written as we are nearing Nagpur. We arrive [at] Wardha this evening.

Love.

Bapu

CWMG, *Vol. LXVI, pp. 296–8*

## 270. Letter to M.K. Gandhi

19 November 1937

Mahatma Gandhi
Maganwadi
Wardha

My dear Bapu,

I wrote to you a few days back about your criticism of the Mysore Resolution of the AICC. I have received a letter on this subject from R.S. Hukerikar, Secretary of the Karnatak PCC. I am enclosing a copy of it for your information.[637]

Yours affectionately,
Jawaharlal

MKG Papers, Pyarelal Collection, *Subject File 165, NMML*

## 271. Telegram to Jawaharlal Nehru

10 January 1938

Mother lived nobly has died nobly.[638] She was a model wife widow and mother. No sorrow. Let our women copy her example.

Love.

Bapu

CWMG, *Vol. LXVI, p. 332*

[637] R.S. Hukerikar had written to Nehru in his letter dated 14 November 1937 that Gandhi was unfair in his criticism of the Mysore Resolution that it 'did not set forth the correct state of affairs'. He pointed out that the Resolution had been unanimously passed after hearing all shades of opinion, of members as well as non-members of the Karnataka Pradesh Congress Committee. See pp. 320–2.

[638] Swarup Rani Nehru died on 10 January.

## 272. Letter to M.K. Gandhi

13 January 1938

My dear Bapu,

Anand Bhawan is full of people today–relatives and others who have come. Yet it has a deserted look and in another day there will not be a soul then. We are all leaving tonight or tomorrow morning. I do not think I shall come back for a fortnight as I do not look forward to living all alone here.

You were perfectly right. Bibi's death was welcome to her and it was in the fitness of things.[639] She had done her life's job and there was nothing to bind her further. In some years past she had quietly taken to *sanyas*. Indeed since her girlhood, when she became a widow, she had lived a hard life.

Neither my mother nor Bibi could have long survived the other.

Bibi used to consider Sarup's second daughter Tara as her धर्म की बेटी.[640]

Tara is disconsolate.

Mahadev has sent me a letter which has touched all of us.

Love.

Yours affectionately,
Jawaharlal

MKG Papers, Pyarelal Collection, *NMML*

[639] Bibi Amma, widowed sister of Swarup Rani Nehru, had lived with the Nehrus in Anand Bhavan. Vijayalakshmi Pandit in her book *The Scope of Happiness* recounts that the shock of Swarup Rani's death was a great blow to Bibi Amma. 'After the funeral we tried to make her drink a cup of tea but she said she wanted to sleep ... lay down on the floor ... when she was not up for hours later ... Bhai went to wake her ... She was dead.'

[640] Dharam ki beti, meaning adopted daughter.

## 273. Letter to M.K. Gandhi

Swaraj Bhawan, Allahabad
13 January 1938

Mahatma Gandhi
Maganvadi
Wardha

My dear Bapu,

You will remember my handing to you the letter I had received from Chander Singh Bhandari, Ex-Havildar Major in the Garhwal Regiment who is at present in the Naini prison here. Ranjit went to see him yesterday. As a local MLA Ranjit has a right of visiting the prisons here. He has given me a note, a copy of which I enclose. I might add that Ranjit was very favourably impressed by the man who struck him as a fine type.

You will notice from Ranjit's note that Chander Singh has been recommended for release by various authorities since March 1936. He has been a model prisoner and has won the goodwill of all he has come into contact with. I understand that military officers who have some time visited him have also spoken highly of him. It appears that according to the rules of the frontier province jails he is actually due for release in another two months' time and in any event his case will be put up for review in October 1938. His colleague Narayan Singh, who was sentenced to 14 years, was discharged a month back after completing seven years. I am told that all the other Garhwali prisoners have been discharged as a matter of course on the completion of half their term. Under the circumstances there seems to be a very strong case for Chander Singh's immediate release. One incident will interest you. Chander Singh told Ranjit of this, and further added that he had made the statement before the Court Martial also. It appears that feeling in the Garhwali Regiment was running high in those early days of Civil Disobedience in 1930. A large number of sepoys and petty officers had resolved not only to refuse to fire on their own countrymen but also to fire at and kill the British officers. This is the average soldier's reaction when he thinks in terms of disobedience of orders. He goes to the other limit. Chander Singh was strongly opposed to any such violence on the part of the sepoys because he realised not only that it was opposed entirely to our movement but was also bound to be followed by disastrous consequences. He explained this to his comrades and told them how the Congress movement was founded on nonviolence. He refused to have anything to do with anything in the nature of violence against the officers. Ultimately after great argument he brought his people round to his viewpoint.

You will notice that the act of disobedience of the Garhwali soldiers was not a sudden and unthought-of act but was the result of full consideration and deliberation.

Chander Singh has a record of long and distinguished service in the field behind him in France and other foreign countries. He has had nothing to do with politics. But he is intelligent and wide-awake.

I do hope that it will be possible to get him released soon. Perhaps a recommendation by the Frontier Ministry might help. We have told Chander Singh that you are interesting yourself in the matter.

Yours affectionately,
Jawaharlal

MKG Papers, Pyarelal Collection, *Subject File 274, NMML*

## 274. Letter to Jawaharlal Nehru

4 April 1938

My dear Jawaharlal,

This is not a final draft.[641] I want you to read it sympathetically. I feel that unless we do some such thing, the tension must continue. Anyway at one o'clock I won't take all of you by surprise. I have discussed the subject with the Maulana at some length.

Yours sincerely,
Bapu

CWMG, *Vol. LXVII, p. 4*

[641] Presumably of the Congress Working Committee Resolution on the CP crisis that was passed later at Calcutta

## 275. Letter to M.K. Gandhi

Anand Bhawan, Allahabad
16 April 1938

My dear Bapu,
I enclose copies of recent correspondence with Jinnah and Nawab Ismail Khan. In view of what Jinnah says I feel that your correspondence with him must also be published.[642] I hope you agree. If so kindly have copies of this sent to me soon.

Yours affectionately,
Jawaharlal

I have sent copies of this correspondence to Maulana Abdullah also.
Mahatma Gandhi
Wardha CP

MKG Papers, Pyarelal Collection, *Subject File 16, NMML*

## 276. Telegram to M.K. Gandhi

19 April 1938

To
Mahatma Gandhi
Wardha
Postponing publication letters but request you send copies correspondence.

Jawaharlal

MKG Papers, Pyarelal Collection, *Subject File 19, NMML*

[642] The Gandhi-Jinnah correspondence was released to the press on 15 June 1938. On 14 June, Jinnah had sent Gandhi a telegram saying: 'Publication correspondence Jawaharlal and myself is breach of confidence. Seems leakages from Congress circles. I must release fully now your correspondence along with the rest. Hope you agree.'

## 277. Letter to Jawaharlal Nehru

Segaon
25 April 1938

My dear Jawaharlal,
Here is a copy of Mahadev's notes on his Frontier Province visit. As I could not go and as we had disturbing news, I felt that he should be sent.[643] I am not circulating the notes among all the members. I am sending copies to the Maulana and Subhas. The notes have made me disconsolate. Mahadev has more to say. I am sending a copy, of course, to the Brothers.[644] I hope you will feel impelled to use your great influence over the Brothers. I am of course in telegraphic communication. I may even visit the Province for a few days, if Khan Saheb wants me to go, in spite of the shock I have received. We seem to be weakening from within. It hurts me that, at this very critical juncture in our history, we do not seem to see eye to eye in important matters. I can't tell you how positively lonely I feel to know that nowadays I can't carry you with me. I know that you would do much for affection. But in matters of state, there can be no surrender to affection, when the intellect rebels. My regard for you is deeper for your revolt. But that only intensifies the grief of loneliness. But I must stop.

Love.

Bapu

CWMG, *Vol. LXVII, p. 47*

## 278. Letter to M.K. Gandhi

Allahabad
28 April 1938

My dear Bapu,
I returned to Allahabad this morning from Lucknow and received your letter together with a copy of Mahadeva's note on his visit to

[643] At Mayar, a village about three kilometers from Mardan, three Sikhs, a boy of 11, an old man of 80 and a young man of 25, were murdered by three Pathans. See *CWMG*, Vol. LXVII, p. 71. Gandhi left for the Frontier Province on 29 April. Mahadev Desai's 'Frontier Notes III and IV' with reference to Gandhi's visit were carried in *Harijan*, May 1938.

[644] Abdul Ghaffar Khan and Dr Khan Saheb

the Frontier. I have read this note and I shall write to Khan Saheb and Abdul Ghaffar Khan. I am not surprised at anything that Mahadeva has written. It is a natural development of what I myself saw. I had hoped, however, that some check might be imposed on the tendencies that were visible then. The only person who can do this effectively, apart from you, is Maulana Abul Kalam. I think it is highly necessary that he should go to the Frontier. Meanwhile I do hope that both the Khan brothers will come for the Ministers' meeting and the Working Committee.

As you know, I have been greatly distressed at the turn events have taken in Congress politics during the last six months. Among the matters that have disturbed me is the new orientation of the Gandhi Seva Sangh. We are developing very rapidly on Tammany Hall[645] lines and it is distressing to find that even the Gandhi Seva Sangh, which might have set a standard to others and refused to become just a party organisation intent on winning elections by hook or crook, has descended to the common level. I feel strongly that the Congress Ministries are working inefficiently and not doing much that they could do. They are adapting themselves far too much to the old order and trying to justify it. But all this, bad as it is, might be tolerated. What is far worse is that we are losing the high position that we have built up, with so much labour, in the hearts of the people. We are sinking to the level of ordinary politicians who have no principles to stand by and whose work is governed by a day-to-day opportunism.

Partly of course this is due to a general deterioration all over the world, partly to the transition period through which we are passing. Nevertheless, it does show up our failings and the sight is painful. I think there are enough men of goodwill in the Congress to cope with the situation if they set about it the right way. But their minds are full of party conflicts and the desire to crush this individual or that group. Obviously bad men are preferred to good

[645] Which was founded in 1789 as the Tammany Society. As a Democratic Party political machine it played a major role in controlling New York City politics and helping immigrants (most notably the Irish) rise up in American politics from the 1790s to the 1960s.

men because the former promise to tow the party line. When this happens there is bound to be deterioration.

For months past I have felt that I could not function effectively in India as things were going. I have carried on of course as one can always carry on. But I have felt out of place and a misfit. This was one reason (though there were others also) why I decided to go to Europe. I felt I could be more useful there and in any event I would freshen up my tired and puzzled mind. I have found it difficult to discuss any matter at length with you because I do not wish to tire and worry you in your present state of health. And then I have also felt that such discussions do not yield any worthwhile results.

I have decided to sail from Bombay on the 2nd June. How long I shall be away I do not know. But probably I shall return in September towards the end.

On the 1st of May I am going for a week to Garhwal. Sarup will go with me and we shall have a short aeroplane flight over Badrinath and the snows. On return from Garhwal I shall go to Bombay for the Ministers' meeting and the Working Committee.

Yours affectionately,
Jawahar

SWJN, *Vol. 8, I Series, pp. 387–9*

## 279. Letter to Jawaharlal Nehru

On the train to Peshawar
30 April 1938

My dear Jawaharlal,
Here is a copy of the brief notes I have jotted down of the 3½ hours' talks with Jinnah.[646] It may be that you and the other members may not like the basis. Personally I see no escape from it. My handicap today is that I do not move about the country, as you do, and a still more serious handicap is the inner despondency that has overtaken me. I am carrying on, but it is galling to me to think that I have lost the self-confidence that I possessed only a month ago. I hope that this is but a temporary phase in my life. I have mentioned

[646] On the Hindu-Muslim question on 28 April. See Appendix IV in this volume.

this to help you to examine the proposals on their merits. I do not suppose the first will present any difficulty. The second is novel, with all its implications. You will not hesitate summarily to reject it if it does not commend itself to you. In this matter you will have to give the lead.

I expect to return on the 11th. Subhas in reply to my telegram suggesting that he should open formal negotiations with Jinnah telegraphs that he will be in Bombay on the 10th. I wish that you could also go there early. I am writing to Maulana Saheb in the same strain sending him a copy of this letter.

Love.

Bapu

CWMG, *Vol. LXVII, p. 56*

## 280. Letter to Jawaharlal Nehru

7 May 1938

My dear Jawaharlal,

What is it in the new orientation of the Gandhi Seva Sangh that has disturbed you?[647] I must own that I am responsible for it. I should like you to tell me unhesitatingly what has disturbed you. If I have erred, you know that I shall retrace my steps as soon as I discover the error.

As to the general deterioration, I agree with you, though we may differ as to the weak spots.

More when we meet.[648]

Love.

Bapu

CWMG, *Vol. LXVII, p. 70*

## 281. Letter to M.K. Gandhi

22 May 1938

My dear Bapu,

I tried to carry out your directions to some extent at least in regard to the Girgaum DCC dispute. I do not know if any step was taken

[647] See p. 331.

[648] They met on 19 May in Bombay.

about this on my return from Bombay. I enclose copy of my note on this subject.[649]

I am leaving Allahabad on the 27th evening and going straight to Poona and Panchgani to see Jal again. I reach Bombay on the 30th morning and sail on June 2nd. My address in England will be:

C/o India League
165 Strand
London W.C. 2

Yours affectionately,
Jawaharlal

MKG Papers, Pyarelal Collection, *Subject File 120, NMML*

## 282. Letter to M.K. Gandhi

Camp Lucknow
23 May 1938

My dear Bapu,

Mahadev has sent me the notes of your conversation with Jinnah.[650] I think Jinnah's demands are preposterous and cannot be acceded to. What does he mean by the Muslim mass contact propaganda being suspended? There is no special propaganda going on anywhere. But in the ordinary course Congress meetings are held and members enrolled—Hindu or Muslim. There is no fuss or noise about it. We cannot stop enrolling Congress members among Muslims, though we have taken care to do so without any aggression, or even criticism of the Muslim League. Jinnah objects to speeches delivered in Bombay but his own speech just before he met Subhas was highly objectionable.[651]

I fear that Jinnah is under some misapprehension as to what the Congress might or should do. Personally, as I have said previously, I am very much distressed at these talks with Jinnah. What is likely

[649] See *Pyarelal Papers*, Subject File 120, pp. 69–73.

[650] On 20 May. See Appendix V in this volume.

[651] During his discussions in May with Subhas Chandra Bose who was Congress President, Jinnah had presented a list of demands on behalf of Muslims, one of which was that Congress should accept the position that Muslim League alone could speak on their behalf.

to happen is that he will get one impression from you and another impression from some one else and he will rightly complain.

Yours affectionately,
Jawaharlal

MKG Papers, Pyarelal Collection, *Subject File 16, NMML*

## 283. Letter to Jawaharlal Nehru

26 May 1938

My dear Jawaharlal,

How very businesslike and prompt you are! I am so glad you were able to go into the Girgaum DCC's affairs. I hope your advice will be accepted by both parties, as it should be.

Today I have your letter about my notes of my talks with Jinnah. I think my second talk with him was inevitable. I hope it won't do any harm. If you have time I would like you to give me a line about Jal after you have seen him. How I wish you will give yourself rest during your European tour and not rush as you have been doing here all the time.[652]

Love.

Bapu

CWMG, *Vol. LXVII, p. 95*

## 284. Letter to M.K. Gandhi

12 June 1938

My dear Bapu,

I enclose a typed copy of a letter[653] I have sent to Kripalani[654] for members of the Working Committee. This voyage has been delightful, chiefly because the passengers are an interesting lot. But I have

[652] Nehru left for Europe on 1 June. Commenting on it, Gandhi in his letter of 22 May to Amrit Kaur had written, 'The European visit will do him good. Of course he is at heart religious, though he denounces religion. He reads the *Gita*. He sports a Buddha head in his bedroom. Whatever he does and wherever he is it is well with him.'

[653] Entitled 'A Letter from the Mediterranean' dated 12 June 1938. See *SWJN*, Vol. 9, I Series, pp. 8–11.

[654] J.B. Kripalani, General Secretary of the Congress

had no news of India still. In two more days we reach Geneva and then probably go off to Spain.

I hope you are keeping well.

Love.

Yours affectionately,
Jawahar

MKG Papers, Pyarelal Collection, *NMML*

## 285. Letter to M.K. Gandhi

The Deanery, Canterbury
3 July 1938

My dear Bapu,

Since my arrival in England—indeed since my arrival in Europe—today is the first day I have had with some quiet and peace. This morning we motored from London to Canterbury to visit the Dean and we are spending the night here. Tomorrow morning we return to London.

I have been having a fairly hectic time. Five days in Barcelona, full of interest and excitement and air raids and bombing. I was deeply impressed by the spirit and nerve of the Spanish people. They are behaving splendidly under adverse circumstances and, whatever happens, I do not think they can be crushed. I wish I had the time to write at length about my visit to Spain. Perhaps I might do so later. Then I spent three days in Paris which were also very full of functions and interviews. Then London.

London has been very tiring and I have had no leisure at all. This kind of thing will go on for another fortnight. I have already had innumerable functions and interviews with all manner of people. I have met Zetland[655] and Halifax[656] and had fairly long talks with them. They were pleasant talks and we were agreeable to each other but they were vague talks. So far as I was concerned

[655] Laurence John Lumley Dundas, Second Marquis of Zetland (1876-1961); Governor of Bengal, 1917-22; Secretary of State for India, 1935-40

[656] Edward Frederick Lindley Wood, Lord Irwin, later First Earl of Halifax (1881-1959); Lord Irwin, 1925-34; Secretary of State, Foreign Affairs, 1938-40; Secretary of State for War, June-November 1935; British Ambassador, United States 1940-6

I told them that they could not solve the Indian problem unless they were prepared to eliminate themselves completely and leave constitution making to the Indian people through a constituent assembly. I laid stress on this and on independence and said that only then could there be a proper treaty of friendship between England and India. I treated Federation as almost a minor issue in this framework but stressed our entire opposition to this scheme.[657] We discussed foreign affairs also and I pointed out how this was entirely contrary to our outlook and was thus another important reason why we should want to sever our connection with them.

International affairs are dominating the scene in Europe and the Chamberlain[658] Government has carried on so incompetently that hardly anyone is pleased with it. Probably it would have broken down already if the Labour opposition had any vision and capacity. I have met many of the Labour leaders also and am meeting them again. About my talks with them I shall write later.

[657] In a confidential note of 1 August 1938 to the Working Committee, Nehru had written that he had discussed the question of federation with many of the leaders. His general line was that it was quite impossible for India to accept federation as it was, or even with minor variations, and any attempt to do so now would be silently resisted ... the only proper and effective way of dealing with the Indian problem was to recognise the right of self-determination and agree to a constituent assembly ... even to work federation, the Congress had laid down that, among other things, it was essential for the Princes federating to have a democratic and constitutional method of election for the federation, approximating to that of the provinces. This in itself was not enough as India could not accept the reserved subjects or 'safeguards'.But if the first point was settled to their satisfaction, there was the possibility of other points being considered in a favourable atmosphere. See *SWJN*, Vol. 9, I Series, pp. 665–71.

See also Gandhi's article 'Federation' wherein he declared, 'On the question of Federation there never has been any difference of opinion between us. And I have made a rule for myself that so far as the Congress is concerned, if there is an unbridgeable gulf between him and me his view should prevail.' (*CWMG*, Vol. LXVII, pp. 384–5).

[658] Neville Chamberlain (1869–1940); British Conservative politician; Prime Minister, United Kingdom, 1937–40; best known for the 'appeasement' foreign policy, particularly the Munich Pact, 1938

My programme is still uncertain. Probably I shall leave London about the 20th July for Paris and then Switzerland, Czechoslovakia, Austria, Hungary, Balkans and may be Turkey. Then I return to England.

I hope you are keeping well. Indu is with me. The Dean here tells me that he wrote to you more than once some years ago but had no acknowledgement. He thinks that the letters must have been stopped en route.

Love. Yours affectionately,

MKG Papers, Pyarelal Collection, JN Correspondence, *NMML*

## 286. Cable to M.K. Gandhi

21 July 1938

Gandhiji
Wardha
Mahadev's letter. Approve draft generally.

Jawaharlal

MKG Papers, Pyarelal Collection, *Subject File 16, NMML*

## 287. Letter to M.K. Gandhi

Grand Hotel, Houlgate
France
1 August 1938

My dear Bapu,
As soon as I got Mahadev's letter sending me your draft reply for Subhas to send to Jinnah I sent you a cable of approval. If I had the chance I might have suggested some changes here and there but the general line had to be what you had indicated. I hope you got my cable in time.

I enclose a long note which I have prepared for the Working Committee members.[659] I am [sending] copies of it to Kripalani

[659] Dated 1 August 1938, the note detailed Nehru's discussions with Linlithgow and other leaders on the question of India. See *SWJN*, Vol. 9, I Series, pp. 93–105.

and to Subhas apart from you and to no others. I want this to be kept entirely confidential. Perhaps you could indicate to me what you think of the various methods referred to in it.

Indu is with me here and we have a swim in the sea daily. It is warm and pleasant here.

I hope your blood pressure is behaving.

Love.

Yours affectionately,
Jawahar

MKG Papers, Pyarelal Collection, *NMML*

## 288. Letter to M.K. Gandhi

Budapest
22 August 1938

My dear Bapu,

It was my intention to go for a few days to Istanbul and to pass Budapest on the way. Then Sarup's coming here made me give up Istanbul but as I was at Prague I decided to come over to Budapest to meet Sarup. Indu and I arrived here on the 19th. Indu was not feeling very well but as that is not usual with her I did not attach much importance to it except to ask her to take more rest. On the 20th she felt very tired and I found her temperature to be 100°. The temperature mounted rapidly in the course of six hours to 104.6°. Our intention to leave Budapest the next day with Sarup had obviously to be given up. Sam came the next morning.

The doctors said it was wet pleurisy and might be complicated with pneumonia. There was an accumulation of fluid round her pleura. Some of it (a little) was taken out for examination and it was clear and watery. The doctor did not think it desirable to extract more as he thought it ought to be given a chance to be absorbed in her system. If this failed after a few days then the question of extraction might be considered.

Yesterday–the 21st–Indu was slightly better and her temperature did not rise beyond 103°F. Today the temperature kept under 102°F. She feels better also and is more cheerful. There are apparently no complications. Pleurisy is bad of course and it will take time for her to be rid of it and even afterwards she will have to be careful. But under the circumstances she is doing as well as can be expected.

For the present I am tied down to this place, much against my will. To some extent Sarup is also. I should like to take Indu to London as soon as I can but that is not possible for a week at least. Even going by air it is a tiring 7½ hours' journey. As soon as she is well enough to travel I shall take her there. Sarup might go earlier.

Hungary is a dull country, very backward, which does not interest me. It is one of the last relics of feudalism in Europe. The peasantry are very poor. Every country has some kind of a national festival in celebration of an event connected with the struggle for freedom. Hungary's national day—we saw the celebration—is in memory of the first Christian King who was made a saint—St Stephen. A shrivelled up thing which is said to be his hand, miraculously preserved, was carried triumphantly in procession. But the crowds were silent and undemonstrative in spite of the Regent and Ministers and big officers being present in the procession. Hungary is a kingdom without a king—the Regent functioning. It is obvious even to the passerby that the Government is not popular and is imposed and kept up by force.

I am entirely cut off from India and get neither letters nor newspapers since I left London. Sarup has given me some scrappy news.

Indu sends you her love to which I join mine.

Yours affectionately,
Jawaharlal

MKG Papers, Pyarelal Collection, *NMML*

## 289. Letter to M.K. Gandhi

Budapest
30 August 1938

My dear Bapu,

Indu has been progressing well and we have decided to leave Budapest for London day after tomorrow by air. I took her for a long drive today.

Central Europe—and for the matter of this all Europe—is tense and there is a sense of anxiety. War hovers and no man knows when it will descend. The decision ultimately rests with Hitler.[660] It is extraordinary how much they depend on the will of one man, and that man a semi-neurotic, also bitter. I have so far refused to admit to myself that war will come soon. I am still doubtful. But every moment seems to increase its chances. September is the critical month. If this passes without war then in all likelihood there will be no war this month.

Czechoslovakia is of course the country which will be affected most by the war. Whatever the ultimate outcome, it will be largely destroyed and its fine cities ruined. The tension there is tremendous and every moment a catastrophe is expected. Yet the people are behaving with extraordinary calm and even carry on cheerfully. I have been greatly impressed by their stoic and determined behaviour.

If war comes very vital decisions will have to be taken by us. I earnestly trust that we shall act wisely and determinedly and above all that we shall be prepared for any contingency that might arise.

Love.

Yours affectionately,
Jawaharlal

MKG Papers, Pyarelal Collection, *NMML*

[660] Adolf Hitler (1889–1945); leader of the Nationalist Socialist (Nazi) Party, 1920–1; dictator, Germany, 1935–45; assumed the twin titles of Fuhrer and Chancellor, 2 August 1934; pursued a policy of exterminating the Jews of Europe for establishing his 'new order'

## 290. Draft Cable for Jawaharlal Nehru

30 August 1938

Wire Indu's health. Love all.

Bapu[661]

CWMG, *Vol. LXVII, p. 294*

## 291. Letter to Jawaharlal Nehru

Segaon, Wardha
31 August 1938

My dear Jawaharlal,

Owing to my limited energy, I have been obliged to repress my desire to write to you.

I await your reply to my wire about Indu.

I note your warning about federation.[662] I discount the news, i.e., if it is more than a rumour. They won't call it without first securing Congress consent. This they can't get.

Then about the Jews.[663] I feel entirely like you. I boycott foreign goods, not foreign ability. And I feel keenly for the persecuted Jews. As a concrete proposal I suggest your collecting the names of the most deserving ones and making it plain to them that they must be prepared to throw in their lot with us and accept our standard of living. The rest from Mahadev.

Love.

Bapu

CWMG, *Vol. LXVII, pp. 297–8*

[661] This was part of a letter to Mahadev Desai, requesting him to wire the text to Nehru.

[662] See p. 337.

[663] For Gandhi's views, see his article of 20 November 1938, 'The Jews', *CWMG*, Vol. LXVIII, pp. 137–41.

## 292. Cable to Jawaharlal Nehru

Wardhaganj
16 September 1938

Just received note. Already wrote Heath.[664] Though our language different we mean same thing. No doubt my mind writing.

Love.

Bapu

CWMG, *Vol. LXVII, p. 345*

## 293. Letter to M.K. Gandhi

112 Route du Chêne, Geneva
16 September 1938

My dear Bapu,

As I was leaving London yesterday by air I received your letter of the 31st enclosing a note for Indu. I do not know why this took so long in reaching me. You mention sending a cable inquiring after Indu's health. I do not remember receiving this cable. Perhaps it was sent to Budapest and missed me.

This evening your cable about Heath and the Federation reached me here. Thank you. I knew you would feel that way but your assurance is very welcome.

Indu has been progressing. The real cause for anxiety has been not so much the pleurisy she got—that was bad enough—but the possibility of this developing into something worse. Because of Kamala and also because of Indu's frail condition, one had to think of this. Her rapid recovery points to her freedom from any complications. The doctors said that so far all indications are favourable but they cannot give a really definite opinion till she

[664] Carl Heath, a Quaker, in his letter to Gandhi, had expressed his concern at the impasse on the Federal question and suggested a common statement being made by Nehru, Subhas Bose and other known leaders on the question so as to make an impression on British public opinion. In his response dated 13 September 1938, Gandhi wrote: 'Let this be made clear that there is no real difference between Jawaharlal and me. Our language often differs but we arrive at the same conclusion. The present British policy seems to be to do nothing through negotiation. There is something to be said for it.'

has completely recovered from the pleurisy and her lungs, etc., are in normal condition and can be examined as such. She is to remain in hospital—it is more of a nursing home—for another two weeks for rest. After that she is supposed to have six weeks of regulated rest and exercise in a healthy place. At the end of this period she should be normal.

I am feeling very unhappy at the way Chamberlain & co. are preparing to betray Czechoslovakia.[665] Nothing is certain yet but the probabilities of a dirty deal grow.

This evening I had a long talk with Del Vayo,[666] the Foreign Minister of the Spanish Republican Government. The way the people of the Republic have stood up against the insurgents aided by Italy and Germany is one of the miracles of the modern age. It has been not only astonishing heroism but also cool determined organisation and a will to persevere whatever happened. The contest has been between the spirit and courage of a people and an enemy with an abundance of modern weapons of war and aeroplanes. The spirit has triumphed and I have no doubt that the Republic will win in the end.

The great difficulty before the Republic is how to feed a starving population. Del Vayo appealed through me to the Congress to help them in this respect by sending food supplies from India. They also lack clothes. Cloth would be welcome but they would prefer raw cotton which they can themselves get spun and woven into cloth. I realise that it is not easy for us with our starving and naked millions to talk about helping others. And yet I am greatly moved by the present plight of the Spanish people and the vast importance of preventing them from being crushed by their foreign invaders. It would be a great thing if a gift of a food ship was sent on behalf of India to Spain. It could be arranged that the cost of freight should not fall on us. We would only collect the articles which are more or less easily available from surplus stocks and hand them over to the

[665] For Nehru's statement to the Press of 20 September 1938, 'The Betrayal of Czechoslovakia', see *SWJN*, Vol. 9, I Series, pp. 159–60; for his signed article written in Paris, 'The Great Betrayal', ibid., pp. 153–4.

[666] Julio Alvarez del Vayo (1890–1975); Spanish Socialist politician, journalist and writer

representatives of the Spanish Government. These articles might be: wheat, rice, sugar, cotton and jute. The energy that we put into this collection would be repaid a thousandfold not only by the actual relief we give to very deserving people but also adding to India's stature in the world. Even if we cannot get a shipload we can have less. I think that an appeal made with your blessings would meet with a big response.

The Spanish Foreign Minister especially asked me to request you to send them (that is to the Prime Minister) a message of sympathy for their cause.[667] I promised to convey this request to you. I do not know how you feel about it but I think that a worthier cause has seldom demanded support. It is not necessary for you to support violence or violent methods, though personally I do not see what other course, except violent armed resistance, was open to the Spanish people under the circumstances of the case. A sudden rebellion financed, organised and largely aided by foreign powers and foreign troops took place suddenly. It was of the most brutal kind and the frightfulness continues unabated. The Republic tried to defend itself. It hardly had an army. It was comic opera, but with a terribly tragic side to it, for many months. Then the Republic tried to build up an army of the people in spite of every conceivable difficulty put in their way by England and the French Government, Germany and Italy were of course openly and aggressively supporting Franco.[668] It is a marvel how this popular army was built up during the past two years. The rank and file are magnificent, both in discipline, training and enthusiasm. Even officers had to be drawn from the common people and trained rapidly. Today two of the most famous and popular army leaders are Modesta and Lister. Two years ago one of them was a mason and the other a tailor. In over five weeks the battle of the Ebro has been going on with

[667] In his message to Juan Negrin, Prime Minister of the Spanish Republic, Gandhi wrote, 'I have been told of the woes of your country and the bravery with which you are meeting the situation. It is needless to say that my whole heart goes out to you in sympathy. May true freedom be the outcome of your agony.'

[668] General Francisco Franco (1892–1970); leader of the nationalist forces that overthrew the Spanish Democratic Republic in the Spanish Civil War; head of the Government of Spain till his death

the most fearful persistence and losses. On Franco's side is a tremendous superiority in heavy and mechanised weapons of warfare and Italian and German aeroplanes. Yet the Republic's army has held them and defeated them repeatedly through sheer courage, enthusiasm and discipline. If foreign help was withdrawn, there is not a shadow of a doubt that Franco would crack up within a few weeks.

You know well how aerial bombardments of open towns and defenceless populations have been going on from day to day for months and years past. All this has been done by the insurgents. The Spanish Government, in spite of every provocation, has refused to retaliate in kind, although they could have easily done so. This bombing from the air both in Spain and China has grown to scandalous and inhuman proportions and your condemnations would be especially welcome.[669]

If you cared to send a message of sympathy to the Spanish people I would suggest your addressing it to His Excellency Senor Negrin, Prime Minister, Barcelona. Or perhaps it will be better to send it to me by air and I could forward it.

The British Government is behaving very shamefully towards Czechoslovakia. It seems almost that there will be another gross betrayal.

I am returning to London soon via Paris where I shall stop for two days to see Nahas Pasha. I expect to return to India, so as to reach there about the end of October. But I am not sure as much depends on Indu and the international situation.

Love.

Yours affectionately,
Jawaharlal

[PS]
In your letter you wrote about our welcoming foreign talent provided the people who came threw in their lot with us and accepted our standards of living.[670] Both the conditions are of course necessary, except perhaps in the case of special experts whom we may have for a time for a particular job. In Central Europe standards

[669] See also p. 347.
[670] See p. 342.

have been far lower than in England and America. But while wages have been low, the actual home standards have been fairly high as the municipalities, etc., provide fine houses with modern comforts at a cheap rent. Even ordinary workers have good houses.

MKG Papers, Pyarelal Collection, *NMML*

## 294. Letter to Jawaharlal Nehru

Delhi
4 October 1938

My dear Jawaharlal,

Just now I can only send you the letter you want me to write. If you approve, please forward. You will see my article[671] in *Harijan* in which there is reference to Spain also.

I hope Indu is rapidly progressing and Sarup is having the full benefit of the change.

What a peace at the cost of honour![672]

I wish I had time to write at length.

Mahadev is staying behind for rest. I leave for the Frontier Province.

Love to you three.

Bapu

CWMG, *Vol. 67, pp. 391–2*

[671] 'Logical Consequences', which Gandhi wrote with reference to the Working Committee's resolution on Czechoslovakia. For the reference to Spain in it, see *CWMG*, Vol. LXVII, p. 415.

[672] The reference is to the Munich Pact signed on 30 September 1938. Chamberlain, describing the Munich Pact, had called it 'peace with honour'. Under the terms of this pact, Czechoslovakia was forced to cede to Germany all those districts of Bohemia and Moravia which had a 50-per cent German-speaking population; see also 'If I were a Czech', ibid., pp. 404–6.

## 295. Letter to M.K. Gandhi

Bexhill
7 October 1938

My dear Bapu,
I have been anxious to get back as soon as possible to India but it is no easy matter to get passages at this time of the year. To go by air is frightfully expensive and I intend therefore to return by sea. I have decided to take Indu with me to India. She is gaining strength but cannot go back to Oxford this term. I do not want her to spend the next winter in England. She can come back early in spring.

With some difficulty I have at last managed to get passages for us two early in November by a P&O boat. This is somewhat later than I wanted it to be but there is no help for it. If I had been alone I would have journeyed back overland but I cannot make Indu face this ordeal.

We propose to leave England about the 24th of this month and proceeding via Paris to Egypt. We shall spend a few days there and catch the P&O Strathuaver at Port Said on November 9th, reaching Bombay on November 17th. I should like to spend two or three days in Bombay and then (if you are at Wardha then) to go to Wardha.

I have brought Indu to Bexhill on Sea to give her rest and a better climate than London offers.

Love.

Yours affectionately,
Jawaharlal

MKG Papers, Pyarelal Collection, *NMML*

## 296. Letter to M.K. Gandhi

London
10 October 1938

My dear Bapu,
Thank you for your letter and for the letter for Negrin.

I wrote to you a few days ago and sent two letters to Wardha. But probably you are in the Frontier Province. I enclose programme of the return voyage. It is difficult to get berths at this time of the year.

You will notice that Indu is accompanying me back. She is doing well but she cannot go back to Oxford this winter and I thought it best to have her in India. She can return in Spring.

What a peace without honour! you truly say.[673] Without honour of course but it is not even peace. The most terrific preparations for war are going on. And as for Czechoslovakia, it is difficult to read the paper without horror and a sinking of heart. Already these shootings going on of those who were opposed to the Nazis and concentration camps have been set up. I am quite convinced that a majority of the people (mostly German) were opposed to the cession of territory to Germany but under the new style of 'self-determination' they have been forced by Britain and France to put themselves under Hitler. Because Hitler said so, the census of 1910 was taken into account, although the world had changed since then. Hundreds of thousands of refugees are fleeing from the Nazis, and the horror of it is that many of these have to be sent back under Hitler's orders, so that they can be shot or tortured. The way the British Government has behaved passes all human standards of comparison. Deliberately they worked for a betrayal for months and months, when a word from them could have ensured peace and honour. And then having arrived at the final stage, with the terrible prospect of immediate war they perpetrated the act of betrayal and posed as the peacemakers. Whatever happens to the world or to Europe, the British Empire is doomed.

My love to the Khan brothers.

Yours affectionately,
Jawaharlal

MKG Papers, Pyarelal Collection, *NMML*

[673] See p. 347, *fn*. 672.

## 297. Letter to Jawaharlal Nehru

Segaon
16 November 1938

My dear Jawaharlal,
I hope both you and Indu have benefited by the voyage. I am expecting you to be in Wardha about 20th.[674] But of course you will come as early as you wish. You have tough problems awaiting solution.

Love to you both.

Bapu

CWMG, *Vol. LXVIII, p. 134*

## 298. Letter to Jawaharlal Nehru

21 November 1938

My dear Jawaharlal,
I do hope you had my note in Bombay. I could not take silence before 2 o'clock. I hope you will have a little quiet till then and enjoy it after the strenuous time in Bombay. Hope Indu is well.

Love.

Bapu

CWMG, *Vol. LXVIII, p. 142*

## 299. Letter to Jawaharlal Nehru

Segaon
24 November 1938

My dear Jawaharlal,
I have your note.[675] I knew that once you were in harness you won't be master of your own time. I shall be satisfied with what I get.

Here is a letter delivered through messenger from Gurudev.[676] I have replied saying my personal opinion was that he needed to be

[674] Nehru who returned from Europe on 17 November arrived in Segaon on the 21st.

[675] Not available

[676] Rabindranath Tagore (1861–1941); poet, novelist, essayist and dramatist primarily in Bengali but also in English; awarded the Nobel Prize for Literature 1913; renounced his knighthood as a protest against the massacre at Amritsar

free from the Presidential work, if he was to rid Bengal of corruption. I have no doubt Gurudev will write to you directly or talk to you.[677] You will give your own opinion.

I hope Indu was none the worse for the journey.

Love.

Bapu

CWMG, *Vol. LXVIII, p. 144*

## 300. Letter to Jawaharlal Nehru

Segaon, Wardha
30 November 1938

My dear Jawaharlal,

The Chinese friends came and instead of five minutes they took thirty-five. I had ultimately to say as gently as I could that they had overstayed their time seven times.

Here is your copy of Agatha's report of the interview with the Viceroy. My message was merely to say that he was to regard me as a friend of the English people, etc. It had nothing to do with politics.

I hope you duly received my letter enclosing Gurudev's letter about Subhas.[678]

[677] Tagore was lobbying for Subhas Chandra Bose's re-election as Congress president. On 28 November he wrote to Nehru, 'I merely wanted to know your own opinion about Bengal whose present condition puzzles me and makes me despair. My province is clever but morally untrained and supercilious in her attitude towards her neighbours, she breaks into violent hysteric fits when least crossed in her whims. ... I cannot passively acquiesce in her doom of perdition. But I am quite willing to ... leave to your Congress organisation to deal with her as it thinks fit.'

[678] The reference appears to be to the letter from Rabindranath Tagore's secretary A.K. Chanda, dated 28 November, clarifying Tagore's position:

'He has been also rather captivated by Dr Saha's ideas of Rational Planning and is hoping much from the Committee. ... He also wants a "modernist" to be the Congress President for the next year, so that the Report when finished would be warmly accepted by the All-India Congress and not just shelved up. In his opinion ... there are only two genuine modernists in the High Command–you and Subhasbabu... and he therefore is very eager to see Subhasbabu again elected as President... he recently wrote to Gandhiji about this.'

Hope you are not killing yourself with work and that Indu is doing well.

Sarup should be relieved of the heavy work she is doing. She should rebuild her shattered body.

Love.

Bapu

CWMG, *Vol. LXVIII, p. 161*

## 301. Letter to Jawaharlal Nehru

Segaon, Wardha
21 December 1938

My dear Jawaharlal,

Maulana Saheb does not want the crown of thorns. If you want to try again please do. If you won't or he won't listen, Pattabhi seems to be the only choice.

Love.

Bapu

CWMG, *Vol. LXVIII, p. 227*

## 302. Letter to Jawaharlal Nehru

Segaon, Wardha
3 February 1939

My dear Jawaharlal,

After the election[679] and the manner in which it was fought, I feel that I shall serve the country by absenting myself from the Congress at the forthcoming session.[680] Moreover, my health is

[679] On 29 January 1939, when Subhas Chandra Bose had succeeded Nehru as President of the INC in 1938. Gandhi was not for Bose's re-election and encouraged the right wing of the Congress to set up Pattabhi Sitaramayya as their candidate. However, Bose won decisively. For Gandhi's statement of 31 January 1939 on the re-election of Bose, see *CWMG*, Vol. LXVIII, pp. 358–9.

For Nehru's statement of 22 February 1939 on the re-election of Subhas Bose, see *SWJN*, Vol. 9, I Series, pp. 485–7. For his eight articles printed in the *National Herald* on 28 February and 1–6 March, 1939, 'Where Are We?', ibid., pp. 485–520.

[680] To be held from 10 to 12 March 1939 at Tripuri

none too good. I would like you to help me. Please do not press me to attend.

I hope the rest at Khali has done you and Indu good. Indu ought to write to me.

Love.

Bapu

CWMG, *Vol. LXVIII, p. 368*

## 303. Letter to Jawaharlal Nehru

5 February 1939

My dear Jawaharlal,

This copy[681] for your information.

Love.

Bapu

CWMG, *Vol. LXVIII, p. 383*

## 304. Telegram to Jawaharlal Nehru

9 February 1939

Jawaharlal Nehru
Anand Bhawan
Allahabad

All things considered I think it would be wise postpone Ludhiana conference till after Congress.[682] Principal work(er)s engaged in struggle going on various states.

Bapu

CWMG, *Vol. LXVIII, p. 398*

[681] Of Gandhi's letter of 5 February to Subhas Chandra Bose; see *CWMG*, Vol. LXVIII, pp. 382–3. For the Bose-Gandhi-Nehru correspondence, see *A Bunch of Old Letters*.

[682] Nehru presided over the All India States People's Conference at Ludhiana on 15 February. For his speech, see *SWJN*, Vol. 9, I Series, pp. 418–31.

## 305. Letter to Jawaharlal Nehru

Segaon, Wardha
9 February 1939

My dear Jawaharlal,
I have your letter. I understand your analysis. Subhas wired saying he wants to come to Wardha.[683] Let us see what happens.

Of course I shall take no hasty decision. I am glad Sarup is coming soon. I am hoping that the quiet of Segaon will suit her.

Love.

Bapu

CWMG, *Vol. LXVIII, pp. 398–9*

## 306. Letter to M.K. Gandhi

Allahabad
9 February 1939

My dear Bapu,
Your telegram about postponing the Ludhiana Conference has surprised me. At this last moment when arrangements have been made and people are coming from distant parts, like Kashmir, a postponement will be deeply resented and will give rise to all manner of suspicion. There will be the charge of autocracy. Factions will rise up in the Conference, one in favour of postponement, the other demanding that it be held. My time and money will be exhausted in sending telegrams all day and in replying to messages of protest. Anyway who am I to postpone it. I have already viewed a strong protest from the Reception Committee in regard to postponement and yesterday I wired to them that there was no question of it. I am quite convinced that there will be a crisis in the affairs of the States Peoples' Conference if a postponement is made. There will be bitter argument and counter-argument and attentions will be diverted from the real struggle to this unedifying spectacle. Even apart from this and many other considerations, I am quite clear in my own mind that this is the right time for a Conference. I do not know what arguments were placed before you and by whom. I am unaware of any valid argument in favour of postponement. And

[683] Subhas Chandra Bose arrived in Segaon on 14 February to have discussions with Gandhi.

even if I was, I would not postpone at this stage when expectations have risen so high and arrangements have proceeded thus far.

I received your letters[684] about resigning from the Working Committee yesterday. It is not for me to advise others but I see no reason whatever why I should resign. Even if Subhas asked me to resign it is not clear to me that I should do so just at this stage. Of course Subhas should have the upper hand in putting forward his policy. Nobody will obstruct him. But surely the questions before us are not personal or individual. They transcend personalities. I think we should forget for the moment Subhas as well as others and consider our problems on these merits. Individual or group relations should be considered later. The position is far too critical and the possible consequences too grave for any other attitude to be taken up.

I understand that the Working Committee is meeting on the 22nd.[685] I hope to reach Wardha on the 20th or the latest 21st morning. I shall come as early as I can after Ludhiana and another engagement.

I have just had a shock. Three days ago[686] I issued a statement in which there was the following sentence: 'Today, as of old, Gandhiji is the soft but iron voice of India challenging this imperialism and preparing for struggle with it.'

What the wretches of the press put in was: 'Today, as of the old, Gandhiji is soft but the iron voice of India', etc., etc.

Is this not terrible?

Sarup did not go to Wardha yesterday as she is not well. But I shall bring her with me.

I am going to Benares today.

Love.

Yours affectionately,
Jawaharlal

MKG Papers, Pyarelal Collection, *NMML*

[684] Not available

[685] Gandhi advised the Working Committee to resign if they were not in agreement with Subhas Chandra Bose. For Bose's references to Nehru's statement of 22 February 1939, see his letter dated 28 March 1939 in *A Bunch of Old Letters*

[686] On 7 February 1939. See *SWJN*, Vol. 9, I Series, pp. 414–15.

## 307. Letter to Jawaharlal Nehru

Segaon, Wardha
11 February 1939

I have your wire[687] and letter. I understand your position about the conference and the WC. I cannot think of causes without the persons who handle them. I wrote about postponement on the strength of what I had heard from Balwantrai Mehta.[688] He is engrossed in the Kathiawar struggle.[689] Achint Ram could not do without him. So I wired to you. I know nothing about the situation in Ludhiana.

I am sorry about Sarup. I was looking forward to her passing a few days with me.

Love.

Bapu

CWMG, *Vol. LXVIII, p. 403*

## 308. Telegram to Jawaharlal Nehru

Rajkot
9 March 1939

Jawaharlal Nehru
Tripuri Congress
(Jabalpur)

It will be first class blunder if resolution not taken to rid Congress of internal corruption.[690] Power should be given to AICC to make

[687] Not available

[688] Balvantrai Gopalji Mehta (1899–1965); one of the founders of the All India States Peoples' Conference; General Secretary, 1928–47; Chief Minister, Gujarat, 1963, till his death in an air crash in 1965

[689] For self-rule

[690] Regretting the large-scale impersonation that took place in the election of delegates for the Tripuri Congress, Gandhi had written in his article of 23 January, 'Internal Decay', 'Besides impersonation there is wholesale tampering with the Congress registers which contain bogus names ... Strife at Congress elections is becoming a common occurrence. The indiscipline of Congress elections is on the increase everywhere. Many of them make irresponsible, even violent, speeches ... Kisans of Bihar are supposed to be Congressmen. Their leaders are Congressmen. But Bihar ministers live in perpetual dread

required changes in Constitution without necessity their being submitted to Congress. Keeping well.[691]

Bapu

CWMG, *Vol. LXIX, pp. 42–3*

## 309. Letter to Jawaharlal Nehru

New Delhi
20 March 1939

My dear Jawaharlal,

Shaukat has just brought your note.[692] The news you give me is astounding. I only hope that there is a misunderstanding. Did you get the name of the Congressman? I am inquiring.

I hope Maulana Saheb is much better. Please give him my love and tell him I am anxious to see him. I shall do so as soon as I can safely leave.

Love.

Bapu

CWMG, *Vol. LXIX, p. 71*

---

of kisan risings and kisan marches. ...Out of the present condition of the Congress I see nothing but anarchy and red ruin in front of the country. Shall we face the harsh truth at Tripuri?' He further observed in his statement to the Press on 31 January 1939, 'My writings in the *Harijan* have shown that the Congress is fast becoming a corrupt organisation in the sense that its registers contain a very large number of bogus members.' See *CWMG*, Vol. LXVIII, pp. 320–1.

[691] According to *The Hindu*, 11 January 1939, an identical telegram was sent to Subhas Chandra Bose. It was read out to Sarat Chandra Bose in the Subjects Committee meeting as the former could not attend it owing to ill health. Sarat Bose said that Subhas Chandra Bose 'whole-heartedly endorsed Gandhiji's view'.

[692] Not available

## 310. Letter to M.K. Gandhi

Allahabad
22 March 1939

My dear Bapu,
Thank you for your letter. I do not know the names of the Congressmen who are supposed to have approached a government official in Delhi.[693] The names have not been mentioned to me.

I received today the following telegram from Subhas from Jharia:

Received your telegram only yesterday. Does it represent your personal views or views of others also and if so of whom?

To this I sent the following reply:

Your telegram. My previous message sent my own behalf but after conversation with Gandhiji who keenly feels Congress work suffering owing lack direction office arrangements. Also national, international crises demand ceaseless vigilance.

Later informed him of my message.

Maulana is much the same. His pain is generally less and the swelling has also partly subsided. He is waiting for your visit here and after that intends to go to Calcutta.

Yours affectionately,
Jawahar

SWJN, *Vol. 9, I Series, p. 526*

## 311. Letter to M.K. Gandhi

Allahabad
24 March 1939

My dear Bapu,
I enclose copy of a letter I am sending to Subhas.[694] As you will notice from it I had another telephone message, this time from

[693] Bhulabhai Desai and some local Congressmen of Delhi met the Home Secretary in February 1939 in connection with the state of prisoners in Delhi.

[694] The letter, dated 24 March 1939, was in fact addressed to Sarat Chandra Bose and a copy of it sent to Subhas Chandra Bose. This was Nehru's

Sunil Bose[695] from Calcutta, on the same lines as the Jharia one. On learning that you had gone back to Delhi he apparently intended sending you a telegram to the same effect.[696]

Yours affectionately,
Jawahar

SWJN, *Vol. 9, I Series, p. 527*

## 312. Letter to Jawaharlal Nehru

New Delhi
30 March 1939

My dear Jawaharlal,
I had your two letters. Both were good.

I send you copies of correspondence.

The events in UP disturb me.[697] My solution is that you should become Prime Minister or dissolve the Ministry. You must get control over the unruly elements.

---

response to Sarat Bose's complaint to Gandhi about the 'mean, malicious and vindictive' propaganda carried on against Subhas Chandra Bose by 'some ex-members of the Working Committee' in Tripuri. Sarat Bose had also cited a number of 'instances of unfairness in the conduct of the proceedings of the Congress' by Maulana Azad. Nehru had written, 'You have used language in your letter which is exceedingly strong and bitter. I have read this with great regret and I failed to find any justification for it. What pains me most is the overshadowing of all political issues by the personal equation. If there is to be conflict among Congressmen, I earnestly hope that it will be kept on a higher level and will be confined to matters of policy and principle.' For the full text of the letter, see *A Bunch of Old Letters*.

[695] (1894–1953); elder brother of Subhas Bose and a well-known cardiologist

[696] For Gandhi's telegram to Dr Sunil Bose, dated 30 March 1939, see *CWMG*, Vol. LXIX, p. 89.

[697] In Lucknow on 29 March 1929, several Congressmen and their sympathizers had been injured when they were attacked by some Europeans and others who had met to protest against the Employment Tax Bill introduced by the Congress Ministry in UP. See 'A Discussion', *CWMG*, Vol. LXIX, p. 93.

I have had three days' heart-to-heart conversations with the socialists who were here. Narendradev will report to you. If he does not of his own accord, you should make him.

Love.

Bapu

CWMG, *Vol. LXIX, p. 92*

## 313. Letter to M.K. Gandhi

Lucknow
1 April 1939

My dear Bapu,

I have your letter of the 30th March together with copies of correspondence with Subhas.[698] Jayaprakash met me yesterday for a short time on his way to Patna. I think that there is little to be said beyond what you have written to Subhas.

The Lucknow Baradari incident was very unfortunate. But still I hope that you will not attach too much importance to it. I am sending you the *National Herald* report of this incident. This is a truthful report by a competent eye-witness. The next day I issued a statement in regard to the incident, a copy of which I enclose also.[699] A letter by Gautam in the Press also helps in understanding the background.[700]

The communal situation is very disturbing. There are certain novel features about it. In past years, when such riots occurred, there was a great deal of emotion and passion in the multitude. For

[698] Gandhi had written to Subhas Chandra Bose on 30 March 1939 that his choice of the Working Committee should be unfettered and the Committee need not be homogeneous in character and may be composed mainly of the members backing Bose's policy. He himself would not be a party to 'self-suppression' by Bose as against 'voluntary self-effacement'.

[699] On 30 March 1939 to the Press. Nehru had stated that while he regretted the behaviour of the organizers, he was more concerned with what the Congressmen and their sympathizers did. He had pointed out that it did not behove Congressmen to attend such meetings and that the policy of nonviolence was essentially a positive policy and a technique with numerous implications and should not be forgotten whatever the provocation.

[700] Mohanlal Gautam had argued that it was an unprovoked attack made on a few Congressmen.

instance, last year the Allahabad riot was clearly of political origin but still large masses of people were affected and were excited. This year it is even more purely political and it is patently superficial. That is to say that there is no passion or emotion visible in the city. There is a certain amount of fear and some resentment. Clearly, these riots tend to be brought about purely to exercise a certain political pressure. It also seems that people are slightly getting used to them and are not quite so frightened by them as they used to be. Today in Allahabad there is no feeling of general panic or suppressed emotion. A fair amount of business is being done. Most shops are open, and yet odd cases of stabbing occur in out-of-the-way places. There are no big crowds or conflict on a mass scale. Generally people are irritated and bored at what is happening. There is no local or religious problem which has to be solved. This forenoon I drove through parts of the city and saw three stabbing cases which had occurred about five minutes before I arrived. In each case the man who had done the deed had disappeared.

In my mind the local leaders of the Muslim League must certainly be held responsible for much that is happening.

I fear this individual violence on a small scale will continue in some of our cities for some days. Gradually it will fade out. It is not easy to deal with it for either the Congressmen or the police.

As for your suggestion about the Ministry, I do not think it is at all feasible. No sudden change will make much difference, while it may well give rise to additional problems. Of course, so far as I am concerned, I am perfectly willing to help the UP Ministry in every way.

Yours affectionately,
Jawaharlal

SWJN, *Vol. 9, I Series, pp. 331–2*

## 314. Letter to Jawaharlal Nehru

New Delhi
6 April 1939

My dear Jawaharlal,
Who can help feeling distressed over the turn things are taking? Let us hope that the cloud would be soon lifted.

The Rajkot Award[701] is but one step towards the objective. I have still to watch the next step. However, I telephoned to Dr Khan Saheb today. He has promised to telephone and tell me if he wants me. I was agitated over the raids that have become a feature there. I have to see the Viceroy today. I might have to go to Rajkot in connection with the Committee.[702]

My love to Indu. I take it that Krishna is also going. This means that you will be in Bombay on 15th?

Love.

Bapu

[PS]

I note what you say about the tension there.

CWMG, *Vol. LXIX, p. 113*

## 315. Letter to M.K. Gandhi

Allahabad
17 April 1939

My dear Bapu,

Pyarelal has been sending me copies of your correspondence with Subhas. I fear that this correspondence has reached a deadlock and I do not see any way out.[703] I am in the unfortunate position of a person who does not agree with either of the viewpoints taken Because of this, I have thought it best to remain silent and not to write to anybody or say anything in public. But it seems to me that it is not good enough for us to drift along in this helpless

[701] Announced on 3 April by the Chief Justice of India, Sir Maurice Gwyer. According to it, Thakore Saheb, the Ruler of Rajkot, was bound to appoint a committee of ten persons who were to be chosen only by Vallabhbhai Patel, and had no discretion to reject names which he did not approve.

The claims made by the Muslims, the Bhayats and depressed classes caused a deadlock in the composition of the committee for suggesting reforms. The talks held in April 1939 between Gandhi and Darbar Virawala, advisor to the Ruler of Rajkot, in connection with the personnel of the Rajkot Reforms Committee failed. Later, on 17 May, Gandhi renounced the award and conceded defeat declaring, 'Rajkot has been a priceless laboratory. My patience has been sorely tried by the tortuous politics of Kathiawar.'

[702] Gandhi was in Rajkot from 27 February to 13 March 1939.

[703] See *fn*. 679 and 681.

manner. The issues are too serious and the consequences distressing to contemplate.

It seems to me that there is no way out unless you are prepared to shoulder the responsibility yourself to a very large extent. You have to give the lead and you cannot wait for things just to happen. Subhas has numerous failings but he is susceptible to a friendly approach. I am sure that if you made up your mind to do so you could find a way out.

I realise the importance of Rajkot, but I think you will agree with me that the larger Congress issue is infinitely more important and is likely to govern all our activities. Therefore, I would beg of you to address yourself to the latter, even at the cost of your not attending to Rajkot affairs for a while. The idea that you may not attend the AICC meeting is alarming. That simply means that conditions should go on deteriorating and that the Congress should go to pieces. The right way is for some settlement to be arrived at before the AICC meeting. To leave this issue to the AICC is to make confusion worse confounded. I wish you could have met Subhas. Quite apart from any feasible outcome of this visit, this would have been helpful in many ways.

The delay in the formation of the Working Committee has been bad. But for us to meet only to quarrel will be worse. It would be preferable, though I dislike it intensely, for the AICC meeting to be postponed by a week or two in order to suit your convenience and to give more chance to have a settlement.

I have just received a letter from Subhas in which he asks me to pay a visit to him for a few hours to discuss the situation. I fear our talk cannot lead to anything definite, for I cannot deliver the goods. Still, I cannot say no to him and I propose to go there in a day or two.[704] What I shall say to him is not clear in my mind. For the moment I think that the only advice I can give him is for him to say to you that he leaves it to you completely to suggest the names of the Working Committee. He may make certain suggestions of his to you but on the clear understanding that you may

[704] Nehru went to Jealgora in Dhanbad district on 19 April 1939 at Subhas Chandra Bose's invitation. For Bose's letter dated 15 April 1939, see *A Bunch of Old Letters*.

accept them or reject them. As regards the programme, this will be governed by the resolutions of the Tripuri Congress, which, among other things, indicate definitely that there should be no break with the past programme.[705]

If Subhas agrees to this course, then responsibility rests with you and you cannot shirk it. I think now, as I thought in Delhi, that you should accept Subhas as President. To try to push him out seems to me to be an exceedingly wrong step. As for the Working Committee, it is for you to decide. But I do think the idea of homogeneity, if narrowly interpreted, will not lead to peace or effective working. Some kind of homogeneity there must of course be. Otherwise we cannot function. I do not think that a few individuals in the Working Committee make any radical difference to the policy. Of course, it is difficult to accept individuals whose bona fides one does not trust at all. But the principle of homogeneity should not be extended to differences in political approach, provided the common background of work is accepted. After all, we must remember that by having a homogeneous executive we do not create a homogeneous Congress. The latter is easier of achievement if we have a larger homogeneity in view.

You have been greatly distressed at developments in the Congress during the last many months and you have condemned corruption, etc. I think every sane element in the Congress, whatever his political views, is eager to deal with this problem. I have been paying a great deal of attention to many factors outside the Congress and I must say that I am alarmed at the trend of events and the development of new forces. I am not merely referring to the communal question. There are deeper forces at work. If, at this juncture, the Congress weakens and disrupts, the consequences may well be disastrous. We must hold together. I would beg of you, therefore, to make up your mind to settle this matter, even though that way of settlement may

[705] A resolution moved by G.B. Pant, stated that 'the Congress declares its firm adherence to the fundamental policies of the Congress which have governed its programme in the past twenty years under the guidance of Mahatma Gandhi and is definitely of the opinion that there should be no break in these policies and that these policies should continue to govern the Congress programme in the future.'

not be to the liking of all of us. Only so can we go in the direction of our choice. Otherwise we are stuck up.

A word about myself. It is my misfortune to be too much of an individualist. I found it very difficult to pull on, in the later days, at the Working Committee meetings and probably I became a nuisance to my colleagues also. And this not through any lack of goodwill on either side. Hence I felt that I should not continue in it. For even more potent reasons I felt it difficult to think of joining a Committee of a different kind formed by Subhas. My feelings are still the same. But in view of this deadlock that has arisen, if a way out is found and my presence in the Committee is considered helpful, I shall agree to serve as such.[706] This is not a prospect that I cherish. But I do feel that I cannot shirk this responsibility if it is offered to me under the present extraordinary circumstances.

Yours affectionately,
Jawaharlal

SWJN, *Vol. 9, I Series, pp. 553–5*

## 316. Telegram to M.K. Gandhi

Allahabad
18 April 1939

Mahatma Gandhi
Rajkot
Am visiting Subhas tomorrow at his request.

Jawaharlal

MKG Papers, Pyarelal Collection, *Subject File 65, NMML*

## 317. Telegram to M.K. Gandhi

20 April 1939

Mahatma Gandhi
Rajkot
Had long talk with Subhas. Feel your guidance control situation essential. Earnestly hope you will agree. Meanwhile trust you will

[706] Nehru, however, did not join the Congress Working Committee constituted by the AICC at Calcutta.

not commit yourself by public statement. Please wire when what route going Calcutta.

Jawaharlal

MKG Papers, Pyarelal Collection, *Subject File 65, NMML*

## 318. Letter to M.K. Gandhi

Allahabad
20 April 1939

My dear Bapu,

I returned this morning from Jealgora. I had several hours' talk with Subhas yesterday. I need not go into this in any detail but two things stand out. One is the absolute necessity of a solution of the present deadlock before the AICC meets.[707] Two, that you are the only person who can do it.

As regards the first, it seems to me clear that if we face the AICC without any constructive suggestion, there will be a continuation of trouble and conflict which would be bad enough at any time, and disastrous under present circumstances and in view of the deepening crisis.

As regards two, I realise fully the difficulties that have arisen and which have been accentuated by the correspondence you have had with Subhas. I feel, however, that it is possible to tone down those difficulties if you are prepared to take a good deal of responsibility. So far as the programme of work is concerned, there are obvious differences between what Subhas says and what many others feel. But in actual practice, it is clear that there should be no basic change in our programme or outlook, as indeed has been decided by the Congress. In effect, it comes to this that the Working Committee should be formed according to your wishes and the programme should be carried through under your guidance. No

[707] Bose had written to Gandhi that since he could not give effect to Gandhi's advice to form a 'homogeneous cabinet' Gandhi should accept the responsibility of forming the Working Committee. At the meeting of the AICC, Bose resigned from the Presidentship of the INC, stating that having failed in his efforts to arrive 'at an informed solution' of the problems he felt that the AICC might be able to settle the matter 'if it can have a new President.' Rajendra Prasad was elected President on 30 April 1939.

one can tell what the future will bring, but for the present there will be general relief, if this is done, and a clearing of atmosphere.

I understood from Subhas that he was agreeable to do this, not in any spirit of resentment but because he felt that it was the right course now. He acts strangely at times and is fond of issuing statements which create difficulties. I hope, however, that this kind of thing will lessen.

I advised Subhas not to publish his correspondence with you, as this would greatly add to our difficulties. May I also suggest to you that no statement might be issued by you committing yourself to any course at this stage? Very soon you will be meeting Subhas, and it will be far better if you issue a statement after meeting him and others.

I should have liked to meet you soon but I do not know how to do so. If you could go to Calcutta early it would be very helpful. I would personally prefer that you meet Subhas at a quiet place other than Calcutta. Perhaps you could break journey to Calcutta somewhere and Subhas could meet you there. If I know your programme I might try to join you en route.[708] I am concerned to read in today's paper that you have got fever.

Yours affectionately,
Jawaharlal

SWJN, *Vol. 9, I Series, pp. 559–60*

## 319. Telegram to Jawaharlal Nehru

Rajkot
21 April 1939

Jawaharlal Nehru
Allahabad
Your wire. Won't make statement. Going via Bombay Nagpur. No fever today.

Bapu

MKG Papers, Pyarelal Collection, *Subject File 65, NMML*

[708] Gandhi had discussions with Nehru and Bose on 27 and 28 April at Calcutta. He had further talks with Bose on the 29th.

## 320. Telegram to Jawaharlal Nehru

Delhi
27 July 1939

Jawaharlal Nehru
Care Congress
G[irgaum], B[omba]y
You have done bravely and spiritedly.[709]

Bapu

CWMG, *Vol. LXX, p. 31*

## 321. Letter to Jawaharlal Nehru

Segaon, Wardha
29 July 1939

My dear Jawahalrlal,
Instead of guiding the Dhami people I have passed them on to you.[710] I feel that you should discharge this burden without any interference from me. The idea in the States seems to be to isolate and ignore the Congress and hence the States Conference. I have already suggested in *Harijan*[711] that no State Association or Mandal should act on its own without reference to your committee.[712] I should act, if at all, through you; i.e., when you refer to me, I should

[709] The Ceylon Government had given notices of dismissal to a number of Indians employed by the Government. The AICC, in its resolution of 24 June 1939 drafted by Gandhi, had chosen Nehru as an ambassador of peace to go to Ceylon to find a way to avoid undesirable and grave conflict and effect a just and honourable settlement between the two countries. Nehru visited Sri Lanka from 15 to 25 July 1939, and reported that he had requested the Ceylon Government not to dismiss the Indian labour already in employment, though fresh recruitment might be stopped, giving preference to Ceylonese labourers in the matter of employment, and the visit had resulted in increasing the goodwill between India and Ceylon.

[710] A deputation on behalf of the Himalayan States People's Conference had met Gandhi at Delhi on 27 July, and apprised him of the firing in the state of Dhami.

[711] Dated 29 July 1939 in the article 'Minority Administration' (*CWMG*, Vol. LXX, pp. 14–17)

[712] Standing Committee of the All-India States People's Conference, of which Nehru was President

give my opinion as I do in respect of the Working Committee. I told the Gwalior people also likewise yesterday. You will have to reorganise your committee a bit, if it is to function properly.

After all I could not go to Kashmir. Sheikh Abdullah[713] and his friends won't tolerate the idea of my being a State guest.[714] Banking on my past experience, I had accepted the State offer in anticipation of Sheikh Abdullah's approval. But I saw that I was mistaken. I therefore cancelled the acceptance of the State hospitality and accepted the Sheikh's. This embarrassed the State. So I cancelled the visit altogether. I was guilty of double stupidity–in daring to think of going there without you and in not getting Sheikh's permission before accepting the State offer. I had thought that I would serve the people by accepting the State offer. I must confess that I was not pleased with my contact [with] the Sheikh and his friends. They seemed to all of us to be most unreasonable. Khan Saheb reasoned with them. But it was to no purpose.

Your visit to Ceylon was glorious. I don't mind what the immediate outcome is. Saleh Tyabji asks me to send you to Burma and Andrews thinks of you in connection with South Africa. For Ceylon the idea of a Congress deputation came to me spontaneously, not so these two even after the promptings. But of these when we meet. I hope you are fresh and that Krishna is enjoying herself.

Love.

Bapu

CWMG, *Vol. LXX, pp. 42–3*

[713] Sheikh Mohammed Abdullah (1905–1982); leader of the National Conference of Kashmir State, 1938; President, All-India States People's Conference, 1946; Prime Minister of Kashmir, 1948–53; dismissed and arrested, 1953; served long terms of imprisonment thereafter; Chief Minister, Kashmir, 1974–82

[714] While Gandhi was in Abbotabad he received an invitation on 17 July from Kailas Narain Haksar, Personal Advisor to the Mahraja of Jammu and Kashmir, to be his guest.

## 322. Letter to Jawaharlal Nehru

Segaon, Wardha
11 August 1939

My dear Jawaharlal,

I was half inclined to talk to you in the presence of the Working Committee (for want of other time) about the Planning Committee.[715] Shankerlal came this morning after his chat with you bringing with him copy of a letter written by him to Kripalani in the matter. I sympathised with him in his objection. I have never been able to understand or appreciate the labours of the Committee. I do not know that it is working within the four corners of the resolution creating the Committee. I do not know that the Working Committee is being kept informed of its doings. I have not understood the purpose of the numerous sub-committees. It has appeared to me that much money and labour are being wasted on an effort, which will bring forth little or no fruit. These are my doubts. I seek light. I know your mind is in China.[716] If you think Shah[717] can express your mind, I shall try to learn from him. Or I shall wait till you return from your great mission. May God protect you and bring you safe to the motherland.

Love.

Bapu

CWMG, *Vol. LXX, p. 86*

[715] Nehru was appointed Chairman of the National Planning Committee in 1938. In a letter to Rajkumari Amrit Kaur, dated 29 June 1939, Gandhi wrote, 'In my opinion the whole of this planning is a waste of effort. But he can't be satisfied with anything that is not big.'

[716] Nehru left for China on 20 August. See Nehru's article 'I go to China', 18 August 1939, in *SWJN*, Vol. 10, I Series, pp. 81–3; see also 'Diary of a Journey', ibid., pp. 84–101.

[717] K.T. Shah, Professor of Economics, Bombay University; Secretary, National Planning Council, 1938–47

## 323. Letter to M.K. Gandhi

Anand Bhawan, Allahabad
14 August 1939

Mahamtma Gandhi
Wardha
My dear Bapu,

Thank you for your letter of the 11th. I am sorry I could not talk to you about the Planning Committee. I had a talk with Shankarlal but he did not tell me anything about a letter that he had written to Kripalani. I do not know what his prticular objection was.

I have today received a letter from Rajendra Babu also.[718] I enclose a copy of my reply[719] to him. I am afraid it is a little difficult to discuss the whole background of the Planning Committee in the course of a brief letter. Perhaps the way I look at it is different from yours. To some extent I tried to place my viewpoint before you at the Working Committee meeting held in Bombay. Whatever the viewpoint, I do not see how even this feeble attempt at planning and gathering information can do other than good. It is something to make people think even. The money spent on this is less than is being spent on any number of odd committees which some of our provincial governments are appointing.

If it is possible for you to discuss this matter with K.T. Shah I would suggest that you might do so, or if you like we can discuss it further on my return.

I have definitely fixed up my departure for the 20th August.

Yours affectionately,
Jawaharlal

MKG Papers, Pyarelal Collection, *Subject File 66, NMML*

[718] Rajendra Prasad in his letter of 12 August had protested that the Planning Committee had given publicity to certain resolutions without placing them before the Working Committee and that it was never intended that the resolutions should go directly to the Provincial Governments for action.

[719] Of 14 August 1939. Nehru had written that the resolution was in the nature of a suggestion and, in order to give effect to this, it was obvious that the Working Committee or its Parliamentary Subcommittee should approve of it. The resolution was, therefore, sent to the Parliamentary Subcommittee in July. It was also communicated for information to various provincial governments and States.

## 324. Letter to M.K. Gandhi

15 August 1939

Mahatma Gandhi
Wardha
My dear Bapu,
I enclose a letter in original which I have received from Sri Prakasa.[720] This will give you some idea of how he is feeling.[721]

I also enclose a cutting from a Hongkong paper which might interest you.[722]

Yours affectionately,
Jawaharlal

[PS]
Last night I received a long cable from the Chinese Ambassador in London conveying his greeting. This cable ended up by saying that

[720] (1890–1971); contemporary of Nehru at Cambridge; Secretary, UP Provincial Congress Committee, 1928–34; Secretary, INC, 1927 and 1931; served as High Commissioner in Pakistan, 1947–9; Governor of Assam, 1949–50, Madras, 1952–6, and Bombay, 1956–62

[721] Expressing his deep distress over the 'drastic action against Subhas Chandra Bose', Sri Prakasa in his letter dated 12 August 1939 to Nehru had written, 'I am too small a person to judge the great man in whose hands is entrusted the destinies of our country at the present juncture. Still when something is done that goes right against the grain of my moral being—and the great attraction of Mahatmaji's movement for me was its moral basis and insistence on self-purification—I cannot but protest ... I am therefore enclosing my resignation from the offices I hold in the Provincial Congress organisation and my membership of the Indian Legislative Assembly.'

[722] In its issue dated 15 July 1939, the paper said, 'Chungking dispatches indicate that Pandit Jawaharlal Nehru is to pay a visit to China to extend a sympathetic hand to a people struggling for life against the juggernaut of Japanese imperialism. Nehru has been called the Truth part of the Indian triad of Good, Truth and Beauty, the other two being Gandhi and Tagore. ... Nowhere else do we find a like spirit of self-sacrifice, a like belief in eternal values, and a like disregard of the material amenities of life on earth as we find in Mahatma Gandhi. ... In her struggle for life, could not China make good use of India's moral leadership? One word from Gandhi could go a long way in exposing the moral depravity of the enemy.'

Winston Churchill requested him to send me his good wishes for success of my mission!

J.

MKG Papers, Pyarelal Collection, *Subject File 66, NMML*

## 325. Telegram to Jawaharlal Nehru

Wardhaganj
18 August 1939

Jawaharlal Nehru
Anand Bhavan
Allahabad
May your Chinese mission be crowned with success. May God be with you and bring you safe home. Regret Sri Prakasa. He should suspend action till after your return.[723] Propose issuing a statement on crisis and war resolution unless you wish otherwise.[724] Send your Chinese address.

Love.

Bapu

CWMG, *Vol. LXX, pp. 96–7*

[723] Later, when Sri Prakasa was persuaded to withdraw his resignation from the Congress, Gandhi sent him the following wire on 26 August: 'Delighted. Just like you. Awaiting letter.'

[724] The Congress Working Committee had passed a resolution on 11 August disqualifying Subhas Chandra Bose from being President of the Bengal Provincial Congress Committee for three years with effect from 30 August. For Gandhi's statement to the press on 23 August regarding his differences with Bose and the AICC resolution on the impending World War II, see *CWMG*, Vol. LXX, pp. 112–14.

Referring to the action against Bose in his article 'The Charkha', dated 9 January 1940, Gandhi wrote: 'the love of my conception, if it is as soft as a petal, can also be harder than a flint. My wife has had to experience the hard variety. My eldest son is experiencing it even now. I had thought I had gained Subhas Babu for all time as a son. I have fallen from grace. I had the pain of wholly associating myself with the ban pronounced on him. ... I maintain I have acted towards them as I have acted towards those who are considered nearest and dearest to me. In all my dealings love has dictated my actions.'

## 326. Letter to Jawaharlal Nehru

Segaon, Wardha
18 September 1939

My dear Jawaharlal,
Here is my letter to Chiang Kai-shek.[725] The letter became longer than I had wanted it to be. Perhaps it will be well to send a typed copy with the original.

Mahadev went to Madras yesterday.

Love.

Bapu

CWMG, *Vol. LXX, p. 185*

## 327. Letter to M.K. Gandhi

Lucknow
23 September 1939

My dear Bapu,
I enclose four articles[726] which I have written. The first one, India and the War, was sent under my name to various papers in India. The set of three articles–War Aims and Peace Aims–has been contributed by me as editorials to the *National Herald*. My name has not been given. I felt it would be better for this subject to be considered impersonally.

I am here for two or three days. After that I do not quite know. I might visit one or two big towns.

Yours affectionately,
Jawaharlal

SWJN, *Vol. 10, I Series, pp. 588–9*

[725] Generalissimo Chiang Kai-Shek, the supreme leader of China; President of the National Supreme War Council of China; Member, Central Executive Committee of the Kuomintang. In Nehru's description he 'embodies in himself the unity of China and her determination to be free'.

[726] See *SWJN*, Vol. 10, I Series, pp. 144–5 and 148–58.

## 328. Letter to Jawaharlal Nehru

Segaon, Wardha
24 September 1939

My dear Jawaharlal,
The enclosed wire[727] for you to dispose of. It is your special department.

I am off to Simla again.[728] I go only to act as intermediary. You will send me instructions if any. I do hope you will be ready to answer invitation, if it comes.

Love.

Bapu

CWMG, *Vol. LXX, p. 197*

## 329. Letter to Jawaharlal Nehru

Segaon, Wardha
25 October 1939

My dear Jawaharlal,
I have gone through the American thing. It is most expensive. In other respects, too, it does not attract me.

I hope you have good news about Indu.[729]

Love.

Bapu

CWMG, *Vol. LXX, p. 294*

[727] Not available

[728] Gandhi left for Simla on 24 September on being invited by the Viceroy for a second round of talks concerning India's role in war efforts, the first having been held on 3 September.

[729] Who was studying in Europe. In her book *With No Regrets*, Krishna Hutheesing explains that Indira went hiking during the autumn of 1939, got soaked and caught a chill which developed into pleurisy. She went tc Leysin, Switzerland, after having been in a Middlesex hospital for some time.

## 330. Letter to Jawaharlal Nehru

Segaon, Wardha
26 October 1939

My dear Jawaharlal,
I could see that though your affection and regard for me remain undiminished, differences in outlook between us are becoming most marked. Perhaps this is the most critical period in our history. I hold very strong views on the most important questions which occupy our attention. I know you too hold strong views on them but different from mine. Your mode of expression is different from mine. I am not sure that I carry the other members with me in the views that I hold very strongly. I cannot move about. I cannot come in direct touch with the masses, not even with the Congress workers. I feel that I must not lead if I cannot carry you all with me.[730] There should be no divided counsels among the members of the Working Committee. I feel that you should take full charge and lead the country, leaving me free to voice my opinion. But if you all thought that I should observe complete silence, I should, I hope, find no difficulty in complying. If you think it worthwhile, you should come and discuss the whole thing.

Love.

Bapu

CWMG, *Vol. LXX, p. 297*

[730] Gandhi wrote in his article, 'The Next Step', on 30 October, explaining his position: 'I have undertaken to guide the Working Committee, but my limitations appal me. My physical condition makes it impossible to move about as I used to before. I am therefore cut off from all outward contact with the masses. Even the present Congress workers I do not know personally. ... I hold the opinion strongly that whilst by their own action the British Government have made it impossible for the Congress to cooperate with them in the persecution of the war, the Congress must not embarrass it in its persecution. ... holding the views that I do, I am in no hurry to precipitate the civil disobedience. ... I swear by the old constructive programme of communal unity, removal of untouchability and the charkha. ... If it makes no appeal to them, either they have no nonviolence in them or I do not know the ABC of nonviolence. If my love of the charkha is a weakness in me, it is so radical as to make me unfit as a general.' See *CWMG*, Vol. LXX, pp. 315–16.

## 331. Letter to Jawaharlal Nehru

Segaon, Wardha
29 October 1939

My dear Jawaharlal,
I wrote to you yesterday. This is to send you a complaint from Meerut.[731] Please inquire and write directly to the correspondent. I have told him I have passed the letter on to you.
Love.

Bapu

CWMG, *Vol. LXX, p. 309*

## 332. Letter to M.K. Gandhi

6 Couper Road, Lucknow
30 October 1939

My dear Bapu,
Mahadev told me in Bombay that you had written to me to Allahabad. As I came here from Bombay I have not yet received your letter. Perhaps it may reach me tomorrow.

I intend going to Allahabad on the night of November 1st. Maulana is still here but probably he will go to Calcutta tomorrow morning.

I enclose some cuttings. There is an article by Bernard Shaw which appeared in the *New Statesman* of London three weeks ago.[732] This created a minor sensation in England. It is worth reading as representing a definite viewpoint held by many people in England. Then there is an editorial from the *New Statesman*. There is nothing special in this. I enclose also a cutting from the *Hindustan Times* giving its London Letter which you may not have seen. This gives a

[731] The reference is, presumably, to the communal riots that broke out in Meerut on 4 October, when the army was called and arrests were made.

[732] On 7 October 1939, under the title 'Uncommon Sense about the War', wherein Shaw had argued that there was no further excuse in continuing with the war.

good account of the reception in England and elsewhere of the Congress statement.

Yours affectionately,
Jawaharlal

MKG Papers, Pyarelal Collection, *NMML*

## 333. Letter to M.K. Gandhi

Lucknow
31 October 1939

My dear Bapu,
I have received your letter forwarded from Allahabad. It is true that in many fundamental respects our views and approach to life's problems differ.[733] I have grown into my present views after many internal struggles and I cannot say that even now the process of change or growth has stopped. If I have to do anything worthwhile in life I must be true to myself insofar as I can. I have tried very hard to adapt myself to others, notably to you, but with little success, I fear. As for the Working Committee you know how badly I fit into it. We all put up with each other because of mutual affection and respect but we think on different planes. You will remember that after the Calcutta AICC I had kept out of the WC and previously before Tripuri, I had written that I had no place in the WC. It is my misfortune that I can find no place elsewhere where I can fit in. I function individually, lonely and weary at heart, disliking much that happens, including myself. I suppose I must play that role since there is no other for me. But I cannot shed responsibility for what is happening, nor can I retire when every fibre in my being calls for action.

I do not know that any talk between you and me will throw any further light on this matter. You know me well enough and I have nothing to add. I talk too much. But it is always good to meet you and talk to you and you can summon me when you will and where you will. Probably we shall meet soon. As far as possible I should like to keep the dates free—Nov. 6, 7, and 8, especially the last two, as

[733] See p. 376.

we have important Congress Committee meetings on the 7th and 8th here.

Love.

Yours affectionately,
Jawahar

MKG Papers, Pyarelal Collection, *NMML*

## 334. Letter to Jawaharlal Nehru

Railway Station, Delhi
4 November 1939

My dear Jawaharlal,

Just after you had gone, Kripalani told me that in United Provinces there was great ferment and preparation for civil disobedience.[734] He told me, too, that anonymous placards had been circulated asking people to cut wires and tear up rails. My own opinion is that there is at present no atmosphere for civil disobedience. If people take the law into their own hands I must give up command of civil disobedience movement. I would like you to read this week's *Harijan*.[735] It deals with my position in this connection. It was this that I had intended to discuss with you. But it was not to be. At this critical time in our history there should be no misunderstanding between us and, if possible, there should be one mind.

Love.

Bapu

CWMG, *Vol. LXX, p. 328*

[734] Nehru had had discussions with Gandhi on 2 November 1939 in Delhi.

[735] See p. 376.

## 335. Letter to M.K. Gandhi

Lucknow
8 November 1939

My dear Bapu,

I enclose for your information a copy of the resolution[736] passed by the Council of the UP PCC yesterday.

All the members were desirous of having an opportunity of meeting you if this was possible during your stay in Allahabad, without inconvenience to you. I wrote to you yesterday.[737]

The Working Committee is likely to last up to the 21st or possibly the 22nd. May I suggest the 23rd for an informal meeting between you and some of our prominent workers in the UP—say about 30 or so? If you think it is possible, kindly have a telegram sent to me to Allahabad.

Zetland's speech puts a lid to all talks between the Congress and the British Government.[738]

Yours affectionately,
Jawaharlal

SWJN, *Vol. 10, I series, p. 475*

[736] Which endorsed the Congress attitude towards the war. It also welcomed Gandhi's leadership at the supreme hour of crisis.

[737] The letter is not available.

[738] In his speech of 2 November 1939, Zetland had referred to the Congress as a Hindu organization which should reach a settlement with the Muslim League. Nehru, in his editorial in the *National Herald* had written, 'Lord Zetland's and his government have put a final seal on the bill of divorce and the gulf that separates us is wider than the many oceans that intervene between his country and ours.' See Nehru's editorial of 20 October 1939, 'Lord Zetland's Apologia', *SWJN*, Vol. 10, I Series, pp. 203–6 and of 8 November 1939, 'Freedom is in Peril', ibid., pp. 232–4.

## 336. Letter to Jawaharlal Nehru

Segaon, Wardha
14 November 1939

My dear Jawaharlal,

Your letters have been coming in regularly. I have seen yours to Rajen Babu.[739] Before I saw it I had written a note[740] on it for *Harijan*, I must try to send you an advance copy.

If you need me longer in Allahabad, you will keep me.

The interested editings in London of our statements here do not worry me.[741] If I find time I shall write out a brief message for the *News Chronicle*.[742] I have prepaid authority from that paper.

More when we meet.[743]

Love.

Bapu

[739] In his letter of 11 November 1939 to Rajendra Prasad, Nehru had written: 'Certain remarks of Bapu's ... seemed to me to be unfortunate. He said he cannot have civil disobedience so long as the Viceroy is carrying on the talks and so long as we have not come to an agreement on the Hindu-Muslim question. ... But a positive a statement of the kind made by Bapu really makes settlements and agreements far more difficult. ... There is no doubt that at the present moment there is complete impasse between the British Government and us. There has been a final and absolute refusal by Zetland and others to meet our demands. He has said that is impossible for the British Government to agree to what we want. Bapu's statement after all this must lead people to think that we are not serious in our demands.' See *SWJN*, Vol. 10, I Series, p. 447.

[740] Entitled 'Unnecessary Alarm', dated 13 November 1939. See *CWMG*, Vol. LXX, pp. 342–3.

[741] Nehru had mentioned to Rajendra Prasad in his letter that 'I have been receiving letters and cables from London which are disturbing. It appears various phrases and sentences extracted from their context are cabled there and produce an entirely wrong impression. The result is confusion at the other end and a belief that Congress is not serious and does not mean business and is only out to bargain here and there.' See *SWJN*, Vol. 10, I Series, p. 447.

[742] Dated 14 November; see *CWMG*, Vol. LXX, pp. 348–9.

[743] Gandhi reached Allahabad on the 19th when he attended the Working Committee. At another gathering where he laid the foundation-stone of the Kamala Nehru Memorial Hospital, he said, 'This work is my sacred duty and I have come to Allahabad specially for it.'

[PS]
Mahadev just reminds me that you complete half a century today. I hope you will complete the other half retaining the same vigour, frankness and robust honesty.[744]

CWMG, *Vol. LXX, p. 347*

## 337. Letter to M.K. Gandhi

Itarsi
24 November 1939

My dear Bapu,
I found a deputation of Kashmiris waiting for me at Itarsi and as we had five hours to spare here, I could give them plenty of time. I have gone through all their papers. Last January I met Sheikh Abdullah and had several talks with him about the Kashmir situation. From many points of view Kashmir deserves our consideration. Apart from being an important state, the movement there has undoubtedly been a mass movement and has been continuing for several years. It began in a somewhat communal way and though not responsible for the riots which occurred in 1931, was indirectly influenced by them. Ever since then it has been trying to wean itself from communalism and has largely succeeded. Sheikh Abdullah struck me as an intelligent person who was trying hard to understand the Indian National movement to adjust himself and the Kashmir movement with it. Frightened by the riots of 1931, the Hindus kept away from this but individuals (and they were worthwhile Hindus) gradually drifted to it. This drift has continued and quite a number of Hindus are associated with it now, though of course there are many who still suspect it and are a little afraid of it. The Hindus having had for many years almost a monopoly of petty offices are apprehensive of being displaced.

[744] 'Your first half century of life has already passed into history, song and legend', wrote Sarojini Naidu wishing Nehru, 'May the early years of the next half century bring you the fulfilment of your great dreams and visions and immortalise you in the chronicles of human progress as one of the Supreme Liberators.'

As a matter of fact the Kashmiri Pandits by virtue of their intelligence and high intellectual level are bound to make good under a progressive government. They would be cramped by minority protection.

The present movement grows more and more national in outlook, though it has to contend with reactionaries on either side. The Punjab communalists—Hindu and Muslim—are an evil influence. I think that Abdul Ghaffar Khan and the Khudai Khidmatgars have indirectly influenced the movement also.

I am naturally interested in Kashmir (provincialism crops up in odd ways!) and I should love to go there some time next year. But my personal predilections apart, I do think that this is an important problem having an all-India significance and affecting our handling of the Hindu-Muslim question.

At present the civil disobedience movement is off there. There is no point in restarting it again during the winter when movements are restricted. So there is a breathing period of three-and-a-half months. How is this period to be best utilised and what is to be done afterwards?

Although responsible government is demanded the CD took place on an issue of civil liberty. A monstrous ordinance was used to crush all activity. This ordinance is worthy of study. Sheikh Abdullah and other leaders are still in prison.

Our friends, who are taking this letter, have foolishly not made an appointment with you. They are going to Wardha to await your convenience and pleasure. They have piles of papers with them. I am advising them to send some of these papers to you and then, when you so desire, they can meet you.

Yours affectionately,
Jawaharlal

MKG Papers, Pyarelal Collection, *Subject File 141, NMML*

## 338. Letter to M.K. Gandhi

Anand Bhawan, Allahabad
4 December 1939

My dear Bapu,
Your note[745] about Jinnah. I wrote to Jinnah three days ago on the subject and I am awaiting his reply.[746] I did not write to him previously as a report had appeared in the press about my writing to him and this put me off. I do not know what action you are thinking of in connection with this.

Indira is progressing slowly.

Yours affectionately,
Jawaharlal

[PS]
I have got a lovely photograph of your being shaved by the barber.

Have you seen the UP Conference resolutions?[747] I am asking Ranjit to send them to you.

Mahatma Gandhi
Sagaon, Wardha

MKG Papers, Pyarelal Collection, *NMML*

## 339. Letter to Jawaharlal Nehru

Segaon, Wardha
7 December 1939

My dear Jawaharlal,
I have not read the Muttra resolutions or your speech.[748] I should like to have both.

[745] Not available

[746] Nehru in his letter of 1 December 1939 had written about meeting to 'discuss various aspects of the communal problem' and also about the visit of Sir Stafford Cripps.

[747] Passed at the UP Political Conference on 28 and 29 November, relating to the Indian States and the Tenancy Bill, and on the Constructive programme.

[748] Nehru spoke in Hindi for 90 minutes. Referring to the war in Europe, he was happly to state that its repercussions in India were most welcome as they succeeded in composing their internal differences in Congress. He emphasized that their demand for swaraj was an old one and had nothing to do with

I note your gentle complaint in Mahadev's letter. What can I do? You have to take me as I am. I know you [do].[749] I know also how gentle you are with me.

You may bring Cripps[750] when you like.

Love.

Bapu

CWMG, *Vol. LXXI, pp. 12–13*

## 340. Letter to Jawaharlal Nehru

Segaon, Wardha (CP)
10 December 1939

My dear Jawaharlal,

What is this cutting about? I should like to see your speech[751] and like you to reply to the article.

---

the present war. The Congress sought clarification from the British Government's war aims in relation to India. He regretted that the British Government's reply to their demand was most unsatisfactory and therefore the Congress Working Committee had no alternative but to call upon Congress Ministries to resign. He reiterated the Congress demand for a Constituent Assembly to frame a suitable constitution for India, and said that he saw no prospect of a settlement between the British Government and India so long as the main Congress demand was not accepted. The communal problem, he said, was not a major issue and was not capable of solution if India's right to be treated as a free country was conceded. ... Concluding, Nehru remarked that they were in no hurry to launch a struggle and would not take the offensive, but at the same time they should prepare themselves from then for future contingencies. See *SWJN*, Vol. 10, I Series, pp. 254–8.

[749] The source has 'are'.

[750] Sir Stafford Cripps (1889–1952); Solicitor-General, Labour Government, 1930–1; expelled from the Labour Party, 1939; visited India after the outbreak of War, 1939; British Ambassador, Moscow, 1940–2; Member, War Cabinet deputed to India, 1942; Member, Cabinet Mission to India, 1946; Chancellor of the Exchequer, 1945–7

Cripps met Gandhi on 19 December 1939 at Wardha.

[751] Presumably Nehru's speech at Agra on 4 December, where he had said: 'We have placed our cards on the table, and no useful purpose can be served by interviews, talks and statements unless the Government is prepared to accept the views expressed by the Congress and Mahatma Gandhi.'

What an extraordinary *fatwa*[752] of Jinnah about Congress Ministries!

Love.

Bapu

CWMG, *Vol. LXXI, p. 21*

## 341. Letter to M.K. Gandhi

25 December 1939

My dear Bapu,

I enclose a letter for you from Chiang Kai-shek.[753] The original is in Chinese but he has sent a translation in English. I hope you will not destroy this Chinese letter. It is worth preserving at Maganwadi. Should you care to answer it, please send me your reply and I shall forward it through the Chinese consul.

The 'deliverance day' did not prove much of a draw in the UP. In fact it was on the whole a failure. Many of the meetings started off in a very small way, but then curious sight-seers, chiefly Hindus, joined them to find out what was happening. Some meetings were held on that day by Muslims, both in mosques and outside, condemning the Muslim League proposal. I enclose a letter to give you one such instance. You can destroy this letter after reading it as I do not want it back.

Yours affectionately,
Jawaharlal

SWJN, *Vol. 10, I Series, p. 417*

[752] A proclamation of religious authority issued on 6 December 1939, in which Jinnah had exhorted 'Mussalmans all over India to observe Friday, the 22nd December, as a day of deliverance and thanksgiving—as a mark of relief that the Congress Governments have at last ceased to function.' For Gandhi's 'Statement to the Press' on this, see *CWMG*, Vol. LXXI, pp. 18–19.

[753] Who had written inviting Gandhi to China

## 342. Letter to Jawaharlal Nehru

Segaon, Wardha
28 December 1939

My dear Jawaharlal,

I have your letter. I shall preserve the Chinese letter.

The deliverance day has received a full-page advertisement in the *Times of India*. But in truth, it seems to have fallen flat everywhere.

Have your read Fazlul Haq's[754] indictment[755]? Should nothing be said or done about it?

You have not sent me Kumarapppa's letters to which you had raised strong objection.[756] He is here. I asked him and he says he sent nothing recently. Do please send me what you may have.

Love.

Bapu

CWMG, *Vol. LXXI, pp. 65–6*

[754] A.K. Fazulul Huq (1873–1962): Member, Bengal Council, 1931–4, and Central Assembly, 1934–6; delegate, Round Table Conference, 1930 and 1931; Prime Minister, Bengal, 1937–41; resigned after heading the Coalition Ministry; headed the United Front Ministry, East Pakistan, 1954; Central Minister, Pakistan, August, 1955 to March, 1956; Governor, East Pakistan, 1956–8

[755] The Huq-Nehru correspondence between 30 October 1939 and 16 December 1939 was released to the Press on 17 December 1939. On 27 October 1939, Huq had stated that he had definite evidence that 'the most inconceivable atrocities' had been committed and the Congress Government would not or, at any rate, did not take any action to protect the Muslims. 'I give a definite challenge to Pandit Jawaharlal Nehru. Let him fix a convenient time and I will take him to a dozen places which I am sure would open his eyes to the atrocities which the Congress has committed on the Muslim minorities.'

[756] J.C. Kumarappa had said that by accepting the Chairmanship of the Planning Committee, Nehru had violated the principle of nonviolence, for the use of machines represented some kind of violence.

## 343. Letter to M.K. Gandhi

3 January 1940

My dear Bapu,

I have just returned to Allahabad and received your letter of the 28th.

I do not quite know what one should do about Fazlul Huq's indictment. It is possible for some Congress ex-minister to deal with the matter.

About Kumarappa's correspondence with the Planning Committee, I was told by Ambalal[757] and Dr Nazir Ahmad[758] that they had approached him for certain information in regard to cottage industries and sought his cooperation on some other matters connected therewith. Both of them were very much hurt at the reply received from Kumarappa which seemed to them to refuse any kind of cooperation or help. Both Ambalal and Nazir Ahmad spoke to me about it in an agitated way and said that it would be very unfortunate if this attitude is taken up, as the information gathered by the Village Industries Association will not influence them in coming to their conclusions.

Yours affectionately,
Jawaharlal

SWJN, *Vol. 10, I Series, pp. 525–6*

## 344. Letter to Jawaharlal Nehru

Segaon
5 January 1940

My dear Jawaharlal,

Your letter makes me sad. You said in indignant tones that Kumarappa was a worthless man. And this you did on the flimsiest

[757] Ambalal Sarabhai, Chairman and Secretary of the Manufacturing Industries Sub-committee

[758] (1898–1951); head of the Department of Science, Islamic College, Lahore, 1925–40; Member, National Planning Committee, 1938–41; Director, Cotton Technological Laboratory, 1931–45; Member, Indian Tariff Board, 1945–7; Secretary, Development Board, Pakistan, 1947–50; Chairman, Tariff Commission, Pakistan, 1950–1.

testimony. I asked you for the correspondence and you said you had not it with you but would send it to me. Now I see you accepted the interpretation of others. My point is not that the interpretation was incorrect but that it was wrong to judge a co-worker on such hearsay. I suggest your securing the correspondence and sending it to me.

Herewith my letter to the Generalissimo.[759] I have not released his to the Press. You will do so if you think it necessary.

Love.

Bapu

CWMG, *Vol. LXXI, p. 77*

## 345. Letter to M.K. Gandhi

Anand Bhawan, Allahabad
10 January 1940

My dear Bapu,

I have just returned to Allahabad after an intensive tour in the rural areas of our north-western districts. Your letter of the 5th followed me about and at last reached me.

I am exceedingly sorry that I should have distressed you. It surprises me greatly that you should think that I said or considered that Kumarappa was 'a worthless man'. Your memory may be better than mine in the matter but I cannot imagine myself saying anything quite so foolish or absurd. I think and have long been of opinion that Kumarappa is a very efficient, strong and hardworking person with strong convictions. He is a rare acquisition to any cause. But I confess to having been irritated at his attitude which, instead of gaining converts, drove people away. You are right that I placed my opinion partly on others' reports. Ambalal and Nazir Ahmad spoke to me strongly and referred to the correspondence which I had myself not read then. I should not have done so. But I was inclined to do so as I had myself felt

[759] Gandhi sent the following letter dated 5 January 1940 to Chiang Kai-shek: 'Many thanks for your very kind invitation. If I could accept it, I would be fulfilling a long-cherished wish. But my present mission forbids my responding to your invitation.'

previously that Kumarappa's attitude had been so unbending and non-cooperative as to hinder the very cause he represents. Anyway I apologise for my misbehaviour and am very sorry indeed for the distress that I have caused you and Kumarappa.

I shall bring the correspondence with me to Wardha. For the moment I cannot trace it but I think I shall find it.

I have read some of your recent articles on khadi, etc., and especially your reference to your old book *Indian Home Rule*. I believe in khadi but I am afraid I am literally unable to accept the economic as well as other organisation of society envisaged in your book. So far as I know the Congress has never considered this, much less accepted it. I fear that if this is pushed to its logical extreme, it will add to the many disruptive tendencies which are at work in the country.[760]

Yours affectionately,
Jawaharlal

MKG Papers, Pyarelal Collection, *NMML*

[760] Emphasizing the importance of khadi in his writings during December 1939 Gandhi said, 'Heart peace among communities and reinstatement of the wheel in every home are my politics, for I expect to gain the freedom of the country from political and economic bondage through these means in the place of red rebellion.' He wrote, again, 'If the village spinners and weavers are to come into their own, and that quickly, every Congressman has to become a master spinner and master weaver. He should be able to teach and guide the poor villagers. He has ... to spin for the sake of the country. ... If Congressmen have this faith, all Congress organisations will become efficient spinning and weaving schools. ... The economics of khadi require that from cultivation of cotton to the manufacture of khadi and its disposal, all the processes should, as far as possible, be gone through in the same village or centre.'

## 346. Letter to M.K. Gandhi

24 January 1940

My dear Bapu,

You asked me at Segaon about Molotov's[761] speech about the war and I said something in reply which was rather vague. Since Molotov's speech was made much has happened and the position has grown very difficult. I have no doubt in my own mind that Russia has acted very wrongly in regard to Finland and she will suffer because of this.[762] But what concerns us even more is the fact that behind the Anglo-French-German war, what is really happening is a consolidation of the imperialist and fascist powers to fight Russia. It is clearer now than it was ever before that the war is a purely imperialist venture on both sides. Fine phrases are being used by politicians as they were used in 1914. It seems to me highly important and vital that we should not be taken in by these phrases and pious protestations. All this has an intimate bearing on our own position in India and any talks with the British Government. The object of the Government is to gain our goodwill for their war. Under existing circumstances, quite apart even from the question of India, I do not see why we should give our moral support to an imperialist war. Of course if Britain changed her attitude radically towards India and acknowledged our independence that in itself would mean that her imperialism has undergone a vital change. But what is more likely to happen is that this imperialism will fundamentally continue and the war will continue to be waged for its sake, though under stress of circumstances some vague declarations are made in regard to India. Even these declarations, it will be said, will be honoured at the end of the war. That seems to me a very dangerous position for

[761] Vyacheslav Mikhailovich Molotov (1890–1986); Soviet politician and diplomat; a leading figure in the Soviet Government from the 1920s to 1957, principal Soviet signatory of the Nazi-Soviet Non-aggression Pact of 1939.

[762] The Molotov-Ribbentrop Pact (Nazi-Soviet Non-aggression Pact), by a secret protocol, provided for the partition of Poland, Finland and the Baltic States between Nazi Germany and the Soviet Union. Molotov was given a free hand in relation to Finland. The Soviet-Finnish war ensued.

us as we shall be involved, whether we want it or not, in supporting British imperialist policy in all manner of nefarious undertakings. I feel, therefore that we must be very cautious and wary and should make it perfectly clear that we are not going to support these imperialist objectives of the war.

As I have mentioned above, the position is likely to grow much more complicated soon if the western powers mobilise against Russia and their intrigue with Italy succeeds. They will call it a holy war against communism and under cover of that not only try to strengthen their own empire but break up the socialist state of Soviet Russia. That would be a calamity from every point of view, quite apart from our agreement with Russian policy or not. I would beg of you to bear this in mind and to view Indian talks in this perspective.

You will notice that one or two optimistic phrases in your article,[763] as well as some minor occurrences like the UP Governor's visit to Anand Bhawan, have led to an extraordinary impression everywhere that some kind of a settlement is coming with Britain and that the Congress ministries will soon be back in office.[764] Jinnah[765] profits by this by making fun of our independence, the Muslim League gets an opportunity to raise its head a little, and as for our newspaper editors, they misbehave as usual.[766] All this creates a wrong impression in the minds of the public in India as

[763] In which Gandhi had said, with regard to the Viceroy's statement of January 1940, offering Dominion status of the Statute of the Westminster variety 'I believe in the sincerity of Lord Linlithgow. In the immediate carrying out of policies it is the individuals who count. I have worked with faith and hope. And I have not lost the hope that we shall have an honourable settlement without a struggle.' For Gandhi's article 'The Independence Day', see *CWMG*, Vol LXXI, pp. 125–7.

[764] Sir Maurice Hallet and his wife had unexpectedly visited Anand Bhawan on 18 January 1940. Nehru was not present.

[765] Who, writing to Gandhi in January 1940, said: 'India is not a nation, nor a country. It is a subcontinent composed of nationalities, Hindus and Muslims being the two major nations. ...Your peculiar doctrines regarding khaddar, ahimsa and spinning are not going to win India's freedom. Action and statesmanship alone will help us in our forward march.'

[766] *The Times of India* editorial of 22 January 1940 had said: 'Mr Gandhi's pronouncement is on the lines hoped for... a settlement is now possible.'

well as England. It makes even a possible settlement far less likely. What will happen again is that the Viceroy will complain that he was misled. *The Pioneer* has come out with a heading 'Congress Ministries' Resignation Bluff Called by Viceroy' and so on. Everywhere there is questioning, what is happening behind the scenes?[767] Everywhere there is expectation of some big and sudden development.

All this not only does not square with the facts and with the existing situation, but creates a wrong atmosphere for any kind of mental or other preparations.

Personally, I feel sure that there is no real chance of a settlement, although the British Government would no doubt like it. But they are very far from agreeing to what is our minimum. The British Government today is more reactionary and imperialist than it has ever been and to expect it to give in to us is to expect something that cannot happen at this stage. To raise false hopes is unfair and inexpedient and may even weaken our position. I would suggest that it is fairer to lay stress on the other side so that the other party may know exactly how matters are and should adjust itself accordingly.

Yours affectionately,
Jawaharlal

SWJN, *Vol. 10, I Series, pp. 310–12*

## 347. Letter to Jawaharlal Nehru

Segaon, Wardha
30 January 1940

My dear Jawaharlal,

Padma Pant of Cawnpore has sent me copy of his letter to you. I hope you will probe the truth.

Love.

Bapu

767 On 22 January 1940, Subhas Bose had said: 'Mr Gandhi's latest statement heightens my worst suspicions, namely, that serious efforts at compromise with the British Government have been going on behind the scenes.'

[PS]
Have you seen the latest pamphlet of the Jamiat-Ulema-i-Hind?[768] They are dangerous friends. I wonder if the Working Committee had a full talk with Moulvi Kifayatulla Saheb![769]
CWMG, *Vol. LXXI, p. 165*

## 348. Letter to Jawaharlal Nehru

On the way to Delhi
3 February 1940

My dear J.L.,
Read the within letter.[770] You know best what to do. These things require attention.
Love.

Bapu

CWMG, *Vol. LXXI, p. 174*

## 349. Letter to M.K. Gandhi

Allahabad
4 February 1940

My dear Bapu,
You will reach Delhi tomorrow and it appears that you are going to stay there for a week or more.[771] I do not know what development

[768] An organization set up in 1919 by Maulana Mohammad-ul-Hasan. It began to associate itself with Congress activities from 1930. In 1939, the Jamiat-ul-Ulema took the initiative of bringing together all Muslim organizations and forming a joint front against the Muslim League.

[769] Mufti Kifayatullah (1872–1952); prominent leader of the Jamiat-ul-Ulema-e-Hind

[770] Dr Satyapal, in his letter to Rajendra Prasad dated 24 January, had described the communal activities of the Akalis, stating that 'unless the High Command includes these also in the list of communalists there is grave danger of the Punjab Congress being entirely under the thumb of the Akalis, and they will be a serious danger for this organisation because of their being neither believers in truth, nor nonviolence, nor nationalism ... nor Purna Swarajya.'

[771] On 10 January 1940, the Viceroy, Lord Linlithgow, had declared in a speech the British Government's 'objective for India' as 'full Dominion

there will be and whether it may become necessary for you to summon any of us. Personally I do not think there is the slightest chance of this happening as I do not see the least bit of a change in the Government's attitude. In any event I wanted to inform you that it is exceedingly difficult for me to think of going to Delhi during the next two weeks. I am fully occupied all this time. Tonight I am going to Lucknow for two days. On the 7th I shall come to Allahabad for a day, leaving on the 8th morning for Bombay, where I have to attend important meetings of the Planning Committee which I have convened specially to consider certain matters. The whole meeting would be completely upset and would become infructuous if I did not go there. I shall be in Bombay from the 9th morning to the 12th night when I leave for Lucknow. On the 14th, 15th and 16th I shall be in Lucknow for our provincial Congress and delegates' meetings. During the next two days I expect to be in Gorakhpur for vast gatherings there. This is for the moment my programme for the next two weeks.

Everything that has happened during the last month or so confirms me in the belief that there is not the slightest ground for hope that the British Government will accept our position. In fact many things have happened which demonstrate that they are following a very definite imperialist policy. You must have seen that the British Parliament has just passed a bill amending the Government of India Act which limits the powers of provincial governments in regard to taxation.[772] This was specially in view of the property tax in the UP which is thus vetoed. Apart from the demerit of such a decision which reduces the powers of the provincial assembly, the time and the method chosen for it are eloquent of the imperialist outlook of the British Government and indicate that this has in no way changed.

---

Status ... of the Statute of Westminster variety'. The speech prompted Gandhi to seek a meeting and they met on 5 February 1940.

[772] The India Burma (Miscellaneous Amendments) Bill sought to restrict the tax imposed by the UP Employment Tax Bill passed by the Legislative Assembly on 14 April 1935 by limiting the amount that might be levied on any one individual in one year. Graduated Tax was imposed on those who derived their income from employment. The Bill was reserved for the Governor-General's assent.

I wonder if your attention has been drawn to a recent social function[773] in London, organised by the Royal Central Asian Society. Lord Zetland presided and a number of cabinet ministers were present. The ostensible object was to establish a centre of Muslim culture and religion in London; the real object was to encourage pan-Islamism and to exploit this sentiment in India and in the Islamic countries to the advantage of the Allies in the war. It is extraordinary how the war is developing along true-blue imperialist lines and how events are repeating themselves.

All this does not fit in with the notion that England is preparing to deliver up her empire. Nor is it at all encouraging to find that we are going to have again a procession of people headed by you to interview the Viceroy. The same old game is played again, the background is the same, the various objectives are the same, the actors are the same, and the results must be the same.

There are, however, some unfortunate indirect results also. An atmosphere of approaching compromise pervades the country when, in effect, there is no ground for it. It is enervating and depressing because it does not come out of strength but, in the case of many individuals, from the excessive desire to avoid conflict at all costs and to get back to the shreds of power which we had previously. Conflict is undesirable but obviously conflict cannot be avoided at all costs, for sometimes such avoidance itself is a more costly and harmful affair. For the moment, however, there is no immediate question of conflict. The question is of maintaining our position with dignity and not weakening it in any way. I fear that the impression is widely prevalent in England as well as in India that we are in no event going to have any conflict and therefore we are going to accept such terms as we can get. This kind of impression is demoralising. I have noticed during the last fortnight that even our Congress delegates' elections have been influenced by this. Many people, who for fear of possible conflict were keeping in the background, have now pushed themselves in front again when the possibility of enjoying the plums of office and power seem to dangle again in front of them. The effort of several months to keep undesirables out of the Congress has partly failed because of this

[773] Held on 30 January 1940

sudden change in the Indian atmosphere which has led them to believe that a compromise was imminent.

The British Government is also reacting in a way unfavourable to us, though it may use soft language. Of course it wants to come to terms with us because it wants our support in the war. But it is much more certain that it does not wish to give up any shred of real power or change its fundamental imperialist policy in order to come to terms with us. It is carrying on and will carry on its old intrigue on the communal issue, though occasionally it uses a few critical words against the Muslim League in order to soothe the Congress. So far as it is concerned, it will try to win us over, keeping its present position intact. If this is possible, well and good for it. If this does not take place, as seems likely even to it, then to carry on from time to time conversations with Indian leaders, to prolong the issue, to make it appear that we are on the verge of a compromise, and thus to soothe both world opinion and Indian opinion. This second policy has the additional advantage, from their point of view, of exhausting our energy and toning us down, so that, if ultimately a conflict does come, the requisite atmosphere is lacking for it. It is the general belief among official circles in England that their policy of parleys and postponement has had this result and the situation in India, which was threatening when the Congress Ministries resigned, is much easier now and no dangers are to be feared.

It seems to me that while we cannot and must not precipitate a conflict and, while we need not bang the door to a possible and honourable compromise, because your methods are never to bang the door, still we must make it crystal clear that there can be or will be no compromise except on the conditions stated by us previously. As a matter of fact even these conditions have to be slightly reviewed from the point of view of developments in the war. We cannot now say, as we then said, that we want to know whether this war is imperialist or not. The British Government's answer to us as well as their consistent policy in the war and in foreign affairs has been one of full-blooded imperialism. We must therefore necessarily proceed on this admitted fact that it is an imperialist war, any profession to the contrary notwithstanding. The war and British policy grow more and more sinister every day and I would hate to see India entangled in any way in this imperialist adventure from which India can only lose, not only materially but spiritually. This point seems to me of vital importance today.

Thus it seems to me that the most important thing for us to do is to make our position perfectly clear to the world, to the British Government and to the Indian people. There is too much misunderstanding on this issue of compromise and this misunderstanding is entirely to our disadvantage and to the advantage of British imperialism which meanwhile is exploiting our resources for the war and even pretending to have a large amount of our goodwill. An approach by us to the British Government or to the Viceroy increases these misunderstandings and leads the British Government even further away from a right compromise.

Some recent speeches of Rajagopalachari have distressed me because they talk too compromisingly of Dominion Status and the like.[774] The Congress speaks with too many voices and it is not surprising that confusion and embarrassment should result. On the question of independence at least there should be only one voice.

I have inflicted two long letters on you today for which I seek your indulgence and forgiveness.[775]

Yours affectionately,
Jawaharlal

SWJN, *Vol. 10, I Series, pp. 319–22*

[774] On 25 January 1940, Rajagopalachari had said: 'We should not allow posterity to say that a great opportunity was spoiled by internal differences. ... Dominion Status today might even be equivalent to complete freedom. It might even be better because we get a navy without paying for it, but, is not the same thing as complete freedom.' Further, on 28 January, he had said that the British people were not satisfied with the present position and desired that Indians should take up the responsibility for the administration. He, therefore, believed that before long they would of their own accord permit Indians to govern themselves.

[775] The other letter is not available.

## 350. Letter to Jawaharlal Nehru

[After 4 February 1940][776]

My dear Jawaharlal,

I have your letter. I know the possibility of misunderstandings.[777] These and ignorant or interested criticism have never influenced me. I know that all would be well, if we are strong within. For the external affairs you are my guide. Your letter therefore helps me.

You have made more than ample amends about Kumarappa. You will like to see his letter. You may destroy it after perusal. Yes, we have very few workers like him.

Love.

Bapu

G-N Correspondence, *JN Papers, NMML*

[776] Inferred from the contents

[777] Gandhi in response to Nehru's letter of 4 February 1940, wrote on 11 February 1940 an article entitled 'The Old Game' which appeared in *Harijan,* 17-2-1940: 'The Warning is sound. Perhaps I did not need it. But such warnings are never superfluous. It is wise to be sure of one's own wisdom. It is healthy to be reminded that the strongest might weaken and the wisest might err. And then, so far as I am concerned, I am so ignorant even of current events that I am thankful when co-workers keep me posted with things I ought to know.

'But whilst I value the warnings given and admit the force of the argument advanced, I do not repent having visited HE the Viceroy and having had a prolonged talk. It has given me added strength. It is of great value to an army officer that its General gains strength. I should therefore repeat the performance every time the Viceroy summons me, i.e., so long as I have faith in his sincerity. And every time I shall come out with greater strength than I go with. The method of satyagraha requires that the satyagrahi should never lose hope as long as there is the slightest ground left for it. For he never despairs of being able to evoke the best in his opponent, his mission being to convert his opponent, not to humiliate or defeat him. He therefore even knocks at his opponent's door if it becomes necessary, as I did often with General Smuts. It so happened that the last opening, when even I had the least hope, proved the prelude to success.'

## 351. Letter to Jawaharlal Nehru

Segaon, Wardha
[On or after 7 February 1940][778]

My dear Jawaharlal,
I like your letters. They give me information which I do not get otherwise. I knew nothing of the pan-Islamic movement. It does not surprise me. You will have seen my statement on the interview.[779] My method you know. I gain strength from these meetings. It is for you and other co-workers to see that the country gets the proper interpretation of what I do. I would like you not to worry about CR. He is absolutely sound. Nevertheless I would like you to share your doubts with him. I leave for Santiniketan on 15th evening and thence on 19th for Malikanda.

Love.

Bapu

CWMG, *Vol. LXXI, p. 195*

## 352. Letter to Jawaharlal Nehru

Sevagram, Wardha
23 May 1940

My dear Jawaharlal,
Read the enclosed and guide me. I have told the writer that his suggestion attracts me and if I see my way clear I shall act up to it in part or wholly.[780]

Love.

Yours,
Bapu

CWMG, *Vol. LXXII, p. 90*

[778] From the contents it is evident that this was written after Gandhi's return to Segaon on 7 February after his meeting with the Viceroy on the 5th.

[779] With the Viceroy. See *CWMG*, Vol. LXXI, pp. 186–9.

[780] Abdul Hai Abbasi of Lucknow had suggested that communal troubles usually started in northern India, and that Gandhi should settle in a village in the UP where Muslims were in a majority.

## 353. Letter to Jawaharlal Nehru

Sevagram, Wardha
29 May 1940

My dear Jawaharlal,
I had your letter[781] enclosing Mr. Spalding's.[782] Thompson's was not in it. I am writing to S generally approving of your reply.[783] That will save my time.

I have also your enclosing reply to Sir Sikandar[784] and your letter [to] the Maulana. Your statements are good and full.[785] I purposely refrain from making statements. But I will when I find it necessary.

I hope you are having a good time in Kashmir.

Love.

Bapu

CWMG, *Vol. LXXII, p. 113*

[781] Not traceable

[782] Henry Norman Spalding (1877–1953), endowed the Spalding professorship of Eastern Religions and Ethics and a lecturership in Eastern Art at Oxford University

[783] Spalding had written to Nehru in his letter of 18 April, 'While freedom and self-government remain a true ideal for every state-independence has become a false ideal. If freedom is to be preserved, statesmanship must aim at a Commonwealth of Man—not of independent but of interdependent states or groups of states.' Nehru had replied: 'I agree with you entirely that the idea of the independent sovereign state has completely broken down. ... While I accept completely this ideal, I am quite convinced that the ideal cannot be realised through groupings as the British Empire, even though that empire may change its imperialist characteristics and become a truer commonwealth. ... So far as India is concerned, it is almost impossible for it to become a really free member of a free British commonwealth but India can much more easily become a member of a wider commonwealth which embraces all countries.'

[784] Sir Sikander Hyat Khan (1892–1942); served in World War I; Revenue Member, Punjab Government, 1932–5; Deputy Governor, Reserve Bank of India, 1935–7; Chief Minister and leader of Unionist Party, Punjab, 1937–42

[785] In a statement to the Press on 24 May 1940, Nehru had said that while India was not out to embarrass at a moment of peculiar difficulty, they were at the same time 'out to assert and gain our freedom and we cannot give that up because the war situation has developed to India's disadvantage', and that the internal policy of India 'must be governed by one consideration only - the freedom of India and the attitude of Britain towards that freedom.' See *SWJN*, Vol. 11, I Series, pp. 45–6; see also Nehru's 'Interview to the Press', Lahore, 24 May 1940, ibid., pp. 46–8.

## 354. Letter to Jawaharlal Nehru

Sevagram, Wardha
15 July 1940

My dear Jawaharlal,
The idea about Urdu is good. You shall have a review of the Urdu writings by Hindus and of Urdu periodicals and books. There should be an Urdu weekly giving a dispassionate reply to the lies. It is uphill work to overtake deliberate lies but it is worth trying.

Love.

Bapu

Shri Jawaharlal Nehru
Lucknow, UP

CWMG, *Vol. LXXII, p. 275*

## 355. Letter to M.K. Gandhi

Lucknow
17 July 1940

My dear Bapu,
I have just received your post card. A great deal can be done on the lines you suggest and, as it happens, we have quite competent men to do it. Unfortunately we have not got enough money for any such work on a big enough scale.

As a matter of fact we have had a Urdu weekly for the last two years. This was not officially started by the Congress but it was sponsored by leading Congressmen in this province. It is called *Hindustan*. I think it is far the best Urdu weekly in India, so far as literary and political contents are concerned. But, as it so often happens, the managerial side was hopelessly incompetent and, in spite of all efforts, the weekly has become an increasing burden. Because of the rise of the cost of paper due to the war, it has become almost impossible to carry it on. Very probably the last issue will come out this week. That will be a pity.

A weekly does not cost very much and it could do a lot of good but the finances must be forthcoming. With a weekly like the one you have mentioned and a number of pamphlets in simple Urdu, I am quite sure that we would create a marked impression on the

Muslims. They are just in the mood to understand and the feeling against the leadership of the Muslim League is growing. In the UP, in spite of everything we have always had some Muslim backing and good Muslim workers. In Delhi the anti-Muslim League sentiment is strong.

Yours affectionately,
Jawaharlal

SWJN, *Vol. 11, I Series, p. 224*

## 356. Letter to Jawaharlal Nehru

Sevagram, Wardha
8 August 1940

My dear Jawaharlal,
Maulana Saheb gave me the Hyderabad preliminary report.[786] It makes fearful reading. There is nothing new in it for me. But one does not want confirmation of worst fears. I have been taxing myself about the remedy. I meet the workers tomorrow. If you have any thoughts pass on to me.

Love.

Bapu

[PS]
Will you send me any authentic evidence you may have of the war exactions?

CWMG, *Vol. LXXII, p. 369*

## 357. Letter to M.K. Gandhi

10 August 1940

My dear Bapu,
I have just received your letter of the 8th. About Hyderabad, I can make no suggestion. So much depends on the strength of the people and their organisation. I think, however, that it is far better for them to concentrate on the rural areas where the chances of

[786] Relating to Ittehad, the Muslim communal organization in Hyderabad. It was headed by Bahadur Yar Khan, which opposed the scheme of reforms announced by the Nizam in 1939.

communal clashes are probably less. I do not see how they can remain passive under the circumstances. Yet it may be perhaps better not to precipitate a big crisis immediately in view of the rapid developments of the political situation in India as a whole. When this all-India situation advances further, Hyderabad people might be in a better position to assert their right.

In a sense I am not sorry at the developments in Hyderabad. The impossible attitude that Bahadur Yar Khan and others have taken up will react on them. It may of course lead to a great deal of trouble and bloodshed. In any event the States Congress people should make it perfectly clear that they cannot reduce by an iota their demand for responsible government.

I understand the Working Committee is likely to meet in Wardha in eight or nine days' time. I hope to meet you then.

About the exaction for war funds, I have written to the secretary of the UP PCC to send you some particulars. Some have been published in the Press and are clear enough. Some others, though equally clear, might be explained differently. For instance, a usual case is for a person to be approached for a donation. He refuses or offers a smaller sum than what is demanded. Immediately or a day or two after, he is arrested on the charge of preventing others from subscribing to the war funds, and thereby coming in the way of war efforts.

I have just had a case like this from Allahabad district. A poor village shopkeeper was asked to give Rs 15/- or Rs 20/-. He said the most he could possibly give was Rs 5/-. He was cursed and sworn at and immediately a notice was given to him to appear to show cause why he should not be proceeded against under the Defence of India Rules.[787] His case is up today in a court here. Usually this kind of thing is not done with full-fledged Congressmen who are expected to refuse anyhow. Another case which has come to me today is from Kasganj in Etah district. A *naib tehsildar* went to the shop of a Congressman on 2nd of August and demanded money

[787] On 3 September 1939 the Governor-General had promulgated the Defence of India Ordinance that curtailed civil liberties. The same day an amendment to the Government of India Act was rushed through Parliament enabling the Central Government to nullify provincial autonomy.

for the war funds. This was refused and the man stated that as a Congressman he could not do so. Thereupon the naib tehsildar threatened to take action and had the name of the person noted down. On the next day this man, who is the nephew of a well-known Congressman in the district, was suddenly arrested for non-payment of a punitive police tax. He was put in the lock-up and for 30 hours he was not given any food or facilities for bathing, etc. This arrest was completely illegal as punitive tax can only be recovered by attachment of property and the person concerned, whose name is Omprakash, has considerable moveable and immoveable property. The amount of punitive tax concerned was only Rs 6/- which could easily have been realised by attachment. Omprakash's uncle, Manpal Gupta, thereupon created a lot of fuss and ultimately Omprakash was discharged. That is how the matter stands now.

Another interesting case is that of Thakur Surendra Bahadur Singh, taluqdar of Simri in Rae Bareli district. He is a Congress MLA. His father, the taluqdar, recently died and thereupon, at his own request, his taluqa was taken under the court of wards. The Deputy Commissioner informed him that he should contribute Rs 1,500/- to the war fund. He refused to do so as a Congressman. He was then told that he held his taluqa on conditions of loyalty and good service and the court of wards has a perfect right to give the donation out of the revenues of the taluqa. Thereupon he sent a registered notice to the Deputy Commissioner protesting against this imposition and saying that it was wholly illegal. His case was that it might or might not be open to the Government to confiscate his taluqa for want of loyalty to them. But it was certainly not open to them to give a donation on his behalf and against his will. In spite of this the Deputy Commissioner has already paid or is going to pay this sum to the war fund and Surendra Bahadur Singh is thinking of bringing a declaratory suit in a court of law.

I am getting complaints from various districts of pressure being brought on kisans to pay eight annas or a rupee or more per plough. It is obvious that they do not want to pay but are compelled to do so.

Petty government servants and minor officials dare not say no when they are asked to contribute. A recent case which came to my notice informally but nevertheless correctly was that of a stenotypist of a district magistrate. He was asked to give Rs 200/-. His salary was Rs 125/- a month. He pointed out hesitatingly that he had a large family and it was entirely beyond his capacity to pay that sum. He was then told that in any event he and his family would have to starve if the British lost the war. So this was a kind of insurance that he had to pay. A curious thing is that one does not hear very much about donations from higher officials. They think it is enough for them to serve the cause by giving their very efficient service at a high rate of payment.

The number of new appointments at high salaries grows from day-to-day. Probably a very large proportion of the funds that are being collected goes towards the payment of these high salaries. Simla, I understand, is crowded with this type of officials serving the great cause by drawing a fancy salary for little or no work. There was a recent case of an English official who was till recently drawing Rs 750/- a month suddenly being pushed into some war work and is being given Rs 2,500/- a month. It was stated that he had accepted this new job at considerable sacrifice to himself.

Yours affectionately,
Jawaharlal

[PS]
I am sending you separately the 2nd number of the UP PCC review of the Urdu Press. This is better than the last one and is illuminating.

SWJN, *Vol. 11, I Series, pp. 275–7*

## 358. Letter to M.K. Gandhi

21 September 1940

My dear Bapu,
There was one matter I forgot to mention to you. On the 17th of September, that is when we were in Bombay, a young boy named Rajni Patel[788] was arrested in Bombay on landing there. I am particularly interested in this young man and I consider him a very

[788] Rajanikanth Patel (1915–1982); President, Bombay Pradesh Congress Committee, 1972–7

intelligent and competent person. He was returning to India after five or six years spent abroad and was greatly looking forward to his homecoming.[789] In particular he had been writing to me that he would come to see me immediately on arrival so that he might take up worthwhile work immediately in connection with the Congress or some connected activities. It was a curious homecoming for him to be arrested on landing under the Defence of India Act. None of his people were present when he landed as the time of arrival was not known previously. In fact I heard of his arrest for the first time from the evening paper in Bombay. I tried immediately to get an interview in the police lock-up but this was refused and we were informed that no interview could be given unless special permission of the Bombay Government was taken. The next morning he was sent to Nasik Jail.

Rajni Patel comes from the village Sarsa near Anand in Gujarat. He was sent to England some five or six years back—I do not know exactly the date—for the Civil Service Examination. He prepared for this and actually went to the examination hall. As he was sitting there, however, he was asked to go out because his political opinions were not approved of by the India Office. He had been expressing these opinions at meetings and elsewhere. I remember this matter being brought up in questions in the Central Assembly at the time.

After that he continued his studies in various places and ultimately became a barrister, though he had no particular desire to practise the law. I had come into intimate contact with him during my visits to England and I found him to be very intelligent and very likeable. In fact he was exceedingly popular among all kinds of people in England, especially among English students. He associated himself with the student movement there, with youth leagues, with the Labour movement and with the India League. In fact these various activities somewhat came in the way of his studies.

When I was in England last I promised him that on his return to India we would try to utilise him for some worthwhile work. I have

[789] For Nehru's article of 29 September 1940 entitled 'Homecoming', see *SWJN*, Vol.11, I Series, pp. 434–6.

been in correspondence with him and in every letter he had told me how he was looking forward to working under my directions.

Sometime last November, that is after the war began,[790] he finally left England and went to America intending to spend a month or two there and then return to India via China. As he was well-known in the British Youth Movement, the American Youth Movement took him up and made him tour all over the country. He spent nine or ten months in America and visited all parts of the United States as a youth representative. He appears to have been very popular there. He delivered, I suppose, rather strong speeches against British imperialism. During his visit there, he was invited to the White House to tea by Mrs Roosevelt.[791]

Ultimately he left America with various letters and messages for the Chinese Youth Movement. To his surprise and indignation he was not allowed to land at Hong Kong by the British authorities and was compelled to proceed to India direct. At Singapore he was not even allowed to land for a short while as other passengers were. Probably this must have happened at Colombo also. On arrival in Bombay he was arrested on the plea that he had many books and papers with him which were objectionable. As a matter of fact the policemen told us that they had been on the lookout for him for a long time and would have arrested him anyhow.

I have no idea what the exact charge against him is or what books or papers he had with him. Returning home after a long absence, he must have got many books which must have accumulated. So far as I have read reports of speeches they have been strong but not very different from the kind of speeches many of us deliver here. He is a frank, straightforward person and not given to underhand work. He is not a Communist, though he has no doubt come into contact with Communists in England and possibly in America. His general outlook is what might be called socialist.

Just before I left Bombay, I spoke to Vallabhbhai about Rajni and also mentioned the matter to Bhulabhai. I asked them to do what they could to help him and also to get into touch with his

[790] In September 1939

[791] Eleanor Roosevelt, wife of the American President, Theodore Roosevelt

people. Rajni Patel's father's address is: Motibhai Venibhai Patel, Sarsa, via Anand (Gujarat).

I have a faint notion, but I am not quite sure of this, that Rajni took part in the civil disobedience movement in the early thirties and also went to prison.

I am writing all this to you to keep you informed and in the hope that possibly you might be able to do something for him.

Yours affectionately,
Jawaharlal

SWJN, *Vol. 11, I Series, pp. 425–7*

## 359. Letter to M.K. Gandhi

23 September 1940

My dear Bapu,

I am enclosing a cutting from the *National Herald* which reproduces two very interesting judgements of the Supreme Court of the USA. These judgements are not only interesting in themselves and very well written, but also raise a point which may well come up for decision in India. Of course there is no urgency about this issue and if you are too busy, you need not read these judgements. But I thought they might possibly interest you.

You might have heard that M.R. Jayakar returned from England a few days ago. I am told he wanted to meet you just before you left Bombay but hesitated to do so as that was your last day there. I did not see him either. It appears that he is thoroughly disillusioned about the British Government's attitude towards India and is convinced that this Government is determined to crush the Congress. One curious criticism he is reported to have made about the AICC decision. He said that mass CD should be indulged in and not individual because, I presume, he wanted us to react in as big a way as possible to the British Government's offensive.

You will be interested to know that the private bank accounts of well-known Congressmen are being examined in detail by the police under orders from the district authorities. The idea apparently is to find out where the money comes from and where it goes to.

An interesting case happened in Lucknow the other day where a Congressman was sentenced for a speech of which there was no proper report. A constable had just noted down a few sentences out of a long speech. When objection was taken to this kind of a report, the magistrate said that we could not expect the police to arrange for the reporting of the speeches that were being made and so he would proceed on that very inadequate basis. This is interesting doctrine.

I have just received a letter from Horace Alexander in which he mentions that the British Government is obdurate in regard to India because Anglo-Indian officialdom has assured them that Congress is weak and Gandhiji's influence is waning.

I am going to Lucknow on the 26th night and I expect to remain there for four days. We are having our Provincial Congress Committee meetings there as well as some other committee meetings.

Yours affectionately,
Jawaharlal

SWJN, *Vol. 11, I Series, pp. 236–7*

## 360. Letter to M.K. Gandhi

Allahabad
2 October 1940

My dear Bapu,
About six weeks ago, when I was in Bombay for the Planning Committee, I had a remarkable experience, which has oppressed me often since then. I should have told you about it when you were in Bombay last but the Working Committee and the AICC filled my mind and I forgot. I did not want to write about it through the post.

I came back from the Planning Committee during the midday interval for food. I had to go back soon after and was pressed for time. Just then a young English boy turned up at my sister's flat. He was dressed in khadi—a shirt and loose pyjamas and cap. He told me that he was an officer in the Army—a Second-Lieut.—and had decided to leave the Army and face the consequences. He produced a copy of a document which he said he had given to his commanding officer and which had been forwarded to Army headquarters at

Simla.[792] I read this and was amazed. It was a fine statement. I enclose a copy of it and you can read it for yourself.

His name was Napier. He was the great-grandson of the Napier[793] who is said to have conquered Sind. The family since then had been intimately connected with the Army. Apparently it had come down in the world. Young Napier joined as a private a few years before the war began. But because he was a bright lad, and possibly also because of his family, he got a scholarship for Sandhurst and later became a commissioned officer. He was sent with his regiment to India a month or two after the war began. He was stationed at Mhow in Central India. Evidently he did not fit in with his brother officers. He was more serious and intellectual and he felt drawn towards India, especially of the poorer classes. He avoided officers' messes and spent his time in the bazaar or elsewhere talking to paltry shopkeepers, labourers, etc. He tried to pick up Hindustani. I think he gave a good part of his salary to the poor.

This was not liked by his brother officers. The CO spoke to him about it and they had many arguments. He began to dislike his profession, and especially service in India, more and more. He wanted to leave it but this was not possible in war time. Ultimately he gave the enclosed note to his CO.

His regiment was transferred from Mhow to Jhansi. This gave him a day and a half or two to join up at Jhansi. He decided to burn his boats whatever the consequences and went and sold his uniform. This was done chiefly to put a definite end to his military career—also to raise some money. He did not particularly want to be sent back from India to England.

He then telephoned to Allahabad to get into touch with me and learnt—found I was in Bombay and got my address. Went straight to Bombay and to my sister's house from the station.

[792] Napier in his note of August 1940, had condemned the British Empire in India in strong terms and put forth his reasons for wanting to leave the Army and join the struggle for freedom and the alleviation of the misery of India's poor.

[793] Sir Charles Napier

This was a novel situation for me and I was completely taken aback. My heart went out to this young and terribly sincere boy of 25 but I did not know what to do. By coming to Bombay he had deserted—and that too in war time. This is the gravest offence in military law and there was not doubt that he would be arrested in a day or two and court-martialled. I found from him that he was due to report at Jhansi the next morning. There was just a chance of his getting back to Jhansi in time if he took the next train which left soon after.

I wanted to have a much longer talk with Napier but already I had kept the Planning Committee waiting. If he had to go back to Jhansi by the next train then there was going to be no other chance. I felt he must go back. To be charged with desertion was to confuse the issue apart from other consequences. He had already made his position perfectly clear to the army authorities and he could face them and fight them on that issue. I could hardly conceive of his remaining in the British Army after his declaration of faith. Nor could I see how he was to get out of it. Army authorities do not permit this kind of thing. What was going to happen to him I could not guess, but it seemed to be clear that he would have a very hard time. Anyway, I felt that this question must not be mixed up with desertion. I advised him therefore to go back by the next train to Jhansi and to report himself to the CO there. I further suggested to him not to go in khadi kurta and pyjamas. He said he had shorts, etc., and he would wear them. I asked him if he had enough money. He said he had quite enough for his purpose.

He accepted my advice and said he would go back. I asked him to communicate with me, if possible, or with my sister, and to let me know what happened. We have had no news of him since. I am told now that every regiment that is sent to Jhansi, goes off soon after to Egypt. I am trying to find out now what has happened to Napier's regiment. It is quite likely that because of his views and his escape he was kept under arrest and prevented from communicating, and later sent out of India.

His face haunts me and I often wonder if I advised him rightly.

Yours affectionately,
Jawaharlal

SWJN, *Vol. 11, I Series, pp. 436–8*

## 361. Letter to Jawaharlal Nehru

Sevagram, Wardha
6 October 1940

My dear Jawaharlal,
I had your two letters. You will tell me more about Rajni Patel when we meet. Your letter about Napier, with enclosure, I am sending to the Viceroy. It is a pathetic case.

I am over head and ears in work. Hence no more.

Love.

Bapu

CWMG, *Vol. LXXIII, p. 81*

## 362. Telegram to Jawaharlal Nehru

Wardhaganj
21 October 1940

Jawaharlal Nehru
Fyzabad
Vinoba arrested early morning.[794] Trial today. Thinking next step.

Bapu

CWMG, *Vol. LXXIII, p. 118*

[794] Vinoba Bhave who began Individual Satyagraha on 17 October for anti-war propaganda was arrested. For Gandhi's statement to the Press of 21 October advising Congressmen not to be impatient, see *CWMG*, Vol. LXXIII, pp. 118–19.

Writing earlier for *Harijan*, 20-10-1940, Gandhi had said that Vinoba was chosen to commence Direct Action for he 'believes in the necessity of the political independence of India. He is an accurate student of history. ... It was necessary to introduce Vinoba at length to the public in order to justify my choice. ...' For Gandhi's article 'Civil Disobedience', ibid., pp. 102–7.

## 363. Letter to Jawaharlal Nehru

Wardha
21 October 1940

My dear Jawaharlal,

So Vinoba has been fixed up. His four days' ministry has been quite successful from my point of view.[795]

I am issuing a note which you will see. Professor[796] telephoned saying you were ready.[797] I have seen your statement[798] too. I would still like to ask you whether you can see anything to commend itself to you in all I am writing and doing. I would not like you to go in merely as a disciplinarian. My present conception requires those who believe in the plan—not in every detail but in the main. *Verb sap.*[799]

Drop me a wire if you can.

Love.

Bapu

CWMG, *Vol. LXXIII, p. 119*

[795] Vinoba Bhave had been making anti-war speeches from 17 October 1940 until his arrest on the 21st, when he was sentenced to three months' imprisonment.

[796] J.B. Kripalani

[797] For Individual Satyagraha

[798] Of 16 October 1940. While referring to Gandhi's announcement that 'direct action will be commenced by Shri Vinoba Bhave and for the time confined to him only', Nehru had said, 'I would have you remember that it has been the Congress way to start big movements in a small and sure way. ... Each one of us therefore must do his allotted task in a spirit of perfect discipline and keep ready for all emergencies whenever they might arise. Instructions issued by Gandhiji should be carefully observed and implicitly followed, without fretting and impatience.'

[799] Abbreviation for Latin *verbum sapient sat est*, meaning 'A word is enough for the wise'

## 364. Draft Telegram to M.K. Gandhi

24 October 1940

Mahatma Gandhi
Sevagram, Wardha

Your letter. Agree generally.

Jawaharlal

MKG Papers, Pyarelal Collection, *NMML*

## 365. Letter to M.K. Gandhi

24 October 1940

My dear Bapu,
I enclose copy of a letter I am sending to Maulana. You will remember that you referred to Mahmud[800] one day. I do not know what your source of information was, but in this matter at least I think Mahmud is not to blame.

On my arrival here today I received your letter dated 21st October. I have sent you a brief telegram in reply. It is difficult of course to express anything clearly in a telegram. My mind is by no means clear as to what the future is going to be. More and more I think about the problem in India in its larger world perspective. I think of this, naturally, from the political point of view. I think that your plan has great possibilities and therefore I would like it to go ahead and to help it in so far as I can. But not knowing exactly how you intend to develop it, I feel a little confused.

I do not know whom you consider to be the spiritual leaders of the world (the phrase you have used somewhere), but if they are the leaders of organised religions or religious groups, I am quite convinced that they are a hopeless lot. It is the common man who might ultimately make a difference and the approach to him will

[800] Syed Mahmud (1889–1971); lawyer of Patna; Minister, Bihar, 1937–9 and 1946–52.

In his letter to Azad, Nehru had written that he had met Mahmud and that he had denied having made any suggestion, direct or indirect, to the Muslim League people. He had met Jinnah and Khaliquzzaman and to the suggestion of the latter that the Congress should agree to the Viceroy's proposals Mahmud had replied that it was impossible.

have to be such that he can grasp it. If that approach is entirely beyond his reach or understanding, it will fall flat. I think the horror of war is bound to lead to a strong reaction. But this reaction will only come when some way out which guarantees individual and national freedom is found. Without this guarantee nonviolence becomes associated in people's minds with submission to slavery and force. That argument applies to India also. I have found a receptive atmosphere among our people, also a certain confusion about the future and as to what they should do.

I have received Mangal Singh's letter. I do not know what you expect me to do about it. I realise all the implications of what he says. Mangal Singh is not a very reliable person, still I think he is right in the main about this matter. I am writing an article for the Press on the Sikhs and the Congress.[801] This will be a fairly frank statement.

During my visit to Sultanpur district I found numerous complaints of forcible realisations for war funds. I enclose a letter about this. On enquiry, I found it to be perfectly correct. Scores of boys came to me and complained to me that they had been forced by their school authorities to pay a monthly sum of 1 anna each for the war fund with their tuition fee, in spite of their protests. It seemed to me a particularly mean thing to do to make these boys pay.

Yours affectionately,
Jawaharlal

SWJN, *Vol. 11, I Series, pp. 186–7*

[801] This was in reply to the Gujaranwala District Congress Committee's representation to the Working Committee to settle the differences between Sikhs and the Congress in the Punjab. On 9 August 1940, Master Tara Singh had written to Gandhi and Maulana Azad asking the Congress not to do anything to prevent recruitment to the army. On 30 September 1940 the All India Sikh League had appealed to the Sikhs to continue to cooperate with the war effort, and on 7 October 1940, the Akali Political Conference called upon the Sikhs not to embrace the creed of nonviolence, which was opposed to the basic spirit of the Sikh religion. See *SWJN*, Vol.11, I Series, p. 245.

## 366. Letter to Jawaharlal Nehru

Wardha
24 October 1940

Dear Jawaharlal,
I was glad to have your wire. If my statement has been allowed, you will have seen it before this.[802]

If you are ready, you may now ceremonially declare your civil disobedience. I would suggest your choosing a village for your audience. I do not suppose they will allow you to repeat your speech.[803] They were not ready with their plans so far as Vinoba was concerned. But should they let you free I suggest your following the plan laid down for Vinoba. But if you feel otherwise, you will follow your own course. Only I would like you to give me your programme.You will fix your own date so as to leave me time for announcing the date and place. It may be that they won't let you even fulfil your very first programme. I am prepared for every such step on the part of the Government. Whilst I would make use of every legitimate method seeking publicity for our programme, my reliance is on regulated thought producing its own effect. If this is hard for you to believe, I would ask you to suspend judgement and watch results. I know you will yourself be patient and ask our people on your side to do likewise. I know what strain you are bearing in giving me your loyalty. I prize it beyond measure. I hope it will be found to have been well-placed, for it is 'do or die'.[804] There is no turning back. Our case is invulnerable. There is no giving in. Only I must be allowed to go my way in demonstrating the power of nonviolence when it is unadulterated.

[802] The reference, presumably, is to Gandhi's 'Statement to the Press' dated 24 October 1940. See *CWMG*, Vol. LXXIII, p. 73.

[803] Presumably, the reference is to Nehru's address at Patti, Pratabgarh District, on 18 October 1940, where he had talked about starting of individual satyagraha. See *SWJN*, Vol. 11, I Series, pp. 181–2.

[804] An expression, which in the years following, was to acquire great potency. On 8 August 1942, presenting the thought process behind it to his countrymen, Gandhi said 'Here is a mantra, a short one, that I give you. You may imprint it in your hearts and let every breath of yours give expression to it. The mantra is "Do or Die". We shall either free India or die in the attempt.'

Maulana Saheb telephoned saying I should choose another man for the second satyagraha. I told him I could not do so if you consented to come in.

I would like your reaction to the step I have taken regarding *Harijan*.[805]

Love.

Bapu

CWMG, *Vol. LXXIII, pp. 126–7*

## 367. Telegram to Jawaharlal Nehru

Wardha
25 October 1940

J. Nehru
Anand Bhawan
Allahabad

Letter posted today.

Bapu

CWMG, *Vol. LXXIII, p. 131*

## 368. Letter to Jawaharlal Nehru

Sevagram, Wardha
26 January 1941

My dear Jawaharlal,

I had your messages about the hospital.[806] Dr Mehta has been to Allahabad and he is of opinion that it should be opened by me on 28th February. All things considered, I agree with him that I should open it and that too on 28th February at the earliest. If I go, the balance of the contemplated sum is likely to be collected and the hospital inaugurated without much anxiety as to the future. I

[805] On 21 October 1940, an ordinance was promulgated prohibiting newspapers from publishing matter affecting the war effort. Gandhi suspended the publication of *Harijan* and allied publications in protest.

[806] The Kamala Nehru Memorial Hospital

know you will all be with us in spirit.[807] I think we need not wait for Sarup and Indu.

If you are permitted to wire your opinion, please do. I shall then go to Allahabad with a lighter heart.

Love.

Bapu

CWMG, *Vol. LXXIII, pp. 300–1*

## 369. Letter to M.K. Gandhi

24 July 1941

My dear Bapu,

...[808] I have been taught self-restraint about my personal feelings and emotions and the habit of confessing to people or taking them into one's confidence is totally alien to me. I live a lonely personal life and the only person who could occasionally peep into it was Kamala. Few people even know or realise how I felt about Kamala. It seems rather silly to say so and the expression is a trite one, but throughout our married life I was very much in love with her. Why this was so, I do not know; such feelings are spontaneous and often utterly unreasonable. It was not just because she was my wife or because she had certain good qualities. Neither of these facts lead to a man's love for a woman. Affection there may be, a feeling of contentment with each other and all that through close associations and mutual interests. But love as I conceived it and as it came to me was something different, something electric, something often painful. It was not the conception of duty owed or an obligation to be discharged. I would hate to have someone feel that it was his or her duty to love me. I want no such purchase ...

My conception of marriage and sex may strike you as odd; they certainly differ from yours. In my own married life there was this unusual fact (I think it is definitely unusual in sedate and long-married people) that while I might be irritated with Kamala or quarrel with her, her touch would always thrill me. I was the worst

[807] Nehru had been arrested at Allahabad on 31 October 1940. There were several other leaders arrested too, in the months following.

[808] Omissions in the letter are as in the source.

possible husband for any woman owing to my intense public activities, preoccupations, absences and jail. Yet always there was a certain magic in our relationship. She was a mystery to me and I was a mystery to her and something of the initial novelty and surprise never wore off, and though we grew older in years, we remained very young in our outlook. It is rather odd that I should make this confession to anyone, and more especially to you, whose ideas of the relationship between man and woman seem very extraordinary to me. I am a pagan at heart, not a moralist like you, and I love the rich pagan culture and outlook on life of our ancients, their joy in beauty of all kinds, in richness of life and a wise understanding of human nature with all its virtues and frailties.

India grows upon me more and more and I am ever discovering something new in her. It is a voyage of discovery which has no end. And yet people call me, because of my ways and outlook, a European and an Englishman. They are right in a way and yet only superficially so. I do believe intensely in India, though it would be hard to define this belief. I have never yet been disappointed in the common people of India perhaps because I did not expect too much from them. But I am irritated and disgusted often enough by our middle classes (my own kind) who have lost all sense of values, of beauty, of what is essential in life. Their vulgarity and weaknesses and limited outlook appal me. Always they seem to be willing to sell their immortal selves for a dirty mess of pottage.

I am at peace here and, as usual, quite fit and feeling absurdly young for my advanced years. The realisation that I am over fifty-one always surprises me. I can't quite believe it! I do not worry at all, or perhaps it would be more correct to say, that I worry seldom. At no period previously in jail have I had this feeling of inner calm. The days pass easily enough with reading, spinning and various other activities. The present does not engage my attention much; whatever I might be doing, my mind tries to probe into the future, to imagine what this mad world will be like tomorrow and how and where India will fit into it. Why do people worry so much about getting something quickly and now, and fear that if they do not get it, it might elude their grasp? Do they not realise that we have come to the end of an age and there is no further room for quibbling and political trickery and manoeuvre and all the arts of the average politician? Only strength counts in this naked age which lays bare all weaknesses. It may be the strength of armed might, which is above law and lawyers, or some other form of inner strength, which also is above law and lawyers. A people or a nation which still thinks in terms of law and lawyers is lost.

With my love to you,

Yours affectionately,
Jawaharlal

SWJN, *Vol. 11, I Series, pp. 658–9*

## 370. Telegram to M.K. Gandhi

Wardha
4 December 1941

Just arrived.[809] Returning Lucknow tomorrow morning for two days then Allahabad. Future programme depending Maulana and your directions. Understand you going Bardoli. Would not Bardoli involve longer journey for Maulana others.

Love.

Jawaharlal

MKG Papers, Pyarelal Collection, *NMML*

## 371. Letter to Jawaharlal Nehru

5 December 1941

My dear Jawaharlal,

It is nice to be able to write to you outside the jail. But the pleasure is only momentary for I cannot reconcile myself to these discharges. However, we meet this new menace.

[809] On 3 December, the Government of India began releasing satyagrahi prisoners. Nehru, Maulana Azad and others were released on the 4th. In a statement on 5 December 1940, Nehru said, 'But it is not good to be in and out of prison at the bidding of alien authority. It is not good to come out of the narrow confines of jail into a larger prison that is India today.' See also Nehru's statement of 11 December 1941 to *News Chronicle*, 'The Meaningless Release of Prisoners', where he had stated that the gesture was 'of little avail if the whole background is one of hostility'. See *SWJN*, Vol. 12, I Series, pp. 1 and 11–12.

This is merely to tell you that I delayed answering your question as the rumour about your discharge was in the air.

I have read your letters most carefully. I agree with your conclusions and I like the very generous manner in which you have treated the whole thing. I had one and only one chat with F[810] and he accepted my proposition that he would not think of marrying Indu without your consent and blessing. Indu wrote to J. that she was coming and seeing me too. Now that you are out and probably will be for a few days if not longer, you will shape this thing as you wish.

I hope you have liked the recent statements issued by me.[811] You will tell me when you are coming. Maulana telephoned today saying he proposed to come after two or three days. I propose to leave here on 9th for Bardoli for one month.[812] Sardar wants me to give one month to Gujarat. He is under treatment, mostly dietetic, I have prescribed the diet. I think his pain is most bearable under that regime. So far as it is possible our talks and meetings should take place in Bardoli. The discharges are a challenge. I feel that we should hold the WC, AICC meetings as early as we can.[813] But of this you and Maulana are the best judges.

I am writing this against time.

Love.

Bapu

CWMG, *Vol. LXXV, p. 133*

[810] Feroze Gandhi (1912–1960); politician and journalist; Member of Parliament; married to Indira Nehru

[811] The release of Nehru, Azad and other political leaders was announced on 3 December 1941. Gandhi had said that it could not 'evoke a single responsive or appreciative chord' in him. Mr Amery's pronouncement, he said, did not 'soothe the festering sore, but are like sprinkling chillies on it.' See *CWMG*, Vol. LXXV, pp. 92–3 and 131–2.

[812] Gandhi was in Bardoli from 10 December 1941 to 9 January 1942.

[813] The Congress Working Committee met at Bardoli from 21–30 December 1941.

## 372. Telegram to Jawaharlal Nehru

Wardha
6 December 1941

Jawaharlal Nehru
Lucknow
Wrote yesterday. Your wire. Come when you can. Sardar had long settled Bardoli programme. His body shattered. I am sole guide on care his body. Would avoid disturbing him but your and Maulana's opinion shall prevail.

Love.[814]

Bapu

CWMG, *Vol. LXXV, pp. 135–6*

## 373. Letter to Jawaharlal Nehru

Sevagram, Wardha
9 December 1941

My dear Jawaharlal,
Your letter.[815] I am off to Bardoli tonight with Rajen Babu.

Do come as early as you can.

Maulana Saheb wires WC is to be held on 18th at Bardoli. If he has not already issued notice I have suggested 23rd as I have heavy meetings[816] on 17, 18, 19. But I have left the decision to Maulana Saheb.

I hope you got my letter.

Love.

Bapu

CWMG, *Vol. LXXV, p. 145*

[814] On the same day Gandhi sent a telegram to Vallabhbhai Patel which read: 'Maulana Jawaharlal disapprove Bardoli for meeting. Am pleading hard but may fail. Wire opinion. Hope you are progressing.'

[815] Not available

[816] Of the All India Spinners' Association

## 374. Letter to M.K. Gandhi

Anand Bhawan, Allahabad
10 December 1941

My dear Bapu,
I was delayed in Lucknow and have only just returned this morning when I received your letter of the 5th December.

I had intended as I wrote to you, to go over to Calcutta for a day to meet the Maulana. But he has told me he intends spending a day with me on his way to Bardoli. So I shall not go to Calcutta. I do not know when he is coming here. I would like him to come early so that both of us can reach Bardoli two days before the actual date of the Working Committee meeting. Probably we shall go via Bombay. I shall inform you as soon as I hear definitely from the Maulana. Indu is likely to accompany me to Bardoli.

Yours affectionately,
Jawaharlal

Mahatma Gandhi
Bardoli
District Surat

G-N Correspondence, JN Papers, *NMML*

## 375. Letter to Jawaharlal Nehru

13 December 1941

My dear Jawaharlal,
I have your letter. I am glad Indu will be coming with you. There is no winter worth the name here. The nights are cool, the days hot.

The questions we have to discuss are many. I trust you and Maulana Saheb will be here before the date of the Working Committee.

I have heavy meetings of the AISA and GSS[817] beginning from 17th. I expect to finish all on 20th.

Sardar is bearing himself well.

Love.

Bapu

CWMG, *Vol. LXXV, p. 168*

[817] Gandhi Seva Sangh

## 376. Letter to M.K. Gandhi

Allahabad
5 January 1942

My dear Bapu,

I arrived here last night. The events at Bardoli have naturally made me, as others, think furiously.[818] I do earnestly hope that by the time we meet at Wardha a satisfactory way out will be found, pleasing to you and to others. It is too sad that at this critical juncture there should be anything leading to confusion in the public mind. I hope to reach Wardha on the 11th evening and to present myself at the Ashram the next day.

In drawing your programme for the journey from Wardha to Benares, I should like you to consider the advisability of breaking journey for a few hours at Allahabad, then taking a more convenient train. This might save you a night's discomfort and arrival at Benares at a very inconvenient hour at night. This is not meant to trouble you in any way in Allahabad where few persons need know about it, but solely in the interest of your comfort and convenience. Possibly I might travel with you from Wardha as I intend going to Benares also.

Indu is in Bombay and will probably reach Wardha about the same time as I do.

Yours affectionately,
Jawaharlal Nehru

SWJN, *Vol. 12, I Series, pp. 73–4*

[818] The Working Committee, which met at Bardoli from 21 to 30 December 1941 was divided on the role of nonviolence. While Nehru, Azad and Rajagopalachari were prepared for conditional support to the war, Rajendra Prasad and Vallabhbhai Patel insisted on no participation because of nonviolence. The Working Committee relieved Gandhi of the responsibility of leading the individual satyagraha, complying with his request in his letter of 30 December 1941 to Azad. The Bardoli Resolution on the political situation had been drafted by Nehru. See *SWJN*, Vol. 12, I Series, pp. 45–55.

On 15 January 1942, however, Gandhi announced to the Congress his choice of Nehru as his heir, despite their political differences. See also *fn*. 870.

## 377. Letter to Jawaharlal Nehru

Sevagram, Wardha
11 January 1942

My dear Jawaharlal,
I have just learnt that both you and Maulana Saheb have arrived. I had told MS that I would take silence at 2. When I said so I had forgotten that I had given an appointment to Prof. Copeland[819] for 4.30 p.m. I could not cancel it. I took silence, therefore, at 5.25 p.m. I should be at your and his disposal after that time. I am sorry but I was helpless.

Please read this to MS.

Indu should be coming tomorrow.

Love.

Bapu

CWMG, *Vol. LXXV, p. 214*

## 378. Letter to Jawaharlal Nehru

Sevagram, Wardha
11 February 19[42][820]

Chi. Jawaharlal,
Why should I not write to you too in the national language after my Kashi speech?[821] I write to Sarup in the national language and to Ranjit in Gujarati. Why should I write to you in English?

[819] The reference seems to be to Dr Reginald Copeland whom Gandhi had met at Oxford in 1931.

[820] The source has '1941', which is a slip, as is evident from the reference to Jamnalalal Bajaj's death.

[821] On 21 January 1942, at the Silver Jubilee Convocation of the Benares Hindu University, Gandhi, speaking in Hindi, had emphasized the importance of Hindi, or the mother tongue, and cited the example of Japan. For the text of the speech, see *CWMG*, Vol. LXXV, pp. 240–5.

Here are the two letters.[822] Pass them on if you approve of them. I shall send a telegram also to the Generalissimo.[823] I am writing this letter at night after returning from the cremation ground so that it may be cleared in the morning.

What should I write about Jamnalalji?[824]

Chandra Singh[825] has settled down here. He is happy. He is learning khadi work on his own initiative. His wife cannot remain calm at the Vikasgriha. She writes letters to Chandra Singh. I have written to Mridu that she may send her when she likes.

The office of the States People's Conference is being shifted here. Should Jamnalalji's death make any difference? The office can, of course, work here with the help of Amrit.[826] But you have to think this over. Now it is getting late and I shall not write more.

Blessings from
Bapu

CWMG, *Vol. LXXV, p. 311* (Original in Hindi)

## 379. Letter to Jawaharlal Nehru

23 February 1942

Chi. Jawaharlal,

Now you may be a little free. What is to be done about the office of the States People's [Conference]? And what about the journal?

822 One of them is not available; the other was his letter to Chiang Kaishek; ibid., pp. 306-7.

823 Ibid., p. 13.

824 Jamnalal Bajaj had died of cerebral haemorrhage in the afternoon. Writing on his death the same day, Gandhi said, 'In Seth Jamnalal Bajaj, death has taken a mighty man. Whenever I wrote of wealthy men becoming trustees of their wealth for the common good I always had this merchant prince principally in mind.'

825 Of the Garhwal Regiment who in 1930 had refused to fire upon the Khudai Khidmatgars and had undergone a long prison sentence.

826 Rajkumari Amrit Kaur (1889-1964); princess of the State of Kapurthala; a close associate of Gandhi, freedom fighter and social activist; Health Minister, Government of India, 1947-57; had also served as Secretary, All-India Women's Conference

Pattabhi writes that he can publish the paper from Masulipatnam.[827] His letter is enclosed. Dr Menon is here. Balwantrai cannot take up the Secretaryship. Nor can Jainarayan Vyas. Rangildas is available. Bapa does not like it. If the office is here, it can, of course, be kept going; but financial arrangements will have to be made.

Blessings from
Bapu

[PS]
I hope you find no difficulty in deciphering my handwriting.

CWMG, *Vol. LXXV, p. 356* (Original in Hindi)

## 380. Letter to M.K. Gandhi

Allahabad
27 February 1942

Dear Bapuji,
Received your letter. You may of course write to me in Hindi but I often find it difficult to decipher your handwriting. In the last letter at one or two places I could not make out what you had written.

The affairs of the *States' People* are in your hands. Whatever you advise we will do now Jamnalalji is not there. Balwantrai did not come and so the difficulty increased. Pattabhi's letter did not come to me. If there is no other alternative then the newspaper can be published from Masulipatnam itself.

I am thinking of fixing 26 March, which is Ramnavami, as the date for Indu's marriage. You might have probably seen the statement which I gave to the Press.[828] Since something about it was published in the newspapers letters and telegrams started coming to me, Indu and Sarup expressing resentments and making complaints. Therefore I thought it proper to issue a statement.

[827] Gandhi wrote on 5 March 1942 to Pattabhi Sitaramayya who was Editor, *States' People*, that in view of financial difficulties following Jamnalal Bajaj's death, publication of the paper should be suspended. See *CWMG*, Vol. LXXV, pp. 383–4.

[828] On 26 February, confirming Indira Nehru and Feroze Gandhi's engagement. The marriage took place in Allahabad with Gandhi's blessing.

I intend to perform the marriage ceremony very simply. But even if only very close friends and relations are invited the number becomes quite large. The list of invitees has already become 250, excluding the people of Allahabad and many more names are still occurring to me. I am unable to decide what to do. Probably most of the people seeing the present conditions will not come. Even so quite a large number of people may turn up.

Indu is happy and well. Krishna will be coming here after a week.

You must have read Chiang Kai-shek's statement.[829] It was not prepared at my suggestion or in consultation with me. I saw it at the eleventh hour—a little before his departure. He had written it on the previous night.

Mahadev wrote to me to Shantiniketan asking me whether or not the telegrams and letters written by you to Chiang Kai-shek should be published. That letter of Mahadev's was received by me day before yesterday after reaching here. I immediately wired to Mahadev saying that in my opinion the telegrams and letters should be published.[830] Now there is no time to ask Chiang Kai-shek, nor do I think it very necessary. It will be well if they are published in the *Harijan*. Then other papers can reproduce from it. Or they can be released direct to the Associated Press.

I came to know about Chandra Singh and Bhagirathi[831].

I had sent Yunus[832] to Prithvi Singh's[833] camp thinking that he could stay there for about a month and then go to Sevagram

[829] Chiang Kai-shek who had visited India from 9–24 February 1942, said in his statement of 24 February that India should give united support to the principles of the Atlantic Charter, but wondered why she should if they did not apply to her.

[830] The correspondence was not released to the Press. For Gandhi's letters to Chiang Kai-shek, see *CWMG*, Vol. LXXV, pp. 306–7 and 313.

[831] A social worker associated with the Mahila Ashram

[832] Mohammad Yunus; Member, Indian Foreign service, 1947–74; Prime Minister's Special Envoy, 1975–7

[833] Prithvi Singh Azad, a Rajput revolutionary; joined the Ghadar Party in 1911; convicted in the Lahore Conspiracy Case and sentenced to life imprisonment; escaped from jail in 1922 but surrendered in 1938 at the insistence of Gandhi and became his follower; was associated with the Mahila Ashram

for a few days. But he is not well at all and is getting weaker every day. I got him examined by Kuvalayanand[834] and one more doctor also saw him. Everybody said that he should take complete rest. I have asked him to come away from the camp. For the time being he will stay in Bombay so that the doctors could observe him carefully. Badshah Khan has written that he should return to the Frontier.

Yours,
Jawaharlal

SWJN, *Vol. 3, II Series, pp. 474–5* (Original in Hindi)

## 381. Letter to Jawaharlal Nehru

1 March 1942

Chi. Jawaharlal,
I got your letter yesterday. I did not intend replying, nor do I want to do so now. I wish to remind you of the hot weather. The heat is severe. I am having a wet-pack on my head. Indu should not come this side during such heat. I would suggest that both of them should go to Khali or Kashmir. They should visit Sevagram and other places only after the rains. But if Indu has the courage to face the heat here, I shall, of course, be happy to meet the two.

One thing more. Khurshedbehn had written to you. She says you have written to her that you are awaiting an invitation from the Mahatma. Why do you need an invitation from me? It is always there for you. There was no special work for which I should put you to the trouble of coming here. I do not understand the implications of an 'open city', that is why I have said: 'I must consult Jawaharlal before I say anything. I depend upon Jawaharlal in such matters.'[835]

[834] Swami Kuvalayanand who was researching in the technique and benefits of *hatha yoga*

[835] Ram Manohar Lohia had sought Gandhi's support for launching an agitation to have the big towns like Calcutta, Bombay, etc., declared 'open cities'. Gandhi, in his reply dated 23 February 1942, had written: 'How far can the term "open" be applied? How can one believe that a town occupied by the enemies is an open town? According to Japan, Hindustan is an enemy country. If Japan declares Tokyo an open city will it be spared by the English?'

We are meeting soon.

Blessings from
Bapu

CWMG, *Vol. LXXV, p. 374* (Original in Hindi)

## 382. Letter to Jawaharlal Nehru

Sevagram, Wardha
4 March 1942

Chi. Jawaharlal,
Received your letter yesterday. Hope you will not find it difficult to read this letter.

About Indu's marriage, I hold the firm opinion that no one from outside need be invited. A few persons who are at Allahabad may, however, be called as witnesses. You can send invitation cards to as many people as you like. Ask for blessings from everybody but make it clear that no one in particular need take the trouble of coming. If one person is asked to come, others cannot be left out.

It has to be considered whether or not Indu likes to go to this extent of simplicity. In case you too do not like to go so far, you can rule out my suggestion.

I have seen your statement about Indu. I like it. I receive letters [concerning her marriage] every day. Some are horrid. I have destroyed all of them. In reply to all these, I have sent a note[836] in *Harijan*, a copy of which I am sending herewith. The note was written on Monday. Since yesterday, letters from Muslims have been pouring in, making Sarup the target of their attack. This will go on.

I will do all that is possible for the Indian States. Funds will be a constant difficulty. Jamnalalji had taken all the responsibility upon himself; how he would have done it was not decided. I am now wondering how to raise the money. I am consulting Pattabhi about the paper. Balwantrai will not be able to come. That will not make much difference. We shall be getting help from here. When

[836] 'Indira Nehru's Engagement'; *CWMG*, Vol. LXXV, pp. 375–6.

you come here, we shall talk over the matter. Menon is going to Bombay today to complete the work there.

I saw Chiang Kai-shek's statement. It was good. Your consent was received but I thought that there was no need now to make that letter public. The subject has become stale.

Bhagirathi has come. It is rather difficult to keep Chandra Singh. He is very much given to indulgence; and she is very weak. He quarrels on petty matters. I will not be surprised if he beats up someone. I, however, find him hard working. You need not worry. If you feel any difficulty in reading my letters, I will try to write more legibly. But it is our duty to start writing to each other in the national language. After some time we will find it easier to do so. It will be of great benefit to the poor.

Blessings from
Bapu

CWMG, *Vol. LXXV, pp. 382–3* (Original in Hindi)

## 383. Letter to Jawaharlal Nehru

Sevagram, Wardha
9 March 1942

Chi. Jawaharlal,

I have your letter. I had promptly replied to your earlier letter. I hope you got it.

Mukerji is a good and honest worker. He has some land. I had asked him. He said he did not seek charity. I have no doubt he will return the entire amount. He was prepared even to pay interest. We have given much aid to other workers. I am clearly of the view that we should lend Rs 3,000 to Bhai Mukerji for six months.

Blessings from
Bapu

CWMG, *Vol. LXXV, p. 401* (Original in Hindi)

## 384. Letter to Jawaharlal Nehru

[After 27 March 1942][837]

Chi. Jawaharlal,

Khurshedbehn is very unhappy. She feels that your heart has dried up towards her. Send for her, give her some affection. You know she adores you.[838]

Today I woke up at two. I was thinking of you and Rajaji only. I am clearly of the view that we cannot accept this 'offer'. If you also agree, then talk to Rajaji and reach a final decision. If you are inclined to agree with Rajaji then the matter deserves further consideration.

Blessings from
Bapu

CWMG, *Vol. LXXV, p. 440* (Original in Hindi)

## 385. Letter to Jawaharlal Nehru

Sevagram, Wardha
15 April 1942

Chi. Jawaharlal,

The Professor is here. He has told me everything. I also heard about your Press interview.[839] Whereas we have always had differences of

[837] This was written on the back of a bill bearing this date. The date is also confirmed by the reference to the 'offer' of the British War Cabinet proposals brought by Sir Stafford Cripps whom Gandhi met on March 27. See *CWMG*, Vol. LXXVI, Appendix VI.

[838] Gandhi started writing this letter while he was being massaged. It appears from a dash here in the source that the following paragraph was written some time later.

[839] Of 12 April 1942. This was on the rejection of Cripps' proposals. Nehru answering the question 'How do you think India can defend itself?' had replied, 'it is our duty and the Congressman's duty and the duty of all other persons to carry out this programme of self-sufficiency to the utmost. Maybe we have to take up guerilla warfare. I don't know what the Congress will decide. But it is this foundation, and the organization we are building up, that will ultimately help us to meet the present situation.' And to the question 'How can the United Nations help India now?' Nehru answered, 'I am prepared to welcome help and assistance from any nation or nations, if

opinion it appears to me that now we also differ in practice. What can Vallabhbhai and others do in such a situation? If your policy is accepted the Committee should not retain its present shape.

The more I think of it the more I feel that you are making a mistake. I see no good in American troops entering India and in our resorting to guerrilla warfare.[840]

It is my duty to caution you.

I hope Indu and Feroze are well.

Blessings from
Bapu

[PS]
I heard yesterday that the Forward Bloc people in Utkal are armed and that the Communists are ready for guerrilla warfare. I do not know how much truth there is in it.

CWMG, *Vol. LXXVI, p. 40* (Original in Hindi)

## 386. Letter to Jawaharlal Nehru

Segaon, via Wardha
19 April 1942

Chi. Jawaharlal,
A letter from the Maulana arrived today. He writes that I have to go to Allahabad. How can I go? I had said even when I was there that I

---

they are prepared to recognize India as an independent nation. ... I am quite convinced that America will like real popular war effort in India.' See *SWJN*, Vol. 12, I Series, pp. 213–27.

[840] Answering a reader's question, 'What will happen to your ahimsa when Jawaharlal openly advocates violence and Rajaji wants arms and military training for the whole nation?', Gandhi said on 19 April: 'I am sorry he has developed a fancy for guerilla warfare. But I have no doubt that it will be a nine days' wonder. It will take no effect. It is foreign to Indian soil. Twenty-two years' incessant preaching and practice of nonviolence, however imperfect it has been, could not be suddenly obliterated by the mere wish of Jawaharlal and Rajaji, powerful though their influence is. I am, therefore, not perturbed by the "apostasy" either of Jawaharlal or Rajaji. They will return to nonviolence with zest strengthened by the failure of their effort. Neither goes to violence for his belief in it. They do so because they think probably that India must have a course of violence before coming to nonviolence. ... Guerrila warfare can take us nowhere. If it is practised on any large scale, it must lead to disastrous consequences.'

was not any more fit for travel. And what shall I do by going there? I have the same one thing to offer and I have called three meetings here. One of them has been planned for a long time. I cannot miss any of them. You must therefore excuse me. Write to Maulana to spare me.

Blessings from
Bapu

[PS]
Janakibehn[841] wrote to you yesterday to hold both the meetings at Wardha. I withheld the letter. Meetings should be held at Wardha when my presence is considered essential.

CWMG, *Vol. LXXVI, p. 53* (Original in Hindi)

## 387. Letter to Jawaharlal Nehru

Sevagram, Wardha
24 April 1942

Chi. Jawaharlal,
Mirabehn agrees that I must take some step and that she will have to make a sacrifice.[842] She wanted to go to Allahabad even if I did not go. I have therefore called her here. I am sending through her my views in the form of a resolution.[843] Maulana Saheb has been urging me to go to Allahabad. I have told him I am helpless. I find travelling difficult these days. What is more, I have called three meetings for

[841] Janakidevi, widow of Jamnalal Bajaj. On her husband's death, she had 'decided to take up the work to which he had dedicated himself' and had 'divested herself of all her personal property valued at two and a half lacs'. She had been elected President of the Goseva Sangh on 21 February 1942.

[842] Mirabehn had written to Gandhi expressing her keenness to go to the AICC meeting to be held at Allahabad and 'plead behind the scenes with the leaders for organising nation-wide nonviolent resistance to the Japanese'.

[843] The AICC at its meeting on 27 April took up consideration of the resolution which Mirabehn carried with her from Wardha to Allahabad, since Gandhi did not attend the meeting, and continued discussion on it till 1 May along with certain amendments proposed by Rajendra Prasad. The text of this revised version is to be found in *The Transfer of Power,* Vol. II, pp. 66–70. See also *CWMG*, Vol. LXXVI, pp. 63–5. The resolution inter alia stated: 'The Congress is of opinion that if the British withdrew from India, India would be able to defend herself in the event of Japanese or any would-be aggressor attacking India.'

the same period. I have therefore asked Maulana Saheb to excuse me and told him that I shall be sending my views in the form of a resolution.

I do not think it necessary to give arguments in support of the resolution. If you do not like my resolution I really cannot insist.[844] The time has come when each of us must choose his own course.

The behaviour of the Government in Feni[845] and other places is simply intolerable. What will such a government do even if it survives? And today it is only trying to save itself. I am now certain that if this Government goes we shall be well able to deal with Japan. It is another matter that after the Government is removed we may fight among ourselves. Even if that should be so, do we want to save ourselves from internal quarrels through the good offices of this Government?

Acharya Narendra Dev has seen the resolution and liked it.

Blessings from
Bapu

CWMG, *Vol. LXXVI, p. 66* (Original in Hindi)

## 388. Letter to Jawaharlal Nehru

Sevagram, Wardha
9 May 1942

Chi. Jawaharlal,

I have been awaiting your letter every day. It has arrived today. You do need a little rest. Many people have given me reports of Indu's work. She will become perfectly fit if she always maintains good health.

They tell me also that Feroze too is doing good work.

[844] Finally, however, on 1 May an alternative resolution proposed by Nehru was passed. See *CWMG*, Vol. LXXVI, pp. 424–5.

[845] In Noakhali, Bengal. The reference is to the scorched-earth measures adopted by the authorities in Feni in the face of anticipated Japanese invasion of East Bengal, dispossessing people of their holdings, including country boats. For Gandhi's article on the situation, 'Scorched-Earth Policy Again', see *CWMG*, Vol. LXXVI, pp. 71–2; also pp.12–13 and *CWMG*, Vol. LXXV, pp. 409–10.

Everything possible is being done for Chandra Singh. Madhavi has got whooping cough. I visit her every day. Chandra Singh and Bhagirathi appear happy. They do not complain much about the heat now. The problem of Chandra Singh's education is difficult. I am going to Bombay for eight days in connection with the Deenbandhu Memorial.[846] I shall do whatever I can on my return. You should not worry.

Maulana's letters come regularly. He too is unwell. He writes to say that he will be coming to Wardha towards the end of this month. Perhaps you too will be coming along with him?[847]

Ba is well.

Blessings to both from
Bapu

CWMG, *Vol. LXXVI, pp. 90–1* (Original in Hindi)

## 389. Letter to Jawaharlal Nehru

Sevagram, Wardha
5 June 1942

Chi. Jawaharlal,
I received your letter.

There is nothing from Maulana. In one letter he had said that he would be accompanying you here.

Fischer[848] has arrived. I do manage to give him an hour every day. He is staying at the Ashram.

Hot winds are blowing here.

Blessings from
Bapu

CWMG, *Vol. LXXVI, p. 185* (Original in Hindi)

[846] See *CWMG*, Vol. LXXVI, p. 118.

[847] Nehru met Gandhi towards the end of the month.

[848] Louis Fischer (1896–1970); Jewish-American journalist; his works include a biography of Gandhi entitled *The Life of Mahatma Gandhi*. For an account of his talks with Gandhi, see *CWMG*, Vol. LXXVI, Appendix V.

## 390. Letter to Jawaharlal Nehru

Sevagram, Wardha
13 July 1942

Chi. Jawaharlal,
I have read the resolution.[849]

I note that you have tried to include some of my points. I do not desire any modification.

But I do desire that, as far as possible, all of us should interpret the appeal in the same way. It will not be good if we speak in different voices.

I stick to the hundred per cent support I gave you in what you said about yourself. I have thought over the matter a great deal and still feel that your capacity for service will increase if you withdraw. And to that extent you will find satisfaction. You may attend the Committee occasionally as I do or as Narendra Dev does. This will ensure your help being available and at the same time your fully retaining your freedom.

This is my plea about Maulana Saheb. I find that the two of us have drifted apart. I do not understand him nor does he understand me. We are drifting apart on the Hindu-Muslim question as well as on other questions. I have also a suspicion that Maulana Saheb does not entirely approve of the proposed action. No one is at fault. We have to face the facts. Therefore I suggest that the Maulana should relinquish presidentship but remain in the Committee, the Committee should elect an interim President and all should proceed unitedly. This great struggle cannot be conducted properly without unity and without a President who comes forth with a hundred per cent cooperation.

[849] The original resolution on the proposal for the withdrawal of British power from India was drafted by Gandhi. For the first draft, all the later versions showing changes after discussions in the WC and the final version passed on 14 July 1942, see *SWJN*, Vol. 12, I Series, pp. 386–400. The 'Quit India' resolution was passed on 8 August. For the four drafts of the resolution and the final version, see Ibid., pp. 436–53. Writing to Amrit Kaur, Gandhi had said, 'The resolution is my draft. Changes have been made for JN's satisfaction, and of course Maulana's.'

Please show this letter to Maulana Saheb. At the moment it is intended for you two only. If you do not like either or both of my suggestions, you may reject them. My motive in writing this is only to help. Whether you approve of it or not, it should not cause any unpleasantness.

The date and venue for the AICC have not been indicated in your draft.

As far as I am concerned, you are free to issue this appeal to the Press.

It is not necessary to come here for a discussion of the resolution. But it has to be as Maulana Saheb's orders.

Blessings from
Bapu

CWMG, *Vol. LXXVI, pp. 293–4* (Original in Hindi)

## 391. Letter to M.K. Gandhi

Anand Bhawan, Allahabad
24 July 1942

Dear Bapuji,

I got your letter of the 21st just now, and also the photographs from *Life*.[850] I have seen these earlier also—I am quite convinced that this article has not gone via a Chinese. This is just impossible. The article is extremely inappropriate. Lots of people work in these large newspaper offices, and often, there are articles in the same issue against one another. This is a failure on the part of some sub-editor.

I have heard that you have written an article in the *Harijan* about fasting.[851] I have not read it yet. But I hope that you will not take a decision in haste about this. In principle it cannot be denied always, and yet, it should not be resorted to unless it is absolutely

[850] In the first week of June 1942, Gandhi had been interviewed by two American journalists, one of whom was Belldon of *Life* and *Time*.

[851] The reference is to the article 'Fasting in Nonviolent Action', *Harijan*, 26-7-1942; see *CWMG*, Vol. LXXVI, pp. 317–19 and 333–5.

the last alternative and no other way seems possible. Therefore I hope that you will not take any decision.

Indu and Feroze are returning from Kashmir tomorrow.

Yours,
Jawaharlal

[PS]
There are certain things in the article in *Life* (for instance my statement[852] regarding Cripps) which could not have been sent by anyone from China.

MKG Papers, Pyarelal Collection, *NMML* (Original in Hindi)

## 392. Letter to M.K. Gandhi

Anand Bhawan, Allahabad
29 July 1942

Dear Bapuji,
I had sent you a short reply to your letter yesterday. When I thought about the matter more deeply I was surprised as to how you thought a Chinese had got it written. There can be no basis for this and it would be unfair to them. There are indications in the article which show that perhaps it was put together in the newspaper office itself, and neither in China nor in India. These days there are two reporters from the magazine here but I do not think that they have written it. Some young novice in the newspaper office must have written it after looking at the photographs.

Kachru[853] has been somewhat perturbed by his child's illness. He is going to Marwar from here. If you have any instructions for

[852] Dated 27 July 1942. See *SWJN*, Vol. 12, I Series, pp. 419–22.

[853] Dwarkanath Kachru, a public worker attached to the States People's Conference. He had been deputed by Nehru to go to Jodhpur to send a report to Gandhi on events there. Kachru was served with an order on 5 July 1942 to depart by the train 'which leaves Jodhpur ... (*via* Marwar Junction) ... and not return to Marwar for a period of one year from the date of this order.' For Gandhi's article 'Pandit Kachru Externed' (*Harijan*, 26-7-1942), see *CWMG*, Vol. LXXVI, pp. 316–17.

In the princely state of Jodhpur, where satyagraha was being offered, there were extreme acts of inhumanity being committed against the people. For Gandhi's article 'Jodhpur Tragedy" (*Harijan*, 21-6-1942), ibid., pp. 220–3.

him, please send them to him there. I think it will be a good thing if he came at the time of the Bombay Standing Committee. Sri Prakasa is tied up in work and writes that he can go to Jodhpur on the 29th.[854]

Yours,
Jawaharlal

MKG Papers, Pyarelal Collection, *NMML* (Original in Hindi)

## 393. Telegram to M.K. Gandhi

15 June 1945

Going Khali. Tomorrow Nainital. Reaching Allahabad Monday evening.[855]

Jawaharlal

G-N Correspondence, JN Papers, *NMML*

[854] Sri Prakasa had been requested by Gandhi to go to Jodphur 'to do whatever he could to ease the atmosphere, interview the authorities and know their version of the affair.' For the contents of his report, ibid., pp. 258–9.

[855] Nehru writes in *A Bunch of Old Letters*, 'The members of the Working Committee of the Indian National Congress were arrested on 9 August 1942 and kept together in Ahmednagar Fort prison till 28 March 1945. Thereafter, they were gradually dispersed and sent to their respective prisons. Narendra Deva and I were sent on the 28th March to various prisons successively in the United Provinces. The others left Ahmednagar Fort on later dates in April.' World War II ended in Europe in May 1945 and consequently all the Congress Working Committee members were released on 15 June 1945.

## 394. Telegram to Jawaharlal Nehru

Express

Panchgani
16 June 1945

Pandit Jawaharlal Nehru
Khali (Nainital)
Your wire. Early meeting working committee necessary.[856] Suggest fix Bombay announce date. Sardar Dev agree. Hope you Maulana Saheb Narendra Dev well.

Bapu

CWMG, *Vol. LXXX, p. 334*

## 395. Letter to Jawaharlal Nehru

Manor Ville, Simla
25 June 1945

Chi. Jawaharlal,
There are several names in the Kasturba Memorial Trust.[857] When the Trust was formed, I had expressed a desire that your name and Sardar's should be included. All the Trustees were agreeable that the names of you two should be included when you were released. I had forgotten to consult you. It occurred to me this morning. Will you agree to be on the Trust? It means working for women and children in the villages and that too in my way. If you can take interest in this, I can send you the papers for your perusal. I have said the same thing to Sardar. He is considering it. I have told him that this is no matter for honour. It is a matter for work.

[856] The Working Committee met on 21 January 1945 after three years and Gandhi approved the leaders attending the Simla Conference, which was to begin on 25 June.

The Simla Conference, held to form a provincial National Government, ended in failure in July. The Viceroy, Lord Wavell, had invited all party leaders to submit to him lists of their nominees for the Council, out of which he would make his own selection and place it before the Conference for review. While the Congress gave its list, Jinnah would not comply with the plan.

[857] Kasturba Gandhi died while in Ahmednagar Fort prison on 22 February 1944.

The same is true about the propagation of Hindustani. I am very keen on having your name for it if you are agreeable. I shall send you the papers if you like, for your perusal about this too. I am scared of placing any more burden on your head as you are already overburdened. But what can I do?

Everyone misses you here.

Blessings from
Bapu

CWMG, *Vol. LXXX, pp. 367–8* (Original in Hindi)

## 396. Letter to M.K. Gandhi

27 June 1945

Dear Bapuji,

Got your letter of the 25th just now. You have rightly written that to be in the Kasturba Memorial Trust or Hindustani Prachar is not a matter of honour but of work. It is obvious that my sympathies are with these works. But at present I cannot definitely say to what extent I have understood them or agree with their methods. Besides this, the fact is that at present I want as far as possible not to bind myself down to any particular work. For some time I want to look about. This is difficult because one willy-nilly does get involved. Even so, for the time being I want to remain somewhat detached. Therefore if you permit I would not like to be on any committee. Later on these problems can be considered carefully at leisure.

Yours,
Jawaharlal

SWJN, *Vol. 3, II Series, p. 476* (Original in Hindi)

## 397. Letter to M.K. Gandhi

Near Gangabal Lake
30 July 1945

My dear Bapu,

For ten days now I have been wandering among the mountains and living the life after my heart.[858] Indira is with me. Our present trip

[858] Nehru was in Kashmir from 20 July to 21 August on medical advice.

is now drawing to a close and by day after tomorrow we shall reach Srinagar. We shall have trekked about 100 miles at altitudes varying from 9,000 ft. to 14,000. We have crossed a rather dangerous pass, seldom traversed, leading from one river valley to another. It was a tricky business, involving a good deal of ice-walk, and a false step would have sent us 400 ft. below. However, we survived and felt rather elated over it all. This mountain trekking, skirting glaciers and going up and down several thousand feet every day, reaching our journey's end tired out but getting up next day fresh and refreshed, has done me an immense amount of good. Both my body and mind feel much better. I feel light-hearted and cheerful and the numerous worries and troubles that surround us seem far away. This is all very selfish I know for it is pure sensual enjoyment of the mountain air and the snow and the forests and the flowers which abound here. I rationalise it, of course, and try to convince myself that it is necessary for my bodily and mental health. There is some truth in that but not as much as I make out. I take refuge in doctors' advice. But the fact remains that I am here when I ought to be elsewhere. This morning I had a dip in the Gangabal, a lake at the foot of the Harmukh glacier. This is considered a particularly holy lake by the Kashmiri Brahmans. The holiness, I am afraid, did not attract me but I was curious to know how I would react to a dip in a glacier lake. Nearly 29 years ago I had bathed in this lake and I wondered how far age had enfeebled me for this purpose. Well, it was very cold, naturally, and I have got into the bad habit of taking warm baths. Nevertheless I enjoyed the dip and felt warm and refreshed afterwards.

Indira has stood this trek very well. She left her babe[859] at Pahalgam. We shall be in Srinagar day after tomorrow on the 1st August and I propose to spend a week there, full of engagements. After that a few days at Pahalgam and then return. (There is, I must confess, a vague idea at the back of my mind to visit the cave of Amarnath from Pahalgam. It is four days rapid journey there and

[859] Rajiv Gandhi (1944–1991); elder son of Indira Gandhi; a pilot by profession, but entered politics after his brother's death in 1980; seventh Prime Minister of India, 1984–9; assassinated by the Liberation of Tamil Tigers Elam in 1991

back.) I hope to meet Maulana in Srinagar and then to fix up my programme definitely. Probably on my return journey I shall make brief halts in Peshawar, Lahore and Delhi. Badshah Khan is likely to be here next week and I shall meet him.

We have been far from post and telegraph offices and newspapers—a welcome change, but nevertheless a handicap. I hardly know what has happened during these days in India or elsewhere. A report has reached me that the Labour Party in Britain has won a thundering victory but I do not know the details yet.[860]

You may have seen in the papers repeated references to the possibility of my going to America. I have not encouraged these in any way and as far as I can see my business lies in India at present and in the near future. What I have said is that it is always possible that I might go abroad if the situation in India permits it. The situation here is so fluid that no one can say what is likely to happen. The surprising and overwhelming victory of the Labour Party in Britain may have little significance for India—certainly most of the Labour leaders there are a poor lot so far as we are concerned. But it does indicate a great turnover of opinion both on domestic and international matters. In a sense it has a revolutionary significance but I doubt if the leaders there have anything resembling a revolutionary spirit.

I am enclosing a copy of an air letter I have received from Krishna Menon.[861] This reached me in the course of my wanderings here. The letter speaks for itself and I have nothing to add to it. There is a mention in it of a previous letter which I have not received so far. Whether anything will come out of this I do not know, but

[860] On 26 July 1945 the Labour Party won the general elections. A cabinet with Attlee as Prime Minister and Pethick-Lawrence as Secretary of State for India took office. For Nehru's reaction to the victory of the Labour Party, see *SWJN*, Vol. 14, I Series, pp. 62–3 and 387–8.

[861] V.K. Krishna Menon (1896–1974); Secretary, India League, London, 1929–47; Borough Councillor, St Pancras, 1934–47; Indian High Commissioner, London, 1947–52; Minister without portfolio, Government of India, 1956–7; Minister for Defence, 1957–62

Nehru had described Krishna Menon ten years earlier as 'very able and earnest' and 'highly thought of in intellectual, journalistic and left-wing labour circles', adding that he 'has the virtues and failings of the intellectual'.

it seems to me certainly worthwhile to encourage this attempt to improve the spinning-wheel. May I request you to ask someone who knows all about our charkha economics and technique to write to Krishna Menon and answer his questions, as well as give such additional information as may be considered necessary? In order to save time, Krishna Menon should be addressed directly by air mail and, if possible, samples of yarn might also be sent by air mail. (I might add that an Air Letter—special forms to be obtained from the Post Office—goes more quickly than an ordinary air mail cover and is cheaper. But space is limited. In order to overcome this paucity of space 2 or 3 Air Letters can be sent.) If it is convenient, I should like to have a copy of the communication sent to Krishna Menon—His address is:

V.K. Krishna Menon
India League, 165 Strand
London W.C. 2, England
Telegraphic address: Krishnamenon, 165 Strand, London.

I am writing this far from a post office, but I hope it will be posted tomorrow.

Yours affectionately,
Jawaharlal

My address till August 8th—c/o Postmaster, Srinagar. From 9th to 15th—c/o Postmaster, Pahalgam, Kashmir.

I have not received any of the plans and specifications referred to in Krishna Menon's letter.[862]

SWJN, *Vol. 3, II Series, pp. 476–8*

[862] The enclosure of letter from Krishna Menon contained a design of an improved *charkha* which would give more output.

## 398. Letter to Jawaharlal Nehru

Sevagram
8 August 1945

Chi. Jawaharlal,
Your letter is beautiful. Come back fully recovered. Indu has done a bold thing. I have written to Menon.[863] I enclose a copy. That is all the time I can spare.

Blessings from
Bapu

CWMG, *Vol. LXXXI, p. 94*

## 399. Letter to Jawaharlal Nehru

On way to Bombay
19 August 1945

Chi. Jawaharlal
I have received your letter.[864] I know a little bit about the Kashmir branch of the Charkha Sangh. I do not know why the dispensary has been closed down. It is just as well that you wrote to me. I have sent a copy of the letter to Jaju.[865] I am on my way to Bombay. From there I shall go to Poona taking Sardar[866] with me. I cannot say how long I shall be staying there. I shall write again when I hear from Jajuji.

The Kashmir trip was bound to do you good.

What was the attack on Maulana Saheb?

Blessings from
Bapu

CWMG, *Vol. LXXXI, p. 143* (Original in Hindi)

[863] See *CWMG*, Vol. LXXXI, pp. 92–3.

[864] Not available

[865] Srikrishnadas Jaju, Secretary, All-India Spinners' Association

[866] Who was to undergo nature-cure treatment at Dr Dinshaw Mehta's clinic, Arogya Bhawan, Poona

## 400. Letter to M.K. Gandhi

Lahore
27 August 1945

My dear Bapu,
I enclose a copy of a letter received from Krishna Menon which may interest you. I wanted to send it to Vallabhbhai but I am not sure where he is. Perhaps you could share it with him.

I have been involved in Frontier and Punjab matters for some days and have hardly had time to glance through a newspaper for a considerable time. So I am much out of date. May I suggest to you to write a line to Badshah Khan asking him to attend the next meeting of the AICC. Maulana is, I believe, inviting him.[867]

Yours affectionately,
Jawaharlal

SWJN, *Vol. 14, I Series, pp. 74–5*

## 401. Letter to Jawaharlal Nehru

1 September 1945

Chi. Jawaharlal,
I have your letter. Menon's information is correct. Sardar has read that letter. Let us see what happens. You have done a lot of work in the Frontier and other places.

Sardar cannot leave Poona on the 12th. He cannot leave Poona for another four weeks if he is to give a fair trial to Dinshaw[868] and his treatment. The climate here also suits him but he has not shown much improvement. His court is always full.

Blessings from
Bapu

CWMG, *Vol. LXXXI, p. 204*

[867] The Working Committee meetings were held in the third week of September 1945 under the leadership of Abul Kalam Azad.

[868] Dr Dinshaw Mehta

## 402. Letter to Jawaharlal Nehru

5 October 1945

Chi. Jawaharlal,

I have long been intending to write to you but can do so only today. I have also been wondering whether I should write in English or Hindustani. In the end I have decided to write in Hindustani.

I take first the sharp difference of opinion that has arisen between us. If such a difference really exists people should also know about it, for the work of swaraj will suffer if they are kept in the dark. I have said that I fully stand by the kind of governance which I have described in *Hind Swaraj*. It is not just a way of speaking. My experience has confirmed the truth of what I wrote in [1909].[869] If I were the only one left who believed in it, I would not be sorry. For I can only testify to the truth as I see it. I have not *Hind Swaraj* in front of me. It is better that I redraw the picture today in my own language. Then it would not matter to me whether or no the picture tallies with that of 1909, nor should it to you. I do not have to establish what I had said before. What is worth knowing is only what I have to say today. I believe that if India, and through India the world, is to achieve real freedom, then sooner or later we shall have to go and live in the villages—in huts, not in palaces. Millions of people can never live in cities and palaces in comfort and peace. Nor can they do so by killing one another, that is, by resorting to violence and untruth. I have not the slightest doubt that, but for the pair, truth and nonviolence, mankind will be doomed. We can have the vision of that truth and nonviolence only in the simplicity of the villages. That simplicity resides in the spinning-wheel and what is implied by the spinning-wheel. It does not frighten me at all that the world seems to be going in the opposite direction. For the matter of that, when the moth approaches its doom it whirls round faster and faster till it is burnt up. It is possible that India will not be able to escape this moth-like circling. It is my duty to try till my last breath, to save India and through it the world from such a fate. The sum and substance of what I want to say is that

[869] The source has '1908' evidently a slip, for Gandhi wrote it in November 1909 on board the S.S. *Kildonan Castle* on his way back to Africa from London.

the individual person should have control over the things that are necessary for the sustenance of life. If he cannot have such control the individual cannot survive. Ultimately, the world is made up only of individuals. If there were no drops there would be no ocean. This is only a rough and ready statement. There is nothing new in this.

But even in *Hind Swaraj* I have not said all this. While I appreciate modern thought, I find that an ancient thing, considered in the light of this thought looks so sweet. You will not be able to understand me if you think that I am talking about the villages of today. My ideal village still exists only in my imagination. After all every human being lives in the world of his own imagination. In this village of my dreams the villager will not be dull—he will be all awareness. He will not live like an animal in filth and darkness. Men and women will live in freedom, prepared to face the whole world. There will be no plague, no cholera and no smallpox. Nobody will be allowed to be idle or to wallow in luxury. Everyone will have to do body labour. Granting all this, I can still envisage a number of things that will have to be organised on a large scale. Perhaps there will even be railways and also post and telegraph offices. I do not know what things there will be or will not be. Nor am I bothered about it. If I can make sure of the essential thing, other things will follow in due course. But if I give up the essential thing, I give up everything.

The other day, at the final day's meeting of the Working Committee, we had taken a decision to the effect that the Working Committee would meet for two or three days to work out this very thing. I shall be happy if it meets. But even if it does not meet, I want that we two should understand each other fully. And this for two reasons. Our bond is not merely political. It is much deeper. I have no measure to fathom that depth. This bond can never be broken. I therefore want that we should understand each other thoroughly in politics as well. The second reason is that neither of us considers himself as worthless. We both live only for India's freedom, and will be happy to die too for that freedom. We do not care for praise from any quarter. Praise or abuse are the same to us. They have no place in the mission of service. Though I aspire to live up to 125 years rendering service, I am nevertheless an old man, while you are comparatively young. That is why I have said that you are my heir.[870] It is only proper that I should at least understand my heir and my heir in turn should understand me. I shall then be at peace.

One thing more. I had written to you about Kasturba Trust and Hindustani. You had said you would write after thinking things over. I find that your name is already figuring in the Hindustani Sabha. Nanavati[871] reminded me that he had approached you and Maulana Saheb and that you had appended your signature. That was in 1942. That was long ago. You know where Hindustani stands today. If you still stand by that signature, I wish to get some work out of you in this regard. It will not involve much running about, but some work will be called for.

The work of Kasturba Memorial Trust is rather complicated. I realise that if what I have said above is going to irk you or is irking you, you will not feel comfortable even in the Kasturba Trust.

The last point concerns the sparks that are flying about in the conflict with Sarat Babu.[872] I have been pained by the episode. I have been unable to trace it to its root. If what you have told me is all there is to it and nothing more remains to be said, then I do not have to inquire further. But if an explanation seems necessary, I very much want to hear it.

If we have to meet to thrash out all these matters, then we should find time for a meeting.

[870] Gandhi had said in his address on 15 January 1942, at the Working Committee session of the Congress at Bardoli, that his successor was neither Rajaji nor Vallabhbhai but Nehru.

[871] Amritlal Nanavati

[872] In his speech of 26 September 1945, Sarat Chandra Bose had criticized Chiang Kai-shek for not coming to terms with Mao Tse-tung and described him as the 'grand fascist of the East'. Nehru in his statement of 29 September 1945 had said: 'I have read with deep regret Mr Sarat Bose's remarks about Generalissimo Chiang Kai-shek and Madame Chiang. Mr. Bose is perfectly entitled to his opinion about persons and things. But no one who occupies a responsible position in public life should make statements or accusations without full knowledge of the facts. This applies more to expressions of opinion in regard to the internal affairs of other countries about whom our knowledge must necessarily be limited.' See *SWJN*, Vol. 14, I Series, pp. 446–7 and 451.

You are working very hard. I trust you are in good health and Indu is well.

Blessings from
Bapu

CWMG, *Vol. LXXXI, pp. 319–21* (Original in Hindi)

## 403. Letter to M.K. Gandhi

Allahabad
9 October 1945

My dear Bapu,
I have received today, on return from Lucknow, your letter of the 5th October. I am glad you have written to me fully and I shall try to reply at some length but I hope you will forgive me if there is some delay in this, as I am at present tied up with close-fitting engagements. I am only here now for a day and a half. It is really better to have informal talks but just at present I do not know when to fit this in. I shall try.

Briefly put my view is that the question before us is not one of truth versus untruth or nonviolence versus violence. One assumes as one must that true cooperation and peaceful methods must be aimed at and a society which encourages these must be our objective. The whole question is how to achieve this society and what its content should be. I do not understand why a village should necessarily embody truth and nonviolence. A village, normally speaking, is backward intellectually and culturally and no progress can be made from a backward environment. Narrow-minded people are much more likely to be untruthful and violent.

Then again we have to put down certain objectives like sufficiency of food, clothing, housing, education, sanitation, etc., which should be the minimum requirement for the country and for everyone. It is with these objectives in view that we must find out specifically how to attain them speedily. Again it seems to me inevitable that modern means of transport as well as many other modern developments must continue and be developed. There is no way out of it except to have them. If that is so inevitably a measure of heavy industry exists. How far will that fit in with a purely village society? Personally, I hope that heavy or light industries should all be decentralised as far as possible and this is feasible now because of the development of electric power. If two types of economy exist in the country either there should be conflict between the two or one will overwhelm the other. The question of independence and protection from foreign aggression, both political and economic, has also to be considered in this context. I do not think it is possible for India to be really independent unless she is a technically advanced country. I am not thinking for the moment in terms of just armies but rather of scientific growth. In the present context of the world we cannot even advance culturally without a strong background of scientific research in every department. There is today in the world a tremendous acquisitive tendency both in individuals and groups and nations, which leads to conflicts and wars. Our entire society is based on this more or less. That basis must go and be transformed into one of cooperation, not of isolation which is impossible [*sic*]. If this is admitted and is found feasible then attempts should be made to realise it not in terms of an economy which is cut off from the rest of the world but rather one which cooperates. From the economic or political point of view an isolated India may well be a kind of vacuum which increases the acquisitive tendencies of others and thus creates conflicts.

There is no question of palaces for millions of people. But there seems to be no reason why millions should not have comfortable up-to-date homes where they can lead a cultured existence. Many of the present overgrown cities have developed evils which are deplorable. Probably we have to discourage this overgrowth and at the same time encourage the village to approximate more to the culture of the town.

It is many years ago since I read *Hind Swaraj* and I have only a vague picture in my mind. But even when I read it 20 or more years ago it seemed to me completely unreal. In your writings and speeches since then I have found much that seemed to me an advance on that old position and an appreciation of modern trends. I was therefore surprised when you told us that the old picture still remains intact in your mind. As you know, the Congress has never considered that picture, much less adopted it. You yourself have never asked it to adopt it except for certain relatively minor aspects of it. How far it is desirable for the Congress to consider these fundamental questions, involving varying philosophies of life, it is for you to judge. I should imagine that a body like the Congress should not lose itself in arguments over such matters which can only produce great confusion in people's minds resulting in inability to act in the present. This may also result in creating barriers between the Congress and others in the country. Ultimately of course this and other questions will have to be decided by representatives of free India. I have a feeling that most of these questions are thought of and discussed in terms of long ago, ignoring the vast changes that have taken place all over the world during the last generation or more. It is 38 years since *Hind Swaraj* was written. The world has completely changed since then, possibly in a wrong direction. In any event any consideration of these questions must keep present facts, forces and the human material we have today in view, otherwise it will be divorced from reality. You are right in saying that the world, or a large part of it, appears to be bent on committing suicide. That may be an inevitable development of an evil seed in civilisation that has grown. I think it is so. How to get rid of this evil, and yet how to keep the good in the present as in the past is our problem. Obviously there is good, too, in the present.

These are some random thoughts hurriedly written down and I fear they do injustice to the grave import of the questions raised. You will forgive me, I hope, for this jumbled presentation. Later I shall try to write more clearly on the subject.

About the Hindustani Prachar Sabha and about the Kasturba Fund, it is obvious that both of them have my sympathy and I think they are doing good work. But I am not quite sure about the manner of their working and I have a feeling that this is not always to my liking. I really do not know enough about them to be definite. But at present I have developed a distaste for adding to my burden of responsibilities when I feel that I cannot probably undertake them for lack of time. These next few months and more are likely to be fevered ones for me and others. It seems hardly desirable to me, therefore, to join any responsible committee for form's sake only.

About Sarat Bose, I am completely in the dark as to why he should grow so angry with me, unless it is some past grievance about my general attitude in regard to foreign relations. Whether I was right or wrong it does seem to me that Sarat has acted in a childish and an irresponsible manner. You will remember perhaps that Subhas did not favour in the old days the Congress attitude towards Spain, Czechoslovakia, Munich and China. Perhaps this is a reflection of that old divergence of views. I know of nothing else that has happened.

I see that you are going to Bengal early in November.[873] Perhaps I may visit Calcutta for three or four days just then. If so, I hope to meet you.

You may have seen in the papers an invitation of the President of the newly formed Indonesian Republic to me and some others to visit Java. In view of the special circumstances of the case I decided immediately to accept this invitation subject of course to my getting the necessary facilities for going there. It is extremely doubtful if I shall get these facilities, and so probably I shall not go.[874] Java is just two days by air from India, or even one day from Calcutta. The Vice-President of this Indonesian Republic, Mohammad Hatta,[875] is a very old friend of mine. I suppose you know that the Javanese population is almost entirely Muslim.

[873] Gandhi, however, did not visit Bengal in November, but spent the whole of December in Calcutta.

[874] Nehru was to go to Java in response to Dr Sukarno's invitation as a representative of the Congress, but did not as the Indian Government refused to grant necessary facilities to enable him to do so.

The Congress Working Committee which met in Calcutta from 7–11 December 1945, passed a resolution on Indonesia emphatically condemning 'the wanton invasion of Java and other parts of Indonesia' by the British and Dutch forces. The Committee while expressing sympathy for the people of Indonesia in their 'valiant struggle in defence of their newly won republic and independence', noted with distress that 'the units of the Indian army were arrayed against the Indonesians and Indo-Chinese'. It added that it viewed 'with deep indignation this mischievous misuse of the Indian forces by the British Government.' See *CWMG*, Vol. LXXXIII, Appendix I.

[875] (1902–1980); first Vice-President, Indonesia, 1945–8; Prime Minister, 1948–50

I hope you are keeping well and have completely recovered from the attack of influenza.

Yours affectionately,
Jawahar

Mahatma Gandhi
Poona

SWJN, *Vol. 14, I Series, pp. 554–7*

## 404. Letter to Jawaharlal Nehru

Poona
13 November 1945

Chi. Jawaharlal,

I was very happy with our talks yesterday. We could not have discussed more yesterday and it is my view that we shall not be able to finish our work at a single sitting. We must meet from time to time. I am so made that if I had the strength to travel about, I would seek you out, stay with you for a day or two, have some talk and then leave. Though I am not in a position to do that now, you may know I have done such things before. I want that people should know us as we know each other. If in the end we find that our paths are different, then so be it. Our hearts will still remain one, for they are one. The talks we had yesterday have given me the impression that there is not much difference in our outlooks or the way we understand things. I want to tell you how I have understood you. If there is any difference you will let me know.

1. The crucial question according to you, is how to ensure man's mental, economic, political and moral development. That is my position too.

2. And in doing so every individual should have equal right and opportunity.

3. From this point of view there should be equality between villages and cities. And therefore their food and drink, their way of life, their dress and their habits should be the same. If such a condition is to be brought about people should produce their own cloth and food and build their own houses. So also they should produce their own water and electricity.

4. Man is not born to live in the jungle; he is born to live in society. If we are to make sure that one person does not ride on another's back, the unit should be an ideal village or a social group which will be self-sufficient, but the members of which will be interdependent. This conception will bring about a change in human relationship all over the world.

If I have understood you correctly up to here, I shall take up the second part. I have had Rajkumari translate the letter which I wrote to you earlier. I am getting this also translated and will send the translation along with this. I serve two purposes by getting the letters translated. First I can explain to you more clearly in English what I want to say and secondly I shall be able to know better whether I have understood you fully or not.

Blessings to Indu.

Blessings from
Bapu

CWMG, *Vol. LXXXII, pp. 71–2* (Original in Hindi)

## 405. Letter to Jawaharlal Nehru

Camp: Mahishadal
Post Sodepur
28 December 1945

Chi. Jawaharlal,

I am enclosing a letter, this as desired by the writer. He might have met me in South Africa, but I do not remember. I have written to him that he has made a tall claim in his address. He seems to be a crazy man.

I could find time only now to read what you said before the students in Bihar.[876] I like it very much.

[876] In his address on 24 December 1945 at the 'Release Jayaprakash Rally' (Jayaprakash Narayan had been arrested in Lahore on 6 October 1943), Nehru had said: 'India will continue to be a prison as long as a single patriot remains encaged in a British prison. ... The justification brought forward by a section of the people for the release of Jayaprakash and other leaders is that the war is over and that peace and amity have returned. I express my strong disagreement with the justification as this amounts to begging the authorities for

You need a little rest. It would indeed be good if you could snatch it.

I had told Rajkumari to write to you about the Communists. Today I find a totally different thing in the newspapers. A clipping is attached herewith. What is this? Can you throw some light?

Blessings from
Bapu

CWMG, *Vol. LXXXII, p. 292* (Original in Hindi)

## 406. Letter to M.K. Gandhi

Allahabad
14 January 1946

My dear Bapu,

I enclose a copy of a letter from an American[877] who was in the American Army as an engineer and planning expert. He was in charge of building up a number of camps. He advised the Sriniketan[878] people also and was put in a committee[879] by the Bengal Government. I was considerably impressed by him. He has the knowledge and training for his job, knows the latest technique, and at the same time understands the background of village India. He is attracted to India in many ways (even philosophically) and has got the urge to do something here without thinking in terms of monetary recompense. Because of this urge he may come back to India.

His idea was to experiment in a number of typical localities with village reconstruction and development, keeping Indian

---

their release. The war might have ended, but our struggle against the British Government will not be over until we win full freedom.' See *SWJN*, Vol. 14, I Series, pp. 278–85.

[877] Albert Meyer, who in his letter of 19 December 1945 had suggested, among other things, the re-planning and re-development of a group of villages, building of houses in villages chiefly with materials locally available, and production of adequately trained technicians in as large numbers as possible for a construction and reconstruction programme.

[878] Twin University of Santiniketan

[879] As a member of the Committee on the Improvement of Higher Technical Education

conditions in view. This was not to consist of just building but of helping in providing a corporate life for the people.

Yours affectionately,
Jawaharlal

SWJN, *Vol. 3, II Series, pp. 479–80*

## 407. Letter to M.K. Gandhi

Allahabad
30 January 1946

Dear Bapu,

Received your letter. I said something about the incidents which took place in Bombay concerning the Communists.[880] These are very wrong things that are happening and I think some people are getting these done from behind the scenes. It is true that these days public opinion is generally very much against the Communists. At several places they cannot hold even a meeting. But such large-scale attacks cannot take place without any special motive.

At the same time it has also to be kept in mind that the Communists have also often indulged in a lot of rioting. In this very month, in Kanpur, they resorted to violence as a result of which several of our people were injured.[881]

Of late the Muslim League has also been indulging in violence but now it is somewhat under control in comparison to the past. There has been some reaction against them among some Muslims too. In Allahabad a number of big processions of nationalist Muslims (that is, against the League) have been taken out.

Yesterday Sarup reached here. Her health is good and she is happy. I was a little indisposed. Now I am getting well.

Yours affectionately,
Jawaharlal

SWJN, *Vol. 3, II Series, pp. 480–1* (Original in Hindi)

[880] On 23 January 1946 the printing press of the *People's Age* in Bombay was badly damaged and 40 Communists were injured in an attack on their headquarters. See also *SWJN*, Vol. 14, I Series, pp. 231 and 547–8.

[881] On 2 January 1946, about a dozen persons were injured in a clash between the Congress and Communist workers of Bhairon Ghat in Kanpur while the two groups were proceeding to join the funeral of a worker of the Muir Mill.

## 408. Draft Reply to Jawaharlal Nehru

New Delhi
[21 June 1946][882]

I and all are of opinion that you presence here is essential above everything else. Remember that you are under an organisation which you have adorned so long. It needs must be paramount for you and me. Remember also that your honour is ours and obedience to the Congress call automatically transfers to it the duty of guarding your honour. The Committee is also equally solicitous with you about Sheikh Abdullah's case and the welfare of the Kashmir people. Therefore I expect you to return in answer to this. You will tell the Maharaja Saheb that as soon as you are freed by the Congress, you will return to Kashmir to retrieve your honour and fulfil your mission.

CWMG, *Vol. LXXXIV, pp. 353–4*

## 409. Letter to M.K. Gandhi

Bombay
9 July 1946

Bapu,

You must have seen that two names for the Working Committee were changed later on and Sarat Babu was taken in.[883] This was

[882] Nehru along with Asaf Ali had proceeded to Kashmir to arrange for the defence of Sheikh Abdullah (President of the Kashmir National Conference) and his colleagues, who had been arrested by the State Government for demanding a democratic set-up. At Kohala, on the border of Kashmir State, an order was served on Nehru prohibiting his entry into the State. On his refusal to comply, he was arrested and detained in a dak-bungalow.

In response to Abul Kalam Azad's urgent summons to return to Delhi, Nehru replied on 21 June, 'that in view of the grave discourtesy offered to me. ... I am unable to return until full liberty of movement ... is accorded to me. I request the Working Committee to proceed without me.'

Gandhi drafted the reply to this on behalf of Azad. Presumably this was the reply referred to by Gandhi in his speech at the prayer meeting on this day as having been sent telegraphically; see *CWMG*, Vol. LXXXIV, p. 355.

[883] The Working Committee nominated by Nehru did not have the names of Kripalani and Sarojini Naidu. See *SWJN*, Vol. 15, I Series, pp. 460–1 for the complete list.

done with the approval of the Maulana. Vallabhbhai also liked it. I hope you will also approve it.

Today in the evening I heard that Sarojini's condition has become serious and her entire head has swollen. It is perhaps not a mere external swelling.The doctors think there might be something wrong inside. She is suffering.

I will go to Allahabad on the 11th night.

Yours,
Jawaharlal

SWJN, *Vol. 3, II Series, pp. 484–5* (Original in Hindi)

## 410. Letter to Jawaharlal Nehru

Panchgani
17 July 1946

My dear Jawaharlal,

I have gone through what Munshi[884] showed me, though I did not have the time to examine it closely.[885] He came today after 4 o'clock and will be going back tomorrow morning. I had a long talk with him about grouping.[886] He will explain things to you. I have advised him to consult other lawyers as well. What he has prepared after seven days' labours may not be placed before the Committee just yet. Once it goes before the Committee, it will become public. I do not see the need of making it public so soon.

Your statement as published in the papers does not sound good.[887] If it is correctly reported, some explanation is needed. It must be admitted that we have to work within the limits of the

[884] K.M. Munshi (1887–1971); founded Bharatiya Vidya Bhavan, 1938; Home Minister, Bombay, 1937–9; Union Minister for Food and Agriculture, 1950–2; Governor, Uttar Pradesh, 1952–7; later joined the Swatantra Party

[885] The reference is to the Rules of Procedure in the Constituent Assembly.

[886] Of provinces in sub-federations in the North-East and North-West zones claimed by the Muslim League for Pakistan

[887] The reference presumably is to Nehru's 'Interview to the Press' of 10 July 1946, in which he was reported to have said that the Congress would enter the Constituent Assembly 'completely unfettered by agreements and free to meet all situations as they arise'.

State Paper.[888] It is clear in Maulana's letters. We have given it our own interpretation. But if the Federal Court gives a different interpretation, we shall have to be firm. I think it necessary to say this clearly. If we do not admit even this much, we will be doing nothing and Jinnah Saheb's accusation will prove true.

Fischer and Jayaprakash have come here today. They too will return tomorrow.

Blessings from
Bapu

[PS]
In regard to Kashmir, Sardar has sent me the Maharaja's[889] speech. It deserves careful study. I think a meeting of the Working Committee should be called to consider it.[890] Let us not be hasty. Let us not endanger the whole thing just for this reason. I am of the view that Maulana Saheb and, if necessary, Sardar too, should go to Kashmir. After all, has not the Working Committee assumed the entire responsibility?

CWMG, *Vol. LXXXV, p. 5*

[888] Of 16 May 1946, proposing a three-tier Constitution that would formally preserve India's political unity and also partly satisfy the Muslim League demand for separate political self-expression for Muslims. See *CWMG*, Vol. LXXXIV, Appendix VII.

[889] Maharaja Hari Singh (1895–1961); was the last ruling Maharaja of the Princely State of Jammu and Kashmir; signed the Instrument of Accession on 20 October 1947. His rule was terminated in 1951.

At an address delivered at a special durbar in the middle of July 1946, the Maharaja was reported to have said, 'The second principle which guides our policy is that so far as our domestic affairs are concerned we must work out our own destiny without dictation from any quarter which is not an integral part of the State.'

[890] The meeting took place in Wardha from 8–13 August 1946.

## 411. Telegram to M.K. Gandhi

Allahabad
18 July 1946

Have received no communication from Kashmir. In view Maharaja's recent speech as reported no change in policy indicated. Please advise about future action. Am going Delhi tomorrow.

Jawaharlal

SWJN, *Vol. 3, II Series, p. 485*

## 412. Letter to M.K. Gandhi

Delhi
20 July 1946

Dear Bapu,

Munshi gave me your letter. The subjects which you do not want to be discussed by the Committee will not be put on the agenda. But every member has already given thought to these matters and they are in everyone's mind. Several members have prepared long notes too. Our proceedings will not be released to the Press at all. When the Working Committee meets, these matters will be considered.

Regarding the Constituent Assembly I am more than ever convinced that we should work in such a manner that the Assembly should in no way be concerned with the British Government. We have to keep it independent and there should be no interference in its working by the Parliament or Viceroy and if possible by the Federal Court. If ever there is an interference by the Federal Court it cannot be helped but the effort should be to prevent it. However, these things cannot be discussed fully in a letter. I shall talk about them when we meet.

After receiving the Viceroy's[891] letter I decided today to go to Kashmir.[892] Vallabhbhai also gave this advice.

[891] Sir Archibald Wavell (1883–1950); Commander-in-Chief, Middle-East, 1939–41; Commander-in-Chief, India, 1941–3; Viceroy of India, 1943–7

[892] Nehru had written to Lord Wavell on 13 July 1946 informing him that he intended to go to Kashmir on 23rd or 24th of the month. The Viceroy in his reply of 20 July had said that if Nehru was anxious to go to Kashmir he could do so and there would be no ban. He had hoped that Nehru would observe the laws of the state.

I, too, want that the Working Committee should meet soon. When and where do you want it to meet?

Yours,
Jawaharlal

SWJN, *Vol. 3, II Series, pp. 485–6*

## 413. Telegram to M.K. Gandhi

New Delhi
20 July 1946

Received letter from Viceroy today about Kashmir. Thereupon decided go there twenty- fourth on brief visit as Abdullah's trial beginning twenty-second.[893] Informed Viceroy Maharaja others my visit. Received your letter later. Consider change in programme not desirable now. Would early August suit you for Working Committee? Please wire suitable date place.

Jawaharlal

SWJN, *Vol. 15, I Series, p. 40*

## 414. Letter to M.K. Gandhi

New Delhi
20 August 1946

Dear Bapu,

Here the situation changes daily and it is not known yet what will be the final decision. It might be known probably in two or three days. In my last talk with you I had said that Rajendra Babu should be the President either of the Constituent Assembly or of the Congress. I had in mind particularly the Congress. Therefore I did not want him to join the Interim Government. But here others felt strongly that he should be in this Government. Then I gave in.

[893] Sheikh Abdullah and Mirza Mohamad Afzal Baig, an ex-Minister, had been arrested in Kashmir following an agitation to repudiate the allegiance of the people to Hari Singh, the Maharaja of Kashmir. More than 450 arrests had been made and soldiers were patrolling Srinagar.

I wanted the Maulana also to join the Interim Government. I pleaded much with him but he did not agree. Then he said that if people wanted he would be ready to bear the burden of the presidentship of the Congress.

This question of the presidentship of the Congress seems to me quite significant.[894] As you know these days the condition of the Congress is peculiar. Any mistake on our part can do much harm to the Congress and there can also be a rift in it. In such a situation when neither Rajendra Babu nor Vallabhbhai would be available I think the Maulana's becoming the President can do much good.

Today I have sent a list of 14 names to the Viceroy.[895] One more name will be sent later.

Yours,
Jawaharlal

SWJN, *Vol. 3, II Series, p. 486–7* (Original in Hindi)

[894] On 6 May 1946 Nehru had been elected President of the Congress, succeeding Maulana Azad.

[895] The list of names for the Interim Government read as follows: Sardar Vallabhbhai Patel, Rajendra Prasad, Asaf Ali, C.R. Rajagopalachari, Fazulul Huq, Sarat Chandra Bose, Dr John Mathai, Sardar Baldev Singh, Sir Shafaat Ahmad Khan, Jagjivan Ram, Syed Ali Zaheer, Cooverji Hormusji Bhabha, a Muslim name to be supplied, and Frank Anthony.

## 415. Telegram to Jawaharlal Nehru

Sevagram
23 August 1946

Express
Rashtrapati Jawaharlal Nehru
18 Hardinge Avenue
New Delhi
Wire[896] received. Leaving Sunday.[897] Staying Bhangi Quarters.[898] Inform Birla Brijkrishen.[899]

CWMG, *Vol. LXXXV, p. 196*

## 416. Letter to Jawaharlal Nehru

New Delhi
3 September 1946

Chi. Jawaharlal,
Dr Shaukatullah Ansari,[900] who was here yesterday, tells me that your health is deteriorating and that there is fear of a nervous breakdown. People say that you keep working till past midnight. I am certain this is not at all good. For the work ahead of you, you need great care. This becomes impossible if you overstrain your mental resources.

Blessings from
Bapu

CWMG, *Vol. LXXXV, p. 252*

[896] Not available

[897] The 25 August 1946 for Delhi. On the 27th Gandhi, accompanied by Nehru, met the Viceroy. He also attended the Congress Working Committee meetings from 27 to 30 August 1946.

Referring to the meeting of 27 August with Lord Wavell, Gandhi wrote to him the following day, 'Your language last evening was minatory. ... You threatened not to convene the Constituent Assembly if the formula you placed before Pandit Nehru and me was not acted upon by the Congress.' See also *CWMG*, Vol. LXXXV, pp. 215–16.

[898] At Kingsway Camp, Delhi. For Gandhi's article 'Why Bhangi Quarters?', *Harijan*, 31-3-1946, see *CWMG*, Vol. LXXXIII, pp. 316–17.

[899] Brijkrishna Chandiwala

[900] Son-in-law of Dr M.A. Ansari

## 417. Letter to M.K. Gandhi

New Delhi
4 October 1946

My dear Bapu,
I am sending you a copy of the Viceroy's reply to Jinnah's nine points;[901] also my letter to the Viceroy.[902]

Bhopal has just come to me and asked me if I would go to his place for lunch today presumably to meet Jinnah there. I said I would do so. The matter has not been settled yet.[903]

Yours,
Jawaharlal

SWJN, *Vol. 3, II Series, p. 493*

[901] As listed on 3 October. They were: 1. Executive Council to consist of 14 members; 2. Of the nominees of Congress one should belong to the scheduled caste; 3. No Muslim should be included in the Congress quota; 4. In case of conflict on communal issues no decision to be taken; 5. Vice-presidentship to be by rotation; 6. Representatives of minorities to be chosen thereafter in consultation with the Congress and the Muslim League; 7. Important portfolios to be equally distributed between Congress and the Muslim League; 8. Arrangements not to be changed without agreement of the two parties and 9. Long-term plan to be postponed till agreements were reached and the Interim Government set up. The Viceroy, Lord Wavell, in his reply of 4 October agreed to points 1, 2, 6 & 8 of the nine points.

[902] Of 4 October clarifying certain points in the Viceroy's replies to Jinnah; see *SWJN*, Vol. 1, II Series, pp. 165–7.

[903] Nehru and Jinnah met the Nawab of Bhopal on 5 and 7 October 1946.

## 418. Letter to M.K. Gandhi

New Delhi
11 October 1946

My dear Bapu,
I enclose copies of correspondence with the Viceroy. I think these letters explain themselves.[904]

Yours affectionately,
Jawaharlal

[PS]
In my telegram to Aung San[905] (which I sent in consultation with my colleagues) I stated that it was our general policy to withdraw Indian troops from abroad but that we would like to have the views of his Government so that any action we might take might not embarrass the Burma Government. Our Defence Member and the C-in-C, therefore, suggested that their views might be communicated to us or preferably that Aung San and the G.OC in Burma might come here for consultation.

I am enclosing a copy of the memorandum[906] on the salt tax which the Finance Department has circulated to us and about which I spoke to you this evening.

SWJN, *Vol. 3, II Series, p. 494*

[904] The UP Government, disapproving of certain steps taken by the IGP of Police, Sir Philip Measures, as also the circular issued by him, had asked that he be replaced. The Governor, Sir Francis Wylie, declined, and invoked his special responsibilities to prevent the Cabinet decision taking effect. This resulted in the Governor and the Government being in direct conflict. While the Viceroy concurred with the Governor's action, Nehru had written that if Measures did not resign, it might result in some serious consequences as any provincial and other Cabinet could not submit to such imposition. See *SWJN*, Vol. 1, II Series, pp. 176–9.

[905] U Aung San (1914–1947); Commander, Burma Independence Army, 1942; President, Anti-Fascist Freedom League, 1945–7; Deputy Chairman, Executive Council that ruled Burma in 1946; negotiated with the British Government for independence; was Premier-designate of the soon-to-be independent government when he was assassinated in July 1947.

[906] Which proposed abolition of excise duty on salt but favoured the continuation of production of salt by the Government. Ultimately, the tax was abolished on 28 February 1947.

## 419. Telegram to Jawaharlal Nehru

[3 November 1946][907]

*Morning News*[908] reports butchery by Hindus of Muslim passengers. Muslims fleeing from mob fury and premier[909] countenancing. Wire particulars.

CWMG, *Vol. LXXXVI, p. 70*

## 420. Telegram to M.K. Gandhi

[After 3 November 1946][910]

Report in *Morning News* grossly exaggerated and vague. Government here doing its utmost but situation tense and grave in many places. Am staying on here with Nishtar. Vallabhbhai and Liaquat Ali[911] going on to Delhi.

Jawahar

CWMG, *Vol. LXXXVI, p. 75*

## 421. Letter to Jawaharlal Nehru

5 November 1946

Chi. Jawaharlal,

The events in Bihar have distressed me. I can clearly see my duty. My bonds with Bihar are close. I cannot forget it. If half of what I hear is true, it means that Bihar has lost all humanity. To say that *goondas* were responsible for whatever happened there would be quite untrue.[912] Although I have tried hard to avoid the fast, I

[907] Inferred from related items in the source

[908] A publication of the Muslim League. It had stated that hundreds of thousands had been killed in the communal riots in Bihar following a hartal on 25 October.

[909] Srikrishna Sinha (1887–1961); lawyer of Monghyr; joined the noncooperation movement, 1920; Chief Minister, Bihar, 1937–9 and 1946–61

[910] Inferred from the contents; see preceding item.

[911] Nawabzada Liaquat Ali Khan (1896–1951); first Prime Minister and Defence Minister of Pakistan; assassinated in 1951

[912] Addressing a prayer meeting the previous day, Gandhi had said, 'We always put the blame on the *goondas*. But it is we who are responsible for their creation as well as encouragement. It is, therefore, not right to say that all the wrong that has been done is the work of *goondas*.'

shall not be able to do so. It is the seventh day today since I gave up milk and cereals. The cough and the boils were responsible for it, but also I was tired of the body. Then Bihar made matters worse. And the cry came from within: 'Why should you be a witness to this slaughter? If your word, which is as clear as daylight, is not heeded, your work is over. Why do you not die?' Such reasoning has forced me to resort to fasting. I want to issue a statement that if in Bihar and other provinces slaughter is not stopped, I must end my life by fasting.[913]

The letter Mohammed Yunus wrote to Shamsuddin[914] is with Sardar Baldev Singh.[915] See it. Is what it says correct? It is our duty to give full report of what happened.

My low diet will continue. There may be delay in undertaking the fast. In Delhi you had asked me about the fast. I had said I had no idea then. Now the situation is not the same. Still you may say what you want to say. If it appeals to me I shall give up the idea of a fast. What I hope is that, knowing my nature, you will appreciate my position. Whatever the issue, I shall advise that all of you continue to do your work. Do not waste time thinking of my death. Leave me in the hands of God and stop worrying.

You can show this letter to the Bihar Cabinet. Is this the Bihar of Brijkishore Prasad?[916]

Blessings from
Bapu

CWMG, *Vol. LXXXVI, pp. 78–9*

[913] In a letter 'To Bihar' written on 6 November (*Harijan* 10-11-1946), Gandhi wrote, 'I regard myself as part of you. Your affection has compelled that loyalty in me. And since I claim to have a better appreciation than you seem to have shown of what Bihar Hindus should do, I cannot rest till I have done some measure of penance. Predominantly for reasons of health, I had put myself on the lowest diet possible soon after my reaching Calcutta. That diet will become a fast unto death, if the erring Biharis have not turned over a new leaf.' On 19 November, Gandhi resumed his normal diet, as Bihar was returing to normalcy.

[914] Shamsuddin Ahmad; Minister for Commerce, Labour and Industries in the Bengal Muslim League Ministry

[915] Then Development Minister, Punjab; Member, Interim Government, 1946–7; Defence Minister in the Nehru Cabinet, 1947–52

[916] A Congress leader of Bihar; father-in-law of Jayaprakash Narayan

## 422. Letter to M.K. Gandhi

Patna
7 November 1946

My dear Bapu,

I enclose a hurried report[917] prepared last night. The news thus far has been fairly satisfactory. We flew over most of the affected areas and found them quite peaceful with people working in the fields but there are still 2 or 3 pockets of trouble. There evidently some people with guns are functioning. This must be the professional dacoit element.

The Viceroy is coming here today.

Yours affectionately,
Jawaharlal

SWJN, *Vol. 1, II Series, p. 79*

## 423. Telegram to M.K. Gandhi

Patna
8 November 1946

Situation generally quiet for two days. No major incident but tension and apprehension continue. Certain criminal elements including...[918] gang causing trouble in some places. Newspaper reports on military action two days ago greatly exaggerated. Am going Delhi Saturday. Rajendra Babu and Jayaprakash staying on.

Jawaharlal

SWJN, *Vol. 3, II Series, p. 495*

## 424. Note to Jawaharlal Nehru

30 December 1946

Your affection is extraordinary and so natural! Come again, when you wish, or send someone who understands you and will faithfully interpret my reactions ... when, in your opinion, consultation

[917] On the disturbances in Bihar; see *SWJN*, Vol. 1, II Series, pp. 80–6.

[918] Dots in this and the following item indicate illegibility in the source.

is necessary and you cannot come.[919] Nor is it seemly that you should often run to me even though I claim to be like a wise father to you, having no less love towards you than Motilalji.

Do not depart from the spirit of the draft[920] you showed me yesterday.... Somehow or other I feel that my judgement about the communal problems and the political situation is true. I have no doubt now about the wisdom of what I had said in Delhi when the Working Committee accepted the Cabinet Mission's statement. [921] This does not mean that what was done by the Working Committee should not have been done. On the contrary, I had completely associated myself with all that the Working Committee did. I could not support with reason what I had felt so vaguely.

This time it is quite different. My reason wholly supports my heart. I notice daily verification. So I suggest frequent consultations with an old, tried servant of the nation.

CWMG, *Vol. LXXXVI, p. 287*

## 425. Telegram to M.K. Gandhi

New Delhi
1 January 1947

Visited Patna. Met minister and relief commissioners. Arrangements for relief rehabilitation appear satisfactory. No communal incidents for many weeks. All agree reports sent to you grossly exaggerated and containing unfounded allegations. Enquiry welcome. Good wishes for New Year.

Jawaharlal

SWJN, *Vol. 3, II Series, p. 495*

919 According to Pyarelal, 'Jawaharlal Nehru's plea with Gandhiji to return to Delhi did not succeed.' This was 'scribbled at 3 o' clock in the morning'.

920 Of the Congress Working Committee resolution of 22 December 1946 on the British Cabinet Mission's Statement of 6 December 1946 on Grouping. See *CWMG*, Vol. LXXXVI, Appendices VI and VII.

921 See *CWMG*, Vol. LXXXIV, pp. 169–72 and 209–11.

## 426. Letter to M.K. Gandhi

New Delhi
1 January 1947

My dear Bapu,
I enclose copy of a letter I am sending to Suhrawardy.[922] I might add that there were probably a few cases of rape and abduction. The number must be small. The nature of the upheaval was such that this did not fit in with it and the whole thing lasted only a few days.

Yours affectionately,
Jawaharlal

SWJN, *Vol. 1, II Series, p. 103*

## 427. Telegram to Jawaharlal Nehru

15 January 1947

Pandit Jawaharlal Nehru
New Delhi
Pathetic telegram received from Peshawar about murder arson and loot. Received similar wire [from Hazara]. Please reply about truth allegations.

Bapu[923]

CWMG, *Vol. LXXXVI, p. 357*

## 428. Telegram to M.K. Gandhi

16 January 1947

Owing to false and exaggerated propaganda about Bihar several serious incidents took place in Hazara district involving attacks on Hindus Sikhs arson and loot. Number of persons killed not considerable. Large numbers refugees. Frontier Government has taken strong action against miscreants also helping refugees. Situation

[922] H.S. Suhrawardy (1893–1963); leader, Muslim League, Bengal; Chief Minister, Bengal, at the time of partition; founder, Awami League, Pakistan; Prime Minister of Pakistan, 1956–7

[923] An identical telegram was sent to Vallabhbhai Patel, who was in charge of Home Affairs in the Interim Government.

now quiet. We are keeping in close touch and will take all necessary steps.

Jawaharlal
Vallabhbhai

SWJN, *Vol. 1, II Series, p. 348*

## 429. Letter to M.K. Gandhi

New Delhi
18 January 1947

My dear Bapu,

I have just returned from Patna.[924] A letter from Shuaib was waiting for me here enclosing a cover for you. This is being sent to you—presumably it contains a letter from the Nawab of Bhopal.

At Patna I had a brief talk with Sri Babu and the Chief Secretary about conditions in Bihar. There have been no incidents worth reporting but the exodus of Muslims has continued—many from areas which had not been affected by the disturbances. It was estimated that about 75,000 had gone to Bengal. Some people are still going while some are coming back. Obviously this kind of thing must have some organised effort behind it but no one knows what this is. Indeed it is being done rather quietly, even somewhat secretly. The Bihar government gets no information and they have no satisfactory method of getting it. The government is far too passive about it all. They work slowly. They are worried naturally but have no conception of what should be done. I am sure Badshah Khan's visit is doing good.[925] I did not meet him there but I shall see him at the Constituent Assembly soon.

It is said that some anonymous notices asking Muslims to quit were distributed in some places—presumably by Hindus. There is a sense of fear and apprehension among the Muslims.

[924] Nehru had visited Patna to receive the honorary degree of Doctor of Science at the Patna University convocation held on 17 January 1947.

[925] Abdul Ghaffar Khan had arrived in Patna on 10 January 1947 for a village-to-village tour, on the pattern of Gandhi's walking tour, in the riot-affected districts of Bihar.

We are following your tour and watching its results from a distance.[926] We all wonder when you will come this way again. You are wanted in so many places.

I hope you are looking after yourself.

Love.

Yours,
Jawaharlal

SWJN, *Vol. 3, II Series, pp. 495–6*

## 430. Letter to M.K. Gandhi

New Delhi
30 January 1947

Dear Bapu,

Thank you for your letter[927] of January 26th.

About the Hindu University[928] matter, I know very little. Radhakrishnan[929] spoke to me about it when I paid a brief visit to Benaras. He mentioned Shyama Prasad's[930] name. I did not

[926] Following Hindu-Muslim riots and atrocities that had started in October 1946 in Noakhali and other districts in East Bengal, Gandhi had undertaken a tour of Noakhali from 6 November 1946. This culminated in his walking tour of the district that began on 2 January 1947 and ended on 2 March 1947.

[927] Not available

[928] Benares Hindu University, founded in 1917 by Pandit Madan Mohan Malaviya and Annie Besant. A premier Central University and a world-class educational institution, it is located in Varanasi, the current name for Benares.

[929] Sarvepalli Radhakrishnan (1888–1975); philosopher and statesman; Spalding Professor of Eastern Religions and Ethics, Oxford University, 1936–52; first Vice-President of India, 1952–62; President of India, 1962–7. 5 September, his birthday, is celebrated as Teachers' Day in India.

[930] Shyama Prasad Mookherji (1901–1953); Vice-Chancellor, Calcutta University, 1934–8; Member, Bengal Legislative Council and Assembly, 1929–37; Minister, Industry and Supply, Government of India, 1947–50; founder-President, Bharatiya Jana Sangh, 1951; Member, Lok Sabha, 1952–3

The names of S.P. Mookherjee and Govind Malaviya were being considered for the post of Pro-Vice-Chancellor that had fallen vacant by the resignation of Rang Bihari Lal.

particularly fancy it chiefly because of his communal affiliations and politics. Otherwise, of course, he was a suitable man. I told Radhakrishnan that he might make a good Pro-Vice-Chancellor and so far as I was concerned I had no objection. I did not wish to interfere in any way in the Benares University affairs which are complicated and intricate.

Later I had a visit from Raman who was very much opposed to Shyama Prasad's appointment. I told him that this was none of my concern and I did not propose to interfere. I found subsequently that my name was being used by both parties. This was annoying. I have had no further part in this affair. I understand that some UP Ministers supported Govind. The election has now been postponed for a year.

I am quite sure that your visit to and tour in Noakhali District has great significance and importance. It is not for me to suggest to you to go against your own inclination. You are the best judge. What I had ventured to put to you however, and would like to repeat, is that conditions all over India to some extent are very unsatisfactory. There is a certain disruptive tendency at work which affects our work in every direction. The whole Congress organisation is suffering from it and we, who are in the Government, have no time at all to give to any work except the immediate problems which confront us. It is difficult to write much in a letter. But I want you to realise that there is in some ways a progressive deterioration in the situation and I feel very unhappy about it. I would not mind so much any number of what I would call external problems however difficult they might be. But when our own approach is not quite clear and there are different viewpoints and pulls, then it becomes even more difficult to deal with any problem.

I know that we must learn to rely upon ourselves and not run to you for help on every occasion. But we have got into this bad habit and we do often feel that if you had been easier of access our difficulties would have been less.

I am worried about Bihar. I made it quite clear to some of the Ministers there that they must ask for a Commission of Inquiry or appoint it themselves even if the Bengal Government got out of it. I thought they had agreed, but nothing has been done since.

I do not know the reason for this, and I am writing to Sri Babu about it.[931]

I have a feeling, for which I have no proof whatever, that there is no strong desire for an inquiry. The Bihar Government anyhow moves slowly. The Government has done a great deal in giving relief and yet it has not done it in the right way and hence the psychological results achieved have not been great. There is a sense of fear and apprehension among the Muslim population. Badshah Khan passed through Delhi the other day and I met him. I did not have time to talk to him about Bihar, but I understand that he is not at all happy at what he found there.

I have found both in Bihar and elsewhere very little regret or remorse among the Hindus for what happened there. There is a feeling almost of justification. Among the Muslims there is definitely a fear, whether justified or not, that there might be further attacks on them.

In Hazara in the NWFP some horrible things were done, though, of course, in point of extent and numbers there is no comparison whatever with Bihar. In quality or lack of it there is little to choose, in my mind, between Noakhali, Bihar, Meerut District and Hazara. They all represent utter degradation and depravity.

You know that there is going to be an Inter-Asian Relations Conference in the last week of March in Delhi. This Conference has assumed an unusual importance and it is going to be very representative indeed. Almost every country of Asia from the West to the East and South, including the Arab countries, Tibet, Mongolia and the countries of South-East Asia as well as the Asian Republics of the Soviet Union, will be represented by leading men. This is going to be a unique event in history. Because of this, various European and American Governments are taking a great interest in this and are even rather apprehensive because they fear the development of

[931] On 31 January 1947 Nehru wrote to Sri Krishna Sinha that the Bihar Government should make clear its demand for a Commission of Inquiry into the happenings of November 1946. He had also asked Sri Krishna Sinha to write to Gandhi on the matter.

an Asian bloc. There is no such idea in our minds, but undoubtedly we want the countries of Asia to cooperate with each other.

I do not usually trouble you about attending any function. I do feel, however, that your presence at this Inter-Asian Relations Conference would be valuable and greatly appreciated by the people who come here from abroad. If it is at all possible for you to be here then, I hope you will come. The Conference begins on March 23rd and is likely to last from ten days to a fortnight.[932]

Yours,
Jawaharlal

SWJN, *Vol. 1, II Series, pp. 110–12*

## 431. Letter to Jawaharlal Nehru

[6] February 1947

The last week of March next is at present for me a far cry. If God wills He will find a way for me to attend the Conference.[933]

CWMG, *Vol. LXXXVII, p. 22*

## 432. Letter to Jawaharlal Nehru

6 February 1947

I know that if I were free I could take my share in trying to solve the various problems that arise in our country. But I feel that I should be useless unless I could do something here. ...[934] We are all in the hands of the Power which we call God.

* * *

Very great pressure is being put upon me to go to Bihar because they all say that things are not properly represented to me on behalf of the Bihar Government. I am watching.

CWMG, *Vol. LXXXVI, p. 437*

[932] For Nehru's inaugural address, see *SWJN*, Vol. 2, II Series, pp. 501–16.

[933] Gandhi attended the Asian Relations Conference on 1 and 2 April 1947. For his address to the conference, see *CWMG*, Vol. LXXXVI, pp. 190–3.

[934] Omission as in the source.

## 433. Letter to M.K. Gandhi

New Delhi
9 February 1947

Dear Bapu,

I have received your letter of the 3rd February regarding the Malaviyaji Memorial Fund.[935] At Radhakrishnan's instance a number of people gathered together here and they started a committee and a fund. They made me chairman much against my will as I do not like assuming any responsibility for this kind of work.

I remember, of course, that nothing of this kind has yet been done about Hakim Saheb,[936] my father and Ansari. It is not for me to move in this matter and I suppose it is rather late now to take any step.

In the circumstances here I found it difficult to refuse and there I am, rather a formal chairman. No target has been fixed, but people are thinking in big terms running into several crores. They expect quite a number of substantial donations of a lakh or over. The object is principally to expand the activities of the Benares Hindu University. The money may be used for other purposes also as the committee decides.

The League resolution[937] was about as bad as it could be. Perhaps there was a virtue in it for it makes the position quite clear. After this resolution it is even more difficult than before for

[935] The letter is not available.

Madan Mohan Malaviya had died on 12 November 1946. Gandhi wrote in *Harijan,* 8-12-1946: 'Malaviyaji has left an imperishable memorial of himself in the Kashi Vishwa Vidyalaya. To put it on a stable foundation, to secure its evolutionary growth, will surely be the most suitable memorial that can be erected by us to the memory of the great patriot. He spared no pains in making a big collection for his pet child. Everyone who reveres his memory can give a helping hand to the labour of continuing the collection.' For his article, 'Malaviyaji', see *CWMG*, Vol. LXXXVI, pp. 147–8.

[936] Hakim Ajmal Khan (1865–1927); well-known physician of Delhi; President, INC, 1921

[937] Which was passed in Karachi on 31 January 1947. The Muslim League Working Committee blamed the Congress party for exceeding the 'limitations imposed by the statement of May 16th on the Constituent Assembly functions and powers' and demanded that the Constituent Assembly should be forthwith dissolved.

us to carry on in the old way in the Interim Government. We are moving in the matter.

Meanwhile we are having talks with the Rulers.[938] Their approach too as a whole is bad.

Yours,
Jawaharlal

SWJN, *Vol. 3, II Series, pp. 496–7*

## 434. Letter to M.K. Gandhi

New Delhi
10 February 1947

Dear Bapu,

This morning I sent you a letter[939] by post. But as Sudhir[940] is going I am sending this note with him.

I have received your letter of February 6th.

I cannot venture to criticise your decision to stay on in East Bengal. But I have an overwhelming feeling that vital decisions are being made and will be made in Delhi, affecting the whole of our future as well as of course the present, and your presence at such a moment is necessary. We are drifting everywhere and sometimes I doubt if we are drifting in the right direction. We live in a state of perpetual crisis and have no real grip of the situation.

As you know, we have informed the Viceroy that in view of the Muslim League resolution passed at Karachi, the League Members cannot continue in the Government.[941] There is really no answer to our charge and demand and the Viceroy realises it. He is awaiting instructions from London. Whatever these may be, our troubles will no doubt continue. What I am worried most about is the rapidly

[938] For detailed information on the negotiations with the Princes regarding their joining the Constituent Assembly, see *SWJN*, Vol. 2, II Series, pp. 198–287.

[939] Not available

[940] Sudhir Ghosh, who had been appointed Public Relations Officer at the Indian High Commission, London; author of *Gandhi's Emissary*

[941] On 5 February, nine members of the Interim Government—all except the five members of the League—wrote a joint letter to the Viceroy that in their opinion the League could not continue in their Government.

deteriorating economic and labour situation. Also the state of the Congress organisation. Those of us who are in Government have given and can give no time at all to Congress work. We are losing touch with our people. I have been unable to go even to Allahabad for a day for months.

The question of the Princes and States entering the Constituent Assembly worked out ultimately a little better than we expected. But of course there are still many hurdles ahead.

Love.

Yours,
Jawaharlal

SWJN, *Vol. 2, II Series, p. 36*

## 435. Letter to M.K. Gandhi

New Delhi
21 February 1947

Dear Bapuji,

I have your letter[942] of the 15th February enclosing a letter from Khurshed Naoroji. There is a great deal of talk in the papers about sending a medical mission to help Vietnam. Nobody, however, seems to be taking any effective step in that direction. Sarat Bose wrote to me asking for permission for a medical mission to be sent as well as for armed volunteers. I told him that we could not give facilities for armed volunteers to be sent as this meant practically declaring war on France. Apart from this, we couldn't possibly give transport facilities.

In regard to the medical mission we promised to try our best to give the facilities and asked for particulars as to who was being sent. No answer has come.

Obviously we cannot deal with individuals who want to go there. There is no regular service to Indo-China from India and the extraordinary French services are hardly likely to cooperate. If, however, some responsible group sponsors a medical mission we would try to help in every way. Khurshed can join that mission. There is no question, as you say, of any recommendation being

[942] Not available

required for her unless the organisers of the group require it. There will be no difficulty at our end apart from normal transport difficulties which are considerable.

Yours,
Jawaharlal

SWJN, *Vol. 3, II Series, pp. 497–8*

## 436. Letter to M.K. Gandhi

New Delhi
24 February 1947

Dear Bapu,

Thank you for your letter[943] of February 18th. I enclose a cheque for Rs 5,000/- from the fund placed at my disposal by the ex-Maharaja[944] of Nepal. He earmarked this for the relief of Gurkhas in distress in East Bengal. I am informing the Gurkha League that I have sent this money on to you.

I have not yet seen what you wrote about the Benares University on Malaviyaji's death.[945] I am rather worried about my chairmanship of the memorial committee. Govind thinks in large terms of getting very big donations. I suppose it will not be difficult to collect 15 or 20 lakhs. But he thinks in terms of crores.

You must have seen my statement[946] on the new declaration made by the British Government.[947] That statement was consid-

[943] Not available

[944] Judha Shamsher Jang Bahadur Rana, Prime Minister of Nepal, 1932–45. He had made a considerable grant from his privy purse for the Gurkha refugees.

[945] See *fn.* 934.

[946] Of 22 February 1947. Nehru had said: 'The Statement made by the Prime Minister Attlee at the House of Commons on February 20th in regard to Indian policy has received and is receiving the earnest attention of all those who are virtually interested in bringing the present transitional period to a satisfactory conclusion. The statement is obscure in some places and requires careful consideration. The outstanding feature of it is, however, in the decision of the British Government to transfer power to Indian hands not later than June 1948.' See *SWJN*, Vol. 2, II Series, pp. 41–2.

[947] Attlee had announced the British Government's decision to hand over responsibility to authorities established by a constitution approved by

ered carefully by all our colleagues in the Interim Government minus, of course, the Muslim Leaguers. We wanted very much to consult Kripalani before a statement was issued and he was to have come here. But then he fell ill at Allahabad. We felt that something should be said soon both for India and abroad. Attlee's statement contains much that is indefinite and likely to give trouble. But I am convinced that it is in the final analysis a brave and definite statement. It meets our oft-repeated demand for quitting India. It may not be so exactly as we would have liked it. But the real thing is that they have finally decided and announced that they are quitting. Whatever their motives might be, they cannot go back on this and everything that happens from now onwards must be governed by it.

The present position is that if the Muslim League comes into the Constituent Assembly, which is very unlikely, then the Cabinet Mission's Statement of May 16th applies. Otherwise the limitations of that Statement go and the Constituent Assembly functions really as a sovereign body without sections and groups and a limited centre. But there is one limitation: that its decisions will apply only to the parts represented in it. More or less this was what you said when we met last. This may result in the Indian Union being first established for the whole of India except Bengal, the Punjab and Sind. Of course the Union constitution will apply to or rather be open to all; but these provinces may not choose to adhere to it. If so the second question that arises is that those parts of Bengal and Punjab which are fully represented in the Constituent Assembly (Western Bengal and Southern Punjab) should be parts of the Union. That means a partition of Punjab and Bengal. It is unlikely that Jinnah or the Muslim League will agree to this truncated Pakistan which can never succeed economically or otherwise.

---

all parties in India in accordance with the Cabinet Mission's plan, though there was yet no clear prospect that such a constitution and such authorities would emerge. As for the Indian States, the British Government did not intend to hand over their powers and obligations under parmountcy to any government of British India. For excerpts from it, see *CWMG*, Vol. LXXXVII, Appendix I.

They will thus have to make a choice ultimately between this and joining the Indian Union possibly on special terms. In other words the position of Bengal and Punjab in such an event approximates to that of an Indian State.

Matters will move swiftly now or at any rate after Mountbatten[948] comes. We do not yet know what special directive has been given to Mountbatten by the British Cabinet. Logically this should be to function as a constitutional head only and to allow the Government to act as a Dominion Government. That would mean the Government having a leader. This again would bring matters with the Muslim League to a head.

The Working Committee is meeting on the 5th March and we shall take no other step till then. Our general outlook at present is to approach privately some of the Muslim League leaders and try to induce them to come into the Constituent Assembly. If they refuse to come in, then the question of their remaining in the Interim Government has to be faced afresh. For the moment we are not pressing for their resignation as this would, of course, put an end to all talk of cooperation. But anyhow this matter should be settled one way or the other in the course of the next month.

We have to go ahead now rapidly with the Constituent Assembly. We shall try to work to a time-table which means finishing the constitution-making by the end of the year.

Your advice at this critical moment would help us greatly. But you are too far away for consultation and you refuse to move out of East Bengal. Still if you could convey to us your ideas on the subject, we would be very grateful.

As I have already written to you, the Asian Conference begins on the 23rd March and will last for at least ten days. We are having a very distinguished and representative gathering then from almost

[948] Mountbatten of Burma, First Earl (1900–1979); the last Viceroy of India; Chief of Combined Operations, 1942–3; Supreme Allied Commander, South-East Asia, 1943–6; Viceroy of India, 24 March–15 August 1947; Governor-General of India, August 1947–June 1948; First Sea Lord, 1954–9; assassinated at Mullaghmore in Ireland by the Irish Republican Army.

He arrived in India on 22 March 1947.

all the countries of Asia. If you do not come to it your absence will be keenly felt by all.[949]

Yours,
Jawaharlal

SWJN, *Vol. 2, II Series, pp. 52–4*

## 437. Letter to Jawaharlal Nehru

Kazirkhil, Ramganj PS, Noakhali Dt.
24 February 1947

Chi. Jawaharlal,[950]
Today being silence day I am writing this. But it will be typed for your easy reading.

I have read Attlee's speech. Lest I might embarrass you by an untoward word or phrase I am not saying anything just now.

Evidently I had anticipated practically the whole of it in my speeches here, i.e., if I am interpreting the speech correctly. My interpretation is this:

Independence will be recognised of those parts which desired it and will do without British protection.

The British will remain where they are wanted.

This may lead to Pakistan for those provinces or portions which may want it. No one will be forced one way or the other. The Congress provinces if they are wise will get what they want.

Much will depend upon what the Constituent Assembly will do and what you as the Interim Government are able to do.[951]

If the British Government are and are able to remain sincere the declaration is good. Otherwise it is dangerous.

Now about Sardar Niranjan Singh Gill. He has been to Bihar and has produced a report which somewhat reflects upon the Ministry.[952]

[949] See pp. 477–8.

[950] The superscription and subscription are in Devanagari.

[951] Nehru was Vice-President, Member-in Charge, External Affairs and Commonwealth Relations in the Interim Government.

[952] Srikrishna Sinha had announced on 13 February 1947 the appointment of a Commission of Enquiry to report on the communal disturbances in Bihar. See *CWMG*, Vol. LXXXVI, pp. 251 and 446.

You should see him and his report. It has gone to Suhrawardy and Sinha under my advice. He and Sardar Jiwan Singh[953] have not hit it off. The whole thing is bad. INA[954] seems to have split up. Probably you know all this.

In view of the above report I might have to go to Bihar. God knows. You may show this to friends.

Hope you are well.

Blessings from
Bapu

[PS]
I take it that you have a cable from Durban about orders against Drs Dadoo and Naicker.[955] I trust you have taken prompt action. I have cabled F.M. Smuts.[956]

Bapu

CWMG, *Vol. LXXXVII, pp. 12–13*

[953] Colonel Jiwan Singh of the Indian National Army. Suhrawardy had written to Zaffar Imam of the Bihar Muslim League recommending Gill for work in the state.

[954] The Indian National Army or Azad Hind Fauj was an armed force formed by Indian nationals in South-East Asia during World War II. The aim of the army was to overthrow the British Raj in India with Japanese assistance. Initially composed of Indian prisoners of war captured by Japan in her Malayan campaign and at Singapore, it later drew large numbers of volunteers from the Indian expatriate population in Malaya and Burma. The first INA collapsed in 1942 and was revived under the leadership of Subhas Chandra Bose in 1943 and proclaimed as Arzi-Hukumat-e-Azad-Hind (The Provisional Government of Free India).

[955] It had been reported that the Government of South Africa had refused passports to Yusuf Dadoo and G.M. Naicker and impounded their certificates of identity.

[956] Field Marshal Jan Christiaan Smuts (1870–1950); Prime Minister of South Africa, 1919–24 and 1938–48

## 438. Letter to M.K. Gandhi

New Delhi
28 February 1947

Dear Bapu,

The Working Committee is meeting here soon and all of us were anxious to have you here on this occasion. We considered the question of sending you a joint telegram appealing to you to come. But we decided ultimately not to send it. We felt sure that you would not come at this stage and our telegram would only be an embarrassment.

But though we are not sending the telegram we feel very strongly that your advice during the coming critical weeks is most necessary. It is possible of course for one or two of us to visit you but that is not a satisfactory way of doing things. It is a full discussion among all of us that we would have liked to have. At present it is exceedingly difficult for any of us to leave Delhi even for two or three days. For several to go together would upset work completely. There is the budget in the Assembly, the Committees of the Constituent Assembly, the negotiations with the Princes, the change in Viceroys and so many other things that demand constant attention. So we cannot go away and if you will not come here, how are we to meet?

You have written to me in the letter Sudhir brought about sharing the same bed with Manu.[957] No one who knows you or has any sense of proportion would normally attach any importance to this. I do not know much about this matter and I would hesitate to say anything outside my own province. Sardar has spoken to me briefly about it and so have some others. I confess I have been greatly troubled not at the propriety of any action that you may think fit, for you are the best judge, but rather at the whole set-up. I dislike intensely people talking about these matters. It is impossible for the average person to understand it all and there are plenty of persons who take delight in distorting and misrepresenting

[957] Manu Gandhi (1928–1969); daughter of Jaisukhlal Gandhi and a grandniece of Gandhi who was in constant attendance on him in his last years, and who also participated in his experiments in *brahmacharya*

anything that you may do. Even our friends are greatly disturbed. Foreign correspondents whisper about it. Obviously all this injures the cause which you have at heart. I do not understand why it should be considered necessary to raise such issues which can do no good and may do much harm.[958]

Apart from this I feel that what may be natural and unexceptionable in you will not be so in others. What you do becomes an example to others and your warnings to them will go unheeded.

I would not have written to you about this matter, if you had not yourself mentioned it in your letter and some of your speeches. I feel a little out of my depth and I hate discussing personal and private matters. You will I hope forgive me.

Yours,
Jawaharlal

SWJN, *Vol. 2, II Series, pp. 620–1*

## 439. Letter to Jawaharlal Nehru

20 March 1947

I would like you...[959] to tell me what you can about the Punjab tragedy. I know nothing about it save what is allowed to appear in the Press which I thoroughly distrust. Nor am I in sympathy with what may be termed by the old expression of 'hush hush policy'. It is amazing how the country is adopting almost the very measures which it criticised during the British administration. Of course, I know the reason behind it. It makes no appeal to me.

* * *

I have long intended to write to you asking you about the Working Committee resolution[960] on the possible partition of the Punjab. I

[958] For Gandhi's explication of the concept of brahmacharya, see *CWMG*, Vol. LXXXVIII, pp. 57–9.

[959] Omissions are as in the source.

[960] Passed at its meeting held in New Delhi on 6, 7 and 8 March. The resolution drafted by Nehru, and its final draft amended by Gandhi, read: 'In regard to the proposals, which I presume Lord Ismay is carrying with him London, our Committee are prepared to accept the principle of partition based on self-determination as applied to definitely ascertained areas. This involves the partition of Bengal and Punjab. As you know, we are passionately

would like to know the reason behind it. I have to speak about it. I have done so in the absence of full facts with the greatest caution. Kripalani said in answer to a question in Madras that it was possible that the principle might be applied to Bengal also. I was asked by a Muslim Leaguer of note ... if it was applicable to the Muslim-majority provinces, why it should not be so to a Congress-majority province like Bihar. I think I did not know the reason behind the Working Committee's resolution, nor had I the opportunity. I could only give my own view which was against any partition based on communal grounds and the two-nation theory. Anything was possible by compulsion. But willing consent required an appeal to reason and heart. Compulsion or show of it had no place in voluntariness.

CWMG, *Vol. LXXXVII, pp. 124–5*

## 440. Letter to M.K. Gandhi

New Delhi
25 March 1947

Dear Bapu,
Thank you for your letters. I am very sorry I have not written to you for a considerable time. I have been overwhelmed with work and anxiety and it is not easy to write briefly about complicated matters. This is one of the reasons why I have been wanting you to come here so that we might have long talks. This has become even more urgent now because of the new Viceroy's arrival and impending developments. He is anxious to meet you and has written to you.[961] I do hope therefore that you will come soon and be prepared to stay here for a week or 10 days.

I feel strongly also that you should meet the delegates of the Asian Conference. Most of them are very desirous of meeting you.

---

attached to the idea of a United India, but we have accepted the partition of India in order to avoid conflict and compulsion. In order to give effect to this partition every effort should be made to meet the wishes and interests of the people affected by it.'

This was sent by Nehru to Lord Mountbatten on 1 May 1947. See *SWJN*, Vol. 2, II Series, pp. 106–12. See also pp. 510–5.

[961] Gandhi met Lord Mountbatten on 31 March and had long talks.

They are a very representative lot coming from almost every country of Asia. This is a unique occasion, historic in the full sense of the word, and your absence would be unfortunate. The Conference lasts till 2nd April.

I would suggest your coming here on Saturday next the 29th March if that suits you. Or else on Sunday. Vallabhbhai is also anxious that you should come about this time.

I cannot write to you about events in the Punjab. It is a repetition of the same ghastly story and the same pattern. The newspapers have given fairly full accounts.

About our proposal to divide Punjab, this follows naturally from our previous decisions. These were negative previously but now a time for decision has come and mere passing of resolutions giving expression to our views means little. I feel convinced, and so did most of the members of the Working Committee, that we must press for this immediate division so that reality might be brought into the picture.Indeed this is the only answer to Pakistan as demanded by Jinnah. I found people in Punjab agreeable to this proposal—except Muslims as a rule. For the present it means an administrative decision without any change in law.

I am writing in haste. You will forgive me. But I do hope you will be able to come here soon to discuss all these matters.

Love.

Yours,
Jawaharlal

SWJN, *Vol. 2, II Series, pp. 77–8*

## 441. Letter to Jawaharlal Nehru

18 April 1947

Chi. Jawaharlal,
Who will now sign the cheques concerning the Jallianwala Bagh[962] since Malaviyaji is no more? As the Sardar happens to be there, consult him and let me know.

Blessings from
Bapu

CWMG, *Vol. LXXXVII, p. 302*

[962] Jallianwalan Bagh Memorial Trust

## 442. Letter to M.K. Gandhi

New Delhi
23 April 1947

Dear Bapu,

I have your note about the Jallianwala Bagh accounts. I have spoken to Sardar. There will be no difficulty about arranging for the signing of cheques. But we do not know who the trustees are. I suggested that Mukherji, the Secretary of the Jallianwala Fund, might come here with the papers when the Working Committee meets and then we can fix this up. I am having a letter sent to him.

You know that the Congress Working Committee is meeting here on the 1st May. I should very much like you to be here about that time. The first week of May is likely to see the formulation of Mountbatten's scheme[963] for the future. This is obviously important and will shape our future. His intention is to have a rough framework ready by then—to discuss this in detail and then finalise it after reference to the British Government. He expects to get through all these processes by the 3rd week of May. According to this programme, the first week of May will be of considerable importance and all of us would like you to be near us for advice and guidance. I hope therefore that you will be able to come here then. You need not come on the 1st or even 2nd, though if you can do so it will be preferable. But I do hope you can be here by the 3rd the latest.

Kripalani is not here and has gone to Jaipur. I am sure he would like you to be here at the time of the Working Committee. I spoke to Vallabhbhai and he agreed with me that you should come.

I hope you are keeping well.

Yours,
Jawaharlal

SWJN, *Vol. 3, II Series, pp. 498–9*

[963] For the draft of which, see *The Transfer of Power*, and for the British Government's official statement of 3 June 1947, see *CWMG*, Vol. LXXXVIII, pp. 474–8.

## 443. Telegram to Jawaharlal Nehru

Calcutta
11 May 1947

Pandit Nehru
Care of His Excellency
Simla
Your wire.[964] Hope reach Delhi sixteenth morning. Have you seen my special letter?[965] Rajkumari knows.

Bapu

CWMG, *Vol. LXXXVII, p. 447*

[964] Requesting Gandhi's presence at the forthcoming meeting of the Congress Working Committee. On 10 May, the Viceroy had announced that a conference of the Congress, the Muslim League and Sikh leaders would be held on 17 May to announce the plan of the British Government for transferring power to Indian hands. The leaders invited were: Jawaharlal Nehru, Vallabhbhai Patel, M.A. Jinnah, Liaquat Ali Khan and Sardar Baldev Singh.

[965] To the Viceroy, Lord Mountbatten, dated 8 May 1947. The points stressed by Gandhi in main were as follows: '...the Interim Government should be composed either of Congressmen or those whose names the Congress chooses or of Muslim League men or those whom the League chooses... referendum at this stage in the Frontier (or any Province for that matter) is a dangerous thing in itself ... if a division is at all to be countenanced.... the partition of the Punjab and Bengal is wrong in every case and a needless irritant for the League. This as well as all innovation can come after the British withdrawal, not before, except always for mutual agreement.... Non-partition of the Punjab and the Bengal does not mean that the minorities in these Provinces are to be neglected. ... If popular Governments cannot placate them, the Government should during the interregnum actively interfere.' See *CWMG*, Vol. LXXXVII, pp. 434–8.

## 444. Telegram to M.K. Gandhi

New Delhi
12 May 1947

Mahatma Gandhi
Sodepur
Owing other developments Working Committee meeting postponed Saturday May thirtyfirst. However would like you come here some days earlier for consultation.

Jawaharlal
Kripalani

SWJN, *Vol. 2, II Series, p. 146*

## 445. Letter to M.K. Gandhi

New Delhi
12 May 1947

Dear Bapu,
Owing to various developments the Working Committee has now been fixed for May 31st. Mountbatten intends to see some of us plus Jinnah & c[o]. on June 2nd presumably to place before us some tentative proposals of the British Government.

As you know the situation is extraordinarily delicate and complicated and we stand on the verge of major conflicts in north India and possibly Bengal. In these circumstances we have to give the most earnest consideration to it. Your presence is therefore essential and I hope you will be able to come here as early as is convenient to you. The more time we have the better. I hope you will arrive here by the 25th. If you will be able to come here as early as is convenient to you. [*sic*] The more the WC meets on the 31st May its members will anyhow be here when you come.

I would like you to invite Jayaprakash to Delhi also about that time so that we can discuss Congress matters with him. He is likely to be in Patna soon.

Yours,
Jawaharlal

SWJN, *Vol. 2, II Series, pp. 145–6*

## 446. Letter to M.K. Gandhi

17 York Road, New Delhi
16 May 1947

Dear Bapu,

You must be following the rapid developments taking place here. Mountbatten is going to London on Sunday next[966] and is likely to be away for nearly 2 weeks. I understand you intend arriving here on the 25th. Vallabhbhai and I feel that it would be a very good thing if you could come to Mussoorie for a few days before coming to Delhi. This would suit us and it would also no doubt give you a few days of rest. Nothing much is likely to happen in Delhi till the Viceroy returns.

I was in any event thinking of going to Mussoorie for 3 or 4 days for a change and to see Indu and her children. I intend going on the 20th morning. I shall return to meet you here. But if you could come to Mussoorie I could stay on a little longer and have leisurely talks with you then. We could come down to Delhi just when it suits you.

Vallabhbhai is also going to Mussoorie.

I do hope you will be able to come to Mussoorie.

Yours,
Jawaharlal

MKG Papers, Pyarelal Collection, *NMML*

## 447. Letter to Jawaharlal Nehru

Patna
17 May 1947

Chi. Jawaharlal,

Your note. I must deny myself the pleasure of going to Mussoorie. I am quite fixed up here and can easily delay coming to Delhi till 31st May or even a day later.

[966] To secure the British Cabinet's approval of the revised draft announcement

Give my love to all at Mussoorie and take full rest whilst you can.

Blessings from
Bapu

CWMG, *Vol. LXXXVII, p. 486*

## 448. Letter to M.K. Gandhi

New Delhi
19 May 1947

Dear Bapu,
I am so sorry you cannot come to Mussoorie. I am leaving tomorrow morning and expect to return on Sunday 25th night or at the latest on Monday 26th morning. I have to be here on Monday anyhow.

I hope you will be able to reach here on Monday. If not then on Tuesday morning.

I enclose some papers received from Dr Julian Huxley[967] of the UNESCO. He mentions a letter for you but he did not actually send it. But the other papers will make it clear what he wants from you.[968]

Yours,
Jawaharlal

[PS]
I enclose a copy of a letter received from Rangoon asking for a message from you for the Burmese Constituent Assembly.

SWJN, *Vol. 3, II Series, p. 500*

[967] Julian Sorell Huxley (1887–1975); biologist and Fellow of the Royal Society; Executive Secretary, UNESCO Preparatory Commission, 1946; Director-General, UNESCO, 1946–8; author of several books including *Man and the Modern World* (1947) and *Soviet Genetics and World Science* (1949)

[968] Gandhi's message printed in the *United Nations Weekly Bulletin* of 17 October 1947 read: 'I have learned from my illiterate, but wise, mother that all rights to be deserved and preserved came from a duty well done.

'The very right to live accrues to us only when we do the duty of the citizenship of the world. From this one fundamental statement perhaps it is easy enough to define the duties of man and woman and correlate every right to some corresponding duty to be first performed. Every other right can be shown to be usurpation hardly worth fighting for.'

## 449. Letter to Jawaharlal Nehru

7 June 1947

I had a long conversation with His Excellency. ...[969] The more I see His Excellency the more I feel that he is sincere. But it is quite possible to damage him if the surrounding atmosphere of which the Indian element is the author overwhelms him, as it may well do any of us.

All the points we discussed at the Working Committee meeting yesterday were touched upon by me and I carried with me the impression that he really appreciated them.

To be wholly truthful requires the highest form of bravery and therefore of nonviolence.

CWMG, *Vol. LXXXVIII, p. 94*

## 450. Letter to Jawaharlal Nehru

7 June 1947

The oftener we met the more convinced I am becoming that the gulf between us in the thought world is deeper than I had feared. He (the Sardar) says that you are largely responsible for the present situation.[970] He is of the opinion that Badshah Khan's ...[971] influence

[969] Omission as in the source

Gandhi met the Viceroy on 6 June 1947 at 4.30 p.m. It appears that the following points were written down by Gandhi and discussed at the Working Committee meeting: '1. Frontier Province—postponement of referendum before Pakistan scheme disclosed, otherwise bloodshed is a certainty. Therefore the Ministry [the Congress Ministry in NWFP headed by Dr Khan Saheb] may make a statement and resign. 2. There must be no coalition Ministry but only the Congress. You may have another Pakistan Ministry, provisional. 3. You should ask Ji[nnah] at this stage to talk to Congressmen and settle all other matters and work as friends excelling one another in well doing. 4. Agreements between the States that each will have identical status and treaty with the British.' See *CWMG*, Vol. LXXXVIII, p. 94.

For Lord Mountbatten's note on the interview with Gandhi, ibid., Appendix X.

[970] Vallabhbhai Patel had had an hour's talk with Gandhi on the night of 6 June.

[971] Omissions are as in the source.

is on the wane. Badshah Khan has not left any such impression on me. Whatever he is today, he was always. There is undoubtedly more steadiness today than before. I also feel that Dr Khan Saheb and his colleagues would be nowhere without the Badshah. He alone counts in so far as the Congress influence is concerned.

If the Qaid-e-Azam[972] does not go to the Frontier and does not woo the Badshah, his brother and his other colleagues, the Frontier Ministry should resign and so also the Parliamentary majority on the sole ground that a referendum at this moment must lead to bloodshed and probably, if not certainly, to a lasting blood-feud, which they should avoid in so far as it is humanly possible. Amrit (Rajkumari Amrit Kaur) tells me that you think to the contrary. You think the referendum should take place now... You are also of opinion that a referendum[973] will not cause bloodshed, indeed that my proposal would be more likely to cause it. I do not share this view. I had told the Badshah that if I do not carry you with me, I shall retire at least from the Frontier consultation and let you guide him. After all, was it not you who brought him to me? You will now decide and tell me.

CWMG, *Vol. LXXXVIII, pp. 94–5*

[972] Jinnah, known as Qaid-e-Azam in the League circles. The first time that Gandhi used the appellation was in a letter to Jinnah dated 16 January 1940.

[973] On the North West Frontier Province

In acting on the clause of the plan for partition Congress was concerned about the North West Frontier Province. Abdul Ghaffar Khan asked if the plebiscite in the NWFP could include the third alternative of independence. Gandhi took Ghaffar Khan to meet Mountbatten who refused to consider the suggestion, pointing out that Nehru himself had strongly objected to the grant of independence to any province. Out of the electorate of 5,72,798, the voting went in favour of Pakistan by a hairline majority of 2,874 votes. For Nehru's note of 8 June 1947 on the position in the NWFP, see *SWJN*, Vol. 3, II Series, pp. 273–9.

## 451. Letter to M.K. Gandhi

9 June 1947

Dear Bapu,

I enclose 2 copies of a note on the Frontier. You will deal with it as you think best. If it is to be sent to Badshah Khan, a messenger will have to take it. In any event Badshah Khan will I hope come here next week.

Yours,
Jawaharlal

SWJN, *Vol. 3, II Series, p. 279*

## 452. Draft of Letter to Jawaharlal Nehru

[9 June 1947][974]

Chi. Jawaharlal,[975]

I have your note which I have read most carefully. If I shared your premises, I should whole-heartedly agree with you.

I am sending your note by messenger to the Badshah with my covering letter[976] of which I enclose a copy herewith.

The more I contemplate the differences in outlook and opinion between the members of the WC and me, [the more] I feel that my presence is unnecessary even if it is not detrimental to the cause we all have at heart. May I not go back to Bihar in two or three days?

Would it be wrong if you insisted that referendum would be wrong without the presentation of the picture of Pakistan?[977]

CWMG, *Vol. LXXXVIII, p. 113*

[974] Square brackets as in the source

[975] The superscription in Devanagari is not in Gandhi's hand.

[976] Wherein Gandhi wrote: 'Here is a note from Jawaharlal. It is the result of a difference of opinion between him and me. In the circumstances I must not guide you. He has put forth his argument as usual in his very able manner. Now you have to act as you think best. His suggestion that you should come to Delhi and discuss the situation before taking any final decision is worthy of consideration.'

[977] This sentence is not in Gandhi's hand. In his letter dated 10/11 June 1947 to the Viceroy, Gandhi wrote, 'Whether he favours the idea or not, Qaid-e-Azam should be asked to give a fair picture of the Pakistan scheme before the simple Pathan mind is asked to make its choice of Hindustan or Pakistan.' For details, see *CWMG*, Vol. LXXXVIII, pp. 126–8.

## 453. Letter to M.K. Gandhi

30 June 1947

Dear Bapu,

You must have got the Viceroy's letter inviting you to come at 10 a.m. tomorrow. He has also agreed to allow us to bring Alladi Krishnaswamy,[978] Gopalaswamy[979] and K.M. Munshi. I had mentioned these names rather casually in my letter to him as some of the people we would like to consult. I had not mentioned the names of our colleagues in the Cabinet as I took them for granted. Now I have written to him that he should permit me to consult them later and should give me a copy of the draft bill to show them. It is very unfair to leave them out of the picture in this vital matter.

I do not know if you can come at 10 tomorrow. This will be inconvenient for you. We are likely to be there for 2 hours or more. If it is more convenient for you, you could come later, say at 11 or after.

I enclose copies of letters I am sending to Badshah Khan and Khan Sahib in a separate envelope.[980]

Yours affectionately,
Jawaharlal

SWJN, *Vol. 3, II Series, p. 286*

[978] Diwan Bahadur Sir Alladi Krishnaswamy Iyer (1883–1953); lawyer; Member, Constituent Assembly

[979] N. Gopalaswamy Ayyangar (1882–1953); Member, Legislative Assembly, 1927; Chief Minister, Kashmir, 1937–43; Union Minister without Portfolio, 1947–8; for Railway and Transport, 1950–2; for Defence, 1952–3

[980] Nehru, at Gandhi's suggestion, had written to Badshah Khan on 30 June 1947, saying: 'A serious situation has arisen in Afghanistan in regard to the Frontier Province.... Afghan radio and Press were carrying on a campaign from India with a view, no doubt, to its incorporation in Afghanistan. To begin with this was not apparently official. But lately it has become official and various demands are made to us and to the British Government.' See *SWJN*, Vol. 3, II Series, pp. 287–91.

## 454. Letter to Jawaharlal Nehru

New Delhi
30 June 1947

Chi. Jawahar,[981]
Your letter. I have the invitation. I shall be at the Viceroy's house at 10 a.m. tomorrow. You or Vallabhbhai can fetch me, if that will save petrol.

Blessings from
Bapu

[PS]
I spoke at the meeting[982] about Badshah Khan.

CWMG, *Vol. LXXXVIII, p. 240*

## 455. Letter to Jawaharlal Nehru

24 July 1947

Chi. Jawaharlal,[983]
I did not say anything yesterday about the Maulana Saheb. But my objection stands. His retiring from the cabinet should not affect our connection with him. There are many positions which he can occupy in public life without any harm to any cause. Sardar is decidedly against his membership in the cabinet and so is Rajkumari. Your cabinet must be strong and effective at the present juncture. It should not be difficult to name another Muslim for the cabinet.

I have destroyed the two copies you sent me yesterday.

Blessings from
Bapu

CWMG, *Vol. LXXXVIII, p. 408*

[981] The superscription and subscription are in Devanagari.

[982] On 30 June. Referring to Badshah Khan's demand for Pakhtoonistan at a prayer meeting, Gandhi had observed that he saw no objection to it. He had further said, 'A serious charge levelled against Badshah Khan is that he is playing into the hands of Afghanistan. ... He will never allow the Frontier Province to be absorbed into Afghanistan.' See also *CWMG*, Vol. LXXXVIII, pp. 248–9.

[983] The superscription and subscription are in Devanagari.

## 456. Letter to M.K. Gandhi

24 July 1947

Dear Bapu,

Received your letter. It is always our duty to pay full attention to your views. But I think that if the Maulana goes out it would harm us much.[984] I fully agree with you that we should take such persons as can do the best possible work. We try to follow this principle. But whether in the Congress or in the Provincial Government it is not acted upon much. So many other factors are taken into consideration on the basis of which decisions are taken. About this matter we all shall talk with you later.

Yours,
Jawaharlal

SWJN, *Vol. 3, II Series, pp. 427–8*

## 457. Letter to M.K. Gandhi

28 July 1947

Dear Bapu,

I have seen the Viceroy's letter.[985] What am I to say about it? I wrote to you this morning that I would not trouble you any more about your programme. That is entirely for you to judge.

I am a little tired of hearing what Pandit Kak[986] feels or thinks. I am not concerned with it. Indeed I think that it would be normally right to do the opposite of what he advises. For many months—ever

[984] The reference is to Abul Kalam Azad's retiring from the Cabinet.

[985] Lord Mountbatten in his letter of 28 July to Gandhi had written that Kak had told him that the Kashmir Government was 'very anxious not to have the visit from a political leader ...' and that although he feared even a visit from Gandhi might provoke violence, the fact that the he was known to preach nonviolence would reduce the risk in Gandhi's case to a greater extent than if Pandit Nehru went, and had requested the Viceroy to inform Gandhi that if he thought the visit was imperative, then his own visit was preferable to Nehru's. Susequently, it was Gandhi who visited Kashmir from 1–5 August 1947.

[986] Ramchandra Kak, an archaeologist and a librarian in a Government college in Kashmir; appointed Minister in waiting to Maharaja Hari Singh; Prime Minister of the State in 1945

since Mountbatten came--this question of your going or mine has been discussed and postponed. I have had enough of this business. This is not my way of doing anything. I hardly remember anything that has exasperated me quite so much as this affair.

It is for you to judge what you should do. Meanwhile I shall go ahead with my plans. As between visiting Kashmir when my people need me there and being Prime Minister, I prefer the former.

Yours,
Jawaharlal

SWJN, *Vol. 3, II Series, p. 265*

## 458. Letter to M.K. Gandhi

28 July 1947

Dear Bapu,
Thank you for your letter. I have also written[987] to the Viceroy informing him that I propose to go to Kashmir about the 4th August for 4 or 5 days. I have not mentioned your name in this connection.

I have nothing to suggest about your Punjab programme or later.

I agree that the Viceroy should move to a smaller house.[988] The only present difficulty is one of finding suitable accommodation and making arrangements for changing over when we are so busy.

Yours,
Jawaharlal

I am asking Badshah Khan to see me today at my house at 2.30.

SWJN, *Vol. 3, II Series, p. 266*

[987] On 27 July 1947. See *SWJN*, Vol. 3, II Series, pp. 264–5.

[988] Writing to Lord Mountbatten on this day, Gandhi said, 'May I say I deeply appreciated your wish to go to an unpretentious house as the chosen Governor-General of the millions of the half-famished villagers of the nation. I hope it will be possible to carry out the wish.'

## 459. Note on Kashmir Visit[989]

6 August 1947

No public prayer was held on the day of arrival but I appeared before them twice or thrice and said that I could not make any public speech, not because there was any prohibition but because I had promised to myself that if I was to make my visit devoid of political significance in so far as it was possible, I must not address public meetings. ...[990] The Prime Minister ... told me that he had no objection whatsoever to public prayers ... Consequently, public prayers were held during the two days following in Srinagar and the third in Jammu.

During the two interviews with the Prime Minister I told him about his unpopularity among the people. ... He wrote to the Maharaja ... that on a sign from him he would gladly resign... The Maharaja had sent me a message... that the Maharaja and the Maharani were anxious to see me.[991] I met them.... The heir-apparent[992] with his leg in plaster was also present ... Both admitted that with the lapse of British Paramountcy the true Paramountcy of the people of Kashmir would commence. However much they might wish to join the Union, they would have to make the choice in accordance with the wishes of the people. How they could be determined was not discussed at that interview...

Bakshi (Ghulam Mohammad)[993] was most sanguine that the result of the free vote of the people, whether on the adult franchise

[989] This was sent by Gandhi to Nehru 'to be shared with Vallabhbhai Patel'.

[990] Omissions are as in the source.

[991] Gandhi had met Maharaja Hari Singh on 3 August 1947.

[992] Yuvaraj Karan Singh (b. 1931); heir-apparent to the throne of Jammu and Kashmir; was just eighteen in 1949 when appointed Regent; for the next eighteen years served the State as Regent, Sadar-i-Riyasat and Governor; Minister for Tourism and Civil Aviation, Government of India, 1967; for Health and Family Planning, 1973; for Education and Culture, 1979; Ambassador, USA, 1989-90, Chairman, Indian Council for Cultural Relations, 2005

[993] Bakshi Gulam Mohammad (1919-1971); Member, Kashmir National Conference; Member, Jammu and Kashmir Assembly, 1951-67; acting President of the Kashmir National Conference; Deputy Prime Minister, Kashmir, after Independence; Prime Minister, Jammu and Kashmir, 1953-63; Member, Lok Sabha, 1967-71

or on the existing register, would be in favour of Kashmir joining the Union provided of course that Sheikh Abdullah and his co-prisoners were released, all bans were removed and the present Prime Minister was not in power.[994] Probably he echoed the general sentiment. I studied the Amritsar treaty[995] properly called 'sale deed'. I presume it lapses on the 15th instant. To whom does the State revert? Does it not go to the people?

CWMG, *Vol. LXXXIX, pp. 7–8*

## 460. Telegram to M.K. Gandhi

21 August 1947

May I offer you my respectful congratulations on the wonderful change in Calcutta.[996] Situation in Punjab still very grave though slowly improving.[997] We are grappling with it with all

[994] Kashmir joined the Indian Union on 27 October 1947.

[995] Signed on 16 March 1846. Based on the provisions of the treaty the British Government transferred and made over for ever in independent possession to 'Maharaja Gulb Singh Dogra and his male heirs, all the hilly or mountainous country with its dependencies situated eastward of the River Indus and the westward of the River Ravi including Chamba and excluding Lahul, being part of the territories ceded to the British Government by the Lahore State according to the provisions of Article IV of the Treaty of Lahore dated 9th March, 1846.' Gulab Singh was to pay 75,00,000 Nanak Shahi rupees (the ruling currency of Punjab) to the British Government as the price for the cessation along with other annual tributes. The Treaty of Amritsar marked the beginning of Dogra rule in Kashmir.

[996] Gandhi who arrived in Calcutta on 9 August 1947 was pressed by the Muslim leaders including Suhrawardy, ex-Prime Minister of Bengal, to stay and prevent the outbreak of communal riots. On 13 August 1947, he moved with Suhrawardy to a house in an area considered unsafe for the Muslims. He preached peace in his prayer meetings and walked with Suhrawardy through streets tense with religious frenzy. Violence subsided wherever they went. Thousands of Muslims and Hindus embraced one another with cries of 'Long live Mahatma Gandhi' and 'Long live Hindu-Muslim unity'. After 14 August, no disturbances were reported in Calcutta.

[997] The Radcliffe Award, announced on 17 August 1947, gave to East Punjab control over three of the five rivers of the Beas, the Sutlej and the upper waters of the Ravi. About thirty-eight per cent of the area and forty-five percent of the population were assigned to it. The non-Muslims of the Punjab, especially the Sikhs, bitterly resented the loss of Lahore and the canal colonies

our might and hope to succeed. Punjab will require your healing presence.

SWJN, *Vol. 4, II Series, pp. 11–12*

## 461. Letter to Jawaharlal Nehru

Calcutta
22 August 1947

Chi. Jawaharlal,
I have your wire. The work here is proceeding well. Yes, I must go to Noakhali. Some days are to be given to Bihar. Under the circumstances, when can I go to the Punjab? Nevertheless, you must tell me when I have to go. No time to write more. I wanted to write in English but the pen went off into Hindustani. See the enclosed; is there any truth in it?[998]

Blessings from
Bapu

CWMG, *Vol. LXXXIX, p. 75* (Original in Hindi)

## 462. Letter to M.K. Gandhi

New Delhi
22 August 1947

Dear Bapu,
Thank you for your letter. I do not ask you to go to the Punjab immediately. We must face the situation now. Later I might request you to go there.

---

of Sheikhpura, Lyallpur and Montgomery, though Amritsar was given to India. As countless numbers of Sikhs from the West Punjab began a mass trek eastwards, their fellow Sikhs in the East, driven by an overwhelming sense of loss and betrayal, had unleashed violence.

Riots of an unprecedented nature had broken out in Jallunder and Amritsar in early August and had continued unabated.

[998] The press cutting from *The Bombay Chronicle* of 20 August 1947 alleged that Vijayalakshmi Pandit wished to furnish her house in Moscow with Swedish furniture estimated to cost £25,000 and Maulana Azad desired to furnish his official residence at a cost of Rs 36,000. It was said further that a proposal from Asaf Ali (India's Ambassador to the United States) for buying new crockery and cutlery had been rejected. See the following item for Nehru's explanation.

The situation there during the last three or four days has been bad, very bad. My visit there on the 17th and 18th produced good results in Amritsar and, to some extent, in Lahore.[999] Amritsar, both the city and villages, has been fairly quiet. But just about that time the southern districts, which had been free from any major trouble, blew up unexpectedly so far as we were concerned. The districts of Hoshiarpur and Jullundur especially have witnessed some horrible deeds and large-scale massacres of Muslims. It is quite impossible to form any estimate of people killed. I imagine, however, that during the last month the number killed in eastern Punjab might amount to 7 or 8 thousand. These figures may be completely wrong as they are guess-work.

In western Punjab probably the number of those killed is much less, may be half the other figure. This, of course, applies to recent weeks only and not to the previous Rawalpindi and Multan killings. There has been far more arson and looting in western Punjab than in eastern.

All this killing business has reached a stage of complete madness, and vast populations are deserting their habitations and trekking to the west or to the east. A large number had left western Punjab in previous months, as you know. Now the process is repeated on both sides.

The present trouble started about thee weeks ago in Amritsar rural areas. The Sikhs were the aggressors. Within a week Lahore retaliated, the Muslims being the aggressors. Since then it has spread on both sides, perhaps more so in eastern Punjab where well-armed bands, chiefly Sikh, partly Hindu, had been roaming about and attacking predominantly Muslim villages. Normally Muslims are safe in a village where they are in a minority. Their neighbours do not attack them. Armed bands go specially to Muslim majority villages in eastern Punjab. Something of this kind happens in western Punjab too, but our information is limited.

[999] Prime Ministers of India and Pakistan, Jawaharlal Nehru and Liaquat Ali Khan, issued a joint statement after their visit to Lahore and Amritsar. For the text, see *SWJN*, Vol. II Series, pp. 5–6.

It appears that most of the petty Government officials join in this business, including policemen. Sometimes soldiers also. The whole thing is revolting in the extreme.

Dr Zakir Husain[1000] tried to go to Kashmir for a holiday three days ago. The train service was not running properly and he had to get down in Jullundur. At the station itself he narrowly escaped being killed by an armed band and some Indian soldiers standing by merely looked on. Ultimately a Sikh captain in the army rescued him at some risk to himself. Zakir Husain returned this morning, safe and unhurt, but minus all his belongings and money. I rather hesitate to write to you about all this as I do not wish to add to your worries. But I think that you should know what is happening. I have no doubt that we shall put an end to this business within the next few days, at any rate, so far as major events are concerned. But what a terrible legacy! The Punjab will be a ruined province, both west and east, and vast numbers of human beings will be destitute.

At present there is no doubt that the Muslim League leaders as well as Master Tara Singh[1001] and Giani Kartar Singh[1002] are trying to stop the slaughter and arson, having previously lighted the fuse.[1003] I am going to Jullundur on Sunday morning.

The Press message you have sent is largely untrue or greatly exaggerated. So far as Maulana Azad is concerned, no request has been made for any grant for furniture. The question of furnishing his new house did arise. When an estimate was made by some firm, he said it was excessive and rejected it.

[1000] (1897–1967); founded Jamia Millia Islamia, National Muslim University, Delhi, with a group of students in 1920; headed the Aligarh Muslim University, 1927–48; Vice-Chancellor, AMU, 1948–56; Governor, Bihar, 1957–62; Vice-President, India, 1962–7; President, India, 1967–9

[1001] (1885–1967); Sikh leader of Punjab; supporter after 1947 of the 'Panjabi Suba'

[1002] (1905–1974); Member, Punjab Legislative Assembly, 1937, 1946 and 1957; General Secretary for many years and President, Akali Dal, 1947

[1003] Tara Singh toured the East Punjab in military transport, appealing to the Sikhs to refrain from violence.

About Asaf Ali,[1004] there has been no special demand for any large sum. Some petty demands come from time to time. As for Sarup,[1005] she is having an exceedingly difficult time in Moscow where apparently nothing is obtainable and everything is frightfully expensive. She intended giving a small party to the diplomats on August 15th. She wanted to invite about 200 persons. The estimate for this party came to 100,000 roubles which means about Rs 36,000. Naturally she gave up the idea. Living in Moscow, for foreigners at least, is quite astonishingly expensive, especially in a hotel which is very second rate. She hopes to move to a house fairly soon. She has been very fortunate in getting a house, and this is supposed to be a very rare privilege which the Soviet Government has accorded to her. Normally ambassadors do not get houses for a year or so. This house, which will function as the Embassy, has to be furnished both for the Embassy offices and for living purposes. The equipment and furniture are not obtainable in Moscow except at very high prices indeed. Normally, therefore, foreign Embassies buy their furniture, etc., from Stockholm which is relatively near. Being a stranger there she consulted the Russians, of course, as well as the Chinese Ambassador who is the doyen of the diplomatic corps. She made it clear that she wanted to do things as simply as possible but tastefully, of course. She was advised that she should get most of the things she wanted in the shape of office equipment and furniture from Stockholm. She was further told that a certain standard has to be kept up in the Embassy, or else the Russians would consider it as a mark of disrespect. She decided, therefore, to go herself to Stockholm to have a look round. She hasn't gone thus far. The estimate prepared by her staff in consultation with people there, for furniture and equipment of the Embassy, was for £20,000/-. The pound, having fallen in value, doesn't buy as much as it used to. We have suggested to her to reduce this sum fairly considerably. As a matter of fact I knew nothing about this till yesterday. Some of my office people were

[1004] Who had been appointed Ambassador to the United States of America on 6 December 1946

[1005] Vijayalakshmi Pandit, who had been appointed Ambassador to the Union of Soviet Socialist Republic on 25 June 1947 dealing with the matter. We made enquiries here from various Embassies and legations who had experience of conditions in Russia and they all told us that the furnishing of a whole building for office and living purposes was a very expensive affair.

In view of circumstances we have cut down our expenditure on the expansion of foreign missions very greatly. Indeed we have stopped expansion. We couldn't very well leave out Russia as Moscow is highly important today, the other two important places being London and Washington. Both the latter places are on a much bigger scale than Moscow. The only other places we are thinking of at present are Iran and Egypt and they have a very special importance for particular reasons.

As you know, Chandralekha has gone with Sarup. I suggested to her to do some regular work and to function as a kind of Public Relations Officer. This is entirely honorary work and she is not paid for it. I mention this as some reference has been made to it in the Press.[1006]

Yours,
Jawaharlal

SWJN, *Vol. 4, II Series, pp. 14–16*

## 463. Letter to Jawaharlal Nehru

24 August 1947

Punjabis in Calcutta have been pressing me to go to the Punjab at once. They tell me a terrible story. Thousands have been killed. A few thousand girls have been kindnapped! Hindus cannot live in the Pakistan area, nor Muslims in the other portion. Add to this the information that the two wings of the army took sides and worked havoc! Can any of this be true?

When do you think I should go to the Punjab if at all? I have still work in Calcutta, then in Noakhali and Bihar. But everything can be laid aside to go to the Punjab if it is proved to be necessary.

CWMG, *Vol. LXXXIX, p. 83*

[1006] The *Hindustan Times* of 12 August 1947 had carried a Reuter report from Moscow of Chandralekha Pandit's appointment.

## 464. Letter to M.K. Gandhi

New Delhi
25 August 1947

Dear Bapu,
I have received your letter of the 24th. Evidently this was written before you received my last letter. I returned this morning from the Punjab after a short visit.

In my last letter I gave you some idea of conditions in the Punjab. The second visit[1007] has depressed me even more. During the past year we have had a pretty full dose of horror and brutality and sadistic violence in Noakhali, Bihar, Rawalpindi, Hazara, etc. The new phase in the Punjab, which might be said to have started about a month ago and to have come to a crisis in the second week of August, has, I think, on the whole surpassed in horror its predecessors. The results also are likely to be far more far-reaching. This is, of course, due to a combination of circumstances among which is the partition of the Punjab and the establishment of Pakistan.[1008] Normally even after the worst riots most people stick to their homes. Now with the coming of Pakistan the urge to get out of it has added to the normal urge to escape from a dangerous zone. On both sides of the border in the Punjab people are affected in this way and mass migrations are taking place on a vast scale. These are largely spontaneous. Inevitably this is resulting and will result in misery for hundreds of thousands of people. It will mean also a tremendous burden on all governments concerned, provincial and central, on both sides.

In my last letter I gave you some kind of an estimate of deaths. It is just impossible to approach accuracy. But there is no doubt that mass massacres have taken place in the most cruel manner in cities and rural areas alike. I imagine that during these last three weeks more people have been killed (Muslims) in eastern Punjab than in western Punjab (Hindus and Sikhs). The Muslims of Amritsar district, that is the survivors, told me that 50,000 of them had perished in the district. This is certainly wild exaggeration. But we should not be surprised if anything up to 10,000 were killed in

[1007] On 24 August 1947
[1008] See also *fn.* 997

eastern Punjab. On the other side the figure might be somewhat lower. We really do not know. There has been widespread killing on both sides and large numbers of refugees have been massacred. In eastern Punjab probably the Akali Sikhs have indulged in killing more than anyone else.

Worse than the killing have been the horrible outrages on women on both sides.

At the present moment major killings have stopped. But this continues in a small way in many places.

It is said and rightly that Lahore and Amritsar are quiet. The fact is that there are not many people left there to be killed. That is to say that Lahore has become almost entirely a Muslim city and Amritsar a Hindu-Sikh city. Not more than 10% of the original Hindu-Sikh population remains in Lahore and perhaps even less than 10% of the original Muslims are now in Amritsar. Large numbers of these people are in refugee camps.

It is not much good my giving you any details. The present problem is to put an end completely to this business of killing and arson and to look after the refugees who are pouring in and out. Arrangements in East Punjab are highly unsatisfactory partly because the government there is still in a formative stage and hardly functions. We are sending immediately Sri Prakasa, our High Commissioner in Pakistan, with a staff to Lahore, to get in touch with all the refugee camps there and help in evacuation and transport. We have also sent a number of other persons to western Punjab to help in this business. In eastern Punjab we are thinking of the Central Government taking charge of the refugees. The Provincial Government is not capable of looking after them.

I have little doubt that the Pakistan High Command is desirous of establishing peace in the Punjab. They are a new state and cannot afford long continuing troubles which sap their strength and ruin their economy. Also they are rather afraid of developments in the Frontier and do not want to get entangled in the Punjab.[1009] They

[1009] The Frontier Province had voted by a narrow majority to join Pakistan and when the Muslim League took over on 15 August, the Khan brothers were arrested, their supporters were hunted down and the influence of the Khudai Khidmatgars was almost wholly broken.

are trying, therefore, in their own way, to stop this lawlessness. But more and more, both in the East and West Punjab, habitually lawless elements are coming to the front and they are not prepared to listen to the leaders. There are internal conflicts also in both Provinces. In western Punjab there is conflict between Mamdot,[1010] the Prime Minister, and Feroz Khan Noon.[1011] Noon appears to be encouraging the wilder elements in the League. In eastern Punjab, there is a good deal of stress and strain between the Sikhs and the Hindus. The Akalis, or some of them, do not hesitate to talk in terms of establishing a Sikh State as a result of this turmoil. Their logic is not very good but there is little doubt that many of them have vague hopes that something advantageous to them might happen if trouble continued. Some of these think that they can force India to go to war with Pakistan. In such a war they imagine that Pakistan is bound to be defeated and then Sikhistan will emerge.

Master Tara Singh and Giani Kartar Singh, however, have been trying to get peace restored. Their influence does not seem to go as far as many people imagined.[1012] The wilder elements among the Akalis have joined hands with some of the RSS[1013] people.

[1010] Iftikhar Hussain Khan, Nawab of Mamdot (1906–1969); Pashtun leader; President, Punjab Muslim League, 1943; Prime Minister, East Pakistan, 1947–9

[1011] Sir Feroz Khan Noon Malik (1893–1970); Defence Member, Viceroy's Executive Council, from 1923; High Commissioner of India to the United Kingdom, 1936–41; Chief Minister, Punjab Province, Pakistan, 1953–6; Prime Minister, 1957–8

There was political rivalry between Feroz Khan Noon and the Nawab of Mamdot. Both contested for leadership of the Muslim League Party in the Punjab Assembly. But Noon, at the time of the election on 5 August 1947, withdrew his name as he was not supported by Jinnah.

[1012] When a vast column of Muslims was about to pass through Amritsar, Indian Army officers tried to get Master Tara Singh to guarantee the safety of the city as the city was full of agitated Sikh refugees from the West. As he could give no such assurance, the column was diverted along another canal road.

[1013] Rashtriya Swayam Sevak Sangh, a volunteer organization founded at Nagpur in September 1925 by Keshav Baliram Hedgewar, for the declared purpose of preservation of Hindu roots in the cultural life of India

An incident, which is symptomatic, occurred two days ago in Amritsar. The Sikhs attacked a Hindu village and are said to have killed some Hindus and raped some Hindu women.

The situation in the Punjab raises a variety of difficult problems. We are dealing with them to the best of our ability. I hope to go back to the Punjab in another three or four days and intend staying some days there.

As for your going there, it is exceedingly difficult for me to advise. This morning, at a meeting of the Joint Defence Council, Mountbatten urged me to request you to go to the Punjab and he hoped that you would repeat your Calcutta miracle there.[1014] I told him that I was myself not clear about this. I feel you should go but not just yet.

We are making special efforts to have news of the Wah camp and to get it protected or evacuated.[1015]

So far as the army is concerned, in the Punjab, there can be no doubt that it is influenced by communal feelings and given the chance has acted up to them. But outwardly and generally it has observed discipline and carried out orders. The police has been much worse.

Yours,
Jawaharlal

SWJN, *Vol. 4, II Series, pp. 20–3*

## 465. Letter to Jawaharlal Nehru

29 August 1947

Herewith is a letter from one Sardar Ajit Singh. You will see he is insistent on my going to the Punjab without a moment's delay. You will judge what I should do. Will it be any use my going after life and property are destroyed to the saturation point? Will it not be a

[1014] For Gandhi's article 'Miracle or Accident?' written from Beliaghata on 16 August 1947, see *CWMG*, Vol. LXXXIX, pp. 48–9.

[1015] On 4 August, Gandhi had visited a refugee camp at Wah in the Gujarat District of West Punjab where 9,000 Hindu and Sikh refugees were awaiting evacuation.

mockery? I put before you for consideration the thoughts welling up within me. I have three wires pressing me to go.

CWMG, *Vol. LXXXIX, p. 108*

## 466. Telegram to M.K. Gandhi

29 August 1947

I still think that the time has not come for you to visit the Punjab but feel your presence in Delhi very desirable so as to keep in touch with the Punjab situation and advise us.

CWMG, *Vol. LXXXIX, p. 108fn*

## 467. Letter to Jawaharlal Nehru

30 August 1947

About my going to the Punjab, I won't move without your and Vallabhbhai's wish. I want to say, however, that every day pressure is being put upon me to rush to the Punjab before it is too late. If you wish I could send you all that comes to me so as to enable you to come to the right decision.

If I am not going to the Punjab, would I be of much use in Delhi as an adviser or consultant? I fancy I am not built that way. My advice has value only when I am actually working at a particular thing. I can only disturb when I give academic advice as on food, clothing, the use of the military. The more I think, the more I sense the truth of this opinion. Left to myself I would probably rush to the Punjab and if necessary break myself in the attempt to stop the warring elements from committing suicide. From a letter I just have from Lord Mountbatten[1016] I get the same impression. He would welcome my immediate going to the Punjab.

On this side I have work which must help you all.

CWMG, *Vol. LXXXIX, p. 117*

[1016] Who had assumed his new office as Governor-General of Independent India on 15 August 1947. In his letter dated 26 August, he had said, *inter alia*, 'In the Punjab we have 55 thousand soldiers and large-scale rioting on our hands. In Bengal our forces consist of one man and no rioting. As a serving officer as well as an administrator, may I be allowed to pay my tribute to the One-man Boundary Force, not forgetting his second-in command, Mr Suhrawardy.'

## 468. Telegram to M.K. Gandhi

31 August 1947

Received your letter[1017] of August 28th. Punjab problem overwhelming in extent and intensity. I feel now that your presence in Punjab is desirable and would be helpful in curing insanity and bringing solace to this ruined and heart-broken province. Am returning to Delhi 4th. After brief stay coming back to Punjab.

SWJN, *Vol. 4, II Series, pp. 45–6*

## 469. Telegram to M.K. Gandhi

New Delhi
2 September 1947

Received your letter 29th. I feel sure now that you should come to Punjab as early as possible.[1018]

SWJN, *Vol. 4, II Series, pp. 47*

## 470. Letter to Jawaharlal Nehru

2 September 1947

Chi. Jawaharlal,[1019]
I replied to your message[1020] of yesterday.

I would have started for Lahore today but for the flare-up in Calcutta. If the fury did not abate, my going to the Punjab would be of no avail. I would have no self-confidence. If the Calcutta friendship was wrong, how could I hope to affect the situation in the Punjab? Therefore my departure from Calcutta depends solely

[1017] Not available

[1018] Nehru had written to Vallabhbhai Patel, 'I hope you will pull up the Punjab states, specially Faridkot, Nabha and Jind. They are centres of trouble and disorders and they must be made to behave. ... I think the time has come when Bapu should be asked to go to East Punjab.' On receiving the wire Gandhi said: 'I now feel happy and at peace because I am doing what my duty requires of me.' But, meanwhile, Gandhi's fast against fresh riots in Calcutta had commenced and he could leave for Delhi only on 7 September 1947.

[1019] The superscription and subscription are in Devangari.

[1020] Not available.

upon the result of the Calcutta fast. Don't be distressed or angry over the fast.

Blessings from
Bapu

CWMG, *Vol. LXXXIX, p. 134*

## 471. Letter to M.K. Gandhi

New Delhi
5 September 1947

Dear Bapu,
I had some talk with Sushila.[1021] Your going to Punjab seems to me proper. But first you should come to Delhi and stay here for a couple of days and then make the further programme. Probably first to Amritsar and then to Lahore. To move about much at this time does not seem proper. From here it would be convenient to go by plane. Otherwise you can go by car also halting on the way. I might probably go with you or meet you there itself.

Yours,
Jawaharlal

SWJN, *Vol. 4, II Series, p. 50* (Original in Hindi)

## 472. Telegram to Jawaharlal Nehru

[On or before 7 September 1947][1022]

Pandit Nehru
New Delhi
God willing leaving for Delhi way Punjab. Inform Sardar Birla Brijkrishna.

Bapu

CWMG, *Vol. LXXXIX, p. 159*

[1021] Dr Sushila Nayyar (1914–2000); younger sister of Pyarelal Nayar; personal secretary to Gandhi and his personal physician; Minister for Health, Government of India, 1952–5 and 1962–7. She had accompanied Gandhi on his Noakhali tour.

[1022] Inferred, as Gandhi left Calcutta on 7 September 1947.

## 473. Letter to M.K. Gandhi

17 September 1947

Dear Bapu,

I am sending you a press clipping giving the resolutions passed by the joint conference at Lahore on September 3rd.[1023] On the second page you will find the reference to forced conversions.

Yours,
Jawaharlal

SWJN, *Vol. 4, II Series, p. 85*

## 474. Letter to M.K. Gandhi

18 September 1947

Dear Bapu,

I enclose a letter from Rajendra Babu and a copy of my reply to him.[1024] Also a note[1025] which I am presenting to the Cabinet today. It is meant to be a draft for a declaration on behalf of Government. This is just a rough draft to be finalised after discussion.

Yesterday we discussed in Cabinet this matter for some time in a rather desultory fashion. While superficially people seemed to agree, there were obviously vital differences in approach and objectives. So we are meeting again this afternoon.

Yours,
Jawaharlal

SWJN, *Vol. 4, II Series, p. 85*

[1023] The Indian and Pakistan Governments agreed to establish law and order, protect all refugees and get them safely across the border, run refugee and evacuee camps, organize evacuation by the military, appoint custodians of refugee property and liaison officers, not to recognize forced conversions and forced marriages, trace and restore abducted women to their families, protect and safeguard property belonging to religious, charitable and cultural institutions and restore at public expense religious places destroyed or desecrated, expedite transfer of stranded government officers and issue reports of occurrences to check wild rumours.

[1024] See *SWJN*, Vol. 4, II Series, pp. 81–4.

[1025] *Aide-Memoire*, prepared by Nehru on 18 September 1947 for his talks with Liaquat Ali Khan on 19 and 20 September. This was sent to Attlee on 24 September 1947. Ibid., pp. 86–93.

## 475. Note to Jawaharlal Nehru

[29 September 1947][1026]

So far as the war is concerned my speeches have been quite clear.[1027] The summaries sent to America and elsewhere may be quite the contrary of what I might have said. I shall deal with the question more fully in my written speech today. As to the deteriorating situation I have told you quite firmly that you should [not] dispense with Sardar, or he you. He won't shoulder the burden without you, hence you should take it up and reform the Cabinet with one mind. Rajen Babu should give up food portfolio. He will do so gladly.

I have always looked upon the wholesale accessions of States with suspicion.[1028] They are probably a liability rather than an asset. This sums up my reaction. We may discuss these things more fully when I can speak.

CWMG, *Vol. LXXXIX, p. 520*

## 476. Letter to M.K. Gandhi

New Delhi
17 November 1947

Dear Bapu,

You will be interested to know that I have just received the following telegraphic message from Radhakrishnan[1029] via Asaf Ali. This is from UNESCO Conference at Mexico:

May I convey to you the remarkable impression which Mrs. Asaf Ali made today by her spirited appeal for the common man. I wish you

[1026] Inferred from the contents

[1027] Gandhi clarified his stand on the War on 29 September, a silence day, in his 'written speech today'. See *CWMG*, Vol. LXXXIX, pp. 259–60.

[1028] Apart from Kashmir, Hyderabad and Junagadh, all other States had acceded to one or other of the new Dominions before 15 August 1947.

[1029] Sarvepalli Radhakrishnan was a member of the Executive Board of the UNESCO and leader of the Indian delegation at the session of the General Conference held at Mexico City from 6 November to 3 December 1947.

were here to share in our joy at her success. We the members of the Indian Delegation are quite proud of her contribution.

Yours,
Jawaharlal

SWJN, *Vol. 4, II Series, p. 590*

## 477. Note to M.K. Gandhi

6 January 1948

The recent correspondence between Sardar Patel and me has raised important issues of vital consequence; and yet the origin of that correspondence related to a relatively minor matter.[1030]

2. It is true that there are not only temperamental differences between Sardar and me but also a difference in approach in regard to economic and communal matters. These differences have persisted for a large number of years, ever since we worked together in the Congress. Nevertheless, in spite of these differences there was obviously a very great deal in common in addition to mutual respect and affection and, broadly speaking, the same national political aim of freedom. Because of this we functioned together during all these years and did our utmost to adapt ourselves to each other. If the Congress came to a decision, we accepted it though there might have been a difference in implementing it.

3. Our political aim having been more or less achieved the other questions, on which we have differed to some extent, come more and more to the forefront. At the same time crises face the country which makes it incumbent on all of us not to stress the differences but rather to emphasise the points of agreement and

[1030] The reference is to the correspondence regarding H.V.R. Iengar's visit to Ajmer on 20 December 1947. Writing to Nehru on 23 December, Patel who had already issued a statement to the Press on Ajmer-Merwara resented 'such visits of inspection'.

A copy of this note was sent as an enclosure to Nehru's letter to Patel of 12 January 1948. Nehru and Patel had wanted to discuss with Gandhi their separate viewpoints, but desisted, as Gandhi began fasting from 13 January. As a last resort, Patel wrote on 13 January, beseeching Gandhi to 'give up your fast and get this question settled soon'. See *Sardal Patel's Correspondence*, Vol. VI, pp. 9–13, 16–17, 21–6.

to cooperate in the face of these crises. So far as the economic and communal matters are concerned, we are bound down by Congress policy and decisions, and both of us, as well as other Congressmen, must necessarily work in accordance with them. On the communal issue, the Congress standpoint has been clarified recently. On the economic issue, the broad lines of policy have been laid down and, no doubt, further details will soon follow. The Cabinet will have to consider these matters soon. We have delayed too long already in laying down an economic policy and this has led to differing interpretations and statements by Ministers.

4. We may therefore, for the moment, leave out of consideration these important matters and come down to the immediate issue. This issue essentially relates to the functions of the Prime Minister. It is something much more than a personal issue and it should be considered, therefore, as a question of principle, whoever the Prime Minister might be.

5. As I conceive it, the Prime Minister's role is, and should be, an important role. He is not only a figurehead but a person who should be more responsible than anyone else for the general trend of policy and for the coordination of the work of various Government departments. The final authority necessarily is the Cabinet itself. But in the type of domestic set-up we have adopted, the Prime Minister is supposed to play an outstanding role. This, I think, is important (again quite apart from personal factors), as otherwise there will be no cohesion in the Cabinet and the Government, and disruptive tendencies will be at work.

6. Speaking for myself, I have at present two functions to perform in Government. As Minister of External Affairs, I function like any other Minister and my Ministry is like any other Ministry. As Prime Minister, however, I have a special function to perform which covers all the Ministries and departments and indeed every aspect of governmental authority. This function cannot be easily defined and the proper discharge of it depends a great deal on the spirit of cooperation animating all the parties concerned. Inevitably, in discharging this function of Prime Minister I have to deal with every Ministry not as head of one particular Ministry, but as a coordinator and a kind of supervisor. Naturally, this can only

be done effectively with tact and goodwill and without in any way diminishing the prestige of other Ministers. Other Ministers must not normally be interfered with and should have freedom to carry out their work without unnecessary interference.[1031]

7. If this position is recognised, then no present difficulty arises, and if at any time a difficulty does arise, it can be resolved by personal contact and discussion between the parties concerned. Because of this I have endevoured in almost every matter of importance to confer with Sardar Patel.

8. The immediate issue arose out of my sending Iengar to Ajmer.[1032] I think that my sending him was not only completely within my competence but also it was eminently desirable thing to do in the circumstances and that undoubtedly it did some good. This opinion of mine has been strengthened by my visit to Ajmer. Iengar had nothing to do with holding any kind of an inquiry or sitting in judgement in any way on the officials in Ajmer.[1033] He was sent as the eyes and ears of the Prime Minister and to convey the Prime Minister's regret for his having had to cancel his visit to Ajmer previously. In Ajmer and elsewhere, we have to deal with psychological problems and mental states. The approach to the people direct is always important when dealing with such problems. The importance of Ajmer has induced me to pay a visit there even at inconvenience. I could not go then because of a death in the family. My not going was variously interpreted in Ajmer and gave rise to all

[1031] Patel in his reply of 12 January 1948, in response to this note, questioned Nehru's interpretation of the Prime Minister's role as inconsistent with the democratic system of government, for it would raise him 'to the position of virtual dictator'. The Prime Minister was no doubt 'first among equals', but he had no overriding powers over his colleagues 'as responsibility for implementing policy decisions rested with the Ministry concerned and on the Minister in charge'.

[1032] However, Patel argued that the issue was not H.V.R. Iengar's visit but related to Gopalaswami Ayyangar directly corresponding with the East Punjab Government.

[1033] Patel reiterated that 'Iengar went to Ajmer, inspected various places, received deputations ... the public mind is bound to associate it with an inquisition. The Chief Commissioner took it in that light and stated that the public also felt it as such.'

manner of suspicions and rumours. Iengar's going helped to lessen these suspicions somewhat among the people by making them realise that the Government was greatly interested in their peace and welfare. My subsequent visit, of course, did much more good. It did not, as it was not meant to, affect the position of the Chief Commissioner, whom indeed I praised publicly for his ability and impartiality. But apart from these facts the question remains: Is the Prime Minister entitled to take such a step and who is to be the judge of this? If the Prime Minister cannot even take this step and is not himself to be the judge of what is proper and what is not in such matters, then he cannot function properly or fulfil his functions.[1034] Indeed he does not function at all as the Prime Minister should. The mere fact that he is Prime Minister presumably leads to the conclusion that he is capable of judging aright and carrying out the policy laid down. If he is not capable of this, then he should cease to be Prime Minister. Indeed, this means abdication of his functions and he cannot in future function with any effectiveness. There will be no proper coordination of governmental authority and, in such circumstances, the administrative machinery weakens and there are rival pulls.

9. If this view is correct, then the Prime Minister should have full freedom to act when and how he chooses, though of course such action must not be an undue interference with local authorities who are immediately responsible. The Prime Minister obviously is as much interested as anyone else in having the loyalty and cooperation of the services.

10. In the event of the Prime Minister not functioning in this way, then he can hardly carry on as a mere figurehead and much harm may be done to the services as well as to the public at large by the enunciation of contradictory policies by Ministers.

[1034] Patel's response was, 'the question is not whether the Prime Minister was entitled to take this step or not or whether he is not to be the judge of the propriety of the action, but whether I, as a Minister, was wrong in pointing out to him the inadvisability of the course he had taken and the probable consequences it entailed.'

11. This is the background. But whatever the theory may be, practical difficulties continually arise. Normally speaking, the best way out of these difficulties would be for some arrangement in the Cabinet to be made which would cast the responsibility on one person more than anyone else. In the present set-up this means that either I should go out or that Sardar Patel should go out. For my part, I would greatly prefer my going out. Of course, this going out of either of us need not and should not mean any kind of subsequent opposition. Whether we are in or out of Government we remain, I hope, not only loyal Congressmen but loyal colleagues, and we will still try to pull together in our respective spheres of activity.

12. Nevertheless, there can be little doubt that if either of us goes out at the present juncture it would create a sensation both nationally and internationally, and the consequences may not be that good. At any time this position would have to be faced; but at the present juncture, with the Kashmir issue and the great problem of rehabilitation facing us, not to mention the States and growth of communal organisations in India, any such parting of ways may well have very serious consequences affecting the good of India. None of us wants to do anything which may be at all injurious to the national good, even though our views of the national good may differ somewhat. After having given very serious thought to this matter during the last fortnight I have come to the conclusion that this as far as possible we must avoid, at this particular juncture, any parting of the ways in the Government. We are too much in the transitional stage and a serious shake-up of Government may well lead to an upsetting of the applecart. I think that we should carry on for some months more till the Kashmir issue is more clarified and other problems have also been tackled to some extent. The way to do this must be the fullest consultation about every important matter. At the same time I do feel that the Prime Minister's function, as defined above, must be appreciated.

13. If, however, this is not to be considered possible, then the only alternative left is for either me or Sardar Patel to leave the Cabinet. As I have said above, I consider this an undesirable alternative in the present context, and I have come to this conclusion

as objectively as possible. If someone has to leave, I repeat, I would prefer to leave.[1035]

14. Latterly there has been a growing tendency towards a lack of cohesion in the various Ministries and departments of Government. This has resulted in members of the services also being affected. This is unfortunate and, in any event, has to be countered, for if the Cabinet and Government do not work jointly, all work must necessarily suffer and a psychology produced in the country which comes in the way of cooperative working.

15. Probably before very long we shall have to consider a refashioning of the governmental set-up in the sense of introducing Deputy Ministers, Parliamentary Secretaries and the like. It may be desirable to put certain departments in charge of Deputy Ministers, each group of such Deputy Ministers being under the supervision of a Minister. This would make the real Cabinet a somewhat smaller body. However, this can be seen to later. At the present moment the allocation of portfolios is not a very logical one for some are very heavy indeed.

16. The States Ministry is a new Ministry which has to deal with vital questions. If I may say so, it has dealt with these questions thus far with remarkable success and surmounted the many difficulties that are continually arising. I feel, however, that many decisions have been taken involving matters of principle without any reference to the Cabinet.[1036] For my part I agree with these decisions, but it seems to me a wrong procedure for these decisions to be taken without reference to the Cabinet or to the Prime Minister. Being a new Ministry, it functions naturally outside normal procedure. To some extent this is inevitable and quick decisions have to be taken. But an attempt should be made to bring this functioning within the terms of our ordinary procedure.

[1035] Patel's response was, '... if anybody has to go, it should be myself. I have long passed the age of active service. The Prime Minister is the acknowledged leader of the country and is comparatively young; he has established an international position of pre-eminence for himself.'

[1036] Denying this Patel said, 'The only instance in which I anticipated a Cabinet decision was that of the merger of Orissa and Chhatisgarh States; subsequent confirmation of my action ... upholds my judgement in anticipating it.'

17. Before the Constituent Assembly meets or sometime during its next session, we have to come to some decision regarding our general economic policy. The problem of rehabilitation may well be tied up with this policy.[1037]

SWJN, *Vol. 5, II Series, pp. 471–5*

## 478. Letter to Jawaharlal Nehru

[*Below is the English translation of a letter which Gandhiji sent me. The original is in Hindi. It was written on the day he broke his fast which had already lasted a number of days and which was undertaken to indicate his unhappiness at the communal tension in Delhi.*

*I was rather upset at events in Delhi as well as Gandhiji's fast and for a day or two I did not take my food. This was not a regular fast but rather a personal reaction to events which hardly anyone knew. Somehow Gandhiji got to know of it and hence his advice to me to put an end to it.*

*The reference to a 'jewel of India' is a pun on my name which means jewel.*

*This was the last letter he wrote to me. Twelve days later, on 30 January 1948, he died at the hands of an assassin.*][1038]

18 January 1948

Chi. Jawaharlal,

Give up your fast.

I am sending herewith a copy of the telegram received from the Speaker of West Punjab. Zaheed Hussain had said exactly what I had told you.[1039]

[1037] Nehru wrote to Patel on 11 January 1947, suggesting that they meet at Gandhi's place to resolve the issues. The meeting, however, was not to be as Gandhi was assassinated on 30 January. See Appendix VI for Nehru's letter to Patel of 3 February 1948 on the aftermath.

[1038] Reproduced here is Nehru's prefatory note to this letter in *A Bunch of Old Letters*.

Gandhi who had begun a fast on 13 January 1948 'by way of protest against some wrong done by society', broke it on 18 January on receipt of a declaration by various groups and organisations in Delhi that they would abide by the seven clauses laid down by him as a precondition to his breaking the fast. After breaking it, when Gandhi learnt that Nehru was also fasting, he promptly wrote the letter in his own hand despite extreme weakness.

[1039] Zaheed Hussain was among those assembled at the meeting where Gandhi spoke before breaking his fast on 18 January. On behalf of the people

May you live long and continue to be the jewel of India.

Blessings from
Bapu

A Bunch of Old Letters, *pp. 517–18*

## 479. Letter to Mahatma Gandhi

New Delhi
20 January 1948

Dear Bapu,
The Chinese Ambassador[1040] has sent me a message he has received from Dr Tai Chi-tao of the Examination Yuan of the Republic of China. The message came by telegram. I enclose a copy of the message.[1041]

Yours,
Jawahar

SWJN, *Vol. 5, II Series, p. 19*

of Pakistan he offered to do all he could towards creating circumstances that would enable Gandhi to break his fast. See *CWMG*, Vol. XC, p. 444.

[1040] Dr Lo Chia-lun

[1041] Of 18 January from Nanking. It read: 'The Chinese people, who are heartily in accord with all which Gandhiji stands for, are feeling anxious in this hour when he is again in the courageous act of mercy and sacrifice. I, for one, pray that his noble mission be fulfilled so that he may end his fast.'

# Appendix I

## Draft Deed of Swaraj Bhawan Trust*

19 September 1931

I, Jawaharlal Nehru, of Anand Bhawan, Allahabad, do hereby declare as follows:

Whereas my father, the late Pandit Motilal Nehru, had expressed a desire to dedicate his old house, formerly known as Anand Bhawan and now known as Swaraj Bhawan, for the general benefit of the people of India as represented by the Indian National Congress, and had announced his intention at a public ceremony, and allowed the use of it in accordance with this wish, but had not the time to execute the necessary document of trust, and whereas on his death the legal ownership of the said house, known as Swaraj Bhawan, now vests in me, the declarant, and whereas I am desirous of carrying out my father's wishes and of transferring the property to trustees for the benefit of the Indian people in the advancement of knowledge, health, social and economic well-being, and specially with the object of promoting unity among all classes and creeds of the Indian people, raising the status of Indian women and the elevation and betterment in all respects of the suppressed classes in India and Indian workers and peasants, and the promotion of social equality among all the peoples and classes of India, I do hereby make this declaration of trust and transfer the said property, known as Swaraj Bhawan, fully described below to Dr Mukhtar Ahmad Ansari of 1 Daryaganj, Delhi, Shrimati Perinbai Captain of Orient Club Building, Chowpatty, Bombay, Seth Jamnalal Bajaj of Wardha CP, Dr Bidhan Chandra Roy of 36 Wellington Street,

* See Item no. 138, p. 150.

Calcutta, and myself, the declarant, as trustees for the objects stated above and subject to the following conditions:

1. The trustees shall form themselves into a Board of Management for the purpose of managing the said property and shall coopt with themselves as members of the said Board of Management, the President and the Working Secretary of the Indian National Congress for the time being.
2. The said Board of Management shall have complete and absolutely unfettered discretion to use the said property in such manner as they think fit for the purpose of carrying out the objects specified above and more particularly may use the said property for the purpose of locating a hospital and also for the purpose of locating the general headquarters of the Indian National Congress. The Board of Management shall, however, act in accordance with the general policy of the Working Committee of the Indian National Congress in relation to the charitable object specified above.
3. The said Board of Management shall elect a Chairman and shall meet as often as may be necessary or transact business by circularisation, and shall frame its own rules for the purpose of regulating its proceedings.
4. The trustees mentioned in this deed of trust shall hold office for life and any vacancy among the trustees caused by their death or retirement or resignation shall be filled by the Working committee of the Indian National Congress.

In token whereof I have signed and sealed and delivered this declaration of trust for charitable purposes.

## Specification of the Property

House and grounds bearing Municipal No. 3 Church Road, bounded on the north by No. 7 Church Road, on the north-west by No. 5 Church Road, on the east and south by Anand Bhawan No. 1, Church Road, and on the west by the Church Road.
Plan attached.

## Note on the Swaraj Bhawan Trust

Jamnalalji has pointed out that the draft deed of trust may not permit sale of the property should necessity for this arise and he wants this power to be given. It is probable that the present draft will not allow this to be done. In any event as the question has been raised it ought to be cleared up, one way or the other.

My own feeling is that it will be very unfortunate if Swaraj Bhawan has to be sold for any reason and I know that father was averse to this also. Swaraj Bhawan has a certain cash value no doubt but its real value is one of association and sentiment. A principal object of creating the trust was that the site itself should remain a national possession and should not go into other hands.

At the same time I feel that I should not allow my sentiment to intrude too much in this matter. It is possible that a contingency might arise when the purposes of the trust might be served better by a sale of the property. As I cannot apply my mind impartially to this question I am requesting the proposed trustees to favour me with their opinions. I am also requesting Gandhiji for his advice in the matter. I am very sorry for the additional delay, but perhaps it is best that the matter be cleared up.

A possible suggestion is the addition of the following clauses to the deed of trust:

'It shall not be open to the Trustees to sell or otherwise alienate the property, but under very special circumstances, if it is clear that the purpose of the trust will be served better by such sale or alienation, the Trustees may do so, provided that no such decision will be arrived at unless the Trustees are unanimous and unless the Working Committee of the National Congress approves of such a decision.

In the event of such sale or alienation taking place the monies realised shall be invested in other properties for the furtherance of the objects of the Trust.'

This is not in legal language but the meaning is probably clear enough.

Jawaharlal Nehru

G-N Correspondence, JN Papers, *NMML*

# Appendix II

## Working Committee Resolution No. 13 of 18 June 1934*

Whilst the Working Committee welcomes the formation of groups representing different schools of thought, it is necessary, in view of loose talk about confiscation of private property and necessity of class war, to remind Congressmen that the Karachi resolution as finally settled by the AICC at Bombay in August 1931, which lays down certain principles, neither contemplates confiscation of private property without just cause or compensation, nor advocacy of class war. The Working Committee is further of opinion that confiscation and class war are contrary to the Congress creed of nonviolence. At the same time the Working Committee is of opinion that the Congress does contemplate wiser and juster use of private property so as to prevent the exploitation of the landless poor, and also contemplates a healthier relationship between capital and labour.

The Encyclopaedia of Indian National Congress, *Vol. Ten, 1930–35, p. 400*

* See Item no. 193, p. 230.

# Appendix III

## Some Notes on the New Congress Constitution on a Fresh Perusal of it*

5 October 1935

Article V (b): A distinction seems to be made between a member of the Congress and one who is entitled under this clause to election to an office or to membership of any Congress Committee. It is not clear how any person can be a member of the Congress without being a member of even a primary Committee. Thus the distinction seems to be meaningless, unless by 'Congress Committee' in the clause is meant the executive Committee or the higher Committee, and every member of these must either fulfil these qualifications or cease to be a member.

As for the qualifications: (i) The khadi clause has hardly been a success so far and has given rise to a great deal of duplicity. There is apparently no change in it. Perhaps it would have been better to confine it to office bearers and executives.

(ii) It is a little difficult for me to understand this clause. The object evidently is to emphasise the necessity and dignity of manual labour and that is certainly desirable. But it becomes farcical when noted Congressmen publicly perform some thoroughly futile operations and pretend they are doing useful manual work. This is common enough. It also seems odd to ask a manual labourer, who works hard enough as it is, to do extra manual work for the Congress in addition to his subscription of 4 annas.

I do not think that either of these clauses will succeed in driving away the undesirable and careerist elements which have become so prominent recently.

* See Item no. 213, p. 258.

Clause (c) I think this is a very desirable addition.

Article VI (e) and following clauses: I am not quite clear yet about the implications and consequences of the division into rural and urban areas.

Article VII (i) and Article IX (f): The mode of electing the President is likely to lead to a person being chosen who has only a minority of votes. Separate provincial groups, meeting independently of each other, propose any number of odd names and then vote on each name. It is quite possible that a large number of names are proposed and the person who gets most votes has really only 25% or 30% of the total votes cast. This seems undesirable, especially when the President has so much power as the new Constitution gives him. The old method was not good but it did serve a useful purpose in dividing the operations in two stages. Some method of eliminating fancy names before the real elections would help.

Clause (i) says that 'the vote of each of the delegates assembled on the proposals' for the presidentship, must be recorded. Does this mean that each voter's name as well as vote has to be recorded? If so why?

Article X: The provision that the delegates of the preceding session of the Congress shall also be the delegates for a special session takes away somewhat from the value of the special session. In a changing and revolutionary situation mass opinion also changes rapidly, usually far more rapidly than that of the leaders. If no opportunity is given to the electorate to change its old delegates, if it so chooses, the new opinions are not reflected in the Congress session. The special session is only an adjourned session of the last Congress with the same performers, however much they may be out of touch with realities. Under the new Constitution there is no way of the electorate making its will felt, if this is contrary to official Congress policy, between two ordinary sessions.

Article XII: Under the old Constitution a convention had grown up for the President to suggest the names of the secretaries and the members of the WC. This is now crystallised into constitutional rules. So far, perhaps, the change is desirable. But as formed, the rule amounts to the formation of the WC without even a subsequent vote of confidence of the AICC. A President may carry on for months with his self-appointed WC without any reference to the AICC. As the President himself is chosen in a manner which may lead to a minority election, this may lead to the dominance of a minority group, with all power concentrated in one man's hands. The checks are few and difficult of application.

The new Constitution is certainly more efficient than the last. It is likely to lead to a more compact and workman-like organisation. But it is certainly not more democratic and it has a number of Fascist elements in it, especially the concentration of power in the hands of a 'leader' who may represent minority factions even in the Congress. The old style democracy need not be made into a fetish and all modern tendencies even in so-called democratic countries like England, France and the USA are for the executive to exercise enormous power, subject only to fear of being kicked out at a subsequent election or having to face a revolution. To some extent this is inevitable under modern complex conditions but it has its dangers, especially in an organisation which has no clear, well-defined policy. The Congress has no such policy. It has today a certain vague outlook, which might be called a non-cooperative outlook, and for the rest it has a certain social reform programme, which is not directly political and with which most people of differing views will largely agree. The real difference will be in the stress laid on various items of this programme. There can be no doubt that during the last year or two the Congress has gone back ideologically almost to the pre-NCO era. At any rate many of its leading members have done so. The present Constitution may tend towards making it, even more than it has been in the past, a political caucus.

These are just a first reaction to a reading of the new Constitution. A further consideration and consultation may vary these reactions and impressions or bring out other doubts. It seems to me that the real trouble of the Congress lies deeper and cannot be [got] rid of by changing constitutions, helpful as such a change might be. Unless the Congress knows its own mind and expresses it clearly it will wobble and prove ineffective, and will be a field for careerists and opportunists who can pose as patriots and the like without having to commit themselves to anything definite or having to face any risk. During our struggles the element of risk was ever present and this to some extent kept out many undesirables. When the struggle ends these people roll in again. Constitutions indeed cannot keep them out, however good they might be. Other things are necessary for this. But constitutions should be as flexible as possible and susceptible to changing ideas. If they attempt to keep in the ...[1] and to freeze ideas, they become a hindrance.

MKG Papers, Pyarelal Collection, *NMML*

[1] Word illegible in the source.

# Appendix IV

## Gandhi's Notes on Talks with Jinnah-I*

30 April 1938

I met Mr Jinnah on the 28th instant at 11.30 a.m. Our talks were finished at 3 p.m. They were quite cordial. I am inclined to think also that Mr Jinnah was as open and frank as I know I was myself. My impression is that the points that have appeared in the Press on behalf of the Muslims are not to be seriously pressed, at any rate not in the form they have been put forth before the public. In the course of the discussions I saw that there were two things about which Mr Jinnah was particular. 1. The Communal Award should be treated as final until an agreed substitute is found for it. 2. Any Hindu-Muslim pact should be between the Congress and the League.

Assuming that the League is the predominant Muslim organisation and that in the legislatures the League has the largest number of Muslim members, the Congress is bound to recognise the fact, so much so that it should induce the other Mussalman groups to merge themselves in the League. It would be better for the country as we are constituted at present, that there is one solid Muslim organisation, than that there should be several struggling for their separate existence. If the Congress is to achieve a living unity, it should promote every tendency towards amalgamation of rival groups under one banner. I say this on the assumption that it is not possible at the present stage to absorb the Mussalmans in the Congress. If we are to achieve this we shall only do so when the Mussalmans can speak with one voice, even as, if we are to achieve

* See Item no. 279, p. 332.

independence the Congress should speak with one voice in the sense that there are no rival organisations worth the name.

After having arrived at the above-mentioned two formulas, Mr Jinnah was prepared to discuss the details, but I suggested that they should be discussed at a formal conference, that anything that I might say will be binding on nobody, and that without consultation with co-workers, I should not give my own individual opinion. Therefore I suggested that a formal conference might now take place, but an intermediate stage was a possibility, and might also be desirable.

That step was a Conference between Mr Jinnah, Maulana Abul Kalam Azad and myself. I told him that I was myself guided by the Maulana in all matters especially relating to the Muslims. I added that the Working Committee too was guided by the Maulana. Mr J. took one hour in trying to persuade me not to insist upon the Maulana's presence at any formal talk, for Mussalmans who were in the Congress could not by the League people be considered as representatives of Mussalmans. I told Mr Jinnah that it was a point of honour with me to have the Maulana at any such conference. We had reached a point when our talks, opened so auspiciously as I had thought, might come to an abrupt end. I therefore said that I might disappear from the scene at least for the time being and a formal conference should take place between the two presidents, where the methods of discussion, the question of Maulana's presence might be discussed. I left the question purposely open, not only because an abrupt end would have been most unfortunate, but also because, on merits the Maulana and the other members of the WC might, for the sake of the cause, think it wise not to make the presence of the Maulana a *sine qua non* of negotiations. During the talks it was agreed between us, that a way to evolve a pact was that accredited representatives of both the organisations should meet, with a determination to bring into being an agreement, which will merely require a formal sanction. If necessary an umpire might be appointed, to give finality in the event of an agreement between the two bodies whilst I have suggested that the President of the Congress should meet Mr J. I have told him that the President might depute some other member to carry on the negotiations, or rather to open them, and he was quite agreeable.

In fact he said that he would willingly confer with any non-Muslim nominee of the Congress. He added that if the Maulana saw him in his individual capacity he was always welcome.

I made it clear to Mr Jinnah that whatever I said at the meeting was not binding upon anybody but myself. It is therefore open to the WC to examine the two broad propositions on merits, and come to independent judgement.

MKG Papers, Pyarelal Collection, *Subject File 16, NMML*

# Appendix V

## Gandhi's Notes on Talks with Jinnah-II*

20 May 1938

At his wish I met Shri Jinnah at his residence at 2.30 p.m. on the 20th inst. The conversation had to be abruptly terminated because I had to catch the train for Wardha at 5.45 p.m. This does not mean that all the topics that Shri Jinnah had to cover were not discussed. At the outset he said that he had hoped to meet me before the exchange of letters between him and Subhash Babu. Then he referred to the speeches made at the recent Bombay meetings by Dr Hamid, Dr Mahmud and a third Muslim whose name just now escapes me. He said that their speeches were inappropriate whilst negotiations for a settlement were going on. I told him I had not read the speeches, but said that if they were calculated to offend the Muslim League they might not have been made. He then said that whilst the negotiations were going on:

1. *Bande Mataram* should not be sung in public institutions or at mixed gatherings, the latter as far as possible.
2. The Congress flag should not be flown over non-Congress public institutions.
3. Hindi should not be imposed as was sought to be done in Madras primary schools in certain areas.
4. Muslim mass contact propaganda should be suspended.

I told him that so far as Muslim mass propaganda was concerned my personal view was that if it was going on it should be suspended. But I told him also that in this matter I did not in any

* See Item no. 282, p. 334.

shape or from represent the Congress opinion, which might even be contrary to mine.

As to Hindi, I was not inclined to believe his information, but I said that I should inquire.

As to the proposal regarding *Bande Mataram* and the flag, whilst I recognised that caution was necessary, I did not think anything more could be done at the moment.

The largest part of the conversation however centred round the Congress repudiation of the claim that the League was the authoritative and representative Muslim institution. I told him that as I myself could not endorse the claim, I could not advise any member of the Working Committee to do so. I told him that he should be satisfied with the fact that the Congress was negotiating with the Muslim League to the exclusion of any other Muslim body. He cavilled at the fact that the right to consult other Muslim bodies was reserved in the letter handed to him, though he said that he could have no objection to the Congress consulting anybody or any organisation it liked.

I told him in the end that I hoped that he would not advise the League Council to break on the point, because it seemed to me to be such an obvious error. He then recalled the previous conversation between us and said that I ought not to insist upon the inclusion of Muslims in any committee that might be appointed to draw up the settlement in conjunction with a similar committee appointed by the Muslim League. I said that so far as I was concerned I could not be party to any such exclusion. I would hold it to be dishonourable to submit to any such exclusion. But I would gladly agree openly that any Mussalman who might be appointed on the committee would not be regarded as representative of Muslim opinion, even as any Hindu who might be a member of the committee would not be regarded as representing Hindu opinion. Any person appointed by the Congress would necessarily and only represent Congress opinion. Hindus, Mussalmans, Christians and others who belong to the Congress were more than mere Hindus, etc. But they were Congress-minded and that they were less so if and insofar as any of them sought to represent his own community in antagonism to any other, and if there was in the Congress a Christian or a Parsi whose all-India authority was unquestioned, I could conceive the Congress appointing him as its sole representative to negotiate with the Muslim League. I said that this function which the Congress had cultivated from its very birth could never be surrendered for any price, and I urged him not to forget this fundamental distinction between the Congress and Muslim League. The Congress was a purely all-inclusive national organisation and the Muslim League, however national its aspiration may be, was an exclusive organisation fighting for Muslim rights.

Shri Jinnah also complained that proceedings were taken against Muslim papers in Bombay for alleged libellous falsehoods circulated by them. He resented the exercise of the law authorising forfeiture of security without any opportunity of a trial. I told him that I knew something about this action. The Bombay Premier had approached Shri Jinnah on the subject and appealed to him to stop such writing. As he said he would want time to deal with the matter, and as the matter was probably urgent proceedings were taken. But I suggested that if Shri Jinnah could even at that stage intervene and give a satisfactory assurance that this lying propaganda would be stopped assuming that it was going on, the proceedings might be withdrawn and security refunded. I suggested his writing to the Law Member.

In the course of the conversations he referred to cases of injustices alleged to have been perpetrated by Congress Ministries or under their aegis. He produced a letter received from Minister Suhrawardy saying that Subhas Babu had engaged a hundred Maulvis and was in league with Maulana Abul Kalam Azad to create a division among Mussalmans and warned him against negotiating with such a person. I told him that I could not believe the statement, as Minister Suhrawardy had no balanced judgement. He had simply passed on to Shri Jinnah hearsay evidence, but in any case it was due from Shri Jinnah to Subhas Babu that the former should acquaint him with the contents later. The other complaints he made I need not deal with here.

MKG Papers, Pyarelal Collection, *Subject File 16, NMML*

# Appendix VI

## Letter to Vallabhbhai Patel*

New Delhi
3 February 1948

My dear Vallabhbhai,

When Bapu was alive we had hoped to meet him together and discuss various matters that had troubled us somewhat. You will remember our correspondence. In my last letter I had expressed the hope that, in spite of certain differences of opinion and temperament, we should continue to pull together as we had done for so long. This was, I was glad to find, Bapu's final opinion also.

Now, with Bapu's death everything is changed and we have to face a different and more difficult world. The old controversies have ceased to have much significance and it seems to me that the urgent need of the hour is for all of us to function as closely and cooperatively as possible. Indeed, there is no other way.

I have been greatly distressed by the persistence of whispers and rumours about you and me, magnifying out of all proportion any differences we may have. This has spread to foreign ambassadors and foreign correspondents; mischief-makers take advantage of this and add to it. Even the services are affected and this is bad. We must put an end to this mischief.

It is over a quarter of a century since we have been closely associated with one another and we have faced many storms and perils together. I can say with full honesty that during this period my affection and regard for you have grown, and I do not think anything can happen to lessen this. Even our differences have brought out the far greater points of agreement between us and the respect we

* See Item no. 477, *fn*.1037.

bear to each other. We have even learnt to differ and yet carry on together.

Anyway, in the crisis that we have to face now after Bapu's death I think it is my duty and, if I may venture to say, yours also for us to face it together as friends and colleagues. Not merely superficially, but in full loyalty to one another and with confidence in each other. I can assure you that you will have that from me. If I have any doubt or difficulty I shall put it frankly to you, and I hope you will do the same to me.

I had hoped to have a long talk with you, but we are so terribly pressed for time that we can hardly see each other in private for long. Some time or other, soon I hope, we shall have this talk and remove any misunderstandings or misapprehensions that may have arisen. Such talks are necessary from time to time. But meanwhile I do not want to wait for this talk and hence this letter, which carries with it my affection and friendship for you.

Yours,
Jawaharlal

SWJN, *Vol. 5, II Series, pp. 479–80*

# Index